The 1st Royal Irish Rifles in the Great War

The 1st Royal Irish Rifles
in the Great War

JAMES W. TAYLOR

with a foreword by
Martin Middlebrook, F.R. Hist. S.

FOUR COURTS PRESS

Published by

FOUR COURTS PRESS LTD

7 Malpas St, Dublin 8, Ireland

email: info@four-courts-press.ie

http://www.four-courts-press.ie

and in North America by

FOUR COURTS PRESS

c/o ISBS, 5824 N.E. Hassalo Street, Portland, OR 97213.

ISBN 1-85182-702-1

A catalogue record for this title
is available from the British Library.

Printed in Great Britain
by MPG Books, Bodmin, Cornwall

Foreword

It would be a foolhardy Englishman who commented on Irish history without the deepest preliminary study. But this book describes just one small element of a war that I have studied intermittently for more than thirty years, so perhaps I can comment usefully on it.

The 1st Battalion, The Royal Irish Rifles, was just one of some 600 infantry battalions which formed the British Expeditionary Force on the blood-soaked Western Front in France and Belgium in the First World War. The battalion strength rarely reached the 1,024 officers and other ranks of its war establishment. It arrived at the front from its peacetime garrison location in Aden on 14 November 1914. It had only missed the first ten weeks of fighting. It would serve continuously for almost exactly four years.

The battalion casualties would number nearly 4,000 men. Of these, 1,275 were fatal, a horrific total by modern standards but no more than average for a Regular battalion of infantry serving on the Western Front. Roughly two thirds of those dead soldiers were citizens of the then undivided country of Ireland. Ireland gave approximately 30,000 of her young men in this way to a cause that they thought worth fighting for at the time. Their country would soon find it convenient to forget that sacrifice.

Britain wallowed in war books between the two World Wars, but Irish history was pre-occupied with its War of Independence, the Civil War, and then the political problems of setting up a new state in a sorrowfully partitioned country and maintaining its neutrality in the 1939 war. In the 1960s, Britain saw a new wave of books about the First World War and a new wave of pilgrimages and study tours of those battlefields just across the English Channel. The thousands of British veterans still alive and active were treated with honour and their reminiscences assiduously recorded before they left us.

But in Ireland it was only in the North that this resurgence of interest was pursued. In the Republic there were few new books and the thousands of surviving veterans had found it prudent to say little of their experiences through their working lives and into their retirement. The National War Memorial in Dublin was allowed to go into disrepair. New generations grew up unaware of the experiences of their fathers and uncles and of their grandfathers and great uncles or the cause of their deaths as young men.

Recent years, however, have seen a welcome change. There came a more liberal, a more charitable, a more understanding view. History fell into its proper perspective. The Irish soldiers who fought in the British Army were no longer seen to have served in an unworthy cause. The National War Memorial was restored. A Peace Tower commemorating soldiers from all of Ireland was erected at a place in Belgium where troops from both North and South had carried out a successful attack in 1917.

But, what of literature? A great gap had to be filled. Parts of the gap would never be filled. The few veterans left were in insufficient numbers to provide adequate coverage of the experiences of the ordinary soldiers from which those British writers like myself had benefited so hugely thirty years earlier.

I agreed to write this recommendation for James Taylor's book although it has not been my custom to accede to such requests. But, not only is the author a good friend, I have become very interested myself in the Irish part in the First World War, viewing it as a subject much neglected. I feel that the academics in Ireland have not adequately filled that gap in their history I mentioned earlier. Mr Taylor, a family man with a full-time occupation, has devoted inordinate amounts of effort to produce a very worthy account of the history of the unit in which his great uncle was killed on the opening day of the Battle of the Somme. He worked to such good effect that he secured a contract for publication. Having once been in the same situation, I felt he should be given all the help I can provide.

Unit histories can be dry reading. This one is not. The official War Diary was kept conscientiously and intelligently and forms a sound and interesting basis for the first part of the book. Extracts from contemporary personal accounts and diaries put flesh on bare bones. But the author has delved deeper than these obvious sources and has discovered much original material that forms the Appendices. The best of these is the 'Biographical Details of the Officers' which takes up half of the space in the book. Sad that similar details for the ordinary soldiers have not survived, but their presence is always there behind the scenes. The reader will gain a good insight into the experiences of all the men in that typical Irish Regular battalion through four years of war. Remember, reader, that there were seventeen other Irish Regular battalions and no less than forty wartime-raised battalions of volunteers who had shorter but no less harrowing experiences in that war.

I know that all students of the First World War will find this book a useful addition to their collections. I hope, in particular, that the people of Ireland will support one of their own who has worked so hard to fill that gap to which I keep referring and has jumped across the periods of dissension and sadness in the history of their island.

Martin Middlebrook
Boston, England
4 October 2001

Contents

PART TWO

Illustrations

CREDITS

6 Brian Fitzmaurice; 7 Sir John M. Forbes; 11, 12 Imperial War Museum; 4 Commander Victor M. Lake; 5 Royal Irish Fusiliers Museum; 1, 2, 8, 9, 10, 14 Royal Ulster Rifles Museum; 3 Tony Whitfeld

Acknowledgements

I could never have finished this work without the understanding and patience of my wife, Maura, and our children, Adam and Emma. To them this book is dedicated.

Special thanks must be conveyed to Commander Victor M. Lake, RN, and Tony Whitfeld, both of whom allowed me to use their fathers' papers, and to Irish Jesuit Archives for permission to quote from Fr Gill's diary. To Martin Middlebrook for his Foreword and guidance. I received a great amount of data and help from the Royal Ulster Rifles Association through their Assistant, Terence Nelson. My researcher, Tom Tulloch-Marshall, Surrey, to whom I am particularly indebted, unearthed all of the information from the Public Record Office and guided me through many pitfalls. Dr Timothy Bowman, Queen's University, Belfast, gave very generously of his time and the list for courts-martial. Bobby Rainey, Dundonald, supplied many useful items from his extensive RIR collection. Laurence Lett, Raymond Quirke, Eamonn Power, and Raymund Kelly for turning the maps into a presentable format. My good friend Larry Gittens provided constant support, help, and encouragement. Thanks also to Michael Adams, Martin Fanning, and Anthony Tierney of Four Courts Press.

Mention must also be made of the assistance given by: *In Éire*: Alice Bonham, Frank Brophy, Geoff Campbell (Assistant Defence Attaché, British Embassy), Derek and Karen Coleman, John Culleton, Myles Dungan, Oliver Fallon, Jarlath ffrench-Mullen, Brian Fitzmaurice, Jim French, Jarlath Glynn, Donal Hall, Fintan and Jim Hoey, Comdt. Victor Laing (Irish Military Archives), Philip Lecane, Revd Fr John Looby SJ (Clongowes Wood College), Dr Pat McCarthy (Military History Society of Ireland), May McDonald, Revd Dermot McKenna, Paul Maguire, Dr David Murphy (Royal Irish Academy), Gerry Murphy, Michael O'Brien, Jack O'Connell (Schull Books), Pat O'Daly, Major-General David N.C. O'Morchoe CB, MBE, David Robertson, Angela Ryan, Liam Ryan, Sam Smyth, Orna Somerville (Irish Jesuit Archives), Cyril Wall, Frank Walsh, the staff of the National Library of Ireland and of the Wexford County Library; *in Northern Ireland*: Editor *Belfast Telegraph*, Lt.-Col. Reginald Harvey Bicker OBE, TD, UD, Dawn Collins (Royal Irish Fusiliers Museum), Major J.M. Dunlop (Royal Inniskilling Fusiliers Regimental Museum), Billy Ervine (Somme Association), Dr R.H. Jordan (Archivist of Methodist College), Paul Minchin McKay, Alan K. McMillen (Presbyterian Historical Society of Ireland), Jonathan Maguire, Amanda Moreno (Royal Irish Fusiliers Museum), R.J.I. Pollock (Headmaster, Campbell College), Major M.B. Murphy (RUR Association),

Robert Thompson, Samuel Troughton, Carol Walker (Somme Association), and Major R.J. Walker MBE (RUR Association); *in Britain*: David Bownes (Royal Welch Fusiliers Regimental Museum), Joy Bratherton (Western Front Association), David Chilton (The Royal Gloucestershire, Berkshire and Wiltshire Regiment Museum), Ronald Clifton (Western Front Association), The Commonwealth War Graves Commission, Jacyntha Crawley, Lt.-Col. P.A. Crocker (Royal Welch Fusiliers Regimental Museum), Philip Dutton (Imperial War Museum), Vice-Admiral Sir John M. Forbes KCB, Dr Peter Liddle (Liddle Collection), Nigel Lutt (Bedfordshire and Luton Archives and Record Service), Jim Parker (Machine Gun Corps OCA), Anthony Richards and Professor Peter Simkins MBE (IWM), Pete Starling (Army Medical Services Museum), S.B. Taylor (PMA RAF), Kate Thaxton (Norfolk Regiment Museum) and Dr P.J. Thwaites (Curator, Sandhurst Collection); *in the USA*: Russell H. Schaller.

To all of these I express my gratitude.

Glossary

ADS	Advanced Dressing Station
ASC	Army Service Corps
AWOL	absent without leave
Bar	additional award of the same medal
Barrage	Artillery bombardment
Bde	Brigade
BEF	British Expeditionary Force
BM	Brigade Major
Bn	Battalion
bomb	hand grenade
Bomber	hand grenade specialist
CCS	Casualty Clearing-Station
CO	Commanding Officer
Coy	Company
CQMS	Company Quartermaster Sergeant
demonstrate	a feint attack
DCLI	Duke of Cornwall's Light Infantry
DCM	Distinguished Conduct Medal
draft	a group of men sent as reinforcements
DOW	died of wounds
DSO	Distinguished Service Order
duck-board	wooden planks used to make walkways in trenches or muddy ground
dug-out	a shelter made in the wall of a trench
enfilade	gunfire directed along a line from end to end
fire trench	front-line trench
FOO	Forward Observation Officer
Gefreiter	German Lance Corporal
GHQ	General Headquarters
GOC	General Officer Commanding
GSO	General Staff Officer
GSW	Gunshot wound
keep	a heavily fortified position in a trench system
KIA	killed in action

13

KOYLI	King's Own Yorkshire Light Infantry
KRRC	King's Royal Rifle Corps
MB	Medical Board
MC	Military Cross
MGC	Machine Gun Corps
MM	Military Medal
MO	Medical Officer
MSM	Meritorious Service Medal
NCO	Non-Commissioned Officer
NYD	not yet diagnosed
OC	Officer Commanding
OCA	Old Comrades Association
OIC	Officer in Charge
OR	Other Rank
OTC	Officers Training Corps
parados	the back of a trench
parapet	the front of the trench
pill-box	a reinforced concrete machine-gun post
POW	Prisoner of War
Pte	Private
RAF	Royal Air Force
RAMC	Royal Army Medical Corps
RDF	Royal Dublin Fusiliers
RE	Royal Engineers
Regt	Regiment
RFC	Royal Flying Corps
RIF	Royal Irish Fusiliers
RIR	Royal Irish Rifles
R. Irish	Royal Irish Regiment
redoubt	a fortified strongpoint
RMC	Royal Military College
RMF	Royal Munster Fusiliers
RWF	Royal Welsh Fusiliers
RWK	Royal West Kent Regiment
RUR	Royal Ulster Rifles
S.A.A.	small arms ammunition
salient	a trench system projecting towards the enemy
sap	a narrow trench extending from a main trench
shrapnel	small metal balls ejected from a shell, usually while still in the air
TF	Territorial Forces
TMB	Trench mortar battery
Town Major	an officer responsible for billeting arrangements in a town
UVF	Ulster Volunteer Force
WO	War Office
Zero-hour	the time for an attack to commence

PART ONE

The history of the 1st Royal Irish Rifles, 1914–19

Introduction

This book has been compiled in two parts. The first covers the history of the 1st Royal Irish Rifles, 1914–19. Part Two gives brief biographical details of the officers and some of the other ranks that served with the battalion during this period. Its purpose is to add some humanity to the story. Histories of this kind normally give the names of the officers who were involved but seldom, if ever, actually tell you who these men were.

To understand this narrative clearly it is first necessary to know the way the British Army was organized. In simple terms, the basic unit was a section – four of these made up a platoon of about fifty men and there were four numbered platoons in a company (which also included a Company HQ) giving a total strength of roughly 230. When a company went into an attack about twenty men were left behind, their grim function being to form a cadre to train replacements for casualties. Of course, as the war progressed, the battalion was seldom up to full strength. Four companies designated A, B, C, and D jointly formed a battalion (Platoons No. 1 to 16). The strength of a battalion was roughly 1,000 men when account is taken of headquarters, transport, supplies, signals, cooks, etc. There were initially four battalions in a brigade and three brigades in a division; which in this instance was the 25th Infantry Brigade of the 8th Division and later, in the spring of 1918, the 107th Brigade of the 36th (Ulster) Division. At that time the strength of a brigade was reduced to three battalions.

Regimental Headquarters was little more than an administrative depot that served its battalions. The Royal Irish Rifles had twenty-one battalions during the Great War. The 1st and 2nd Battalions were the old regular units and had been formed by the amalgamation in 1881 of the 83rd (County of Dublin) and the 86th (County Down) Regiments of Foot. The 3rd, 4th, 5th, 17th, 18th, 19th, and 20th were Reserve Battalions; the 6th to the 16th were Service Battalions (for active service on a fighting front), and last was the 1st Garrison Battalion in India.

The usual rankings and abbreviations were:

Rifleman	Rfn
Lance Corporal	L/Cpl
Corporal	Cpl
Lance Sergeant	L/Sgt
Sergeant	Sgt

Company Sergeant Major	CSM Warrant Officer 2nd Class
Regimental Sergeant Major	RSM Warrant Officer 1st Class
Second Lieutenant	2/Lt.
Lieutenant	Lt.
Captain	Capt.
Major	
Lieutenant-Colonel	Lt.-Col., the CO of a battalion

Although volumes have been written about the Great War, there are few references to this regular unit. Most attention is concentrated on the fate of those volunteer battalions of Kitchener's Army. This disregards the fact that most members of regular units were, by the summer of 1915, of a similar ilk, as the *Old Contemptibles* (the regular soldiers who formed part of the original British Expeditionary Force) had long since ceased to exist in any appreciable numbers.

Cyril Falls wrote *The History of the First Seven Battalions: The Royal Irish Rifles in the Great War* in 1925. This excellent history is, by its nature, quite general dealing as it does with seven battalions. It has been quoted liberally throughout this book with the kind permission of the past Curator of the Royal Ulster Rifles Museum, Major M.B. Murphy.

The Royal Irish Rifles was a Belfast-based regiment but its regular battalions always included many members from all over Ireland.[1] There was a religious mix of Catholics, Protestants, and Dissenters, which was certainly not the case with the RIR Service Battalions of the 36th (Ulster) Division for most of the war. That division originally consisted of elements of the Ulster Volunteer Force (UVF) which was opposed to the imposition of Home Rule for Ireland. The Irish National Volunteers was set up in response to defend Home Rule and mainly joined the 10th and 16th (Irish) Divisions. Conscription was never introduced in Ireland. A remnant of the Irish Volunteers refused to follow the lead of their political leaders and was eventually to take the main role in the Easter Rebellion of 1916.

When one visits the 36th Division's memorial, the Ulster Tower, at Thiepval today it is hard to imagine that any Roman Catholics or Nationalists ever had a part in Ulster's military achievements in the Great War. This is the fault of both parts of the island of Ireland and, until recently, suited the objectives of each side. Northern Ireland was keen to display Britain's debt to her loyal subjects. The Irish Republic hardly acknowledged that her people took any part in the war and concentrated its historical education on the War of Independence. Inordinate amounts of people in the south were keen to claim that they had a relation in the General Post Office in Dublin during the Easter Rising of 1916. Few boasted the memory of kin who died in France, Belgium, Turkey, Egypt, Greece, and many other foreign lands. With an estimated 300,000 Irishmen in the British Forces during the Great War (roughly 30,000 of whom never returned) it is almost impossible, given our population, that there are any families who did not have at least one member involved in that conflict.

1 Fr Henry Gill SJ, DSO, MC, chaplain of 2nd RIR, December 1914: 'There was plenty to do as there were nearly 1,200 Catholics in the Brigade. About 70 per cent of the men of 2nd RIR were Catholics. Chiefly from the North of Ireland, but with a large sprinkling from the other parts of the Provinces.'

Over the intervening years, successive generations of schoolchildren in the Republic learned about Ireland's struggle for freedom from oppression. They never learned that, at times, the dreaded British Army included a large amount of Irish soldiers. It was inconceivable that the oppressors of the glorious heroes of Dublin in 1916 actually contained many Irish regimental units. Indeed, the Irish had always formed a disproportionate percentage of the British Army.

My grandmother's brother, 3/8826 Rifleman Edward Donnelly, No. 9 Platoon, C Company, was killed in action at Ovillers on 1 July 1916. Being very close, I knew that she never got over his loss. She had a few tattered letters that she read regularly and, when she died in 1970, they passed on to me. They were barely legible and I put them away safely and nearly forgot about them.

A few years ago I took out the letters again. It was obvious that he had just recently arrived at the front and the Somme offensive was to be his one and only contribution to the war effort. I started to correspond with various people enquiring as to the fate of his unit during the day's fighting. Regrettably, there was not a lot of information readily available. It soon became an obsession of mine to put together all the data I could find. Reading Martin Middlebrook's excellent *The First Day on the Somme* clarified much that was confusing to the beginner. Eventually I had garnered enough information and decided to compile a record of the battalion's activities for the entire war.

Edward Donnelly was born in the heart of the 'Monto' at 19 Beaver Street, Dublin, on 8 November 1891. He was the youngest of a family of six children. His father was a labourer with the Dublin Glass Bottle Works and his mother reared pigs in their back yard and sold seconds of military equipment purchased from the Junior Army and Navy Store in D'Olier Street. They all resided at 50 Railway Street in one of the poorest areas of the city and notorious for its red-light district. Ned, as he was known, had a typical hard life in the disease-ridden tenements of the inner city. When he was fifteen he went to Philadelphia, having been invited over by an uncle. This was Ned's chance for a better life but he was too homesick and returned to Dublin within eighteen months. He trained as an electrician and became great friends with James Thompson Taylor who lived just around the corner in Foley Street. James was the son of Scots Presbyterian immigrants and his father worked as an engineer at Dublin Port. Over time James became infatuated with Ned's sister, Nora, but she would not allow him to court her, as she was a Roman Catholic. Secretly, James took religious instruction and was baptized at Gardiner Street Church in 1910. His father created a furore with the church authorities over this as James was only nineteen and had not received his parent's permission to convert. Eventually a settlement was reached, James and Nora being married on 8 January 1911. Ned was the best man and Nora's friend, Katie Devereux, was bridesmaid. It wasn't long before a romance struck up between Ned and Katie and they eventually married. Katie had two miscarriages and remained childless. Ned continued with his work and, in the autumn of 1915, he and two friends were sent by their employer to complete an electrical contract in Govan, Glasgow. One evening in a bar, while they were well under the influence, they were approached by a group of women who handed them white feathers. This was an accusation of cowardice and the three men responded by immediately enlisting. Ned had no fondness for his employer and it did not take much for him to consider another option. Indeed, in a letter to James sent from the trenches, he advised:

> If I was you I would stick the job you are in. I have been in the other one and I know it does not pay. You know the way the Gaffers in it treated me. I was never out of trouble. You can never do enough work day and night for less money than the job you have. When this war is over I am not going to work for him again.

In October 1915 he went to 3rd RIR at Portobello Barracks, Dublin, for training. This battalion was one of the main sources of replacements for the active service units of the regiment. The barracks were intended for use by two battalions but, at the time of the rebellion, quartered about 600 men, half of whom would have been on duty outside the barracks. Ned got caught up in the Easter Rising in Dublin from 24 to 30 April 1916. Many soldiers from various regiments flocked to the barracks for duty and protection. This resulted in confusion and a lack of communication due to unfamiliarity. The Royal Commission of Enquiry described the atmosphere at the time:

> On the 24th and 25th April various alarming rumours were current as to an impending attack on the barracks, and as to various alleged successes of the rebel forces, and undoubtedly at the time both officers and men thought that they were in serious peril, which could only be averted by taking strong measures for the safety of the troops and the barracks.

It was in these barracks on 26 April that Capt. J.C. Bowen-Colthurst, 3rd RIR, murdered three innocent civilian prisoners. His trial started on 6 June at Richmond Barracks, Dublin. Statements were made by two of the seven members of the firing squad, 5643 Fred McFuigan and 6900 Michael Ireland, both of 3rd RIR, and their Sergeant, 7149 John Maxwell, gave lengthy evidence at the trial. Eventually Colthurst was found guilty but insane and imprisoned at His Majesty's pleasure. Two years later he was freed on pension and emigrated to Canada, dying there in 1965.

After the rebellion 3rd RIR moved to Belfast but Ned went to France. A comrade reported that he was hit by shrapnel in no-man's-land during the attack of 1 July 1916 and lost part of his foot. He was placed in a shell-hole but was buried alive by a subsequent explosion and officially reported as wounded and missing. His body was not recovered and he is remembered on the Thiepval Memorial. His wife was later to die in the influenza epidemic of 1918 and was buried in a pauper's grave.

A brother, 42638 Pte John Donnelly, survived service with 99 Company, Machine Gun Corps, although his wife also died in the epidemic. Their brother-in-law, 9461 Pte George Wolfe, 2nd Royal Dublin Fusiliers, died in Belgium, 10 May 1915, a week after he had arrived in the trenches for the first time. They had all resided at the same address.

Lt.-Col. G.B. Laurie wrote to his wife, 30 November 1914: 'My mind is so full at present that I cannot say if I shall be able to write ours [the Regimental History of the War], even if I come through all right. However, I keep an official War Diary, which will always help greatly.'

The primary source for a history of this kind is the War Diary. In May 1918 a small book was published called *Hints for Adjutants in the Field*. It noted that there was actually no military manual that explained the duties of an adjutant. The chapter on the War Diary states:

> This important document is known as Army Form C 2118. It is usually in the keeping of the adjutant, though some Commanding Officers prefer to keep it to themselves; and as it is in many battalions the only record of an historical nature which is kept at all, it is essential that it should be written up fully and accurately. I regret to record that I have met adjutants who consider the War Diary to be one of the monthly returns. True it has to be forwarded to Brigade monthly by a certain date, but it is not a return. It is History! The War Diaries of battalions will be the only accurate histories available after this war of the part played by each Infantry Regiment engaged in it, and an adjutant must bear in mind that unless he keeps this daily record carefully and describes the events of each day, no matter how monotonous they may seem, accurately, he will be defeating the object of the whole thing and possibly depriving future generations of a mass of historical facts. Especially after an action must he write up his War Diary when the events of the battle are fresh in his mind, copies of the Operational Orders issued before the battle should be attached, names of all casualties should be entered, and by no means least the Honours awarded to the battalion and to whom awarded. Historians complain that it will be almost impossible to write the history of this war when it is over. They would have no such complaint if War Diaries had been kept as they ought to have been kept.

Unfortunately, the War Diary of 1st RIR was not as detailed as it could have been and much information has, therefore, been lost to posterity. A good effort was made when Col. Laurie was commanding in the early phase of the war. But, in general, it omitted to record many details: for example, officers are noted as being struck off the strength but there is no note of their arrival or return, and many awards for bravery were omitted. Details of what the battalion was doing while not actually in the firing line are scant. This is by way of explanation rather than criticism. It should be remembered that, at times, the diary was written up in atrocious conditions or while the orderly room was under fire. An adjutant was not someone who stayed behind during attacks. In the course of the war two of the adjutants were killed in action and some of the others had several narrow escapes. A comparison shows that the diary of 2nd RIR was nearly twice as long although they were abroad only two months longer.

The 8th Division was the last of the Regular divisions to cross to France in 1914. In his Foreword to the division's history in 1926 Earl Haig wrote: 'In the major offensives in which it took a direct part the 8th Division, despite unfailing gallantry, was signally unfortunate.' It will be seen that 1st Royal Irish Rifles had very little success during the war although they were wiped out several times.

Early days

Apart from a short spell in Burma, the 1st Battalion of the Royal Irish Rifles had been stationed in India since the turn of the century. Lt.-Col. G.B. Laurie arrived from England to take over command in 1912 and, the following year, the battalion moved from Kamptee to the port of Aden, now in Yemen. Aden commanded the entrance to the Red Sea and was then a part of British India. It was their job to defend vital points against sabotage – the power station, the condensing plants, and the cables from the forts to the station at the top of Shum-Shum. During this time Col. Laurie finished writing his history of the regiment.

The battalion mobilized on 6 August 1914 when the war stage of the Aden Defence Scheme was ordered. Headquarters, and companies that were located at the Crater, marched to Steamer Point and, joining with the detachment there, occupied the British infantry barracks. At this time C Coy was stationed at Kirkee, near Poona, in India. The battalion occupied its place in the Harbour Defence Force and was actively employed in strengthening the defences of the fortress over the next few weeks.

> We had by night patrolled the beaches to guard against a surprise landing by the German cruiser *Konigsberg*, and as soon as we had come off patrol we practised our marching powers round Aden in preparation for the trek through Germany. We had furnished prize crews for German ships which, deficient of wireless, had innocently entered the harbour on what they thought were their lawful occasions, and we had had a little jaunt up to Perim to capture the truculent ship's company of the SS *Lindenfeld*, an 8,000-ton Hansa Line cargo boat.[1] This operation entailed a surprise boarding of the ship in the dark, the securing of the crew, and working the ship down to Aden with the help of a navigator and two engineers from the Indian Marine Guardship *Dalhousie*.
>
> In the course of this private war, conducted by 'Jacko' (Captain A.J. Biscoe) and myself with thirty of the toughest nuts we could find (RSM Clarke being amongst them), the German wireless operator's jaw connected with the fist of

1 Perim is now called Barîm and is an island located at the narrow junction of the Red Sea with the Gulf of Aden. All the quotations in this chapter about the voyage home come from an anonymous article, *The Cruise of the Dilwara*, that appeared in *Quis Separabit*, vol. 3, no. 1, May 1932. I suspect this was written by F.R.W. Graham.

Map 1: The Western Front

Rifleman Hutcheson, producing a sound sleep of nearly twenty hours. I must say the back of the man's head hit the iron deck as well, although Hutcheson was heavyweight champion of India.

The German engineers nearly sank the ship by opening the seacocks, and had to be induced, none too gently, to close them again, and I sat on top of a hatch containing 20,000 dozen bottles of Lager Beer all the way from Perim to Aden lest the thirsty ones should quench their thirst. We arrived in Aden with a list of ten degrees, six feet of water in the hold, and rather relieved to find ourselves on dry land again.

A squad, under the command of Lt. J.W. Foley, then escorted all of these prize ships to Bombay.

C Coy rejoined on 16 August and an officer, with 116 men of this company, was dispatched to reinforce the garrison of Perim. The battalion was detained in Aden until anxiety about the problems in Somaliland was allayed. On 27 September, under special orders for home, they embarked on HM Transport *Dilwara* that had brought 1st Lancashire Fusiliers from Karachi to relieve them at Aden.

At last the great day arrived, and the old *Dilwara* was signalled – and she was old: her sister ship, the *Dunera*, took the 1st Battalion to the Cape in '97, and she wasn't new then. She was one of those funny old ships with three masts and one funnel – the saloon aft and the cabins opening out of it. On board she had 178 officers' wives and children belonging to the Indian contingent, and they had been waiting in Karachi for nearly a month before sailing. Many of these poor ladies were already widows by the time they had landed at Liverpool.

We had just got on board about 6 p.m., when a cable arrived from England saying that the *Dilwara* was to load all available S.A.A. surplus in Aden. I don't know how many hundreds of boxes we stowed that night – from the derricks to the ammunition room, on both sides of the ship, we formed two lines and passed the ammunition down by hand. In that heat we all, officers and men, worked stripped to the waist and with only a pair of shorts on. By 11 p.m. we had the whole lot on board, and went ashore for a last farewell at the Club.

The following day they sailed for England with a strength of 19 officers and 999 men, including the prize guard from Bombay and four Reservists from India.

The half hour before Mess in the salon used to be perfect pandemonium. We subalterns used to volunteer to look after the children whilst their mothers dressed for dinner. Every few minutes a child, having been placed on the table and ordered to 'stay put' until such time as its temporary nurse had obtained a pink gin for himself, would fall with a thud on the deck. The piercing howl that followed brought the entire pack of mammas from the surrounding cabins in all stages of undress and like a swarm of angry bees, buzzing to see whose offspring was in trouble. However, after a little experience, we found that gin judiciously administered in small quantities to our charges, added greatly to the peace of the ship. They 'stayed put' better, and the volume of sound emitted on hitting the deck was greatly reduced.

A man we all felt sorry for on that ship was the Chief Steward. He had a rotten time. Perhaps his worst trial was when the cold store went wrong. He tried his best to disguise the fact, but when some of the ladies complained of the bad smells about the ship and then looked sideways at us as if they thought the battalion might be responsible for them, something had to be done. All fresh food went overboard in the night, and we lived mostly on bread and jam until we got to Port Said ... Except for the next ahead (the *Gurkha*, with, I think, the Rifle Brigade on board, who suddenly turned out of the line with defective steering gear and did her best to ram Arabia) all went well; and we hurtled through the Red Sea throwing up clouds of spray from our bows at nearly 8 knots.

Two days out of Suez, however, the doctor appeared with a face as long as a horse to say we had eight cases of suspected Berri-Berri. Amongst them, as far as I remember, Colour-Sergeant Kendrick and Sergeant Motum. Again we had visions of quarantine on arrival and not getting to the war in time. As it turned out, even if we had cholera on board, we should have been pushed straight into it.

On arrival at Suez we said goodbye to our escort, the *Swiftsure* and *Black Prince* ... A night which few of us who saw it will ever forget, was our convoy of 42 ships passing through the Canal in batches of five and anchoring in Port Said harbour. Each unit manned ship and the band played its Regimental March and the National Anthem as she anchored. The harbour was packed with warships and craft of all nations. We got a tremendous reception. Every foreign ship capable of producing musical noises played its own and our National Anthem on every known instrument from a single concertina upwards to a full band.

The next day, one of our poor fellows having died the day before, we paraded and buried him at the Port Said Cemetery, the whole Battalion turning out and doing a route march round the town afterwards.[2] This walk at an ultra rifle step was most trying. It is astounding how even a week on board a ship softens one's feet.

At this stage of the voyage we did not yet know whether we were going home first or going direct to Marseilles. All we knew was that we remained at Port Said for forty-eight hours, and having got leave to go ashore that night, we proceeded to make the most of it, and decided to dine at the Casino Palace Hotel ... The next morning we sailed [with the French battleship *Bouvet* as escort], and incidentally got our first impression of the realities of war. Not five miles outside Port Said and just clear of the Channel, sticking up out of the water were the masts and a funnel of a ship sunk by a submarine three days previously. From then onwards it was a case of darkened ports and no smoking on deck between dusk and dawn.

We made another discovery that morning. To our amazement we saw under the forecastle head seven animals. On closer inspection they turned out to be

2 I was unable to identify this soldier.

seven shadows of cows. On making further inquiries, we were told that as it had been impossible to mend the cold store we had to eat these animals gradually. Each night one was murdered by the Regimental butcher and his assistant ghouls, all evidence of the crime being concealed before daybreak. Death, even at the hands of the Regimental butcher, must have been a merciful release: for many years these cows had been turning the water wheels of Egypt.

From now onwards the voyage became uneventful. We, with three other ships, were switched off from the convoy in the Gulf of Lyons and proceeded home, the remainder going direct to Marseilles. Ten days later the *Dilwara*, in a dense fog, fetched up three hundred yards off the Mersey Bank. As our skipper said, 'I can see nothing, I don't know where I am. So I think I had better drop the hook.' When the fog cleared, that's where we were.

HMS *Euryalus* had escorted the battalion, together with 2nd Rifle Brigade, 1st Suffolk Regt, and 2nd Berkshire Regt, as far as the English Channel. Two Riflemen had died on the journey home and one was hospitalized at Gibraltar. Having voyaged in company with the transports of the Indian Expeditionary Force as far as Malta from Gibraltar, the Irish Rifles landed at Liverpool, 22 October.

We landed the unfortunate Berri-Berri cases, and were preparing to disembark ourselves when disaster overtook us – a dog was seen! 'No', said the Port authorities. 'No dog is to be landed at any price – couldn't be done.' We told the Port authorities what fine fellows they were, we begged and we blustered – they had their orders and nothing would move them.

The only thing then to be done was to form a committee and find a formula which would save their faces and ours, and so allow the pets to be landed.

Now the most important livestock consisted of *Hermes*, an Arab pony, the winner of many races in India, and in later years the charger of successive adjutants; *Ugly*, a cross-bred harrier, the last survivor of the Maymo pack, and owned by Charles Newport; and last but not least, *Nellie*, a Spaniel bitch, the mother of literally thousands of pie puppies, and owned by Jimmie Gartlan. He it was who eventually found the formula. 'Land them as war dogs', he said, and as war dogs they were landed.

The battalion immediately departed that evening for Hursley Park Camp, Winchester, in two trains, arriving early the next morning with a strength of 19 officers and 996 men. At this time the composition was 77 per cent Irishmen with the remainder coming from Great Britain. 1st RIR, together with 2nd Rifle Brigade, 2nd Lincolnshire Regt, and 2nd Royal Berkshire Regt, formed the 25th Infantry Brigade under Brigadier-General A.W.G. Lowry Cole, and, joining with the 23rd and 24th Brigades, the 8th Division was born. The division commenced refitting immediately and was destined to join the British Expeditionary Force for Europe with the 7th Division in IV Corps under the command of Sir Henry Rawlinson. Some difficulty was experienced in obtaining new equipment, harnesses, and the like. The camp was a quagmire of mud though, fortunately, the weather was mild. A draft composed of about 200 men, from 3rd RIR and the Reserve, together with twelve attached officers was waiting for them. The reservists were found to be very indifferently drilled and seemed to have poor musketry training. They also had to become acquainted with a new (to them) short service rifle. During this period of refitting the Brigade Parades somewhat hindered the process and the men, after nearly a year in Aden and a long sea voyage, were not in marching trim. On 5 November the battalion marched by road to Southampton in the rain and embarked on SS *Anglo-Canadian* with a strength of 31 officers and 1014 men. The details and the first reinforcements were left behind. Having arrived at Le Havre at 2 a.m., after a smooth crossing, they remained in the outer harbour until early next morning, disembarking at 9 a.m. and marching through the town to No. 1 Rest Camp. Col. Laurie recorded on 8 November:

> The sun is finally dispersing the fog, so we shall get an opportunity of drilling together. We have practically never done so yet; and I am really appalled at what might be the consequences of going into action with the men unpractised. Few of them have been on active service before, and it will all have to be taught under fire.

Shortages in equipment were made up there and, over the next two days, marches and manoeuvres took place. The CO noted that his men were very willing but very troublesome – they lost themselves and fell out on every pretext. On the night of 9 November they left Le Havre aboard a train with fifty carriages and moved north via Rouen, Abbeville, and Calais, then south-east via St Omer and Hazebrouck to Strazil, arriving at about 1.30 a.m. on the 11th, and rested in two barns for the night. That morning at 9 a.m. they marched to billets in the vicinity of Vieux Berquin; A and B Coys, together with Headquarters, were located near La Brionne Farm; D Coy and one platoon of C were located on the Vieux Berquin–Neuf Berquin Road. Col. Laurie wrote:

> In the hay barn I have 50 men, 100 men and 11 horses in the stables, and 16 officers in the house, with all the remainder somewhere near me. It is colder and has been blowing up a gale up to now, but I expect it will turn to rain again when the wind drops. I was inspected this morning by a superior General: am rather tired of inspections! From where we sit we can see the flash of the shells bursting in front of our position. We hear all sorts of reports as to what is happening. I fancy it is fairly even balanced fighting of a very hard sort ... I only wish that something would happen to end the war with honour to ourselves.

Their stay here was pleasant enough with the French inhabitants being very ready to do everything to assist them. One farm, occupied by HQ, had been looted by the Germans who had practically cleared the house of food but the occupants did a great trade with the troops in the way of bread, etc. Deficiencies in equipment were still being made good here within sound of the German guns for the first time. Advantage was taken during the available time to practise a little manoeuvre and route marching. Orders were received on the 13th for the whole division to advance by marches to Laventie (3.7 miles south-west of Armentieres, 6.8 miles north of La Bassée, and 2.5 miles north of Neuve Chapelle). They arrived there, in their second billets, the following night. This town, including a fine church, had been partially destroyed by German shellfire, and the battalion was now within range of enemy guns and occasional shells were falling to the south-west. The troops marched off to take their place in the trenches for the first time during the afternoon of 15 November. They were now a little over a mile north-east of Fauquissart in the flat country between Armentieres and La Bassée Canal, the only front it was to know until the opening of the Somme battle in the summer of 1916. The 8th Division was to relieve the Lahore Division (Indian Army) in the Laventie area, near the scene of 2nd RIR's bitter fighting during the previous months. They came under fire when advancing along the road, but this appeared to have been directed against one of the British batteries that was in action close by. At about 9 p.m. they entered F Lines of the division at Rue Tilleloy where they were to stay for the next seven days. Two men were killed while occupying these trenches, the battalion's baptism of fire in this war, 6795 Rfn Hamilton Orr of B Coy, age 30, from Newtownards, Co. Down, and 9838 Rfn Robert Sparrow, age 21, from Dublin. A new cemetery was established by the battalion at Laventie that was called Red House Cemetery.[3]

The front line, at that time, consisted of a series of scattered posts joined by trenches that were mere scratchings in the ground and already flooded. During this tour they were subjected to continual sniping by day and night and A Coy suffered from the fire of high explosive shells. 'At the end of twenty-four hours there was an outcry that rifles were clogged, and insistent demand for paraffin and old socks to clean them.'[4] Col. Laurie arranged with the Medical Officer to have one man trained in the use of morphine so that those who were badly wounded might die in peace. The German VII Corps opposed them in this position. Minor attacks were made on the British line, but without any real vigour, and a sap was pushed out by the Germans against A Coy's trenches. Officers' patrols visited the German trenches at intervals during the night and obtained valuable information: principally that the Germans kept very few men in their front trenches at night. Great difficulty was experienced in communicating with A Coy's trenches on the right owing to the length of the position allotted to the battalion and the absence of telephone communication. This was subsequently established but was generally unreliable. The front held by 1st RIR was so long that messages took ninety minutes to be received at Battalion HQ from its furthest company. In one part of the line there were only 50 Riflemen to 250 yards of trench. A great deal of improvements was made in deepening the trenches and making traverses but, in spite of this, men were frequently hit by snipers. On 18 November a Rifleman was shot out of a tree where he was posted as a sentry, protected by sandbags, but the German sniper was also hit. Owing to a report that the German VII Corps had vacated their trenches, officers' patrols went out that night and found that the enemy trenches were actively held, losing one man in the process. Col. Laurie:

3 Red House Cemetery was renamed (13th) London Graveyard after it was taken over for burials by that battalion, the Kensingtons, in December 1914. Another cemetery started by 1st RIR at this time was the Royal Irish Rifles Graveyard, Rue du Bacquerot, Laventie.   4 Falls. All quotations attributed to Falls come from the Regimental History and not the 36th Divisional History.

November 20th … I am now in the trenches in the snow, and it was very cold indeed last night. Can you picture such conditions, lying out in it after dark? All my poor men feel the change very much, coming from the heat of Aden. However, it is business … Fifty Germans attacked a few of our men; I stood revolver in hand and watched it, as we gradually drove them back. This morning at daybreak our men are reported to have shot two men of a burying party, so there must have been casualties. Still, one is sorry for the burial party.

November 21st … This procession was a walk with stooping heads, bullets raining in through the loopholes, and frantic runs along ditches beside hedges. I crawled completely doubled up. Suddenly a sniper would see some part of me showing, and would then let drive at me. I had to duck, and then run like a hare until I got to a bank which gave some protection.

During these seven days the men's feet suffered severely from the wet in the trenches followed by three days frost with snow on the ground. Total casualties for this tour were 10 men killed, 29 wounded and 2 missing. Col. Laurie:

November 23rd … Such a business as it was getting out of the trenches. Of course, my men could not leave until the others were in place; then they had to change back to their roads through the trenches, practically so narrow that they could not pass without stepping over each other, and these three miles long. Well, the result of all that was, moving off at 4.30 p.m., we collected at a road two miles back at two in the morning. Just think of it! There was snow and 15 degrees of frost, and we were awfully cold. We got back to our billets at 3 a.m. … Did it ever occur to you how difficult it is to feed 1,000 men in a trench three miles long when you can only get in at the ends? It took from 5 p.m. to 10 o'clock to get and give them their teas, and then from 3 a.m. to half-past six to give them their breakfast and their food for the day, whilst all the time the enemy was fighting and shooting, and one has to judge to a nicety where to keep everyone until the rations were issued, so that in case the Germans should suddenly rush us we should have enough to repel them.

Having been relieved by 2nd Lincolns in the early hours of the 22nd, they marched into billets not far to the rear of the trenches. During this period the Divisional Commander, Major-General F.J. Davies, inspected them, and Major J.W. Alston, Capt. E.B. Jones, and Lt. P.J.L. Davies, were transferred to 2nd RIR.

The battalion returned to the same trenches on the afternoon of 24 November for three days and was subjected to continuous sniping from the Germans. Time was spent on improvements to the communication trenches, but great difficulty was experienced in keeping a telephone connection to A Coy on the right owing to the line being badly laid. Not much happened this time beyond night reconnaissances and midnight shooting; the Germans were not inclined to attack but actively shelled localities to the rear of the trenches. A furious Laurie noted that 'A man looked into one of my loopholes during the night, and told my men that he was an Engineer mending our wire, and the silly fellows thoroughly believed him. I am certain he was a German.' Casualties on this tour were 3 men killed and 7 wounded. During the evening of 27 November the battalion went into billets at Ft D'Esquin, which consisted of ruined farms immediately behind the front line, leaving C Coy in reserve at Rue Masselot and D at the reserve trenches in the rear of F Lines. Nothing special was recorded during the time spent there except that the enemy continually shelled the vicinity of their billets, particularly those of A Coy. A French woman was suspected of being a spy and of directing the fire of the Germans, but the General Staff would not allow civilians to be arrested due to the objections of the French authorities. At this time the Army started to distribute goatskin coats to the troops in order to ease their suffering from the cold. Apart from the Colonel, men were only allowed 35 pounds of kit, which meant that heavier clothing could not be kept.

On the afternoon of 30 November they reoccupied the trenches in F Lines. Many men were left behind this time with trench foot – a complaint that was very prevalent throughout the division. This was caused by the wet conditions in the trenches and manifested itself by the sufferer's feet and ankles becoming swollen and discoloured until they looked like lumps of raw meat. The men wrapped their legs in straw, tied sandbags around them and rubbed them with whale oil when that became available.

Instructions were received that special efforts were to be made to capture a prisoner in order to identify the German regiments opposing the division, as it was thought that the enemy's VII Corps had been withdrawn. All attempts were unsuccessful due to bright moonlight in which the Germans kept strictly to their trenches at night. Several patrols were sent out to supplement the information obtained; the enemy to the right front was wearing dark blue uniforms, those opposite the centre and left were wearing the German service uniform. Before leaving Ft D'Esquin each company selected two NCOs and Riflemen per platoon as company sharpshooters to keep down the fire of the enemy snipers which had been accounting for most of the casualties. These men undoubtedly restrained the enemy's sniping and the casualties were reduced accordingly. The principal item of interest this time was the advancing of a German sap opposite B Coy, which was brought to within 40 yards of the Irish trenches. Machine gun fire was directed on to the wire entanglements placed in front of the sap to keep the enemy at bay. On this tour 6 men were wounded.

Having been relieved, 3 December, the battalion was detailed as Corps Reserve and marched six miles to new billets in Estaires. One group of 400 men was lodged in a granary that was four stories high; there was only one ladder and it took half an hour to get them out each morning. This was the first time since 10 November that they were not under fire and, also, the first time since they landed in Le Havre that they could sleep with their boots off. The whole battalion attended the Divisional Bath; the men marched there by companies and received a complete change of clothing. It was noted in the War Diary that, in one or two of the billets, the French people with whom particular companies and units were located showed a decided aversion to having them there, and in one case were all 'out for trouble'. In others, however, they were very ready to do anything they could to help. This difficulty was the first that the troops had met with from occupants of houses in which they had been billeted. They returned to F Lines, 6 December, having to change their route to avoid Laventie Station and the surrounding roads due to the shellfire being directed against it. Capt. B. Allgood, the first officer to be killed, was shot through the heart while taking his men into the trenches. The time normally taken for the relief to be carried out was two hours. It commenced at 5.30 p.m. and, generally, relieved companies were clear between 7 p.m. and 9.30 p.m. except when the trenches were very wet. The first reinforcement of seventy men arrived, coming straight into the trenches. These were mostly made up of 1st and 3rd RIR men that had been left behind at Winchester. Other casualties were one man killed and 6 wounded.

The battalion arrived in billets on 9 December leaving A Coy in Local Reserve at Rue Masselot and B in Local Reserve at Picantin. Since leaving Le Havre, they had now been one month in the field. Total losses, inclusive of all ranks, were 18 killed, 47 wounded, and 167 sick. It can be seen that almost 72 per cent of the total were lost, not as a result of enemy action, but nearly all from frostbite and sore feet. Owing to persistent rain, the state of the trenches was very bad and knee deep in mud when the battalion returned on the 12th. One Sergeant of the Lincolns had to be dug out of a communication trench running between A and B Coys; faggots were used extensively to reduce the mud in places, but the general length of the firing trenches was very bad. The Germans adopted a trick of firing volleys, by three or four men, at the loopholes and were a little more active in shelling where they thought the guns might be. The 24th Infantry Brigade was withdrawn, 14 December, and 25th Brigade took over D Lines in addition to F Lines. One company from each battalion of the brigade was now in reserve. In the case of 1st RIR, A Coy from the right moved into the farmhouse next to that known as Corner Farm in Rue du Bois. HQ was removed from the dug out near the support trenches, 400 yards back to Corner Farm, a small three-roomed public house built in 1779, which was 1,100 yards from the German line. Orders were received that the brigade was to adopt a more aggressive attitude to give the enemy the impression that the trenches were held in great strength. During the afternoon of the 14th, and throughout 15 December, the opportunity was taken to train the reinforcements and bursts of rapid fire were kept up against the German trenches. The gunners also vigorously shelled the enemy. The first result of this was to keep down the German sniping which had become too lively. Activity on the part of patrols at night was hampered by the appalling state of the ground; trenches and dugouts collapsed in some places and the men were nearly up to their thighs in muddy water and liquid mud. Rain fell at intervals during the day and all efforts to improve the trenches were wasted. A relieved Laurie wrote home, 14 December, that 'this morning I was lucky in getting hold of a German helmet. The Divisional General has been screaming for one for days, as we wish to find out what troops are in front of us. I have had patrols prowling about everywhere at nights trying to catch a prisoner.'

On 15th orders were received to change dispositions in the trenches due to the withdrawal of 24th Brigade towards Armentieres. Three companies were in the trenches with one in reserve in Rue du Bois. The rate of fire, particularly artillery, was kept up uniformly throughout the 16th. A draft of one officer and 93 men arrived the following day and one of these was wounded while marching into the trenches. A small proportion of this group had never even fired a rifle, which indicated the severe pressure that the BEF was now under. During an attack by 23rd Brigade against the German trenches in front of Neuve Chapelle, 18 December, the battalion was employed in demonstrating against the enemy's trenches opposite its own lines. Col. Laurie:

> In the morning, when the troops returned, the Germans caught the company moving with shell, and only that Major Baker and myself flew for our lives and hurried people about, we should have lost a lot. I have seldom used worse language! It had its comic side, too, for several of the men got so frightened that they fell into a cesspit in trying to take cover, and two were knocked over and wounded … Two more of my fellows were badly hit at the same time, and I had to send a man to give them morphia while awaiting the doctor.

On withdrawal to Ft D'Esquin on the 21st, one company was left in local reserve in Rue du Bois and another in Rue Masselot, out of range of rifle fire but well within range of shell fire. Casualties were 5 men killed, 24 wounded and one missing.

2

The Christmas truce

During the afternoon of 23 December the battalion moved out to the trenches again to relieve 2nd Lincolns. They occupied E Lines for the first time, with HQ situated on Rue Tilleloy near the junction of Rue Masselot and Rue Tilleloy, where a draft of 64 men arrived.[1] The report by the Company Officers on this draft was that their physique was fairly good and their general efficiency fair but their musketry skills were not up to standard. Regular Reservists were rusty and Special Reservists could not work their rifle bolts well, but they improved with special instructions in the trenches; their discipline was, however, very poor.

On Christmas Eve, Col. Laurie told his men that they were not to fire on the enemy the following day unless they came under fire first, but not to trust them in any way. He recorded: 'One of my men there had to be carried away with his eye knocked out by a bullet which had come through the parapet.' The German front line trench was only 100 yards away and nothing of major importance occurred until 8 p.m. when, heralded by all sorts of celebrations from their trenches, the Germans placed lamps on their parapets and commenced singing Christmas carols and other songs. The 13th London Regiment (Kensingtons), attached to 25th Brigade, was on the left of the battalion. Their regimental history noted:

> We were a little embarrassed by this sudden comradeship and, as a lasting joke against us, let it be said that the order was given to stand to arms. But we did not fire, for the battalion on our right, The Royal Irish Rifles, with their national sense of humour, answered the enemy's salutations with songs and jokes and made appointments in no-man's-land for Christmas Day.

The Germans shouted out 'Do not shoot after twelve o'clock, and we will not do so either.' Then, at about 11 p.m., they called 'If you English come out and talk to us – we won't fire.' One Rifleman ventured across and was not fired at; instead he was given a cigar and told to go back. A German officer came out next, and asked for a two-day truce but the Irish Rifles only agreed to one. The Riflemen then came out and both they and the Germans met half way between their respective trenches and conversed. A large number of the Germans spoke English, were well clothed, clean shaven, and of a good

1 HQ was 400 yards from the front line and, at this point, it was another 400 yards to the German line.

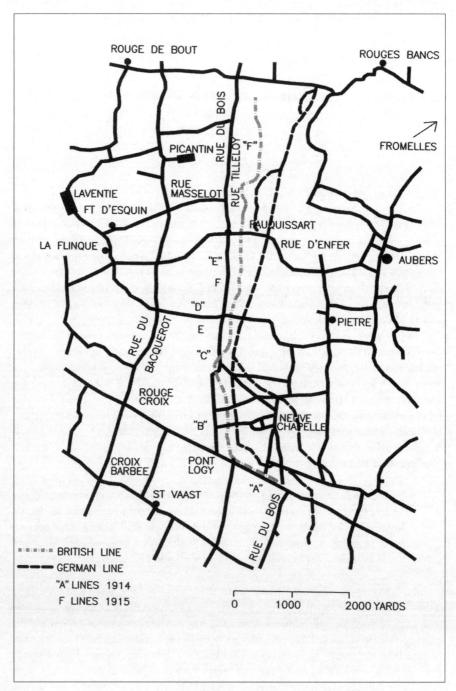

Map 2: Laventie area

physique but rather inclining to extremes of age. The Kensingtons were hesitant to venture forward until they saw the RIR greeting the enemy 'in the friendliest possible manner'. Col. Laurie:

> December 25th … Then we saw both sides, English and German, begin to swarm out to meet each other; we thought it wiser to keep our men in, because we did not trust the Germans, so I rang up the General to tell him this. We had to station sentries on the trenches to keep the men back; they were so eager to talk to the Germans. Then I offered to go across myself and learn what I could, and finally the German General asked me to send one of our officers over to them. This I did, and gave the latter, as an ostensible reason, the *Daily Telegraph* of December 22nd, which I had got hold of, and which contained a very fair account of the troubles in Austria–Hungary and Berlin. He went out with this paper, met some German officers, and discovered a certain amount.
>
> They were very anxious to know if the Canadian Division had arrived, whether our trenches were very muddy, and told him that our rifle fire was good. We said that our rifle fire in general was our weak point, etc., etc. … You have no idea how pleasant everything seems with no rifle bullets or shells flying about. I need hardly tell you that we have kept our men ready in the trenches all the same, as we do not trust our friends further than we can see them.

The following signals were exchanged between Col. Laurie and Brigade HQ on this curious situation:

> 8.30 p.m. Germans have illuminated their trenches, are singing songs and are wishing us a Happy Xmas. Compliments are being exchanged but am nevertheless taking all military precautions.

Message from Brigade:

> 9 p.m. Following instructions from GHQ for information and necessary action begins. It is thought possible that enemy may be contemplating an attack during Xmas or New Year. Special vigilance will be maintained during this period.

From OC 1st RIR:

> 11.45 p.m. Germans before my Regiment state they will not fire until midnight 25th/26th unless we fire. No shot has been fired since 8 p.m. A small party of one company met Germans half way and conversed. 158th Regiment [25th Brigade, VII (Westphalian) Corps], fine men, clean and well clothed. (They gave us a cap and helmet badge and a box of cigars. One of them states the war would be over in 3 weeks as they had defeated Russia!) A large number of Germans came out of their trenches, which appeared quite as strongly held as ours. Digging and erection of wire continued. All Companies have been cautioned to be doubly alert. German trenches still illuminated.

From Brigade:

> 12.35 a.m. No communication of any sort is to be held with the enemy nor is he to be allowed to approach our trenches under penalty of fire being opened.

This situation continued throughout a very cold night. At dawn on a frosty Christmas Day, the Germans shouted out 'Merry Christmas' from their trenches and danced and sang in front of their parapets.

  Message from Brigade:

> 8.40 a.m. 8th Division message begins – so long as Germans do not snipe, there should be no sniping from our lines today but greatest vigilance must be maintained, as Germans are not to be trusted. Our guns will not be firing today unless asked to do so by Infantry or unless German guns fire.

From OC 1st RIR:

> 11.30 a.m. Progress report. All very quiet along my front. Has been no sound of sniping on either flank even for some time. Situation seems evolving into a kind of mutual armistice ending at 12 midnight tonight. The restrictions are being observed by both sides. Germans are moving about on their parapets doing odd jobs which seem quite harmless. At dawn this morning enemy came out on their parapets and cheered and danced and called out 'Merry Xmas', etc. Reconnaissance last night points to conclusion that enemy's trenches and advanced posts were strongly held apart from those who were fraternising and singing. Position in our trenches is – careful guard by those held on duty while allowing those off duty to relax. This seems to be the German attitude also. (Later) Germans are now walking up and down outside their trenches. Our men are mostly in their trenches – those out are in rear of their parapets. Actual communication with the enemy is forbidden.

The War Diary recorded the following comments:

> It is very doubtful how one should regard this curious soldier's truce. The German soldiers themselves are probably simple minded enough about the thing but only time will show whether there is not something behind all this and whether we have not made a mistake in permitting this to take place.
>   The following notes are recorded:
>
> 1. The truce is sought entirely by the enemy.
> 2. The enemy have asked for two days of this which has been refused by the officers of the battalion in the firing line.
> 3. The mutual arrangement is that if either side construct works or carry out repairs to works that the other consider not playing the game, they will fire shots over the other side's heads.

4. Captain O'Sullivan, commanding B Coy of the battalion, will fire his revolver at 12 midnight tonight (25th/26th) at which signal the truce ends.

Only a few shots were fired by the enemy after the midnight signal was fired by Capt. O'Sullivan from our trenches. Shortly before midnight a party of Germans came over towards B Coy's trenches and were ordered back. During the morning of the 26th, the enemy fired very few shots. Some of our sentries were above their parapets and the Germans, throughout the morning, appeared to have no intention of opening fire on us.

The main concern was that the German infantrymen had been able to guarantee, the night before the truce, that there would be no firing by their artillery. Col. Laurie:

December 27th. Our strange sort of armistice continued throughout yesterday. The Germans told us they were all Landwehr men, and therefore not obliged to fight outside Germany except as volunteers, and that they did not intend to fight at present. Sure enough, though we shelled them and fired at them with rifles, they paid not the slightest attention. Whilst the shelling was on, they dodged down in their trenches, and popped up again when it was over. We hit one with a rifle, but they would not reply, we felt rather mean and fired over their heads.

At 4.45 p.m. the battalion, having been relieved by 2nd Lincolns, moved into Divisional Reserve near Laventie Station. A telephone message was received from Brigade HQ, 11.45 p.m., that a German deserter to the Kensington Rifles had stated that a German attack along the whole of the front was planned for 12.15 a.m. The Irish Rifles were ordered to turn out and take up a position at La Flinque crossroads; men were later placed in farms nearby and awaited further orders while passing an uncomfortable night. British guns opened a vigorous fire for about twenty minutes and that appeared to be all that happened; the Germans had, in fact, no plans for an attack that day. At 7 a.m. the following morning, the battalion received orders to move back to Laventie and the remainder of the day was spent in scraping off the trench mud and making up for lost sleep. A note in the War Diary recorded that 'the deserter who caused the alarm on the night of 26th/27th *unfortunately* did not fall into the battalions hands'. On the 28th they went to the Divisional Baths in Estaires where, the diary noted, 'Baths duly appreciated.' The following day the battalion returned to E Lines again for three days where the German 25th Infantry Brigade still opposed them. During this tour Capt. R.P. Miles, King's Shropshire Light Infantry attached to 1st RIR, was killed. Col. Laurie wrote home, 30 December:

They are up nearly to the waist in water, with little islands here and there for the men … Poor Capt. Miles, attached to me, was shot through the head. Being close by, I waded to him, but it was hopeless from the first. Such a place to die in! … I had plenty of morphia given to him, and he is now dying without any pain quite peacefully.

Drainage in the area could not be resolved, particularly where the ground frequently did not fall a yard in a mile. The year ended with a policy of building breastworks above ground level and that considerably improved the situation. Col. Laurie, in a letter to his wife, 18 January:

> I really sent the account of our Christmas luncheon to you. It was an RA Captain who lunched with us, and afterwards wrote to his people about it. They published the letter, and I found it in *The Times* I got from you.

The Times, 1 January 1915:

> An officer in the RFA writes on December 27th: On Christmas Eve things were very much as usual. It was a glorious afternoon and several aeroplanes were up which were duly shot at by the Germans. I went down to pass the time of day with an Infantry regiment down the road. The battery was firing but it was on a particular place which I could not observe. About 8 o'clock things went positively deaf; there was not a sound. Even our own pet sniper went off duty. As a rule he is relieved at 9.15 and sends what the telephonists call 'a good night kiss' at 9.15. We sat around a fire all evening, and about 11 o'clock a very excited Infantry officer came along and told us that all fighting was off, and his men were fraternising in between the trenches. We had seen lights flashing on the parapets earlier in the evening and there had been a good deal of noise going on. Shouts from the Germans – 'You English, why don't you come out?' and our bright knaves had replied with yells of 'Waiter' [a reference to the occupation of many Germans who worked in Britain before the war], but that had all been a good deal earlier. I walked down to the trenches with the man – we did not worry about walking down a communication trench, we just walked across a couple of fields, jumped over the parapet of our fire trench and went out beyond our own barbed wire. By that time all the men were back in their trenches and there was nothing much doing. They had lights on the parapets, and there was still a certain amount of noise, but no shooting. It had been agreed between the soldiers on both sides that there would be no firing until midnight Christmas Day.
>
> We went back to bed about 12.30 a.m. and stood to arms as usual on Christmas morning. I had a look round, and as nothing seemed to be doing, went along to see some other people, they confirmed the news of the truce. It was all arranged privately, and started by one of our fellows going across. I think he was rather brave to be the first to do it. I arranged to go down to their trenches after breakfast, as they have a place where they are only about 70 to 80 yards apart. Then the colonel and X came out to see the fun. They arrived about 11 o'clock and I was on my way back. You can hardly imagine it; the only sentries were two unarmed ones to keep the men from straying out beyond the barbed wire. All our fellows were digging in the open and theirs were doing the same. The only thing forbidden was to make any improvement to the barbed wire. Further, they agreed that if by any mischance a single shot were fired it was not to be taken as

an act of war, and an apology would be accepted; also that firing would not be opened without due warning on both sides.

Finally we all walked out and one of their officers came to meet us. We all saluted, shook hands, and exchanged cigarettes. Unfortunately they understood no French or English and we could not muster a word of German between us. You will rather gather that conversation languished. Finally they got a man out of the trenches who had lived in America and he acted as interpreter. The officers were little more than boys, and one of them had already been wounded. They were intensely polite and there was any amount of clicking of heels. The soldiers all seemed rather young, but they did not appear very despondent or underfed. One man informed us that they had been told that Russia had been defeated, and that the war would be over in three weeks. Another begged an officer on our side to send his photograph to his sister, who lives in Liverpool. I know that is true because the officer showed me the photo. Seems a strange idea to take a packet of ones photos on active service, but there you are! One thing we did notice was that some of them were shy of uniforms, but that may have been merely owing to the fact that they were in the trenches and trying to save their uniforms. The Germans were all for the truce lasting for 48 hours but we stuck out for midnight on Christmas.

Then we had lunch – pheasant and partridge, plum pudding, and paté de fois grace, washed down by rum and hot water, eaten in a house which really as a house was wasting its time. The upper floor has simply gone, and certainly half one wall of the room they live in. The pictures you see give a fair idea of what the places are like, and I suppose there is a risk in inhabiting them. They all have 'funk holes' dug close at hand and if Johnson gets busy everyone clears out. After lunch I went back to the observation post. The road along there is honestly, as a rule, rather infested with bullets; it seemed so strange to walk along it and never hear the whisper of one. X brought the sergeant-major out in the afternoon, and we walked along the front of our trenches for nearly two miles! The sergeant-major has not got over it yet; his remarks were 'It is 'ardly credible' and 'I never would 'ave believed it'.

3

1915

The New Year started with the battalion moving to Ft D'Esquin while two companies were left in Local Reserve at Rue Masselot and Picantin. The normal routine was one of three days in the line, three in Brigade reserve at Ft D'Esquin and three in Divisional reserve at Laventie which was no comfortable refuge, but there were opportunities to have baths in the brewery at La Gorgue. On 3 January a High Mass was held in a barn for the Roman Catholic members of the battalion and a draft of 55 men arrived. The War Diary commented indignantly:

> This draft apparently had practically no training, cannot even handle their arms and some cannot load their rifles properly. Altogether a slow, badly set up and untrained body of men – certainly not Riflemen.

After spending the next three days at E Lines, they moved back to Laventie where the last two drafts were collected and given a good stiff day of drill and musketry that improved them to the level where they could at least use their rifles. Col. Laurie returned to England for seven days leave on 6 January and Major Baker assumed temporary command.

> [Laventie] was repeatedly shelled, particularly on nights of relief, of which the enemy always had accurate knowledge, possibly from overhearing telephone conversations, possibly through spies. Leave was now regular, though the allowance was small.[1]

Having returned to the line, 10 January, time was spent constructing the new parapets in the rear of the original trenches and some companies were occupying the high command parapets. These trenches were almost under water and even platoons were divided up into as many as four groups by flooded sections of the trenches. As a result, a large portion of the troops was accommodated in the ruined houses of Rue Tilleloy, from where it could quickly reinforce in the case of an attack.

> At this time the trenches in this area were full of water, even the roads leading to Battalion HQ's being flooded, but the battalion had only eight pairs of short gumboots, which were handed over by one battalion to another on relief. However, the

1 Falls.

Ordnance Department were doing their best to cope with the matter, and issued sand bags which the men wore round their legs like puttees, and with the straw, of which at this time there was a large quantity in the trench area, the conditions were slightly alleviated. On 4th January 1915, Headquarters 4th Corps notified Units that 23,000 pairs of large rubber boots were expected to arrive shortly, and 270 pairs of these were drawn by the battalion on 24th January.[2]

During the 11th, Battalion HQ was shelled out of their farm; fifty shells fired over it, most of them bursting close to the dugouts in which the men were sheltered. The following day HQ moved 150 yards north to another farm and a few more shells were put close to the new base shortly after being occupied. The French woman suspected of being a spy was still in the vicinity. On the 13th they moved to Ft D'Esquin, with one company at Rue Bacquerot (returned from Rue Masselot) and one at Corner Farm on the right of Rue du Bois. A draft of 60 men under the command of Lt. N.H. Hutcheson joined from the Transport Lines where they had been kept since their arrival two days earlier, instead of being sent right out to the trenches. It included several re-enlisted men of 1st RIR, some of whom had left the battalion at Calcutta, Meerut, Fyzabad, Winchester or Liverpool. The two latter places represented men who had been left behind sick and this group, on the whole, were considered quite a useful addition. Brigadier-General Lowry Cole and the CO inspected them before being distributed among the companies. QM Edwards:

This was a period of experiments in trench weapons, and it was now that the jamtin bomb was evolved and practised with, often causing severe casualties, and rockets, bomb bags, etc., were articles to be daily met with.

Col. Laurie detailed events at this time:

January, 16th … this morning I have been practising bomb-throwers. This Christian device is made of a jam-tin or crock filled with gun-cotton and nails, and has a fuse attached to it. The fuse is lighted and thrown by hand into the enemy's trench … Another plan of mine was rather unpleasant. I told you that I pumped the water out of our trenches into the German ones, and that they replied, and then dam-building began. Finally, we burst their dam, and some men working in it fled. Our people were about to fire, seeing them running, when an old soldier called out: 'Do not shoot, for they cannot run far in that mud.' The poor things finally stopped, panting, and they had to be shot down as they stood. Such is war. Very hideous, and I loathe it, but what will you do?

January, 17th … We dug away hard whilst the Germans sent occasional bullets amongst us and threw rockets to try to show us up: we lay down to prevent having machine guns turned on us. But now that we are making the dry parapets I advocated, things are much better in every way, and everyone is more cheery.

2 G.W. Edwards, the Quartermaster. All his quotes come from an article in *Quis Separabit*, vol. 36, June 1965.

In building these parapets, the materials have to be carried across drains and even disused trenches, the ground in places being seamed with old diggings. Last night I saw two men fall into these ditches in the dark, and we had to fish them out. One fell about six feet into about four feet of water. The whole thing was most weird, with the rockets flying and the bullets going, and working parties shovelling for dear life in the darkness. We all tumbled about into shell-holes or ditches in turn where the water is very cold.

The new trenches at E Lines, 600 yards from the Germans, were nearing completion during the tour of 16–19 January, but the work was very much hampered by bad weather and the appalling state of the ground, there being a heavy snowstorm on the 18th. According to Col. Laurie:

My Sergeant-Major, Master Cook, and Sergeant-Bugler, all trembling with cold shut themselves up last night with a charcoal fire, and we found them about four o'clock insensible from the fumes, and had a certain amount of difficulty in bringing them round.

While in Laventie, 19–22 January, training for the men of the new drafts took place every day. The next tour in E Lines passed without any unusual incident. On 25 January information was received that an attack was expected at points along the Allied Front within the following 24 hours; this did not, however, materialise until after the Irish Rifles had been relieved. Lt. T.F. Ingram and reinforcements of 84 men arrived at the billets on the 26th and were posted to companies – this was a good draft consisting principally of returning old 1st RIR men. Next day the artillery of the 8th Division bombarded the Neuve Chapelle area on the Kaiser's birthday. Starting with the tour of 28–31 January, the trenches alternatively occupied by 1st RIR and 2nd Lincolns were now to be known as F Lines, while those occupied by 2nd Rifle Brigade and 2nd R. Berkshires would be called E Lines. The company that had been in local reserve on Rue Bacquerot was billeted at Picantin from the 31st. Training for the new men continued every day in Laventie from the end of January to 3 February. Casualties for January were 13 men killed and 26 wounded. The War Diary had 'Nothing special to record, except that several enemy shells fell near Bn HQ – one shrapnel bullet coming through the window.' QM Edwards:

The Ordnance and Supplies were fairly regular at this time – railhead being at Merville – a percentage of the battalion being able to get clean clothing at each Divisional Reserve tour, and other sorts of jam than 'plum and apple' were coming along occasionally, but there was a shortage of rum, and that was a real hardship in the sodden state of that country.

There was at this time, too, a considerable shortage of engineer material, for riveting and wiring trenches, but sufficient was available to occupy a good proportion of the troops in the working parties. Whale oil for frostbite was a daily issue to troops in the trenches.

The German guns shelled Ft D'Esquin on the night of 3 February, putting one blind shell through the front door of the CO's billet but it failed to explode – fortunately for him he was at the front. That same night the 8th Divisional Artillery, on information furnished by two deserters, bombarded the approaches to the German trenches from Aubers with the intention of catching the enemys' reliefs between 9.30 p.m. and 10 p.m. The enemy guns replied by bursting shells accurately on Rue Tilleloy and sharp rifle fire was opened up from E Lines on the right. Col. Laurie observed:

> How close the fire is here is shown by one of my companies having had two periscopes hit. Periscopes are four inches wide or less, and probably only five inches shows above the parapet, so you can see the German marksman at 100 yards anyhow is not to be despised.

The night of 4 February found 45th Royal Field Artillery Brigade shelling the approaches to the German trenches again, opposite F Lines, based on information garnered from the deserters. The Germans made no reply to this, as the bombardment was not very intense. After a rest in Ft D'Esquin the Irish Rifles again returned to F Lines on the 9th. Col. Laurie recorded the death of 9276 Rfn James Hodgins from Co. Louth:

> 12th February. One of my poor men died also this morning; it was astonishing that he was alive at all, for yesterday a bullet hit him in the head and blew the back of his head off, and yet he remained alive and quite conscious without pain till 2 a.m.

That night the battalion went into Divisional reserve. German shrapnel burst in a barn near Laventie Station, occupied by one platoon of D Coy, and two men were wounded. A good draft of 75 men arrived from England on the 15th; over half of these were either 1st or 2nd Bn or Regular Reservists. When 1st RIR returned to the front line that day, a message from 25th Brigade HQ stated that reports from all brigades in the 8th Division pointed to unusual quietness on the part of the enemy. A request was made that patrols be sent out to check if the German trenches were held more tightly than usual. The battalion patrols found that the trenches opposite F Lines were held, as far as could be ascertained, with the normal strength. Company wire cutting parties were exercised while the troops were in Ft D'Esquin, 18–21 February, before returning to the front line. During the morning of the 23rd several German shrapnel shells burst just in front of the new Battalion HQ. Reinforcements of 20 men had arrived from England on the 22nd and remained in the Transport Lines until the battalion returned to billets two days later. The men of all drafts were divided into three squads A, B and C for training – A being the squad from which the men were passed out to duty. There was active shelling by German artillery on the 28th; the support billet of A Coy was set on fire and two men in the building were wounded, one of them being badly burned and died on reaching 24th Field Ambulance. He was 13922 Rfn John Munster, age 34, from Dublin and Col. Laurie told what happened:

Yesterday we were once more under heavy fire. One shell exploded beside two men who were trying to make some tea. I am sure the poor fellows, without thinking, gave away their position by having too large a fire. Anyway, this shell burnt everything round them, including the flaps of a barn door standing upright, with nothing inflammable near, but the doors were in a blaze in a moment, and also their clothes. One man had 18 holes in him; the other was dreadfully scorched and hurt. I gave him morphia tablets, but I'm afraid they did not do him much good; it was a mercy that the doctor arrived soon to give him a proper hypodermic injection. In one place we found a piece of shell about the size of a half pound iron weight which had forced its way right through, and was just under the skin on the other side. We got that out but he died shortly after.

On 28 February orders were received that 22nd Brigade, 7th Division, would relieve 25th Brigade. Casualties for February were 6 men killed and 28 wounded. The trenches were taken over by 2nd The Queens on the evening of 1 March and 1st RIR occupied billets in Le Franc's Factory near Estaires. Col. Laurie:

If you saw my men in a spinning mill sleeping under engines, etc., you would wonder how we exist! Of course, Spring is coming on, and we shall then have to go in for business of the worst type; so whilst someone else is holding the lines, we are trying to get our men fit for this work.

Instructions were received to exercise the men in physical training, running across ploughed fields and route marching. The instruction of machine gun detachments, bomb throwers and wire cutting parties was to continue while six blocking parties were to be trained in holding sections of captured trenches to secure the flanks. This was carried out over the next three days. During that time the CO and Company Commanders visited the trenches of B Lines opposite Neuve Chapelle. 1st RIR, together with the other battalions of the brigade, formed night digging parties for these lines from 2–6 March. Laurie wrote home on 4 March: 'I lost two NCOs killed yesterday by one bullet through their heads, and another of my poor men had his tongue cut out.'

Other casualties amounted to one man killed, 6 wounded, and a Sergeant was accidentally drowned in the canal running by the factory. 2nd Lincolns and 2nd Rifle Bde billeted at La Gorgue while 2nd R. Berkshires was at Riez Bailleul; the 13th London Regt was in the same factory as 1st RIR. Orders were received on the 6th that all surplus kit, gum boots, and fur coats were to be stored the following day at La Gorgue. The battalion was to be prepared to move at short notice, carrying only baggage in accordance with the Field Service Manual, and ammunition was to be increased to 170 rounds per man. All COs met the Brigadier at his HQ on the morning of 7 March. The battalion was ordered to move into Close Billets that evening and surplus kit was to be stored at once. Col. Laurie expressed his frustration:

Next came the orders to move into fresh billets tonight in the dark. This with 1,000 men and 70 horses, whilst I must send a working party of 400 men to a

place 5 or 6 miles off at 10.30 p.m. tonight. How it is all to be done I have not
been informed, but you can imagine the chaos that can ensue.

At 5.20 p.m. they marched to Pont Riquel, occupying new billets and, fortunately for
Col. Laurie, the working party ordered for that night was cancelled. Secret orders were
received, 8 March, for 1st RIR to carry out operations over the next two days. The
weather was varying between flurries of snow and bright sunlight. Lt. D.A. Browne, and
one officer from each company, left at 7 p.m. for B Lines to reconnoitre their assembly
trenches. Two NCOs and four Riflemen accompanied this party to clear any impeding
wire and make holes in hedges and any other obstacles. The men's packs were stored at
a shoe factory at La Gorgue and regimental entrenching tools were despatched to sites
near the forming-up points. Col. Laurie observed:

> These Irishmen are most amusing fellows; they can't be treated like the English
> soldier: one has to be much more strict with them, and ride them at other times
> with a much lighter hand. For the next few months, unless Germany collapses at
> once, there will be heavy fighting for us.

On 9 March two sandbags and two extra bandoliers per man were issued. The battalion paraded at 10.45 p.m. in battle order and marched from Pont Logy to the assembly trenches and breastworks to the right of 23rd Brigade, south of Sign Post Lane, B
Lines, for the attack on Neuve Chapelle. There was a certain air of anxiety among the
troops that was mixed with a sense of enthusiasm. For it was here that 2nd RIR had suffered severe casualties when the village was lost to the Germans the previous October in
the Battle of La Bassée. Now was their chance to even the score. QM Edwards:

> All ranks were in good spirits as it had become known that we had a large artillery
> concentration in position, and the troops, weary of trench work, were eager to
> get to grips with the Boche ... [The battalion] was composed of fine seasoned
> soldiers, and the casualties which had occurred during its period in France had
> been made good principally by men who were on the Reserve when war broke
> out and had been at Mons and on the retreat with the 2nd Battalion, and then
> home, sick or slightly wounded. Many men who had previously served with the
> 1st Battalion in Burma and India had thus rejoined it, and at Neuve Chapelle it
> comprised material of which any Commander might well have been proud.

4

Neuve Chapelle

This was to be 1st RIR's first action since the Indian Mutiny of 1857–9.

> Neuve Chapelle was a new type of battle, which was for long to be the model for the attacks of trench warfare. A great concentration of artillery was obtained to crush out all resistance in front before the infantry attack was launched. Its objective was Aubers Ridge, for which there had been a struggle so fierce in the previous winter, the capture of which might eventually involve the German evacuation of Lille.[1]

At 12.50 a.m., 10 March, the battalion halted for an hour, had a hot meal near Croix Barbee and then moved off after picks and shovels had been allocated. By 3.45 a.m. they had arrived in the support trenches and took up their allotted positions in an orchard just east of Rue Tilleloy, 600 yards north of Pont Logy. The strength for the attack was 22 officers, 890 other ranks, and 2 machine guns. They were also provided with the assistance of a Stokes gun, a 2-inch trench mortar, and one 1.5-inch Trench Mortar Battery that were to be used to keep down flanking fire from the Germans. An intense 35-minute bombardment by the British artillery commenced from 7.30 a.m. QM Edwards remembered:

> There were 350 guns in action and the bombardment was terrific. It was spoken of by the Infantry long afterwards as the heaviest bombardment experienced; that on the Somme on 1st July 1916 was not considered equal to it. It was most effective too, and when the Brigade advanced at 8 a.m., 2nd Lincolns and 2nd Royal Berkshires forming the first wave, there was practically no opposition, and the enemy's first and second lines fell at once.

2nd Lincoln's place on the breastwork should have been taken over by 1st RIR but, due to the speed with which the Lincolns advanced and took the trenches, the Irish Rifles filed out at once and moved towards the German line. At 8.35 a.m., 1st RIR advanced through the German trenches and attacked the second objective; A Coy was on the right and B on the left, supported respectively by C and D. Both machine guns

1 Falls.

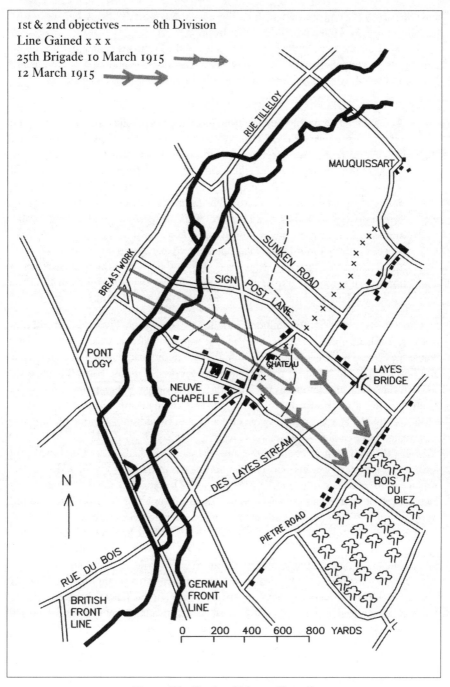

1st & 2nd objectives ------ 8th Division
Line Gained x x x
25th Brigade 10 March 1915 ➔
12 March 1915 ➔

RUE TILLELOY

MAUQUISSART

SUNKEN ROAD

BREASTWORK

SIGN POST LANE

PONT LOGY

CHATEAU

LAYES BRIDGE

NEUVE CHAPELLE

DES LAYES STREAM

N ↑

BOIS DU BIEZ

PIETRE ROAD

RUE DU BOIS

GERMAN FRONT LINE

BRITISH FRONT LINE

0   200   400   600   800 YARDS

Map 3: The Battle of Neuve Chapelle

and two parties of bombers were with B. The assault was led by Capts A.J. Biscoe, A.M. O'Sullivan, F.R.W. Graham, and Lt. W.A. Burges.

B Coy advanced successfully but, as D came up, the Germans opened with machine gun fire from the left flank. There were many casualties, including Lts Burges and Barrington killed. Rfn James Scott wrote that in the attack on the German second line they

> were met with a murderous fire from a machine gun which for an instant made our men waver. An officer, Lt. Burges, leading our platoon, No. 8, B Coy, dashed into a stream of water which reached to his neck, and which ran parallel to the second German line wire entanglements. He called out as he plunged into the water: 'Follow me, No. 8; be quick and we will capture that machine gun.' Straight away every man followed this gallant officer. Once across the stream, 'Form up, No. 8', and away we went towards the machine gun like hounds after the hare. We followed this officer over the German third line of trenches, and away in full cry towards the village of Neuve Chapelle, in our efforts to capture the accursed machine gun, which was playing the deuce with our men. Dashing forward to a wood on our right where the gun was concealed, our gallant officer received a bullet wound in the neck, which ended in his death.[2]

Capt. Biscoe was seriously wounded and died two days later. The battalion still continued towards its objective in two lines and, at 8.40 a.m., after advancing with considerable speed, reached the line running from the fork in the road, in front of the chateau, and north to the crossroad on the brigade boundary at Sign Post Lane. This was the western side on an area known as the Triangle. As the British 6-inch guns were not due to lift their fire from this road until 9 a.m., the two leading companies had to retire 100 yards and wait. The road was re-taken at 9 a.m. and the advance continued; direction was changed from east to south-east, in fact a right wheel. They pushed on through the Triangle, through orchards and houses and, by 9.40 a.m., had secured the line to the fence east of the chateau garden. Having occupied and improved some old trenches, which had been occupied by 2nd RIR the previous October, they joined with 2nd Rifle Bde on the right. It was here that Capt. O'Sullivan rapidly reorganized the leading troops of the battalion that had got slightly mixed during the rapid advance.

Owing to 23rd Brigade being held up, the left of 1st RIR had to be thrown back to guard their own left flank. Two platoons under Capt. Galwey fortified the left Brigade line facing north-east and got in touch with the Scottish Rifles at that point. This was a precaution well taken as the Germans counter-attacked at 10.50 a.m. but were beaten off. About thirty prisoners were captured passing through the Triangle. Small parties of the enemy were seen to the east, mostly unarmed, and making away towards the Bois de Biez. The Irish Rifles kept firing at these causing many casualties. Patrols were pushed out and a few prisoners were taken, but the bulk of the enemy had gone and the rest of the day was spent in consolidating the line from east of the chateau garden. The battalion remained in its positions throughout the night and a certain amount of sporadic shelling went on. QM Edwards:

2 de Ruvigny.

Some heavy hand-to-hand fighting took place in the village in rooms and cellars, but eventually all the enemy were either killed or captured. At this stage there was not a single German anywhere within sight of the Brigade, and men walked about on top of the ground without having a shot fired at them. This continued for over two hours when the first sign of the enemy reserves was seen. There would have been nothing to prevent the battalion going forward, but the attack was held up further to the left.

Their casualties for the day were:

	Killed	*Wounded*	*Missing*	*Total*
Officers	2	6	–	8
Other Ranks	22	88	99	209

The village had been very heavily shelled – so much so that even the bodies in the cemetery had been scattered all over the place. A grisly scene met the troops when they found that the bodies of 2nd RIR men, killed the previous October, were mixed among the recent dead of 1st RIR. The battalion was relieved by the West Yorkshire Regt at 9 a.m. the next morning and moved to the old German trenches where they spent the day. While making this move 2/Lt. A. Gilmore, who had just taken over command of A Coy, was shot dead. Major Baker: 'On the 11th we did little except get shelled, as we tried to sleep in some German trenches.' During the whole night there was a continuous heavy bombardment by the enemy and rest was impossible.

The day's casualties were:

	Killed	*Wounded*	*Missing*	*Total*
Officers	1	–	–	1
Other Ranks	8	30	17	55

An exhausted Col. Laurie wrote a last letter home:

March 11th. I have had some very hard fighting since I wrote to you. Of course I knew it was coming off, but could not tell you exactly. We lost a certain amount. I am too busy, though, to write much, and I am out in the open feeling very cold, and will be in the mud all night, where, by the bye, I've been for the past three nights. A few of my officers have been killed, I regret to say. Can you imagine me charging down with the regiment shortly after dawn into Neuve Chapelle? I will write more about it all if I am spared. There is heavy fighting before us.

At 3 a.m., 12 March, orders were received to attack the enemy's trenches east of the chateau at 4.45 a.m. but, at about 4 a.m., this was altered to 10.30 a.m. – a fatal delay. Major L. Oldfield, RFA, attached 1st RIR, gave this account to Mrs Laurie:

I rushed over to arrange with him, and went into his trenches and among his men. All were very exhausted. He said they simply could not go on. We arranged to attack in the morning. I went to the Brigadier to say so, but found that he was ordered to attack at once. Col. Laurie knew it was almost impossible, but ran off to obey.

The battalion took up preparatory positions at 9 a.m. at orchards in the Triangle. Due to fog the preliminary bombardment was not carried out at 10 a.m. as arranged; it also proved exceptionally difficult for the artillery to locate their targets. The Germans, however, continuously shelled the Triangle with large calibre guns from about 9.45 a.m. until noon and the Irish lost heavily. The British bombardment began at noon and at 12.30 p.m., under heavy fire, the battalion occupied the trenches it had dug on the 10th; the West Yorkshires were also there. The companies moved in the following order: C on the right and D on the left, supported respectively by A and B. The order to advance was given at 12.45 p.m. and the enemy at once opened a heavy fire from the flanks and the front. Anyone who attempted to advance was shot down before they were clear of the parapet, including Capt. O'Sullivan who was wounded. Capt. E.B.R. Colles volunteered to cut the barbed wire and was killed while doing so. The left half of D Coy crossed to the north of the road and attacked due east, led by Lts N.H. Hutcheson and G.J. Laing. They made for a small trench, lightly held by Sherwood Foresters, but only about six men succeeded in getting there. Lt. Laing and the CSM were killed on the way and, while in this trench, Lt. Hutcheson was shot through the head by a bullet that had passed through the parapet.

Col. Laurie, considering the advance to be impossible, ordered the rest of the battalion to stand fast. The troops remained in their positions until 5 p.m. when the British heavy artillery reopened fire. Orders were received to attack again at 5.15 p.m. and take the position at all costs. The 8th Division history tells us that

> The living were well-nigh dead from physical exhaustion. At every halt, men fell asleep from sheer overmastering fatigue and could only be aroused by violence.

Col. Laurie ordered the companies to advance in four successive lines, B leading followed by C, A, and D. During the bombardment volunteers were sought to cut the wire in front of their trenches, but they were nearly all killed. The bombardment ceased at 5.15 p.m. and the enemy again opened very heavy gunfire. Col. Laurie then gave orders for the leading company to advance. All who got up to do so were knocked over at once by rifle and machine gun fire. At 5.20 p.m. Major Baker, who had charge of the right of the line, came across to the left to enquire as to why the charge was hanging fire and found that Col. Laurie had just been killed and that Major H.C. Wright was wounded. The intensity of the fire had increased and, there being no sign of an advance by other units on the flanks, Major Baker gave the order to stop their assault, reporting his action to the GOC. The GOC then issued orders postponing the attack and troops were ordered to return to their former positions. QM Edwards:

On the 12th a further advance was attempted but with little success. It was here that Rifleman Bradshaw and Donnolly gained the DCM for advancing under heavy shell and machine gun fire and cutting the enemy's wire to make a passage for the advance.

This was the first big battle since the trench period set in, and the services behind the line were put to the utmost strain. The battlefield was served by only one good road, the Estaires–La Bassée Road, and the congestion on it was fearful. It was heavily shelled day and night, and it says much for the organisation behind the line that all through the operation, rations, including hot meals, ammunition, etc., were got up to the troops and the wounded were cleared.

At 7.30 p.m. the Irish Rifles were withdrawn to reoccupy the line of Chateau Garden where Capt. C.H.L. Cinnamond arrived with 33 men and reinforced them. The day's casualties amounted to:

	Killed	*Wounded*	*Missing*	*Total*
Officers	4	4	–	8
Other Ranks	50	72	13	135

The battalion remained at Chateau Garden, 13 March, consolidating its position while the enemy shelled throughout the day. At 5.30 a.m. Capt. and Adjutant A.O'H. Wright was shot dead while going round the trenches with Major Baker. 1st RIR was relieved at 6.30 p.m. by 2nd Lincolns and moved to the old German trenches where 2/Lt. A.W. Bourke and 70 men joined them. Casualties for this day were one officer killed, 3 men killed and 2 wounded. The casualties for 10–13 March inclusive were 9 officers killed and 9 wounded; Other Ranks: 106 killed, 270 wounded and 15 missing. Total of all losses for the battle amounted to 409, which was a casualty rate of 45 per cent.[3]

During 14 March the battalion remained in the trenches that they had occupied the previous night and there was still some shelling by the enemy. At 7 p.m. they moved to the old British breastworks while A and B Coys occupied the old trenches. Lt. Browne was appointed Adjutant. Casualties were one killed and 2 wounded. They remained in position throughout the following day subjected to random enemy shelling and, that evening, moved to trenches on Rue Tilleloy, north of Sign Post Corner, where one man was wounded. At 7 p.m. on the 16th they relieved 2nd Lincolns in the front line. Lt. Gartlan occupied a detached post at the crossroad with a machine gun and 40 men of A Coy. The whole place was littered with the bodies of both British and German dead. It was found to be extremely difficult to bury them as the enemy sniping was intense and two men were wounded. However, three wounded Germans were rescued and sent to the rear.

3 10–13 March 1915: Officers killed: Lt.-Col. G.B. Laurie, Capts A.J. Biscoe, A.G. Colles, and A.O'H. Wright, Lts N.S. Barrington, W.A. Burges, and N.H. Hutcheson, 2/Lts A. Gilmore and G.J. Laing. Officers wounded: Major H.C. Wright, Capts A.W. Galwey, F.R.W. Graham, A.M. O'Sullivan, and L.G.B. Rodney, Lts G.G. Adeley and R.F.A. Gavin, 2/Lts D.F. Hubert and T.F. Ingram.

At 3 p.m., St Patrick's Day, A and C Coys were heavily shelled with *woolly bears*, which killed 3 men and wounded 22. Some of these shells fell near Battalion HQ. The War Diary noted that 'The ground in front of these trenches is heaped with German dead. Impossible to bury them all.' During the 18th the enemy sniping had improved, being very close and accurate. Burial parties worked at night clearing both the German and British dead, but 3 men were killed and 2 wounded in the process. The next day passed uneventfully, there was some shelling but no casualties; more dead were buried and the area was certified clear. 2nd Lincolns relieved 1st RIR at 7 p.m., 20 March. HQ, A and B Coys moved to billets near Rouge Croix and formed Brigade Reserve, while C and D moved to support trenches on Rue Tilleloy, one man being wounded. Six officers and 145 men arrived as reinforcements. Major A.H. Festing joined from 2nd RIR to take over the duties of senior Major.

The Irish Rifles remained near Rouge Croix and, on the 22nd, some enemy shells fell close by but did no damage. Four men, however, were wounded while working in the front line and a shell hit the nearby Brigade Office the following day. The battalion moved to La Gorgue on the evening of the 24th and, next morning, moved to billets at Tron Bayard, marching off to Rue Biache, near Fleurbaix, and into Divisional reserve on the evening of the 26th. Over the next few days reinforcements of 8 officers and 112 men arrived. A working party of 100 men was attached to 2nd Field Coy, Royal Engineers, on the evening of the 28th, and, three days later, a fatigue party of 50 men from B Coy joined them. One man was wounded.

Total casualties to date:

	Killed	Died of Wounds	Wounded	Missing
Officers	10	1	9	–
Other Ranks	139	17	445	26
Total	149	18	454	26
Grand Total	647			

According to QM Edwards 'Reinforcements had already reached the Battalion, which had now 25 officers and 700 men.'

5

Fromelles

April was a relatively quiet month for the battalion. On the 1st it moved from Divisional to Brigade reserve on Rue du Quesnes and relieved 2nd Rifle Bde in the trenches near La Cordonnerie Farm on the evening of the 4th. The next morning Capt. W.M. Lanyon was killed, sniped over the parapet, and on the 6th, Capt. Cinnamond was wounded at dawn putting up barbed wire in front of his company. The routine of moving in and out of the trenches continued. A special event occurred on 17 April when the Irish Rifles were inspected by the Commander-in-Chief, Field Marshal Sir John French, at Bac St Maur. The battalion was drawn up in three sides of a square and received him with a General Salute. He congratulated the CO, Major Baker, on the fine work done by 1st RIR at the battle of Neuve Chapelle. He then made a speech to the men congratulating them on their gallantry during the battle and referred to the deep loss they had suffered by the deaths of Col. Laurie and Capt. Wright. He concluded his speech by referring to the marked percentage of losses among officers which, he said, showed that they were always ready to be the first in a charge and as long as the men followed their officers, as apparently they had done, there would be no doubt as to the ultimate victory. On the conclusion of his speech the battalion gave three cheers for the C.-in-C. and then marched back to billets.

The state of discipline in the battalion was considered by Brigade to be very poor at this time, drunkenness and men going AWOL being particularly prevalent, and strenuous efforts were being made to improve the situation. Capt. Browne fractured his leg in a riding accident, 19 April, and Lt. Gartlan took over the duties of Acting Adjutant. On 27 April, Lt. MacIlwaine, 2/Lt. Soulby, and 4 men were wounded while putting up wire entanglements at night within 70 yards of the enemy. The next day, the three left companies interchanged with two companies of 1st Londons and one company of 1/6th West Yorks and took up their old positions on the right of F Lines. The battalion was then occupying the same front as it held from December 1914 to the Battle of Neuve Chapelle having, in the interval, fought at the battle and occupied four different sections of the line. The casualty losses for this entire period amounted to 22 officers and 454 other ranks. F Lines were now known as FA Lines, which was constructed by 1st RIR with the help of 2nd Lincolns, and were the most complete and comfortable trenches they had occupied to this date. From 5 May the battalion was in billets at Bac St Maur. They departed at 11 p.m. on the 8th and marched to the assembly trenches at La

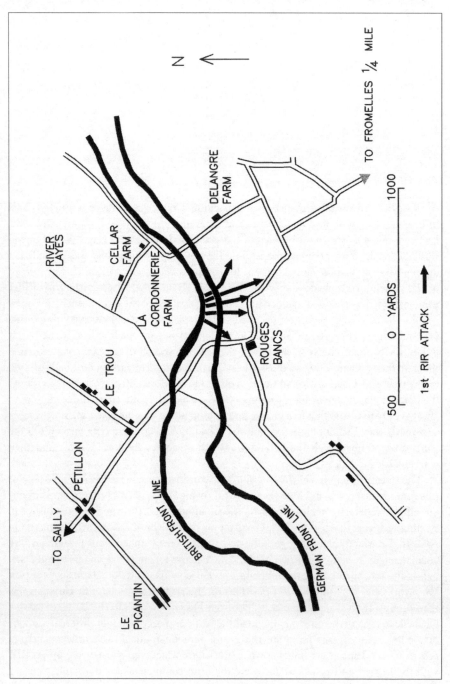

Map 4: Fromelles, 9 May 1915

Cordonnerie Farm, arriving three hours later, to take part in an attack against the German trenches at Rouges Bancs.

The operation was part of another attempt to take Aubers Ridge in concert with the French attack at Souchez. This effort was made in two separate attacks, known respectively as the Battles of Fromelles and Festubert. It was in the former that the battalion was to be destroyed for a second time in as many months. The task of 8th Division was to break through the enemy's lines in the area near Rouges Bancs, south of the Des Layes stream, and gain a position from the old line in the neighbourhood of La Cordonnerie Farm through Fromelles and Le Clerq. 1st RIR was to attack with 2nd Rifle Bde and capture the German front-line system and the road behind them running from Rouges Bancs towards Fromelles. At 5 a.m. the artillery commenced their 40-minute bombardment, 15 of which were devoted to wire cutting with the balance concentrated on the German trenches that were to be assaulted. This was hopelessly inadequate due to the shortage of guns and the time allotted. Indeed, brass mortars dating from 1840 had to be pressed into service. Even at the height of the bombardment, the volume of effective fire was not sufficient to compel the German garrisons to keep under cover and this failure was to prove fatal to the success of the operation.

At 5.40 a.m. C (Capt. Newport) and D (Lt. Gartlan) Coys advanced in lines of platoons at about thirty paces distance and rushed the front German trenches, advancing beyond it to a portion of the road beyond. 2nd Rifle Bde was on the right and 13th London Regt (Kensington) on the left. A (Capt. Tee) and B (Capt. O'Sullivan) Coys followed in the same formation immediately behind C and D (less two platoons). They were subjected to very heavy machine gun and rifle fire obliquely from both flanks by Germans who had remained in portions of their trench on either side of the line of the advance. Of the two platoons mentioned above, one section of twenty men advanced to the right under Col. Baker, and another under RSM W. Carroll to the left, to check and stop the crossfire. All of these men were killed except the RSM, who had several bullet holes in his clothing and a slight wound in his hand. The remaining sections of these two platoons spent the day holding part of the British front line in front of the left flank. At 8.30 p.m. they withdrew having received orders to do so.

In the meantime the remainder of the battalion was holding the portion of the road, mentioned above, under machine gun and rifle fire and were expecting another battalion to go through them and continue the advance. 7095 Sgt Simner captured a machine gun that was used in repelling several later counter-attacks. The relief battalion failed to appear and, after waiting half an hour beyond the time appointed for its appearance, the order was given at 7 a.m. to retire, as they could make no effective reply to the enemy's fire and were losing heavily in officers and men. It was at about this time that Brigadier-General Lowry Cole was mortally wounded while trying to reorganize the attack. What was left of this party returned to the captured portion of the German front line trenches and established defences there. It was placed under the command of OC 2nd Rifle Bde, Lt.-Col. R.B. Stephens, who was also in the trench, having assumed command of 25th Brigade. The strength remaining at this stage was about 150 men of the Rifle Bde and 50 of the RIR. They remained there all day and, at 7.50 p.m., the enemy made a determined counter-attack which was easily repulsed – the captured machine gun being used very effectively by 2/Lt. Gray of the Rifle Bde. At 8.30 p.m. Col. Stephens, on leaving for the Brigade Report Centre, handed over command of the detachment to Capt. Newport. At about 3 a.m., 10 May, the British remnants were driven out by bombs and heavy fire and returned to their original trenches. In the retirement Capt. Newport was badly wounded and lay on the battlefield for fifteen hours before being rescued. The Irish Rifles had lost all its officers either killed, wounded, or missing, and were brought out of action by the RSM and returned to their billets at Bac St Maur at about 5 a.m. During the entire war this was the blackest day for the battalion. Losses amounted to 23 officers and 454 men out of about 600 who had gone into the attack, a rate of almost 80 per cent. The only other officers of the battalion who went into action were 2/Lt. G.W. Panter with the reserve platoons and Lt. J.P. Stallard, the Medical Officer. There was no officer left who could make a report on the action to Brigade HQ and a compilation of statements from senior NCOs had to be made instead. According to QM Edwards:

> The battalion took all its objectives and consolidated the position, but owing to supports not forthcoming and being left with both flanks in the air it eventually had to retire, the enemy counter-attacking, not as usual under cover of heavy fire, but gradually outflanking and bombing until retirement or capture were the only alternatives.
>
> Many gallant deeds were performed on this occasion, among others by Lts McCausland and Dixon, and Corporal Peter O'Brien (all killed) and Rfn Campbell. One Company (D) did not retire with the rest of the battalion, and all hope of their return had been given up when they were brought in by CSM Simner and CSM Driscoll – all officers having been killed.[1]

Capt. A.J. Ross assumed temporary command of the remains of the battalion and, on 17 May, they marched to Estaires-la-Sarque in Divisional Reserve. Major A.D.N. Merriman arrived that day and took command. One man was killed and 3 wounded on the 22nd while with a working party behind the lines. The battalion returned to the trenches two days later, taking over D Lines from the Notts and Derby Regt, and a draft of 5 officers and 146 men joined them there. Casualties were 2 men killed and 6 wounded. The War Diary recorded 'Enemy all quiet along our Front.' They were relieved on the night of the 28th by 1st London Regt and proceeded to Ft D'Esquin. Having returned to the trench-es on the 31st, they took over Lines D.1 and D.2 from 1st Londons and part of Line D.3 from 2nd Rifle Bde. This was a short move northward to the Fleurbaix trenches.

The Germans were active throughout 2 June shelling the trenches with shrapnel and trench mortars, killing 2 men and wounding 12. 2nd Rifle Bde relieved 1st RIR the next day and, while in Ft D'Esquin, one company was in reserve to the left sector of D Lines and billeted at La Flinque. The battalion took over the left of D Lines from 2nd Rifle

---

1 The casualties among the Officers were: Killed or died of wounds: Lt.-Col. O.C. Baker, Major A.H. Festing, Capt. A.M. O'Sullivan, Lts R.A. Finlay, A. Hellmers, G.M. La Nauze, J.S. Martin, J.E.B. Miller, and R.L. Neill, 2/Lts A.W. Bourke, L.A.F.W. Dickenson, C.G. Dixon, D. Hamilton, A. McLoughlin, O.B. Macausland, and C.E. Windus. Wounded: Capts C.C. Tee and C.J. Newport, Lts G.H. Coey, G.I. Gartlan, G.M. Mew, H.P. Parkes, and A.C. Soulby.

Bde, 6–12 June, and the enemy was active during the 10th using a trench mortar and firing rifle grenades. A Coy replied with rifle grenades and the duel was kept up for about an hour. Casualties were one man killed and 13 wounded. Having being relieved, they returned to billets with the same arrangements as before and Lt.-Col. R.A.C. Daunt arrived and took over command.

During the next tour they remained in the trenches for seven days until the night of the 25 June. War Diary: 'Enemy very quiet along our Front during this Tour.' Lt. L.J. Arnott was wounded on the 24th. Three men were killed and 9 wounded in addition to 2 men who were accidentally wounded by picking up a German rifle grenade. This time relief was provided by the Jullunder Brigade (A Coy) and the 754th Brigade (C and D Coys). The night was spent in billets north-east of Laventie and they moved to Brigade Reserve, north-west of Fleurbaix, the following day. One company was in immediate support to the trenches held by 2nd Rifle Bde at La Croix Marechal. July began with a move into Divisional Reserve, which was also north-west of Fleurbaix. HQ and A Coy remained where they were while B, C, and D moved to billets in Rue Bataille. The battalion relieved 2nd Rifle Bde, 2 July, which in turn relieved them six days later. The enemy was very quiet during this tour, casualties being 2 killed and 5 wounded. After six days in Brigade Reserve they returned for a further six days in the front line. The enemy was more active than usual on this occasion: the portion of trenches held by B Coy was shelled, 18 July, and considerable damage was done to the parapet and parados. Lt. E.D. Dent was wounded, 8 men were killed and 16 wounded. The battalion went into Divisional Reserve at Bac St Maur for seven days on the night of 20 July. It had a relatively quiet tour in the trenches for the last four days of July, 2 men being killed and 5 wounded. The following four days were spent in Fleurbaix, HQ and three companies billeted in Rue du Quesnes, while the support company was at Elbow Farm. Then came another quiet tour in the trenches, 4–8 August, 2 men being wounded. 12th Rifle Bde was attached to the battalion for instruction, 9–16 August, while they were in reserve at Rue du Quesnes, then 1st RIR moved into Divisional Reserve in Rue du Quesnoy until 1 September. While there, 4 men on working parties were wounded. The battalion moved into Brigade Reserve for four days and, during the next three-day tour, only one man was wounded. After three days back at Rue du Quesnes, they returned to the line 9–13 September, casualties being 3 men killed and 5 wounded.

During the time spent at Rue du Quesnes, Col. Daunt had it declared to all ranks that L/Cpl P. Sands was to be executed on 15 September for desertion. The battalion took over a trench line further north that same day: two companies were in the trenches, the remainder in billets, and one man was wounded in the process. From 17–20 September the two companies replaced each other. Capt. J.W. Field was accidentally wounded on the 20th and died later that day. Three men were also wounded during this tour. Two companies were relieved by 2nd Northampton Regt, moving into billets, while the others went to Bois Grenier Work.

6

Bois Grenier

The attack to be carried out by the 25th Brigade had a similar object to the attack at Hooge, and two others, by the Indians north of Neuve Chapelle and the 2nd Division at Givenchy; that is to say, it was designed purely to pin down German reserves and serve as a diversion from the affair at Loos. But it was perhaps on the smallest scale of any of the holding actions. All that was hoped from it at best was the capture of the German front-line trench upon a front of about 1,200 yards, after which it was intended to join it up to the existing British line. In order to allow the consolidation of the front line, when taken, the second was also to be captured, and the troops withdrawn as soon as the front had been put into a state of defence.[1]

The line in this sector that had been selected for the attack, between Well Farm salient and Le Bridoux Road salient, ran back in an almost complete semi-circle. Across the front of this area lay a ditch which was dry in summer but flooded and wet in winter. It was decided to use this ditch as the jumping off point and link the two salients to the German front, between Corner Fort and Bridoux Fort, which included two other particularly strong points, the Angle and the Lozenge. Having captured this front the attack was to proceed and take the German second line but only to allow time for the consolidation of the previous gain and, once this was done, to withdraw. Operation Orders issued by Col. Daunt included the following: 'Coys will "Stand to Arms" at 3.45 a.m. when they will receive an issue of rum, which is to be carefully supervised by Coy Officers.'

C Coy moved at 6.20 p.m. on the evening prior to the attack via Rue Delettre, Rue des Charles, Bois Grenier, to Shaftesbury Avenue, taking over the trench from 2nd Northants. D followed fifteen minutes after C had left Bois Grenier. A and B started out at 6.30 p.m. and moved via Rue Bassieres, Rue Lombard, Croix Marechal, Elbow Farm, Bois Grenier, to Shaftesbury Avenue. They were ordered to halt near Croix Marechal from 7.20 p.m. until 2 a.m. on the 25th, when they moved into their select-ed position in Rue des Layes. At 3.30 a.m., A and B, under the command of Major Merriman, had taken up their position about 900 yards to the rear of C and D.

1 Falls.

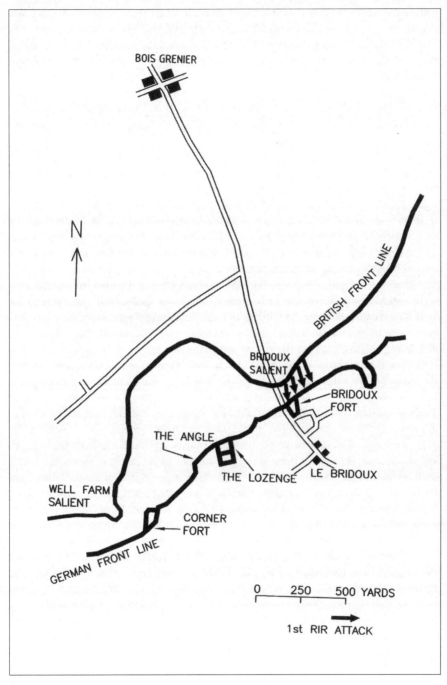

Map 5: Bois Grenier, 25 September 1915

Fifteen minutes later Col. Daunt left his HQ and joined them. The plan of attack was that Corner Fort was to be assaulted by 2nd Rifle Bde, the Angle and the Lozenge by 2nd R. Berkshires, and Bridoux Fort by 2nd Lincolns. The extreme left of the attack was to be made by the two leading companies, C and D, of 1st RIR. According to QM Edwards:

> This was the first time in which the precaution was taken of leaving a pro-portion of officers and senior NCOs out of the fight, in order to re-form the unit in case of heavy casualties.

The attack, which was preceded by an intermittent bombardment that lasted for four days and by a concentrated bombardment starting at 4.25 a.m., was launched at 4.30 a.m. On the right, Corner Fort was captured at once; in the centre, 2nd R. Berkshires captured the Lozenge but, below it at the Angle, were beaten back by heavy machine gun fire. On the left, 2nd Lincolns took Bridoux Fort and advanced to the second line. This, however, was heavily manned by the Germans and a pro-tracted bombing engagement ensued.

Meanwhile, C and D Coys of 1st RIR had been provided with a Stokes gun, a 2-inch trench mortar, 1,000 smoke candles, and eight catapults with 1,000 threffallite bombs to create smoke in the left flank of the attack. An 18-pounder field gun had been brought up and put in a parapet emplacement on the night of the 24th, its pur-pose being to fire directly at the enemy parapet. Two mines were to be exploded: one at Corner Fort at the moment of the attack, and the other, a much shallower one, at Bridoux Fort after the wave had gone over. The latter was to be blown in no-man's-land, which was very narrow at this point, and its objective was to form the basis of a communication trench. Owing to the wind being unfavourable, the smoke candles were not used and were subsequently set on fire by a German shell, killing 2/Lt. R.H. Andrews. The 2-inch trench mortar jammed having fired only two rounds. Worse still, a Stokes bomb burst setting all the others on fire and, moments later, a shell ignited the threffallite bombs. The resultant large column of smoke rising from the breastwork drew heavy fire from the German artillery and actually hampered the British artillery observation. The 18-pounder gun only fired during the bombard-ment and was not detected.

C and D were heavily shelled from 4.30 a.m. to 3.30 p.m. but suffered compara-tively slight casualties. At 6 a.m. the bombers of C Coy were sent by the CO to assist the Lincolns who had asked for bombs. Thirty minutes later 2/Lt. F.C. Wallace and 24 Brigade bombers were also sent to assist. When he reached the German trenches he found that they were being abandoned by the Lincolns and attempted to bomb out the enemy. On finding that they could outrange his bombers, he returned to the breastwork for his eight catapults and did excellent work clearing the German trenches with them, driving the enemy back 300 yards. Most of his men and cata-pults were lost in this action.

A telephone message was received by Battalion HQ at 8.05 a.m., from the 25th Brigade, ordering up A and B Coys to support the Lincolns left flank as they were in urgent need of reinforcements. This was passed on to Major Merriman and he acted on it at about 8.15 a.m. A and B advanced via Emma Post and Safety Alley. B was ordered to remain in the seventy yards line while A proceeded to the breastwork. At 10 a.m. Major Merriman led two platoons of A across to the German trenches just east of Bridoux Fort. The mine here had been a comparative failure, not having broken deeply enough into the ground, and proved small aid to communication. The Lincolns were found on the British side of the enemy parapet as the second line trench was full of Germans and rifle fire was brisk. Eventually, under an avalanche of bombs, the Lincolns withdrew with the Irish Rifles, and in this retirement Major Merriman was severely wounded, losing an arm. 2nd R. Berkshires were now attacked from both flanks and had to retire. 2nd Rifle Bde had done very well and had established itself firmly at Corner Fort, beating off many counter-attacks, but had to withdraw at 4 p.m. as the overall attack had been a failure. The four machine guns, under the command of Capt. Gartlan, had been in action all day. A and B Coys returned to their first position in Rue des Layes at 4 p.m. Col. Daunt reported to Brigade HQ:

> I left my Adjutant at my report centre in the 250 yard line all day, while I was in the breastwork, and I experienced considerable difficulty in getting communications as all telephone wires were soon cut, but the orderlies worked well though communication was slow, however nothing of an urgent nature arose.

The operations were greatly spoiled by the heavy rain, the weather having broken on the 23rd. Brigadier-General Stephens made the following observations in his report to Division:

> The weather was bad, with much mist and heavy rain late in the day. It was impossible to see what was going on. Artillery observation was very difficult, but in spite of this the artillery support was splendid and made no mistake.
> Most of the casualties were caused by shell fire or by bombs, and few by rifle fire. Consequently a large proportion of the wounded were slightly injured. The arrangements for getting the wounded away worked admirably and very few were left behind in the German trenches.

The chief reason for the failure to hold the German trench was the superiority of the enemy bombers, who threw a larger and heavier bomb than the British could throw. At 6 p.m. orders were received to remain in position for the night. Other casualties on the day were 2/Lt. J.H. Butler (slightly wounded), 11 other ranks killed, 76 wounded, and 15 missing. Brigade Order No. 722, 10 October 1915:[2]

> The unexpired portion of the sentences of the following men undergoing Field Punishment has been remitted by the G.O.C., 8th Division, from

2 WO95/1725.

September 25th, 1915, for gallant conduct in action on that date: Rfn
Johnstone, 1st RIR, 28 days F.P. No. 1 and Bugler Lee, 1st RIR, 28 days F.P.
No. 1.

HQ, with A and B Coys, moved to Bois Grenier Work about 1,500 yards to the
rear of the firing line on the afternoon of 26 September, while C and D remained in
the breastwork. The following day D was shelled and had 6 men wounded. During
the night of the 28th, A and B relieved C and D while HQ moved to Moat Farm. 5th
Black Watch relieved A and B Coys in the breastwork and one company of 2nd
Northants relieved C and D in the Bois Grenier Work on the night of the 30th. The
battalion moved to billets at Pont Mortier, 1 October, and Major-General Hudson,
the 8th Division Commander, inspected them the following day. Lt-General Sir W.P.
Pulteney, Commanding III Corps, carried out a further inspection during the afternoon of the 4th. 1st RIR relieved 2nd Rifle Bde, 7 October, in the trenches at Well
Farm Salient and the line extending to the left. The next day one NCO was killed
and one man wounded. Relieved by 2nd Rifle Bde, the battalion proceeded to billets
around Fleurbaix on the evening of the 10th. The following afternoon a German
aeroplane was shot down by British aircraft north-west of Fleurbaix and it fell near
Rue Bataille. The Irish Rifles captured the two-man crew, one with a broken leg. The
War Diary described 'A good new machine. Very well found and not very much damaged.' One man of the advanced company was wounded at Elbow Farm Work.

During the night of 13 October 2nd Lincolns, who were holding the trenches, sent
an SOS signal. It was a false alarm but there was a good deal of trench mortaring and
rifle fire opposite Bridoux and Well Farm Salients. 2/Lt. A.C. Workman, who was
attached to 2nd Home Counties, RE, was wounded along with nine men of the working party. Having relieved 2nd Rifle Bde on the 14th, three platoons of C Coy took
over an additional line to the right. It was very quiet in the trenches with practically
no sniping the next day but one man was wounded. Lt. W.O.F. Darling and Cpl Wall
were killed by rifle fire while out on patrol during the morning of the 16th. Between
3.30 and 4.30 p.m. heavy artillery and trench mortar fire was opened by the enemy,
chiefly between Marble Arch and the line about 100 yards to the left. A large gap was
made in the parapet to the right in Well Farm Fort by a heavy trench mortar, otherwise very little damage was done. Two men were wounded by shell fire and two by
rifle fire, while 2/Lt. A.J.J. Gwynn and two men were shocked by shell fire. After
being relieved by 2nd Rifle Bde on the 18th, they proceeded to Brigade billets near
Fleurbaix. Four men were wounded by rifle fire over the next four days.

It was at this time that 8th Division was restructured to take account of the arrival
of New Army units at the front. 24th Brigade changed places with 70th Brigade,
which had been part of 23rd Division. For a few weeks 2nd Lincolns and 2nd Rifle
Bde were replaced in 25th Brigade by 11th Sherwood Foresters and 8th KOYLI.
Having relieved 2nd Rifle Bde on the 22nd, 1st RIR took over about 190 yards more
of trench to the left from 8th Middlesex Regt. On this tour three men were wounded by rifle fire. Relieved on the 27th by 2nd Scottish Rifles, with 2nd Middlesex taking over the 190 yards section, the battalion went into Divisional Reserve at Rue du

Quesnoy and remained there until 4 November. Sgt Palmer drowned in the River Lys on 28 October.

Total casualties for the year ended 5 November 1915 were 1,410:

	Killed	*Wounded*	*Missing*	*Died of Wounds*
Officers	26	25	2	4
Other Ranks	216	887	200	50

It must be remembered that these are figures compiled by the battalion. Many of those who were wounded died after having been struck off the strength. As has been pointed out earlier, the number who had left the battalion for reasons other than wounds was also high but now no longer constituted the greater percentage due to the terrible battle losses during the year. Allowing that most sick men and a large amount of the wounded recovered and returned to the battalion (some being wounded more than once) it is still clear that experienced officers and men were at a premium. It will be recalled that the original strength was 31 Officers and 1,014 men when the battalion joined the BEF.

Billets were handed over to 2nd Middlesex and 1st RIR proceeded to Brigade Reserve at Fleurbaix for four days where billets were taken over from 2nd Scottish Rifles. The battalion relieved 8th KOYLI, 8 November, and HQ moved from Temple Post to Wye Farm. The diary recorded an 'Uneventful tour' and, having been relieved on the 12th, they returned to Fleurbaix. The next tour, 16–18 November, was very quiet, after which they moved to Rue du Quesnoy. During the 22nd they marched to billets via La Couronne and Vieux Berquin to Pont Rondin and, the next morning, marched twelve miles to Sercus via La Motte and Morbecque and billeted north-west of the town. The battalion was now in GHQ Reserve and about to enjoy a long period of badly needed rest and training. QM Edwards: 'This was the first time the battalion had been out of the trench area since arrival in the country more than a year before.' There followed a course of 24 days training in open warfare starting on 25 November. Classes began under Brigade arrangements for machine gunners, signallers, bombers, NCOs, and trench mortars. During the period of this intense training eight men were wounded by rifle fire.

> Games and sports of every kind were also instituted, and the men speedily began to show the results of a pleasant change. Not least valuable was the moral tonic of returning, if only for a while, to civilisation and unspoiled country from the abomination of desolation near the line.[3]

At the beginning of December the War Diary had noted: 'Weather very bad – tremendous rain and wind. Took over camp from 2nd R. Berks and they took over billets round Sercus. Camp of huts and bell tents. Mud indescribable.' On the morning of 20 December the battalion left Sercus to take part in Divisional training in the

3 Falls.

area south-west of Aire. They formed part of the main guard of the advanced guard of the division during the march to Delette. B Coy and one platoon of D formed part of the out-post line south-west of the village, while the remainder of the battalion stayed in the village. On the 21st they billeted at Enquin les Mines as training continued. Operations terminated at 3 p.m. the next day and the battalion marched to billets at Marthes. 'It returned to Sercus on the 23rd, and there spent Christmas – a very happy occasion when it chanced to fall when troops were out of the line, as can easily be guessed.'[4]

From 9 a.m. to 1 p.m. on the 29th, Brig.-Gen. Stephens carried out an inspection. This took the form of an attack from Le Romarin on Ridge 5 of Bois des Huit Rues due east of Sercus, and the general declared himself satisfied with what he saw. Major-General Hudson was also present. In December 139 reinforcements arrived, including 10 signallers.

4 Ibid.

7

1916

The battalion was still in the Fleurbaix area at the beginning of 1916, where it had been, except for several moves of a few miles, since its arrival in France a little over a year before. The sector was, generally speaking, a very quiet one, and occasions did occur when, during a tour of three days in the front line, not a single shell fell in their area. This was due in the most part to the fact that both sides were short of ammunition and the British were accumulating a reserve for the great Somme offensive in the coming summer.

> The trenches were found in a deplorable condition, wet and ruinous. And, as in such circumstances was always the case, the German snipers were active and troublesome. One, who did great damage, was for long unlocated, and seemed to be able to hit men even when behind a parapet. The secret was revealed when at last some movement was detected in a tree behind the German lines. A rattle from a machine gun, and a body pitched out to the ground. The Brigadier at once set about the reorganisation of our snipers, who improved with practice in the use of their telescopic sights, till at last it was their pride that no German periscope could remain ten minutes with its glass whole.[1]

On 9 January the battalion handed over their camp to 10th Rifle Bde and marched sixteen miles to Estaires. The next day they moved off and relieved 7th DCLI (61st Bde, 20th Div.); 2nd R. Berkshires were on their right and 2nd East Lancs (24th Bde, 23rd Div.) on their left. The diary reported: 'Uneventful tour. Trenches in very bad state. Very wet and parapets in a ruinous condition.' A new arrival at this time, 2/Lt. W.V.C. Lake, described the area:

> The Battalion was out of the line and back in billets. A few days later we found ourselves in the Laventie sector where long 'breast-work' communication trench-es with duck-boards underfoot led up to the reserve line and onwards to the front line. Ration parties had a long trail each night with their loads and very often a man would slip off the duck-boards and go into the smelly mud. One becomes accustomed in such situations to 'bad' language but it was never richer than in the dark of those breastwork trenches.

1 Falls.

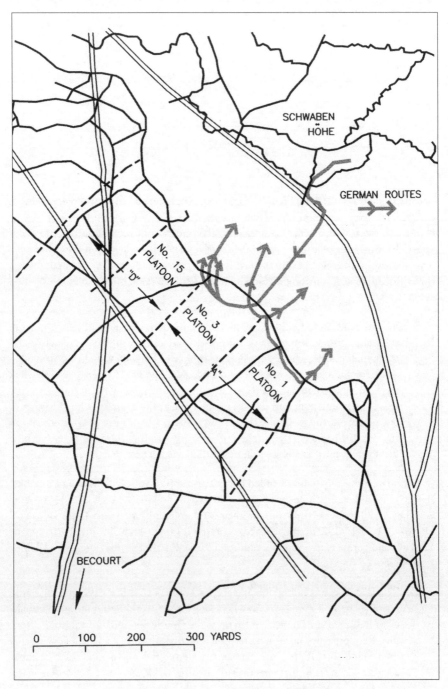

Map 6: The raid at La Boiselle, 11 April 1916

The 'season' was getting late by this time and there was little fierce fighting going on. But always vigilance was required. 'Stand-to' at dusk and again at dawn was strictly observed and between whiles through the night filling of sand-bags and repairing of damaged parapets went on.

Occasionally a subaltern was detailed to take an NCO with him and creep out into no-man's-land on patrol. On my first venture of this sort, when we had got beyond our wire, my little Corporal tugged at my sleeve and whispered in my ear: 'Don't do anything rash, Sir. I have a wife and family at home.' He had been through it before and I had not and I was just as scared as he was but dare not show it. We encountered nothing and came back in.

Having spent three days in Brigade Reserve at Fleurbaix, with the advanced company (B) at Elbow Farm, the battalion moved on the 18th to Divisional Reserve near Steenwerck. The next day 2 officers and 34 men were transferred to the Brigade Machine Gun Company, which was being formed by withdrawing the machine gun section from each of its four battalions. The Vickers machine guns were replaced by four Lewis guns per battalion, these being gradually increased as they became available in greater numbers, until a Lewis gun section formed part of each platoon.

At this point the War Diary gives interesting statistics for the number of admissions to hospital from all causes except wounds from April to December 1915: April 43, May 51, June 75, July 103, August 91, September 38, October 90, November 60, December 54, total 605. During the afternoon of 26 January they returned to the trenches only to find Battalion HQ in flames, having been hit by the enemy with incendiary shells. There followed a very disturbed night with shelling at short intervals until dawn. On the afternoon of the 29th the new HQ had three large shells dropped close to it; Rue du Bois and VC Corner were shelled daily. Having been relieved the next day, they moved to Brigade Reserve on Rue du Quesnes; Battalion HQ was at Weathercock House, but was relocated the next day to Rouge de Bout crossroads. Reinforcements of 74 men arrived during the month. Casualties were 5 men killed and 12 wounded. In addition, 57 were admitted to hospital for other reasons.

Throughout the next tour, 3–7 February, there was a lot of hostile shelling on the trenches along Rue du Bois, particularly at VC Corner. During the 6th, the advanced billet of the left support battalion, about 150 yards from Battalion HQ, was shelled. The next day these same billets were set on fire by a direct hit from a 5.9 shell. The War Diary recorded 'A very disturbed tour, much shelling by both sides; the enemy chiefly with field guns and 4.2 and 5.9 howitzers.' Two men were killed and 2 wounded on this occasion. If one was to think that Brigade Reserve was a safe area they could not be more wrong. Consider the experience of the battalion as they spent the period of 7–11 February in this area. The advanced company was D. On the afternoon of 8 February, B Coy's billet and work, Windy Post, was heavily shelled and partially destroyed by 5.9 shells, receiving about twenty direct hits. C's billet at Weathercock House was also shelled by 15-pounders and some damage was done. Two men were killed and 6 wounded. 2/Lt. Lake, B Coy, recorded this incident:

We were in a billet known as 'Windy Farm Post' which was quite some distance behind the Line in flat country and quite isolated and it held the entire company. One morning our Company Commander and his Second-in-Command were summoned to Battalion HQ. The only other officer beside myself was detailed for Orderly Officer, so I was left in sole command of the men.

We occupied ourselves in scraping off the mud of the trenches and generally having a good clean up. The whole place needed cleaning too. The farmhouse was a solid red brick building with cow-byres, stabling and so forth on either side of a large and overfilled 'midden'. It hadn't been cleared for ages. The front of the square, facing to the approach road, was a solid archway with a huge gate.

About 11 o'clock we heard the sound of distant gunfire, then the whistle of shells coming over. It was a salvo of three shells which exploded short of the road. We had our orders to move out to shelter trenches to the side of the farm if this sort of thing happened. But before we could get organised we heard again the three distant booms followed by the whistling. I ordered everyone to crouch down behind the huge slabs of slate that formed the sides of the byres. The second salvo hit the buildings at the front of the farm and soon we were enveloped in smoke and dust of bricks and mortar. My knees began to shake, but I dare not show my fear as the men depended on me. I ordered an NCO to lead a batch of men out through the side opening to the shelter trenches. As soon as the guns sounded again, I made the rest crouch down as before. This time it was the main building that got it, one shell exploding in the midden, which raised a ghastly stink. But still we escaped. Each time, immediately after an explosion, we followed the same routine.

All the men with me got out to the trenches without much damage, but the cook who was boiling up a big stew in a field kitchen that had been hidden in the kitchen of the house was killed outright. The stew for the whole company was scattered in all directions. When it was safe to do so, I returned to my room to see what damage had been done there. The stairs were still intact, but my room was a shambles. A shell had landed on the window-sill – there was no glass in any of the windows – and had swept my kit and everything, including the door, across the passage and into the opposite room. I went back to the chaps in the shelter trenches a sad and sorry man, but thankful that we had come through the ordeal as well as we did.

A Sergeant offered me a 'Woodbine'. I had given up smoking at the outbreak of war but never have I smoked anything as consoling as that cigarette. We got nothing to eat for the rest of the day but the rations came up as usual in the evening.

A Coy's billet at Charred Post was hit with 5.9 shells on the 9th and burned to the ground. With the exception of a few rifles all arms, stores, and equipment were destroyed. All companies moved to billets near Rue de Bout. Windy Post was also shelled and two 5.9 shells fell near Battalion HQ shattering the windows of the billet. Two men were killed and 2 wounded. Throughout the 10th, there was a good deal of shelling in their vicinity but no damage was done. Although the artillery on both sides was active on the 11th, the billets were not targeted. Compare this with the next tour, 11–14 February, when the battalion had no casualties in the front line and practically no shelling.

Lake described another incident that occurred about this time:

> Sometimes when out of the Line we were able to run our own little Company Mess. This was usually in a farmhouse where we could use a round mahogany table on which to have meals. Spiers, the Captain's batman acted as cook and waiter. One evening as he waited at table the Captain noticed that the man was crying. He turned and asked 'What is the matter, Spiers? What are you crying for?'
>
> Spiers stopped what he was doing and proceeded to tell us of his adventure an hour or so previously. He had been having a lonely drink in an estaminet when a transport driver in the ASC came in. He ordered his drink and the two men began to talk. Asking where he came from our man replied 'From Dublin. Where do you come from?' 'Oh,' replied the driver, 'from New York but I was actually born in Dublin.' They got down to details and it transpired that they were brothers and had been born in the same house but they had never met before. The driver was the elder man and, as a baby, had been taken out to the States by his grandparents because of overcrowding at home. Our man was born later. It can be well imagined how overcome the two men were at such a meeting.

Having been relieved by 21st Northumberland Fusiliers (Tyneside Scottish), 1st RIR moved into Divisional Reserve north of Sailly for a week. One man was wounded by rifle fire on the 18th while on a working party. Three days later they relieved 21st Northumberland Fusiliers in the right area of the Brigade Reserve. HQ was at Rouge de Bout and A Coy was in the advanced area. A (Windy Post) and D (Weathercock House) were shelled during the 24th, about sixteen and twelve shells fell respectively. Of the sixteen, no less than fifteen were blind and no damage was done. The battalion had a quiet tour, 25–9 February, although there was some shelling and trench mortaring, seven men being wounded. Col. Daunt took ill on the 26th and was temporarily replaced by Major Mayne. Having been relieved, the battalion moved near to Rouge de Bout for four days, leaving B Coy in the advanced area. Reinforcements of 3 officers and 18 men arrived during the month. There were 31 admissions to hospital in February for all causes except wounds. The next tour was from 4–8 March. Heavy batteries bombarded the enemy trenches on the 5th and the Germans retaliated on A and B Coys with about fifty shells. Two bombs were dropped by an aeroplane on B Coy but no damage was done.

Lt. G.H.P. Whitfeld joined No. 1 Platoon, A Coy, on the 10th. As far as this history is concerned he was a most important source of additional information. From July 1916 until November 1917 he was Adjutant and kept a personal diary throughout his time with the battalion.

There was some shelling and a lot of long distance machine gun fire at night during the next tour of 12–16 March at Rouge de Bout. C Coy was in the advanced area.

During the night of the 15th a German aeroplane flew over their trenches heading towards Fleurbaix and returned five minutes later, dropping five pairs of green lights. A 4.2 howitzer shelled the battalion between 9.15 p.m. and 10.30 p.m. but no damage was done. HQ at Rifle Villa was shelled on the morning of the 16th, there were four direct hits and some structural damage was done; Brigade advanced HQ dugouts nearby also received a direct hit. D Coy was in the advanced area on the next return to Rouge de Bout, 20–4 March, but the tour was very quiet with 16th Rifle Bde, having just arrived from England, being attached for training. A Coy was in the advanced area from the 24th and one man was wounded by rifle fire during this period. On the 27th the battalion moved to billets at Cul de Sac in the Sailly area and, the following morning, marched seven miles to Merville via La Gorgue and Beaupre. After leaving Merville by train, they proceeded via St Pol and Amiens to Longeau (two miles south-east of Amiens) and then marched to billets at Montonvillers (seven miles due north of Amiens). The length of this march was 14 miles owing to their guide showing them the wrong route and they did not arrive until 3 a.m. on the 28th. Brigade HQ was based at Flesselles. An impressed Lt. Whitfeld noted that 'The Adjutant, Dominick Browne, was wonderful the way he found the way. It was pitch dark and rained very heavily.' Casualties for March were 6 men killed and 20 wounded, nearly all of them by rifle fire. There were 65 admissions to hospital for all causes except wounds in the same period.

Brig.-Gen. Stephens, having assumed command of the 5th Division on 1 April, was replaced by Brig.-Gen. J.H.W. Pollard. The battalion left Montonvillers on the morning of 4 April and marched to St Gratien via Frénchencourt and Behencourt. Whitfeld: 'That scoundrel Dornan, A Coy's cook, produced a chicken from somewhere – I think I know where.' On the way they joined a column at Villers Bocage, consisting of 25th Brigade HQ, 25th M.G. Coy, and 2nd R. Berkshires, then marched to Millencourt on 5 April and went into Divisional Reserve. Whitfeld wrote:

> While we were in billets during these days, the CO, Adjutant, and Company Commanders went up to look at the new line which we would take over on the 9th. I remained at HQ and 'answered' for Browne. I gathered from Browne on his return that the place was not healthy. ffrench-Mullen confirmed Browne's view when I went back to my billet for dinner.
>
> The position which the battalion would take over was on the ridge beyond Albert and its left was at the village of La Boiselle which, it turned out later, was a veritable fortress. The enemy, as was usual, was in possession of the higher ground and obtained a fairly good observation into our trenches ... The regiment we would relieve were not, I gathered, very impressed with the position. It was certainly rowdy. What a difference from the peace of the sector we had just left.

During 9 April they marched for four hours from Millencourt and relieved 2nd West Yorks in the trenches opposite Schwaben Höhe, a few hundred yards south of La Boiselle, placing their HQ in Bécourt Chateau. B Coy was on the right, A in the centre, D on the left, and C in support in the second line. Two companies of 2nd Rifle Bde were holding Bécourt Redoubt, around the chateau, in Bécourt Wood. The new line was on the ridge above Albert. Whitfeld described the new positions: 'What a difference to the North. No breast work, shoulder high, just a low battered-in trench. The wire, what we could see of it, seemed good. I did not like the place.' Lake commented:

> The trench system was largely in chalk and good red soil. This presented a new set of problems. Whereas before we had dug-outs down underground with only sacking for doors, now we had to get used to the Nissen type of dug-out surrounded on all sides by chalk with only a minimum of chalk on the roof, just sufficient to preserve the level of the ground. We had not been in this position long when the enemy decided to ascertain who the new inhabitants were.

On the evening of 10 April the battalion handed over a portion of trench on their left to 2nd R. Berkshires.

> In those days reliefs were frequently talked about on the telephone, a most dangerous proceeding, as was subsequently proved when the German apparatus for tapping telephone conversations was better understood. There is no doubt that in this case the enemy was aware that there was a change in the troops opposite him.[2]

From 6 a.m. to 3 p.m. that day the enemy was active with field guns, howitzers (5.9 and 4.2), trench mortars, and oil cans. The cans, in particular, caused great alarm as their likes had never been seen before. Some damage was caused to the wire and trenches. Whitfeld recorded:

> In the evening, when we were having dinner and things had got quieter, Sgt D'Arcy came in and reported to ffrench-Mullen that he thought the Germans were cutting the wire opposite his platoon front which was on the left of mine. We were rather amazed at the idea but went up with Sgt D'Arcy to have a look. We could see nothing so returned. Sgt D'Arcy was right as we afterwards found out to our cost.

At 6.55 p.m. on the 11th, the Germans laid down a very heavy bombardment from guns and howitzers of all calibres and trench mortars. This lasted for almost eighty minutes and included a heavy gas attack. It was mostly directed on 1st RIR's reserve, communication and front lines but also on the battalions to their right and left, being most intense on the centre held by A Coy. A German raiding party, estimated at about forty picked men divided into four groups, entered the trenches. They were under the command of four officers named Böhlefeld, Freund, Stradtmann, and Dümas. They took 24 prisoners, killing and wounding several others. The bombardment lifted off the front line at about 7.45 p.m. but remained intense on the other lines until about 8.10 p.m. The raid was made just as it lifted. Whitfeld: 'After the bombardment the front trench, as such, did not exist and it was dangerous, owing to snipers, to go over it as there was no

2 Ibid.

cover.' The British artillery was slow in replying and not much damage, if any, was caused to the raiding party as no dead were seen or found. Twenty-seven unexploded grenades were found later. All was quiet by 8.15 p.m. Telephone communication with all companies except the right broke down at about 7 p.m. but lines to the right company, Brigade HQ, and artillery remained intact. 2/Lt. P.M. Harte-Maxwell and 9 other men were killed, 39 were wounded and 28 missing, of whom the majority were prisoners. Lake described events from his perspective:

> As we were getting ready for 'Stand To' one evening, they laid on a heavy artillery barrage, under which a strong raiding party appeared in the front line. The wire was breached and the communication trenches were filled with broken chalk.
>
> Four of us were just putting on our equipment when it all started, and immediately our exit was plugged with heaps of chalk in the dug-out doorway, jamming the door. Shells came thick and fast and the sacking on the window blew in at every explosion. All we could do was lie low and wait for the end. Our orders had been that in the event of attack we were to rush up to the front line with all speed. But how was this to be done? It does sometimes happen that orders cannot be obeyed.
>
> I had been appointed Lewis Gun Officer by this time and the Germans had captured one of my guns, together with the crew. I had to face a Court of Enquiry because of this, but the Court accepted my account of the raid and I was not punished.

According to Whitfeld:

> The battalion received very severe criticism for their night's work, but some allowance must be made for what appeared to be such a poor fight put up by them. First of all, it was the first occasion that they had ever been subjected to such a bombardment, either in intensity or length. Secondly, it was the first occasion on which gas shells had been used against them in any quantity. Thirdly, those that survived the bombardment were forced to fight in gas helmets (sack type) and being night-time they had no idea where they were themselves or where the enemy was coming from.
>
> The full German account of this raid was afterwards found during the battle of the Somme. In this pamphlet the Germans paid a tribute to the regiment in the following terms: 'The Regiment of Royal Irish Rifles created a most favourable impression both by their physique and their mode of repelling assault. Had it not been … ' and then goes on to explain that things would probably have not happened as they did if they had not used so much gas. It is a glowing tribute and one in which the regiment may well be proud.

Capt. ffrench-Mullen was court-martialled for neglect over this incident but was completely exonerated. Sgt McIlwaine and two men were tried for cowardice; he was found not guilty but the others were sentenced to death, this being commuted to suspended sentences of fifteen years penal servitude each.

At 10 p.m. C Coy relieved A in the front line and A withdrew to support. On 13 April 2/Lt. W. Macky was wounded and one man was killed by trench mortars. Having been relieved by 2nd Rifle Bde that night, HQ, M.G. section, A and D Coys proceeded to billets in Brigade Reserve at Dernancourt. B and C garrisoned Bécourt Redoubt in close support to 2nd Rifle Bde. Casualties for the tour were 2 officers and 87 men. Whitfeld noted: 'We were glad to be out. We had a really bad time of it and my nerve, like most of the other officers, was considerably shaken.'

Major G.H. Sawyer, 2nd R. Berkshires, took over command from Major Mayne on 14 April. During the evening of the 17th, A and D relieved B and C Coys in Bécourt Redoubt and, on the night of the 21st, the battalion relieved 2nd Rifle Bde in the trenches as before, placing HQ at Chapes Spur. At 9.30 p.m. on the 22nd, in conjunction with the divisions on their right and left, a heavy bombardment was opened on the enemy's line in selected places. Under cover of this fire a party of twenty experienced men under 2/Lt. J.L. Muir went out and raided the German trenches. The point selected was in the German line opposite B Coy's front, it being the company nearest to Bécourt Wood. A few Germans were killed but the party got caught by two machine guns and had to retire without taking any prisoners or obtaining an identification. One man was missing, four wounded, and all was quiet again by 10.45 p.m. Whitfeld noted that the raid failed because:

> Not enough time was given to prepare the men (only two days). The men did not combine and did not back the officer up although all old soldiers. Our Artillery fired short. The Hun replied very heavily and it was hard getting back to our own lines again.

Having been relieved on the 25th, the battalion proceeded to Divisional Reserve at Millencourt. The casualties for this tour were 24 men wounded and one missing. There were 42 admissions to hospital for all causes except wounds in April and 3 officers and 116 men arrived as replacements. By this time the battalions' ranks contained roughly 48 per cent from what is now Northern Ireland with 29 per cent from the rest of Ireland and 23 per cent from Britain, many of the latter bearing Irish surnames.

8

Somme

The battalion moved from Millencourt to huts in Hénencourt Wood during 3 May and was attached to 23rd Infantry Brigade. A detachment, consisting of B Coy and two platoons of C, was sent to Dernancourt where they formed large working parties for a new railway. Preparations were now being made for the Somme offensive and, with the French close to collapse at Verdun, the plan was being pushed forward with the utmost urgency. On 8 May the remainder of the battalion returned to Millencourt where their time there was almost entirely employed on working parties making roads, dumps, etc. The detachment returned on the 11th and was replaced by D Coy and the other two platoons of C for work under 110th Railway Coy. The remainder of the battalion rejoined 25th Brigade. They moved to the right Brigade Reserve billets in Albert, 19 May, where the detachment rejoined. The battalion was now back up to full strength but was still short of officers, especially good Company Commanders. Whitfeld observed that

> Our Gunners are good at times and our heavy guns do great damage, especially the 8 inch Howitzer which makes brilliant shooting – unfortunately many of its shells do not explode. For example, the 8-inch fired 190 shells and only 13 exploded which sounds very bad, but I believe they are using up the 100 second fuse (American) – useless stuff. The gas helmet is splendid and perfectly proof against gas.

Four days later they took over trenches in the right sub-sector north of La Boiselle, Dorset Street to Waltney Street opposite the village of Ovillers, one of the strongest fortresses on the whole Somme front that was to be attacked. Three companies were in the front line and D was in support near Donnet Post together with HQ. Major C.C. Macnamara arrived 25 May. Having been relieved after four days, the battalion proceeded to Camp No. 4 Hénencourt Wood, in Divisional Reserve, where training continued until the end of the month. A recent arrival, 8826 Rfn Edward Donnelly, No. 9 Platoon, C Coy, described the nearby Albert Basilica:

> I just came out of the trenches this morning and I feel very tired. We did not have a very bad time, only for the mud and rain I would not mind it. I wish you'd seen this place where we were. There is a chapel and it had a spire of the Blessed

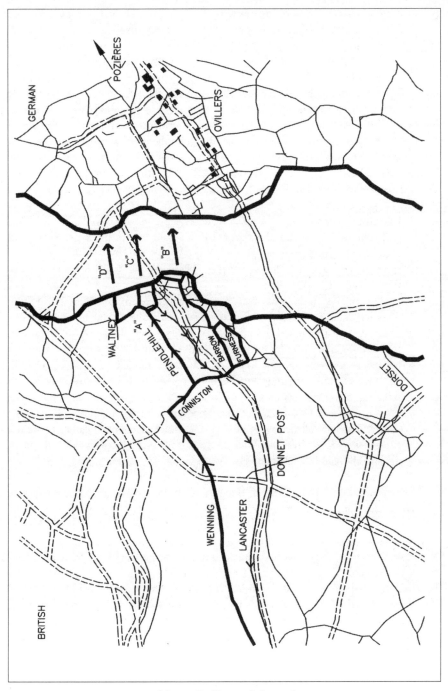

Map 7: Ovillers, 1 July 1916

Virgin holding our Lord in her arms. The Germans shelled it and the Blessed Virgin got struck. She is bent over with her face towards the ground still holding our Lord.

Throughout the 31st all officers went over a plot of ground beyond Bazieux, marked out by flags representing the German trench system that the brigade was to attack. There were 60 admissions to hospital during May for all causes except wounds, while reinforcements of 2 officers and 94 men arrived. Casualties amounted to one man killed and 6 wounded – the best month of the war. During 1 June the division carried out a tactical scheme over the ground gone over the previous day and it was considered a success. The battalion moved to No. 5 Camp Hénencourt Wood on the 4th and to the right reserve billets at Albert on the 12th. Rfn Donnelly described the environment at that time:

> I am still alive thank God. We had a very bad night on Saturday. We were out digging when the Germans shelled us. I don't want you to think that they were bursting all around me; none came near, no. You should have seen our artillery at them. It was interesting looking at the shells going over to them. We could see them going through the air.
>
> This place is nothing like what I expected. There are times you would think there was no war on at all. Just now there is some artillery firing but it is over our heads. Fellows that have been here a long time say this place is one of the worst. It is nothing like what you would read in the newspapers; but maybe I have not been here long enough for to see it. The only thing I miss is dry ground. Everywhere, without telling lies, is covered with mud. In the trenches we are standing in about 2 foot 6 inches of it … They had a great time at home. They saw an aeroplane. I wish you had seen the Germans trying to hit one of our aeroplanes. They are all deserving of a vc for the chances they take … I found a Scotch woman's address in a stocking I was given and a Glasgow fellow wrote to her and she sent him a big parcel of grub.

One man was killed while with a working party on the 14th. Major Macnamara took over command from Major Sawyer (who returned to his own unit) on the 18th and, the following evening, the battalion moved to the Division Centre subsection trenches, its position being Goose Dubs junction on the front line to the junction of Long Ridge Street with the front line. This area is open countryside, perfect for machine guns, and the Germans held the higher ground. Two men were wounded on the 23rd and, having been relieved that day by 2nd Rifle Bde, the battalion moved to bivouac in Long Valley. The twenty-fourth of June began with the commencement of the great bombardment of the enemy positions that was to continue until the start of the battle. The attack had originally been planned for the 29th but, because of poor weather conditions, was postponed until 1 July. Whitfeld wrote, 26 June:

> Battalions move to the trenches. I went up with the CO, Col. Macnamara, a very fine soldier indeed, and poor Browne, the Adjutant. I said goodbye to them both

at Crucifix Corner. I never saw either of them again. After seeing the battalion go into the trenches I returned to the Transport Lines as I was left out of this attack, being Assistant Adjutant. I hated leaving my friends and my platoon but, I suppose, fate ruled that I should.

The German retaliation caused many casualties: 27 June, one man was killed, 2/Lt. F.W. Deane and 3 men wounded; 28th, one man killed and 19 wounded; 29th, 19 wounded and, 30th, 5 men were killed and 23 wounded. According to Major Fitzmaurice: 'During the preliminary bombardment the battalion suffered casualties to the amount of 4 Officers and 114 ORs including sick, killed, and wounded.' Reinforcements of 4 officers and 57 men arrived that month. On the evening before the attack the battalion moved to the assembly trenches and companies were distributed as follows: B on the right in Cartmael Street; C in the centre; D on the left in Pendlehill Street, and A in support in Coniston Street. Lake remembered:

On the last evening of June our battalion moved up to shelter trenches that had been dug on both sides of the communication trench. The Higher Command had ordered that the Lewis Gun Sections were not to be used separately but were to be dispersed among the companies and their officers were to go back to their original platoons. And this after weeks of highly successful training that brought officers and men into a very close partnership together with a very effective fire power.

On the eve of the battle I sat in a shelter with some of my men and tried to keep up their spirits by playing my tin whistle to them. But it was a long night. I had orders to appoint a personal 'runner' who was to stand by me through thick and thin. I asked my Sergeant about it and he chose a keen young chap who had recently joined us. As I gave the lad his instructions his face lighted up and I could tell that he regarded the job as a great honour. Oh Dear! How short was his task.

Lt.-Col. Macnamara had issued the following General Instructions to his officers on 25 June, before the date of the attack was changed:

I

In the offensive operations on the 29th June, the first line of attack will consist of 2nd Royal Berks on the right, 2nd Lincolns on the left, supported by Detachments of the Brigade M.G. and Bomb Companies.

The above battalions will take the first objective as explained, east of Ovillers. The 1st R. I. Rifles supported by Detachments of Bde M.G. and Bombing Coys will pass through the 2nd R. Berks and 2nd Lincolns at the first objective and will take the second objective as explained, including north end of Pozières.

The 1st R. I. Rifles will be supported in attack on second objective by two Coys R. Berks following in rear of their right, and by two Coys 2nd Lincolns following in rear of their left. The two Coys 2nd R. Berks and 2nd Lincolns remain at and consolidate the second objective. The third objective as explained, to East of Pozières, will be taken by 1st R. I. Rifles on the right, and by 2nd Rifle Bde on the left. The third objective will be consolidated by 1st R. I. Rifles and 2nd Rifle Bde.

The 1st R. I. Rifles will consolidate strong points at Walled Garden at X.4.b.1.6½ (Belfast) and at junction of communication trenches at R.34.d.1.0 (Hollywood).

II

The battalion will advance to first objective with B, C, and D Coys in the first line in column of platoons with 50 yards distance between platoons and about 150 yards interval between columns of platoons.

A Coy in same formation will follow 100 yards in rear of centre of first line. B Coy on the right will direct and will have as its first point of direction Ovillers Church. B Coy will then advance with its right on Ovillers Main Street to right of first objective. B Coy will then move on second objective keeping Pozières Church about 300 Yards to its right flank.

III

During advance to second objective, the advance will not be delayed for 'clearing up' trenches.

IV

B Coy will move off from assembly trenches at 10 minutes before zero hour, via Barrow, Furness, and Ulverstone.

D Coy will move off at 10 minutes before zero hour, via Long Ridge and Waltney.

C Coy will follow immediately in rear of D Coy and move via Pendle Hill.

A Coy will leave junction of Coniston and Pendle Hill at zero hour, and follow immediately in rear of C via Pendle Hill.

Headquarters follow A Coy.

Coys will vacate assembly trenches as quickly as possible.

The parapet will be crossed at once on arriving at front fire trench and Column of Platoons formed in the open beyond our wire.

V

General compass bearing of second objective from our front trenches is about 75°.

VI

Each Coy will carry 5 Boxes of S.A.A. and 10 Boxes of bombs, which will be taken from dumps in brigade area as explained.

VII

27 Flares will be carried by each Coy, to be taken from dumps in brigade area.

VIII

In the event of iron rations having to be used, only 1 tin in 3 will be opened at one time to avoid waste, which must be carefully avoided.

IX

The following maps only will be carried: Map S and map of German trenches 1/20,000, Sheet 57d SE Edition 2B. No Operation Orders to be carried in attack.

X

Dumps in our lines to which it may be necessary to send back are marked thus:
S.A.A. – Red flag
Bombs – Yellow flag
Rations and Petrol tins – location follows.[1]

Falls commented:

As a fact, though the concentration of artillery seemed very great to the troops that witnessed it, the British had even yet by no means sufficient weight of metal for such an enterprise. Above all, they were short of field artillery, and as a consequence the German wire at several points was inadequately cut. The effect of heavy artillery upon the German dug-outs, frequently thirty feet down in the chalk, had been extraordinarily overestimated ... The 8th Division was attacking with all three brigades in line, the 25th in the centre. The right flank of this brigade was to be on the north of the ruined village of Ovillers. The final objective was to run through the eastern portion of Pozières. Beyond Ovillers the ground dropped away to a slight valley, rising again to Pozières.

Zero hour for the attack was at 7.30 a.m., 1 July. The division was opposed by the 180th Infantry Regiment of the German Army, with two battalions holding the front defences, and the third battalion in reserve in the neighbourhood of Pozières, the final

1 See Appendix IV for details of the instructions issued by 25th Brigade.

objective of 25th Brigade that day. The brigade attacked with 2nd R. Berkshires on the right and 2nd Lincolns on the left. 1st RIR was supporting and 2nd Rifle Bde was in reserve. The 23rd Brigade was on the right with its left flank at Ovillers and the 70th Brigade was on the left. The 34th Division was on 8th Division's right and 32nd Division on the left. 1st RIR covered the brigade front and if the attack had been successful would have gone through the two preceding battalions to the objective that was assigned to it. On moving from the assembly trenches the company positions were: B on the right, C in the centre, D on the left and A in support. The battalion went into the attack with 21 officers and 600 men. Hopes of success were very high, so much so that the Quartermaster, Capt. Edwards, had orders to be prepared to serve teas to the battalion in Pozières that afternoon. Whitfeld: 'After allowing for battalion reserves, there were, therefore, ten companies of German troops, approximately 1,800 men, to oppose the three brigades of the 8th Division, about 8,500 bayonets.'

Lake described the situation from the perspective of B Coy:

> Punctually at Zero hour next morning, the artillery barrage opened up. Never before or since have I heard such a din. It was accurate fire too and it was lifted after half an hour according to plan. This was the signal for the Infantry to go 'Over the Top'. We were supporting another company and were able to see how gallantly they leaped to it. But they got nowhere. The German machine guns had not been eliminated and at once they opened up accurate fire on our parapets. The men simply got up and fell back into the trench, either killed outright or badly wounded. Those who did get further were never seen or heard of again, as far as I know.
>
> Presently Captain Ross, our Company Commander, came crawling along the trench quite oblivious of the groaning bodies that were under him. There was a glazed look on his face which was streaming with blood and in his mouth was a cigarette that would never light because of the blood on it. I said something as he passed but he made no answer, he just continued on his way on all fours like a wounded animal. I never saw him again and don't know how far he got.
>
> Soon after that there was a heavy explosion just behind me somewhere but fortunately not in the trench, otherwise this would not have been written. I hunched my shoulders as a load of earth landed on my tin helmet. But alas! my runner had gone, he was blown to pieces. Near by, another man lay bleeding from a nasty wound in his thigh. I went over to him and could tell that his femoral artery had been severed and so first-aid was of little use. I moistened his lips from my water bottle and assured him he would soon be out of pain, and so he died.
>
> I became conscious then of a man who was making horrid noises like a trapped animal and with his mouth wide open. My Platoon Sergeant was standing next to him and fearing lest panic should spread, I said to him: 'Dump him on the jaw, Sergeant.' He was a very heavy man with big biceps and he dealt that man a punch that would have knocked out any boxer in the ring. But it made no difference, so stepping over to the man, I pointed down the trench and shouted in his face: 'Go'. He turned and fled and we never saw him again. He was paral-

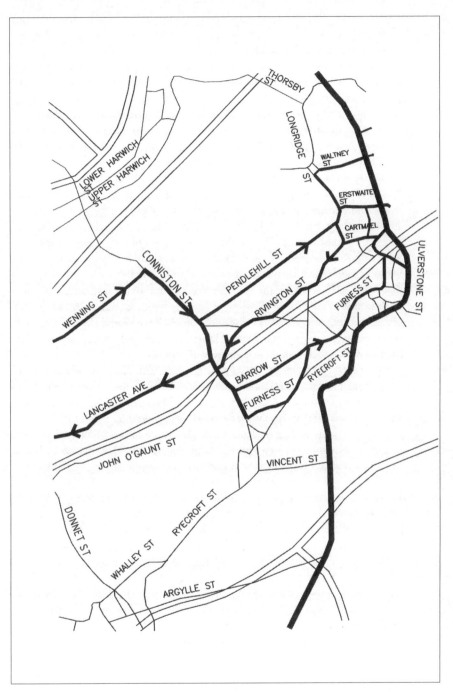

Map 8: Attack route of 1 July 1916

ysed by fright. The instinct of self-preservation said 'Run' and his military training said 'Stand Fast'. It was a clear case of conflict between desire and duty and
I was to come across it again later.

Soon after this a chap named Bentley, who had come overseas with me,
appeared. He brought a chit of paper with him on which was scribbled: 'We will
attack again with you at noon. OC Rifle Brigade'. Bentley was highly suspicious
of this note and so was I. What action were we to take? We decided that one or
other of us must try to make contact with HQ. There was no field telephone
available as far as we knew. We tossed for it, so Bentley remained in charge of
what few men we had and I set off for Battalion HQ.

The Communication trench was clear and all was quiet so I made good time.
Presently my eyes began to sting and my throat became dry and sore. I realised
that I had run into a tear gas barrage. By the time I reached HQ tears were
streaming down my face and I was speechless. The CO was there together with
two or three other senior officers. One of them brought me a small bottle of soda
water and that restored my voice. They ordered taking no notice of the scribbled
note and told me to return to the men, informing them that we should be relieved
that evening. I sought out the stretcher-bearer's dug-out and although they were
all dead beat, I got four of them to come along with me. But really two stretchers were of little use. Eventually we were relieved by the Royal Berkshires and the
first subaltern I ran into was Frank Masters, my chum of college days who later
became my brother-in-law. So is the way of things.

Of twenty-two officers who had gone into action on that eventful day only five
of us remained on our feet by evening. The Second-in-Command, Major
Fitzmaurice, assembled us in a dug-out and told us that we had been awarded a
Military Cross for that day's work and asked who should we give it to. There was-
n't one of us who held up his hand and said: 'Give it to me. I'll take it.' I think it
was given to a junior officer who had been wounded and had got home, but we
never heard what his gallant action had been.[2]

A and B were, owing to the extremely heavy and accurate barrage put up along the communication trenches and the front line, unable to leave their own trenches and only numbered about fifty men on arrival at the fire trench. A Coy lost very severely moving from
the assembly trenches. Capt. G.I. Gartlan, A Coy Commander, was wounded and made
the following report to Lt. Whitfeld (No. 1 Platoon) after the attack:

The attack commenced at 7.30 a.m. after an intensive bombardment of five to ten
minutes. The Berks and Lincolns went over first and were met by a terrific fire
which appeared to paralyse the attack. Our attack following faired no better, only
two companies getting over and no one appeared to come back.

2 The only officers I could identify who had survived unscathed were Major A.J.W. Fitzmaurice, 2/Lts
W.V.C. Lake, M.A. Mulock-Bentley, and A.F.J. Steele-Nicholson. The other officer would have been
T/Capt. C.I..G. Powell (RAMC). This reconciles the figure of 21 officers involved in the attack and
Lake's figure of 22. The MC was awarded to 2/Lt. W.S. Maitland.

Our company, coming up the communication trench, came right into the retaliation and your platoon, I hear, got two 5.9's right into the middle of it and hardly anyone escaped. Your servant was killed.

The CO was terribly wounded – I saw him sitting down, he had lost an eye and was badly hit in the leg. He would not go until he had handed over command to Fitzmaurice. Dear old Dominick [the Adjutant] died in no-man's-land, shot through the femoral artery, so 'the faculty' told me. I believe Carroll [the RSM] knows where he is buried. I know he was brought in.

Major Fitzmaurice had only been on active service for twenty-four days, never before having experienced trench warfare, when he found himself in command under the most difficult of circumstances.[3] Whitfeld commented in his diary:

Ovillers was a veritable fortress. The German heavy gun shooting was good and A Company that commenced coming up the trench 121 strong reached the top with 24 men.

Capt. Gartlan also wrote a letter to Col. Macnamara's family:

We came upon a very heavy artillery barrage from 8-inch and 12-inch howitzers. Colonel Macnamara was just in front of my company at the start (I was the supporting Captain to the battalion); the communication trench we had to go down from our assembly trench to the front line became so congested that the CO and the Adjutant got out and walked down to the trench in the open. After that I lost sight of them.

2nd R. Berkshires report to Brigade:

At about 7.15 a.m. the enemy opened rifle and machine gun fire on our line. This fire was probably drawn by the 2nd Devon Regt which at about this time attempted to line up in front of their parapet. At 7.30 a.m. the three assaulting Coys advanced to attack the German line. They were met by intensive rifle and machine gun fire which prevented any of the waves reaching the enemy line. A little group on the left of the battalion succeeded in getting into the German trench but was eventually bombed out. At about 7.45 a.m. the parapet was swept by rifle and machine gun fire which prevented any exit from our trenches. The enemy replied to our intensive bombardment by barraging the front line from about 6.35 a.m. onwards. At about 11 a.m. the order came from Brigade HQ to

3 The following names were forwarded for gallant conduct by Major Fitzmaurice: Capt. D.A. Browne, T/Capt. C.L.G. Powell (RAMC), Lt. S.D.I. Smith, 2/Lts E.V. Burke-Murphy, H.M. Glastonbury, W.S. Maitland, and J. Marshall, RSM W. Carroll, 5420 CSM J. Driscoll (C Coy), 6823 CSM W. Martin (A Coy), 7323 CSM C.E. Stovin (B Coy), 7270 CSM J. Tonge (D Coy), 9493 Sgt W.J. Fee, 7095 Sgt R.H. Simpson, 9889 Sgt J. Walsh, 9405 L/Sgt D. McCourt, 6543 Cpl W.J. Patterson, 8148 Rfn R. Anderson, 8368 Rfn W. Flanagan, 9257 Rfn J.J. McGuigan.

stand by and await further orders. At about 12.30 p.m. news was received that the brigade would be relieved. Steel helmets proved very reliable and in many cases saved men's lives.

In the meantime C Coy advanced under very heavy fire but it is not known if they ever entered the German front line owing to the severe machine gun fire. It appears that they were annihilated before getting very far and the wounded were killed by shell-fire where they lay. 2/Lt. H.M. Glastonbury, the Company Commander, was shot in the leg crossing no-man's-land and had his wound bandaged. His men were unable to bring him back to the British lines and he died where he fell.

D Coy went over the top at about 7.45 a.m., formed up in no-man's-land in columns of platoons, advanced and entered the German first and second lines. They linked up with Lt.-Col. R. Bastard and the remnants of 2nd Lincolns. Lt. S.D.I. Smith, the Company Commander, had been injured by a bayonet wound to the chest at the second line, but continued on towards the third line throwing grenades as he went, but was killed by machine gun fire at this stage. In order to conform with the movements of the troops on the left and right, the company was then forced to retire. They had experienced much hand-to-hand fighting during the attack and withdrawal. War Diary: 'The German trenches had been completely buried by our bombardment but excellent use had been made of the cellars in Ovillers; his trenches were thickly manned.'

2nd Lincolns report to Brigade:

At 6.25 a.m. the intensive bombardment commenced. To which the enemy retaliated on our front line and assembly trenches with high explosive shrapnel. At 7.25 a.m. companies started to move forward from their assembly positions preparatory to the assault.

The three assaulting companies, getting their first two waves out into no-man's-land, and their third and fourth waves at zero hour. The Support Company got into our front line trench but suffered a lot of casualties from shell fire. At 7.30 a.m. as soon as the barrage lifted the whole assaulted.

They were met with very severe rifle fire and in most cases had to advance in rushes and return the fire, this fire seemed to come from the German second line, and the machine gun fire from our left. On reaching the German front line they found it strongly held, and were met with showers of bombs, but after a very hard fight about 200 yards of German line was taken at about 7.50 a.m., the extreme right failing to get in and also the extreme left, where there appeared to be a gap of about 70 yards, although bits of platoons of the 70th Brigade joined them.

The Support Company by this time joined in. The few officers that were left gallantly led their men over the German trench to attack the second line, but owing to the rifle and machine gun fire, could not push on. Attempts were made to consolidate and make blocks, but the trench was so badly knocked about that very little cover was obtainable, from the enfilade machine gun fire and continual bombing attacks which were being made by the enemy the whole time, and one frontal attack from their second line which we repulsed.

By about 9 a.m. this isolated position became untenable, no supports being able to reach us owing to the intense rifle and machine gun fire. And our left was being driven back, the remainder which by now only held 100 yards, had to withdraw.

On reaching our own line all the men that could be collected were formed up and tried to push on again, but the heavy machine gun and rifle fire made the ground quite impassable. About 1 p.m. I received orders from the brigade to withdraw.

The German perspective from Ovillers was described in *Die Schwaben an der Ancre* by Gerster:[4]

The intense bombardment was realised by all to be the prelude to the infantry assault at last. The men in the dugouts therefore waited ready, a belt full of hand grenades around them, gripping their rifles and listening for the bombardment to lift from the front defence zone onto the rear defences. It was of vital importance not to lose a second in taking up position in the open to meet the British Infantry, who would be advancing immediately behind the artillery barrage. Looking towards the British defences through the long trench periscopes held up out of the dugout entrances, there could be seen a mass of steel helmets above their parapet, showing their storm-troops were ready for the assault. At 7.30 a.m. the hurricane of shells ceased as suddenly as it had begun. Our men at once clambered up the steep shafts leading from the dugouts to daylight, and ran singly or in groups to the nearest shell craters. The machine guns were pulled out of their dugouts and hurriedly placed into position, their crews dragging the heavy ammunition boxes up the steep steps and out to the guns. A rough firing line was thus rapidly established. As soon as in position, a series of extended lines of British Infantry were seen moving forward from the British trenches. The first line appeared to continue without end to right and left. It was quickly followed by a second line, then a third and fourth. They came on at a steady even pace, as if expecting to find nothing alive in our front trenches.

The front line, preceded by a thin line of skirmishers and bombers, were now half-way across no-man's-land. 'Get ready!' was passed along the line from crater to crater, and heads appeared over the crater edges as final positions were taken up for the best view, and machine guns mounted firmly in place. A few minutes later, when the leading British line was within 100 yards, the rattle of machine gun and rifle fire broke out along the whole line of craters. Some fired kneeling so as to get a better target over the broken ground, while others, in the excitement of the moment, stood up, regardless of their own safety, to fire into the crowd of men in front of them. Red rockets sped up into the sky as a signal to the artillery, and immediately afterwards a mass of shells from the German batteries in rear tore through the air and burst among the advancing lines. Whole sections seemed to fall, and the rear formations, moving in close order, quickly scattered.

4 See *Quis Separabit*, vol. 3, no. 1, May 1932.

The advance rapidly crumbled under this hail of shells and bullets. All along the line men could be seen throwing their arms into the air and collapsing, never to move again. Badly wounded rolled about in their agony, and others less severely wounded crawled to the nearest shell-hole for shelter.

The British soldier, however, has no lack of courage, and once his hand is set to the plough he is not easily turned from his purpose. The extended lines, though badly shaken and with many gaps, now came on all the faster. Instead of a leisurely walk they covered the ground in short rushes at the double. Within a few minutes the leading troops had reached within a stone's throw of out front trench, and while some of us continued to fire at point blank range, others threw hand grenades among them. The noise of the battle became indescribable. The shouting of orders and the shrill cheers as they charged forward could be heard above the violent and intense fusillade of machine guns and rifles and the bursting of bombs, and above the deep thunderings of the artillery and the shell explosions. With all this were mingled the moans and groans of the wounded, the cries for help and the last screams of death. Again and again the extended lines of British Infantry broke against the German defence like waves against a cliff, only to be beaten back.

It was an amazing spectacle of unexampled gallantry, courage and bull-dog determination on both sides.

1st RIR suffered such severe casualties that it was not possible for the Assistant Adjutant, Lt. Whitfeld, to establish for certain what exactly had happened. Major Fitzmaurice reported: 'During the action two Lewis Guns were lost and most of the equipment belonging to them.' The 25th Infantry Brigade's diary recorded:

> The progress of this battalion through our trenches was rendered exceedingly difficult by the wretched conditions of our trenches, which were moreover blocked by dead and wounded men, and by men of the assaulting battalions who had been unable to go forward, or had been driven back. The Commanding Officer was very seriously wounded and his Adjutant killed.

At 11.50 p.m. the whole of the 8th Division was withdrawn and returned to bivouac in Long Valley. Officer casualties in the attack were 5 killed or died of wounds and 12 wounded.[5] Losses among other ranks were 17 killed, 348 wounded, 27 missing, 8 wounded and missing. It should, however, be noted that the figure for those wounded refers to the numbers passing through Dressing Stations, a considerable proportion of whom died later. Total casualties for June and 1 July were 433: Officers: 5 killed, 14 wounded. Other Ranks: 19 killed, 360 wounded, 27 missing, 8 wounded and missing. An analysis of those killed on 1 July shows that over 78 per cent have no known grave and are commemorated on the Thiepval Memorial.

---

5 Officers killed: Lt.-Col. C.C. Macnamara (died of wounds, 15 July), Capt. D.A. Browne, Lt. S.D.I. Smith, 2/Lts H.M. Glastonbury, and W.H. Gregg. Wounded: Capts G.I. Gartlan and A.J. Ross, Lt. G. Lawler, 2/Lts E.V. Burke-Murphy, D.B. Hill, H.J. McConnell, A. McDowell, E.A. Mahoney, W.S. Maitland, J. Marshall, M.A. Palethorpe, and W.U. Tyrrell.

9

Le Transloy

BORDER REDOUBT AND ZENITH TRENCH

Lt. Whitfeld took over as Adjutant: 'I am beginning to see how much religion plays its part in an Irish Regiment. I fear that I have made some errors of judgement already but I hope no evil consequences.' At 5 p.m., 2 July, the battalion left Long Valley and moved to Dernancourt where they entrained at midnight. The next evening they arrived at Ailly-sur-Somme and billeted there for the night before moving to Le Mesge via Breilly, Foudrinoy, and Cavillon. Having set off early on the 6th and entraining at Longeau, 5.30 p.m., they arrived at Pernes (via Amiens), at 1.30 a.m. the following day and then marched to Allouagne (via Marles) for a week's rest.

On 14 July the battalion moved to the forward area and was billeted in Béthune for another week. This town was the men's favourite in the British sector having good billets and well-stocked shops. Major E.C. Lloyd, Royal Irish Regiment, arrived on 20 July and took over command. Lloyd was to prove himself a most stern and unpopular CO. At 12.30 p.m. the following day they moved to Brigade Support (Hohenzollern Right Subsector) in front of Vermelles. According to Falls:

> The dug-outs were good and deep and the whole region had the indescribable dirtiness and sordidness of an old battleground, lying like a pall upon a countryside unattractive at the best of times. Outside the front line, with its mortars and constant threats of mine explosions, which shook men's nerves, there was nothing of which to complain, there being little or no long range artillery fire.

At 9.30 a.m. on the 26th the battalion relieved 2nd R. Berkshires in the front lines; the 8th RDF, 16th (Irish) Division, was on their right and 2nd Lincolns on their left. Whitfeld described the area:

> We were now about to enter on a new type of warfare among craters. This area, the Loos Salient, was famous for this. German artillery is not violent as I fancy most of the guns have gone south, but he is very strong in trench mortars, aerial darts, etc. Bombing fights are frequent. The famous Fosse 8 looks right down into our position. It is a great fortress as was proved in the battle of Loos. The

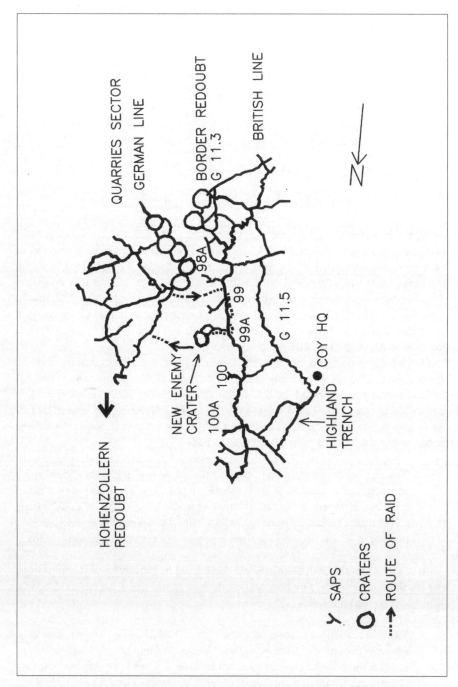

Map 9: The raid at Border Redoubt, 21 August 1916

dugouts are very good here and deep but are infested with mice and rats, the latter run all over the parapet.

The War Diary entry for the first four days of this tour recorded:

A comparatively quiet four days. The enemy does not appear to have many guns
in front of us but he has free use of trench mortar and aerial darts. On the 27th
and 28th we sprung two mines and the enemy sprung one. These did not alter
the general situation.

2/Lt. B.J. Hodson was wounded by gunfire on the 27th, 2/Lt. J.L. Millar was killed
on 29 July, and 2/Lt. C.N. Champney was wounded on 2 August. During this tour 5
men were killed and 30 wounded, while reinforcements for July totalled 19 officers and
130 men. The battalion was relieved on the evening of 7 August and moved into
Divisional Reserve at Labourse. During the 15th they relieved 2nd Northamptonshire
Regt in the left Sub Section of the Quarries Sector in Border Redoubt. On the afternoon of 20 August the Germans blew a mine that overlapped a mine blown by the
British the previous day. This destroyed the wire around the sap and in front of the
trench nearby. An Officer's patrol went out at 12.15 a.m. the next day to examine the
two new craters. They reported that the British crater was about 40 yards from their
front-line trench, being roughly 60 feet broad and 40 feet deep. The crater blown by the
enemy was about 20 feet to the left of the British crater and there was a channel about
6 feet deep running between the two. The enemy crater was about 60 feet broad and 50
feet deep. Neither of these was occupied but, as the patrol approached the enemy crater,
about six bombs were thrown at them. They came either from the far lip of the enemy
crater or from a sap just behind the lip but the patrol returned safely.

At 3.20 a.m. that same day, after a short preliminary bombardment with heavy trench
mortar shells and aerial darts, the Germans rushed that part of the battalion's trench
being held by C Coy. They entered near Sap 98A and proceeded down the front line
trench, visiting Sap 99 en route, and departed by Sap 99A. The front line between Saps
98A and 99A was very narrow and completely blocked with spoil bags, and consequent-
ly was not manned. The trench, at the time, was occupied by a spoils party of the
Northamptons, but these men were necessarily unarmed. There was a certain amount
of confusion, and any independent action was nullified by the congestion in the narrow
trenches arising from the presence of these men. The enemy, numbering about twenty,
did not remain long, probably only five minutes. Casualties of the battalion amounted
to 2 killed, 3 wounded, and 8 taken prisoner. In addition, 2 miners and one man of the
spoils party were killed and another 4 were taken prisoner. 2/Lt. Lake, the Lewis Gun
Officer, described this attack:

The raid was evidently carried out by a working party which had been at work
inside the enemy crater. This was preceded by a trench mortar bombardment
lasting about 15 minutes. The trench mortars fell in front of the line on the left
and right of Sap 99 and around the wire in front of Rabbit Run.

One Lewis Gun was posted to the left of Sap 99. The team was made up as follows: 8176 L/Cpl Scott, 1570 Rfn Nixon, 9603 Rfn Norris, 7453 Rfn Black, 9017 Rfn Murray. The two men on sentry at the time were Rfn Norris and Rfn Black.

For some reason L/Cpl Scott appears to have been round the next traverse to the left and the remaining two men were asleep in a disused mine shaft in the same bay as that in which the gun was. The two men on duty could not have kept on the look-out during the short bombardment. The men asleep in the shaft had just been awakened for 'stand to' when two or three Northamptons and the two men on duty crowded in upon them because the Germans were coming along the trench from Sap 99. Rfn Norris and Rfn Black were dragged out and made prisoners as also were the Northampton men. A scuffle ensued and L/Cpl Scott came round the traverse and fired two or three revolver shots. He was then wounded and taken prisoner. The enemy then shouted down the shaft to find out if there were any more men but Rfn Nixon and Murray lay low and did not answer as they were unarmed. Immediately the enemy had gone these two men came out and manned the gun but could see no sign of the enemy.

Another Lewis Gun was posted at Sap 98A. Owing to the repair work going on in the sap, the team had to post the gun in the trench about six yards to the right of the sap, where it could command the wire in front of Rabbit Run equally well. There is no fire step at this point which makes it difficult for men to pass along the trench when the gun is mounted there.

During the bombardment several men congregated here and forced the gunners still further to the right. L/Cpl Manson who is in charge of the team was actually knocked over by the onrush of men and had his knee cut. Rfn Geraghty of the team was buried by a trench mortar and had to retire. Otherwise this team is intact. A look-out was kept on the wire at Rabbit Run the whole time but owing to the black smoke and white chalk dust, observation was difficult. From this point it is not possible to see Sap 99 owing to the pile of sand-bags on the trench. This team saw nothing of the enemy.

Evidently the raiding party quickly slipped over the near lip of the crater into Sap 99, thus exposing themselves for very few seconds. A whistle was sounded when the party retired. This sound was not thought to be unusual, as it is often blown when our trench mortars go over.

Major Lloyd reported to Brigade:

He entered 98A Sap and captured the post, those that were not captured left the post. The enemy proceeded down the trench moving west and scattering bombs (which did not explode). Killed 3 men on his way, entered 99 Sap and took the garrison prisoners, continued down the trench to 99A Sap which he also entered and captured the garrison, passed a Lewis Gun on his way which was in position but could not come into action; the Corporal in charge of the team appears to have put up a fight with his revolver but is missing. The enemy left the trench at

99A Sap and returned to his line by the mine crater. The garrison of the saps appears to have left their saps. The NCOs in charge are under arrest.[1]

The front line trench between the saps mentioned is entirely indefensible owing to spoil bags which have blocked the trench to such an extent that it is almost impassable. The craters are so close to the sap heads that the enemy held the advantage so far as the ground is concerned.

9894 Pte Taylor stated:

> The first I heard about the raid was when a man came running down the trench saying that the Germans were coming. I was between two parties – three RIR and three 58th. The three 58th got down the mine and I was following when a German officer pointed his revolver at me and told me to come out. I came out and they beckoned me to get up over the parapet. I got up and one man followed me. Directly I was over I ran along between our parapet and our wire. The Germans fired at me but missed. I got back into our trench near the North Border Crater.

Nothing eventful happened again until, at about 10.50 p.m. on the 24th, the Germans attempted to enter the Northern Crater. Bombs were thrown opposite Boyal 98 to distract the attention of 1st RIR. A party of between twenty and thirty of the enemy attempted this raid but were discovered when within 20 yards of their objective, rapid fire was opened and bombs were thrown. The Germans scattered and were seen to carry back some of their men. In this action 2/Lt. W.K. Adrain was killed while helping to dig men out that had been buried in the debris when their trench was hit. During the night of 25 August the battalion was withdrawn into Brigade Reserve at Curley Crescent for three days. They then moved into the Centre Sub Section of the Quarries sector where they had a very quiet but wet tour. In August drafts totalling 4 officers and 28 men arrived. The following casualties occurred 16–30 August: 7 men were killed, 49 wounded and 8 missing. Four men were also killed in action on 30 August while attached to 25th Trench Mortar Battery. The battalion was relieved by 2nd Middlesex (23rd Brigade), 1 September, and marched to Divisional Reserve in Fouquereuil. They returned to the trenches and relieved 2nd Northamptons (24th Brigade) in Brigade Support on the 9th and relieved 2nd Rifle Bde in the Hohenzollern Redoubt, Left Sub Sector, on 13 September. It was here that 2/Lt. J.N. McMillen was buried alive for over an hour after the explosion of a trench mortar and lost the power of speech for nine days. Whitfeld commented:

> This was a noisy part of the line, the Germans making free use of their heavy trench mortars concealed behind Fosse 8. It is all craters, and mining work is most active. They are interesting fellows and, I think, exceedingly brave, and I

---

1 Cpl J. Simpson and L/Cpl J. Richardson were tried by FGCM at Vermelles, 26 August 1916, on a charge of quitting their post. The former was reduced in rank and the latter was sentenced to two years hard labour.

don't envy them their job. They, however, don't envy us our job, so we are quits. They have been most accurate in their calculations as to when the Hun is going to blow up a mine. It is wonderful how they find these things out. I don't like this Crater Warfare, very nerve racking at night going round as the sentries being so near the Hun are 'windy'. So was I.!!

This four-day cycle between Brigade Reserve and the Hohenzollern Sub Sectors continued until 10 October. Casualties for September were 2 officers wounded (2/Lts I.C. Cooke and J.N. McMillen), 3 men killed, and 10 wounded. Replacements amounted to 6 officers and 42 men. At 3 a.m., 9 October, 2/Lt. G.J.H. Palmer, with twelve men, carried out a raid against the German trenches. He and five of his men got to within five yards of the German parapet but were detected; nevertheless he shot two Germans and several bombs were thrown before withdrawing. He suffered multiple grenade wounds in this venture. The Rifles were relieved in broad daylight on the 10th and moved into billets at Nœux les Mines, going the next day to billets in Allouagne.

The battalion entrained at Lillers on the morning of 14 October, arriving early next day at Pont Renay, and proceeded to Ville-sur-Somme by bus. They moved into bivouac in Trônes Wood on the 19th, going into support on the 22nd prior to battle. According to Falls:

> Here the Allies had bitten deeply into the German positions, the British right being ten miles from the old front line in the same latitude. All the three main German lines of defence which had existed in July had been penetrated but, the advance having taken upwards of four months, the Germans had had time to dig any wire as they fell back, and now had equally strong defences in front. The object of the attack in question was to get within striking distance of the village of Le Transloy, on the Bapaume–Peronne Road, from the present position between Morval and Lesboeufs.
>
> The 8th Division was to attack with all three brigades in line, the 23rd on the right, the 25th in the centre, and the 24th on the left. The 25th Brigade had two successive objectives, the first partly represented by a trench known as Zenith Trench, and partly represented by an imaginary line prolonging this trench to the left (and north-west) to another trench known as Misty Trench (in the British line). The second objective was 300 yards beyond the first. The advance to these objectives was to be carried out by the 2nd Lincolnshire on the right and the 2nd Rifle Brigade on the left. Somewhat unfortunately, 'zero', originally fixed at 9.30 a.m., was postponed five hours, till 2.30 p.m.

This delay was due to poor weather conditions. Two companies of the leading battalions advanced towards Zenith and Eclipse trenches, keeping as close as possible to the creeping barrage and suffering some casualties in the process. As soon as the barrage lifted, the Lincolns were met with such intense machine gun and rifle fire from Zenith Trench that the attack ground to a halt. The platoon of 2nd Rifle Bde that attacked the junction of Zenith and Eclipse Trench were also stopped in similar circumstances. To

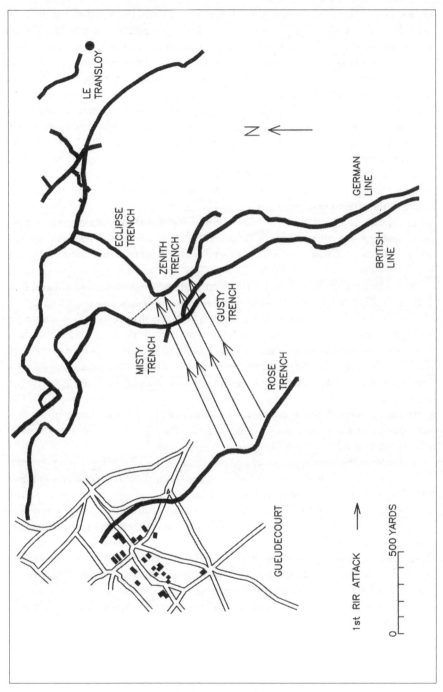

Map 10: Le Transloy, 23 October 1916

the left of this point, on the line between Zenith and Misty, the objective was attained. 1st RIR, being the supporting battalion, was initially ordered to occupy Spider Trench and Rainbow Trench that had been vacated by 2nd R. Berkshires. At zero hour they advanced by platoons, at fifty paces interval in single file, through a heavy barrage that the Germans put up across the valley between Rose Trench and the Quarries. This was, however, crossed with little loss and was carried out in very good order. In crossing the Sunken Road, which was under heavy artillery fire, the casualties incurred were heavy, 3 officers and 130 men. Owing to the narrow communication trenches and blocking that ensued it was necessary to occupy the support trenches by going over the open ground; these trenches were occupied, however, without further loss. At 3.15 p.m. they were in position to attack Zenith Trench and, at 5.15 p.m., due to the situation in front, one company was ordered to occupy the support trench in the rear of Gusty Trench. The attack of the assaulting battalions had been held up with severe losses. All the trenches occupied were under continuous artillery fire and, because of the shallowness and expo-sure, further losses were incurred. These trenches were only 4 feet deep and 2½ feet wide. At 8 p.m. orders were received to attack Zenith Trench; zero hour being set at 3.50 a.m. on the 24th.

Rain fell that evening and during the night, making the ground more difficult than ever. Two companies, A and B, were in line at 25 paces distance on the left of 2nd R. Berkshires. Because of the state of the terrain, both assaulting battalions commenced leaving the front line before zero in order to be able to advance close behind the bar-rage. After 70 yards they were met by heavy rifle and machine gun fire from Zenith Trench, which was strongly held by the enemy. The attack was held up and failed, and severe losses were incurred during the retirement, 2/Lt. G.F. Wolfe and 50 per cent being casualties. Orders were received to hold the line, which was occupied by three companies with one in support. The casualties for 23–6 October were one offi-cer killed and 8 wounded.[2] Among other ranks the figures were 20 killed, 143 wound-ed, and 43 missing.

At daybreak the situation was that 2nd Rifle Bde was holding a line running out from Misty Trench and a small party of 2nd Lincolns was in Zenith Trench on the left of 23rd Brigade. The attack elsewhere had failed leaving a gap of trench 250 yards long still held by the Germans. 1st RIR was ordered to hold the front line with three companies, having the remaining company and two companies of 1st Sherwood Foresters in sup-port. The remaining battalions were withdrawn further to the rear for reorganisation. After three days of heavy and continuous bombardment, 1st RIR was relieved at noon on 26 October and moved into camp at Trônes Wood (where the bivouacs were full of water), moving to Needle Trench in Brigade Reserve the following afternoon. During the evening of the 28th, the battalion went to close support in Spider Trench being only two companies strong. Falls explained:

> A new attack to secure the still uncaptured portion of Zenith Trench had been planned for the next day. It had, however, rained incessantly, and the ground was

2 2/Lt. J.V. Gault killed, 2/Lts G. Benson, A.J.E. Gibson, G.C. Holt, A. Howard-Nicholson, E.W. Lennard, V. Noonan, G.S. Sinclair and G.F. Wolfe wounded.

becoming well-nigh impassable. According to the report, the attack was for this reason postponed. Actually it would appear that the commanding officers in the front line decided it would be madness and wanton throwing away of lives to attempt it under these conditions, and announced their respectful refusal to do so. It was necessary to leave the half-done job to be finished off by someone else.

At 1 a.m. the next day, they went into the front line at Misty Trench but were withdrawn back into Spider Trench by 5 p.m. On the night of the 30th, after being relieved by 10th Sherwood Foresters, they moved into camp in Trônes Wood and went into Citadel Camp near Carnoy the following day. Whitfeld was not impressed:

> A poor place in tents with no bottoms and water runs through my tent under my bed. At about midnight a draft, quite unexpected, of 6 officers and 425 ORs arrived. They were wet through and had no tea or supper. A nice job for Edwards and CQMSs. E.C.L. [the CO] very angry. The draft are mostly Londoners.

Replacements for the month totalled 9 officers and 462 men. The Brigadier-General reported to 8th Division:

> Throughout the operations of October 19th–30th, the men suffered greatly owing to the wet, the condition of the trenches, and continuous shell fire. Movement was extremely difficult, but rations and water were successfully got up by night. The exhaustion produced by the labour of getting about, lack of sleep and rest, lack of hot food, etc., obliged me to report that no unit was fit for an offensive, until opportunity had been given to reorganise and rest.

The battalion moved to billets at Méaulte, 2 November, to North Camp, Carnoy, on the 8th, and into Guillemont in Brigade Reserve on the 9th, but Details remained in North Camp. They relieved 2nd R. Berkshires in the Right Sector on the afternoon of the 11th. That day the battalion said goodbye to RSM Carroll who was promoted to 2/Lt. and posted to the East Yorkshire Regt. CSM J. Driscoll was appointed acting RSM until a permanent replacement could be found. The Left Sub Section was opposite Le Transloy and the battalion front was heavily shelled with gas throughout this tour. After being relieved by 2nd R. Berkshires they moved into Brigade Support in Hoggs Back Trench on the night of 13 November. The next days' events were described by Whitfeld: 'Heavily shelled all day, most unpleasant and protection very bad. They had the trench marked to an inch. One of the Coys was also badly shelled and lost several men.'

The battalion was relieved on the 15th by 2nd South Wales Borderers and marched to Sandpit Camp near Méaulte. On the morning of 19 November they marched to Edgehill Station, Dernancourt, entrained at 4.15 p.m. for Airaines where they arrived at 11.30 p.m. and marched to billets at Laleu.[3] A long period of training commenced in this

---

3 Whitfeld: '19th November, 11.30 p.m. Detrain at Airaines. E.C. Lloyd in a vile temper as one or two officers were asleep when the train stopped. As no one knew where we were I can't see it was their fault.'

pleasant small village. During the month 18 men were killed, one was missing and 56 were wounded. In the same period one officer and 567 men joined as reinforcements. Training continued throughout December and Major-General Heneker took over command of the division. The battalion won the Brigade Soccer Cup on 16 December. They moved from Corps Reserve, Laleu, to Camp 13 near Bray-sur-Somme on the 28th and marched next day to Camp 107 at La Plateau. Five hundred men of the battalion relieved 1st R. Irish Fusiliers in the trenches in front of Combles, 30 December, while 150 men relieved the detachment of 1st RIF in Combles, 140 remained with the Transport in Hardicourt. Whitfeld described the new area:

> The line ran partly through Saillisel and going north keeping east of Sailly-Sail-lisel and the Bapaume–Peronne Road which had been nearly shelled out of recognition. The line was quiet but one could not visit it by day however, because there were no continuous trenches and it was all in view of the Hun. At night time it was equally horrible as there was nothing to guide one to the various posts.

During December 2 men died of wounds and one died from self-inflicted wounds. Six officers and 218 men arrived as reinforcements.

10

The German retreat

1917

As 1917 commenced 1st RIR was in the front line at Sailly-Saillisel with details at Combles and Maurespas. According to Falls:

> The front here was now comparatively quiet, but it was very exposed and the outposts could not be visited by day. There were no continuous trenches. If the posts could not be visited by day, they were not very pleasant to visit by night, for officers inspecting, or reliefs, or ration carriers, for then the visitors stumbled blindly about amid shell-holes and tangled wire, with about equal chance of being shot by their friends or walking into the lines of their enemies.

The character of the battalion was changing rapidly with the fall in the level of recruitment in Ireland. Irishmen no longer formed the majority of the troops as 52 per cent now came from Britain. Most of these were transferred from the London Regt, the RASC, and 110th T.R. (Training Reserve) Bn. The Rifles were relieved, 3 January, by 12th King's Regt and proceeded to Camp 14 near Bray-sur-Somme. Sgt W. Ward, 4th Coldstream Guards, arrived on the 5th and took over the duties of RSM. There was great resentment among the Warrant Officers at his arrival for several reasons: it was seen to reflect on their abilities, he was not a Rifleman, he had been promoted from the rank of Sergeant, wasn't particularly tactful, and arrived wearing only Sergeant's chevrons. In fact RQMS Corrigan had declined the position and, although the CSMs were considered excellent candidates in their own right, it was felt essential that a rigorous drill instructor was needed in view of the poor level of training that the new arrivals had received. The battalion left Camp 14 on the 9th and proceeded by march and rail to Laleu for a period of training.

During 24 January the battalion moved to the forward area at Camp 124 near Sailly-Laurette and to Camp 21 near Suzanne on the 26th. They went into Brigade Reserve in Maurespas Ravine relieving 18th Welsh Regt on the 27th. Three days later they moved into the front line in the Rancourt Left Sector, south of Sailly-Saillisel on the Bapaume Road, with two companies in advance. The ground was so hard it was impossible to dig. HQ was right in front of Bois St Pierre Vast. The next day two men were wounded. Replacements of 8 officers and 109 men arrived during the month. Falls continued:

Snow had begun to fall and there was setting in one of the bitterest six weeks that Northern Europe has experienced for many years. The fiercest cold of all was between February 1st and 18th. On one occasion 32 degrees of frost were recorded. The frost also had certain advantages with regard to the work necessary to improve the position. Digging was impossible; so was wiring. Neither spade, pick, nor iron picket could be driven into the ground. But the engineers' stores, so hard to bring up over swampy ground, could now be easily dumped near the front line.

Seven horses were killed in the Transport lines at Maurepas Ravine, 1 February, and three men were wounded on the 3rd. The men bore the cold very well and there were only seven cases of frostbite. Having been relieved by 2nd Rifle Bde on the 3rd, they moved back to Brigade Support in Albowy. Six men were wounded at Detail Camp, Maurepas, on the 5th, and one died later. The battalion relieved 2nd Rifle Bde in the Rancourt Left Sector of the front line, 7 February. During this tour 3 men were killed and 12 wounded. Having been relieved by 18th Welsh Regt on the 11th, they proceeded by route march and lorry to Camp 13 near Bray for Brigade training. Nine officers and 500 men went on Divisional Works parties in the Bouchavesnes North sector on the 19th, after a thaw had set in. The remainder of the battalion moved to Camp 17 near Suzanne two days later. Three officers and 37 men relieved 1st Somersets at P.C. Messimey, 22 February, while details of 6 officers and 60 men were based at Curlu. The battalion reassembled on the 24th at Junction Wood less one officer, 40 men and the transport, which were at Curlu.

Five men were wounded, 26 February, and the next day the battalion relieved 2nd Rifle Bde in support at Bouchavesnes cellars. The line ran immediately east of the village, which was a complete ruin, and lay just off the Bapaume–Peronne Road with rising ground in front. Whitfeld observed:

> The Nurlu Ridge can be seen from the front line and, I imagine, will be a nasty place to tackle. In the valley lies Moislains with the Canal du Nord and the Tortille River running through. A little north is Manancourt where the Kaiser stayed for the Somme offensive. The country here is pretty, or would be if war wasn't on.

1st RIR relieved 2nd Lincolns on the 28th in Quarry Farm Sector where 2 men were killed and 7 wounded. Five officers and 36 men had joined during the month. The battalion was relieved by 2nd R. Berkshires on the night of the 2 March; HQ, A and D Coys moved to Linger Camp, Curlu, while C and B went to Junction Wood. On the 3rd, HQ and C moved to P.C. Messimey, B to Marrieres Wood, A and D to Junction Wood relieving C and B.

The 8th Division carried out an attack against Pallas and Fritz Trenches on the morning of 4 March. The Divisional Commander wanted to test the troop's fighting spirit prior to larger operations. The 25th and 24th Brigades attacked and the 23rd Brigade was in reserve. Of the 25th Brigade, 2nd R. Berkshires attacked while 1st RIR

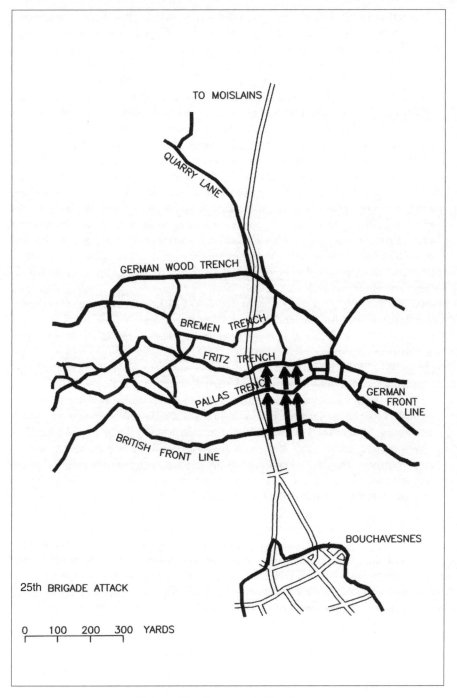

TO MOISLAINS

QUARRY LANE

GERMAN WOOD TRENCH

BREMEN TRENCH

FRITZ TRENCH

PALLAS TRENCH

GERMAN FRONT LINE

BRITISH FRONT LINE

BOUCHAVESNES

25th BRIGADE ATTACK

0   100   200   300   YARDS

Map 11: Bouchavesnes, 4 March 1917

was in reserve with its HQ at Messimey. Falls commented that 'It was quite a small operation, which had for object the capture of ground from which the enemy has close
observation of the Bouchavesnes Valley and the valley north-west of it to Rancourt.'

The attack began at 5.30 a.m., the same time that the artillery bombardment commenced, and ten minutes later the German front line at Pallas Trench was captured. By
6.10 a.m. news was received that Fritz Trench, the objective that was at a distance of 500
yards, was captured. At noon orders were received to send a company of 1st RIR to carry
up stocks of bombs and S.A.A. to 2nd R. Berkshires. Two Lewis Gun teams were also
dispatched to be at the disposal of 2nd R. Berkshires. At 6 p.m. orders were received for
1st RIR to move up and relieve 2nd Lincolns and the supporting companies of 2nd Rifle
Bde; 2nd R. Berkshires was to maintain its position in the captured trenches. 1st RIR
moved into the old British front line and support between 6 and 10 p.m. The shelling
during the night was severe. In the afternoon the enemy counter-attacked and gained a
footing in a part of the trench. Three men, belonging to 1st RIR Lewis Gunners that
had been lent to 2nd R. Berkshires, were killed. At noon on the 5th, orders were received
that 1st RIR would relieve 2nd R. Berkshires in the front line that night while 2nd Rifle
Bde would take over the old front line. Whitfeld wrote: 'We pushed up "London Lane".
Many dead about and still lying in the trench. Not pleasant.' The shelling was again
heavy; one man was killed and 3 were wounded. D Coy held the new front line at Fritz
Trench, C was in Pallas Trench, A was in a new trench leading from Pallas to the old
British front line, while B was in the old British line. For the rest of this tour shelling
was still severe but consolidation continued. During 7 March five men were killed and
19 wounded and, on the 8th, Capt. G.W. Calverley and 2/Lt. L.M. Bayly were wounded, 5 men were killed and 18 wounded. The battalion was relieved that night and moved
to a base in Bouchavesnes and Lock Barracks; HQ was just off the Béthune Road.

On the night of the 11th, 1st RIR relieved 2nd Rifle Bde in the same sector, which
was considerably quieter. During this tour one man was killed and 23 wounded. The
battalion moved into Brigade Reserve at Junction Wood, 13 March, with C Coy in
Marrieres Wood. They moved back to the front line relieving 2nd Rifle Bde, 16 March,
when two men were wounded. The enemy was very quiet and it was believed that he
was about to retire from this front. Falls explained:

> It had for some time been apparent to the British command that the enemy was
> about to carry out an important retirement. In February he had evacuated his
> positions west of the line Le Transloy–Loupart Wood and north of the
> Albert–Bapaume Road. Hurried by successful attacks he was now preparing to
> move back to the famous Hindenburg Line, which ran from south-east of Arras,
> across the Bapaume–Cambrai Road about half-way between the two towns, east
> of St Quentin, through La Fère.

At 2 p.m., St Patrick's Day, 1st RIR patrols moved forward and discovered that
Bremen Trench was unoccupied and found a machine gun left behind in a dugout. The
division on the right pushed forward and the new line was stabilised. Orders were
received to push a patrol into Moislains and, at 4.30 a.m. on the 18th, the village was

first entered by 2/Lt. G.S. Sinclair and 20 men. Posts were established later in the day on the Canal du Nord and one man was wounded on 19 March. According to Falls:

> With the best will in the world the British could do little. Every possible device to hinder them had been employed. At every crossroad huge craters had been blown, while trees had been cut down and thrown across the roads. On the Bapaume–Cambrai Road there must have been thousands of the big poplars that so often flank national roads in France dealt with in this manner. The villages outside the shelled area had been systematically destroyed.

The battalion was relieved that evening and moved to Bouchavesnes Cellars and Lock Barracks, and to Asquith Flats near Maurepas, 23 March, and then to bivouacs in Riverside Wood, Manancourt, on the 26th. Orders were received at 5 p.m. that three companies were to move to the valley near Sorel and Fins that were held by the Germans. The next day patrols pushed forward continuously to these villages and came under fire. Battalion HQ was near Nurlu and orders were received, 28 March, that companies should return to Riverside Wood. They moved again on the 30th to a rendezvous in Ecquancourt Wood. No. 5 Platoon was ordered forward to move south of the Fins–Gouzeaucourt Road and parallel to it, to cover the advance of 2nd Rifle Bde who were attacking Desart Wood, east of Fins. The movement commenced at 4 p.m. by which time No. 5 Platoon was in position south of the road but was being held up by the fire of two enemy machine guns: one on the road, the other north of the road. 2/Lt. J. Brown, in command of this platoon, had orders to engage any opposition that might threaten the right flank of the attack. On being held up by these guns he went forward with his Lewis Gun team and engaged them. The one on the main road managed to withdraw but the other, on the north of the road, failed to extricate itself and, after the crew had been either killed or captured, was taken in its entirety by 9222 Cpl S. Massey who was in charge of the Lewis Gun. The right of the attack was then clear and Desart Wood was captured. Later in the day, B and C Coys were ordered forward to occupy the ground north of Revelon Farm. The remaining companies and HQ were in Sorel-le-Grand. One man had been killed and 9 were wounded. Whitfeld was wary:

> The Hun had lain booby traps all over the place and nothing seems safe to touch. He has also destroyed all fruit trees, etc. We found a good dug-out in Sorel but as it probably has an acid time fuse mine, we shall get out and live in a hut put up by Byrne.

During March reinforcements of 2 officers and 23 men arrived. Total casualties for the month were 3 officers wounded, 13 men killed and 78 wounded.

At the beginning of April the battalion was holding the outpost line 3,000 yards west of Gouzeaucourt. Time was spent in defence and outpost work where 7 men were killed and 10 wounded. Whitfeld wrote on 1 April:

> We must be careful as the Hun may easily hop out of the Hindenburg Line and we should have a small chance. I was nearly killed in the line today. I went to see

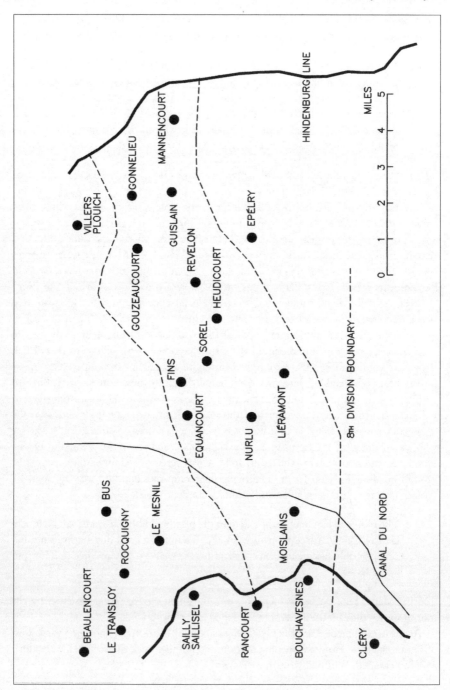

Map 12: The German retreat, Spring 1917

Fitzmaurice and was sitting with him in a hut in a sunken road when the Hun let fly two whizz bangs and hit the corner of the hut. A very close shave for all of us.

On the 3rd, the two companies in Sorel were relieved and moved, with HQ, to Riverside Wood where 2/Lts Ennis and Doherty joined them. The battalion moved forward, 4 April, and took up a position in the valley west of Sorel-le-Grand. They were in reserve for an attack to be carried out by two battalions of the brigade against Gouzeaucourt Wood and the ground south of it. At 6 p.m. orders were received for three companies and HQ to move forward to Bichecourt Wood; one company (C) was to take up the original Outpost line in front of Dessart Wood. At midnight orders were received for two companies to move back to Riverside Wood and HQ moved to Sorel-le-Grand. In the morning C Coy rejoined from Outpost line, the attack having been successful, and HQ moved to Riverside Wood. The next day HQ and companies assembled in Sorel-le-Grand and took up permanent billets where they were employed in working on the line of defence until the 15th. During that time reinforcements of one officer and 28 men arrived, while another 11 men joined on the 16th. The battalion then moved forward and took up a position east of Gouzeaucourt in the Outpost line for a three-day tour. One man was missing at the end of this period. Having been relieved, 18 April, they moved to trenches 2,000 yards west of Gouzeaucourt with HQ in Sunken Road, 400 yards north of Heudecourt. One man died of wounds and one was wounded.

Two companies were ordered to move to the original Outpost line, east of Gouzeaucourt, on the night of the 19th and to hold the line during an attack that was to be made by 2nd Lincolns on Gonnelieu. This attack was carried out at 4.20 a.m., 21 April, and the village was taken with over 100 prisoners. 1st RIR was then ordered to take over the new Outpost line east of Gonnelieu having suffered losses of one man killed and one wounded. After relieving 2nd Rifle Bde in the left sub sector in front of Gonnelieu that night, two companies were placed in front and two in support, one man being wounded. The 40th Division attacked Villers-Plouich and Beaucamp during the 24th in conjunction with 119th Infantry Brigade on 8th Division's left. The 8th Division advanced their line about 600 yards to get in touch with 18th Welsh Regt, and dug in. Four men were wounded, while a draft of 2 officers and 36 men arrived.

One man died of wounds and 12 were wounded before the battalion was relieved on the night of 24 April and moved to support in Blue Line–Quinton Mill and Gouzeaucourt Station, with HQ located at Sunken Road north-east of Heudicourt. One man was killed and another wounded, 25 April, and HQ moved forward near to the Quarry at Quinton Mill. The battalion then moved into the left Sub Sector on the night of the 27th and relieved 2nd Rifle Bde. Lt.-Col. R.A.C. Daunt DSO, and Capt. T.H. Ivey arrived the following day, the former assuming command of the battalion. Five men were wounded on this tour. Having been relieved early on the morning of 2 May, the battalion proceeded to Heudicourt South in Division Reserve. During its stay there a draft of 2 officers and 52 men arrived. 1st RIR relieved 1st Worcestershire Regt in Brigade Reserve at Vaucellette Farm, Villers Guislain Sector, on 10 May and relieved 2nd Rifle Bde in the right sub sector three days later, where one man was wounded. The battalion was relieved by 12th Suffolk Regt, 15 May, and proceeded to camp at Nurlu where the division was now in Corps Reserve. Over the next ten days a draft of 4 officers and 55 men arrived. One man was killed and 3 were wounded, 22 May. The battalion won the Brigade Boxing Championships in lightweight (L/Cpl Houlton), and featherweight (L/Cpl Lawlor), 27 May. The following day, 2/Lt. G.S. Sinclair died of wounds received accidentally while instructing men in bombing techniques; three men were also wounded in this incident.

The battalion moved to Moislains, 29 May, and to Camp 19 at Suzanne relieving 1st Worcesters in billets two days later. June commenced with the Irish Rifles moving to Méricourt L'Abbé. They entrained at Heilly, en route for Caestre, on the afternoon of the 3rd and, next morning, detrained and marched to the Strazeele Area and were bivouacked. Training was carried out under Company Commanders until 10 June. The next day they moved to Hondeghem, then to Caestre two days later and, on the 14th, to a camp four miles south-east of Poperinghe. They were now in the Ypres area of Flanders and company training continued. During the period 5–19 June, a draft of 2 officers and 100 men had arrived.

11

Pilkem Ridge

The battalion moved to billets in the Steenvoorde Area, arriving at 9 a.m., 19 June. Capt. Ivey took over the duties of Second-in-Command after Major Fitzmaurice had returned to England suffering from trench fever.[1] Training consisted of carrying out dummy attacks on trenches each morning and specialist lessons in the afternoon. Four officers and 108 men joined as reinforcements during this time. Throughout 27 June the brigade practised an attack: 1st RIR was on the right of the brigade with two battalions taking part. D, B, and A were the leading companies, while C engaged in 'mopping up' operations. The attack was carried out under creeping barrage working at 100 yards in three minutes. The Division Commander, at a conference afterwards, remarked that the practice was carried out in a successful manner. They moved from the Steenvoorde area to Dominion Camp, four miles south-west of Poperinghe, two days later. Whitfeld confided to his diary:

> The Hun bombs these camps nightly – very unpleasant. In early mornings he pots at them with HV Guns. Daunt has gone home. He didn't hit it off with Heneker. I am sorry. Tom Ivey commanding.

Seven men were wounded on working parties while in the forward area and June ended with the arrival of 2 officers and 11 men. Falls noted:

> The Salient, which had been comparatively quiet during the height of the Somme battle, had now flared up again, and its back areas were certainly more dangerous and unpleasant than at any time since the beginning of the war. The cause of this was the great increase in long-range shelling, with high-velocity guns, and in the number and size of bombs dropped by aeroplanes. There was, therefore, little rest in the camps, which were generally bombed at night and shelled during the daytime.

The battalion moved on the evening of 5 July and proceeded to the Ramparts at Ypres with its HQ based in the Esplanade. Whitfeld described his impression:

[1] Trench fever was a prevalent problem. It had flu-like symptoms and it could take years for the victim to fully recover.

Thrilling first experience of Ypres. We approached it by the lower road and via Lille Gates. After leaving Kruistraathoek I came with the Battalion HQs to the bridge over the Canal. They were shelling it hard as usual and Shrapnel Corner beyond. What a place. Dead horses everywhere and such a smell of these and gas. We waited for a quiet moment and then nipped past and on past Shrapnel Corner and into Ypres pretty quickly. Ypres was burning in places, and it is a sight that I shall never forget, with ruins standing out against the red glare.

6th July. In the afternoon Tom [Ivey] and I went up to the line to have a quick look round and, being new to the place, chose the quickest route, which was up the Roulers railway. When we told the CO of the Sherwoods which way we had come he was amazed and said we were damn lucky to be living. 'Ignorance is bliss.' Companies went off at ten and we intended going off at 11.30. No luck. Violent shelling and we simply couldn't get out. However, we had to make an effort, and choosing a quiet minute we nipped out and across Ypres as fast as we could go and out into the Roulers railway. The Hun was shelling the Ramparts very heavily and it was a magnificent sight. We got in safe. HQ Railway Wood. Trenches right up Ypres–Roulers Railway.

7th July. Not so quiet as we were led to believe. At 5 a.m. heavy TMs commenced falling above where I was lying down. Suddenly there was a fearful flash and explosion and a yell from my orderly room Sgt and the electric lights went out. We lit candles and a nasty sight presented itself. Two dead bodies were lying at the bottom of the stairs; the wood ceiling had been rent off and lay all over the place. The papers, defence schemes, were rent in pieces and lay about the place. Apparently a large TM had landed actually in the mouth of the dug-out and blown it in. The orderlies were sitting up there probably asleep at the time. Sgt Kenny, who was sleeping in the orderly room opposite where I was, was blown through the table but was more alarmed than hurt.

8th July. Major A.D. Reid, Royal Inniskilling Fusiliers, arrived to take over command. He arrived with the BM and got to work at once. Rather frightened us all and sacked some of the HQ Staff right away. I liked him very much. He was very thorough indeed.

Six men were killed and 3 wounded during this tour. The Irish Rifles were relieved at midnight, 9 July, and moved to Dominion Camp where a draft of 10 men arrived; Battalion Transport moved via Cassel en route to the training area at Tournehem, 10 July. The battalion left Dominion Camp, 11 July, and, just before they boarded the train at Ouderdore, a German plane came over and shot down five observation balloons. Having reached Audricq they marched to Andrehem, arriving at midnight; HQ was based in the hamlet of Le Poirier. For three days an attack was practised together with other regiments. They then moved to Zougfques Training Area on the 19th after receiving a draft of 29 men. From 20–28 July, the attack was practised in conjunction with troops on their immediate left and right, as it would be in the coming battle. There was a steady improvement by all ranks of keeping close to the barrage and keeping together. Whitfeld noted that 1st RIR 'was in first class trim and would have stuck at nothing'.

The battalion marched to Audricq, 24 July, where they entrained at 10.15 a.m. and arrived at Hopoutre 2.15 p.m., then marched to bivouacs in a field near Busseboom. Four days later they moved to Scottish Lines, Dominion Area and, on the 29th, to Pioneer Camp, which was not far from Den Groenen Jaeger crossroads, and three miles west of Ypres. Transport and Details remained in the Dominion Area. The War Diary for 30 July recorded: 'The battalion proceeded by overland train to the positions of assembly at Halfway House and China Wall arriving there at 3.15 a.m. on the 31st. 4 ORs wounded.' Lt. Whitfeld, who made this entry, had more to say in his personal diary:

On the afternoon of July 30th, the Colonel saw the battalion by two companies at a time and wished them the best of luck and mentioned that he was sure that all would do their level best to keep up the reputation of a famous regiment and division. The men liked this, for although the CO had only been with us a month, they saw in him a brave and exceedingly just man. At 7.30 p.m. we sat down to our last meal together – I remember it well – the Colonel as grave as ever – he never smiled, Brown, the Intelligence Officer, Major Ivey and myself. If I remember rightly, no one spoke very much and the jokes that were made fell distinctly flat. I remember wondering what we should be doing two days hence and whether we should sit united again at dinner. Dinner finished, I went to my room to put on my battle array, taking good care to adjust my box respirator, for I knew only too well that I should need it before the night was past ... Our route took us right through the heavy batteries just north of the Kruistraathoek–Ypres Road. We reached this place at 12 midnight and were floundering along in the dark in single file – the CO and myself leading while there were blinding flashes all round us – the great counter-battery bombardment had opened. The 'going' was frightfully slow owing to the weights the men were carrying and the fact that we had the whole of the 2nd Lincolns in single file in front of us. We, however, pushed on and crossed the canal at 12.30 having taken 3½ hours to do four miles – we still had four to go. Soon after crossing the canal a message came back to say that the Germans were shelling Shrapnel Corner. I knew this corner of old – it was one of the most terrible places on the Ypres Salient. It was on the main route and is situated about ¼ mile from Lille Gate on the Ypres–Messines Road. On arrival at this dreaded spot we were fortunate, as owing to a lull, the whole battalion got past with only one casualty. Then commenced one of the most terrible marches I ever experienced: try and imagine for yourself a dark night, a shell-swept track, the stench of dead horses (for no man dared wait in that region), and the sickly smell of asphyxiating gas, then perhaps you can realise, more or less, what that night was like. It is a horrible sensation to be floundering along in the dark with a gas helmet over one's head and falling into shell holes. I got so fed up I removed my helmet from my eyes, keeping, however, the tube in my mouth. At last we reached our destination – Halfway House – where it had been previously arranged that all men would be under cover; this, however, was not the case and the men just flopped down and fell asleep –

regardless of gas and HE shells that came over at frequent intervals. The Colonel, Brown, and myself then went down into the dug-out, which was half under water, and full of troops, and got into a small recess which had been reserved for us. All three sat on a bed and in five minutes were asleep, but only for one hour – I never remembered an hour passing quicker.

The battle was set for 31 July: 25th Brigade was to pass through 23rd and 24th Brigades on the Westhoek Ridge, along which ran the Frezenberg–Westhoek Road. Its own objective was the Green Line, an imaginary line running west of Zonnebeke village and through the western edge of Polygon Wood. 1st RIR went into the attack with 20 officers and 620 men. At 6 a.m. they moved from Halfway House, in artillery formation, to the Westhoek Ridge passing over the original front lines that had been taken by the other brigades at zero – 3.50 a.m. They met with little shellfire until their arrival on Westhoek Ridge at about 8.30 a.m. The situation was not quite what was expected because the division on the right had been unable to take the Black Line – the high ground near Polygon Wood. 25th Brigade War Diary:

> In addition to the machine-gun fire from Glencorse Wood, enemy machine guns and snipers were firing from the neighbourhood of Kit and Kat, and from the Westhoek crossroads. A large number of houses on the Westhoek Road were evidently held by enemy machine guns and snipers.

At zero plus 6 hours 20 minutes, the battalion advanced in perfect order to close up with the new barrage. On leaving the Black Line, the left company (D) was met with withering machine gun and sniper fire from the front and right flank; these Germans were located west of the line where the barrage had fallen. The Company Commander therefore ordered section rushes but that cost so many casualties that he decided to withdraw to the original line and consolidate. Here he got in touch with 2nd Rifle Bde on his left. The right company (A) made an attempt to advance but this was found impossible owing to the division on the right being held up. The line was therefore consolidated and several counter-attacks were driven off. The centre company (B), pushed forward all the way to the Hannebeke Stream, but finding that the enemy were working around the right flank, the officer commanding this company ordered it to withdraw until each flank was safe and in touch with companies on his right and left. At about 3 p.m. the Germans made a determined attack against the centre company and reached the trench they were holding but a vigorous counter-attack was immediately launched and the enemy was driven out leaving many dead. A machine gun was captured in this incident. No gained ground was lost during the operation and the battalion was relieved at 11 p.m. and moved to the old German front line. The casualties were 6 officers killed and 7 wounded;[2] 30 other ranks killed, 145 wounded and 18 missing.

Whitfeld described the events:

2 Officers Killed: Lt.-Col. A.D. Reid, 2/Lts H. Brown, V.C. Byrne (A Coy Commander), P. Doherty, J. Furniss, and R.K. Pollin. Wounded: Capts G. Mockett and C.H.R. Reed (C Coy Commander), 2/Lts P.A. Breen, E.V. Burke-Murphy, E. Daniel, H.M. Jeffares, and R.A. Veitch.

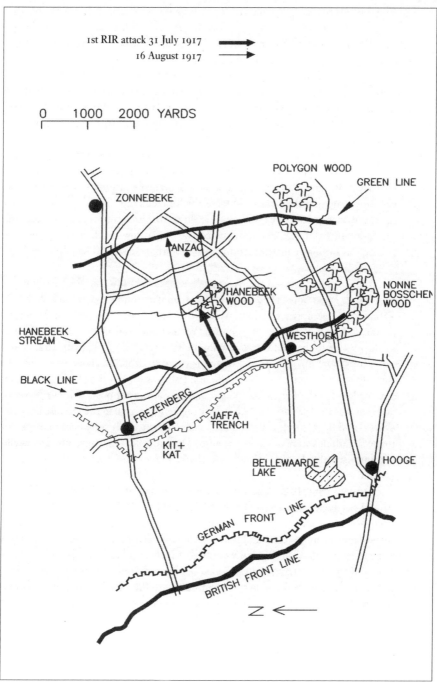

1st RIR attack 31 July 1917

16 August 1917

0   1000   2000 YARDS

POLYGON WOOD

GREEN LINE

ZONNEBEKE

ANZAC

HANEBEEK WOOD

NONNE BOSSCHEN WOOD

HANEBEEK STREAM

WESTHOEK

BLACK LINE

FREZENBERG

JAFFA TRENCH

KIT+ KAT

BELLEWAARDE LAKE

HOOGE

GERMAN FRONT LINE

BRITISH FRONT LINE

N

Map 13: Westhoek Ridge

The actual task which was allotted to my brigade was to attack at 10.15 a.m., after having passed through the 23rd and 24th Brigades. Our objective was an imaginary line just west of Zonnebeeke, the left of the brigade resting on the Ypres–Roulers Railway. The order of battle was as follows: 2nd Rifle Brigade on the left, 1st Royal Irish Rifles the centre, and the 2nd Lincolns on the right. The Commanding Officers of the brigade were to meet General Coffin, on Westhoek Ridge at 9 a.m., in order to ascertain the exact positions of the battalions. The CO, therefore, left Halfway House at about 5.45 a.m., and handed over to Captain G. Mockett.

At 6 p.m. the order to move was given and the battalion went forward in Artillery formation. Two Liaison Officers reported to me and with them and my Orderly (Rfn James) we started. The hostile artillery was not too active and, by carefully watching the bursts, we were able to reach our original front line safely, where owing to the wire and craters, slower progress was made. On reaching the German front line I was surprised to find so few dead, showing that the enemy was evidently distributed in depth and that we should have a tough time when we attacked.

At 9 a.m. I had crossed the Bellewarde Ridge and I saw that the battalion was well ahead. I therefore called a halt to my small party and lay down in a shell hole watching the aeroplanes – there were dozens of them. The shelling from now onwards increased hourly in volume. We therefore moved forward again and made our way to the spot where Battalion HQ was. This was at about 10 a.m. and the troops were lined up ready for the barrage to drop. At about 10.05 the CO went up to see if everything was right, and that was the last time I saw him. I then gave orders for the Signalling Officer and his 'advanced post' to move forward, and that was the last time I spoke to Brown. At 10.15 a.m. to the minute, the guns opened and the second phase of the attack commenced. It soon became apparent to me that things were not going right for I heard violent machine gun fire, which was unmistakably Boche, on our right flank, and as the Colonel did not return I became anxious.

A runner came back from one of the companies at 10.40 a.m. and this confirmed my belief that the attack had been held up and that our casualties had been heavy. At about 11 a.m. a wounded NCO informed me that the Commanding Officer was dead and that Brown had been hit in the stomach and was lying in no-man's-land. Several wounded officers and men now passed me and I gathered that our barrage had dropped behind a nest of German machine gunners instead of in front, owing (it is supposed) to the 24th Brigade thinking that they had taken the Black Line when they had not. The day wore on and it was evident that an attempt to commence the attack again would be hopeless. The shelling now became violent and for the remainder of the day was extremely unpleasant. Rain set in heavily at about 5 p.m. During the afternoon we had repulsed the enemy in four local counter-attacks and captured a machine gun.

At about 4 p.m. I began to get very tired indeed, and even amidst the explosions I kept dozing off until a shell would burst unpleasantly near, and I would suddenly awake to reality – my thirst too was horrible.

At about 7 p.m. my present Headquarters became too hot so I therefore moved up the side of the ridge into a deep shell hole near Brigade Headquarters. At 9 p.m. I received orders that the battalion was to be relieved by the 2nd West Yorks. It was impossible to send the message round to the Company Commanders because there was no definite line and the orderlies would in all probability walk into no-man's-land and be captured. How that relief was completed I do not know to this day. The order was, that on relief the battalion was to take up its position in the old German front line, this I was unable to communicate to the NCOs but I fancied I should find them at Halfway House next day, and I was right. I however, went to the old German line and sat in it for the remainder of the night in pouring rain, and was so chilled that I could hardly stand in the morning. At about 6 a.m. on August 1st I was joined by Captain Ross who had been acting liaison officer to the 2nd Lincolnshire Regiment. We ate a little 'Bully' and then trecked for Pioneer Camp which we reached at 1 p.m., on receipt of orders from General Coffin.

On the morning of the 1st August we received orders to move to Dominion Camp and from there the following Thursday we moved by motor bus to Steenvoorde Area.

The following order was published by General C. Coffin, Commanding 25th Brigade (who was awarded the Victoria Cross for his part in the battle):

I wish to thank all ranks of the 25th I.B. for what they did in the Battle of 31st July and 1st August. On arrival behind Westhoek the situation which met the Brigadier was not quite the one anticipated but all ranks acted to the changed conditions. The line reached was held against numerous enemy counter-attacks and was handed over intact upon relief. The enemy attacks were taken full advantage of by the brigade and the enemy casualties must have been heavy.

Major-General W. Heneker, Commanding 8th Division, stated:

I wish to thank all ranks for their splendid efforts yesterday. The attack was magnificent. The Blue and Black lines were taken without a hitch. The 25th Infantry Brigade's attack went well until held up by cross fire from the high ground. The Army Commander recognizes this.

12

Langemarck and Passchendaele

A draft of 11 men arrived on 3 August and the battalion entrained on the Vlamen-tinghe–Ouderdom Road two days later, moving to billets in the Steenvoorde Area. Whitfeld recorded:

> Orders came in that all deficiencies were to be made up forthwith which showed at once that another attack was pending and that we should (25th I.B.) take a prominent part in it. This turned out to be true as there was only one assaulting brigade and that was the 25th, the objective being the Green Line on the heights immediately West of Zonnebeeke. The assaulting battalions being 1st Royal Irish Rifles and the Royal Berkshire Regiment. On the 9th August the new Commanding Officer arrived – Major H.W.D. MacCarthy-O'Leary MC, Royal Irish Fusiliers. The remainder of the battalion, which numbered 500, seemed to me to be in excellent spirits considering they knew they had to face the enemy again. For myself, if I remember rightly, I paid little thought to it as I had a great quantity of work. On the afternoon of the 14th August we marched on to the main Steenvoorde–Wormhoudt Road and awaited motor buses which duly arrived at 7 p.m. and which were to take us to the main Vlamertinghe–Ouderdom Road.
>
> We arrived at our de-bussing point at 9 p.m. and started forward in rear of the Royal Berkshire Regiment. We kept our route as laid down as far as Belgian Chateau; we then should have gone by the canal and Shrapnel Corner – in fact, the same way as we moved on the 30th. The corner was, however, being heavily shelled and the Commanding Officer and I, after consultation, decided to go on via Kruistraat. The gas shelling was exceedingly heavy near the canal and after crossing it I became violently ill and continued to be so at intervals. To add to my discomfort I was forced to act as guide being the only one who knew the way. We finally arrived at Lille Gate dugouts at 12 midnight. The next day (August 15th) was spent in distributing stores and finding the way on to the Menin Road through a sally port through the ramparts, which route we should have to take that night. And now the last meal is served and the Quartermaster, Captain Edwards, and Transport Officer join us. The Doctor procured two bottles of 'Fiz' and we drank success to the show and luck to the doctor.

9 p.m. arrived and it was time we should start our march to the assembly positions on Westhoek Ridge. We had allowed six hours to do this trip which I suppose was four or five miles but it was over such country that the troops could not move more than about one mile per hour. We led off therefore towards the Sally Point near Menin Gate which gate I am very thankful we had not to go through as it was always heavily shelled. (This was just by St Martin's Church).

We were unfortunate, for one of the companies (D) passing an open space received a direct hit with a 5.9" shell knocking out thirteen. We finally reached the Menin Road, a distance of 400 yards after much shouting of 'Get closed up'. The Germans, as luck would have it, were exceedingly quiet on our front, having, as I found out from the FOO, received three hours gas on his batteries. The 'going' on the Menin Road was good and we made quite fair progress as far as Birr Cross Roads where we were to meet guides from the 2nd Rifle Brigade and start our journey across three miles of mud and shell craters. After waiting half an hour, finding the guides we heard the cheerful news that only one out of sixteen knew the way. We started, and from 10 p.m. to 3.45 a.m. were trying to cover those three miles. If I did the journey once I did it five times, for the CO and I would hear the message come up to say 'So and so Company have lost connection' and so it went on until at last I saw Westhoek Ridge in front and knew that we were at last there.

Now came the job of getting the companies into position. We only had three quarters of an hour to do it in. At this moment someone reported to me that one of the companies was missing. The rear of the preceding company had seen them, they said, about an hour before but had lost sight of them. At any rate, finally only half turned up and the other half went 'over' with the 23rd I.B. The Colonel assembled the battalion in a very able manner whilst I went to Brigade Headquarters and reported to the Brigadier. I then gave Battalion Headquarters men some cover against the pending Boche barrage and finally made my way to Rifle Brigade Headquarters. In doing so, I passed the companies lined up already, a few were muttering to each other but most were too excited to speak. We probably all had that extraordinary feeling which only those who have 'been over' have experienced. On arrival at the 2nd Rifle Bde Headquarters I found the Colonel waiting, and as the barrage was timed to commence in three minutes, I went outside again to see the commencement.

The first streaks of a summer dawn were already showing in the east when suddenly the whole sky lit up behind me with dull red flashes and the roar of guns commenced. In less than half a minute the German line was lit up with marvellous colours – green, red, blue, gold and silver, intermingled with the short red glare of our bursting shrapnel. The German barrage dropped within three minutes – it was then time to take cover. The Colonel had decided that he would, in company with the FOO and myself, move on to our forward Battalion HQ immediately we heard that the first objective had been taken.

The 25th Brigade Diary noted:

> The leading Company of the 1st Royal Irish Rifles did not arrive until later, and
> the Assaulting Troops were not finally formed up in position until about 4.15
> a.m. One or two small parties of the 1st Royal Irish Rifles probably never reached
> the forming up positions, but as the battalion had several casualties on the way
> up this cannot be stated for certain.
>
> Troops formed up in shell holes approximately on the tape line to avoid any
> possibility of detection by the enemy just before zero. Each company boundary
> was marked by a circular disc, and a tape was run forward for about 50 yards
> from this point along the main bearing of the attack, so as to give the troops their
> direction at the start.
>
> At about 4 a.m. when it appeared doubtful whether all the 1st Royal Irish
> Rifles would be in position in time, an order was issued to the 2nd Rifle Brigade
> to provide one company to assist them in mopping up, thus leaving the 2nd Rifle
> Brigade only one company to follow on in support.

At 4.45 a.m. the barrage dropped and the troops, who had moved forward to get in
touch with the barrage a few minutes before zero, advanced. The Irish Rifles moved in
excellent formation and little resistance was met with as far as the Hanebeek Wood. The
casualties were also light except for the centre company, which suffered severely from
machine guns firing from their right flank. The pill-box, known as Anzac Farm, held up
the advance for about ten minutes but was finally over-run after working round the
flanks and some prisoners were taken. The Green Line was captured at about 6.20 a.m.
and an attempt was made to consolidate it but, owing to the lack of men and the heavy
sniping from their left rear, this was found impossible. At about 7.50 a.m. the enemy was
seen to be working around the right flank. The position on the left was far from satisfactory and the line, therefore, had to fall back. Later in the day the Germans brought
up fresh forces in considerable strength – the left company saw these troops arrive in
trucks near Zonnebeeke. Owing to the superior numbers of the enemy, and the effects
of 1st RIR losses, they were forced to withdraw during the afternoon to the Black Line
(the front line of that morning). Whitfeld recorded the scene from his perspective:

> A message came in at 6.45 a.m. per Royal Berkshire Regiment that all had gone
> well and that we had captured the Green Line – in fact, had gone beyond it but
> at a heavy cost. We therefore started forward – five of us I think we were – and
> made our way straight for the Hanebeek Wood. The shelling at this time was not
> too bad as the German gunners were uncertain as to our position, but the
> machine gun fire was heavy, especially from the high ground SE of us (Polygon
> Wood) which made us keep low and resort to trenches, such as were left, for pro-
> tection. At this period I lost sight of the Colonel but caught sight of him again a
> few minutes later. Entering the Hanebeek Wood the FOO and myself moved
> forward but were driven into the trench again by a German airman who swooped
> down upon us. We again went forward and crossed the stream which by now had
> been reduced to a series of small lakes.

No officers could be found, and very few men, and it was reported to me that all had been either killed or wounded. I have never seen so many dead as there were in that Hanebeek Valley – both Boche and British – the majority of whom were the former.

About half an hour later I met the Colonel coming back and could see at once that he had been hit, for his right arm was hanging limp and blood was all over his coat. He decided that we must go back at once and report the situation to the Brigadier, which we did, having again been chased by bullets all the way.

It was at 9 a.m. that the CO and Adjutant visited 25th Brigade HQ. Col. MacCarthy-O'Leary told how the enemy were counter-attacking in great force on the left of his battalion and that his forward companies, without a single commissioned officer remaining, were putting up a stubborn fight against overwhelming odds and were gradually giving ground. As a result of this report 2nd Rifle Bde was ordered to send up its remaining company in support of the two that had been following up the attack. Whitfeld noted:

> The CO was by this time very weak and the MO ordered him to go back at once to the rear Dressing Station. He therefore handed over command to me and I again proceeded forward. The shelling now became very heavy (far worse than on the 31st July) and I took cover in a shell hole where some more men were, and which I soon found out was 'marked' by the German Gunners.

25th Brigade War Diary:

> A message was received from the 23rd Infantry Brigade, timed 10.20 a.m., stating that their troops had been driven out of the Zonnebeke Redoubt and were holding a line about Hanebeek Wood. The remnants of two companies 2nd Rifle Brigade and 1st Royal Irish Rifles were also apparently on this line (about 100 yards east of the Hanebeek) where they maintained their position until compelled to withdraw in the afternoon ... For some hours after this there was no change in the situation. There is no doubt that the enemy suffered very heavily in the course of these counter-attacks, and but for the continuous losses incurred from enfilade machine gun fire from the right, and the danger of the right flank being completely turned, the frontal attacks could have been dealt with without much difficulty.

Whitfeld's report continued:

> From then on the shells came pouring in without cessation. Shrapnel and HE – mostly the latter – kept bursting with a deafening roar. I might have guessed that this bombardment was nothing less than an attack by 'Storm Troops' and this was the case. They came – six battalions in six lines – and owing to our heavy casualties we were forced back nearly to our original position.
>
> At 8 p.m. I sent up the SOS signal and this was replied to by, as I heard afterwards, about 980 guns. Dusk at last came and, except for a violent barrage from both sides at 8 p.m., comparative quiet set in.

Just before dusk I had met the doctor for the first time that day and he informed me that I was the sole survivor of all the officers and therefore again in command of the battalion. At 9 p.m. I received orders to take the remnants of the battalion back to Birr Cross Roads – just NW of Hooge on the Ypres–Menin Road. After much tripping and stumbling in shell holes I and my orderly arrived safely at 1 a.m. and went down into the deep dugout where I was given some food and drink and then slept.

Two days passed in this dugout but on the third we left for Halifax Camp [Halifax Area, Vancouver Camp] and a day later for billets in the Hazebrouck Area well out of reach of shells and so far as I (or the battalion) was concerned, the summer battles were at an end.

Casualties were 7 officers killed and 3 wounded, 27 other ranks killed, 170 wounded, 63 missing, 7 wounded and missing.[1] Whitfeld remarked:

When we were in Halifax Camp, we were inspected by our Corps and Divisional Commanders. Both expressed their pleasure in the way in which the battalion had fought, and the Corps Commander, Lt.-General Sir C. Jacob, on hearing that I had commanded the battalion, shook hands with me and said: 'Well, Whitfeld, you realise now the responsibility of command.' I was very pleased with myself but more so with the praise the battalion received. It was well deserved.

The remnants of the battalion entrained on the Vlamertinghe–Ouderdom Road and proceeded to Caestre billeting area on 19 August; HQ was located at La Brearde. August 21 was a good day for Whitfeld:

When we went back to the Hazebrouck Area, another inspection was in store for us. The Field Marshal Commanding in Chief, Sir Douglas Haig, had shown his appreciation of the Division's work by saying that he would inspect them. The Parade was arranged in a hollow square and we were the last but one battalion on the right wing. The 'Chief' at last came to us. When opposite the CO and I, who were standing in front of the battalion, General Coffin, I think it was, said 'May I bring to your notice this young officer who commanded his battalion in the last two battles and was, in the last one, the only surviving officer.' Sir Douglas Haig then came up to me and, taking my right hand, shook it and said 'I congratulate you Sir, how long have you been Adjutant?' I answered him and then, turning to his Staff, said 'He looks very young, doesn't he?' I was, needless to say, frightfully pleased and felt very honoured that the C.-in-C. should have shaken hands and spoken to me.

1 Killed: Capts J.F. Clery, A.F.J.S. Nicholson, A.J. Ross; 2/Lts R.J. Ennis, W. Kingston, E.A. Mahoney, and J.E.G. Wilson. Wounded: Lt.-Col. H.W.D. MacCarthy-O'Leary, Capt. J.K. Boyle and 2/Lt. C.D. Quilliam.

By the end of the month a further draft of one officer and 51 men had arrived. The battalion moved, 27 August, to De Seule Camp four miles east of Bailleul. Whitfeld recalled: 'Quite a nice Camp. The Bombing in this area was unpleasant and went on all night. Most annoying.'

At the beginning of September Lt.-Col. J.H.M. Kirkwood DSO, from the Household Battalion, joined and assumed command. Whitfeld was impressed: 'A top hole fellow. He brought tons of kit. Mine, always big as I thought, was a drop compared to his.' On the afternoon of the 3rd, the battalion moved from De Seule Camp to Bulford Camp, half a mile to the north, and the new CO went on leave. Eight days later they moved to Le Romarin Camp. Whitfeld recorded an event on 14 September:

> The Orderly Room was burnt to the ground and all my valuable records were destroyed. All through a fool of a signaller who fell asleep when on duty and upset a candle. Whelan, who by the way, has replaced Kenny as Orderly Room Sergeant, saved M.M.L. [Manual of Military Law] and Pay Warrant. I am very sorry to lose Kenny, a real good fellow. Whelan seems good.

1st RIR relieved 2nd Lincolns in the 'Plugstreet' area during the night of 19 September. Their boundary was the River Douve on the left to Corn Post on the right. Falls:

> Here a dummy attack, with stuffed figures in khaki and trench helmets, and a liberal amount of smoke, was arranged to make the enemy believe that offensive operations were being renewed on this front. The Germans put down a heavy barrage, while their machine guns made accurate shooting against the dummies, knocking most of them over.

A weary Whitfeld wrote on 27 September:

> I find my nerve none too good after that dose at Ypres ... Enemy raided one of our posts and took two men who made no effort to fight. They were not proper RIR men but 'combed out' ASC people.[2]

That night 1st RIR was relieved by 1st Notts and Derby Regt and moved to billets at Waterlands Camp, near Niepe. During the time that the battalion was in the line Lt. G.C. Robb was wounded, 4 men were killed, 22 wounded, and 2 were missing. Whitfeld's entry for 28 September:

> Apparently Kirkwood had noticed that my health was none too good and he had a talk with Heneker about me. The latter suggested six months at home at a Cadet School or something. Fortunately this did not come off but I was granted a month's leave.

2 Falls: 'Many battalions had trouble about this time with "combed out" men from safer avocations, who did not relish the change in their existence. To do them justice, all but a negligible proportion speedily acquired the proper spirit, particularly when they found themselves in a really good battalion.'

During September replacements of 5 officers and 169 men arrived. Col. Kirkwood fell ill and was evacuated to England, 9 October, and Major Ivey assumed command. 2/Lt. A. McClelland died of wounds, 13 October, and the battalion moved to Red Lodge.

They relieved 2nd R. Berkshires in the left subsector of the Basse Ville Sector on the 21st. The 8th Division history recalled the following event:

> Yet even the small change of daily trench warfare was not without its piquant and exciting incidents. Take, for instance, the adventure which befell an unnamed officer and NCO of the 1st Royal Irish Rifles when out on patrol on the night of the 25th/26th October. These two became detached from their patrol and being uncertain of their position, although they knew that they were somewhere on the German line, were forced to take cover in what appeared to be a sniper's post. A sniper's post, indeed it was, and with the dawn there came along the German occupier. Quite unsuspicious, and not unnaturally, of such unlikely tenants, he blundered straight on – into the path of a revolver bullet. Whereupon the two made off at top speed in the glimmering dawn and, despite the noise of the shot, succeeded in getting clear. At about 11 o'clock they managed to regain our lines where they had long since been given up, and indeed had been officially reported as missing.

2/Lt. A. Howard-Nicholson was wounded on the 27th. At the end of an eight-day tour the battalion was relieved by 2nd East Lancs and moved back to Waterlands Camp for resting, training, and working parties. During October reinforcements amounted to 10 officers and 141 men; casualties totalled one officer killed and one wounded, while among other ranks 6 had been killed and 19 wounded. Whitfeld was re-assigned:

> On my return however, I learnt that I was not to return to the battalion but was to proceed to take over a company in the 8th Division Training Wing as it was then called. All drafts from the Base went there first before joining their battalion. My faithful servant, Lawrence, is still with me.

2/Lt. E. Patton took over as Adjutant, 9 November. The battalion moved by route march, on the 12th, to billets in the La Motte–Caudescure area for rest, training, and reorganisation. Three days later they marched to Caestre, then moved by rail to Ypres, and marched east to D Camp, St Jean.

The 25th Brigade relieved 116th Canadian Infantry in the Brigade Reserve Line at Capricorn and Spree Farm on 16 November. Troops were used for working and carrying parties to the front line. During this short tour 3 men were killed and 12 wounded. Having been relieved by 2nd North Hants on the 19th the battalion marched to camp at Wieltje, where they remained until midnight, and then moved by train to Ridge Camp near Vlamertinghe. There they learned that they were due to make another attack and engaged in a further period of training. 2/Lt. P. Windle and one Rifleman were wounded by shrapnel, 27 November. The battalion proceeded by route march to Haslar Camp, St Jean, on 29 November and, the next day at 3.30 p.m., moved by platoons via Wieltje and the plank road, to occupy a sector of the line north-east of Passchendaele. At 5.30 p.m., while still en route, they came under the fire of enemy 'heavies' on the plank road east of Somme Redoubt. Capt. W.R.L. Patterson (A Coy Commander) and 2/Lt. A.B. Wilkie were wounded, the latter dying of his wounds three hours later. About 30 men were also killed or wounded, C Coy in particular suffering heavily. Capt. G.C. Robb (C Coy Commander) was wounded later, before the line was reached, and several other casualties were sustained. Having taken over the brigade's left line it was found that the right post of 32nd Division on the left, at Teale Cottage, and with which it was C's duty to maintain contact, had been lost during the afternoon and was strongly held by the Germans with machine guns. 2/Lt. E.W. Lennard, who had been sent to command C Coy, was mortally wounded during a reconnaissance to consider retaking Teale Cottage. HQ was in a pillbox at Meetcheele, C and D were in the front line, A and B being in close support. There was heavy shellfire on the front line and supports between dusk and midnight. Total casualties for the day among the ranks were 16 killed and 30 wounded. During November reinforcements of 6 officers and 17 men had arrived.

The attitude of the Germans on 1 December was not aggressive, sniping and machine gun fire being pretty general. Plenty of enemy movement was observed and fire was opened on them causing some casualties. After covering the forming up of the remainder of the brigade for the attack, the battalion moved back into Brigade Support in trenches and shell holes near Meetcheele. The two companies in Brigade Reserve dug in and suffered no casualties. A Coy was in close support holding four strong points. D remained in the outpost line replacing C Coy of 2nd Lincolns (which was caught in the enemy barrage on the way to the trenches and arrived only 20 strong), and held the line during the fight that followed. Casualties were one man killed, 14 wounded, and 4 missing. The assault was planned as a night attack near Venison Trench at 1.55 a.m., 2 December. According to Falls:

> The object of the attack was to gain possession of two important redoubts, one three-quarters of a mile due north of Passchendaele, the other a thousand yards north-east. The attack was launched at 1.55 a.m. behind a very heavy barrage. At once the inevitable blast of German machine gun fire burst out. Despite it, however, the three battalions fought their way forward, and almost everywhere reached their objectives.

The battalion remained in immediate support the next day until the brigade was relieved that evening. One man had been killed, 9 were wounded and one was missing. Casualties for the tour were 10 killed, 74 wounded, and 17 missing – a huge rate for a unit that did not actually take part in the battle. Having entrained at St Jean the battalion proceeded to Wizernes and then by road to billets at Noir Carme and Zudausque (near St Omer) where a period of rest followed. Whitfeld considered that he needed a change:

> I am keener than ever on flying. I think I shall make an effort to go to the RFC. Most of my friends, even if I was with the battalion, have now gone. I have taken

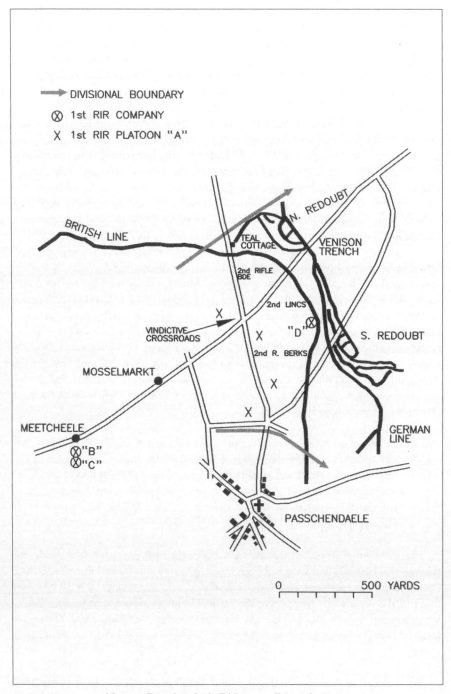

Map 14: Passchendaele Ridge, 1-2 December 1917

one or two drafts up to the battalion. They seem well up there and have been in the line at Passchendaele.

Four officers and 35 men arrived as replacements. The battalion celebrated Christmas on 20 December because of an anticipated early move to the Forward Area. The companies enjoyed Christmas dinner and indulged in sports during the afternoon. The War Diary reported:

> During period in Zudausque Area most of the time was devoted to training in the morning and games – boxing, football and cross country running – in the afternoon and evening, culminating in brigade and divisional competitions, in which the battalion acquitted itself creditably.

The battalion marched to Wizernes on 26 December and entrained for the front area, detraining at St Jean and marching via Wieltje to dugouts at California and Capricorn Trenches. One man was wounded by shellfire. California Trench was the old Black Line of the summer attacks, a little further north of where the battalion had been engaged. The brigade was in support, and the men were employed in carrying and working parties. Lt.-Col. MacCarthy-O'Leary returned on the 29th and resumed command. The battalion moved into the line in the unpleasant Goudberg Sector, north of Passchendaele, 30 December. Dispositions were: front line posts, right to left, A, B and C Coys; D was in close support at Virile Farm. HQ was based at Pill Box 83 and the Aid Post at Waterloo Farm. One man was wounded. The year ended quietly and the troops were engaged in the erection of shelters and improvement of the line.

13

1918

The final year of the war began for the battalion in a lively manner: an attempted patrol to obtain identifications was frustrated by brilliant moonlight on 1 January. At about dusk the Germans tried to raid A Coy's post and were driven off easily, one being killed, several wounded, and valuable unit identifications obtained. At about 5.30 p.m. another raid on C Coy's posts was attempted, 5 Germans were killed and several wounded by a Lewis Gun team under the command of Cpl Hanna, only one Rifleman being wounded. At about 5.30 p.m., 3 January, HQ's pill-box was subjected to a prolonged bombardment of 5.9s; this was continued until 7.45 p.m. and many direct hits were registered. During this time the battalion was in the process of being relieved by 2nd Middlesex Regt and then moved to Brigade Reserve in Brake Camp, Brandhoek. Four men had been wounded and four were reported missing on this tour.

A further move to Junction Camp was made on the 7th. For the next three days the troops worked on the Divisional Reserve Line, from Dump House to Berlin, while company officers carried out daily reconnaissance of the Left Sub-Sector Line. A draft of 38 men arrived. The battalion returned to the same positions in the front line during the 15th and two men were wounded in the process. Conditions had deteriorated in these trenches owing to a thaw and melting snow. The next day a prisoner was captured by C Coy and the battalion was relieved by 2nd Rifle Bde, moving into Brigade Reserve positions at Bellevue. Casualties for this short tour were 5 men killed, 6 wounded, and one missing. Many men suffered from exposure and exhaustion during this time and several were partially buried in mud and shell holes. They were extricated with great difficulty, a party from D Coy under 2/Lt. J.C. Thompson and Cpl Quigley did much good work in digging buried men out. The next day was spent in consolidating and improving their reserve positions. Capt. G.A. Chatterton and 12 men became casualties with trench foot, and 2 men were wounded.

The battalion was relieved on 18 January by 1st R. Guernsey Light Infantry and entrained at Wieltje. They arrived at rest billets near Abeele about 2 a.m. the following morning and, over the next week, 88 men arrived as reinforcements. Orders were received, 2 February, that the battalion was to transfer to the 36th (Ulster) Division – they would now form part of 107th Brigade together with 2nd RIR and 15th RIR. Whitfeld was not impressed:

Definitely settled that the battalion will leave that fine division, the 8th, and go to the 36th Ulster Division – the political division as we know it. The 86th have already joined it I believe. Everyone seems very sick over the move. Heneker made a very nice farewell speech today. I believe he really rather likes us. We had great respect for him and at the same time felt that he had made the division. I never saw a better turned out division in France. They were magnificent and fought very well indeed.

Fr Gill described how 2nd RIR considered their move to the division in his diary entry of 15 September 1917:

Our repose was disturbed by some bad news which reached us. We were to be transferred into the 36th (Ulster) Division. This news came as a surprise and dis-agreeable shock to almost everyone in the Battalion … The prospect of a change into a political division was not pleasant, nor did the outlook appear very bright. Everything possible was done to have the decision changed, but without success … there were not many Catholics in the other battalions except the 1st RIR.

In fact the character of the 36th Division had changed utterly from its original composition by the time 1st RIR joined and was now more representative of the whole of Ulster. Later on Fr Gill noticed:

A marked change had come over the constitution of the 36th Division to which we belonged. Battalions like the 2nd Royal Irish Rifles were moved out of other divisions and put into the Ulster Division – which had failed to obtain recruits – in order to keep it up to strength. Out of the nine battalions for sometime before March 21st no less than five were old regular battalions which had no sort of sympathy whatever with the religious or political aims of the original Ulster division. Those set free by the arrival of the new battalions became Pioneer Battalions … A census of religions at this time showed that in the Ulster Division, at the time of the German advance, there were between 3,000 and 4,000 Catholics. When this division came from Ireland their boast was that there was not a single RC in their ranks. The four RC Chaplains were SJ's [Jesuits] and the three interpreters were French priests.

1st RIR left the 8th Division, 3 February, entraining at Hopoutre where Capt. Whitfeld rejoined as Second-in-Command. They detrained at Ham on the 4th and marched five miles east to billets in Cugny. Whitfeld last entry while with the battalion:

Detrain at 11 a.m. on the Somme; and so goodbye to the 'Iron Eight'. And so we joined the Ulster Division and said goodbye to the 25th Infantry Brigade and the 8th Division. It all seemed very strange mixing with other battalions of the regiment. The 8th Division was a great division with a great leader. The brigade had some of the finest regiments of the British Army and we were indeed sorry to bid farewell to the Rifle Brigade.

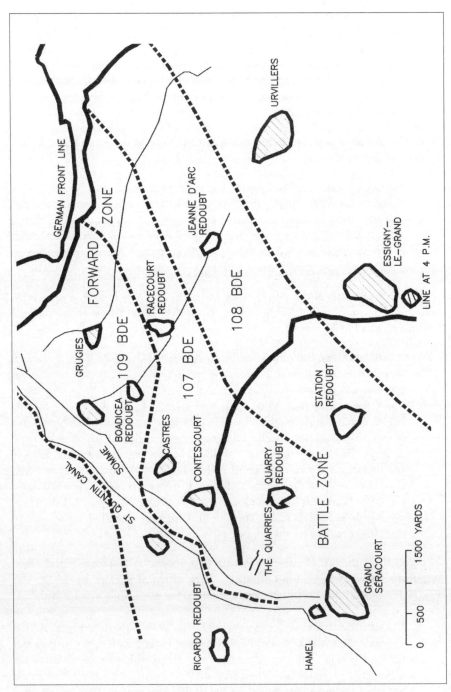

Map 15: Quarry Redoubt, 21 March 1918

Fr Gill noticed that 'there was not much fighting, the country was open and dry and, on the whole, the weather was good'. This was a time of major reorganisation in the British Army. Due to the shortage of reinforcements being released to the BEF, brigade strength was reduced to three battalions. Many units were being disbanded or amalgamated. 8/9th RIR was one such unit being disbanded and 8 officers and 200 men were transferred to 1st RIR on 6 February. The Irish troops were once again in the majority, albeit at a mere 51 per cent. Due to the political problems in Ireland, especially in the south, recruitment had dried up and most of those that did volunteer were either kept in Britain or used to shore up the regiments of their own regions. Only 8 per cent of the total strength then came from what is now the Irish Republic where they had once made up to 30 per cent.

The area had recently been taken over from the French Army and the defences were not up to British standards. There were no reserve trenches and these had to be made. A new system of defence was being prepared for the anticipated German offensive, now that the enemy was being heavily reinforced by troops coming from the Russian front. This involved a three-tier line consisting of a Forward Zone, a Battle Zone, and a Reserve Line, one battalion of the brigade being allocated to each area. The Forward Zone would, in effect, be the old front line and be manned in the normal way. It was designed so that the enemy would have to assault it to make progress and was expendable. The Battle Zone was now the main area of defence and was quite a distance to the rear of the Forward Zone. It was lightly manned but could be quickly reinforced in the case of an attack – this allowed most of the troops to shelter in billets. It had strong redoubts and defensive positions within its area. The Reserve Line held reinforcements that could be directed to assist the areas most under threat in the Battle Zone. It was hoped that this system would hold the enemy until French troops arrived in force. That was the theory; Fr Gill observed the true situation:

> Another cause of disquiet was the system of defence. There were very few troops in reserve. As far as my personal observations went during visits to Divisional and Corps HQ there were practically no reserves to be seen. It was indeed announced that the main shock would have to be withstood by the divisions actually holding the trenches. The line was held as follows. Of each of the three brigades, one battalion was in the forward trenches, one in reserve, and the third in support between the two. Each battalion of the brigades took their turn in each of these positions. Conditions were not satisfactory in the trench system.
>
> The front line was not held as a continuous line manned all along as was the usual case, but was held by a series of detached posts. These posts were supposed to command the gaps between them, and chiefly by machine guns. Each of these posts was an independent unit. Two companies of the battalion were in positions a little behind these forward positions and were to come up if necessary in support. There was no cover but rather ill-constructed trenches. These positions were more or less surrounded by barbed wire. The support positions were arranged on somewhat the same plan. The battle zone consisted of strong points some three thousand yards behind the forward positions. These were surround-

ed by barbed wire, so that there were only a few places in which one could leave or enter.

There was no system of communication trenches between the forward area and this position. In fact there was no question or possibility of the battalion holding the front line being supported or relieved – or of getting away – except at night. I understood that the forward battalion was expected to hold out at least forty-eight hours before there would be any question of relief! It is not surprising that the people in the front trenches had anxious views on the whole position, and as the time of the attack was, of course, unknown, everyone in the division had an interest in the matter.

Shortly before the attack I felt it my duty to make arrangements with the other chaplains as to the best positions to take up. Three of the chaplains lived with battalions and the fourth with an Artillery unit. Now it was quite clear to me that anyone who might happen to be in the front line when the attack took place would never get back alive. But the chaplain's duty was with the brigade as a whole and he therefore had to make arrangements so as to avoid being killed without necessity! I mention this fact as typical of the mental attitude of those who were obliged to face realities. It was a toss up as to which battalion of each brigade would be sacrificed. Whatever be the rights or wrongs of the method it is true that one third of the Fifth Army was killed or captured by the Germans in their initial onslaught.

The 107th Brigade had the centre of 36th Division's sector. In the Forward Zone, HQ and one company would occupy a fortress known as Racecourse Redoubt that was one mile to the rear of the advanced posts.[1] The Reserve was in the village of Grand Séracourt. 1st RIR moved into Brigade Support on 7 February and relieved 15th RIR in the front line the next day, placing their HQ at Grugies. Casualties over the next week were one man killed and 5 wounded. Having been relieved, 15 February, the battalion moved to dugouts at Essigny Station in Divisional Reserve. The next five days were spent working on the Battle Zone G Sector. Two officers and 54 men joined as reinforcements. Having moved to the Quarries Battle Zone on the 22nd, with HQ in deep quarries near Grand Séracourt, the troops worked on the Battle Zone F Sector. The battalion and 1st Line Transport were inspected by Major-General O.S.W. Nugent, GOC 36th Division, 24 February, and a draft of 35 men joined. 1st RIR moved into the front line in relief of 15th RIR on the night of the 28th, with HQ at the Quarries.

At 8.20 p.m., 1 March, a heavy trench mortar and artillery barrage was put on Auvergne Trench. The bombardment lasted about twenty minutes and then lifted to further in the rear. Sentries in St Bruno Trench saw a large body of Germans crawling under, and in some cases lifting and cutting, the British wire. They immediately opened fire and then manned the junction of Auvergne Trench and St Bruno Sap. Heavy rifle and Lewis Gun fire was directed on the enemy for about ten minutes. Moments later, while intermittent fire was ongoing, a few bombs were thrown into the post from

---

1 Racecourse Redoubt was on a railway embankment south of Grugies. It was here that 2/Lt. E. de Wind, 15th RIR, earned a posthumous Victoria Cross for his defence of the redoubt on 21 March 1918.

behind. A large party of the enemy, numbering about eighty, was seen to the rear of Auvergne Trench. They rushed forward, throwing bombs, one of which fell on the Lewis gun and broke it in two pieces. The officer in command of the platoon, Lt. H.D. Sinclair, was severely wounded, one man was killed and 7 were wounded. The parados was too high for the men to use their rifles and, after throwing at least fifty bombs, they retired right and left down the line. The raiders then entered the trench and threw bombs into dugouts. The Lance Corporal in charge of the Lewis gun, who was last seen standing beside his gun, was killed and taken away by the attackers. The enemy left no dead or wounded, but it was certain that he suffered heavy casualties. Working parties continued on the front posts and, by the time they were relieved on the 6th, a further eleven men had been wounded. The battalion then marched to billets: HQ in Grand Séracourt with B and D Coys, A in Hamel, and C in Somme Dugouts. Over the next few days reinforcements of 43 men arrived and time was spent at cleaning kits, refitting, and training.

On the 13th, the battalion relieved 15th RIR in the Battle Zone at Quarries in front of Grand Séracourt. HQ remained at Grand Séracourt, handing over to 2nd RIR. Work continued on the Battle Zone over the next three days and 12 new men were posted to companies. St Patrick's Day was observed as a holiday. 1st RIR was holding the Battle Zone and 2nd RIR was in reserve at Séracourt. The Roman Catholics of both battalions were united at Mass by Fr Gill for the first time since 1854 and shamrock was distributed throughout the division. Strangely enough, Fr Gill did not mention this in his diary but did record:

> I buried a Sergeant and we had sports on high ground from which we could clearly see St Quentin, and no doubt the Germans were watching us at play. The 'tag' was approaching. Adopting the tactics of a prize fighter we hurled defiance at the foe! Typewritten notices were distributed and ordered to be placed by patrols in front of the German trenches! I never heard which department of the Higher Command was responsible for this childish device.

A football match was played in the morning and 1st Battalion won 2–1. The team was: Goal – Cpl Dixon; Backs – Rfn Moorhead, Sgt Styles; Halves – Rfn Conroy, Sgt Meredith, L/Cpl Convery; Forwards – Lt. J. Kerr, Rfn Spence, L/Cpl Barr, Cpl Malone, Rfn McAdams. Battalion sports were held in the afternoon. 1st RIR won the open cookers competition in an event open to the whole Fifth Army, near Ham. Work then resumed on trenches in the Battle Zone and at cable laying near Bray St Christophe. On the 20th, work was also ongoing at Artemps. Battalion HQ moved to the Battle Zone Dugouts in the Quarries. The long-awaited German offensive was expected to open the following morning, after information had been received from prisoners and deserters. Fr Gill wrote:

> Wednesday, March 20th: Information had been received by the authorities which they looked on as reliable. It appeared that two soldiers had come in from the German trenches – Alsatians, it was said – bringing the news that the attack was to begin about midnight that night.

14

St Quentin

At 4.40 a.m., 21 March, there was a heavy bombardment of the Battle Zone, Forward Zone, redoubts, and gun positions by artillery of all calibres. Gas shells were extensively used and the order to man battle positions was received at 4.50 a.m. A Coy (Capt. C.H.R. Reed) occupied the right Battle Zone trenches, B (Capt. J. Brown) the left Battle positions in the Contescourt section, C (Lt. J. Kerr) the counter-attack trenches, and D (Capt. L.M. Bayly) the Quarry Redoubt to the right of Battalion HQ in the second line. Quarry Redoubt was three large wired-in forts to the east of the Quarries and had several smaller semi-isolated keeps.

It was unlucky for the defenders that a dense fog made it impossible for them to see any of the enemy troop movements until they were upon the Forward Zone; the British Artillery was firing blind in most places. Fr Gill moved forward:

> There was a most unusual and dense fog, which made it almost impossible to make our way. With shells falling all round, the journey was not a pleasant one. Soon we had to put on our gas masks, which made things much worse. We had great difficulty in locating ourselves, and after many false moves reached the headquarters of the 1st RIR. We got directions here and soon reached 2nd RIR at the other side of the road. The 15th RIR were in the front trenches and were consequently either killed or taken prisoners – quite according to plan. This part of the programme worked well. We found our people in dug-outs made in the side of a chalk quarry. An indication of the way the Germans had mapped out the ground it is interesting to note that, at the very beginning of the attack, this quarry was heavily shelled. Although, up to this time, it had escaped attention. The shells fell with an accuracy which proved that the range had been carefully taken beforehand. Then began an anxious time of waiting. Gas shells were falling all around.

The Fifth Army, in the southern area of the attack, was seriously undermanned and the forward areas were quickly overrun. The Germans reached the Battle Zones with alarming rapidity. Falls explained:

> Unfortunately, the platoon of B destined to occupy Contescourt ran into a large shell on the way up and was almost totally destroyed. This was not learnt till

1. Officers of the 1st Royal Irish Rifles, Kamptee, India.

(*Back row*) Lt. A.W. Galway, Lt. J.W. Foley, Lt. I. French, Lt. R.M. Rodwell,
Lt. G.I. Gartlan, Lt. F.R.W. Graham, Lt. C.J. Newport, Lt. D.A. Browne,
Lt. G.G. Adeley, Capt. & QM B. Foster.
(*Front row*) Capt. C.H.L. Cinnamond, Capt. H.L. Gifford, Major J. Alston,
Major O.C. Baker, Lt.-Col. G.B. Laurie, Major H.C. Wright, Lt. &
Adjutant A.O'H. Wright, Capt. A.J. Biscoe, Lt. C.C. Tee.

2. (*left*) Lt.-Col. G.B. Laurie

3. (*right*) Lt. G.H.P. Whitfeld

4. (*right*) 2/Lt. W.V.C. Lake

5. (*left*) Lt.-Col. H.W.D. MacCarthy-O'Leary

6. (*left*) Major A.J.W. Fitzmaurice

7. (*right*) Capt. R.H. Forbes

8. (*above*) Major A.H. Festing
9. (*above right*) Major A.D.N. Merriman
10. (*below*) Lt.-Col. G.I. Gartlan

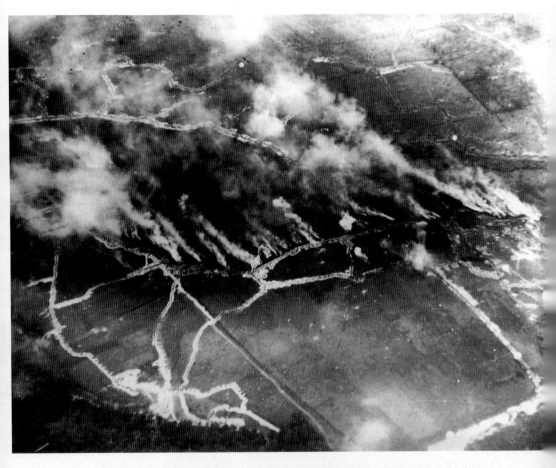

11. Aerial view of the trenches at Ovillers. The British trenches are on the lower
half of the picture and a gas attack is in progress. The main trenches in the
bottom right corner are Conniston and Pendlehill. Ovillers village is in the
top right corner.

12. RIR ration party, Somme, 1 July 1916

13. RIR regimental cap badge

14. Gravestone of 1st RIR

afterwards, and it was at Contescourt that the enemy made the only serious hole in the Division's Battle Zone. The counter-attack company made later in the morning an attempt to regain the village, but was held up by very heavy machine gun fire.

Intense shelling of the Battle Zone developed about 9 a.m., particularly on B and C Coy's trenches. The attack here was intensifying by 12.30 p.m. and the redoubt was reinforced by one company and the remainder were withdrawn to the rear of the dug-outs. The fog was only starting to clear by this time. At 12.50 p.m. the Counter-Attack Company (C) moved forward to meet the enemy who had just entered the front line of the zone. At 3.15 p.m. C was reported to be hanging on at the crossroad. An hour later a reserve company was brought forward to reinforce Quarry Redoubt. By 7 p.m. the enemy was trying to advance towards the redoubt on the west side of the Grugies–Grand Séracourt Road. The situation at 8.05 p.m. was that the Right Company Keep was held by one officer and 34 men; the redoubt by one and a half companies that were weak in strength, and the remainder of the unit was in front of Battalion HQ, with a strength of only about 70 of all ranks. Being almost surrounded, the Right Company Keep was abandoned at 8.15 p.m.; its strength was 23 men. The remnants of 1st RIR were ordered to retire on Hamel at 11 p.m. Capt. J. Brown was wounded and missing; Lts B.J. Hodson, J. Kerr, P. O'Kane, 2/Lts J. Kennedy, and J.C. Thompson were killed; 2/Lts J. Aiken, H. Oliver, and T.A. Valentine were wounded. General Gough had decided that it was more important to keep together the remains of Fifth Army rather than hold ground.

Positions were taken up at Hamel on 22 March. By 3 a.m. their strength was 5 officers, 180 men, and 2 machine guns. At 11 a.m. Capt. Tayler brought up reinforcements for both 1st and 2nd RIR. These were, however, kept at Brigade HQ. The right flank was on scrub and a copse on Sommebank. Large bodies of the enemy and transport were seen moving south along the St Quentin–St Simon Road. The battalion engaged them until it was ordered to fall back to a position 600 yards west of Happencourt at 12.45 p.m., where it hung on till dusk, when the right flank was seriously threatened and orders were received to retire on the line Sommette–Eaucourt–Cugny behind the canal. Capt. Tayler's party covered the withdrawal. At 11 p.m., 1st RIR moved across country, crossing the canal at Pithon by the light railway bridge, and proceeded to billets at Eaucourt, arriving at 3 a.m. on the 23rd. 2nd RIR were also in the vicinity.

At 5 a.m., amid heavy ground mist, picquets were put out around the village. Five hours later the village was shelled with 5.9 guns and the battalion moved out north-west and west and dug in. Falls described the general situation:

> The great breakthrough had begun, and was to be completed the moment the Germans forced the line of the Somme and the Crozet Canal, as they did early on the 23rd … Owing to an error on the part of a brigade on the left of the 36th Division and of some engineers, not only was the main bridge at Ham not properly demolished, but the crossing of the river at this point was not guarded. The enemy speedily crossed here, and was also across the Crozet Canal at several points at 11.30 a.m.

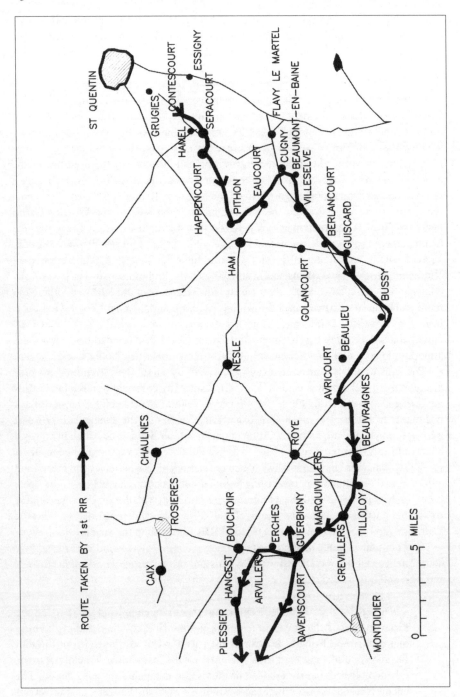

Map 16: The retreat from St Quentin, 21–7 March 1918

Heavy fighting was heard in the direction of Ham and Esmery-Hallon. Orders were received at 11.30 a.m. for both battalions to move to Cugny, where they arrived about 3 p.m. 1st RIR occupied the high ground south of the village in a position facing east and dug in. 2nd RIR occupied a defensive position east and north-east of the village astride the Cugny–Flavy-le-Martel Road. 1st RIR made contact with French dismounted dragoons on the right, 2nd RIR and the 14th Division were on their left prolonging the position southwards. The enemy, in large numbers, proceeded to occupy woods on the opposite height and, at about 3.45 p.m., their advance commenced. This was preceded by intense machine gun fire that continued until the light began to fail.

Large numbers of men, belonging to a battalion in front, commenced a somewhat disorderly withdrawal through the left of 1st RIR at about 4.30 p.m. Col. MacCarthy-O'Leary went forward to find out what was happening and met the Colonel of this battalion being carried back on a stretcher in a dying condition. His men were retiring hastily. It was now dusk and getting dark quickly, while the noise of musketry and German shouting and cheering was great. The enemy attacked at 7 p.m. but were repulsed; a further attack was made at 7.45 p.m. but the line held. At 10 p.m. an enemy patrol succeeded in getting round the left flank of 1st RIR and the HQ in the sunken road was rushed. Fortunately there were no casualties. They had broken through on the left of 1st RIR's front, there being no troops remaining there to stop them, and were firing in enfilade at short range. At 11 p.m., with 14th Division on the left falling back and the Gloucester Entrenching Bn retiring on the right, the line was rushed by the enemy and over-run. The CO ordered a retirement south along the road. 2/Lt. W.N. McNeil and Lt.-Col. MacCarthy-O'Leary were wounded in this attack but he remained in command. A few hundred yards back he was able to collect together the majority of the men and then decided to withdraw to the next high ground which was in the vicinity of Beaumont-en-Beine. The battalion reassembled there at about 1 a.m. on the 24th and dug in. Col. MacCarthy-O'Leary later reported to General Davies:

> On the outskirts of the village I met an infantry officer of another regiment and an artillery officer. As I was the senior I gave instructions for a defensive position to be dug NE of the village. The infantry officer, a Major, had about 250 men of his battalion already in position. His regiment was a north-country one (I thought the York and Lancaster Regiment belonging to or attached to the 14th Division. I understood that they were a Labour battalion and at the time was under the impression that they were the battalion that had withdrawn earlier from in front of Cugny).
>
> The men had no rest since the 20th and were very tired; however they fell to and before long had made passable an attempt at digging isolated holes. About 2 a.m. the acting Brigade Major arrived with rations. He told me to move my battalion in support of the 2nd Royal Irish Rifles who had been forced through Cugny and were now astride the main Villeselve–Cugny Road. I pointed out that we had consolidated an excellent position; that the men were 'done', and that I believed we would be of greater use where we were. He returned to Brigade HQ in Villeselve. Dawn was breaking when he came back with orders to move at once to a position astride the main road.

It was daylight before I was able to collect the battalion but luckily a thick mist covered the ground and we were able to reach and consolidate, after a fashion, the position allotted to us. Some French machine guns were in position in my right rear.

At 4 a.m. the battalion marched to Montelimont on the Villeselve–Cugny Road and dug in south of the road about 700 yards in the rear of 2nd RIR's position taken up the previous night. The HQs of 1st RIR and 10th Rifle Bde were in the sunken road in the trenches to the rear of and north of the battalion. The German artillery opened up as soon as the mist cleared; a general engagement commenced and large reinforcements approaching from the rear were badly shelled in the village at 1 p.m. The French, to the right on the wooded heights near Beaumont, retired and 30th Division around Eaucourt did likewise. At this time messengers from the Right Company brought word that the enemy had got in behind them through the woods on that flank and that the French machine gunners had retired. 1st RIR remained and two messages were sent to 2nd RIR to retire through 1st RIR, at 3 p.m. No answer was received and 10th Rifle Bde was ordered to retire. Runners sent to 2nd RIR had been either killed or wounded. Machine gun fire from the high ground south of Cugny had now become heavy. By this time, after a heroic stand, 2nd RIR had been all but annihilated. The Germans were known to be behind 1st RIR on their right while, to the left at a distance of about 300 yards, they were in strong force and had commenced to fire at them in enfilade. At 3.30 p.m. the battalion was practically surrounded and had to retire on Villeselve, where a defensive position north and west of the village was taken up. From this point two large columns of troops were seen following the Canal north of Cugny. The hostile troops formed part of the 1st Bavarian, 10th, 34th, and 37th Divisions.

The 107th Brigade Major reported back at 4.35 p.m.:

All troops are retiring in disorder except 1st and 2nd R. Irish Rifles. 2nd R. Irish Rifles appear to be cut off, and it is doubtful if the 1st Battalion can get away as the troops on both flanks have retired.

He was sent back to the line to assist in rallying men retiring on the right. Col. MacCarthy-O'Leary:

Hearing heavy firing from Beaumont en Beine and from the NW of Villeselve, I decided to retire still further and to get in touch with other units of the 36th Division. Marching through Villeselve a Colonial Cavalry Officer, dressed as a Lt.-Col., stopped us. He told me he was a Brigadier and being a Cavalryman suggested that I should help him regarding the infantry dispositions. He showed me on his map where many other units of the 36th and 14th Divisions were. I then placed my battalion in position facing NW and rejoined him in the village.

Meanwhile other battalions commenced to fall back and I assisted this officer in sending them to various positions. Later Lt.-Col. M.J. Furnell (CO 1st Royal Irish Fusiliers) joined me. The village was now being heavily shelled. It was reported that Golancourt on our left was in the enemy's hands and that he was south of Beaumont on our right.

A Lt.-Col. on the staff suddenly appeared on the scene. We debated whether we should retire and decided to issue orders for the move back to the high ground near Guiscard. The troops however did not wait for orders and fell back in confusion through the village. Two officers went ahead in an ambulance and formed up the remnants of the division as far as possible by units. The Royal Inniskilling and Irish Fusiliers on the south side of the road, the Royal Irish Rifles and other troops on the north of the road. We formed up in quarter column with a screen of cavalry in front facing Villeselve. Two flights of hostile aeroplanes circled round us for some time. They did not fire at us nor did they direct artillery fire against us.

It was now about 4 p.m. Brigadier-General W.F. Hessey (Commanding 109th Bde) arrived as we were forming up and ordered us to withdraw. I understood that the French were in position on the high ground east and west of Guiscard. Gun detachments (Pompoms) of their troops covered our retirement through Berlancourt. I now had charge of all Royal Irish Riflemen that I could gather.

The high ground was occupied by our infantry. There were also French troops and several batteries of French artillery. It was getting dusk when I reached the outskirts of Guiscard and not meeting anyone of authority I placed the Royal Irish Rifles under cover of a quarry and went into the village to look for Brigade HQ which was said to be there. I was returning from a fruitless search when a staff officer of the 36th Division came galloping down the street. He told me that everyone had gone further back (in a southerly direction) and thought I should do likewise.

The place was now being heavily shelled so I moved as soon as possible and together with the French artillery set out in darkness along the Noyon Road. Some two miles further back an officer of the 36th Division had been posted to guide us to where the division was re-forming. This was another two or three miles further back. It is off the map and I do not recollect its name.

The covering position was held until 6.30 p.m. when the battalion retired through Guiscard, St Martin, and Bussy, to Sermaize (near Noyon), where the brigade came under the orders of the French Army GOC. As the troops moved back and bivouacked for the night at 3 a.m., 25 March, large columns of French guns were passed going up to the firing line. The battalion moved at 9 a.m. via Gredenville to Avricourt, meeting the Transport at noon, where it prepared to bivouac. Accompanying them was a force of fifty officers and men, which was all that could be found of 2nd RIR. Fr Gill recorded on 25 March:

> The 1st Royal Irish Rifles had not suffered so heavily, and a good number of them returned, the line was now definitely held by the French, according to the original plan. There were very few of the brigade remaining.

They moved off at 2 p.m. via Beauvraignes, Tilloloy, Grivillers, and Marquivillers, to Guerbigny, arriving at 1 a.m. on the 26th. Brigade HQ was based in the town. Falls outlined the situation:

> This last move was a nightmare. The men had reached a condition of fatigue when they seemed lost to all sense of what was happening about them. In some cases their boots were giving out. The roads were choked with pitiful columns of refugees, carrying their goods piled high on country carts, the poorest actually pushing wheel-barrows. It is certain that a proportion of the men simply could not have completed the march had it not been that a few lorries were placed at General Withycombe's disposition, which took the most footsore to their destination and then returned to meet the slowly advancing column and pick up a second load.
>
> There now followed the most desperate moment for the Allies of the whole war. The British were retiring due west, the French south-west, being preoccupied by their lines of communication and the safety of Paris. The inevitable gap appeared at Roye on the morning of the 26th, and the enemy pushed into it with extraordinary speed. To close it there were no available troops but the tired and depleted 30th and 36th Divisions. The 36th was ordered to turn out instantly and take up a line, represented over much of its length by old French trenches of 1916, from the River Avre, at l'Echelle St Aurin, to the Amiens–Roye Road north of Andechy. The task of holding this line was allotted to the 109th Brigade on the right and the 108th on the left. The 107th remained for the time being in reserve.

At 10 a.m. the battalion moved out of the town and manned a position two miles to the east, north of the River Avre. Col. MacCarthy-O'Leary was placed in command of a group: 1st RIR, 2nd RIR under Capt. P. Murphy, and 15th RIR under Capt. Miller. At 5 p.m. a fresh position was occupied 700 yards west of the village of Erches. 2nd RIR was on the right, 1st RIR in the centre, and 15th RIR on the left. The battalion was posted in old French trenches and gun pits and old ammunition dumps along the Bouchoir–Guerbigny Road. The French dismounted cavalry screen was being withdrawn and the 109th Infantry Brigade on 1st RIR's quarter right front was in action. At about 8 p.m. the line of 108th Brigade was broken and the Germans advanced on 107th Brigade. Two hours later the enemy, 1st Guards Division, approached the village and secured posts using French uniforms. In one case they kidnapped the occupants. Random fire commenced and later developed into bursts of machine gun fire of some intensity. Having made good the village, light trench mortars were brought up and 1st RIR positions were bombarded. On two occasions the white flag was used to distract attention while machine gun crews operated on the opposite flank. Considerable use was made of the presumed presence of French soldiers in 'Don't fire. We are French' until it became necessary to warn the troops to fire on all soldiers to the front of them.

At dawn, 27 March, the Germans brought up 5.9 calibre guns and the companies on the gun pits were blown out at point-blank range. At 10 a.m., a counter-attack was made on the enemy who rapidly retired and this enabled the battalion to withdraw in fighting order. In this action, Col. MacCarthy-O'Leary, Lt. E.V. Manico, 2/Lts T. Enright, R. Moore, and F.W. Hoyle were wounded. Detachment 4 (Capts E. Patton, L.M. Bayly, 2/Lt. T.H.R. Browne, and 68 men), on retiring to Arvillers, dug in facing east and remained fighting all night. The following morning it kept the enemy in check by its fire, with no other troops in its vicinity. On relief at 11 a.m. on the 28th, they moved east of Hangest via Fresnoy, Mézières, Villers-aux-Erables, Moreuil, and Mailly to Sourdon arriving at 7 p.m. In the meantime, Detachment 3 (Capts C.H.R. Reed and R.O.H. Law, Lt. E.B.R. Colles, 2/Lts J.J. O'Sullivan, I.H. Turkington, T. Farley, and 98 men), having left the gun pits at 10.15 a.m. on the 27th, retired fighting a rearguard action. On receipt of orders a further position south of Hangest was taken. The French relieved them the same day and the party reached Sourdon via Hangest, Le Plessier-Rozainvillers, Moreuil, and Mailly.

Earlier in the day, at 2 a.m., the CO had ordered Detachment 1 (2/Lts S.M. Jamison, P.R.G. Fennell, the MO Lt. J.R. Cameron, and the Orderly Room staff), to proceed along the main road to Arvillers. They went through Hangest, Le Plessier-Rozainvillers, Le Hamel, Pierrepont, Hargicourt, and Aubvillers to Sauvillers arriving at 5 p.m. on the same day. Capt. Tayler, the Second-in-Command, left at about 4.45 a.m. to 107th Brigade HQ. He was then joined by the Assistant Adjutant 2/Lt. Leeper, 2/Lt. Greene, and 16 specialists with 2 German prisoners (Detachment 2) and moved via Davenscourt, Contoire, Pierrepont, Hargicourt, Malpart, and Grivesnes, arriving at 2 p.m. They joined the Transport and proceeded immediately to Sauvillers where Detachment 1 was met. At 10 a.m. on the 28th, both parties moved to Sourdon. Detachments 1, 2, and 3, with a strength of 118 men, moved from Sourdon at 1.30 p.m. via Esclainvillers to Coullemelle, where they dug in on the east of the village and manned these posts during the night.

An attack from hostile forces located at Mesnil-St Georges, west of Montdidier, was anticipated. All troops that could be collected from 107th and 109th Brigades were therefore sent to Montdidier on the 29th and placed themselves to the south and east of the village. The French requested that they move forward to Villers-Tournelle. General W.M. Withycombe, in view of the condition of his troops, decided to check this area first. So, at 4 a.m. on the 29th, a patrol of twenty men under Capt. H. Tayler was sent to check for the presence of Germans in that village. Finding it unoccupied, the party moved on to Cantigny and found French troops there. Their officers told Capt. Tayler that the line out in front was holding firmly, and that there was no cause for anxiety. Though no one knew it, the German advance was, for all practical purposes, now held up. The patrol then withdrew to Sourdon.

Orders were now received for the 36th Division to withdraw for reorganisation. At 2 p.m., the brigade moved off via Folleville to Chaussoy-Épagny, arriving at 5 p.m. and meeting Detachment 4 under Capt. Bayly, which had arrived from Sourdon via Chirmont. Two hours later the battalion paraded and moved to Valennes via Berny, Jumel, Oresmaux, and Lœuilly to near Poix arriving at 4 a.m. on the 30th, where billets were occupied. The battalion rested until 4 p.m. when it marched via Taisnil to the Saleux railhead (south of Amiens) arriving at 11 p.m., and camped on the roadside. They had travelled a total of 105 miles. During these operations casualties were 31 killed, 248 wounded, 155 missing, 9 wounded and missing. The battalion entrained on the morning of 31 March at Saleux Railhead, detrained at Gamaches (near Le Tréport) and marched to billets. The Transport was located at Hocquelus, companies at Frettemeule, and HQ at Monchelet.

15

The advance in Flanders

A draft of 4 officers and 160 men of 10th RIR and 14th RIR arrived from entrenching battalions on 2 April. This brought the strength up to 25 officers and 406 men. At 3 p.m. on the 3rd, they entrained at Fouquieres on a tactical train, detrained at 1 a.m. the following morning and proceeded by lorry to No. 6 Siege Camp, near Brielen, for refitting. Major Ivey assumed command and Capt. Whitfeld left to join the RAF. The battalion relieved two platoons of the South Wales Borderers and 2nd Welsh Regt in the Langemarck–Poelcappel Trenches on the 6th, HQ being located at Hubner. Falls gave the general situation:

> On April 9th the troops in line heard a tremendous bombardment to the south, over their right shoulders. The second great German offensive, of the Lys, had been launched. It met with astonishing initial success. Within forty-eight hours of the assault, the German front at a point fifteen miles south of Passchendaele was fifteen miles west of it. The 108th Brigade, of the 36th Division, was hurriedly carried by bus and lorry to Kemmel, and was in action in the early hours of April 11th. In the Salient there was no fighting, but a withdrawal was absolutely necessary, and was delayed only long enough to evacuate artillery and as much ammunition as possible, tear up the light railways, blow up concrete dug-outs, and blow huge craters at every important crossroads.

The battalion moved to the Pilkem Line with HQ at Mousetrap Farm on 15 April. For the first two weeks of this month, further reinforcements of 4 officers and 266 men had arrived; one man had been killed and 5 wounded. 2/Lts T. Farley and H. De Vine were wounded during the 17th – by a strange coincidence both of these officers had been teachers at the same school. On the 19th the battalion moved to Canal Bank until relieved the next day. Casualties among other ranks were 3 killed, 9 wounded, and one missing. Having moved back to No. 6 Siege Camp, Lt.-Col. J.P. Hunt, Royal Dublin Fusiliers, took command of the battalion. Lt.-General Nugent visited and addressed the battalion on 21 April. They moved into Pilkem trenches the next day, with HQ at Foch Farm, relieving 15th RIR. 2/Lts H.C. Greene and F.H. Lewis were killed and 2/Lt. E.B.R. Colles was wounded on the 29th. Major J.A. Mulholland arrived and assumed the duties of Second-in-Command. By the end of the month another 7 officers and one man had joined while casualties in the ranks were 7 killed, 19 wounded, and 5 missing.

137

Early May found the battalion working on trenches and training at Wagram Farm. Two companies were in huts and the others were in the trenches. They returned to Canal Bank, 6 May, where they were subjected to heavy shelling. During the 10th they moved into the left sub sector and were relieved on the 16th, moving to Hospital Farm. The rest of the month was spent on cleaning up, refitting, training, and recreation; much time was also utilised working on the 'Green Line'. The battalion moved into Brigade Support trenches with HQ at Canal Bank, relieving 12th RIR on 29 May. During the month 3 officers and 113 men joined; casualties were 9 men killed and 23 wounded. Major-General Coffin assumed command of the division and Brigadier-General E.J. Thorpe took command of 107th Brigade.[1]

On 1 June the battalion was in the line in the Left Sub Sector, with its HQ at Hill Top Mine. They were relieved on the night of the 5th by 3/1st Grenadier Regiment of the Belgian Army and moved by rail from Reading to Road Camp, near St Jean der Biezen (three miles west of Poperinghe on the Proven Road), for training and refitting. The officers of the battalion were inspected on 9 June by Lt.-General Sir Claud Jacob, Commanding II Army Corps, and he inspected the entire brigade the following day. 1st RIR moved by road to Pekin Camp, 13 June, relieving 1st RIF and began working on the East Poperinghe Line. They billeted at Tunnellers Camp on the 21st before moving to Bois St Acaire Musketry Camp, where they trained on the shooting range for several days.

The battalion sports were held on the 27th, the winner being C Coy. An inter-platoon musketry competition was held the following day and No. 16 Platoon came out on top. The officers played a rugby game against 153rd Brigade RFA at Houtkerque, winning 34–0. At the end of the month they moved back to Tunnellers Camp. During June one man had died and 11 were wounded, while reinforcements of 6 officers and 66 men had arrived. The 36th Division horse show was held at Proven Aerodrome on 1 July. 1st RIR was awarded more prizes than any other infantry battalion in the division. The following competitions were won: 1st Prize for two limbers (four light-draft horses); 2nd Prize for an officer's charger (style and appearance) to Lt. T.M. Tate, Transport Officer; 3rd Prize for both a travelling kitchen and water carts.

The battalion and transports moved by road to St Marie Cappel, near Cassel, 3 July, and then by road to Oxelaere the next day. They were to move to St Sylvestre Cappel on the 6th, but the order was cancelled on arrival at St Marie Cappel, and they returned to Oxelaere, less D Coy. This company continued to St Sylvestre Cappel and billeted there, having started independently. The battalion relieved the 42nd Regiment of the French Army on the night of 7 July in the St Jans Cappel Sector, HQ being situated in La Manche Copse. A Coy was at Vanilla Farm, B and C at La Manche Farm and D at St Jans Cappel. The Commandant of the 42nd Regiment presented the battalion with a cow.[2] The brigade was situated as follows: 1st RIR in Brigade Reserve, 15th RIR in the front line, and 2nd RIR in support. During this period a working party of 2 officers and 100 men were sent up nightly to the line.

---

1 A sentry of 15th RIR accidentally wounded Brig.-Gen. Thorpe on 13 September 1918. His successor was Brig.-Gen. H.J. Brock. 2 Falls: 'There was, indeed, a large amount of stray livestock in this area, owing to the speed with which the unfortunate civilians had been compelled to evacuate it. There was also plenty of vegetables growing in the gardens right up to the front line.'

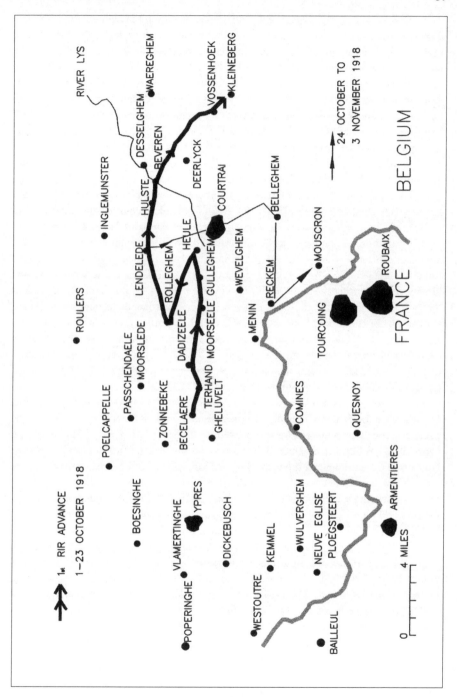

Map 17: The final advances

1st RIR relieved 15th RIR in the Right Brigade Sector on the night of the 15th. The dispositions were: A Coy, right front at Benedict Farm; B, left front at Salvo Farm; C, in reserve at Punkah Farm; D, the Counterattack Company, and HQ at Kopje Farm. The 9th Division was on the right and the 108th Brigade was on the left. The 9th Division, under cover of a heavy bombardment, took Meteren on 19 July. Zero hour was 7.55 a.m. Two platoons of D Coy, under the command of Lt. D.J. McCullough and Lt. J.G. Branford, made an unsuccessful diversionary raid on the enemy trenches in co-operation with that division. C and D Coys relieved A and B respectively that night. 2/Lt. W.E. Parke and 14 men had been wounded. CQMS (a/CSM) J. Leverett DCM, D Coy, went out with a patrol and succeeded in penetrating the enemy wire but, at this juncture, a machine gun opened fire and killed him. A daylight patrol of A Coy, under 41558 Sgt F. Arnold, succeeded in capturing a prisoner. During these eight days that the battalion was in the front line very active patrolling took place with a view of obtaining identification, but they met with very little success; the forward companies sent out day as well as night patrols.

The battalion was relieved on the night of 23 July and, on completion of the relief, moved into Brigade Reserve. The deployment was: HQ at Rifle Range Wood, A Coy at Roberts Farm, B at Noote Boone, C at Tibet Farm, and D at Senlac Farm. HQ was heavily shelled during the night of the 24th by 8 and 12-inch guns. B Coy relieved A as the Nucleus Garrison of the Blue Line late on 27 July. For eight days the battalion worked on the Blue Line, between Schaexken and Fontaine Houck, from 10 p.m. to 2 a.m. nightly. They moved into support in relief of 15th RIR on the 31st. HQ was at La Manche Copse, A Coy at Vanilla Farm, B at La Manche Farm, C at Roberts Farm, and D at Fontaine Houck. During the month replacements of 6 officers and 48 men arrived. Casualties were one officer wounded, 8 men killed, and 22 wounded.

1st RIR relieved 15th RIR in the line, 8 August. A and B Coys were in the front line, C was the Counterattack Company, D was in reserve, and HQ was at Kopje Farm. The next day, after gas cylinders were projected by L Special Coy, Royal Engineers, on Mural Farm, A Coy patrols entered the farm and found it unoccupied. D and C relieved B and A in the front line on the 11th, B moved into reserve and A became the Counterattack Company. There was heavy mustard gas shelling around St Jans Cappel and Schatken on the 13th. The next day 2/Lt. F.R.H. MacAulay was wounded on patrol and Revd W.H. Hutchison, the Presbyterian chaplain, was gassed.

During 16 August Col. Hunt was wounded at Punkah Farm, on the way to Support Battalion HQ after the relief, and Major Mulholland took over command with Capt. Tayler as Second-in-Command. Dispositions were D Coy at Vanilla Farm, C at Hermitage Farm (Nucleus Garrison of Blue Line), B at Roberts Farm, A at Fontaine, and HQ at La Manche Copse. This area was heavily shelled by gas on the 20th and, the next day, the battalion relieved 2nd RIR in 108th Brigade Sector. A Coy was on the left front, B the right front, C was the garrison of the Blue Line, and D became the Nucleus Garrison. B withdrew to reserve and A took over the whole front line on the 23rd. 9th RIF advanced through 1st RIR the next day and gained all its objectives; 60 prisoners and 5 machine guns were captured and the line was advanced to the Haagedoorne–Dranoutre Road. 9th RIF held the new front and 1st RIR remained in position and became the support.

The battalion was relieved, 25 August, and went with 108th Brigade into Divisional Reserve with HQ located at Boeschepe. They moved to St Marie Cappel, 27 August, and then to the Mont Noir area on the 31st. HQ remained at Boeschepe. The Divisional Commander selected 1st RIR to represent the division in the IX Corps Horse Show, which assembled at Terdeghem that day. They won first prize for the best Infantry Transport turnout consisting of a travelling cooker, a watercart, two limbers, and two pack animals. The Commander, Sgt Clarke, was presented with a silver cup and each driver with a silver medal. Replacements for the month were 6 officers and 192 men; casualties came to 3 officers wounded, 6 men killed, and 75 wounded – the bulk of these being gassed. Falls explained:

> The British were now only 1,000 yards from Bailleul, and had pierced its main defences. An attack upon the salient would now have resulted in a victory like that on the Marne. The enemy, however, did not await it. On the morning of August 31st, when the 107th Brigade had gone back to the Cassel area for a rest, it was suddenly discovered that he had slipped away from in front of our positions ... The 107th Brigade was accordingly moved up to the area of Mont Noir and Mont des Cats, to be in readiness to follow up the pursuit.

The battalion proceeded to the Neuve Eglise area in Divisional Support, HQ being at Rag Farm, 1 September. Having relieved 2nd RIR in the Brigade Support Line on the night of the 5th, D Coy was sent forward under Capt. P.J. Cullen to support 2nd RIR in an attack. Their War Diary recorded:

> By 3.30 p.m. 6 September 1918, half an hour before zero, the troops were in position. Three companies in the firing line: A, B, C, 2nd RIR. Two companies in support: D Coy 1st RIR; D Coy 2nd RIR. These two Coys were concealed behind bushes on or near the jumping off line. At scheduled time the guns opened and troops that were not exactly in their places moved from their concealment to get there ready to advance when the barrage lifted. According to time table the barrage lifted and the troops advanced in small wormlike columns picking their way through the undergrowth and uncut wire moving steadily forward until their objectives were reached when Battle Outposts were pushed forward as near as possible to the standing barrage line, the troops consolidating Hanbury Support Trench. When darkness came on patrols were pushed forward to gain touch with the Boche. He was found to be holding a piece of trench in the trench system U.d.Central. At the same time a considerable amount of machine gun fire was coming from the direction of: The Crater in (a) U.1.a. (b) Mortar Farm in N.36.d. (c) Trench system T.6.b.
>
> A good deal of the latter was taking the men in rear and naturally they began to think the Boche was surrounding them. To counteract this I ordered my left supporting company (D Coy 1st RIR) to form a defensive flank between the support and front line – this was done in a very efficient manner by Capt. P.J. Cullen.

7th September. The battalion holding newly captured line as above. As the enemy showed no sign of counter-attack the company of the 1st Royal Irish Rifles withdrew to their own battalion.

1st RIR relieved 24th RWF, 94th Infantry Bde, on the 8th, in the line between Hyde Park Corner and the Douve and also one platoon of 2nd RIR in the front line between Douve and Gooseberry Farm. Lt.-Col. Hunt rejoined and resumed command, 10 September. The next day 2/Lt. J.C. Haigh was wounded. The battalion was relieved in the Hill 63 Sector during the 12th and then relieved 2nd RIR in the Neuve Eglise Line (Old GHQ Line) Support. After three days they moved to the Piebrouck-Berthen Training Area, with HQ situated in Berthen Chateau. Major Mulholland left for duty at home and was replaced by Major E.R.H. May.

There now followed a series of moves by the battalion: 19 September to Terdeghem, 20th to Bissezeele, 26th to Tunnellers Camp, 27th to 'P' Camp (on the Poperinghe–Woesten Road), 28th by rail to the White Chateau Area (east of Ypres on the Ypres–Menin Road), 29th to Westhoek in Divisional Support and occupying pill-boxes in this area, and to the Becelaere area (North), still in Divisional Support, 30 September. That same day they moved to a position 600 yards east of Terhand, HQ was in a pill-box, companies and HQ personnel took up positions along hedges in support of 2nd RIR. Replacements for the month totalled 3 officers and 189 men, while casualties were one officer wounded, 15 men killed, and 82 wounded.

During this time, from 28 September, II Corps (to which 36th Division was attached) had been engaged in a remarkable series of advances. The Germans were being beaten back so fast that 36th Division, which had been in reserve, was called forward to keep up the momentum. 109th Brigade went ahead, engaged the enemy, and made further advances. 108th Brigade passed through 109th Brigade on the 30th and renewed the attack. By this time, however, there was no artillery support as it had been found impossible to bring up the guns at the same speed as the advance. This gave the German machine gunners a major advantage and it was extremely difficult to neutralise them. At 1.55 p.m., 2nd RIR was ordered to move up on the right of 108th Brigade and attempt to seize Klythoek. They had made two attempts by the following dawn but were stopped by withering machine gun fire. 1st RIR moved up, 1 October, to take over the line south of Dadizeele from 2nd RIR and HQ was situated in Cavander House pill-box.

A minor operation was carried out by the battalion on the 2nd, supported by 15th RIR. It succeeded on the left flank and failed on the right owing to intense machine gun fire. Dibsland and Somerby Farm were attacked by B Coy, with C in support on the left, and Claraborough House was attacked by D Coy, supported by A on the right. The left withdrew to the old position owing to the right not having reached its objective; 2/Lts J.C. Haigh and R. Murphy had been killed, 2/Lt. W.C. Gardiner and Capt. H. Tayler were wounded, 2/Lt. A.W. Walker was wounded and missing, and 2/Lt. A.A.L. Mc-Manus was missing. At 6 a.m., 4 October, one platoon of A Coy under 2/Lt. F. Lamont, made an unsuccessful attack on two pill-boxes that were strongly held by enemy machine guns. The Germans counter-attacked but were repulsed. The battalion had captured, during these four days, four heavy machine guns, one light machine gun, and one anti-tank gun. Falls explained:

As a fact, further advance under present conditions had become all but out of the question. The very speed with which the Anglo–Belgian Armies had advanced, over the worst ground upon the whole of the Western Front, was now proving a handicap. They had outrun their services of supply. Across the Ypres Salient there were three roads only, the Menin, the Zonnebeke, and the Poelcappelle, of the slightest value for heavy transport, and these three were blocked with the mass of wheeled vehicles of all kinds struggling forward.

Having been relieved by 15th RIR they proceeded to positions in the Terhand Area, joining 2nd RIR. Both battalions moved on the 7th to the Reutel Area, near Becelaere, where 2/Lt. A.M. Bourke wounded himself accidentally that day.

The battalion moved to assembly positions at Worthington Farm during the evening of the 13th in support of 15th RIR. Dispositions were D Coy on the left front and A in left support; C on the right front and B in right support, with Battalion HQ established at Mail House. Up to this time in October the casualties had been 2 officers killed, 4 wounded, one wounded and missing, and one missing, the Germans having captured the latter two. Among other ranks there were 24 killed, 115 wounded, and 34 missing. Replacements of 2 officers and 31 men arrived. According to Falls:

> The first objective of the II Corps was the important Tourcoing–Courtrai–Inglemunster railway line, upon which the 36th Division was to be directed from the Lys on the right at Courtrai to the northern outskirts of the town of Heule. There were two other towns, Moorseele and Gulleghem, on the front of the attack, lying in almost a straight line from west to east, at equal distances. Moorseele was about two and a half miles from the line now held, Gulleghem a mile and three-quarters further on, Heule a mile and a half beyond that ... The 107th Brigade's attack was to be carried out by the 15th Irish Rifles. After Moorseele had been captured, a line east of it was to be consolidated, and the 1st Irish Rifles was to pass through the leading battalion and advance with the road from Gulleghem to Wevelghem and the southern houses of the former town as objective.

The attack commenced at 5.35 a.m., 14 October. Very few casualties had been caused by the German counter-bombardment as the troop assembly took place in positions that were seldom shelled. It was a fine morning with a heavy ground mist. Prisoners taken by 1st RIR were identified as being from 1st Bavarian Reserve Division and they stated that the attack was not expected. Moorseele was entered at 9.45 a.m., consolidation began and 1st RIR started to take over the lead. At 10.35 a.m. the battalion passed through 15th RIR east of Moorseele and attacked Gulleghem without artillery support. All went well at first and a mile of ground was gained but they were held up by three belts of barbed wire and heavy machine gun fire about 500 yards west of the village. At 5 p.m. they attacked again, attempting an outflanking movement, but only progressed about 200 yards. In this attack Capt. J.C. Leeper, Lt. A. Howard-Nicholson, and 2/Lt. H.M. Jeffares were wounded; casualties among other ranks were 23 killed, 92 wounded, and 8 missing. They did, however, bring down a German reconnaissance aeroplane with rifle fire and captured the crew (an officer and Gefreiter of 16th Flieger Abteilung). Twenty-four other ranks joined as reinforcements. The GOC of II Corps sent the following message to Brigade:

> The Army Commander wishes me to convey to you, and all commanders and troops engaged today, his congratulations on the successful results achieved on what has been a long and arduous day.

1st RIR spent the night 300 yards west of Gulleghem in touch with units on both flanks. The battalion attacked Gulleghem again the following day at 9 a.m., in conjunction with an artillery barrage, and reached their objective, which was 1,000 yards east of the village, by 10 a.m. Prisoners taken were from 181st Infantry Regiment, 40th (Saxon) Division, and a few of the 9th Ulahnen Regiment, 6th Cavalry Division. Progress had been slower than expected because they lost the barrage, having been delayed by heavy wire west of and in the town. 2nd RIR passed through them and reached the line of the Corp's objective at Heule. A gap occurred between 2nd RIR on the right and 9th Division on the left and was filled by 1st RIR, thus bringing it into the front line again at 8.15 p.m. During these attacks they had captured a howitzer but Lt. E.J. Williams was killed, Capt. W.F. Hogg, 2/Lts J.A. Maxwell, and J.G. Branford were wounded. In addition, 3 men were killed, 24 wounded, and one was missing. 2/Lt. W.C. Whelan took over the duties of Acting Adjutant.

The next day the battalion was relieved by 9th Division on the right and 2nd RIR on the left, and moved into billets at Rolleghem Cappel where the Transport rejoined them. During 18 October they marched to comfortable new billets at Lendelede. At 5.30 p.m. on the 19th, they moved to assembly positions 1,000 yards east of Hulste and billeted for the night. The 107th Brigade was in support of 109th Brigade. At 2 a.m. the following day they commenced crossing the River Lys and formed up on the Beveren–Desselghem Road. They advanced until 5 p.m. in support of 15th RIR who had reached a line 500 yards south-east of the Deerlyck–Waereghem Road. According to Falls:

> The 15th Irish Rifles had considerable casualties from machine gun fire, and lost their Commanding Officer at an early stage. But the advance was very rapid. By 9 a.m. we were across the road from Deerlyck to Waereghem, or two miles beyond the Lys. A mill, in which were several machine guns, gave great trouble at this point, and a platoon of the 1st Irish Rifles was brought up to capture it, and succeeded in its task. By this time, however, our field guns across the Lys were firing at extreme range. It was decided to call a halt, to allow the French to cross that evening, while the 108th Brigade came into line on the left of the 107th.

1st RIR went through 15th RIR and reached the Gaverbek Stream during the night. The battalion captured a 6-inch naval gun and a Daimler tractor. 2/Lt. W.J. Linton and Revd Hutchison were wounded. The battalion continued the advance the next day, attacking in a south-easterly direction and reached the line north-west of Knock to the

Gaverbek Stream, dug in and held the position occupied. This had been achieved with great difficulty and no artillery support, the area being well suited to long-range machine gun fire. Lt. E. Daniel was killed, 2/Lt. J.T. Gardiner and Capt. L.M. Bayly were wounded. The battalion continued holding the line on 22 October. Capt. Bayly died from wounds in a CCS and Capt. J.R. Cameron, RAMC, was wounded.[2]

2 Major E.R.H. May was awarded the DSO: 'For consipcious gallantry and good leadership during the attack on Moorseele and Gulleghem on 14–15 October 1918. After zero on the 14th he walked through a heavy barrage to visit his battalion. He organised his companies, and, despite a thick fog, ensured that correct direction was kept. For two days he worked unceasingly during the heavy fighting, and by his clear orders and personal example greatly assisted his battalion to reach its objective.'

16

War ends

Congratulations were received from Marshal Foch, Commanding Allied Forces, and the Divisional Commander, Major-General Coffin, on the splendid work done by the 36th Division in the recent operations.

The battalion continued advancing throughout the 23rd. Falls recorded:

> There were signs that the enemy's resistance was weakening, and it seemed possible that he might be about to retire to the Scheldt. Two companies of the battalion, with a squadron of the 28th French Dragoons, were ordered to form an advance guard and move towards the river.

Passing through 2nd RIR on the Klijtberg Ridge, they took Vossenhoek and advanced as far as the Hulsbosch Ridge but were unable to reach Kleineberg as it was heavily defended by machine guns. They therefore dug in and held the line until relieved by 109th Infantry Brigade, moving into billets at Desselghem that night, where the Battalion Transport rejoined. 2/Lt. F. Lamont and six men had been wounded.

Congratulations and thanks were received from the II Corps Commander, Lieutenant-General Jacob, on the splendid work done by the 36th Division:

> The 36th (Ulster) Division has been fighting continuously since the 28th September in the operation in Flanders. The spirit, dash and initiative shown by all ranks have been splendid and beyond all praise. The leadership displayed by yourself and your brigade and other commanders could not have been better. The conditions under which the men have had to fight have been and are still very trying, but nothing seems to stop your gallant division.
>
> I have also been much struck with the good Staff work of the division and it is very creditable to all concerned. Will you kindly express to the commanders, Staffs and all ranks of the division my heartfelt congratulations and thanks for their work.
>
> When the history is written of what the division has done in Flanders during the past month, it will prove to be a record of magnificent fighting and wonderful progress, for, during this period an advance has been made of about 25 miles over the worst of country and under the heaviest machine gun fire ever experi-

enced in this war. This advance has entailed constant fighting but the 36th Division has overcome every obstacle and has proved itself one of the best fighting divisions in the Army, well commanded and well staffed.

Capt. Leeper rejoined on 24 October and resumed the duties of Adjutant. Although they did not know it, the war was over as far as 1st RIR was concerned. On the 26th they marched to Lendelede accompanied by the Battalion Transport and continued the next day to the Belleghem area, south of Courtrai. During the period 14–31 October replacements of 4 officers and 73 men arrived. Casualties during this time were 3 officers killed and 10 wounded. Among other ranks, 30 men were killed, 163 wounded, and 12 were missing. On the evening of 1 November the battalion moved to the Reckem Area and made a final move to Mouscron on the 3rd. This town is on the Belgian side of the border near Tournai. The battalion held a sports meeting on the 5th and, two days later, took part in the 107th Brigade Sports Meeting which was a great success.

At 11 p.m., 10 November, the official news of the signing of the Armistice by Germany was received. 'The Buglers of the battalion sounded the Cease Fire' was the only comment entered in the War Diary. On 17 November there was a great thanksgiving service in the central square of Roubaix. During the month the strength had been reinforced by the arrival of 17 officers and 94 men. The battalion remained in the Mouscron area throughout the rest of their time with the BEF. The troops were kept occupied by military, educational, and recreational training. In addition there were regular inspections and lectures, especially by the Medical Officer on the 'Dangers of Venereal Disease'.

Christmas Day was celebrated by the battalion holding a Christmas dinner that was thoroughly enjoyed by all ranks. The Brigade Commander visited the dinner of the NCOs and Riflemen and wished them all a Happy Christmas. At 5.30 p.m. the officers held their dinner in the Convent at Mouscron. Christmas greetings were received from Gen. Sir H.H. Wilson, GOC 5th Army, GOC 36th Division, GOC 107th Infantry Brigade, and OC 3rd RIR.

Since I last sent you a Christmas Greeting the British Army has emerged triumphantly from the supreme crisis of the war. It has never been put to a more searching test and it has never responded more magnificently. The greatest war in the history of the world has ended in the most complete victory for the British and Allied arms. The British Army has maintained its glorious reputation.

As your Colonel I have always watched with interest the doings of all the battalions of the Royal Irish Rifles and I am proud of the distinguished part they have played. They have maintained the fighting tradition of Irish Soldiers.

Some of you will shortly be returning to civil life. To these I wish God speed and hope that the lesson of comradeship that you have learned in a great regiment in time of war will serve you in good stead all through life. To those of you who remain in the Army I send warm greetings and hope that you will maintain in peace time the high standard you have attained in war.

Officers, Warrant Officers, Non-commissioned Officers and Men, I wish you all happiness in the coming year on the conclusion of your great task and the return of peace.

> Henry Wilson, General.
> Colonel of The Royal Irish Rifles.

During December reinforcements of one officer and 70 men arrived. The Prince of Wales visited the battalion on New Year's Eve and was introduced to all officers present. The time had now come for the troops to return home. In January one officer and 10 men joined, while 4 officers and 84 men proceeded to the Concentration Camp prior to demobilization. According to Falls:

> Orders were received in February that one service battalion of the Royal Irish Rifles was to be sent to the Rhine, to form part of the newly created Light Division. The 12th Battalion was selected. All men who did not desire to volunteer for the service or who were shortly due for demobilization were demobilized or transferred as quickly as possible, and the strength made up from volunteers and men not due to go for some time of the three other battalions of the Regiment in the 36th Division.

From early February a bus service was provided for the benefit of officers and men who wished to visit Lille. Another attraction was the shows given by Miss Lena Ashwell's Concert party. Capt. J.C. Leeper went to the UK, 10 February, and 2/Lt. W.C. Whelan took over the duties of Acting Adjutant, while Revd Hutchison and Lt. W.C. Gardiner were appointed Educational Officers to the battalion. The Regimental Band arrived, including Mr. W. Allan, the Bandmaster, and 29 boys on the 15th. Lt. Gardiner took over the duties of Acting Adjutant, 17 February. Major May was transferred to 12th RIR on the 19th and took over as Second-in-Command of that unit. Later in the week a further 6 officers joined him. On the 24th, 155 men were transferred to 12th RIR, which was to form part of the Army of Occupation. The Regimental Band played this group off and Col. Hunt addressed the men before leaving. In addition to these changes, there were the following movements during the month: 8 officers joined 2nd RIR, another 3 officers and 55 men transferred to 12th RIR, 2 men joined 7th R. Irish Regiment, 4 men moved to 15th RIR, while one officer and 301 men were demobilized. A draft of 2 officers and 22 men arrived. Orders had been received on 25 February for 1st RIR to be reduced to cadre strength.

During March, 2/Lt. J.G. Stokes went to Calais to take up train Conducting Duties; Capt. P.J. Cullen was appointed CO of No. 855 Area Employment Coy, Calais, and Lt. C.K. McCauley was transferred sick to the UK. One officer and 13 men transferred to 12th RIR; 15 men went to the Depot in the UK, 6 were moved to various units, and 5 actually joined the battalion. Two officers and 66 men were demobilized. On St Patrick's Day the cadre of 2nd RIR left Mouscron for the UK and was sent off by the bands of 1st RIR and 2nd R. Inniskilling Fusiliers. Major G.J. Apperson took over command, 14 April, when Col. Hunt went to the UK on leave. Four men transferred to 12th RIR; one officer and one man returned to the Depot; 3 men were evacuated, sick, to the UK, one transferred to the Royal Engineers, while one officer and one man were demobilized. Another man joined the battalion. Col. Hunt resumed command on 2 May. Capt. Gardiner transferred to 5th Area HQ on the 19th and Lt. S.M. Jamison took over the duties of Acting Adjutant. Col. Hunt assumed command of No. 43 Labour Group, 23 May, and Major Apperson took over command of 1st RIR. Three men joined the unit while one transferred to 12th RIR; one officer and 12 men moved to 15th RIR; 3 men were demobilized and one returned, sick, to the UK. By 23 May the cadre strength was 3 officers and 34 men together with the band of 31 men. They left Mouscron at midday by train for Dunkirk but were held up at Steenwerck by the explosion of a large ammunition dump. Having finally arrived at midnight, they were billeted in huts at 'A' Camp. During the 24th they passed through the Delousing Camp and moved to No. 3 Embarkation Camp where they remained until 28 May. On that day the Transport was loaded on the SS *Mogileff* and all members of the cadre sailed from Dunkirk on the 29th. Since the spring of 1918, in view of the disturbed state of the country, the War Office had moved all Irish troops out of Ireland. The Cadre, therefore, went to Rugeley Camp, Staffordshire. According to Graves:

> This was dispersed on leave pending re-forming in August when, officially termed the 3rd Battalion, it absorbed so many officers and men under Lt.-Col. H.R. Charley CBE, that it temporarily reached the bloated strength of one hundred and eighty-seven officers and two thousand three hundred ORs. The vast bulk of these were rapidly demobilized. After the 1st Battalion had been re-formed, a cadre was furnished from both the 1st and 3rd Battalions to form the Depot which moved to Victoria Barracks, Belfast. The re-formed 1st Battalion then moved to Parkhurst, Isle of Wight, where it remained until 1923.

The following article appeared in *Irish Life* magazine on 12 September 1919:

> All Dubliners have a soft spot in their hearts for the Royal Irish Rifles, who have so brilliantly upheld its past fighting traditions in the Great War. The 1st Battalion, which was raised at the Custom House in 1793 by Colonel Fitch as the 83rd (County of Dublin) Regiment, and whose cadre returned from Belgium last June, has recently been reformed at Rugeley Camp. This reconstruction, may we explain to the uninitiated, is known as 'Changing Over', and the interesting procedure is as follows: the 3rd (Reserve Battalion), to which the cadre of the 1st Battalion had been attached, paraded in 'close column of companies'; while the Permanent Staff 3rd Battalion and those of the 1st Battalion paraded on the right flank, facing inwards so as to form two sides of a square. Lt.-Col. H.R. Goodman DSO, commanding 3rd Battalion, then addressed the troops, after which the 3rd Battalion regimental flag was slowly hauled down, the battalion presenting arms, and the band playing *Auld Lang Syne*. The two commanding officers then shook hands, and Lt.-Col. H.R. Charley assumed command of the battalion, which then became the 1st Battalion. Their flag was then

hoisted, the band playing the salute and the buglers sounding the 1st Battalion regimental call. After Lt.-Col. Charley had addressed the men and the 1st Battalion had been loudly cheered, the Permanent Staff of the 3rd Battalion marched off, the band playing their 'March Past' and the 1st Battalion presenting arms. This concluded the ceremony, which is historical in the annals of the 1st Battalion, Royal Irish Rifles – and some ceremony too, is it not?

The title of the Regiment was changed to The Royal Ulster Rifles on 1 January 1921. At the time it was not a welcome decision, as Graves explained:

> When the news leaked out, every possible action was taken by the Regiment to prevent the change, but when Field-Marshal Sir Henry Wilson, then Chief of the Imperial General Staff and himself Colonel of the Regiment, announced privately that even he was unable to intervene successfully ... there was nothing to be done about it ... In England the 1st Battalion accepted the situation with the best grace that it could muster. But this did not prevent a curious ceremony taking place on New Year's Day, 1921 ... Interested spectators saw a funeral procession in which the whole battalion took part, headed by the regimental band playing Chopin's March. Behind the band came two strangely attired parsons, wearing dark glasses, top hats, and flowing white surplices.[1] Each had his hands clasped over a book with his head bowed. Immediately behind them came a coffin borne by NCOs. It was draped with the Union Jack. Behind them, in turn, came a firing party with arms reversed. Gradually the procession made its way to a spot in the recreation field behind the Orderly Room where it halted beside a small newly dug grave. By this time it was clear that the battalion was burying its old regimental name. The 'ashes' were enclosed in an orange box. One of the two 'parsons' pronounced the committal sentence: 'For as much as it has pleased the almighty War House of its great wisdom to take upon itself the name of our dear regiment here departed, we therefore commit its ashes to the grave without the slightest hope of resurrection.' The orange box was then placed in the grave ... Three volleys were fired and the Last Post sounded. A few shovelfulls of earth were put on the coffin and a tin hat hung over the top ... The wooden cross itself bore the inscription 'Sacred to the memory of the Royal Irish Rifles. Departed this life on 1st January, 1921, after a brief but glorious existence, aged forty years – RIR, RIP, RUR.'

A small gravestone was afterwards erected on the spot with the inscription: 'To the memory of the 1st Royal Irish Rifles who departed this life on Jan 1st 1921 after a brief and glorious existence. Age 40 years. RUR.' This remained in position for many years until it came within the complex of HM Prison, Albany, and was removed for safekeeping to the Regimental Museum in Belfast.

1 Lt.-Col. M.J.P.M. Corbally: 'In rear of the Band, with heads bowed, paced two strangely attired "parsons" ... The senior of these, and the celebrant at this curious ceremony, was the Adjutant, Lieutenant Whitfeld. A coffin was there too, containing a copy of the Regimental History.'

Appendices

APPENDIX I: OFFICER CASUALTIES

This list contains only those officers who were killed while serving with the battalion. They were all members of the regiment unless otherwise stated. There were several others who were killed after they had transferred to another unit. The battalion's war ended on 23 October 1918 and, up to that time, 276 officers had served on various occasions. Of these 73 were killed – a rate of 27 per cent.

2/Lt. William Kearns Adrain, Royal Irish Regt	24.8.1916
Capt. Bertram Allgood	6.12.1914
2/Lt. Robert Hutchison Andrews	25.9.1915
Lt.-Col. Osbert Clinton Baker	9.5.1915
Lt. Noel Scott Barrington	10.3.1915
Capt. Lancelot Myles Bayly MC	22.10.1918
Capt. Arthur John Biscoe	12.3.1915
2/Lt. Albert William Bourke, Royal Irish Fusiliers	9.5.1915
2/Lt. Hugh Brown	31.7.1917
Capt. John Brown MC	21.3.1918
Capt. Dominick Augustus Browne	1.7.1916
Lt. William Armstrong Burges	10.3.1915
2/Lt. Vincent Connel Byrne	31.7.1917
Capt. John Francis Clery, Royal Dublin Fusiliers	16.8.1917
Capt. Arthur Grove Colles, Royal Dublin Fusiliers	12.3.1915
Lt. Ernest Daniel	21.10.1918
Lt. William Oliver Fortesque Darling	16.10.1915
2/Lt. Lawrence Aubrey Fiennes Wingfield Dickenson, Bedfordshire Regt	9.5.1915
2/Lt. Charles George Dixon, Royal Irish Regt	9.5.1915
2/Lt. Patrick Doherty	1.8.1917
2/Lt. Reginald Joseph Ennis	16.8.1917
2/Lt. Thomas Enright	20.4.1918
Major Arthur Hoskyns Festing CMG, DSO, FRGS	9.5.1915
Capt. John William Field	20.9.1915
Lt. Robert Alexander Finlay, Royal Dublin Fusiliers	9.5.1915
2/Lt. James Furniss	31.7.1917
2/Lt. James Tatton Gardiner	1.11.1918
2/Lt. John Victor Gault	23.10.1916
2/Lt. Andrew Gilmore	11.3.1915
2/Lt. Harold Mynett Glastonbury	1.7.1916
2/Lt. Harry Caldwell Greene, Royal Munster Fusiliers	29.4.1918
2/Lt. William Henry Gregg	1.7.1916
2/Lt. John Caleb Haigh, Royal Dublin Fusiliers	2.10.1918
2/Lt. Douglas Hamilton	9.5.1915
2/Lt. Percival Maxwell Harte-Maxwell, Connaught Rangers	11.4.1916
2/Lt. Alfred Hellmers	11.5.1915

Lt. Bertie John Hodson, Royal Irish Regt   21.3.1918
Lt. Norman Heber Hutcheson   12.3.1915
2/Lt. James Kennedy   21.3.1918
Lt. James Kerr   21.3.1918
2/Lt. William Kingston MC, Royal Munster Fusiliers   16.8.1917
2/Lt. Gilbert James Laing, Indian Army   12.3.1915
Lt. George Mansfield La Nauze   9.5.1915
Capt. William Mortimer Lanyon   5.4.1915
Lt.-Col. George Brenton Laurie   12.3.1915
2/Lt. Edward Wood Lennard   30.11.1917
2/Lt. Frederick Homer Lewis   29.4.1918
2/Lt. Alfred McClelland   13.10.1917
Lt. Arthur M. McLaughlin   9.5.1915
2/Lt. Oliver Babington Macausland, Indian Army   9.5.1915
Lt.-Col. Charles Carroll Macnamara   1.7.1916
2/Lt. Edward Archibald Mahoney   16.8.1917
Lt. John Sinclair Martin   9.5.1915
Capt. Robert Patrick Miles, Shropshire Light Infantry   30.12.1914
2/Lt. James Lytton Millar   29.7.1916
Lt. Joseph Ewing Bruce Miller   24.5.1915
2/Lt. Robert McConnell Moore MM   27.3.1918
2/Lt. Robert Murphy   2.10.1918
Lt. Robert Larmour Neill   9.5.1915
Lt. Paul O'Kane   21.3.1918
Capt. Arthur Moore O'Sullivan   9.5.1915
2/Lt. Robert Kelly Pollin   31.7.1917
Lt.-Col. Alexander Daniel Reid DSO, Royal Inniskilling Fusiliers   31.7.1917
Capt. Arthur John Ross   16.8.1917
2/Lt. George Stanley Sinclair   28.5.1917
Lt. Samuel Donard Irvine Smith   1.7.1916
Capt. Alfred Francis James Steele-Nicholson   16.8.1917
2/Lt. John Crawford Thompson   21.3.1918
Lt. Ernest Joseph Williams   15.10.1918
2/Lt. Alexander Buchan Wilkie   30.11.1917
2/Lt. John Edward Goodwin Wilson, Royal Welsh Fusiliers   16.8.1917
2/Lt. Charles Eric Windus   9.5.1915
Capt. Allan O'Halloran Wright   13.3.1915

APPENDIX II: CASUALTIES IN THE RANKS

This list hereunder is as complete as I could reasonably make it. It has been compiled from the database of the Commonwealth War Graves Commission and *Soldiers Died in the Great War*. These records are incomplete and not entirely accurate, especially in terms of the battalion with which men served, the date of death, and whether they were killed in action or died of wounds received on an earlier day. I know that all are not included, as I could not always match the listings to the numbers of casualties given in the War Diary and other sources. Men were often moved between battalions, especially when they returned from sick leave. Thus, you can find a man killed with 1st RIR yet listed in all the records as being from 2nd RIR, etc. In some instances I could find a name to fit a particular date but the battalion was, say, 2nd RIR and the burial was in the wrong battle zone. Later in the war, 1917 onwards, men were transferred in from other regiments or corps, for example the London Regiment and Army Service Corps, but they are recorded as only having served with their original regiment, etc. In some instances they are shown as attached to the Royal Irish Rifles but the number of the battalion is not stated.

A rough analysis of those who are recorded as having previously served in another unit shows that the largest group came from the London Regiment and may generally be identified by five-digit numbers beginning with 43, 44 or 45. RASC men usually had their five-digit number beginning with 472, 473 or 474; 110th T.R. (Training Reserve) Battalion with 423 or 424; North Irish Horse with 408 or 409. The four-digit numbers of the other men are problematic. It was not unusual for these numbers to have been recycled; others would originally have had a prefix such as 3/ (for 3rd RIR) to denote the battalion with which they originally served. It is not, therefore, safe to make assumptions based on the numerical sequences.

I have identified 1,202 deaths of other ranks up to the end of the war on 11 November 1918. Total deaths including officers are 1,275 and, of these, roughly 800 (63 per cent) were Irishmen. The format I have used is the date on which men died – the alphabetical and cemetery orders are already available elsewhere.

September 1914
21st   6508 Sgt H. Wingrove (buried at Aden.)

October 1914
11th   8502 Rfn David Reid (buried at Malta.)

November 1914
15th   6795 Rfn Hamilton Orr, 9838 Rfn Robert Charles Sparrow.
16th   5039 Rfn Samuel Baird, 10440 Rfn John Byrne, 9465 Rfn Joseph Dodd, 7489 Rfn Richard John Dunbar, 8427 Rfn John Joseph McGibney, 7401 Sgt Francis William Wright.
17th   9147 Rfn William John Molloy (*Laurie*: 'A man died after 12 hours of great pain with both legs gone.')

18th   8982 Rfn John Carolan (*Laurie*: 'I have just had a man shot out of a tree where he was posted as a sentry, protected by sandbags.')

19th   9623 Rfn Robert Dempster (*War Diary*: 'while on a reconnaissance patrol.'), 8777 Rfn James Lucas.

26th   9565 Rfn John Aspey (*Laurie*: 'This pointed German bullet does strange tricks. For instance, one of them yesterday must have struck something, turned at right angles, and gone on, killing an old soldier of mine by striking him on the left temple.')

27th   9110 Rfn Patrick Cummins.

28th   8362 Rfn Richard Cooper (died of a disease.)

December 1914

7th   8145 Rfn Joseph Killops (died of wounds.)

9th   9769 Rfn James McCann.

10th   8896 L/Cpl R. Scott.

14th   12487 Rfn William Robert Bell.

16th   9798 L/Cpl Patrick Broghan.

18th   8936 Rfn John Archer (*Laurie*: 'This morning one of my men was shot through the lungs, not far from our room, and he died at once.')

21st   9202 Rfn David Millar.

25th   8363 Rfn Arthur Bell (*War Diary*: ' … went out to join his standing patrol in front of B Coys trenches and, apparently, stumbled against a German picquet. On Xmas day, when conversing with the Germans, Rfn Bell was reported as wounded and captured by them and not far behind their lines.')

30th   9673 Rfn Charles Byrne, 9001 Rfn George Smyth.

January 1915

1st   6882 Rfn Henry Flynn, 9240 L/Cpl John Warnock McLean.

4th   9588 Rfn William Chapman.

5th   9602 Rfn Hugh Flynn, 9411 Rfn David Loughins, 6317 Sgt John McIlwrath.

6th   6421 Rfn William Crumlish.

13th   5221 Rfn James Boy (died of wounds), 9791 L/Cpl John Hunter Gordon Sangster.

14th   9873 Rfn James McClurg.

16th   9248 Rfn William Burns.

17th   8939 Rfn Arthur Corbett.

29th   9341 Rfn Henry Barham (died of wounds), 9236 Rfn Peter Sharpe (*Laurie*: 'I had one man killed and another wounded by the same bullet.')

30th   14908 Rfn John Horace Keelan.

February 1915

6th   6587 L/Cpl Robert McMullan (*Laurie*: 'The poor man was shot dead just before leaving the trenches.')

10th   14460 Rfn Percival George Bullock (age 18. *Laurie*: 'I am just waiting to go to one of our own men's funeral. He was shot yesterday, poor boy, and I was able to get his body out.')

12th   9276 Rfn James Hodgins. (See main text.)

17th   *Laurie*: 'One of my very good boxers, poor chap, was hit in the jaw and died at once. I suppose it dislocated his spine.' No relevant name is recorded for this day.

21st   9324 Rfn Alfred Hudd.

23rd   9299 Rfn Louis Peck. (*Laurie*: 'I had two killed yesterday, through either their own or their comrades' faults. One man was watching our guns shelling the enemy's trenches. He was told to lie down or he would be shot. He did so, and the moment he saw a favourable opportunity he popped up again, and was promptly shot dead. The other was in front of the trenches mending wires, and his comrades, seeing that their NCO was out, joyfully seized the occasion to stoke their fire and have a big blaze. The result was the unfortunate man showed up against it and was shot through the head; and their fire was kicked bodily into the water by an irate NCO.' I cannot locate another casualty this day and assume one of those recorded as died on the 24th is relevant.)

24th   9017 Rfn John Austin, 8233 Rfn Michael Maguire, 8940 Rfn Hugh O'Grady.

28th   13922 Rfn John Munster. (See main text.)

March 1915

3rd   8889 L/Sgt Joseph Gaffney, 6594 L/Cpl Samuel Roy. (*Laurie*: 'I lost two NCOs killed by one bullet through their heads.' *War Diary*: ' … night digging parties for B Lines.')

5th   9417 L/Sgt John Farrell, 9871 L/Cpl Patrick Joseph Keenan. (*War Diary*: ' … night digging parties for B Lines.')

10th   9398 L/Cpl Thomas Anderson, 7955 Rfn Hugh Andrews, 9141 Rfn William Boston, 9140 Rfn Alexander Brickley, 6100 Rfn John Campbell, 9294 Rfn James Carnduff, 18349 Rfn James Clare, 7124 L/Cpl Patrick Clarke, 9061 L/Cpl Henry Crossey, 9380 Rfn Thomas Crymble, 8954 Rfn Michael Curtis, 12378 Rfn Thomas Daly, 8599 Rfn Robert Davenport, 6284 Rfn Francis Doran, 8100 Sgt Thomas Doyle, 13566 Rfn Alexander Elliott, 9400 Rfn Hugh Fitzsimons, 8221 Rfn Philip Fitzsimons, 8849 Rfn George Gallagher, 9206 L/Cpl Arthur Aitken Gardiner, 7916 Cpl John Gordon, 9122 L/Cpl William Gray, 14477 Rfn Allen Hamilton, 6941 L/Cpl Samuel Harper, 9185 Rfn John Harris, 9169 Rfn Andrew Hemphill, 16305 Rfn Samuel Henry, 8779 L/Cpl Thomas Henry, 2616 Cpl Hugh Holmes, 8435 Cpl Arthur Hughes, 2866 Rfn James Hughey, 8982 Rfn William Hunter DCM, 9476 Rfn John Johnston, 9318 Rfn John Kearney, 9014 L/Cpl Joseph Martin, 5556 Rfn Thomas Meighton, 6730 CSM William George Motum (C Coy), 8709 Rfn Alexander Murray, 9246 Rfn Robert McBride, 9389 Cpl Joseph McClean, 6930 Rfn Isaac McCoo, 9248 Rfn James McCoy, 9509 Rfn William McGrath, 6749 Sgt Christopher Riordan, 10309 Rfn Michael Joseph Roche, 13324 Rfn Thomas Scott, 10391 L/Cpl Hugh Ernest Stanley, 9993 Rfn William Harvey John Sugg, 8923 Rfn John Tyrrell, 9102 Rfn James Worsfold.

11th   9775 Rfn Charles Edward Baker, 2445 Rfn William Barker, 9543 Rfn Harold George Brown, 9183 Rfn Edward Collins, 9663 Rfn William Collins, 8924 Rfn Frederick Cullen, 1581 Rfn James Dignan, 7079 Rfn Alexander Gibson, 5057 Rfn

Thomas Graham, 8480 Rfn Herbert Hegan (died of wounds), 8179 L/Cpl Frederick Hunter, 8536 Rfn Edward Jones, 6143 Rfn Henry Kennedy, 6813 Rfn Alfred Laverty, 8375 Rfn John Lynch (his brother William, 4455 8th RMF, was KIA 26.5.1916), 10310 Rfn Robert Law McCartney, 7544 Bugler William J. Mawhinney, 8637 Rfn Henry John Moore, 6979 Rfn William Mulholland, 8237 Rfn William McAuley, 9599 Rfn William John McFall, 9387 Rfn Alexander Pritchard, 9323 L/Cpl Robert Ross, 7190 Rfn John Wesley Small (served in the South African War), 6551 Rfn John Smith, 9556 Rfn Patrick Smith, 5295 L/Cpl Robert Thompson, 6992 L/Cpl Harry Vine.

12th 8303 Sgt Charles Armstrong, 9092 Rfn John Blair, 9819 Rfn Eugene Brennan, 8955 Rfn Patrick Cross, 7229 Rfn William Davies, 16812 Rfn Thomas Davison, 4510 Rfn Christopher Fisher, 7191 Rfn James Fisher, 9812 Rfn William Johnson (died of wounds), 4215 CSM Ernest Kendrick LSM, GCM (died in the UK), 9848 Rfn Henry Joseph MacLoraum, 6988 Rfn James Magee, 9770 Rfn Thomas Mahurters, 8817 L/Cpl Martin Meleady, 9929 L/Cpl James Naylor, 6595 Sgt Thomas O'Leary, 17214 Rfn Joseph Percy Penfold, 9761 Rfn Michael Reilly, 9033 Rfn John Shields, 8827 Rfn William Sturgeon, 6521 Rfn Joseph White, 6949 Rfn William Wade, 14448 Rfn John Watkins.

13th 8759 Rfn Robert J. Arthur, 9472 Rfn Charles Brown, 6563 Rfn George Cooke, 7152 Rfn Thomas Hazel, 9813 Rfn James Kelly, 8181 Rfn John McMinn, 6664 Rfn Stephen William Morris, 9959 Rfn Alexander Wilson.

14th 9744 Rfn Charles Hill, 8470 Rfn Francis Augustine Sherry.

15th 9450 Rfn Patrick Farley (died of wounds), 9179 Rfn Hugh Murphy, 9682 L/Cpl Harry Nelson.

17th 8438 L/Sgt Peter Darby, 9452 Rfn John Hawthorne, 6451 Rfn Frederick John McCluskey, 7975 Rfn John McConnell, 4229 Rfn Samuel Smyth.

18th 7168 Cpl J. Kilpatrick, 8240 Rfn Bernard Mullan (died in the UK).

19th 18363 Rfn Robert Haran.

21st 8918 Rfn Robert Diamond, 8013 Rfn Samuel Gorman (died of wounds in the UK), 6855 Rfn James Moorhead (died of wounds in the UK).

23rd 8566 Rfn James Caldwell, 9353 Rfn John Lavery (died of wounds. Served in the South African War.)

25th 8965 Rfn William Curry.

26th 7507 Rfn William McClelland (died of wounds in the UK).

April 1915

3rd 8738 Rfn James Seawright.

4th 8863 Rfn James Magee, 8727 Cpl William Snowden (died in the UK of wounds received at Neuve Chapelle).

6th 10414 L/Cpl Walter Francis Keating, 8405 Rfn John McCann.

15th 8951 Rfn Joseph O'Neill.

17th 9683 Rfn Thomas Lee.

21st 5414 Rfn John Campbell (died of wounds received on 10.3.1915. Served in the South African War.)

24th   5529 Rfn William Patton.
25th   5537 Rfn John Cochrane.
28th   9789 Rfn James Sexton.
30th   16793 Rfn James Cooke, 6940 Rfn James Wherry.

May 1915

5th   8298 Rfn Frank Orr, 10017 Rfn William Henry Peers, 3358 Rfn John Steele
       (recorded as died on 4 May but the battalion had no casualties that day and had
       three killed on the 5th).
6th   6399 Rfn John McCormick.
9th   9249 Rfn John Adams, 3364 Rfn William Henry Adams, 4791 Sgt John Arlow,
       2602 Rfn George Attley, 1362 Rfn Frank Ball, 1336 Rfn John Barker, 16133 Sgt
       James Barron, 1544 Rfn Clifford Barrow, 8855 Rfn William Bell, 4870 Rfn
       Roberts Bingham, 9629 Rfn Ernest William Blakemore, 7277 Rfn Thomas
       Boland, 6695 Rfn James Brady, 9025 L/Cpl George Henry Brookfield, 4917 Rfn
       Henry Brown, 9457 Rfn William Henry Brown, 7137 Sgt Arthur Burgess, 9342
       Rfn William Byers, 9649 Rfn John Byrne, 9858 Rfn Michael Byrne, 9249 Cpl
       Herbert Cairns DCM, 6796 Rfn Alexander Campbell, 9408 L/Cpl Joseph
       Campbell, 1385 Rfn George Carlin, 12380 Rfn Patrick Carr, 8061 Rfn Chris-
       topher Casey, 9816 L/Cpl Alexander Cassells, 8830 Rfn William Cherry, 8962
       Rfn Charles Clarke, 9176 L/Cpl William Coates, 2595 Rfn Patrick Collins, 8114
       Rfn Denis Coogan, 1585 Rfn William Cooper, 9778 Rfn Walter Cornish, 1266
       Rfn George Corrigan, 9679 Rfn Thomas Crothers, 6080 Rfn John Crozier, 8553
       Rfn Michael Cunniffe, 9810 Rfn Patrick Cunningham, 9937 Rfn Gerald Dalton,
       9743 Rfn Patrick Daly, 2282 Rfn John Deery, 2460 Rfn Samuel Dewhurst, 1322
       Rfn Timothy Donovan, 9433 L/Cpl Francis Dornan, 15291 Rfn Alfred Dowsell,
       6397 Rfn Patrick Doyle, 1314 Rfn John Robert Draper, 1271 Rfn Thomas
       Drinkwater, 1685 Rfn Charles Frederick Elcombe, 6709 Rfn William Ennis, 7928
       Cpl John Eustace, 10259 Rfn Thomas Farrell, 9768 L/Cpl Joseph Fitzpatrick,
       1838 Rfn Martin Fitzpatrick, 1332 Rfn Robert Fleck, 6903 Rfn John Foster, 6943
       Rfn Michael Gavin, 2448 Rfn Henry James Gerrard, 14904 Rfn James Gibbs,
       2293 Rfn John Graham, 1792 Rfn William Griffiths, 7312 Rfn Thomas Stanley
       Groves, 5558 Rfn Thomas Hall, 8540 Sgt William Hanna, 10036 L/Cpl Martin
       Harney, 8359 Rfn Michael Harrison, 9383 Rfn Thomas Hastings, 18367 Rfn
       James Haveron (aged 16), 5241 Rfn John Hawthorne, 9805 Rfn John Healy, 8966
       Rfn Arthur Heenan, 8186 Sgt Thomas Hegarty, 9617 Rfn John Higgins, 9911 Rfn
       Christopher Hogan, 9880 Cpl Hugh Hughes, 16984 Rfn Joseph Hurley, 6359
       L/Cpl Robert Johnston, 6728 Rfn Robert Johnston, 8517 Cpl James Kearney,
       5588 Rfn Patrick Kearney, 10271 Rfn Matthew Keeshan, 771 Rfn Edward Kelly,
       9161 Cpl Philip Lemon, 1570 Rfn James William Lewis, 8257 Sgt Lloyd Lewis,
       8150 Rfn Frank Logan, 1539 Rfn Frank Lomas, 9720 Rfn William Lynch, 7407
       Cpl John McBride, 2272 Rfn James McCafferty, 8774 L/Cpl Robert Henry
       McCallum, 5922 Sgt Thomas McCoubrie, 7578 L/Cpl David McDonald, 8711
       Rfn Thomas McDonnell, 19978 Rfn Walter McDowell, 1738 Rfn Patrick
       McGarraghy, 8683 L/Cpl Robert McGeady, 8382 Cpl Patrick McGlone, 7045

Rfn Hugh McGrady, 6079 Cpl John Hill McKibbin, 7502 Rfn John McMahon, 4912 Rfn Thomas McMeekin, 7681 L/Cpl William Madden, 9149 Rfn James Magill, 7187 Rfn John Maguire, 5995 Rfn Samuel Mahaffey, 14913 Rfn Patrick Malone, 1315 Sgt Matthew Mansell, 6911 Rfn Maurice Mansfield, 9559 Rfn Patrick Masterson, 7659 Cpl David Matier, 1442 Rfn Oswald Mattimore, 8476 L/Cpl Michael Molloy, 1798 Rfn Robert Moore (brother of 3216 Rfn W. Moore, 2nd RIR, KIA 27.4.1916), 7276 Rfn Thomas Morris, 9074 L/Cpl James Morrow, 2515 Rfn John Murphy, 1321 Rfn Joseph Murphy, 7475 Rfn Frank Murray, 6605 Rfn Thomas Murray, 9363 Rfn William Murray, 8871 Cpl John Murtagh, 9274 Rfn Hugh Nabney (five of his brothers also served), 1662 Rfn James P. Neville, 8313 Rfn James Nixon, 10419 Rfn William James Norris, 8463 Rfn James Norwood, 8600 Rfn Michael O'Brien, 8170 Cpl Patrick O'Brien, 14474 Rfn Thomas O'Connor, 6445 Rfn Patrick O'Hanlon, 11301 Rfn Thomas O'Hara, 1526 Rfn Patrick O'Neill, 8287 Rfn James Owens, 1256 Rfn George William Palmer, 1865 Rfn Albert Porter, 9671 Rfn Herbert Purdon, 5780 Cpl Joseph Patrick Quinn, 9914 Rfn William Quinn, 8577 Rfn Henry Reavey, 4543 Rfn John Reilly, 2283 Rfn William Roberts, 1402 Rfn Alfred Rogers, 7131 Rfn William Savage, 1374 Rfn John Shannon, 2511 Rfn Thomas Sharry, 1382 Rfn William Shaw, 19975 Rfn William Shields, 8321 Rfn John Simpson, 8759 Rfn John William V. Simpson, 9731 Rfn John Sleater, 8913 Rfn James Smith, 3653 Rfn Robert Smith, 2377 Rfn Thomas Smith, 8448 Rfn George Smylie, 6437 Rfn Hugh Smyth, 7172 Rfn William Spence, 9326 Rfn Alfred Steen, 6676 Rfn Charles Steenson, 13561 Rfn Thomas Stitt, 14450 Rfn William Stock, 7217 William Stone, 1269 Rfn Harry Sumner, 9419 Rfn Patrick Sweeney, 9241 Rfn Robert James Todd, 6915 Rfn Peter Tohill, 1867 Rfn James Vickers, 12492 Rfn Thomas Walker, 18359 Rfn David Wallace, 9957 Rfn Patrick Walsh, 1384 Rfn James Walton, 8921 Rfn Patrick Joseph Ward, 8962 Rfn Joseph Weir, 8878 Rfn James Wetherall, 8754 Rfn Alexander Whitcroft, 8738 Rfn James Whyte, 8143 Rfn Samuel Wilson, 2399 Rfn George Arthur Wyatt.

10th 9974 Rfn J. Alfred Clegg, 8057 Sgt Thomas John Keating (served in the South African War), 7156 Rfn Thomas Thompson.

11th 7943 Rfn Richard Hutton, 9357 Rfn James Stewart (both died of wounds).

12th 8548 Rfn David Thompson.

13th 5390 Rfn John Power.

16th 9375 Rfn John Howell (died in the UK).

17th 6228 Sgt Anthony Walter Buckley (died of wounds), 9658 Rfn Michael Cullen.

19th 8404 Rfn Michael O'Toole.

22nd 7503 Bugler Patrick McKenna (*War Diary*: 'while working behind the trenches with a working party.').

23rd 1387 Rfn Joseph Bertram (died of wounds, age 17).

25th 6921 Rfn Charles Frederick Wright (died of wounds in the UK).

26th 3376 Rfn Henry Dowling (killed in the trenches).

27th 9557 Rfn John Leggett (killed in the trenches).

29th 3973 Rfn William Close.

June 1915

2nd   1822 Rfn Richard Bennett (shell fire).

3rd   1436 Rfn James Brown (shell fire).

6th   7163 Rfn Charles Rainey (died of wounds in the UK).

9th   1353 Rfn Hugh Ryan (killed by trench mortar or rifle grenade).

11th   4131 Rfn Joseph Jennett.

14th   5257 Rfn Robert Hampton.

16th   10005 Rfn John Bradley, 9488 Rfn Thomas Willis Fraser, 4717 Rfn John
       Johnston, 5714 Rfn James Mayes, 8690 Cpl William Herbert Rogers, 5018 Rfn
       William John Spratt.

18th   7326 Rfn James Keenan (died as POW).

20th   1350 Rfn Alfred C. O'Rourke.

22nd   11379 Rfn Thomas Moore.

24th   7904 Rfn Patrick Brown.

25th   1868 Rfn John Berry.

July 1915

2nd   16130 Rfn James Pender.

5th   9371 Rfn David Hill.

8th   6584 Rfn John Thompson.

16th   9381 L/Cpl Stanley Harris Booth.

18th   2628 Rfn Thomas Caffrey, 10278 Rfn Thomas Elliott, 7213 Rfn Alexander
       McVeigh, 5729 Rfn William Millar, 3404 Rfn Daniel O'Halloran.

19th   4935 L/Cpl Moses Cummins.

20th   6257 L/Cpl John Quinn.

22nd   4775 Sgt Robert John McCleary (died of wounds).

23rd   8046 Rfn Patrick Boland.

29th   10409 Rfn George Jamison, 9023 L/Cpl Frederick William Miller, 5203 Rfn
       William George Pews.

August 1915

4th   1569 Rfn James Brady.

10th   1370 Rfn Frank Whitfield (died of wounds).

13th   5050 Rfn Henry Green, 1696 Rfn Michael Meehan, 2954 Rfn William
       O'Donnell.

September 1915

9th   10173 Rfn Neill Stewart.

12th   2664 Rfn Patrick Stickley (died of wounds).

13th   1553 Rfn Martin Doyle, 2981 Rfn Patrick McNella, 3831 Rfn William H. Owen.

15th   8225 L/Cpl Peter Sands (executed at Fleurbaix).

25th   13549 Rfn Thomas Ashe, 8751 Rfn John Boylan, 6925 Rfn Robert John Connolly,
       9216 Cpl James Earls, 4756 Sgt Patrick Finlay, 13925 Rfn Ernest Franklin, 2976
       Rfn Bernard Furey, 8868 Rfn Henry Frederick Gallery, 9628 Rfn Robert John
       Graham, 8478 Rfn James Kelly, 3963 Rfn Owen Kerr, 6860 Rfn Owen McGill,

     2958 Rfn Joseph O'Connell, 2362 Rfn John Queenan, 9866 Cpl John Ryder, 5543 Rfn David Steele.

26th   2387 Rfn Lincoln Holden, 1/8415 L/Cpl Charles McKenna.

28th   5041 L/Cpl Ernest Herbert Hayward.

October 1915
8th   8347 Sgt Edward McLean.

15th   6997 Rfn Robert James Gallagher (died of wounds).

16th   6322 Cpl John Wall (*War Diary*: 'killed on patrol by rifle fire about 7 a.m.').

28th   8014 Sgt John Palmer (drowned in the River Lys).

November 1915
12th   9891 Rfn Robert Smyth.

18th   7460 Rfn Edward Roberts (died of wounds in the UK).

December 1915
16th   7025 Rfn William Boyd.

25th   9414 Cpl William Printer.

January 1916
8th   13117 Cpl David Morrison.

14th   7005 Rfn Andrew Byrne (rifle fire in trenches).

15th   7282 Rfn W. Nathaniel Graham.

16th   979 Rfn John Hegarty.

24th   G/51 Rfn H. Clark (died in the UK).

29th   7471 Rfn Hugh George Lowry.

31st   15/12084 Rfn Thomas Moore.

February 1916
7th   16803 Cpl Sydney Herbert Abraham, 16802 Cpl Reginald James Hinksman. (*War Diary*: 'Two Corporals killed. Shell fire in trenches.').

8th   9570 Rfn Thomas Hanvey, 9176 Rfn Edward Moore. (*War Diary*: 'Shell fire in billets.').

9th   9343 Rfn James Norton, 9891 Rfn Robert Smyth. (Both shell fire in billets).

March 1916
10th   7385 Rfn Thomas Briggs.

12th   3/8496 Rfn John Keogh (rifle fire in trenches).

13th   8234 Rfn Dan Moynihan (rifle fire in trenches).

14th   8192 Rfn James Weir (rifle fire in trenches).

20th   9266 Rfn William Walsh (rifle fire in trenches).

21st   2347 Rfn James Kelly (rifle fire in trenches).

22nd   11457 Rfn Hugh Allen, 9765 Rfn Patrick Dempsey.

April 1916
10th   3/8885 Rfn Richard Gilbertson (born 26.1.1881. Enlisted 26.10.1915, joined 1st RIR 11.3.1916.), 16139 Rfn John Lynch. (Both killed by grenade and mortar fire).

11th   5796 Rfn William Dodds, 6488 Rfn Henry Holmes, 5745 Rfn William J. Majury, 6694 Rfn Patrick Mullen, 7892 Rfn Francis Parkes, 5454 L/Cpl John Rankin, 1365 Rfn Harry Shaw, 11537 Rfn Thomas Todd. (All during a German raid on their trench.)

12th   7515 Rfn William John Higgins.

13th   5405 Rfn James Love (died of wounds), 8216 Sgt Archibald Russell.

19th   4629 Rfn Valentine Whitty.

20th   10072 Rfn Patrick McGillicuddy (while on a working party).

21st   9355 L/Cpl William Bradshaw.

23rd   9119 Rfn Hugh Farmer.

26th   6600 Rfn John Hart.

27th   6765 Rfn William Fitzpatrick.

28th   6831 Rfn Edward O'Neill (died of wounds).

May 1916

3rd   8948 Rfn Thomas Boyd.

June 1916

3rd   16123 Rfn W. Fanning.

14th   7424 L/Cpl John Couser.

27th   11224 Rfn Samuel Troughton (shellfire. Born 1886. Enlisted August 1914. His son Samuel later served with 2nd RUR. Brother-in-law of 4579 L/Cpl W.J. Frazer, 1st RIR, KIA 7.7.1917.).

28th   3223 Rfn James Noble (shellfire).

29th   9535 Rfn Pierce Butler.

30th   9780 Rfn James Eugene Cleary, 5602 Rfn Patrick Diamond, 7878 Rfn Thomas Hornibrooke (died of wounds), 1843 Rfn Fred Rustige, 7655 L/Cpl Edward Sutherland. (All by shell fire.)

July 1916

1st   8563 Rfn William Anderson, 7542 Rfn Thomas Beatty, 8494 Rfn Joseph Bohan, 7621 Rfn Joseph Bond, 8858 Rfn William John Buller, 3872 Rfn Arthur Byrne, 5704 Rfn William Cadden (age 17, joined the BEF in 1915), 4604 Rfn Patrick Cairney, 7067 Rfn Patrick Canning, 7016 Rfn John Clarke, 2874 Rfn William Clarke, 3073 Rfn Peter Collins, 7295 Cpl John Conners, 4995 Rfn Thomas Deegan, 3/8826 Rfn Edward Donnelly (see *Introduction*), 7201 Rfn John James Fenton, 3/8849 Rfn William Norris Givens (born 16.6.1898. Enlisted 16.10.1915, joined 1st RIR in March 1916. His brother, 42963 L/Cpl G. Givens, Rifle Brigade, was KIA 27.10.1918.), 8925 L/Cpl Joseph Gorman, 4812 Rfn James Gribben, 8811 Sgt Albert Herron, 6952 Rfn Robert Hughes, 1395 Rfn Thomas James, 1345 L/Cpl Fred Jennings, 8819 Rfn Laurence Keating, 4/6687 Rfn James Kelly, 6177 Rfn Joseph Leckey, 4760 Rfn Francis Lowe, 9022 Rfn William McDonald, 9685 Rfn Thomas McEvoy (served as Thomas McDonald), 6174 Rfn William McFadden, 7200 L/Cpl Joseph McShane, 9178 Rfn Joseph Magee, 7616 Rfn John Martin, 3269 L/Cpl Samuel Martin, 6360 Rfn Thomas Matthews, 2326 Rfn John Joseph Meehan, 7445 Sgt Robert Millar, 8379 Rfn Michael Mills, 3990

Rfn Thomas Murphy, 7601 Rfn John Murray, 8972 Rfn Robert Mussell, 7294 Rfn Robert Nixon, 11475 Rfn Arthur O'Hara, 4541 Rfn Denis O'Neill, 2862 Rfn George O'Reilly, 9984 Rfn John O'Reilly, 6702 Rfn Albert Pollett, 8763 Rfn Robert Power (aged 16), 9047 Rfn Joseph Price, 1546 Rfn Harry Swan, 2328 Rfn George Alfred Tanner, 6512 L/Cpl Robert Thompson, 9615 Rfn William James Tipping, 7270 CSM John Tonge, 8824 Rfn Leo Vickers, 7479 Rfn William Walker, 8801 Rfn Arthur Whelan, 5116 Rfn Joseph Wilson.

2nd   1921 Rfn Andrew Higgins.

3rd   4970 Rfn Thomas Brown (died of wounds), 8418 Rfn James Totten.

17th   9126 L/Cpl Charles Cahoon.

21st   9907 Rfn John Mason.

24th   9818 Cpl Samuel Bell, 10317 Rfn Henry Chalkley (died in the UK).

27th   9931 L/Cpl George John Hoey.

29th   5592 Rfn Edward Clement O'Reilly (died of wounds, age 17), 9067 Rfn Edward Rutledge.

August 1916

5th   2987 Rfn Michael Kelly (died of wounds in the UK).

6th   8476 Rfn Michael Hughes, 7618 Rfn Patrick Leonard.

7th   6008 L/Cpl James Butler.

18th   1589 Rfn Patrick Flanagan, 7210 Rfn Dennis Hanna.

21st   2385 Rfn Samuel Thomas, 7613 Rfn Frederick Wilson.

23rd   7173 Rfn Robert Stratton.

24th   6647 L/Cpl Andrew Clarke.

26th   9080 Rfn William M. Pentland (died of wounds in the UK).

29th   10169 L/Cpl William McDowell (died of wounds).

30th   8638 L/Cpl Patrick Byrne, 14462 Rfn John Frederick Davies, 6741 Rfn Alexander Dynes, 8422 Rfn Robert Telfor. (All attached 25th Light TMB.)

31st   9076 Rfn Samuel Wallace Nelson (died of wounds).

September 1916

13th   15288 Rfn John Deane (Hohenzollern Right Sub Sector).

14th   10999 Rfn William Kavanagh (Hohenzollern Right Sub Sector).

16th   10117 Rfn David John Keilty (died in the UK).

22nd   7659 Rfn Sidney John Bakewell (Hohenzollern Right Sub Sector).

October 1916

9th   7474 Rfn Peter Sherry.

12th   2775 L/Cpl Patrick Fitzmaurice.

23rd   1378 L/Cpl Fred Barrow (died of wounds in the UK), 2688 Rfn John Henry Boardman, 9618 Rfn John Brady, 1401 Rfn Richard Browne, 9453 L/Cpl John Burns, 11211 Rfn William Carlisle, 1333 Rfn Thomas Patrick Hagan, 9761 Rfn Thomas Hegarty, 5369 Rfn George Hoey, 4605 Rfn John McGuigan, 7494 Rfn John McLean, 3225 Rfn James O'Brien, 6202 Rfn Matthew O'Brien, 7828 Rfn James Rea.

24th 7439 Rfn Charles Gorman, 9018 Rfn Peter McGonagle, 10678 Rfn James McWilliams (died of wounds).

25th 7003 Rfn James McGeagh.

26th 8877 Rfn Joseph Blain, 8319 Rfn Bernard Finn, 6573 Sgt John Gracie, 8630 Rfn Peter Henley, 7813 Cpl William Hood, 9225 L/Cpl William John McCartny, 8850 L/Cpl Thomas McComb, 9220 Rfn Hugh McKinley, 9046 Cpl Hugh O'Connor, 108 Rfn J. O'Neill, 2440 Rfn John Sinnott, 8599 Rfn David Spence, 11108 Rfn John Walls, 9117 L/Cpl Thomas Watson.

28th 8706 Sgt James Parkhill (Orderly Room Sgt), 6485 Rfn Francis Short.

31st 9794 Sgt Alexander Hamill, 7869 Rfn John Hayes.

November 1916

9th 2995 Sgt Stewart Gordon Dykes (19th London Regt attached).

10th 8907 Rfn James McIvor (attached 25th Coy MGC).

12th 5077 L/Cpl Herbert Thomas Matthews MM (died of wounds, gas), 4722 Sgt Ross Neill.

14th 3958 Rfn Phelim Brien, 40630 Rfn Daniel Devine, 40618 Rfn Fred Lambert, 40653 Rfn William Herbert Lawson, 40619 Rfn Peter McGurk.

15th 43865 Rfn Gerald William Hughes, 779 Rfn H.E. Nunney (1/21st London Regt attached), 7714 Rfn James Henry Pumford, 40627 Rfn John Smith.

29th 724 Rfn Thomas Shaw (died of wounds).

December 1916

13th 9153 L/Cpl Robert McCourt (died of wounds).

16th 8436 L/Cpl Hugh Murphy (died from suffocation).

19th 4405 Pte Albert Edwin Twort (1/22nd London Regt. Suicide. Overseas service from 8.10.1916 with the London Regt until he was attached to 1st RIR 29.10.1916.)

23rd 609 Rfn Joseph Chambers.

January 1917

15th 44080 Rfn Percy Edmund Boon (died of disease).

February 1917

7th 43831 Rfn Charles Henry Flear.

8th 43770 Rfn Francis Collins 13541 Rfn John Orr, 43971 Rfn Cornelius Quinlan. (All in the Rancourt Sector).

9th 43871 Rfn Arthur James Hardy.

13th 41198 Rfn Edward Hewetson Reynolds.

15th 43901 Rfn Paul Kiely.

16th 4761 Bandmaster Harold James Matthews (died in the UK).

18th 104 Rfn John Campbell.

20th 43837 Rfn Benjamin Hassey Glass (bronchitis).

25th 8625 Rfn James Joseph Dempsey (died of wounds).

28th 9178 Rfn John Connor, 7393 Rfn Frank Fitzpatrick, 9582 Rfn Christopher Michael Masterson, 43938 Rfn Edward Anthony Millington (died of wounds), 43968 Rfn Douglas Perkins.

March 1917

2nd   44075 Rfn Arthur William Bennett.

3rd   43828 L/Cpl Edward Westwood Flack (died of wounds, gas), 8123 L/Cpl Ernest Porter.

4th   6875 Rfn Harry Forbes, 2967 Rfn George Savage, 44169 Rfn Henry Suff. (*War Diary*: 'Three ORs belonging to our Lewis Gunners lent to 2nd R. Berks were killed.')

5th   8956 Rfn Alfred Groves, 43927 Rfn Albert Edward Mead, 43955 Rfn Herbert Albert Owen, 44016 Rfn Henry Sharpe, 44003 Rfn Frederick Dudley Smith.

6th   44079 Rfn Frederick William Boon, 43765 Rfn Harry Arthur Cross, 43879 Rfn Arthur Horsefield, 40837 L/Cpl John McSparran, 40906 Rfn William Nixon, 6096 Rfn Joseph Scott, 6721 Rfn Percy Tilesley.

7th   40907 Rfn John Nixon Gibson, 40842 Rfn Thomas Hall, 5886 Rfn Patrick McKeever, 13923 Rfn Patrick Maxwell, 43949 Rfn William Newman, 43976 Rfn Robert George Robbins, 9174 Sgt Ernest Vass, 17956 Rfn James Wright.

8th   10938 L/Cpl William Blair, 43791 Rfn Frederick Clarkson, 43800 Rfn Charles Daniel Dwyer, 44013 L/Cpl William Sullivan.

9th   8785 Rfn Andrew Farley.

10th   7857 Rfn Martin Odlum (died in the UK), 9592 Rfn Robert Sweeney.

11th   43908 Rfn George Beale Mortimore Lang (died of wounds).

24th   44078 Rfn Arthur Bendel.

27th   18/538 Sgt John Porter (died in the UK).

April 1917

1st   40665 Rfn William Blaby, 7286 Rfn Thomas Lowe, 5114 Rfn William John Mitchell, 40908 Rfn Robert O'Hara (died of wounds in the UK), 8712 L/Cpl Joseph Palmer, 4937 Rfn James Tipping, 4007 Rfn Frederick Turner.

2nd   10061 Rfn Jeremiah Cleary, 1833 Sgt Thomas Grant, 9478 Rfn Henry H. Rand, S/62 L/Cpl R.W. Walker.

6th   3052 Rfn John O'Hagan.

8th   9944 Rfn Marshall Cowan (aged 17).

10th   8743 Rfn Robert John Bell (died of wounds).

18th   10314 Rfn Myles Brennan (died of wounds).

21st   4992 Rfn William Orr.

24th   8797 Rfn Thomas Gallagher.

25th   40685 Rfn Robert Marsden, 44018 Rfn William Alfred Sewell.

May 1917

8th   40601 Rfn George Henry Bayles.

25th   9541 Rfn William Curtin.

June 1917

1st   43721 L/Cpl Reginald Agates (died of wounds in the UK).

14th   5585 L/Cpl Bernard Conlon.

30th   6/7423 Rfn John Cougans.

July 1917

7th   10202 Rfn David Broderick, 4579 L/Cpl William John Frazer. (Both by Heavy Trench Mortar. See main text.)

8th   42394 Rfn Henry Arthur Jobson, 4792 Rfn William Hugh Price.

12th   8475 Rfn William J. Johnston.

26th   6703 Rfn John Fitzpatrick.

29th   44043 Rfn Edward George Wiltshire (died of wounds).

31st   43737 Rfn Frederick Amphlett, 10205 Rfn Edward Barron, 42458 Rfn Clarence Edward Bolton, 10553 Rfn James Charles Boyce, 7439 Rfn Albert Victor Browne, 10403 Rfn David Campbell, 42381 Rfn Stanley Arsenius Carrel, 8205 Rfn John Dalton, 42392 Rfn Charles Elliott, 43814 L/Cpl George Henry Emms, 9200 Rfn John Farrell, 42397 Rfn Frederick Samuel Gibbs, 42404 Rfn Charles Gillespie, 13551 Rfn Robert Henry Graham, 40603 Rfn Norman Hirst, 42461 Rfn Henry George Holt, 42402 Rfn Albert Edwin Hopkins (born 18.7.1891. Baker by trade. Enlisted 8.3.1917, joined 1st RIR 29.5.1917.), 43897 Rfn Robert Ernest Jones, 43913 Cpl Joseph Edward Lascelles, 10603 Rfn William Lee, 5213 Rfn John Love, 9882 Rfn James McCabe, 9272 Rfn Patrick McGugan, 7865 Rfn Patrick McReynolds, 9131 Rfn Thomas Magill, 9159 Rfn James Maher, 9717 Rfn James Moloney, 7721 CSM Thomas Nannery, 6867 Rfn Stephen O'Neill, 8768 Rfn James O'Toole, 43966 Rfn William Phillips, 42425 Rfn James Pool, 42428 Rfn George Albert Priddle, 10418 Rfn Samuel Ross (enlisted in 16th KRRC September 1914. His cousin Edward Ross, 10th RIR, was KIA 7.6.1917.), 43987 Rfn Henry Russell, 42435 Rfn Arthur Fisher Simmonds, 44028 Rfn George James Tanner, 44033 Rfn Henry Thomas Tarr, 3932 Rfn John Turley, 9141 L/Cpl Thomas Walsh, 42451 Rfn Harold Walton, 10683 Rfn Thomas Ward, 7521 Rfn John Whittle, 10634 Rfn Baskerville William Wills, 9610 Rfn Walter Arthur Woodward.

August 1917

2nd   14550 Rfn William V. Clode (died of wounds).

11th   40841 Rfn Neason Henry Hale (age 22, enlisted March 1916).

13th   1658 Rfn Martin McIlwraith.

14th   42373 Rfn William Percy Mitchell (died of wounds in the UK).

15th   7470 Rfn Paul Francis Blake, 43941 Rfn Frederick George Musselwhite.

16th   7941 Rfn William Aitken, 8731 Rfn James Allen, 40638 Rfn Charles Baker, 40854 Rfn John Baxter, 9955 Rfn William Bell, 43754 Sgt Edward James Brierly, 43741 Rfn Albert Burrage, 42386 Rfn George William Challenger, 9564 Rfn William Clark, 40862 Rfn John Connell, 9480 Rfn Michael Connell, 3/5926 Rfn Denis Connors, 42387 Rfn James Ernest Constable, 40609 Rfn Francis Joseph Cook, 8497 CQMS Alfred Copeland DCM (enlisted 1907 in 1st RIR. DCM: 'For conspicuous gallantry and coolness at Neuve Chapelle on 10 March in repeatedly carrying messages under heavy fire between the firing line and supports, a distance of 80 yards.' Member of the Orange Order.), 5754 Rfn Edward Corrigan, 8818 Rfn Henry Coughlin, 42384 Rfn Charles Edward Cozens, 42457 Rfn Henry

Debnam, 9620 Rfn Terence Doherty, 4476 Sgt William John Doherty LSM, GCM, 10322 Rfn John Doyle, 7530 Rfn Patrick Doyle, 43809 Rfn Percy Everett, 3/10773 Rfn John Fitzgerald, 42398 Rfn Josiah Gibbons, 42393 Rfn John Samuel Gookey, 2462 Rfn John Alexander Gourley, 10040 Rfn Walter Albert Green, 4787 L/Sgt William Gribbin, 43863 Rfn Frederick James Hatchman, 10033 Rfn John Hipwell, 40880 Rfn Alexander Johnston DCM, 9744 Rfn John Jordan, 8214 Rfn Thomas Kearney, 7264 Rfn John Kennedy, 40886 Rfn Armour John Knox, 7582 Rfn Henry Robert 'Bobbie' Leech (born 17.3.1897), 9487 L/Cpl Thomas Lonergan, 7668 Rfn Edward Lowbridge, 6940 Rfn George McCune, 9247 Rfn James McDowell, 6260 Rfn Michael Marley, 8196 Rfn Fred Maydew, 40933 Rfn Cyril Aubrey Morrison, 8263 Sgt John Murphy, 2980 Rfn Patrick Murray (served as Patrick Berney), 5828 Rfn John Nolan, 8019 Rfn Patrick O'Brien, 9670 Rfn Edwin O'Connell, 43957 L/Cpl Edward Clifford Porter MM, 8360 Sgt Thomas Reid, 40839 L/Cpl William John Robinson DCM (born 19.2.1897. Joined NIH November 1915 and 1st RIR December 1916. DCM, *London Gazette*, 26.2.1918: 'For conspicuous gallantry and devotion to duty. When all his company runners had become casualties he acted as Runner all day, taking messages, under severe conditions, to advanced posts, or shell holes. His successful efforts in performing this extremely dangerous and most important work, contributed greatly to the repulse of two subsequent counter-attacks.'), 10737 Rfn Thomas Russell, 44008 Rfn Henry Tait Seabrook, 9672 Rfn Patrick Shields MM, 43996 Rfn Charles Henry Smith, 42437 Rfn Herbert George Smith, 44010 L/Cpl Charles Spanswick, 44004 Rfn Charles Thomas Spillard, 43999 Rfn Albert Edward Standing, 44023 L/Cpl Frederick Walter Stevens, 40919 Rfn Ernest Augustus Stevenson, 40847 L/Cpl Thomas Stevenson, 43998 L/Cpl Ernest William Summerfield, 44046 Rfn Henry Wallington, 9124 Rfn John Watson, 44047 Rfn Albert Weston, 9511 Rfn Patrick White, 9310 Rfn Ernest Thomas Wicks, 12371 Rfn Henry Wiseman, 10303 Rfn William Robert Yarr.

17th   42409 Rfn George Arthur Morgan (died of wounds).
18th   42401 Rfn Eugene Edward Hill.
24th   8928 L/Cpl James Treanor.
26th   10373 Rfn Edward Caraher.

September 1917
1st   8851 L/Cpl Thomas Quinn.
6th   8300 Rfn David Barnes, 40917 Rfn John Smith.
21st   42374 Sgt Gordon Stanley Howell, 42456 Rfn John Henry W. Roberts.
22nd   43972 Rfn Herbert Frederick Rands, 3270 L/Cpl Robert Scott.

October 1917
15th   47267 Rfn Edward Carrick.
24th   47464 Rfn William Hunter.
25th   47465 Rfn Patrick Browne, 7943 Cpl Henry Corlett.
26th   47213 Rfn Cecil Thornton Ellerbeck.
28th   47437 Rfn Francis Dean.

29th   5702 Rfn Thomas Gallagher, 6013 Rfn John Semple.
31st   317358 Rfn Patrick Melia.

November 1917
10th   47300 Rfn John Grover.
16th   10203 Rfn Harry Toner.
18th   5856 Rfn James Lundy, 47240 Rfn Victor Moule.
19th   10913 Sgt Michael Boyle.
21st   44035 Cpl Edward Edwin Tyler.
22nd   47442 Rfn George Cooke, 47448 Rfn Thomas Simms.
30th   47410 Rfn Daniel Boulton, 47422 Rfn George Cobb, 11377 Rfn Thomas Connolly, 9074 Rfn William Conroy, 5228 L/Cpl John Day DCM, 9168 Rfn Patrick Gilmore, 47300 Rfn John Glover, 47421 Rfn Andrew Hawkins, L/7355 Rfn Edward Kaye, 5675 Rfn Thomas McLoughlin, 42426 Rfn Robert William Parry, 43958 Rfn Edward James Pittman.

December 1917
1st   10664 Rfn John Gilligan, 43844 L/Cpl Clarence Francis George Gough, 10646 Rfn Samuel Green, 47430 Rfn James Herkes, 42423 Rfn William Peploe (died as POW).
2nd   9554 Sgt James William Adams, 3956 Rfn Michael Condron MM (25th TMB), 7712 Cpl Henry Dunn, 4253 Rfn John Hickey.
13th   47262 Rfn Joseph Broome (died of wounds).
18th   6135 CQMS William Alexander Waugh (drowned).
19th   47481 Rfn Thomas Snoddy (attached to Divisional Wing, died of wounds caused by an aeroplane bomb. Noted in the War Diary as the 12th.).

January 1918
1st   6033 Rfn John Pelan (died as POW).
2nd   42438 Rfn Louis Arthur Shirley (died as POW).
12th   47362 Rfn John Thomas Banks (died of wounds in the UK).
16th   42388 Rfn Soloman Cohen, 47462 Rfn Edward James McNamara, 11449 Rfn William Robb, 47331 Rfn Arthur William Wright.
29th   8549 Rfn Thomas Hughes (died of wounds in the UK).

February 1918
9th   20646 Rfn John Galligan.
11th   3/9987 Rfn William McCoy (died in the UK).
21st   47312 L/Cpl George Henry Myers.
22nd   11/2045 L/Cpl Alexander Bruce.
28th   7437 Rfn James Joseph Clifford (died as POW).

March 1918
1st   47266 L/Cpl James Clegg (See main text).
5th   43942 L/Cpl William Mitchell.
6th   7175 Rfn James McLoughlin (served as J. Smith, died in the UK).

10th 7315 Rfn Samuel Duke (died in the UK).

21st 47275 Rfn William Apps, 41355 Rfn James Harry Bass, 1370 L/Cpl Robert Boyle, 11355 Rfn John Burns, 812 Rfn Benjamin Cinnamond, 9709 L/Cpl Patrick Confrey, 9167 Rfn Alexander Courtney, 9759 Rfn William Vance Crockett, 43760 Rfn Sidney Cumming, 43466 Rfn Ernest Frederick Davis, 47361 Rfn Sidney Day, 5002 Cpl Peter Duncan, 6853 L/Cpl Archibald Fallon, 43832 Rfn George Francis Fardle, 20529 Rfn John Garland, 47164 Rfn James Glendining, 47286 Rfn Hubert Griffiths, 43862 Rfn Albert Edward Harling, 43851 Rfn Frederick William Harris, 9301 Sgt John Richard Houlton, 40691 Rfn Herbert Hutchinson, 3096 L/Cpl Joseph Johnson, 10990 Rfn Edward Lowe, 605 Rfn Hugh Milliken, 8819 Sgt James Mulholland, 11378 Rfn Richard Mussen, 13223 Rfn Henry McCartney, 8973 Rfn Christopher O'Neill, 6669 Sgt William Alexander Duncan Patterson (born 17.2.1892. Enlisted 25.5.1915, joined 1st RIR 10.8.1917. B Coy. Killed by shell explosion.), 47250 Rfn William Quine, 25 L/Cpl Joseph Quinn, 10949 Rfn Edward Reid, 47379 Rfn Frederick Ricketts, 6974 Rfn Patrick Rocks, 12425 Rfn Alexander Skillen, 9441 Rfn William John Smyth, 6480 Rfn Hugh Stevenson, 43253 Rfn George Arthur Tyerman, 10382 Cpl Patrick Walsh, 13868 Rfn Hugh Wilson, 13907 Rfn Robert J. Young.

22nd 11/6493 Sgt Matthew Lyness.

23rd 44 Rfn William Henry Breen, 47278 Rfn William Paul Cuthbert, 1300 Rfn Alexander McClements, 1817 Rfn Arthur Reid, 47360 Rfn John Wills.

24th 2162 Rfn William Barker, 20187 Rfn Cecil Charles Hunter Barr, 16328 Sgt William Caswell, 20067 Rfn John Craig, 1137 Rfn William Craig, 47409 Rfn Thomas Walter Doughty, 42868 Rfn Charles Fletcher, 43836 Rfn Frederick Gibbins, 47433 Rfn James Graham, 587 L/Cpl Elias John Harrison, 20583 Rfn Robert Hutchinson, 1462 Rfn Robert McClements (born 13.7.1897, attested 10.6.1916. C Coy.), 26 Rfn Andrew McWilliams, 9558 Rfn John Phillips, 1165 Rfn Hugh Reid (aged 19), 6444 Sgt William Renwick, 44906 Rfn William James Wayman.

25th 9185 L/Cpl George Doherty Armstrong, 47351 Rfn Cecil Gordon Bean, 20225 Rfn Francis Devlin.

26th 20850 Rfn Edmund Jackson.

27th 47257 Rfn George Henry Barker, 43894 Rfn John William James MM, 20124 Rfn Alexander McNeilly, 46 Rfn Alexander Mawhinney, 47412 Rfn Thomas Edward Phillips, 1642 L/Cpl William Edward Thompson (died of wounds).

28th 47457 Rfn William Adams, 5362 Rfn John Cameron, 9817 Rfn Henry Dagens, 8821 Rfn John Gladdery, 9931 Rfn Peter Grimes, 44281 Rfn Albert Stewart Healey, 43997 Sgt Charles Styles, 47470 Rfn Arthur James Walker.

29th 47249 Rfn Edward Robshaw.

April 1918

8th 20259 Rfn Francis Lowry (died of wounds).

10th 8743 Rfn Robert Bell (died of wounds), 6100 L/Cpl Robert Crawford.

15th 20258 Rfn Christopher Murphy.

20th 45090 Rfn Frederick Blackwell, 2354 Rfn Robert Booth, 41424 Rfn Edward George Youngman.

27th   1938 Rfn Joseph McMann.

29th   18/925 Rfn Frederick Honer, 11056 L/Cpl Bryce Longmuir, 257 Rfn Albert
McDonald, 4637 L/Cpl John McKee, 44217 Rfn George Putman, 10878 Rfn
Philip Henry Thomas (age 16).

30th   20843 Rfn Alfred Haslam (died of wounds), 5903 L/Sgt James Kavanagh, 11029
Rfn David Peden, 42443 Rfn Arthur John Symons.

May 1918

5th   47733 Rfn George Alfred John Self.

7th   20000 Rfn James Cruickshank, 18/1738 Rfn Joseph Diamond (enlisted 12.5.1916.
His father, 2803 Rfn Joseph Diamond, served with 12th RIR and died 9.2.1918.)

11th   47415 Rfn Walter Blaber, 11257 Rfn John Cairney, 43528 Rfn John Chipperfield,
47292 Rfn Joshua Hornblower, 40889 L/Cpl William Leckey.

29th   1699 Rfn James Brown.

June 1918

3rd   45858 Rfn Robert Stirling.

8th   9980 Rfn James Andrews.

15th   44987 Rfn George Albert Belson (died as POW).

18th   19695 Rfn John Miller (died in hospital, pyrexia).

21st   45512 Rfn Garnet Augustus Wilton.

25th   44089 Rfn Arthur Edward Blacker (died of wounds in the UK), 14818 Rfn Ferris
Jackson Hall (died as POW).

26th   20459 Rfn Kenneth Malcolm Agnew (died as POW).

28th   14/3751 Rfn Robert Lappin.

July 1918

5th   10514 Rfn John Whelan.

6th   6895 Rfn Patrick Hughes.

15th   834 L/Cpl George Black.

20th   1346 Cpl James Boland, 1568 Rfn John Brown, 43779 Rfn Frederick Joseph
Cannon, 44341 Rfn William Henry Green, 167 L/Cpl David Holmes, 5707 CSM
John Leverett DCM (see main text), 20202 Rfn John Toner, 40272 Rfn James
Wallace.

26th   42454 Rfn George Broughton Larkins.

31st   43781 Rfn James Archer Clarke.

August 1918

21st   11412 Rfn James Jamison, 47095 Rfn Henry William Jones, 1757 Rfn Samuel
Stevely.

23rd   1536 Rfn Bob Dempsey, 45666 Rfn Ernest Walter Leivesley, 50135 Rfn Harold
Alfred George Partis, 42747 Rfn Sidney Harold Ruck.

24th   42412 Rfn Harry Mitchell.

29th   20021 Rfn Robert John Todd.

30th   5536 Rfn George Godden.

September 1918

2nd   8723 Rfn William Dunlop.

4th   16692 Cpl George McCaughan MM (age 27. Joined 1st RIR 29.4.1915. 25th TMB. Awarded a certificate for gallantry in March 1917: 'During operations at Moislin's Ridge on the 4th–5th March 1917, while in the German trench which was being attacked, his section officer was wounded. He carried him back across no-man's-land under heavy fire, reported to his Officer Commanding, and returned to his gun. This Rifleman has always shown great courage and determination during the many months he has been in the field with this battery.' After this he was appointed L/Cpl. Awarded the MM for gallantry and devotion to duty, 15–17.8.1917. His brother John served with 7th RIR), 10354 Cpl Patrick O'Connor.

5th   47411 Rfn James Stevens.

7th   20846 Rfn Charles Davitt, 17647 Rfn William Fordyce, 8846 Sgt William John Gibson, 40874 Rfn Thomas McCready Henderson, 45174 Rfn Albert Charles Lucas, 10178 Rfn John Mahoney, 21659 Rfn Patrick O'Halloran.

10th   43537 Rfn Arthur Frederick Hill, 42710 Rfn Edward Francis Hogg.

11th   20484 Rfn Henry Dornan, 7645 Cpl Joseph Henry Walton.

13th   45041 Rfn Maurice James Dingle, 10983 Rfn Alexander Dougan.

15th   43142 Rfn John White.

17th   10851 Rfn James Hogan.

26th   45472 Rfn William Thomas Horton.

28th   89 Rfn Daniel Heaney, 1/15253 Rfn John McDonald.

30th   14512 Rfn A. McIlroy.

October 1918

1st   14/16213 Rfn James Joseph Bailey, 5021 Cpl Ernest Gibbons, 14708 Rfn James Glencross (died of wounds), 201 L/Cpl William Gould, 22346 Rfn Anthony O'Neill (aged 16).

2nd   47157 Rfn Alexander Baird, 42677 Rfn Arthur Henry Burke, 42468 Rfn Howard George J. Burnett, 47839 Rfn William Frederick Burton, 43788 L/Cpl William Cant, 44269 Rfn George Good Chapman, 300 L/Cpl Edmund Clarke, 7506 Rfn Houston Clements, 19/49 Rfn William John Hillis Croft, 52405 Rfn George Fall, 10052 Rfn Alexander Ferrin, 22007 Rfn William Gray MM, 11036 Rfn James Hamilton, 20927 Rfn William Henry Hart, 9492 Rfn William Hayes (107th TMB), 52307 Rfn Alfred Hilling, 41612 Rfn Wyndham Walter Valentine Hopkins, 45852 Sgt Jesse Jeans, 20529 Rfn Robert George Knowles, 47179 Rfn Frank Love, 16800 L/Sgt George Lucas MM, 52328 Rfn Alfred Joseph Mills (born 27.1.1899. Solicitor's clerk. Enlisted 17.5.1917 in R. Warwickshire Regt, joined BEF 29.3.1918.), 47919 Rfn David McBride, 20318 Rfn John McDonald, 20227 Rfn John McGrady, 448111 Rfn Harry Charles Norris, 52081 Rfn Leslie James Perks, 50139 Rfn Samuel Reginald Philpott, 42830 Rfn William Henry Preen, 20318 Rfn J. Shirley, 47314 Rfn William Sedgwick Shuttleworth, 52460 Rfn Ernest Radford Sidney, 50149 Rfn William John Skelley, 41378 Rfn William Isaac Stannard, 1733 Rfn James Wallace.

4th   3/5532 Rfn Peter Barry, 44067 L/Cpl G.H. Belton, 14/2736 Rfn David Burge, 10327 Rfn David Coey, 43835 Cpl William Geary, 498 Rfn Alfred Johnston, 405 Rfn Andrew McCullough, 1499 L/Cpl John McCully, 50121 Rfn Frederick Mitchell, 47413 Rfn Wilfred Thomas, 18822 Rfn Samuel George Thompson, 41420 L/Cpl Herbert Ernest Youells (died of wounds).

5th   47277 Rfn David Bow DCM (died of wounds).

10th   7926 Rfn Thomas Warren (died in the UK).

13th   5946 Rfn William Black (sickness).

14th   22296 Rfn Andrew Bennett, 42469 Rfn Frederick Ernest Berry (born 31.8.1899. Enlisted 24.7.1916, joined 1st RIR 20.5.1917.), 41538 Rfn Harry William Bradshaw, 503 Rfn George Byng, 606 Rfn James Campbell, 42023 Rfn Fred Cheesman, 42685 Rfn Samuel Henry Chidwick, 41597 Rfn William Henry Clarke, 5365 Rfn Robert Dennison, 44378 Rfn Frank Hamlyn, 52376 Rfn Alfred Harrold, 47429 Rfn William Henry Heal, 43085 Rfn Albert Jackson, 47887 Rfn Charles J. Jenner, 6103 Rfn Robert Kirk, 20128 Rfn John Maguire, 5264 Rfn James Merritt, 975 Rfn John McCartan, 10718 L/Cpl Frederick McCurdy, 15707 L/Cpl Patrick Nixon, 10609 Rfn William O'Brien, 18588 Rfn Frederick Parkes, 20115 Rfn Joseph Reid, 40838 L/Cpl William J. Reid, 20428 Rfn John Reilly, 20654 Rfn Alexander McDonald Simpson, 44032 L/Cpl James William Thompson.

15th   52262 Rfn John Henry Hands, 52163 Rfn George Hoolton, 1451 Rfn James Lawrence Howard (died as POW), 52310 Rfn Bert Harold Humphris.

21st   20707 Rfn John Branigan, 41358 Rfn Henry Cross, 1567 Rfn Joseph Jess, 19189 Rfn Samuel Reid, 10986 Rfn Robert Andrew Richardson, 45853 Cpl Robert Woodruff.

23rd   41955 Rfn Herbert Bailey, 47354 Rfn William Ogilvie Kessack, 201 Rfn James Laird (died of wounds).

26th   43751 L/Cpl Ernest C. Beck.

29th   9487 Rfn T. Richardson (died in the UK).

November 1918

3rd   9216 Rfn David George Hobson.

5th   45671 Rfn Cyril Preston Marston (died of wounds).

8th   9134 L/Cpl Herbert Gordon (influenza).

18th   8691 Rfn M. O'Neill (died in the UK).

26th   50008 Rfn Walter Samuel Radford (died in the UK).

December 1918

5th   23191 Rfn Samuel Sloan.

14th   8396 Cpl C. Stewart (died in the UK).

February 1919

6th   8780 Rfn John Mullen (died in the UK).

21st   6532 Rfn J. O'Shea (died in the UK).

April 1919

9th   20489 Rfn Alexander Crouth (died of wounds in the UK).

15th   G/654 Rfn B. Lynas (died in the UK).

May 1919

2nd   3208 Rfn W. Graham (killed accidentally in the UK).

10th   6672 Sgt William Love (died in the UK).

28th   1862 L/Cpl J. Bannon (died in the UK).

APPENDIX III: MEDAL ROLL

The following list of awards and decorations was compiled from the War Diary, the Divisional, and Regimental Histories. It includes those made after the diary ended or awarded after the person had left the battalion. I have excluded awards that were obviously received while serving with another unit.

OFFICERS

Capt. L.M. Bayly	MC 31.5.18.
Capt. W.R. Bell	MC 30.11.18.
Capt. A.J. Biscoe	Mentioned in Despatches 13.3.15.
2/Lt. J.K. Boyle	MC 26.9.17.
2/Lt. J. Brown	Bar to MC 31.3.17.
Capt. E.V. Burke-Murphy	MC 1.1.17.
Lt. W.A. Burges	Mentioned in Despatches 13.3.15.
2/Lt. C.E. Cooke	Mentioned in Despatches 17.2.15.
Capt. P.J. Cullen	MC 1.10.18.
Lt.-Col. R.A.C. Daunt	Mentioned in Despatches 15.6.16.
Capt. G.W. Edwards	Mentioned in Despatches 22.6.15, 1.1.16, 25.5.17, 25.4.18 and 20.12.18. Belgian Croix de Guerre 4.9.19.
Lt. G.I. Gartlan	DSO 1.1.19. MC 23.6.15. Mentioned in Despatches 22.6.15, 11.12.17 and 20.12.18.
Capt. F.R.W. Graham	DSO 8.3.19. MC 23.6.15. Mentioned in Despatches 22.6.1915, 6.12.16, 21.7.17, 14.6.18 and 11.6.20. French Croix de Guerre 17.8.18.
2/Lt. J. Haslett	MC 11.1.19.
Revd W.H. Hutchison	MC 1.9.18.
Capt. T.H. Ivey	DSO 3.6.18. Mentioned in Despatches 24.5.18.
Capt. P.W. Keating	Mentioned in Despatches 3.2.20.
2/Lt. F. Lamont	MC 30.11.18.
Lt.-Col. G.B. Laurie	Mentioned in Despatches 17.2.15 and 22.6.15.
Capt. R.O.H. Law	Bar to MC 31.5.18.
Capt. J.C. Leeper	Mentioned in Despatches 28.12.18. Belgian Croix de Guerre 4.9.19.
2/Lt. W.J. Linton	MC 30.11.18.
Lt.-Col. H.W.D. MacCarthy-O'Leary	DSO 26.9.17. Bar to DSO 16.9.18. Mentioned in Despatches 21.12.17, 28.12.18 and 17.7.19.
2/Lt. H. McIntosh	MC 8.3.19.
2/Lt. J. McKenna	MC 30.11.18.
Capt. W.A.S. Macpherson	MC 2.12.18.
Lt.-Col. C.C. Macnamara	Mentioned in Despatches 25.10.16.

2/Lt. W.S. Maitland	MC 22.9.16.
Major E.R.H. May	DSO 30.11.18.
Major A.D.N. Merriman	DSO 3.6.16. Mentioned in Despatches 1.1.16, 15.6.16 and 9.9.21.
2/Lt. J.L. Muir	MC 24.6.16. Bar to MC 10.8.21.
Capt. C.J. Newport	Mentioned in Despatches 1.1.16.
Capt. A.M. O'Sullivan	Mentioned in Despatches 22.6.15.
Lt. G.W. Panter	Mentioned in Despatches 1.6.16.
Capt. E. Patton	Bar to MC 31.5.18.
Lt. C.L.G. Powell, RAMC	Mentioned in Despatches 15.6.16.
Lt. T.M. Tate	French Croix de Guerre (Bronze Star) 19.6.19.
Capt. H. Tayler	MC 15.2.19. Mentioned in Despatches 15.6.16.
Capt. A.C. Taylor	Mentioned in Despatches 4.1.17 and 21.12.17.
Lt. F.C. Wallace	MC 1.1.18. Mentioned in Despatches 15.6.16.
Lt. G.H.P. Whitfeld	MC 1.1.18. Mentioned in Despatches 25.5.17.
Capt. A.O'H. Wright	Mentioned in Despatches 22.6.15.

OTHER RANKS

41158 Sgt F. Arnold	MM 31.7.18.
4942 Rfn W. Arnopp	MM 28.9.17.
2254 Rfn E. Ashe	MM 17.6.19.
9335 Sgt J. Bacon	MM 28.9.17.
16231 Rfn J. Bailey	MM 14.5.19.
9661 CSM J. Baines	DCM 3.9.18.
79 L/Cpl W.J. Bankhead	MM 17.6.19.
8778 Rfn T. Barr	MM 13.3.18.
40855 L/Cpl W. Baxter	MM 14.5.19.
47277 Rfn J. Bow	DCM 12.3.19.
9348 Rfn A. Bowers	DCM 5.8.15.
9097 L/Cpl J. Bradshaw	DCM 3.6.15.
8164 Sgt P. Breen	Mentioned in Despatches 22.6.15.
1666 Cpl J.H. Brock	MM 9.11.16.
9314 Sgt S. Brock	MM 9.11.16.
40664 Rfn A. Brown	MM 17.6.19.
2360 Rfn R. Browne	Mentioned in Despatches 22.6.15.
4964 Rfn R. Bullock	MM 13.3.18.
7436 Rfn W.J.A. Campbell	DCM 5.8.15. Bar to DCM 15.3.16.
9249 L/Cpl H. Cairns	DCM 30.6.15.
10736 Cpl A. Carolan	MM 14.5.19. Bar to MM 23.7.19.
5710 RSM W. Carroll	MC 23.6.15. Mentioned in Despatches 22.6.15. Russian Medal of St George, 1st Class, 25.8.15.
47469 L/Cpl J. Carton	DCM 4.3.18. Belgian Croix de Guerre 4.9.19.

47168 Cpl J. Chambers	DCM 3.6.19.
8519 CSM W. Clarke	DCM 3.6.18. Croix de Guerre 12.7.18.
9364 Sgt W. Clarke	MSM 18.1.19.
8082 L/Cpl C. Coleman	MM 2.11.17.
3956 Rfn A. Condon	MM 9.11.16.
8497 Rfn A. Copeland	DCM 30.6.15.
7146 RQMS L.C. Corrigan	Mentioned in Despatches 25.5.17 and 21.12.17. MSM 17.6.18. French Croix de Guerre (Bronze Star) 19.6.19.
14319 Sgt W. Courtney	MM 17.6.19.
6487 Sgt P. Coyle	DCM 30.6.15.
2329 Sgt J. Cromie	DCM 3.6.19.
5228 Rfn J. Daly	DCM 16.8.17.
8223 L/Cpl J. Darcy	DCM 30.6.15. Russian Medal of St George, 4th Class, 25.8.15.
7603 Sgt C. Delaney	MM 9.11.16.
8998 Sgt P. Devine	DCM 22.10.17.
6550 Rfn J. Dickson	MM 6.1.17.
20156 Sgt J.A. Doherty	DCM 3.9.18.
25322 Rfn J. Doherty	MM 14.5.19.
8383 L/Cpl J. Donnolly	DCM 3.6.15. Russian Cross of Order of St George, 3rd Class, 25.8.15.
4653 Rfn J. Downey	MM 2.11.17.
5420 CSM James Driscoll	DCM 14.1.16.
5495 L/Cpl D. Dunlop	MM 13.3.18.
14538 QMS A.G. Ervine	MSM 18.1.19.
9493 Sgt W.J. Fee	Mentioned in Despatches 4.1.17.
85 L/Cpl J. Ferguson	MM 17.6.19.
8368 Rfn W. Flanagan	French Medaille d'Honneur avec Glaives en Bronze 17.3.20.
3835 CSM S. Fowles	DCM 14.1.16 and MSM 22.2.19.
8695 Rfn J. Gaskin	MM 21.12.16.
8796 Rfn J. Graham	MM 1.9.16.
22007 Rfn W. Gray	MM 29.3.19.
8719 CSM J. Greene	MM 13.3.19. Bar to MM 6.12.20.
9562 Sgt C.H.D. Henniker	French Medal Militaire 15.12.19.
16549 L/Cpl R. Herdman	DCM 5.12.18. Belgian Croix de Guerre 4.9.19.
16138 CSM W. Hill	Mentioned in Despatches 9.7.19.
14924 Sgt J. Holmes	MSM 17.6.18.
14927 Sgt J. Hooks	French Croix de Guerre (Bronze Star) 19.6.19.
47307 Rfn W. House	MM 17.6.19.
7254 Sgt R. Houston	MM 13.3.18.
2260 Rfn W. Humphreys	MM 17.6.19.
8982 Rfn W. Hunter	DCM 3.6.15.
9790 L/Cpl P. Hyland	MM 9.11.16.

43894 Rfn J.W. James   MM 2.11.17.
41052 Rfn E. Jeacock   MM 29.8.18.
43893 Sgt L.T. Jeffcott   MM 20.8.19.
1516 Rfn R. Johnson   DCM 5.8.15.
40680 Rfn A. Johnston   MM 2.11.17.
6824 Cpl B. Kavanagh   Mentioned in Despatches 21.12.17.
10856 Rfn J. Kearney   MM 13.3.18.
10225 L/Cpl G. Keeling   MM 13.9.18.
4957 Bdsn. P. Kelly   Mentioned in Despatches 22.6.15.
8716 Rfn A. Kennedy   MM 9.11.16.
7264 Rfn J. Kennedy   French Croix de Guerre 1.5.17.
103 Sgt J. Lanigan   Mentioned in Despatches 28.12.18. MM 17.6.19.
9876 Sgt C. Lawrence   MM 11.8.19.
6177 Cpl J. Leatham   MM 17.6.19.
9550 Cpl W.R. Lees   DCM 3.6.16.
4872 L/Cpl J. Lennon   Mentioned in Despatches 22.6.15.
5707 Sgt J.W. Leverett   DCM 22.10.17
8887 L/Cpl D. Lowe   MM 11.11.16. Bar to MM 17.9.17.
16800 Cpl G.A. Lucas   MM 13.3.18.
43917 L/Cpl P.T. Ludkin   Mentioned in Despatches 28.12.18.
8447 CSM T. Lunn   DCM 20.12.16.
9876 Rfn W. McBratney   MM 14.5.19.
8619 Rfn T. McCarthy   MM 7.10.18.
16692 L/Cpl G. McCaughan   MM 2.11.17.
8729 L/Cpl C. McCoughey   DCM 3.6.19.
9405 Sgt D. McCourt   MM 9.11.16.
13177 L/Cpl W. McCullough   Mentioned in Despatches 9.7.19.
8773 Rfn C. McDonnell   MM 2.11.17.
5399 Sgt J. McDowell   Belgian Croix de Guerre 4.9.19.
7359 L/Cpl W. McFarlane   Mentioned in Despatches 17.2.15.
9280 CQMS W. McFaull   French Croix de Guerre (Silver Star) 19.6.19.
15414 Cpl A.C. McGuigan   MSM18.1.19.
9604 Cpl J. McKeown   MM 29.8.18.
18393 CSM J.J. Mackey   DCM 12.3.19.
9577 CSM J. Magee   DCM 4.6.17.
5256 Cpl J. Magill   MM 13.3.18.
7265 Sgt J.P. Maguire   Mentioned in Despatches 21.12.17. Belgian Croix de
                                Guerre 12.7.18.
10404 Cpl J. Malone   MM 13.3.18.
5320 Sgt E.A. Manderson   MM 7.10.18.
9006 Rfn W.J. Martin   MSM 1.7.18.
9222 Cpl S. Massey   MM 25.5.17.
5077 L/Cpl H.T. Matthews   MM 6.1.17.
7737 Sgt J. Meredith   Belgian Decoration Militaire avec Croix de Guerre
                                24.10.19.

6798 Sgt G. Miskimmons   MM 13.3.18.
12211 L/Cpl J. Montgomery   MM 29.3.19.
25311 Rfn J. Morgan   DCM 11.3.19.
45899 CSM F. Murphy   MSM 3.6.19.
5820 Rfn S. Murphy   DCM 3.6.16.
7750 CSM J. Murray   DCM 1.1.19.
7274 Sgt R. Ness   MSM 17.6.18.
9479 L/Cpl E. Noone   MM 13.11.18.
1284 Rfn J. Nunn   MM and Serbian Gold Medal 21.10.16.
7284 L/Cpl A. Osbaldeston   DCM 1.4.15.
6543 Cpl W.J. Patterson   MM 2.11.17.
5099 Sgt W.S. Poole   DCM 22.10.17.
43957 L/Cpl E.C. Porter   MM 28.9.17.
8160 L/Cpl E.C. Poulton   MM 11.5.17.
8175 Cpl J. Quinlan   Mentioned in Despatches 22.6.15.
44265 Rfn A.W. Ray   MM 7.10.18.
6348 Sgt H. Rees   DCM 30.6.15. Russian Cross of the Order of St George,
                                4th Class 25.8.15.

20428 Rfn J. Riley   MM 13.9.18.
1444 Cpl J. Roberts   MM 13.3.18.
43978 Sgt F. Robertson   MM 11.2.19.
40839 L/Cpl W.J. Robinson   DCM 22.10.17.
20229 Rfn W. Savage   MM 17.6.19.
44009 Rfn W. Seibert   MM 14.5.19.
8914 Cpl C. Sexton   Mentioned in Despatches 22.6.15.
9672 Rfn P. Shields   MM 6.1.17.
7095 CSM W.H. Simner   DCM 5.8.15. MM 1.9.16.
12366 Sgt A.J. Simpson   MM 2.11.17.
18800 L/Cpl J.H. Smith   MM 20.10.19.
8487 Rfn W. Smyth   MM 11.11.17.
8900 Rfn J. Spence   MM 13.3.18.
8794 Rfn W.R. Spence   MM 28.9.17.
6775 L/Cpl J.A.W. Stanley   MM 13.11.18.
5952 Sgt J. Steele   MM 29.8.18.
8875 L/Cpl J. Stevenson   French Croix de Guerre (Bronze Star) 19.6.19.
7323 CSM C.E. Stovin   Mentioned in Despatches 22.6.15. DCM 1.1.17.
8722 Rfn J. Traynor   Mentioned in Despatches 15.6.16.
9258 Rfn H. Tumelty   MM 2.11.17.
42448 Rfn F.A. Vile   MM 17.9.17.
9889 Sgt J. Walsh   MM 21.9.16.
10733 RSM W. Ward   Mentioned in Despatches 21.12.17. French Medal of
                                Honour 29.1.19.

13817 Rfn J. Warnock   MM 17.6.19.
8193 Cpl J. Willott   MM 17.6.19.

40926 Rfn J.J. Wilson	MM 20.10.19.
41678 Rfn W. Woodruff	MM 30.9.18.
9098 Cpl W.H. Woods	Bar to MM 23.7.19.
40615 L/Cpl W. Yardley	MM 29.9.18. DCM 12.3.19. Belgian Croix de Guerre 4.9.19.

Divisional Complimentary Cards awarded in December 1918

5671 Rfn N. Allen	16992 Cpl R. Beattie
16184 Cpl A. Bell	1316 Rfn J. Black
1115 Rfn J. Brown	42927 Rfn J. Brown
115 L/Cpl J. Campbell	6884 L/Cpl J. Campbell
47168 Cpl J. Chambers	44639 Rfn C. Clayson
119 Rfn W. Coates	41674 Sgt E. Cole
20393 L/Cpl B. Curran	9151 Cpl F.R. Dixon
8778 Sgt P. Donnelly	5966 Rfn R. Grant
21160 L/Cpl W. Hall	9562 Sgt C. Henniker
47315 Cpl M. Hill	9218 Rfn B. Jackson
40879 Rfn W. Jackson	45851 Cpl W. Jarvis
588 Rfn J. Kinkaid	18100 Rfn D. Linton
500 Rfn R. Lomas	9280 Rfn J. McKay
45523 Rfn H. McManee	10588 Cpl J. Patterson
50248 Rfn J. Patterson	9933 a/CQMS J. Power
10569 Cpl H. Proctor	44265 Rfn A. Ray
9370 Rfn M. Reilly	2155 Sgt L. Taylor
44040 Rfn W. Vincent	1356 Rfn J. Wilson

APPENDIX IV

These are the instructions issued by 25th Brigade to the battalion commanders for the attack on 1 July 1916:

25TH INFANTRY BRIGADE

Preliminary Operation Order No. 100. Reference Maps R, S, & T.

I   Offensive Operations will be carried out by the 8th Division on a date to be notified later, as part of operations by the 4th Army. The 34th Division will attack simultaneously the German trenches on our right and the 32nd Division on our left.

II DIVIDING LINE BETWEEN BRIGADES – 8TH DIVISION

The 8th Division will attack with three brigades in the front line, the 23rd on the right, the 25th in the centre and the 70th on the left. The boundaries between brigades will be as shown on Map S, already issued.

III OBJECTIVES

   1. The first objective of the 8th Division on the first day, is the line (mauve on Map S) from about X.5.c.O.5 through the eastern outskirts of Pozières (about X.4.b.7.5) R.34.d.o.9 (inclusive) R.34.a.9.1 (inclusive) R.34.a.7.4, R.34.a.6.5 to about R.28.c.2.o. Of the above described line the 25th Brigade front extends from X.4.b.2.7½ to R.34.a.9.1. This line will be consolidated as soon as it is reached.

   2. The capture and consolidation of this objective will terminate the first phase of these offensive operations. There are in addition to this, other intermediate lines which are to be consolidated as soon as captured. They are shown in green and yellow on Map S.

IV DISPOSITION OF UNITS

The disposition of units at the commencement of bombardment will be as follows, and the battalion holding the line will be changed periodically according to the duration of the bombardment.

   (a)   One battalion holding the line.
   (b)   One battalion in Long Valley less one Coy which will be in the Albert– Bouzin-court Line.
   (c)   One battalion in Long Valley.
   (d)   One battalion in Millencourt.
   (e)   Brigade HQs at Orchard W.21.d.2.5.
         Brigade M.G. Coy. ⎤
         T.M. Batteries   ⎬ → Long Valley
         Grenade Coy.   ⎦

On the morning of the assault the troops of the brigade will be formed up as follows:

2nd Royal Berkshire Regiment:

   8 Platoons in new and present front line from Goosedubs to Cartmael Street (both inclusive).

   8 Platoons in Furness (north of Goosedubs) and in Broughton and Ulverstone and in present front line between Broughton and Goosedubs.

   Battalion HQ at Furness near junction with Ulverstone.

2nd Lincolnshire Regiment:

   8 Platoons in front line between Cartmael and Longridge.

   4 Platoons in Pendle Hill and Cartmael.

4 Platoon in Waltney.

Battn. HQ in Waltney.

1st Royal Irish Rifles:

12 Platoons in Pendle Hill.

4 Platoons in Coniston.

Battalion HQ at junction Pendle Hill and Coniston.

2nd Rifle Brigade:

8 Platoons in Ribble Street between Lancaster Avenue and Wenning.

8 Platoons in Ribble Street between John O'Gaunt and Melling Street, in Melling and in Donnet Street.

Battalion HQ in Donnet Post.

25th Bde Machine Gun Coy:

2 Sections in Ribble Street next to Wenning Junction and Wenning Street.

8 Guns in battle emplacements at approximately the following points:

X.7.c.9.52. X.7.c.9.4. X.7.d.15.5. X.1.a.3.37.

X.1.a.5.3. X.7.b.18.75. X.7.b.18.8. X.7.c.9.15.

From which positions they will co-operate with the bombardment and the assault.

25th Bde Grenade Coy:

In Barrow Street between Coniston and Furness and in Furness between Barrow and Goosedubs.

T.M. Batteries:

T.M. Batteries will occupy emplacements at the end of tunnels as follows:

23/5 T.M. Battery: running from junction of X.7.5. & 6.

1 Sec. 25/1 Battery – Rivington Tunnel.

1 Sec. 25/1 Battery – Waltney Tunnel.

The hour and full details as to route each unit is to move by will be issued later.

v The operations will be divided into three phases, as shown on Map S.

(a) First Phase.

The assault will be delivered by two battalions. The 2nd Royal Berkshire Regt on the right and the 2nd Lincolnshire Regt on the left. To these two battalions is allotted the task of capturing the first intermediate objective (coloured green on Map S). The dividing line between these two battalions is the sap at X.8.a.1.4, the communication trench from Point 846 to Point 888. Point 810 and the communication trench running there from Point 244, all inclusive to the 2nd Lincolnshire Regt (Map S).

In close support to these two battalions there will be one platoon of the Bde Grenadier Coy to each and one Section Bde M.G. Coy.

The 1st Royal Irish Rifles, one Section Bde M.G. Coy and one platoon of the Bde Grenadier Coy will be in support.

The 2nd Rifle Brigade and two sections of the Bde M.G. Coy (withdrawn from the front line, detailed in Para 4) and one platoon of the Grenadier Coy will be in reserve.

Each battalion will assault with three Coys in the front line, in depth, on a front of one platoon per Coy. Platoons to be at not less than 50 paces distance.

The remaining Coy of each battalion, together with one platoon of the Bde Grenadier Coy will follow the assaulting Coys at 200 yards distance.

At -05 the assaulting battalions will, if circumstances permit, commence getting out of our trenches and into no-man's-land in front of our wire; the leading two waves being out by zero hour. The remainder following at zero. At zero hour these two battalions will advance over the open, rush the enemy front line, and move straight on the first objective (green on Map S), following in the wake of the Artillery barrage lifts as close as possible. (See Appendix B).

The two leading waves of the assaulting troops will not delay their advance for slight opposition or for the purpose of 'cleaning up' trenches and dugouts; these will be dealt with by the two supporting waves, the battalion reserve Coy and the platoon of the Grenade Coy attached to each battalion.

The special task of the bombers being to look after the flanks of the Bde and to join up with the Bdes on either side.

On reaching the first objective the assaulting battalions will at once commence to consolidate this line by means of strong points, and one section of the Bde M.G. Coy will move up to assist in holding it.

The strong points to be consolidated will be in front line, Point 44, 47, 78. Also in rear Point 10 and 56. Points 62 and 05, on the flanks, are being consolidated by the 70th and 23rd respectfully.

The H.C. Field Coy R.E. will be sent forward later to assist battalions in this work of consolidation.

The strong point at the captured line generally will be held by two Coys of the Royal Berkshire Regt on the right and two Coys of the Lincolnshire Regt on the left. The remaining two Coys of each battalion will be re-organised in readiness for a further advance. The platoons of the Grenade Coys having 'cleaned up' will reorganise for a further advance with 2nd Rifle Brigade.

It is to be remembered that to assault in mass or to crowd men into trenches when checked, will result in considerable and unnecessary losses.

In carrying out the assault therefore, not more than two waves, as a general rule are to be together in one line of trenches, the following two waves being, at that time, in support, in the line of trenches next in rear. A study of Map S will enable battalion and subordinate commanders to grasp this instruction.

(b) Second Phase.

At zero hour the 1st Royal Irish Rifles will commence moving up from their assembly trenches into the front line and will follow the assaulting battalions at a distance of 500 yards.

1 platoon of the Grenadier Coys and one Section M.G. Coy will accompany this battalion.

The 2nd Rifle Brigade (in Bde Reserve) will move forward and occupy our front line trenches as soon as they are vacated by the Irish Rifles. From this Point this battalion will receive orders from Bde HQ as to when it will advance.

The 8 guns of the M.G. Coy occupying Battle Emplacements will be withdrawn into Bde Reserve when the enemy's trenches have been taken and covering fire is no longer practicable.

The attack on the second intermediate objective will be carried out by the 1st Royal Irish Rifles, supported by 2 Coys of the 2nd Lincolnshire Regt on the left rear and by 2 Coys of the Berkshire Regt in rear (see (a) First Phase, one section M.G. Coy and one platoon Bde Grenadier Coy.)

The second intermediate objective, having been gained, will at once be consolidated. The strong points will be 22, 28, 46, 43. Point 95 on the right flank of the 70th Brigade will be consolidated by that Brigade. The line will be garrisoned by two companies of the Royal Berks and by two companies of the 2nd Lincs Regt, with the above mentioned sections of the Bde M.G. Coy. The 1st R. Irish Rifles will re-organise in readiness for an advance to the final objective, as below.

One section M.G. Coy from the brigade reserve will be detailed to push on to this line, extra to the section already detailed to move in support to the 1st R. Irish Rifles.

(c) Third Phase.

The assault on the final objective will be carried out by the 2nd Rifle Brigade on the left, with one section M.G. Coy and the two platoons Bde Grenadier Coy who originally supported the first assault, and by the 1st R. Irish Rifles on the right, supported by one section M.G. Coy and one platoon Bde Grenadier Coy, operating on the right. The final objective will be consolidated as quickly as possible, the strong points being 48, 44 trench junction near point 80 and east corner of orchard near Point 97.

VI   The Trench Mortar Batteries will be posted as in Para 4. At -08 they will open a hurricane bombardment upon the enemies front line covering the deployment and assault of the assaulting battalions. As soon as the assault has entered the hostile trenches the battery will follow and support the advance to the first intermediate objective, and subsequently support the 1st R. Irish Rifles to the second intermediate objective. Four guns will be kept in brigade reserve.

VII PREPARATION FOR ASSAULT

The assault will be prepared by:

(a)   An Artillery bombardment; lasting five days. First day being U day. The assault will be carried out on Z day.

(b)   The discharge of Gas and Smoke.

Details of this will be communicated in Appendix C and D. Eight minutes before the hour for the assault the enemies front trench will be subjected to a hurricane bombardment from 3" Stokes Mortar Batteries. After the assault of the enemies front line the subsequent movement of the infantry will be assisted and regulated by a system of barrages which will move back slowly in accordance with the table given in Appendix B.

As the infantry advance progresses, the barrages become heavier until when the final objective is reached a barrage of the whole of the available artillery will be formed in front of it while it is being consolidated.

VIII GAS

Gas will be liberated during the night of V/W on the front X.13.b.3.7 to X.1.d.1.0 see Appendix C.

IX SMOKE

The instructions for the liberation of smoke are contained in Appendix D.

X MACHINE GUN AND RIFLE FIRE

During the Artillery bombardment rifle and machine gun fire will be brought to bear on the enemies wire to prevent him mending it, and on selected places in the rear of the enemies front trenches. Enfilade and indirect fire is to be used as much as possible. Rifle and Lewis guns will deal with the front line and the Vickers Guns with selected places and trenches behind. The brigade reserve of S.A.A. 500 boxes is not to be used for this purpose.

XI CUTTING WIRE

The battalion in the line is responsible for cutting lanes in our own wire the second night before the assault, and leaving on the far side Chevaux de Frises (if available) which can be easily moved away.

XII COMMUNICATIONS

There will be a Centre Divisional Visual Signal Station at Lavieville (D.10.b.6.9) which will be in communication with Brigade Headquarters. Two Brigade Visual Stations will be established, one about W.12.d.7.4 which will be in communication with the Divisional Stations and the other about X.7.c.3.2; this latter station and the Divisional Station, will during the advance, be on the lookout for Helio or Lamp signals from the advancing troops and can be seen as far as Pozières.

Details of the signalling scheme will be issued to battalions by the Brigade Signal Officer. Supply of carrier pigeons will be given to each battalion.

Contact patrol aeroplanes will work throughout the day picking up the positions of our own troops and also messages from battalions and Brigade Headquarters. Brigade and Battalion Headquarters will use the special brown sheets issued for the purpose.

Battalions will arrange for flare signals to be lighted as follows:

(a)   At each line of enemy trench captured.

(b)   At five minutes past every fourth hour after zero.

No. 14 Kite Balloon Section will also be available to pick up and possibly send messages to the various headquarters. When signalling to the balloons, the lamp or helio must be laid on the basket, not the gas bag.

XIII PRELIMINARY MOVES

Separate brigade orders will be issued to move to their positions for the bombardment and also to their assembly places.

XIV EQUIPMENT TO BE CARRIED

The following equipment, ammunition and bombs will be carried by each infantry soldier:

Rifle, equipment including water-proof sheet (less pack and great coat). Haversacks to be carried on the back. Water bottles to be full. Packs and great coats will be labelled and stored under a guard on the day previous to units moving to their assemble places. Two bandoliers in addition to equipment ammunition (total 220 rounds per man). Bombers and Pioneers will carry equipment ammunition only and Machine Gunners 50 rounds only. Bombers may discard their pouches and carry two bandoliers instead. Iron rations and unexpended portion of days ration. Not less than two sandbags. Not less than two grenades. Smoke helmets. Every third man a pick and shovel of which 50 per cent will be picks.

The following will be carried by selected men.

130 wirecutters with lanyard per battalion. 130 wirebreakers per battalion. 64 billhooks per battalion. 100 pairs hedging gloves. 48 bridges for assaulting battalions. 415 flares per battalion for signalling to Aeroplanes.

Each Bomb Squad, of which there will be one to every platoon, will carry not less than 90 grenades.

XV BDE STORES OF S.A.A., GRENADES & STOKES MORTAR BOMBS, RATIONS AND WATER

The positions of these have already been notified to all units by this office. No. B.M. c/297/12 and Map T.

Divisional are as follows:

Reserve Ration Stores (1) Where the Tram line cuts Wenning Street. (2) Tram Base W.22.c.5.1. (3) Emergency Tram Base W.22.d.8.1.

S.A.A. at Tram Base at W.22.c.5.1.

Bombs at end of Wenning Street W.12.c.3.3.

XVI R.E. DEPOTS   No. 2 X.7.b.5.2.

No. 4 Main R.E. Depot W.18.b.4.5.

No. 5 Main R.E. Depot X.7.a.0.2.

Reserve R.E. Depot W.23.c.2.0.

Mobile R.E. Depot Long Valley.

When units require R.E. Stores, it is only necessary for them to send back guides to the dumps with a list of requirements, as carrying parties are provided by R.E.

XVII   Prisoners will be passed back under escort retailed by battalions to battalion immediately in rear, down to the Prisoners Collecting Station at Brickworks W.22.d.6.8. on the Albert–Aveluy Road where they will be handed over to the A.P.M. or his representative. After handing over prisoners, escorts are to rejoin their units at once. Escorts should not exceed 1 man to every 10 prisoners.

XVIII   Dressing and Collecting Stations are established as follows:

24th F.A. No. 1 Camp Henencourt Wood.

26th F.A. No. 4 Camp Henencourt Wood

25th F.A. Millencourt.

Divisional Collecting Station:

24th F.A. near North Chimney W.22.a.8.8.

25th Brigade. (25th F.A.)

(a)   Advanced Dressing Station in Lancaster Avenue at junction of Ribble Street North of Donnet Post.

(b)   Medical Shelters at:

(1)   Crucifix Corner W.11.d.9.2.

(2)   At entrance to Preston Avenue W.18.a.1.9.

Battalion First Aid Posts have been notified to units.

XIX   MISCELLANEOUS

(a)   No papers or orders are to be carried by officers or men taking part in the attack, except the new 1/5,000 German trench map and the 1/20,000 Map, Sheet 57.D S.E. All messages or reports will refer to one or other of these maps. The numbers on the 1/5,000 Map are only to be used within the 3rd Corps.

(b)   Hand Grenades are difficult to replenish and are not to be thrown indiscriminately.

(c)   Any guns captured, which are in danger of being lost must be rendered useless by damaging the sights and breech mechanism. This is best done by damaging the thread of the screw. Captured machine guns must be collected or broken.

XX   Acknowledge.

H. Lloyd, Capt.

Brigade Major, 25th Inf. Bde.

APPENDIX C.

1.   12 cylinders White Star, and 8 cylinders Red Star, per emplacement will be installed. Gas will be discharged as follows:

0–04   Four cylinders (White Star) simultaneously per bay.

04–1.20   One cylinder (Red Star) per bay every ten minutes.

1.20   All remaining cylinders to be turned on.

2.   The following rocket signals will be fired from Donnet Post commencing at 1.28. Three pairs of Red Rockets from each post at 30 seconds interval between pairs. Responsibility

for firing these rockets will rest as follows, according to which night gas is discharged.

Night of 25th/26th   OC 2nd Rifle Brigade.

Night of 26th/27th   OC 1st R. Irish Rifles.

Night of 27th/28th   OC 1st R. Irish Rifles.

The rockets will only be fired provided the discharge of gas has taken place.

Substituted for obsolete Appendix C, 22/6/1916.

APPENDIX D: INSTRUCTIONS FOR THE DISCHARGE OF SMOKE.

(1)   If the wind permits, smoke will be discharged on W, X and Y days.

(2)   It will be discharged all along the line at the following times:

W day 10.10 a.m. to 10.20 a.m.   2nd Rifle Brigade.

X day 5.40 a.m. to 5.50 a.m.   1st R. Irish Rifles.

Y day 7.10 a.m. to 7.20 a.m.   Right Bde front by 1st R. Irish Rifles ...
                                    Left by 2nd Lincs.

(3)   For this purpose 'P' Bombs and Candles will be required as follows:

	P Bombs	Candles
2nd Rifle Brigade	88	220
1st R. Irish Rifles	132	330
2nd Lincs	44	110

(4)   (a)   On each brigade front smoke will be discharged from 22 points, distributed evenly along the front. (Average interval 33 yards.)

      (b)   At each discharge the following will be thrown from each of the above points: 4 'P' Bombs and 10 Candles.

      (c)   The programme for each discharge will be:

Minutes	'P' Bombs	Candles
0	2	0
1	–	1
2	1	1
3	–	1
4	1	1
5	–	1
6	–	1
7	–	2
8	–	2
9	–	–
10	–	–

(5)   The smoke at each point will be discharged by a group of 1 NCO and 2 men (Infantry). The NCO of every group should be supplied with a copy of the above programme, and a watch. Steps should be taken to ensure that the groups are in position and ready before zero for each discharge so that the discharge will be simultaneous along the whole front.

(6)   Matches or fuses, for lighting the candles, will be issued to units by the Staff Captain. Precautions should be taken to keep them dry.

(7)   Smoke candles are quite harmless. They burn for two minutes. Each 'P' Bomb gives a thick smoke for one minute and fair smoke for about 15 minutes. The fuse burns for about 9 seconds.

(8)   The candles and bombs should be stored in dry dugouts and the candles should only be moved from them wrapped in waterproof sheets.

(9) Bombs and candles will be thrown as far as possible.

(10) In addition a smoke barrage will be formed on Z day on the left flank of the 70th Bde as follows:

    (a) 100 'P' Bombs will be thrown over the parapet from trench X 1/3, commencing at 5 minutes before zero. The GOC 70th Bde will arrange for this and will draw the 100 'P' Bombs from the Divisional Bomb Depot. The 'P' Bombs will only be thrown over if wind is from any point between SW and W, both inclusive.

    (b) Four 4-inch Stokes Mortars will open fire from the vicinity of York Street at 4 minutes before zero and will continue firing till 10 minutes after zero. The approximate line the bombs will be fired is up the road running through squares X.1.b and R.32.c. The OC M Sec., No. 5 Special Bn is making all arrangements for this. The four-inch mortars will fire only if the wind is blowing from any point between SW and NW, both inclusive.

    (c) There will be no smoke barrage on the right flank of the 8th Division.

25TH INFANTRY BRIGADE

The following will be added to Brigade Preliminary Operation Order No. 100

V. (d) The strong points detailed in paragraph V (a), (b), and (c) to be consolidated and held will be garrisoned by 1 platoon, 1 Lewis gun and 1 Vickers gun each (but see below), detailed from battalions as follows:

2nd Lincs, Points 47, 44, 10 (in first line) Point 22 (in second line).

2nd R. Berks, Points 78, 56 (in first line) Point 46, 43 (in second line).

1st R. Irish Rifles, Points 28 (in second line) Point 97 near 80, and such others northward as may appear necessary (in final objective).

2nd Rifle Brigade, Points 91, 09 and such others as may appear necessary (in final objective).

A general plan of what work will probably be required should be prepared before Z day by Commanding Officers concerned, in consultation with OC Home Counties, Field Coy R.E., and names of these several posts will be decided upon by Commanding Officers concerned. Please notify this Office before Z Day as to the names in question. Note. There will be no Vickers Gun in position at Point 56 (Front Line).

The following addition to Appendix C Programme for discharge of gas, will be made. The following Rocket Signals will be fired from Ovillers and Donnet Posts, commencing at 1.28:

Three pairs of Red Rockets from each Post at 30 seconds interval between pairs. The Officer Commanding the 1st R. Irish Rifles or 2nd Rifle Brigade (according to which night the discharge takes place) will be responsible for the firing of these rockets. They will only be fired provided the discharge of gas has taken place.

The OC Grenade Company will draw rockets for this purpose and hand them over to the OC Donnet Post.

H. Lloyd, Captain,
25th Inf. Bde.
16th June 1916.

25TH INFANTRY BRIGADE
OPERATION ORDER NO. 107.

TIME   Zero hour on Z day has been communicated to all units in this office No.
                        B.M.c/297/85 dated 29/6/1916.

REPORTS   2. (a)   All units will report to Brigade Headquarters their progress, and the sit-
                        uation at least once every hour, and at all times when there is any special
                        information to communicate to the Brigade Commander.

             (b)   All units will report to Brigade Headquarters when final movements prior
                        to zero have been completed. A wire or message using the code word
                        'Montigny' with the time will be sufficient.

             (c)   All battalions will also report when they have moved forward from their
                        assembly positions, and the 2nd Rifle Brigade will report when they are
                        clear of our present front line trenches.

DISTINGUISHING BADGES

             3. (a)   Brigade Observers will wear a black and white armband on both arms.

             (b)   All runners both brigade and battalion will wear a black armband with a
                        large R in white on the right arm. These men are to be allowed to go up
                        and down any trenches and are not to be stopped by the battle police.

             4.   After the divisional objective has been captured, the Centre Brigade
                        (25th) may possibly be withdrawn, if the situation permits, into Divisional
                        Reserve. In this event the 70th Brigade will extend to their right and the
                        23rd Brigade to their left.

WATCHES

             5.   Watches will be synchronised with Brigade Signal Office daily at 12.30
                        p.m. in addition to the usual checking at 8 a.m.

             6.   Brigade Advanced Headquarters will open at Ribble Street at 8.30 p.m.
                        30/6/1916.

             7.   The Brigadier wishes everyone the best of luck, and is confident that,
                        before we have done with him, the enemy will be sorry that he ever found
                        himself opposite the British Army.

Dated 30th June 1916   H. Lloyd,
Issued at 2.30 p.m.   Captain, Brigade Major 25th Inf. Bde.

APPENDIX V: COURTS MARTIAL AND DISCIPLINE

Abbreviations:

FP1	Field Punishment No. 1
FP2	Field Punishment No. 2
HL	Hard labour
PS	Penal servitude
SO	Superior officer
S	Sections of the Manual of Military Law:
S9.1a	Disobedience to a superior officer.
S11	Neglect to obey an order.
S18	(1) Malingering. (2) Wilfully injures himself or another soldier. (3) Delaying recovery. (4) Stealing, embezzling, or receiving stolen money, goods or property. (5) Any other offence of a fraudulent nature or any other disgraceful conduct.
S37.1	Strikes or otherwise ill-treats any soldier.
S40	Conduct, disorder, or neglect to the prejudice of good order and military discipline.

Field general courts martial

Date	Name	Charge	Sentence
19.11.1914 Laventie	Rfn Rogers	Drunkenness.	56 days FP1.
	Rfn Murphy	Drunkenness and theft.	2 years HL.
	Rfn Robinson	Drunkenness.	5 days FP1.
20.11.1914 Laventie	Rfn McCardle	Putting the success of an operation at risk.	3 months FP1.
	Rfn Barnes	do.	3 months FP1.
	Rfn McKay	do.	3 months FP1.
24.11.1914 Laventie	L/Cpl Gorman	Disobeying a SO.	21 days FP1.
26.11.1914 Laventie	Rfn Massey	Quitting post.	5 years PS.
	Rfn T. Rice	Quitting post.	5 years PS.
29.11.1914 Laventie	Rfn W. Dougan	Drunkenness and plundering.	3 years PS.
	Rfn P. McDermott	Asleep at post.	3 years PS.
	Rfn G. Smith	Being in search of plunder.	42 days FP1.
	Cpl J. McLoughlin	Drunkenness.	60 days FP1 and reduced in rank. Commuted to reduction in rank.
	Rfn J. Casey	Leaving post.	3 years PS commuted to 3 months FP.
	Rfn S. Massey	Leaving post.	do.
9.12.1914 Laventie	Rfn Sturgeon	Drunkenness.	2 months FP1.
	Sgt Maxwell	Drunkenness.	Reduced in rank.
	Sgt Thompson	Drunkenness.	Reduced in rank.
	Cpl Mannery	Drunkenness.	Reduced in rank.
11.12.1914 Laventie	L/Cpl J. Smith	Drunkenness.	2 months FP1.
	L/Cpl A. Gardiner	Drunkenness.	2 months FP1.
	Cpl W. Snowden	Drunkenness.	Reduced in rank and fined.
	Rfn W. McDowell	Sleeping at post.	3 years PS.
	Rfn R. Rogers	Disobedience.	5 years PS.

Date	Name	Charge	Sentence
16.12.1914 Laventie	Rfn J. McGuigan	Sleeping at post.	3 years PS.
	Rfn J. Warring	do.	3 years PS.
	Rfn M. Murray	Quitting post.	2 years HL.
18.12.1914 Laventie	Rfn J. Green	Sleeping at post.	3 years PS.
21.12.1914 Rouen	Rfn F. Toman	Drunkenness and desertion.	2 years HL. 18 months remitted.
	Rfn J. Brown	Desertion.	do.
	Rfn P. Kearney	Desertion.	do.
	Rfn J. McCarthy	Desertion.	3 months FP1. Guilty of absence only.
	Rfn J. Duffy	Desertion.	do.
22.12.1914 Laventie	L/Cpl G. Hill	Maiming himself.	2 years HL. Sentence quashed.
31.12.1914 Laventie	L/Cpl A. Maguiness	S40.	1 month FP1.
4.1.1915 Laventie	Rfn W. Scott	Sleeping at post.	5 years PS commuted to 2 years HL.
	Rfn A. Boyliss	Losing property and S9.1a.	3 years PS commuted to 1 year HL.
16.1.1915 Laventie	Rfn P. Duffy	Sleeping at post.	5 years PS commuted to 90 days FP1.
20.1.1915 Rouen	Cpl J. Kilpatrick	Desertion.	28 days FP1 and reduced in rank. Guilty of absence only.
3.2.1915 Laventie	L/Cpl D. Wilson	Drunkenness, disobedient and S40.	28 days FP1 and £1 fine.
13.2.1915 Laventie	Rfn W. McGrath	Quitting post and deserting.	15 years PS commuted to 3 months FP1.
	Rfn J. Collins	do.	do.
14.2.1915 Laventie	Rfn J. Hughes	do.	2 years HL commuted to 84 days FP1, guilty of absence only.
6.3.1915 La Gorgue	Rfn H. Andrews	Striking a SO.	5 years PS commuted to 84 days FP1.
9.3.1915 La Gorgue	Rfn F. Darcy	Quitting post.	3 months FP1, quashed.
16.3.1915 Havre	Cpl J. Reilly	Drunkenness.	Reduced in rank.
20.3.1915 In the field	Rfn J. Sheppard	Sleeping at post.	10 years PS commuted to 84 days FP1.
29.3.1915 Havre	Cpl J. Carroll	S11.2.	Reduced in rank.
Sailly	Rfn J. Kelly	Insubordinate and striking a SO.	2 years HL commuted to 3 months FP1.
	Rfn J. Stewart	Quitting post.	28 days FP1.
10.4.1915 Sailly	Rfn J. Hughes	Disobedience.	2 years HL.
20.4.1915 Fleurbaix	Rfn C. Skelt	Sleeping at post.	Not guilty.
	Rfn J. Kelly	S40.	84 days FP1. 14 days remitted.
26.4.1915 Havre	Rfn C. Sproule	Quitting post.	6 months HL commuted to 84 days FP1.
27.4.1915 Rouen	Rfn E. Kelly	Drunkenness and striking a SO.	3 months FP2.
1.5.1915 Laventie	Rfn J. Draper	Sleeping at post.	2 years HL.
3.5.1915 Laventie	Rfn J. Brennan	Drunkenness and striking a SO.	84 days FP1.
13.5.1915 Laventie	Rfn J. Reid	Desertion and breaking out of camp.	2 years HL commuted to 3 months FP1, not guilty of desertion.
	Sgt J. Cranston	Drunkenness and S40.	84 days FP1 and reduced. FP remitted.
14.5.1915 Laventie	Rfn W. Anderson	Sleeping at post.	Death commuted to 3 months FP1.
20.5.1915 Etaples	Rfn J. Scott	Drunkenness.	42 days FP2. Not confirmed.
21.5.1915 La Gorgue	Rfn T. Coglan	Desertion.	Death. Commuted to 5 years PS.
	Rfn J. Deeds	Insubordinate and threatening.	5 years PS commuted to 3 months FP1.
	Rfn W. Robinson	Drunkenness and striking a SO.	Death. Commuted to 3 months FP1.
5.6.1915 Laventie	Rfn J. McCarthy	Desertion.	Death. Commuted to 2 years HL.
	Rfn J. McIlroy	Desertion.	84 days FP1.
	Rfn T. Wilson	Desertion.	42 days FP1, guilty of absence only.

Date	Name	Charge	Sentence
	Rfn J. Eppleston	Desertion.	84 days FP1.
	Rfn J. McSherry	Desertion.	28 days FP1, guilty of absence only.
	Rfn J. McDowell	Desertion.	do.
15.6.1915 Havre	Cpl J. Scourgal	Drunkenness and breaking out of camp.	Reduced in rank.
	Rfn J. McCann	Insubordination.	42 days FP1.
19.6.1915 Laventie	Rfn J. Smith	Desertion.	28 days FP1, guilty of absence only.
	Rfn J. Deeds	Drunkenness and escaping confinement.	Not guilty.
22.6.1915 Laventie	Rfn J. Heffernan	Disobedience to a Cpl and S40.	42 days FP.
29.6.1915 Fleurbaix	Rfn H. Kennedy	Disobedience.	2 years HL.
2.7.1915 Fleurbaix	Rfn E. McAllister	S40.	28 days FP2.
13.7.1915 Fleurbaix	Cpl L. Carter	Drunkenness.	Reduced in rank.
24.7.1915 Fleurbaix	Rfn J. Hoey	Insubordinate and threatening.	56 days FP1.
	Rfn J. Royle	Quitting post.	56 days FP1.
	Rfn J. Reid	Absent and breaking out of barracks.	2 years HL, suspended.
	Rfn W. Dougan	Desertion.	3 years PS, suspended.
	L/Cpl J. Ryan	Drunkenness.	56 days FP1.
28.7.1915 Fleurbaix	Rfn C. Andrews	S40.	60 days FP1, 42 days remitted.
	Rfn D. Redmond	Sleeping at post.	Death. Commuted to 56 days FP1.
29.7.1915 Fleurbaix	Rfn J. Reid	Absent, insubordinate and breaking out of barracks.	84 days FP1.
5.8.1915 Fleurbaix	Cpl W. Bickerton	Absent and breaking out of camp.	Reduced in rank.
13.8.1915 Fleurbaix	Rfn J. McIlroy	S40.	84 days FP1.
	Rfn A. Johnston	Sleeping at post.	Death. Commuted to 2 years imprisonment, suspended sentence.
19.8.1915 Sailly	Rfn J. Coogan	Drunkenness.	28 days FP1.
	L/Cpl P. Walsh	Drunkenness.	42 days FP1, 14 days remitted.
20.8.1915 Havre	Rfn C. Sproule	Offence against inhabitant.	90 days HL.
27.8.1915 Calais	Rfn J. Robinson	Drunkenness and absent and breaking out of barracks.	84 days FP1.
30.8.1915 Sailly	L/Cpl P. Sands	Desertion.	Executed.
	Rfn T. Coughlan	Desertion and losing property.	Guilty of absence only and losing property. 84 days FP1 and fined £7.50.
10.9.1915 Fleurbaix	Rfn T. Owens	Absent and breaking out of camp.	56 days FP1.
	Rfn J. Epplestone	do.	do.
17.9.1915 Fleurbaix	Rfn G. Harrison	Drunkenness.	28 days FP1.
	Rfn W. Thompson	Theft.	Not guilty.
22.9.1915 Fleurbaix	Cpl J. Johnstone	Drunkenness, insubordinate, threatening and losing property.	28 days FP1, reduced in rank and stoppage of pay. Stoppage of pay remitted.
9.10.1915 In the field	Cpl W. Atkinson	S40.	Reduced in rank.
16.10.1915 Fleurbaix	Rfn G. Hoey	S40.	84 days FP1.
	Rfn H. Lindsay	S40.	do.
	Rfn W. Richardson	S40.	do.
	Rfn H. Hoey	S40.	do.
21.10.1915 Fleurbaix	Rfn E. Weir	Drunkenness.	56 days FP1.
2.11.1915 Sailly	Rfn J. Sheppard	Drunkenness and absent and breaking out of barracks.	2 years HL commuted to 84 days FP1.
	Rfn G. Harrison	do.	1 year HL commuted to 84 days FP1.
10.11.1915 Fleurbaix	L/Cpl J. Smith	Drunkenness.	56 days FP1.
	L/Cpl M. Brennan	Drunkenness.	70 days FP1.

Date	Name	Charge	Sentence
7.12.1915 Lercus	CSM W.H. Simner	Drunkenness.	Reduced to Sgt.
	CSM J. Tonge	Drunkenness.	Reduced to Sgt.
9.12.1915 Calais	Rfn J. Coogan	Striking a QM Sgt and drunkenness.	Not guilty.
11.12.1915 Lercus	Rfn H. Fitzpatrick	Desertion.	15 years PS commuted to 2 years HL, suspended sentence.
14.12.1915 Lercus	Rfn R. Bradley	S40.	84 days FP1.
27.12.1915 Lercus	Rfn J. Graham	Drunkenness and absent and breaking out of camp.	56 days FP1.
	Sgt J. Molloy	Drunkenness.	Not guilty.
	L/Cpl T. McManus	Drunkenness.	28 days FP1.
8.1.1916 Sercus	Rfn W. Sterrit	S40.	Not guilty.
	L/Cpl J. Steele	Drunkenness.	56 days FP1.
17.1.1916 Fleurbaix	Sgt J. Molloy	Absent, breaking out of camp and S40(2).	7 days stoppage of pay.
	Sgt F. Lloyd	do.	Not guilty.
	Sgt H. Ransley	Drunkenness.	Reduced in rank.
21.1.1916 Avie	Rfn J.N. Shannon	S40 and S18.2.	Not guilty.
1.2.1916 Fleurbaix	Rfn A. McKitterick	Desertion.	6 months HL commuted to 84 days FP1, absent only.
5.2.1916 Fleurbaix	Rfn J. Bowers	Desertion.	2 years HL, sentence quashed.
	Rfn O. Roberts	S40.	84 days FP1.
17.2.1916 Sailly	Rfn T. Latimer	Desertion.	6 months HL commuted to 3 months FP1, absent only.
22.2.1916 Fleurbaix	Rfn E. Reilly	Striking a SO.	3 years PS commuted to 2 years HL suspended sentence.
	Rfn T. MacDonald	Striking a SO and drunkenness.	18 months HL.
	Rfn I. Donaghty	Drunkenness.	35 days FP1.
	L/Cpl P. Dempsey	Absent and breaking out of barracks.	6 months HL commuted to 84 days FP1.
12.3.1916 Fleurbaix	Rfn W. Steed	Absent and breaking out of camp.	90 days FP1.
15.3.1916 Fleurbaix	Rfn W. Ball	Drunkenness and resisting escort.	2 years imprisonment commuted to 90 days FP1.
18.3.1916 Fleurbaix	CQMS J. Leveritt	Drunkenness.	Reduced in rank.
	Rfn P. Walsh	Quitting post.	3 years PS commuted to 2 years HL suspended sentence.
31.3.1916 Flesselles	L/Cpl C. O'Neill	Absent and breaking out of camp.	9 months HL, suspended sentence.
	Rfn W. Murphy	Sleeping at post.	1 year HL, suspended.
20.4.1916 Dernancourt	Rfn J. Gribbon	Cowardice.	Death. Commuted to 15 years PS, suspended sentence.
	Rfn J. Kane	Cowardice.	do.
	a/Sgt S.J. McIlwaine	Cowardice.	Not guilty.
25.4.1916 Vielle Chapelle	Rfn P. Mullen	Drunkenness and S40.	1 year HL and £1 fine.
	L/Cpl J. Graham	Absent and breaking out of camp.	9 months HL.
28.4.1916 Havre	Rfn W. Day	Disobedience.	14 days FP2.
2.5.1916 Havre	Rfn J. Broion	Absent and breaking out of camp and drunkenness.	35 days FP1.
6.5.1916 Millencourt	L/Cpl T. Carey	Absent and breaking out of camp.	6 months HL. Suspended sentence.

Date	Name	Charge	Sentence
10.5.1916 Millencourt	Rfn L. Keating	Cowardice.	1 year HL.
	L/Cpl W. Gribbin	Cowardice.	Not guilty.
In the field	Rfn P. Duggan	Cowardice.	3 years PS.
18.5.1916 Millencourt	L/Cpl J. Hill	Striking a SO and drunkenness.	1 year HL.
	Rfn D. Boardman	do.	1 year HL.
27.5.1916 Hénencourt	Rfn H. Coughlan	S40.	2 months FP1.
6.6.1916 Havre	Rfn T. Donnelly	S40.	56 days FP1.
9.6.1916 Hénencourt	L/Cpl J. Martin	Drunkenness.	18 months HL commuted to 3 months FP1 .
	Rfn J. McNamara	Drunkenness.	1 year HL commuted to 3 months FP1.
	Rfn J. Daragh	Drunkenness.	do.
7.7.1916 Havre	Rfn J. Brown	Absent and breaking out of camp and drunkenness.	63 days HL.
17.7.1916 Hazebrouck	Rfn W. Roach	Drunkenness.	42 days FP1.
21.7.1916 Béthune	Rfn T. Rodgers	Absent and breaking out of camp.	1 year HL.
14.8.1916 Labourse	Rfn P. Beake	Desertion.	7 years PS, suspended.
21.8.1916 Vermelles	Rfn G.W. Barton	Desertion.	Death. Commuted to 3 years PS, suspended.
26.8.1916 Vermelles	Rfn P. Massey	S18.	84 days FP1.
	L/Cpl J. Richardson	Quitting post.	2 years HL.
	Cpl J. Simpson	Quitting post.	Reduced in rank.
10.10.1916 Havre	Sgt D.P. Kelly	Drunkenness.	Reduced to Cpl.
12.10.1916 In the field	Rfn E. Kelly	Insubordination and drunkenness.	3 months FP1 and £1 fine.
18.10.1916 Arriares	Sgt J. Dowling	S.37.1.	Reduced to Cpl.
24.11.1916 Sailly	Sgt P.L. Fitzsimmons	Drunkenness.	Reprimanded, quashed.
	Cpl J.W. Leverett	Drunkenness.	Not guilty.
5.12.1916 Sorel	Rfn P. Blake	Offence against inhabitant.	84 days FP1.
9.12.1916 In the field	Rfn W. Day	Absent, breaking out of camp, drunkenness and resisting escort.	56 days FP1.
15.12.1916 Havre	Rfn E. McGrath	Disobedience.	84 days FP1.
In the field	Cpl H. Steele	S40 (2). Quashed.	3 months FP1 and reduced in rank.
21.12.1916 Laleu	Cpl J.F. Geraghty	Drunkenness.	Reduced in rank.
30.12.1916 Hazebrouck	Rfn W. Roach	Drunkenness.	90 days FP1.
25.1.1917 Havre	Sgt P. Ryan	Drunkenness.	Reduced in rank and fined £1.
29.1.1917 Le Foret	Rfn H. Coulter	Absent and breaking out of camp.	1 year HL, suspended.
1.3.1917 In the field	Rfn M. Maguire	S40.	Not guilty.
	Rfn M. English	Threatening and S40.	3 years PS.
8.3.1917 Havre	Rfn R.H. Graham	Theft and S40.	Not guilty.
11.3.1917 Havre	Rfn J. Brown	Drunkenness.	90 days FP1.
12.3.1917 Clery	Rfn M. Gargin	Disobedience and S40.	28 days FP1.
22.3.1917 In the field	Rfn D. Day	Theft.	Not guilty.
?.3.1917 In the field	Rfn A. Fairley	Disobedience and S40.	28 days FP1. Not confirmed.
5.4.1917 Manancourt	A/Sgt J. Thompson	Absent and breaking out of camp.	Reduced in rank.
	Cpl D. Broderick	do.	Reduced in rank.
	L/Cpl J.G. Cook	Theft.	3 months FP1.
11.4.1917 In the field	Rfn T. Thompson	Absent and breaking out of camp and S40.	84 days FP2.

Date	Name	Charge	Sentence
12.4.1917 Aizecourt	Sgt G. Lamb	S40 and S11.	28 days FP1 and reduced in rank. FP remitted.
	Rfn R. Davies	S40.	90 days FP1.
16.4.1917 In the field	Rfn W. Day	Drunkenness and theft.	Not guilty.
23.4.1917 Heudicourt	Cpl J. Graham	Desertion.	Not guilty.
1.5.1917 Heudicourt	Rfn W. Day	Offence against inhabitant, insubordination and escaping confinement.	9 months HL.
	Rfn C. Andrews	Desertion (2).	Death. Commuted to 5 years PS, suspended.
9.5.1917 Sorel le Grand	Rfn M. Gargin	Desertion and escaping confinement.	2 years HL. Guilty of absence only.
27.5.1917 Nurlu	Rfn M. Kenny	S40.	1 year HL. Commuted to 3 months FP1.
	Rfn W. Kertland	Absent and breaking out of camp.	5 days FP1.
31.5.1917 Havre	A/Cpl J. Watson	Absent, breaking out of camp, drunkenness and resisting escort.	Fined £1.
1.6.1917 Méricourt	CSM P. Madden	Drunkenness.	Reduced in rank.
8.6.1917 Strazeele	Cpl E. Stokes	Drunkenness.	Reduced in rank.
	L/Cpl H. Conroy	Drunkenness.	90 days FP1.
	Rfn T. Broaders	Violence to SO and disobedience.	10 years PS. Commuted to 2 years HL, suspended.
10.6.1917 Strazeele	L/Cpl J. Kennedy	Drunkenness.	42 days FP1. 28 days remitted.
21.6.1917 Steenvoorde	Rfn W. Morton	Striking a SO and insubordination.	2 years HL.
26.6.1917 Near Steenvoorde	Cpl M. Dunne	Absent and breaking out of camp.	Reduced in rank.
	Rfn W. Simpson	Drunkenness.	35 days FP1.
3.7.1917 In the field	Rfn J. Ward	Drunkenness and S40.	56 days FP1.
9.8.1917 In the field	A/Sgt W. Benson	Drunkenness, S40 and S37.1.	Reduced in rank.
10.8.1917 Rouen	Rfn J. Clarke	S40.	6 months HL, 1 month remitted.
13.8.1917 In the field	Rfn A. Whiteside	S40.	Not guilty.
26.8.1917 Borre	Cpl A. Murray	Absent and breaking out of camp.	Reduced in rank and 28 days pay stopped.
	Rfn H. Light	Desertion.	84 days FP1, guilty of absence only.
7.9.1917 In the field	Rfn J.G. Hagan	Desertion.	2 years HL, suspended sentence.
14.9.1917 Havre	Rfn J. Brown	Drunkenness and losing property.	3 months FP1 and stoppage of pay.
	Rfn M. Flynn	Drunkenness.	60 days stoppage of pay.
20.9.1917 In the field	L/Cpl P. McCarthy	S40.	Not guilty.
22.9.1917 In the field	L/Sgt J. Dunn	S40.	Reduced in rank.
1.10.1917 St Omer	Cpl R. Gaw	Drunkenness.	90 days FP1 and reduced in rank.
2.10.1917 In the field	Rfn P. Diamond	Theft.	Trial discontinued.
5.10.1917 Havre	Rfn P. Lavery	Drunkenness and S11(2).	90 days FP1.
6.10.1917 In the field	Rfn G.H. Culham	Cowardice.	Not guilty.
	L/Cpl W. Armour	S40.	14 days FP1.
15.10.1917 In the field	Rfn G. Harding	S40.	90 days FP1.
17.10.1917 In the field	L/Cpl H. Buston	Absent and breaking out of camp.	90 days FP1.
	Rfn M. Kenny	Insubordination.	42 days FP1.
18.10.1917 In the field	Rfn J. Smyth	Drunkenness, theft, absent and breaking out of camp.	1 year HL.

Date	Name	Charge	Sentence
25.10.1917 In the field	Rfn H. Jeswood	S40.	42 days FP1.
31.10.1917 In the field	Rfn D. Flanaghan	Desertion.	Not guilty.
7.11.1917 In the field	Rfn R. Bullock	Insubordinate and S40.	2 months FP1.
15.11.1917 In the field	Rfn J. Clinton	S40.	Not guilty.
26.11.1917 In the field	Rfn F. Fitzsimmons	Desertion.	28 days FP1, guilty of absence.
28.11.1917 In the field	Rfn J. Gibbons	Desertion.	Death. Commuted to 15 years PS.
1.12.1917 In the field	Rfn W. Roach	Theft and S40.	1 year HL, 4 months remitted.
13.12.1917 In the field	Rfn J. Willott	Desertion.	Not guilty.
	Rfn A. Hooten	Drunkenness.	56 days FP1.
	Rfn W. Lee	Drunkenness.	56 days FP1.
	Rfn W. Hamilton	Desertion.	Not guilty.
14.12.1917 In the field	Rfn S. Cohen	Desertion.	28 days FP1, guilty of absence only.
15.12.1917 In the field	Rfn J. Phillips	Desertion.	Not guilty.
	Rfn H. Wilson	Desertion.	28 days FP1, guilty of absence only.
16.12.1917 In the field	Rfn W. Liebert	Desertion.	Not guilty.
	Rfn J. Totten	Desertion.	42 days FP1.
17.12.1917 In the field	Rfn A. Johnston	S40.	28 days FP1.
19.12.1917 In the field	L/Cpl D. Dunlop	S40.	Not guilty.
31.12.1917 In the field	L/Cpl H. Heatley	S40.	42 days FP1.
1.1.1918 In the field	Rfn F. Grindy	Absent and breaking out of camp.	28 days FP1.
13.1.1918 In the field	L/Cpl P. Cantwell	Desertion.	90 days FP1, guilty of absence only.
25.1.1918 In the field	Rfn J. McConville	Desertion.	18 months HL, commuted to 90 days FP1, guilty of absence only.
27.1.1918 In the field	Sgt J. Robert	Absent and breaking out of camp.	Reduced to Cpl.
29.1.1918 In the field	Rfn G. Hegarty	Theft.	6 months HL.
3.2.1918 In the field	Rfn E. Quirke	S40.	3 months FP1.
3.3.1918 In the field	Rfn J. McKendry	Absent and breaking out of camp.	56 days FP1.
	Rfn J. Thompson	Insubordinate and threatening.	2 months FP1.
7.3.1918 In the field	Rfn M. Lindsay	S40.	90 days FP1.
	Rfn A. Fowler	Desertion.	42 days FP1, guilty of absence only.
11.3.1918 In the field	Rfn G. Roache	Offence against inhabitant and drunkenness.	56 days FP1.
24.3.1918 In the field	L/Cpl T. Kelly	Striking a SO.	1 year HL, 6 months remitted.
6.4.1918 In the field	Rfn W. Morgan	Quitting post.	3 months FP1, commuted to 56 days FP2.
15.4.1918 In the field	Rfn J. McConaghey	Insubordinate and threatening.	42 days FP1.
22.4.1918 In the field	Rfn H. Jerwood	Absent and breaking out of camp, escaping confinement.	90 days FP1.
6.5.1918 In the field	Rfn A. McCaw	S40.	56 days FP1.
13.5.1918 In the field	Cpl T. Egan	Drunkenness and theft.	Reduced in rank and fined £1.
	Rfn J. Totten	Desertion.	10 years PS. 3 years remitted, suspended sentence.
16.5.1918 In the field	Rfn J. Johnston	Losing property.	28 days FP1 and stoppage of pay.
20.5.1918 In the field	Rfn A. Munday	Desertion.	6 months HL. Commuted to 90 days FP1, guilty of absence only.
3.6.1918 In the field	Rfn J. McClean	Drunkenness.	Fined £1.
1.7.1918 In the field	Rfn W. Fitzsimmons	Offence against inhabitant, absent and breaking out of camp, drunkenness.	6 months HL. Commuted to 90 days FP1.

Date	Name	Charge	Sentence
8.7.1918 In the field	Rfn J. McKeown	Violence to a SO, threatening.	28 days FP1.
	Rfn F.E. McCann	Absent and breaking out of camp.	50 days FP1.
	Rfn W. Fitzsimmons	Offence against inhabitant, absent and breaking out of camp.	6 months HL. Commuted to 90 days FP1.
	Rfn J. English	S40.	6 months HL. Suspended sentence.
12.7.1918 In the field	Rfn F. Trickett	S40.	Not guilty.
23.7.1918 In the field	Sgt W. Morris	S40.	Not guilty.
3.9.1918 In the field	Rfn P. Hughes	Disobedience.	Not guilty.
	Rfn T. Doherty	Disobedience.	Not guilty.
	Rfn T. Hardman	Disobedience.	Not guilty.
	Rfn J. Rankin	Disobedience.	Not guilty.
	Rfn D. Watson	Disobedience.	Not guilty.
	Rfn J. Ryan	Disobedience.	Not guilty.
	Rfn J. Casey	Disobedience.	Not guilty.
	Rfn J. Conroy	Disobedience.	Not guilty.
	Rfn S. Caughey	Disobedience.	Not guilty.
	Rfn H. Caulfield	Disobedience.	Not guilty.
	Rfn D. McMillan	Disobedience.	Not guilty.
	Rfn T. Finan	Disobedience.	Not guilty.
	Rfn W. Dullan	Disobedience.	Not guilty.
	Rfn H. Griffiths	Disobedience.	Not guilty.
	Rfn E. Dolan	Disobedience.	Not guilty.
	Rfn P. Craney	Disobedience.	Not guilty.
	Rfn J. Megraw	Disobedience.	Not guilty.
	Rfn T. Hamil	Disobedience.	Not guilty.
11.9.1918 In the field	Rfn L.R. Phelps	Desertion.	56 days FP1. Guilty of absence only.
18.9.1918 In the field	Rfn H. Macree	Desertion.	9 months HL. Guilty of absence only.
	Rfn J. Gumbrell	Escaping confinement.	72 days FP1.
25.9.1918 In the field	Rfn W. Kelly	Self inflicted wound.	21 days FP1.
10.10.1918 In the field	Rfn W. Aicken	Absent and breaking out of camp, resisting escort.	1 year HL. Suspended sentence.
21.10.1918 In the field	Rfn W. Fitzsimmons	Drunkenness and escaping confinement.	56 days FP1.

General courts martial

Date	Name	Charge	Sentence
2.11.1915 Rouen	Lt. C.R.B. Dawes	Drunkenness.	Severe reprimand.
2.6.1916 Hénencourt	Capt. E. ffrench-Mullen	S40.	Acquitted.
1.3.1918 In the field	2/Lt. H. McIntosh	Drunkenness.	Forfeiture of seniority and severe reprimand.
10.5.1918 Boulogne	2/Lt. T.H.R. Browne	Drunkenness.	Severe reprimand.

A rough analysis of the Field General Courts Martial produced the following:

OFFENCE	AMOUNT	PERCENTAGE
Offences against an inhabitant	3	1.0
Cowardice	7	2.3
Desertion	44	14.6
Absence	22	7.3
Striking or violent	10	3.3
Insubordination	7	2.3
Disobedience	24	7.9
Quitting post	13	4.3
Drunkenness	53	17.6
Loss of property	2	.7
Theft	9	3.0
Resisting escort	1	.4
Escaping confinement	1	.4
Misc. and multiple offences	103	34.2
Self-inflicted wound	2	.7

The Battalion had 301 men court martialled on the Western Front. The cases above show the offences that were considered of serious concern and warranted deterrent action by the CO. This list excludes cases that were settled by agreement between the CO and the person concerned without recourse to a formal trial. *Laurie*, 8 February 1915: 'We have certain worries with some of our men who have not been brought up in the strict discipline really required for a continental war.' The final sentences, or results, of these courts-martial are summarized below:

Death	1
Penal Servitude	13
Hard labour	30
FP1	132
FP2	5
Reduced/reprimanded	37
Fines	4
Quashed/not confirmed	6
Suspended sentence	20
Not guilty/acquitted	48

Trial of 8225 Rfn (L/Cpl) Peter Sands

Battalion Routine Order 369 of 25 February 1915 granted leave to the UK, from 26 February 1915 to 1 March 1915 inclusive, to 6250 Sgt Marshall, A Coy, 6820 Sgt Kettle and 8138 Sgt W. Whelan, B Coy, and 8225 L/Cpl Sands, D Coy. Battalion

Order 562 of 1 April 1915: '8225 L/Cpl Sands, D Coy, having deserted from 1st March is struck off the strength of the battalion.'

Sands, the husband of Elizabeth Sands, 74 Abyssinia Street, was apprehended at Belfast on the afternoon of 7 July 1915 by Police Constable Joseph W. Clarke of Roden Street Barracks. Based on information received, Clarke made the arrest on a charge of being absent without leave from 1st RIR. Having been cautioned, Sands admitted the offence. The report noted that he was aged 26, dark brown hair, blue eyes, 5 foot 9 inches tall, fresh complexion with a sandy moustache, tattoos on both arms and had joined the Army at Belfast, 24 July 1906. It is unclear why he was not tried at Belfast.

He was sent under escort from the Depot at Belfast to 3rd RIR at Dublin on 11 July. From here he was sent under escort to France with a draft for 2nd RIR and handed over at the Base. Having rejoined 1st RIR, Lt.-Col. Daunt charged him under Section 12 (1a), 27 August: 'When on Active Service deserting His Majesty's Service in that he, at Estaires, on 2nd March 1915, was absent from 1st Bn The Royal Irish Rifles until apprehended at Belfast on 7th July 1915 by the civil power.' That same day Brig.-General R.B. Stephens ordered that Sands should be tried by FGCM.

The trial took place, 30 August, at Sailly. President of the court was Major F.W. Greatwood, 2nd Lincolnshire Regt, the other members being Capt. A.J. Ross, 1st RIR, and Lt. R.B. Leslie, 2nd Lincolnshire Regt. The plea was not guilty.

Witnesses for the prosecution:

2/Lt. J.J. Hart, a/Adjutant, 1st RIR, produced evidence of Sands arrest at Belfast, the paperwork regarding the leave granted and the extract from Battalion Orders where he had been struck off as a deserter.

8138 Sgt W. Whelan, 1st RIR, stated: 'At Laventie on the 25th February 1915, the accused, L/Cpl Sands, and I were granted four days leave to proceed to the United Kingdom. We proceeded home together and he should have returned with me on the 1st March. He did not report himself on that date at Victoria Station.'

Sands made the following statement in his defence: 'On the 2nd March 1915 I reported myself at Belfast Depot, as I had lost my warrant and I needed a fresh one to get back to France. Cpl Wright (No. 7663) whom I saw said he knew nothing about me. I then went away. Had I intended to desert I would have worn plain clothes, but up to the time I was arrested I always wore uniform.'

Evidence as to character: 2/Lt. J.J. Hart stated: 'I produce A.F. B122, Temporary Conduct Sheet of the accused; the original is not forthcoming. His date of enlistment is 24th July 1906.' Sands was found guilty and sentenced 'To suffer death by being shot.' Brig.-Gen. Stephens confirmed the sentence but reserved a decision.

He wrote to HQ, 8th Division, 3 September:

With reference to the sentence of death passed on No. 8225 Rifleman (Lance Cpl) P. Sands, 1st Royal Irish Rifles, I beg to report:

1. His Commanding Officer gives him a very good character both in ordinary behaviour and as a fighting man.
2. It is not possible to say that his offence was deliberate to avoid a particular duty, but he was absent during the fighting on May 9th and he was away over four months.

3. The state of discipline in the battalion is improving but has not been very satisfactory. As, however, this offence took place four months ago, it has nothing to do with the present state of the battalion.

4. I consider this a bad case of desertion and I recommend that the sentence be carried out.

Major-General H. Hudson, 8th Division Commander, 4 September, forwarded the recommendation to HQ III Corps with the following note: 'I concur with the remarks of the Brigadier-General Commanding, 25th Infantry Brigade, and recommend that the sentence be carried out.' Lt.-General W.P. Pulteney, Commanding III Corps, 6 September, to 1st Army: 'I see no reason why the extreme penalty should not be carried out.' General Douglas Haig, Commanding 1st Army, 7 September, to A.G., GHQ: 'This is a bad case and I recommend that the extreme penalty be carried out.'

Adjutant General, GHQ, to GOC, 1st Army, 12 September: 'In confirmation of my telegram No. A (b) 966 of today, please note that the C-in-C has approved of the sentence … The return of the proceedings direct to Deputy Judge Advocate General at GHQ after promulgation is requested.'

DAAG, HQ, 1st Army, to HQ, III Corps, 13 September: 'The C-in-C has confirmed the sentence of Death in the case of No. 8225 Rifleman (L/Cpl) P. Sands, 1st Bn Royal Irish Rifles. Please return after promulgation. Will you inform me of the date, time and place of execution.' HQ III Corps to 8th Division, the same day: 'For action and report in due course.'

Lt.-Col. Daunt promulgated the courts' findings, 14 September. 8th Division to III Corps, the following day: 'Necessary action taken and proceedings returned herewith. The sentence was carried out at Fleurbaix at 5 a.m. on 15th September.'

8th Division to III Corps, that day: 'With reference to your No. C.M./152/15, dated 13th instant, forwarding proceedings of FGCM in the case of No. 8225, Rifleman (L/Cpl) P. Sands, 1st Bn R. Irish Rifles, which have been returned to you today under separate minute – I forward herewith minute from the A.P.M. of this Division notifying that the sentence had been carried out and also the certificate of death. Will you kindly acknowledge receipt.'

Report from Major Ronald M. Heath, a/A.P.M., 8th Division, 15 September: 'The sentence on No. 8225 Rfn (L/Cpl) Sands, P., 1st Royal Irish Rifles, was carried out under my supervision at 5 a. m. 15/9/15. Certificate of death is attached herewith.'

Lt. C.L.G. Powell, RAMC, MO I/C, 1st RIR: 'I hereby certify that this morning, September 15th at 5 a.m., I attended the execution of 8225 Rfn Sands, 1st Royal Irish Rifles, and that I afterwards examined him and found him to be dead.' III Corps forwarded these papers to 1st Army the next day. PRO reference O71/4320.

Trial of 8335 Rfn Thomas Coughlan

The files of FGCM have mostly been destroyed except in circumstances where the accused was executed.

Rfn Coughlan was tried along with L/Cpl Sands and his papers have therefore survived.

Charge Sheet signed by Lt.-Col. Daunt, OC 1st RIR, 24 August 1915:

'The accused, No. 8335 Rifleman Thomas Coughlan, 1st Bn The Royal Irish Rifles, a soldier of the Regular forces, is charged with

'1st Charge "When on Active Service, deserting His Majesty's service" in that he, at Rue du Quesne, on 12th August 1915, absented himself from the 1st Bn The Royal Irish Rifles, until he reported himself at Trench Headquarters on 15th August 1915. Section 12(1a) A.A.

'2nd Charge "Losing by neglect his equipment" in that he, at Rue du Quesne, on or about 12th August 1915, was deficient of one Government bicycle, value seven pounds, ten shillings (£7/10/0). Section 24(2) A.A.'

The plea was not guilty on both charges. Witnesses for the prosecution:

7418 L/Cpl A. Jenkins, 1st RIR: 'On the afternoon of the 11th August 1915, I personally ordered the Signallers to parade outside their Billet the following morning at 10 a.m. I don't know if the accused was present when I gave this order. On the 12th August the accused was absent from parade at 10 a.m. I did not see him again until 9.30 a.m. on the 16th August at Trench Headquarters. About a fortnight previous to this I placed a Government Bicycle in charge of accused and, when he rejoined on 16th August, he was deficient of this bicycle.'

9405 L/Cpl D. McCourt, 1st RIR: 'On 12th August 1915, I was Acting Orderly Sgt of the Head Quarter Party. L/Cpl Jenkins reported to me that the accused was absent off 10 a.m. Parade. On the evening of the 11th August I read out, at the Signallers Billet, that the battalion would proceed to the trenches on the evening of 12th August. The accused was present when I read out this order.'

5710 RSM W. Carroll, 1st RIR: 'At Trench Head Quarters at 6 p.m. on 15th August 1915 the accused, who had been reported absent since 10 a.m. on 12th August 1915, reported himself to me. I had him confined in the HQ's Guard Room.'

The accused, in his defence, made the following statement: 'On the 12th August 1915, at about 9.30 a.m., I went on my bicycle, which was in my charge, to see a friend of mine at D Coy's billet. I left the bicycle outside the billet and went in myself. When I came out about five minutes later the bicycle was gone. I asked the sentry if he had seen anyone take away a bicycle and he said he had seen some soldier take a bicycle and go in the direction of Fleurbaix. I then went in search, not wishing to lose the bicycle. I hunted round Fleurbaix, next to Bac St Maur, and when darkness came I slept in a farm. Next morning I continued my search and went to Estaires. I wandered all round the place hunting for the bicycle as I did not want to return without it. I had no intention of going absent at all. On the 15th August I had to give up hope of recovering the bicycle and then returned to the Battalion.'

2/Lt. J.J. Hart, a/Adjutant, 1st RIR, was the character witness: 'I produce A.F. B.122 which shows the accused enlisted on 22nd October 1906. There is only one entry on his sheet – for "Desertion on Active Service".'

Coughlan was found not guilty of desertion but guilty of absence without leave and guilty of losing the bicycle. He was sentenced to 84 days FP1 and to be put under stoppages of pay until he had made good the sum of £7.50 in respect of the bicycle. Brig.–Gen. Stephens confirmed the sentence.

PART TWO

Officers who served with the Battalion during the war

Abbott Capt. Cuthbert Sackville MC. Born 8.10.1893. Gazetted a 2/Lt. in 1st Norfolk Regt, 15.8.1914, and promoted Lt., 15.4.1915. He was attached to 1st RIR and rejoined from sick leave, 28.8.1915. While serving as a T/Capt. he transferred to his own corps and was struck off the strength of 1st RIR, 14.3.1916. Wounded during the course of the war and promoted to Capt., 9.1.1921. Put on half pay, 4.12.1921, and on retired pay, 3.12.1923. Entitlement to the 1914 Star with clasp indicates that he served early in the war. Closed file, ref: (34412).

Adeley Major Gerald Graham. Born 22.11.1887 at 4 Chichester Terrace, Belfast, the son of William James and Sarah Anne Adeley, later of Ben Eadan, Cavehill, Belfast. His father was a stockbroker and member of the Belfast Stock Exchange, trading at 32 Rosemary Street, Belfast.

Attended Campbell College until April 1903. Appointed a 2/Lt. in 3rd RIR 26.3.1908. Applied for a commission in the Regular Army, 11.8.1912, and received his commission, 5.2.1913. Single, residing at Ben Eadan, height 5 foot 7 inches, chest 34–37½ inches, weight 138 pounds. Served with 1st RIR in India. Joined the BEF in 1914 with the rank of Lt. Wounded during the battle of Neuve Chapelle, 10–13 March 1915. Promoted Capt. 28.11.1915. Later appointed acting Major and served with the RAF. Retired with the rank of Capt. in 1920. His address in 1938 was Pennfields, Penn Road, Beaconsfield. File ref: WO339/8623 83 (18012).

Adrain 2/Lt. William Kearns. Born 27.1.1896, the son of Robert Adrain, Ballyclare, Co. Antrim, and Mrs Jane Adrain, 5 Donard Villas, Belfast. Educated at the Model School, Belfast; the Royal Belfast Academical Institution, and was a member of Queen's University OTC. Applied for a commission 14.9.1915. Single, residing at 25 University Avenue, Belfast. Requested infantry, 'any unit'. Posted to 5th R. Irish and ordered to report to the School of Instruction, Palace Barracks, Holywood, 2.10.1915. Departed for the front 10.7.1916.

Attached to 1st RIR 18.7.1916. Killed in action 24.8.1916. A WO telegram was sent to David Kearns, Alderslyde, Cyprus Avenue, Belfast, 31 August. A short list of effects included a wallet with photographs and letters, and a 'wrist watch (no glass)'. Mrs Adrain wrote a letter to the WO, 29.9.1916, and declared that William was her son but that dealings should be made through his uncle and guardian David Kearns.

Irish Life 24.11.1916: 'He met his death while heroically helping to dig out men who had been buried in the debris when their trench was hit.'

Vermelles British Cemetery, Pas de Calais, III.P.17. File ref: 113738.

Aiken 2/Lt. John. Born at Belfast, 25.6.1896, the son of Mrs Maggie Aiken. Enlisted as Rfn 5/5356 in 5th RIR, 20.8.1914. Height 5 foot 3½ inches, weight 102 pounds, chest 30–32½ inches, religion Wesleyan, farm labourer, unmarried.

Appointed L/Cpl, 29.4.1915, and joined the BEF, France, 8.12.1915. Granted leave 22–9.2.1916. His file notes, without explanation, that he rejoined from a Field Ambulance 14 April. Wounded 15.7.1916, GSW to his right thigh and left forearm. Evacuated to the UK, 20 July, where he remained until discharged to a commission. Promoted Cpl 11 August, appointed L/Sgt 26 August, awarded a third class certificate at Holywood, 22 September, and qualified as an instructor in range finding at the School of Musketry, 28 October. Reduced to Cpl, 28 November, for 'misconduct' but appointed a paid L/Sgt, 4 December. Married Margaret Abigail Elliott, 21.12.1916, and was sent to No. 7 Officer Cadet Battalion at Fermoy, 5.5.1917, being discharged to a commission as a 2/Lt. in 4th RIR, 28 August.

Embarked for France, 29.10.1917, and was posted to 1st RIR, joining 8.11.1917. Wounded, 21.3.1918, 'GSW right wrist slight'. Embarked for the UK, 25 March, and granted leave 5–26 April. A MB at Durrington Camp, 13 May, noted that he was then recovering and fit for general service. He was ordered again to France but this was cancelled, 27 July, on account of his being transferred to the RAF. Arrived at the School of Aeronautics 3.8.1918. A letter, 18.1.1919, from the OC of No. 1 School of Aeronautics, Reading, noted that he had been struck off the strength upon being transferred to 3rd RIR at Durrington Camp, Salisbury Plain.

Placed under arrest, 19.9.1919 to 29.10.1919, having gone AWOL from the Right Wing Repatriation Camp, Morn Hill, Winchester, 9.9.1919 until arrested by the civil powers in Belfast. Sentenced to a reprimand, 29 October, and demobilized, 19.11.1919, medical rating A1. At that time he was farming and residing at 3 Deacon Street, Belfast.

A letter from the Ministry of Finance, Government of Northern Ireland, to the Army Records Office, Droitwich, 22.12.1948, stated Aiken was in the Government's employment. File ref: WO339/92516 4/83 & RAF 178626.

Allgood Capt. Bertram. Born 11.2.1874, the second son of Major-General George Allgood CB (1837–1907), Indian Army, latterly Chief Constable of Northumberland, and Elizabeth Allgood (died 1874). Educated at Eton and received his commission in the RIR from the militia, 15.5.1897, being promoted Lt., 10.8.1898, and Capt., 6.2.1904. At the time of the South African War he was serving with 1st RIR at Calcutta and so did not take part in that campaign. Continued to serve in India until 1905, when he reported for duty to the Depot at Belfast. Returned to India but again came back to Belfast, and then served for a time with 2nd RIR at Dover.

Appointed Adjutant of 4th RIR, 19.12.1911, keeping this appointment until retirement from the Army in February 1914, joining the Reserve of Officers. At the outbreak of the Great War he was called up for service and joined 3rd RIR, 14 August, but later went to the front with 1st RIR, 7 November. He was the first officer serving with 1st RIR to be killed during the war. Shot while taking his men into the trenches, 6.12.1914.

Laurie: 'I had ordered everyone to return, wished them good luck, and was waiting to see that they were all in whilst the Germans were sniping at us, when someone came and reported to me that a man had been shot through the shoulder by the same bullet which I afterwards heard was believed to have killed Capt. Allgood. The stretcher-bearers brought the latter in, and I sent for the doctor at once, but he could only pronounce him to be dead also! He was shot through the heart, and fell down remarking: "I am hit, but I am all right", and never spoke or moved again. He leaves one little daughter and a young wife ... He looked so peaceful lying on the stretcher.'

Bond of Sacrifice: 'He was very fond of hunting, polo, and all sport, and was a member of the Naval and Military Club. Captain Allgood married in April, 1913, Isa Cochrane, daughter of the late Arthur Bayley and Mrs Herbert Lyde, and left a daughter, born August, 1914.'

Estaires Communal Cemetery, Nord, I.B.2. File missing.

Alston Lt.-Col. James William. Born in 1873, the son of Robert Douglas and Margaret Elizabeth Alston. Attended the RMC and gazetted a 2/Lt. in the RIR, 10.10.1894. Promoted Lt. 3.2.1897, Capt. 17.10.1902, and Major 28.10.1912. Served in India and France with 1st RIR. Transferred to 2nd RIR, 22.11.1914, and took over command at Westoutre three days later.

Fr Gill, at the Kemmel Front: 'The "headquarters" of the battalion was, at this time, in a little ruined cottage a short distance from the front line. This place was inscribed in the official trench maps as *Alston House* after the CO, who was unfortunately killed later on.'

On leave to the UK, 10–17.1.1915. Killed 15.4.1915.

War Diary 2nd RIR: 'At 3.30 a.m. Major J.W. Alston proceeded to the trenches for the day, to observe the enemy's position. At 5 p.m., while observing with a trench periscope, a bullet obviously aimed for the top glass of the periscope, struck a sandbag on the parapet and, being deflected, struck the Major in the head above the left ear. He never recovered consciousness or spoke, and died at 5.15 p.m.'

The Burgoyne Diaries: 'Alston spent the day with Hutchison in his trench and, only a few minutes before he was killed, he was writing to his wife in H's dug-out and he remarked "today is the third anniversary of our wedding". He had an awful wound in his head ... [17 April] We buried

Major Alston at 6.30 p.m. A party of 100 men, besides a firing party, followed, and of course all the officers. He was laid in a little military cemetery at Dichebusche, and we four officers (Company), the Second-in-Command and the Adjutant lowered the coffin into the grave. The firing party presented arms at the end of the service. We could not fire volleys or sound bugles as we were within sight and hearing of the German lines.'

Lt. R.B. Hutchison, C Coy Commander, sent the following message to HQ: 'At about 5 p.m. a man came and told me the Commanding Officer was hit. I and Mr Whitmore rushed up to him where he was lying ... He was moaning and bleeding profusely from the head. He was very badly hit on the left-hand side of his head above the ear. I was with him until he died at about 5.15 p.m. He never spoke.'

Fr Gill: 'He was a kindly man and was greatly missed. His body was brought back to Dickebusch at midnight.' His wife was Daisy Adela Alston. Dickebusch New Military Cemetery, Ieper, D.11. He is named on a memorial tablet at Sandhurst. File missing.

Anderson Capt. David Mitchell. He was a member of 5th RIR rugby team in 1914. First went overseas 23.3.1915 and joined 2nd RIR, 28 March. Wounded 16.6.1915. On leave 5.6.1916. Joined 1st RIR, 4.9.1917, and was transferred to England, sick, 1.11.1917. Later served with the Indian Army. In 1928 he attended the 36th (Ulster) Division Officers OCA annual dinner. File missing.

Andrews Capt. David Ernest. Gazetted a 2/Lt. in 17th RIR, 4.10.1915, and joined 1st RIR from the base, 2.4.1916. Admitted to hospital 30 June.

Irish Times 5.7.1916: 'Information has been received that Second Lieutenant D.E. Andrews, Royal Irish Rifles, has been wounded ... Andrews, who is a son of Mr George Andrews, Glenburn Park, Belfast, obtained his commission from the ranks early in the present year.' Closed file, ref: (114763).

Andrews 2/Lt. Robert Hutchison. Born in 1889 at Ballybrick, Banbridge, Co. Down, the younger son of David and Essie Andrews. Enlisted, 10.8.1914, as Trooper 994 in the North Irish Horse. At that time he was a civil engineer, aged 25 years 2 months, height 5 foot 10½ inches, weight 157 pounds, chest 33½–37 inches, single, Presbyterian.

Sent to France 20.8.1914. The attestation form stated no previous military, militia, or naval service. The overseas date therefore appears most unusual. Appointed Trumpeter 9.1.1915. Sent to Cadet School, St Omer, for course of instruction, 28.7.1915. (His file, at this stage, has a contradictory entry showing home service 10.8.1914 to 29.8.1915, but the previously stated overseas dates are shown on the same page. There is then a note showing his medal entitlement to the 1914 Star. See confirmation from *Irish Life* below.) Commissioned into 1st RIR, 25.8.1915, and joined the battalion 4 September. Killed by shellfire at Bois Grenier, 25.9.1915. Next of kin was his father, residing at Fernhill, Ballynafern, Annaghlone, Banbridge. Cox & Co. forwarded Robert's field kit to him. The estate was left to his mother. There is also a reference to his sister, Mrs Carson.

Irish Life 26.11.1915: 'On the outbreak of the war he resigned an appointment in the West of Ireland under the Congested Districts Board and joined the North Irish Horse as a trooper. He accompanied his regiment to France in September, 1914 and was subsequently gazetted to the 1st Royal Irish Rifles.'

Bois Grenier Communal Cemetery, Nord, F.1. File ref: WO339/41974 110047.

Arnott Capt. Sir Lauriston John, Bt. Born 27.11.1890 at Stoke Bishop, Westbury, Bristol, the second son of John Alexander Arnott (1853–1940), a ship owner (Bristol Steam Navigation Co.), and Caroline Sydney Arnott, eldest daughter of Sir Frederick Martin Williams MP, Tregullow, Cornwall. The family lived at 12 Merrion Square, Dublin, and Woodlands, Cork. Siblings were John, Robert, Thomas, Margaret, and twins Mary and Lina. (According to *Thom's Directory* for

1912, his father was a Lt.-Col., 4th Cheshire Regt, JP and DL for Co. Cork and JP, Co. Dublin. He was also proprietor of the *Irish Times*, Arnott's department store, and the Phoenix Park Racecourse, Dublin. Succeeded his father as 2nd Baronet, 28.3.1898.)

He was living at 12 Merrion Square when he applied for the Royal Military Academy, 25.4.1909, and received his commission in 1910. A 1913 report on his standards reported that he was 'not satisfactory'. He had been dealt with by the GOC Lowlands Division, 24 June, on a charge of misconduct through heavy drinking at Stobbs Camp. All leave was stopped for one year and no clemency was to be shown for any repetition. Also strongly recommended for a court martial. He was a Lt. in 1st Cameronians (Scottish Rifles) when he was placed under arrest by the OC, 19.3.1914, having been witnessed as being 'Drunk and was misbehaving himself' in the Alhambra Theatre the previous night. List of potential witnesses for the prosecution were 2/Lts E.L. Ferry, C.D.W. Rooke, and J.H.C. Minchin, all of 1st Cameronians. There was no witness for the defence. An application for a General Court Martial was submitted 26 March. A report by the OC Lowland Division, to HQ Scottish Command that day, stated that he had been visited in Dublin by Arnott's father, Sir John Arnott, 2nd Bt., the proprietor of the *Irish Times*. He had made a 'most urgent appeal' that his son should be allowed to resign his commission in order to avoid a trial and the disgrace to the family. He also stated that after the South African War he had donated £18,000 to the orphans and widows fund and had received the personal thanks of HRH The Duke of Connaught. The OC also stated that he was concerned for the good name of the Cameronians and therefore recommended that Arnott should be allowed to resign. The GOC Scottish Command acceded to the resignation request 30.3.1914. The Army Council agreed the following month. Lt. Arnott submitted his resignation application, 13 April, and the WO approved, 1 May. His total service with the Scottish Rifles was noted as 7½ years.

Enlisted as Rfn 1312 in 3rd RIR at Dublin, 3.11.1914. Single, 5 foot 11 inches tall, chest 35–37½ inches, and weight 147 pounds. Appointed an unpaid L/Cpl, 6.11.1914, and a/Sgt, 9.11.1914. Went overseas and joined D Coy 2nd RIR two days later.

The Burgoyne Diaries: ' ... my acting Sergeant Major is young Arnott, son of Sir John Arnott, an ex-lieutenant of (I think) the Scottish Borderers.'

Wounded in the leg at Kemmel, 27.12.1914. Capt. Burgoyne gave some extra details of this incident: 'Early about 5.30 a.m. I woke up my Sergeant, who shared my dug-out and told him to go out and serve each man with a tot of rum, before it got too light, as during the day we cannot move along the lines at all. He went off, the Company Orderly Boyd, carrying the rum jar; and returned about three-quarters of an hour later smelling strong of the stuff, having done one half of the company. He was very talkative and chatted on to me till about 6.30, when the sky was getting quite pink and everything showed clear; I told him to hurry up and serve out a tot to the other half of the company, and to be careful. Off the two of them went; an hour later Boyd burst in on me "Sergeant X has been hit Sir". Apparently the two of them were crossing an open bit of ground, hidden from the Huns immediately in front, but in full view of a sniper's post to our right. A bullet hit the Sergeant in the calf of the leg, another drilled a neat hole through the welt of Boyd's boot, never even reddened the skin of his foot. Boyd dropped the demijohn and dragged X into the trench, to be at once abused by the frozen men for letting go of the rum. However, X was not badly hit.'

Returned to the UK on leave 3.1.1915 until 24.3.1915 when he was promoted to a commission. Wounded, 24.6.1915, at Laventie, while serving with 1st RIR. He left the unit that day and embarked Dieppe–Dover 29 July.

Irish Times 2.7.1915: 'He was struck by a bullet, and has sustained a compound fracture of the right arm. Lieutenant Arnott had not long returned to the front after his recovery from another wound which he received some months ago in the trenches. Sir John Arnott's first and third sons, Captain John Arnott, of the 15th Hussars, and Second Lieutenant Robert John Arnott, of the

King's Royal Rifle Corps, are also on active service with their regiments at the front.' Capt. John (Punch) Arnott MC, was killed in action, 30.3.1918, at Narfuste, France, aged 32.

A MB awarded three months leave from 23.8.1915 and, on 8.2.1916, declared him unfit for twelve months, his injury being thought likely to be permanent. Promoted to Capt. 18.9.1915. He was returned to the front in March 1918 and arrived at Le Havre Base, 25 May. The MB at Le Havre declared him a medical category B3 three days later and, 12.3.1919, declared that his service was no longer required due to his wound disability. He succeeded as 3rd Baronet on the death of his father, 26.7.1940.

Irish Times 3.7.1958: 'We regret to announce the death yesterday of Sir Lauriston John Arnott, of Shearwater, Baily, Co. Dublin, a director of the *Irish Times Ltd.*, since 1919, and a former managing director. He was in his 68th year.

'The third baronet of the creation of 1896, Sir Lauriston was a son of the second baronet, Sir John Alexander Arnott, and succeeded to the title in 1940. He was educated at Wellington College and at the Royal Military College, Woolwich. He served throughout the First World War with the Royal Irish Rifles, reaching the rank of Captain, and was wounded twice. He was a grandson of the first baronet, Sir John Arnott, who was a liberal MP for Kinsale from 1859 until 1863, and was the first of his family to have connections with the *Irish Times*.

'On his return to Ireland from the First World War, Sir Lauriston became a director of the *Irish Times Ltd.*, and was its managing director from 1940 until 1954. After that date he remained on the board as a director and took an active interest in the newspaper. A keen sportsman, he maintained the Arnott family connection with the Phoenix Park Race Club, of which he was chairman for many years. He was also interested in golf and was a former chairman and president of the Leinster Golfer's Alliance. He devoted a lot of his time to charitable institutions, and particularly, service charities. He was an active member of the council of the Help Society and Lord Roberts Workshops in Dublin. For a time he was honorary general secretary of that body, with which he was associated for many years ... Sir Lauriston was a member of the Dublin Diocesan Council and of the General Synod of the Church of Ireland and was one of the instigators of the People's Collection for special Church charities. He was also a past-president of the Foreign Mission Supply Association and a member of the board of Christ Church Cathedral. A keen worker in his own parish of Howth, he was a parochial nominator and honorary treasurer of the Select Vestry. For some years he had been a member of the board of the National Children's Hospital, Harcourt Street, Dublin.

'Sir Lauriston devoted a good deal of his time in support of charities connected with the welfare of animals and was an official of the North County Dublin Society for the Prevention of Cruelty to Animals. The benevolent institution of the Masonic Order, too, occupied much of his time and attention. He was a past Grand Deacon of the Grand Lodge of Freemasons of Ireland. It was the Adelaide Hospital, however, which claimed most of his interest in recent years. He joined the board of management of the hospital in 1942 and was its chairman from 1947 until 1949. For some years after that he was its honorary treasurer and since 1953 had been its vice-president. During his years on the board he saw the hospital improved and modernised, and paid particular attention to the organisation of the hospitals *Shilling Fund* which helped to pay for some of the work.

'During the second World War he was an officer in the North Co. Dublin Battalion of the Local Defence Force. Sir Lauriston was unmarried. His successor to the title is his brother, Robert John Arnott, born in 1896. He is also survived by his sister, Victoria, Lady de Freyne.

'Mr Maurice Dobbin, a former chairman of the board of management of the Adelaide Hospital said yesterday: "Sir Lauriston will be sorely missed at the Adelaide Hospital board, which he joined in 1942. But the mere recital of the offices he held there does little to convey the deep and abiding interest he took in the work of the hospital, where week by week his familiar and well-loved figure was to be seen hurrying to its committees. There his experience and balanced judgement was brought to bear on many problems and his services were willingly offered to deal with routine administration. Again, on public occasions, whether general meetings or functions designed to raise money for funds for the hospital, he was often to be heard speaking on behalf of the board with that courteous and charming humility that was so characteristic of him. Only two weeks ago he presided at the nurses' prize distribution, and the theme of his address on that occasion he may well be said to have made his own guiding star, for he spoke about the joy of service to one's fellow-man".'

Irish Times 9.7.1958: 'In the course of a long life I have met few men who did more for others than Laurie Arnott. He was not, I think, blessed with very good health and I often wondered how he managed to do all he did. At our frequent meetings he generally seemed to be in a hurry to get away to attend some charitable gathering. He was a man of even temperament and never appeared depressed or unduly elated. But he had a kindly word and smile for everyone and a good sense of humour. He did excellent work in the First World War and was wounded on two occasions. The Forces' Help Society and Lord Roberts' Workshops will never forget his self-sacrificing and outstanding work as secretary for many years. He will indeed be hard to replace. E.C.S.'

Quis Separabit, vol. 24, no. 2, 1958: 'The regiment has suffered a severe loss by the death, suddenly, as a result of a severe heart attack on 2nd July, at his home in Co. Dublin, of Sir Lauriston Arnott. He was indeed a pillar of the Regimental Association in the South of Ireland and a Rifleman through and through. From the time of his service with the Royal Irish Rifles in the First World War until his death, he took the keenest interest in all matters affecting the development of regimental affairs and the welfare of retired members, especially those who needed a helping hand ... The truth was that he dedicated himself to the service of his fellow men and in no aspect did he enjoy himself more than in the work he did for the regiment. As Chairman of the Southern Ireland Branch for many years he laboured with immense zeal to ameliorate the condition and outlook of his comrades, many of whom were in distress.

'The Dublin Annual Dinner will seem strange without him. Many of us will recall the care he took to ensure that it was as successful as it notoriously has become. Year in, year out, as I went there I could see what he meant to the Rifleman and what the Rifleman meant to him. Year in, year out, he journeyed North in all weathers to take part in our Regimental Committees and ceremonies. Laurie Arnott meant a lot to me ... It was a great privilege to be his friend. I never can forget the days we had together two years ago on the Pilgrimage to Thiepval. No one got greater joy and satisfaction out of that visit to the old battlefields than he. What pleasure he gave to everyone else. — General Sir J.J. Steele.'

Dictionary of Irish Biography: 'During World War II he served as an L.S.F. company commander at Howth. Asked how he reconciled his former career in the British Army with his role as an officer in the L.S.F., he replied, "My house out in Shearwater in Howth, that's my home ... If I saw a British Tommy walking across my meadows, I'd simply have to shoot the bugger, wouldn't I".'

File ref: 26 83 15777.

Baker Lt.-Col. Osbert Clinton. Born 25.9.1869 at Bayfordbury, the third son of William Clinton Clinton-Baker and Edith Mildmay Ashhurst (daughter of the Revd Henry Lewis Majendie, Vicar of Great Dunmow, Essex) of Bayfordbury, Hertfordshire. Educated at Winchester and Sandhurst, from which he was gazetted to the RIR, 1.3.1890. Promoted Lt. 18.11.1894, Capt. 24.2.1900, and was Adjutant for three years from 1.1.1896. Served in the South African War with 2nd RIR and also commanded the 21st Bn, Mounted Infantry. Present at operations in the Orange River Colony from May to November 1900, and in the Transvaal, Orange River, and Cape Colonies between November 1900 and May 1902. Mentioned in Col. Williams' farewell order,

21.4.1901. Received the Queen's Medal with three clasps and the King's Medal with two clasps. Col. Rochfort reported: 'During the whole of my time in South Africa I did not command better or more mobile troops than the two mounted infantry companies of the Royal Irish Rifles under Capt. Laurie and Capt. Baker.'

Commanded a detachment of forty men to guard the country residence of the Commander-in-Chief in Ireland, Lord French, at Drumdoe House, being stationed at Boyle, Co. Roscommon. From February 1905 to 21.9.1906 he was Adjutant of 5th Connaught Rangers (Militia), receiving his majority the day after relinquishing that appointment. Served with 1st RIR in India and Burma. Granted ten days leave 22.1.1915. *Laurie* 14.2.1915: 'Major B. has been decidedly ill several times on this campaign, and I have literally ordered him to stay in bed to get better, as he would not do so otherwise.'

He was one of four out of 22 officers who passed unhurt through the action at Neuve Chapelle and took over command of the battalion, 15.3.1915. He was personally congratulated by Field Marshal Sir John French, 17 April, for the fine work done by the battalion during that battle. Promoted Lt.-Col., 8.5.1915, and killed in action the following day.

Roscommon Herald, 22.5.1915: 'In a recent list of wounded from the fighting at Ypres is the name of Lt.-Col. Clinton Baker of the Royal Irish Rifles. He spent five years in Boyle as Adjutant and was most popular in these counties and very great sympathy is felt with him now, as he was an officer of remarkable intelligence and ability.'

The Times, 29.5.1915: 'He was a good cricketer, fine shot and keen polo player, he with other officers won for his regiment the King George's Cup for Polo at Aden in 1914.'

Belfast Telegraph, 29.5.1915: 'It appears that after the Rifles had carried the front line of trenches allotted to them, and had advanced to the road beyond, the enemy concentrated a terrible fire on them. The General in charge of the brigade was killed, and a battalion, which was to have come up and relieve the Rifles was not sent forward. The Rifles held on to the position, and were being enfiladed when Col. Baker took a party to the right flank to prevent this, a similar party being sent to the left. It was when he was with this party, which was practically annihilated, that Col. Baker was shot.'

He was unmarried and resided at Bayfordbury. Ploegsteert Memorial, Comines-Warneton, Hainault. He is named on a memorial tablet at Sandhurst. File missing.

Barrington Lt. Noel Scott. Born 22.5.1892 at 73 Bruntsfield Place, Edinburgh. His parents, who married 30.1.1891 at Walcha, New South Wales, were Fourness and Christina Brydon Barrington *née* Scott, he being their only son. His father was a surgeon residing in Australia, MS (Edin) and FRCS (Eng); a lecturer in obstetrics, University of Sydney, Surgeon at the Royal Hospital for Women and Royal Prince Alfred Hospital. Educated at Mostyn House and Worcester College, Oxford (1912).

Registered for a commission in the Regular Army, October 1912, gazetted a 2/Lt., 23.1.1914, and nominated for a Regular commission, 7.8.1914, being promoted to Lt., 15.11.1914. Killed in action by machine gun fire, 10.3.1915, while serving with 1st RIR. He was a bachelor and the administratrix of his estate was Mrs Frances Twyman Ryman-Hall, 8 Hazelwood Road, Northampton. A letter was sent to Mrs Barrington, c/o Mrs Ryman-Hall, 14 June, notifying that the burial took place at map reference Sheet 36 Belgium, square M.35. A list of his effects that were recovered included 'one ring (damaged)', two pipes, a silver cigarette case and a silver flask. The Commonwealth War Graves Commission records note his mother as Mrs Christina Hughes of 62 Queensborough Terrace, Hyde Park, London. Royal Irish Rifles Graveyard, Laventie, Pas de Calais, III.D.16. File ref: 83 40529.

Bayly Capt. Lancelot Myles MC. Born 7.8.1884 at Coole Abbey, Knocklofty, Clonmel, Co. Tipperary, the second son of Edward Crosbie Bayly JP and Isabel Georgina Bayly (daughter of

Charles Edward Davison), same address. Father's profession, 'gentleman' – he was a magistrate for Cork and Waterford, residing at Killough Castle, Holycross, Thurles, Co. Tipperary, and 30 Grosvenor Place, Dublin. *Irish Times* 6.12.1918: ' ... was educated at the High School and was well known in football circles, playing on Lansdowne 1st XV, for Cup matches in 1904 and 1905.'

Went to India, September 1909, and returned soon after the outbreak of war. Applied for a commission 2.6.1915. At that time he was residing at Killough Castle, occupation 'banking', educated at the High School, Dublin, currently serving as a L/Cpl with the Bombay Volunteer Rifles, but had taken leave to try to obtain a commission. Height 5 foot 10 inches, single, chest 35–38 inches, weight 167 pounds. Sent to the School of Instruction, Cork Barracks, 7.7.1915. Gazetted a 2/Lt. in 3rd RIR, 3.7.1915, and joined 1st RIR, 13.9.1916. Wounded, 5.3.1917, and admitted to No. 14 General Hospital at Wimereux, 7 March, with a severe GSW to his right hand. Embarked for the UK, 12 March. *Irish Times* 16.3.1917: 'A brother, Lieutenant C.M.C. Bayly, late of the Royal Irish Fusiliers, is serving with the Royal Flying Corps.'

The MB at Caxton Hall, London, 22 March, noted that he was 'healing well' but was likely to be unfit for five weeks from the date of wounding. The same MB, 30 June, granted 21 days leave and ordered that he was then to report to Belfast for light duty. Promoted Lt. 1.7.1917. MB, 3 August, declared him fit for general service and he rejoined 1st RIR on 28 September. Promoted Capt. 6.2.1918. Wounded again, 21.3.1918, in the redoubts to the right of HQ while commanding D Coy and continued fighting until 28.3.1918.

Awarded the MC in May 1918 (*London Gazette* 16.9.1918): 'For conspicuous gallantry and devotion to duty. He commanded a company through a week's heavy fighting, taking part in rearguard actions, and counter-attacks, in which he set a fine example. On one occasion he carried a Lewis gun the whole of a long march.'

Sent with 80 men to 36th Divisional Training Camp at Bonninques, 25.7.1918. He was shot through the body by a sniper, 21.10.1918, and died at a CCS the next day, being reported 'brought in dead' by OC, No. 36 CCS.

de Ruvigny: 'His CO wrote: "Throughout the past 13 months served with the battalion, he has always distinguished himself both in and out of the line, and at all times was held as a gallant and courteous officer, full of sympathy for the men under his command".'

His effects included 'heather' and a 'medal ribbon'. The next of kin and the sole beneficiary to his estate was his widowed mother. Duhallow Advanced Dressing Station Cemetery, Ieper, IV.J.21. File ref: WO339/55776 184770.

Beatty Lt. Eugene Lawrence. Born 1894 at Rathmines, Dublin, the son of Michael Beatty, 27 Dartmouth Road, Leeson Park, Dublin. Attested to the Irish Guards as Pte No. 5356, 19.9.1914. He had been a clerk in the Department of Agriculture, Dublin. No previous military service. Height 5 foot 10 inches, weight 142 pounds, chest 32½–34½ inches. Joined at Caterham, Surrey, 22.9.1914.

Awarded eight days confined to barracks, 31.12.1914, for overstaying his leave by 15 hours 30 minutes. Appointed an unpaid L/Cpl, 8 February, and an unpaid L/Sgt, 20 July. Left to join 2nd Irish Guards in France, 16.8.1915. Promoted Sgt, 4 October. Severely reprimanded, 18 December, for neglect of duty as the Sgt in charge of a Lewis Gun, 'accidentally discharging a round and wounding a man and horse'. Granted ten days leave, 26.5.1916. Acting CQMS, 22 July. Promoted to permanent Sgt, 2 September. Sent to the Cadet School at Blendecques, 29.11.1916. Granted a temporary commission in 14th RIR, 12.2.1917. Joined 1st RIR, 2.4.1918, and left 30 June. Embarked for the UK, 15 July, Boulogne–Dover. Admitted to Cawdor House Auxiliary Hospital, Glasgow. Internal haemorrhoids, 'evacuated for operation'. Address in the UK, 18 Church Avenue, South Circular Road, Dublin. The MB at 3rd London General Hospital, Wandsworth, 2 August, declared him unfit for general service for six weeks. Promoted Lt.

13.8.1918. The MB at Yorkhill War Hospital, 27 September, noted that he had much improved and was fit for general service. Granted three weeks leave. Released from military service, 24.1.1919, 3rd RIR. Medical category A. File ref: WO339/91918 14/83 177663.

Bell Capt. William Rosylin MC. Gazetted to 15th RIR, 6.1.1916, and promoted Capt., 7.9.1917. Appointed Capt., 1st RIR, 23.3.1918. Joined 1st RIR, 2.4.1918, and awarded the MC in November 1918. Transferred to 12th RIR, 22.2.1919, joining the Army of Occupation in Germany. Closed file, ref: 20/83 (121704).

Benson Lt.-Col. Geoffrey OBE. Born 13.12.1897 in Guernsey, Channel Islands. Entered Trinity College, Dublin, 1914, joining the OTC. At the RMC, August 1915 until he obtained his commission in the RIR, 7.4.1916. Left for the BEF 16.7.1916. Joined 1st RIR, 22.7.1916, and was severely wounded, 23.10.1916. In hospital until September 1917. Promoted Lt. in 1917 and attached to 3rd RIR. Attached RIF in France, July 1918, but invalided home the following month. Posted to 2nd RIR in December 1918. Attended a signals course 1919.

By 1935 Capt. Benson was Commander of B Coy, 2nd RUR. Promoted to Major, 14.10.1937. Resided at 54 Broadway Parade, Belfast, 1950.

Blackthorn, vol. 1, no. 4, 1970: 'Geoffrey Benson died in hospital near his home in Pembridge, Herefordshire, on July 14, 1970, at the age of 72 plus. He was commissioned into the Royal Irish Rifles from Sandhurst in April 1916 when not quite 19. Within six months he had been through the mill with a vengeance. First of all he ran into the Easter Rebellion in Dublin; then he joined the 1st Battalion Royal Irish Rifles in France in July and was seriously wounded within a month. These war wounds kept him in hospital for more than a year, and although he returned to France in 1918 to serve with the Royal Irish Fusiliers he was soon invalided back to the UK because of his wounds.

'He was to suffer from their effect for the rest of his thirty years of service. He set aside this considerable disability by sheer force of will, determination, and courage. His outstanding character can be classed as indomitable. He was never subdued. After the First World War his service alternated with periods of regimental duty, mostly with 2nd RUR (1919–26 and 1932–40) and in the Sudan or Abyssinia and 1941–5 when he commanded units of the Sudan Defence Force. He was awarded the OBE in 1939 and retired in 1946.

'I first met Slippy, his affectionate regimental surname, nearly 50 years ago in Mesopotamia and we served side by side in the 2nd RUR for about six years in Egypt and in India and in Cairo he took his full part in the fun and games which we had in that city in 1921–3. An outstanding memory is his performance in the dining room of SS *Marglen* on the journey from Suez to Bombay. He, regularly, went through the menu and there may still be in existence a cartoon sketch of "Slippy slipping it down" – a sight to remember.

'Very soon after arrival in India at the beginning of 1924 he began to demonstrate his prowess in rifle shooting. He won the South India Rifle championship in 1925 and in his first period of service in the Middle East he won the Sudan championship in 1932 – the Governor General's Gold Medal. For the next few years he had a notable record at Bisley. He represented Ireland there 1933–6 and in France during the phoney war period 1939–40. It was in Palestine that his courage and determination not to give in to his old war wounds was so signally shown. He kept "cracking on" without respite and his example in the battalion became legendary. Gerald Whitfeld, his Commanding Officer there and again in France, speaks of him as the most loyal and courageous officer one could ever wish to have.

'After he retired he took up gliding as a hobby and it soon became a mania. If you didn't watch out you would be up aloft with him before you knew where you were. His enthusiasm for the sport was unbounded and in the Gliding Club he made many friends who had a deep respect for his courage and skill.

'He and his wife Dorothy settled down in Herefordshire where they made friends and he helped a lot of people quietly and unobtrusively. On the day when he went into hospital for the last time Dorothy became seriously ill. She died a week after Geoff on July 21 [1970] unaware that he had predeceased her. Thus came to an end a happy partnership in many ways the out turn of events could hardly have been more appropriate. He served his regiment well. They, together, served the community no less faithfully. — General Sir James S. Steele.'

Mentioned in Despatches, GSM Iraq, Palestine 1939–45 Star, African Star, Defence War Medal. Closed file, ref: (132535).

Biscoe Capt. Arthur John. Born 23.6.1880 at Southend, Essex, the elder son of Frederick William and Alice Biscoe of 3 Vanbrugh Park Road East, Blackheath, London SE. Educated at Cheltenham College, where he was in the Cricket XI in 1898, and at the RMC. Joined 1st RIR in Fort William, Bengal, and gazetted a 2/Lt., 12.8.1899, being promoted to Lt., 1.2.1902, and Capt., 28.6.1908. He was in the winning teams of the All India Hockey Tournament in 1901 and 1902. Also a member of the Conservative Club. While in Aden, he led the raiding party on the SS *Lindenfeld*.

Slightly wounded by a shell splinter 27.11.1914. He was one of the officers leading the assault of 10.3.1915, and died in hospital at Boulogne, 12 March, of wounds received in that attack. Mentioned in Despatches 4.4.1915. Boulogne Eastern Cemetery, Pas de Calais, II.B.12. He is named on a memorial tablet at Sandhurst. File missing.

Bourke 2/Lt. Augustus Mary. Born 12.10.1896. His father was a motor dealer. Attested, 18.1.1917, as Pte 4/6802 in the Connaught Rangers and was placed in the Army Reserve. Height 5 foot 10 inches, chest 34–37 inches, weight 140 pounds, address 29 Clonliffe Road, Dublin. Applied for a commission, 14.4.1917. His first choice was the Mechanical Transport Branch of the ASC. A second choice of the Connaught Rangers was added in a different hand. Mobilized and posted to No. 3 Officer Cadet Battalion at Bristol, 28.9.1917. Commissioned a 2/Lt. and posted to 4th Connaught Rangers, 26.2.1918. Home service shown as 18.1.1917 to 26.2.1918. Joined 1st RIR from the Connaught Rangers, 9.9.1918, and wounded himself accidentally, 7.10.1918. Embarked Calais–Dover, 12 October. Cause shown as 'GSW in left foot (acc)'. Address given as Clare View, Streamstown, Westport, Co. Mayo. The MB at 1st Western General Hospital, Liverpool, 6 November, stated that he had accidentally shot himself while handling a rifle, the wound was then healed but the foot was tender and he could not wear a boot. The C.-in-C., Eastern Command, wrote to the WO, 23.2.1919, and wondered if they knew where Bourke was. Declared unfit for further military service, 31.3.1919, and was to be discharged. File ref: WO339/102374 4/88 193037.

Bourke 2/Lt. Albert William. Born 1.5.1892 at 156 Newtownards Road, Belfast, the only son of Charles Edward and Sophia Bourke, *née* Hargreaves, of *Killala*, Cyprus Avenue, Bloomfield, Belfast. (Methodist College records state that he was born at 213 Newtownards Road.) He was the grandson of Lt.-Col. E.A. Bourke, RAMC, and a grand-nephew of Surgeon-General Joynt. His father was a draper. Educated at Methodist College and Queen's University, Belfast. Matriculated at the Royal University of Ireland, June 1908. Medical Student. Served with Belfast University OTC for five years, became Colour-Sergeant and passed the WO examination.

Applied for a commission in the infantry, 5.8.1914, and was gazetted into 3rd RIF. He went to the front in February 1915, being attached to 1st RIR. A WO telegram to his father, 12.2.1915, advised that Albert had been admitted to No. 2 British Red Cross Hospital at Rouen with tonsillitis, 6 February, and that he was progressing favourably. His father wrote to the WO, 22 February, saying he was concerned and had heard nothing since the telegram. A note from the WO, 26 February, advised that a further report was received on the 16th, and that he was 'progressing favourably'. WO telegram to his father, 2 March, stated Albert was discharged to duty 20.2.1915.

He was shot through the head during the attack of 9.5.1915. A telegram from the WO to his father, 15 May, 'deeply regrets' and sends Lord Kitchener's sympathy. Mr Bourke wrote to the WO, 17 May, asking for any news of how Albert died and where he was buried. Both he and his wife were suffering great grief at the death of their only son. He apologised 'for troubling you when you are having such a terrible time'. The WO replied, 22 May, stating that they had no further news.

Irish Life 30.7.1915: 'He was killed in action near Ypres on May 9th whilst gallantly leading a bomb party of the 1st Royal Irish Rifles to which he had been attached.'

Bond of Sacrifice: 'A Private in the Royal Irish Rifles wrote expressing deep appreciation of 2nd Lieutenant Bourke, who was shot at his side, calling, "Come on, boys; we will soon get them on the move".'

Died a bachelor, intestate. A list of his effects included a bunch of nine keys on a ring, two cheque books, an ID disc, and a cigarette holder. All these were sent to his father. A letter to his father from the WO, 8.11.1916, advised that news had just been received from Army HQ in the field that Albert was buried between Fromelles and Petillon. A letter from the WO to Mr Bourke, 16.11.1918, requested instructions regarding the issue of the plaque and scroll. He replied giving his new address as Kensington House, Kensington Road, Knock, Belfast.

Le Trou Aid Post Cemetery, Fleurbaix, Pas de Calais, Special Memorial 4. File ref: WO339/22333 3/87 42241.

Boyle Capt. John Kemmy MC. Born in 1897, the son of Michael and Nora Mary Boyle, 12 Upper Gardiner Street, Dublin. His father was employed in the Veterinary Branch of the Department of Agriculture. Attended the Officer's Instruction School, Trinity College, Dublin, and joined the RDF in September 1915, being afterwards transferred to the RIR. He was serving in Dublin during the rebellion of Easter Week 1916.

Wounded at Ginchy, September 1916. Gazetted to 7th RIR and joined 1st RIR 22.6.1917. Promoted Lt. 1.7.1917. Appointed a/Capt., 12.8.1917, wounded 16.8.1917, and awarded the MC 26.9.1917.

Irish Life 23.11.1917: 'He is the elder son of Mr M.F. Boyle, DATI, 80 Pembroke Road, Dublin, and was educated at the Christian Brothers School, North Richmond Street, and Blackrock College. He has been twice wounded in action.'

He returned to the front, 29.1.1918, and joined 2nd RIR, 6.2.1918 (noted as 7th RDF). *War Diary 2nd RIR*, at Cugny, 23.3.1918: '10 a.m. A defensive position north-east of the village was taken up. The remnants of D Coy, together with reinforcements under the command of Lt. J.K. Boyle MC, who rejoined the battalion that morning, were in reserve north-west of the village.'

Wounded again, 24 March, and taken prisoner. He was in three POW camps, finally moving to Cologne on 8 October. He died of pneumonia following influenza after two days illness, 21.10.1918, and was buried at Cologne Southern Cemetery, Germany, VII.C.21.

Branford 2/Lt. John George. Born 25.7.1884 at Canterbury and educated at Christ's Hospital. Applied for a commission to the ASC, 1.11.1916, and was attested Pte 764628 in 2nd Bn Artists Rifles (28th London), 10.1.1917. (The regiment is shown as 16th City of London over-stamped by Artists Rifles. The original attestation was 10.12.1915, but he was not actually called up – to Army Reserve, and mobilized 10.1.1917). Single, 5 foot 9¾ inches tall, chest 33–36 inches and weight 168 pounds. His next of kin was his mother, Annie, of Wrigham, Canterbury. Applied for a commission in the Artillery, 12.2.1917, later changing his option to the infantry. He gave his address as 56 Louisville Road, Tooting Common, London; employed as a clerk at Coutts Bank. Present address Hut 12, C Coy, 2nd Bn Artists Rifles, SW OTC, Hare Hall Camp, Romford, Essex. His father was listed as deceased. Moved to No. 16 Officer Cadet Battalion at Rhyl, 5.5.1917, and granted a temporary commission in 19th RIR, 29.8.1917.

His medical case sheet, 23.12.1917, is rather confusing: he had complained of lumbago and there is a reference to his having been discharged from hospital, but he had not received any treatment at the Depot. He had been in France two months, including two or six weeks at the front, references were made to both. The MB at Lezarde Valley Camp, Le Havre, 27.12.1917, noted his attachment to 14th RIR. He was complaining of rheumatic pains which 'he has suffered from for years'. He confirmed that he did not mention this at his medical examination when he applied for a commission. The Board noted that he was in fine condition and that they could detect no sign of rheumatism: 'perfectly fit for general service'.

Joined 1st RIR, 28.5.1918, and made an unsuccessful raid on the German trenches, 19.7.1918. Wounded 15.10.1918, GSW. Embarked Boulogne–Dover, 18 October. His address was given as 440 Strand, London. Examined at No. 1 Western General Hospital, Liverpool, 4 November, and released from service, 2.2.1919, medical category A1. Last unit shown as 3rd RIR. File ref: WO339/86291 19/83 169477.

Breen Capt. Patrick Augustine. Promoted to 2/Lt. from CQMS, 1st RIR, 22.11.1916, and wounded 31.7.1917. He later served with the MGC. Promoted Lt. 22.5.1918. 'Capt. P.A. Breen, having attained the age limit of liability to recall, ceases to belong to the Reserve of Officers.' – *London Gazette* 11.5.1935. Closed file, ref: 1/83 MGC (164067).

Brown 2/Lt. Hugh. Born 27.7.1895 in Belfast, the son of John Brown of *Duncairn*, 5 Bond Road, Bitterne Park, Southampton. Educated at the Royal Belfast Academical Institution and enlisted as a Private in 1/5th Hampshire Regt at Southampton, 7.8.1914. At that time he was single and had an elder brother Robert James, aged 20, and a sister Mary Elizabeth who was 26. Prior to joining up he had been a Quartermaster/Seaman with the American Line. Height 5 foot 7 inches, and an expanded chest measurement of 37½ inches. 'Good physical development' is noted in the medical report. Served in the UK up to 8.10.1914 when he embarked for India, serving there until 13.10.1915. His conduct sheet shows that he was charged with being 'Out of bounds without a pass' at Allahabad, 26 June, and was given eight days confined to barracks, again coming to the attention of the CO, 15 September, when he was late on parade and got another four days confinement. He had formally applied for a commission to the RIR on 14 June. Struck off the strength, 13.10.1915, he returned to the UK to attend cadet school, and was commissioned into 3rd RIR. Joined 1st RIR 25.11.1916. He was the Battalion Intelligence Officer and was killed in action, 31.7.1917, shot in the stomach, in no-man's-land.

A telegram was sent to his mother, 5 August. Personal effects returned to her were a religious medal, a mascot, and a leather wallet containing photographs, correspondence, etc. His father was Commander J. Brown, RNR, who, at the time, was commanding HMS *City of Oxford* in the eastern Mediterranean. His remoteness caused Mrs Brown some difficulty with regard to the release of her son's estate of £63.18 as the WO insisted that they would only deal with his father. Ypres (Menin Gate) Memorial.

Brown Capt. John MC. Born at Belfast in 1894, the son of Samuel Stuart and Agnes Brown of 3 Ailsa Terrace, Strandtown, Belfast. He was single and had a sister called Betsy. Enlisted in 8th RIR, 10.9.1914, as Rfn 14151, giving his age as 20 years 5 months. Height 6 foot 1 inch, weight 174 pounds, and an expanded chest measurement of 44 inches. Occupation linen warehouseman. Promoted to Sgt, 12.9.1914, and discharged to receive a commission, 11.11.1914. A note on his file says that all other documents were destroyed in a fire, April 1916.

Wounded, by a rifle bullet to the right shoulder, while serving with 8th RIR, 1.7.1916. Moved to 17th RIR, 11.9.1916, until he was cleared by the MB as being completely recovered, 10.10.1916. During his recuperation he was awarded the Royal Humane Society's Bronze Medal and Certificate for saving a life from drowning at Belfast, September 1916.

Joined 1st RIR, 11.12.1916. Commanded No. 5 Platoon. See main text for 30.3.1917. For his action near Fins he was awarded a Bar to his MC. Took over command of B Coy 20.8.1917 until 5.10.1917. Killed in action, 21.3.1918, while commanding C Coy. Reported wounded and missing, his file contains statements from the following who were all repatriated POWs: 20375 Rfn G. Fleming, interviewed 29.3.1919, stated that he saw Capt. Brown dead in a trench; 9257 Sgt McGuigan saw a German Officer throw a bomb and kill Brown; 161 Rfn J.M. Fall stated that he saw Brown dead in a trench 'shot through the head'. Pozières Memorial.

Browne Capt. Dominick Augustus. Born 28.6.1888 at 47 Raglan Road, Dublin, the eldest son of Frank W. and Mary Maude Browne, *née* Worthington, Killadreenan, Newtownmountkennedy, Co. Wicklow. His father was a solicitor. He attended Marlborough College, Wiltshire, from 1901 until August 1906. As of 30.8.1906 he was living at 6 Carlton Terrace, Bray, Co. Wicklow. At this time he applied for admission to the RMC, and was a Gentleman Cadet, January 1907 to September 1908. During the summer of 1907 he was a member of the RMC Revolver Team. Commissioned a 2/Lt. in 1st RIR, 19.9.1908, and promoted Lt., 8.3.1910.

Quis Separabit, vol. III, no. 1, May 1932, described the voyage home from Aden:

'Another fellow who had perhaps the worst job of the lot was poor Dominic Brown; told off as Baggage Officer, some of the senior ladies, especially, thought that he was there solely for the purpose of hunting in the Baggage Room at all hours of the day and night for their "wanted on voyage" gear. As a visit to the baggage room (average temperature 140°) meant a complete change of clothes, he used to be a bit terse with them at times. He was an extremely smart, well dressed and well groomed fellow, and getting through his clean gear at the rate he was doing positively hurt him.

'A rhyme made up about him annoyed him even more than the ladies did:

> Oh Dominic Augustus, to whom the ladies pray
> For change of clothes and other things on each and every day.
> Deal gently with their failings, Smile sweetly if you can,
> And fetch their knicks and undies, As becomes a nice young man.'

At Port Said: 'From the Casino we went to the Union Club, where we fell in with Dominic Brown entertaining some French officers of our future escort, the *Bouvet*. We were introduced in his best French, adding "Il bouvait too", which wasn't very kind.'

Appointed Adjutant 14.3.15. Returned to the UK, 19.4.1915, with a fractured left fibula sustained at Fleurbaix in a riding accident. Promoted to Capt. 27.5.1915. Leave was granted 20 May to 19 June, being later extended until 30 July and again to 20.8.1915. The MB declared him fit for general service, 23.8.1915, and he rejoined the battalion, 30.8.1915. *Whitfeld*: 'What a funny fellow Browne is. I can quite understand why he is not liked by the Warrant Officers and NCO's. The RSM, however, I gather, likes him … Browne was a great friend of mine but he was far from popular among the NCO's. He had a tongue like a razor and took a lot of knowing … I miss him as a friend and also his knowledge and guidance generally.' Recommended for gallantry for his part in the Somme attack of 1.7.1916, during which he was killed. See main text.

A WO telegram was sent to his sister, Miss Ada Browne, 3 July. Estate valued at £509.99. His medals were despatched to his brother. He is named on a memorial tablet in the RMC Chapel and also on the Bray War Memorial in Co. Wicklow. Thiepval Memorial.

Browne 2/Lt. Thomas Hay Ritchie. Gazetted a 2/Lt. in 3rd RIR 31.10.1917. While serving with 1st RIR he took part in the defensive actions against the German attack of March 1918. Court-martialled at Boulogne, 10.5.1918, for drunkenness and received a severe reprimand. Closed file, ref: 83 (217174).

Buchanan Lt. William John. Gazetted a 2/Lt. in 3rd RIR 26.4.1917. Joined 1st RIR 24.6.1917. Struck off the strength having been found medically unfit while on sick leave in the UK, 6.10.1917. Promoted Lt. 26.10.1918. Employed by the Ministry of Labour 1918. File destroyed.

Bulloch Lt. Ronald Alexander Nevin. Promoted to Lt. in 3rd RIR, 8.5.1915, and joined 1st RIR, 9.7.1915, with a draft of twenty men. Rejoined the unit, 18.12.1916, there being no mention in the War Diary of his earlier departure. Struck off the strength, 19.1.1917, no reason given. Joined 4th RIR from sick leave, 27.3.1917, and was posted to E Coy, being assigned for temporary duty with 3rd Garrison Bn Northumberland Fusiliers at Lenan Fort, Co. Donegal, 29.3.1917. Left 4th RIR, 14.6.1917, and rejoined 1st RIR, 22.6.1917, being struck off again, 3.8.1917, no reason given. He returned to 1st RIR, 14.7.1918, but was transferred to England, sick, 5.10.1918. Closed file, ref: 1/83 (80390).

Burges Lt. William Armstrong. Born 3.6.1889, the second son of Francis Lockyier Burges and Esther Burges *née* Potts, at Irwin House, Irwin River, Western Australia. European descent, Irish family. Educated at the Royal School, Armagh, Sept 1904 to July 1908. Applied for the RMC 21.9.1908. Address given as The National Bank House, Belfast. Application counter-signed by his stepfather, Frederick Scroope, 'Station Owner' of Irwin House.

Having passed out of the RMC, he was gazetted a 2/Lt. in 2nd RIR, 20.4.1910, transferred to 1st RIR, 20.4.1911, and promoted Lt., 15.10.1914. Killed in action by machine gun fire, 10.3.1915, being one of the four officers who led the assault. Mentioned in Despatches, 4.4.1915, for gallant and distinguished conduct in this action. The WO sent a telegram to his sister, 13 March, advising 'wounded 10th March nature or degree not known.' She wrote to the WO, 15 March, asking for details of his wounding as she would have to telegram their mother in Australia.

Irish Life 14.5.1915: ' ... son of the late Mr Francis L. Burges of Irwin House, West Australia, and of Mrs Scroope, stepson of Mr Frederick Scroope and grandson of the late Francis Carleton Burges MD, of Fethard, Co. Tipperary. His school career began at the Grammar School, Clonmel. He was at Campbell College, Belfast for a short time [September 1903 to July 1904] and the remainder of his school days were spent at the Royal School, Armagh, where he was immensely popular with his masters and school fellows alike. Lieutenant Burges' brother (Irwin) is on his way home with the West Australian Light Horse, and his younger brother has, since December, been at the front with the Irish Guards.'

See main text. A WO letter to his sister, 14.6.1915, gave the grave location as Sheet 36 Belgium, Square M.35. A list of personal effects included two silver cigarette cases and a wrist watch. The effects form dated 2.3.1916 shows William as unmarried with no children. His sister was 23 years old and he had two brothers, Irwin (aged 27) and Francis (aged 22), the latter two both in Western Australia. His closest living relative 'residing in the United Kingdom' was his sister, Miss Temple Burges, of the National Bank at Belfast. A graves registration letter to the WO, date stamped 25.9.1919, advised that William was buried 'about 600 yards north of Neuve Chapelle' and the grave was marked with a durable wooden cross. He is named on a memorial tablet at Sandhurst. Royal Irish Rifles Graveyard, Laventie, Pas de Calais, III.D.17. File ref: WO339/7574 83 15425.

In 1945 his brother Irwin wrote from Australia to the new headmaster of Campbell College: 'I was born in this district being the first male child born around Irwin, hence my name. My parents, or rather my mother, decided to send my brother and myself home to school, and my father being Irish and, having two great-aunts near Portora, that school was chosen before leaving here. However, some friends recommended the then-new school of Campbell, and I arrived at Campbell in September 1903.' (Irwin Carleton Temple Burges was born 25.5.1888 and attended Campbell College, September 1903 to July 1906; ward of Frederick Scroope, National Bank, Belfast. Represented Western Australia at hockey and polo. During the Great War he enlisted as a Trooper in the 10th Australian Light Horse and rose to the rank of Capt. in the 16th Bn, Australian Imperial Forces. He was a stock breeder at Irwin Park.)

Burke-Murphy Lt.-Col. Edmund Victor OBE, MC. Born 17.5.1897, the eldest son of Mr Burke-Murphy of Cultra Lodge, Holywood, Co. Down, and was one of the first pupils to attend Rockport Preparatory School, Craigavad. He later went to Mourne Grange School near Kilkeel, Co. Down, and then on to Bradfield College where he excelled as a cross-country runner.

Commissioned into the RIR, 3.10.1914, and served on active service with 1st RIR in the Battles of the Somme (being recommended for gallantry by the CO for his part in the attack on 1.7.1916), Messines, and Ypres from 18.5.1915 until he was wounded 31.7.1917 in the attack on Westhoek Ridge. Awarded the MC for gallantry in the 1917 New Year Honours List. Promoted Lt. 4.4.1918. From May to September 1919 he was with the Allied Invasion Force in North Russia and took part in the capture of Murmansk and Archangel. After this campaign he was Mentioned in Despatches.

When the war ended he rejoined 1st RIR and was with them in the Isle of Wight as Assistant Adjutant and Master of the Regimental Beagles. Promoted to Capt., 1.4.1926. He was also an accomplished yachtsman. From August 1925 to August 1928 he was Adjutant of the battalion in Germany and was well known for his smartness of turnout and his prowess as a horseman. He next became Adjutant, September 1928 to September 1932, of the London Irish Rifles at the Duke of Yorks Headquarters, London. After a year as a Major with 1st RUR in Hong Kong he joined the staff of the Shanghai Volunteer Corps whose commandant was Col. Fergus Graham, his previous CO in the RUR, and served with them from November 1934 until the outbreak of World War II in 1939, when he returned to the Depot at Ballymena.

In May 1940 he arrived in France as a reinforcement for the BEF just in time to be evacuated back to the UK from Dunkirk in a fishing boat, 29.5.1940. During the invasion scare he commanded 30th (Northern Ireland) Bn, RIF, in the area of Kilkeel, Co. Down, until that unit was disbanded in June 1943. At this time he was living with his wife at 3 Golf Links Road, Newcastle, Co. Down. He then commanded a stores depot near Larne and, shortly after the invasion of Europe in June 1944, became the commander of a POW holding unit in Normandy. He set up a compound behind the 3rd Canadian Divisional area and at one time had over 74,000 German prisoners in his charge. On the recommendation of the Canadian Force commander he was awarded the OBE for his distinguished services. At the end of the war he became one of the four quadripartite commandants of Spandau Prison in Berlin. He retired from the Army 1.1.1948.

During 1952–7 he was the officer in charge of the Army Recruiting Office in Belfast. He then went to live in Dorset until 1976 when he returned to live in Holywood with his sister, Miss Muriel Burke-Murphy. For the remaining years of his life he worked at Regimental HQ, Belfast, in a voluntary capacity as honorary archivist. On four days a week he travelled to Belfast and researched and indexed the regimental muniments and photograph albums. Each year on 1 July he laid the wreath on behalf of the officers of 36th (Ulster) Division at the Somme Day ceremonies at the City Hall, Belfast. Also each year he laid the wreath for the RUR on Remembrance Sunday and on other occasions. He died peacefully in hospital, 14.4.1985, aged 87. His son Peter, a partner in a London firm of Chartered Surveyors, survived him. Mainly taken from his obituary in the *Blackthorn*, vol. 4, no. 21, 1985. Closed file, ref: (50782).

Butler Capt. James Humphry. Born in 1897. Member of 5th RIR rugby team in 1914. A letter from OC 5th RIR to OC Belfast Garrison, 27.2.1915, stated that Butler had 26 weeks training and that his appointment as a 2/Lt. was recommended for confirmation. Posted to France, 13.5.1915, and joined 1st RIR five days later. Promoted to Lt. 22.5.1915. Slightly wounded 25.9.1915. Seconded for duty with the 25th Brigade Machine Gun Company, 19.1.1916. Granted leave to England 21–8.2.1916 and 30.5.1916 to 8.6.1916.

Wounded at Ovillers, 26.6.1916, and admitted No. 5 CCS the next day. GSW left arm. Sent to No. 2 British Red Cross Hospital at Rouen, 29 June. Embarked Rouen–Southampton, 1 July, on the *Aberdonian*. Another report gives the embarkation date as 30 June. Arrived Countess of Pembroke's Hospital, Wilton House, Salisbury, 2 July.

Irish Times 5.7.1916: 'Lt. J.H. Butler, RIR, who is reported wounded, was attached to a machine gun company. He is 20 years of age and is the eldest son of Mr C.R. Butler, Mount Leinster Lodge, Co. Carlow, and a kinsman of Sir Richard Butler, Bt., of Garryhundon, Carlow. This is the second time he has appeared in the Casualty List.'

The MB at Tidworth, 22 July, recommended three weeks leave. There had been no bone damage and he was certified unfit for general service for three weeks. Address at this time was Mount Leinster House, Borris. The MB at the Military Hospital, the Curragh, 15 August, noted that he had completely recovered and was fit for general service. Arrived MGC Training Centre at Grantham, 18 August, and was attached to No. 2 Cadet Battalion MGC at Pirbright. He asked permission to be attached to the RFC, 7.2.1917. The application was forwarded by the OC No. 2 Cadet Battalion to the WO, 8 February.

The Director of Air Organisation wrote to the OC, School of Military Aeronautics, at Reading, 15.2.1917, saying that Butler was to report there for a course of instruction in aviation 'forthwith'. 'I am to say that this is a special case.' The MB at Reading War Hospital, 1.3.1917, stated that he 'conforms in every respect' to the medical requirements. A letter from OC 5th RIR to HQ Northern District, 12.9.1917, stated that Butler was currently serving as a T/Capt. with the RFC and recommended his promotion to Capt. He was serving with No. 99 Squadron in India by September 1919. File ref: WO339/24464 83 MGC 45145.

Byrne 2/Lt. Vincent Connel. Born at 12 Wellington Road, Dublin, 14.4.1896, the second son of George Byrne JP (a flour merchant at 4 Cope Street) and Anastasia Byrne, *née* Hoey, of 36 Elgin Road, Dublin. Educated at Belvedere College, Dublin; Clongowes Wood College, Co. Kildare (1909–12), and Trinity College, Dublin. He was a solicitor's apprentice and had three sisters and two brothers. Gazetted a 2/Lt. in 3rd RIR 8.10.1915. He left 4th RIR for the BEF, 12.5.1916, and joined 1st RIR, 12.7.1916. Killed in action, 31.7.1917, while commanding A Coy. A telegram was sent to his father, 5 August. His file notes 'No record of this officer's body having been recovered'.

Clongownian 1919: 'He was educated at Belvedere College and at Clongowes, and won distinction in the Intermediate. On leaving college he took up the study of law, and was serving his apprenticeship in the firm of Messrs Hoey and Denning, of Tullamore, when the war broke out. He obtained a commission in the Royal Irish Rifles in October, 1915, and went to France the following May. He was in several engagements, and was slightly wounded in the battle of the Somme, when he was in charge of ten guns. His Colonel spoke highly of his gallantry on this occasion. When leading his company in an attack over very difficult wooded country close to Ypres, on the morning of July 31st, he was struck by a machine gun bullet. Death was almost instantaneous.

'The life-story of Vinnie Byrne is that of many another gallant young Irishman who has fallen in this war. At the dawn of a promising career, just when the powers of mind and body were in their prime, there came the loud crash of war. With one all-absorbing idea in his mind – to stand between Ireland and the invader – he took up the work of a soldier. Military training served to develop and perfect his natural qualities. But infinitely more important was the working of war on his soul. His courage and efficiency, his cheerfulness for others, and, above all, his close union with the will of God are well illustrated by the two following letters which we publish with the permission of Mr Byrne:

'The Protestant chaplain writes: "Dear Mr Byrne, It was with great sorrow I heard on my return from hospital that your son had been killed. He was one of my greatest and oldest friends, and many a time in trenches I have been cheered on a muddy night by his hearty welcome to share a meal. I don't suppose anyone hated war more than he did, but he realised the greatness of the cause in which we all face the misery and suffering of this campaign. He was one of the most thoughtful officers for his men, and was greatly beloved by them – they would have gone anywhere with him – his courage and consideration inspired confidence, and everyone knew that what he asked another to do he would have been willing to do himself. His unfailing cheerfulness in the most depressing circumstances helped everyone around him, and he will be a great loss to his battalion. Before he went into battle in October he gave me your address and asked me to write you if anything happened to him. I regret that I was in hospital myself when he was hit, and so can only send this belated note expressing my personal sympathy with you in your loss. I suppose you know that by applying to a chaplain you can have a photo of the grave sent to you. I am sure Father Nolan would be glad to make application on your behalf to the proper quarter. With sincere sympathy, yours very truly, Revd J.E. Hamilton, CF, Attd. 2nd Lincolnshire Regt, BEF."

'The following letter to his father was written by Vinnie two days before his death:

"My Dearest Old Dad. I expected to be home by now, but my leave has been temporarily held over as I have been given command of a company. By the time this reaches you I think you will probably have seen in the papers the reason why my leave has been cancelled – the poor old Boche! It is a sort of honour, but at the same time a bit of a responsibility steering a company through, especially as, you know, I have been doing specialist work for such a long time. It is A Company which I am commanding. Reed has now got C Company so we will pray away and not bother. All my men were at Communion this morning, so they will be all right. Of course, I know you won't worry, as you and I understand the eternal omnipotence of God, and so we say whatever God wills will happen; so we pray for grace, get God to sanctify our hearts with Himself, and then cheery O! and off we go. I am not where you mentioned, but opposite a famous town more to the south where many battles have already been fought. I always tell you quite honestly when any extra stunt is coming off, because then we can all put a barrage on heaven, not to seek for safety, but to show that we recognise God's will. It is not for myself that I care, but I know that it would grieve you – grieve you far more than it could possibly affect me, so it is right that you should know so that you can get your battery to open fire on the Gates of Heaven. I expect that our part will be finished in a couple of days, so I expect to be home in about a week. So for the present, cheery O! Vincent. PS – Please warn Phillips to have a complete uniform ready for me."

'We may confidently trust that God, on the festival morning of the soldier-saint of Loyola, sanctified the heart of this young Irish officer, and that the soul of Vinnie Byrne sped swiftly from the tangled wooded country around Ypres to a better world.'

Tyne Cot Memorial.

Calverley Lt. Geoffrey Walter DSO. Born 22.2.1896 at 72 Lower Mount Street, Dublin, and spent his first ten years in Ireland. His parents were Walter C.B. Calverley, a 'private gentleman' who died in 1906, and Edythe Agnes Calverley. His father was from Yorkshire and his mother was Irish. Educated at St Michaels, Westgate, 1906–10; Charterhouse 1910–12, and Loudwater, Westgate, 1912–13. Served in the Charterhouse OTC until August 1912. Entered the RMC as a gentleman cadet, 8.7.1913, applying for a regular commission, 14.9.1914, giving his order of preference as Royal Fusiliers, RIF, and KOYLI.

The Burgoyne Diaries, 3.12.1914, described the experiences of a draft for 2nd RIR: 'On board the boat I found awaiting me 50 men and young Calverley of the 3rd Battalion, who are quartered at Dublin. Col. M'Cammon, Jack Curran, and several other officers of the 3rd Battalion were at the quay to wave their Au Revoir to us. Detrained at Southampton.'

Arrived at Rouen, 8.12.1914, and joined 2nd RIR at Locre, 19.12.1914. Promoted to Lt., 15.3.1915, and went to hospital, 1.4.1915. A telegram was sent to his sister, 2 April, stating that he had been admitted to an Officer's Convalescent Home suffering from debility. Another message, 14 April, advised that he had been admitted to No. 2 British Red Cross Hospital at Rouen, 6 April, with diarrhoea. Evacuated to the UK, 22 April. Joined 4th RIR from sick leave, 30.7.1915 until 15.8.1915. A letter on his file, 1 September, noted that the WO believed they had ordered him to join 3rd RIR in Dublin 26.5.1915, 'however he failed to do so until 31st July'. The Army Council expressed 'dissatisfaction' and instructed that he should 'be warned to be more careful in future'. The OC 3rd RIR had formally posted him as AWOL, 26 May to 28 July, but informed the WO that he personally had not issued the verbal warning as Calverley had by then left Dublin to rejoin his unit. Calverley wrote to the WO to explain his absence and his excuse appears to have been accepted without any formal punishment or reprimand being issued. He explained that he had been told to attend hospital on 25 May in order to have a blood test and, the sample having been taken, was told to wait in the hospital until the result was available. After one hour 'I was told that the test was not completed and that I should hear the result in due course'. The MB at the hospital seemed to be of the opinion that what they had actually told Calverley was to return to 3rd RIR and that any significant result would be sent there, so this is what they advised the WO. The WO, therefore, believed that Calverley was in Dublin and simply waited for some notification from OC 3rd RIR to the effect that he was fit to rejoin a line battalion, and the OC did nothing as he assumed (no one having told him anything to the contrary) that Calverley was still unfit in England.

During the period May to July 1915 Calverley was living at the Imperial Hotel at Hythe and it was not until 27 July that the WO, having queried his status with the OC 3rd Bn and found to their surprise that he had never arrived in Dublin, sent a telegram ordering him to report for duty at once. He then seems to have made only a brief stopover in Dublin before returning to France and rejoining 2nd RIR, 29.8.1915. The WO's main complaint seems to have been that Calverley, regardless of any confusion which may genuinely have existed, had apparently been quite happy to leave hospital and then make no effort at all to contact either the WO or his unit and ask what he should do next despite the fact that he had heard nothing for two months. Wounded at Bellewarde, 25.9.1915, while serving with 2nd RIR. A telegram to his sister, 1 October, stated that he had been admitted to No. 1 Red Cross Hospital at Le Touquet 26 September with severe gunshot wounds to his back and buttocks. The wounds were actually from shrapnel. Arrived in the UK, 2 October, and a telegram dated 6 October advised his sister that he had been admitted to the Hon. Mrs Guests Hospital, 26 Park Lane, London. The MB declared him fit for light home duties, 21.12.1915, and leave was granted until 25.1.1916. Left 4th RIR for the front, 5.6.1916, and joined 2nd RIR at Bailleul aux Cornailles, 10.6.1916.

His DSO was gazetted, 25.8.1916, for actions at La Boiselle, 7–16 July 1916. Admitted to No. 1 Red Cross Hospital at Le Touquet, 7.8.1916, with a dislocated right shoulder due to a fall resulting from his horse rearing the previous day. Returned to the UK, 11 August. Joined 1st RIR, 1.12.1916, and was Mentioned in Despatches, 4.1.1917. Having been slightly wounded by gas poisoning (shells), 8.3.1917, he was admitted to No. 8 General Hospital, Rouen, and later evacuated to the UK. The MB at No. 3 Southern General Hospital, Oxford, 27 March, declared him likely to remain unfit for ten weeks.

Applied for flight training at the School of Military Aeronautics, Reading, 18.4.1917, stating that he had some flying experience. Joined No. 1 Squadron at Reading, 1.5.1917, and was gazetted a Flying Officer, 30.6.1917. The MB, 4.7.1917, noted that he had recovered. Died in a flying accident, 7.1.1918, in a Sopwith Scout number B5933 from the Royal Flying School near Upavon, Wiltshire: 'got into a spin at too low altitude to recover'. He was single and the only next of kin was his sister Miss Sybil Mona Calverley, Clontarf, Brockhill Road, Hythe, Kent. Among his effects were two revolvers in cases, his DSO decoration in a case, two wrist watches, badges of the RIR, a bedstead, and a primus stove.

Died intestate leaving an estate valued at £14,708.96. His file contains the original bill from Richard Charles Hawkins, a local builder, to frame the grave with moss and flowers, 'materials, labour and attendance £2 12s 6d'. The bill from the Clerk of Upavon Church was £1 for the digging of the grave, No. 15, and attending the funeral. 'Unpolished coffin, best brass fittings, engraved plate, best linings, shroud, etc., £6 10s 0d.' He is named on a memorial tablet at Sandhurst.

Carruth Lt. John. Married to Vera Maude Louise Carruth of Bona Vista, Stewartstown, Co. Tyrone. They had no children. Gazetted into 6th RDF, 15.10.1915. His brother, 2/Lt. Matthew Carruth, 6th R. Irish, was killed in action, 9.9.1916, while attached to 6th Connaught Rangers.

Joined 1st RIR on attachment as a 2/Lt., 13.8.1916, being struck off the strength of the battalion, 18.11.1916, suffering from trench fever. Died of wounds, 10.10.1918, at Tincourt CCS. A WO telegram was sent to his wife 12 October.

Irish Times 18.10.1918: '... was the fourth son of Mr E. Carruth, The Haven, Mallusk, Belfast. He obtained his commission through Queen's University Officer's Training Corps in September, 1915, and served in the battle of the Somme, 1916. Invalided home with trench fever, he acted at the Curragh as bombing officer until November 1917, when he was ordered to Palestine to rejoin his regiment. He came back in August last, and was only in action for a few days when he received fatal wounds. In July, 1916, he was married to Vera, only daughter of Mr J.E. and Mrs M. Vicker, Stewartstown.'

A letter from his widow to the WO, 13.11.1918, asked for details of his last three days as a letter from his Colonel said that he was wounded by shell-fire on the night of the 7th and taken away to a dressing station and then to an unspecified hospital. The WO replied, 20.11.1918, and stated that John was wounded on the 8th and taken to No. 50 CCS where he died. 'The Military Secretary much regrets that the words "attached Royal Irish Rifles" should have been added to the report. This was a clerical error which is much regretted, as Lieutenant John Carruth was apparently serving with his own battalion at the time he was wounded.'

The list of effects included a gold ring, a watch, and a New Testament Bible. A letter from solicitors to the WO, 22.2.1947, stated that Vera Carruth received a pension until 2.4.1931 when she married Capt. Ernest Newton Powell of the RDF (commissioned 5.4.1915). Capt. Powell died, 29.1.1947, and Mrs Powell requested the reinstatement of the original pension. Her address was given as 28 Rostrevor Road, Rathgar, Dublin. Tincourt New British Cemetery, Somme, VIII.B.13. File ref: WO339/43825 6/102 112408.

Champney Lt. Cecil Nelson. Promoted to 2/Lt. from the ranks of 1st RIR, 29.7.1915, and rejoined the battalion 20.8.1915.

Irish Times 25.3.1916: 'Lieutenant C.F.I. Bethell, Royal Engineers, recently killed in action in France, was a nephew of Mr Bethell, Royal Irish Rifles, who died in Dublin some years ago. Lieutenant Bethell's two cousins have both won distinctions in the present war, one being Mr N.D. Champney, of the New Zealand Cavalry, who was mentioned in General Hamilton's despatches from Gallipoli, and Mr Cecil N. Champney, who was promoted from the ranks to Lieutenant in the 1st Royal Irish Rifles for service in the field.'

Having been wounded, 2.8.1916, he relinquished the temporary rank of Capt. that day. On 23.5.1917, he joined 4th RIR from sick leave from the BEF and was posted to A Coy for duty. He proceeded to Clandeboye to take over the duties of Assistant Adjutant of 5th RIR, 31.7.1917. 2/Lt., HP, 1920. Closed file, ref: 1/83 (105867).

Chandler Lt. Harold Francis. Born 11.2.1894 in Coventry and educated at Rossall School, near Fleetwood. Next of kin were his father William Thomas, and his sister Doris. Home address Hawthornden, Queen Victoria Road, Coventry. Applied for a commission 5.11.1914. At that time he was single and serving with 15th RIR, Ballykinlar Camp, Co. Down. Previously served with Rossall OTC. Height 5 foot 9 inches. Gazetted a 2/Lt. in 15th RIR, 14.11.1914.

Left 15th RIR, 29.12.1915, and embarked Rouen–Southampton, 5.1.1916, on the Hospital Ship SS *Copenhagen*. Cause of return, hernia. There are various references on his file to MBs during the following months, but no paperwork. The OC 19th RIR wrote to the WO, 14.6.1916, saying that he had received a copy of instructions issued to Chandler to report to Annesley Barracks, Newcastle, Co. Down, but he knew nothing of the man. He wrote again the next day to say that Chandler had just reported for duty.

Medical Boards seem to have continued throughout 1916, and a letter to the C.-in-C., BEF France, 21.12.1916, stated that due to Chandler's continued ill-health there was no alternative but to discharge him from the Army, and that he had been so informed. Chandler wrote to the WO, 3.1.1917, and said that he had received notification about relinquishing his commission from the Adjutant, 19th RIR, but 'I feel sure there must be an error somewhere, as I hold an order to attend a medical board at Warwick on the 11th inst, and now being quite fit I shall be returned to duty'. The WO replied, 13.1.1917, stating that if he could obtain a certificate of fitness from an RAMC officer then an application for reappointment to a commission would be considered. Chandler replied, 15.1.1917, and enclosed a medical certificate and letter of support from OC 19th RIR. This letter was dated 30.1.1916, so presumably this had been in Chandler's possession for a year. The WO replied, 7.2.1917, and say another MB would be arranged. Chandler wrote to the WO, 5 March, stating that he had heard nothing further about the proposed MB. He advised the WO, 18 March, that he had been examined by the Board the previous day and was passed fit for general service. Asked to retain his seniority. He again wrote 8 April: he had heard nothing since his last letter. The WO replied, 20 April, saying he should try to get a nomination from the OC of either 3rd, 4th, or 5th RIR for an appointment to their unit.

WO to Irish Command, 22 May, advised that Chandler had been re-appointed and ordered to report to OC 19th RIR for duty. Promoted Lt. 1.7.1917. Served with 15th RIR in France. Left unit, 5.9.1917, and embarked Le Havre–Southampton on the *Carisbrook Castle*, 9 September, for treatment of stiff joints. He joined 1st RIR, 30.8.1918, but left on 26.9.1918. Embarked Calais–Dover, 29 September, to get treatment for a hernia. Discharged from 1st RIR, 28.8.1919. Occupation in civil life shown as 'Nil'. He wrote to the WO, 19.12.1921, asking how he should go about applying for a position in the Turkish Police. The WO replied, 11.1.1922, saying that such appointments were restricted to Regular officers. File ref: WO339/14172 18/83 30296.

Chatterton Capt. George Alleyn. Served in the South African War 1901–02, receiving the Queen's Medal with five clasps. Gazetted a 2/Lt., 30.4.1902, and promoted to Lt., 12.4.1906. Retired on appointment to the Special Reserve, 5th RIR, 2.4.1910. Promoted Capt. 12.9.1914. Joined 2nd RIR at Locre, 1.11.1914. Reported sick 16 November.

According to W.V.C. Lake, who had been a subaltern with 5th RIR at Holywood Barracks in May 1915: 'My own Company Commander was a Captain Chatterton, who in peace time had been a Gentleman Jockey and had ridden in the Grand National. He owned a very high-spirited pedigree mare, which took some handling at the head of our company and behind the band. One night, when Captain Chatterton became rather boastful as a result of imbibing much liquor, he was challenged to ride one of the Transport mules from the stables into the Mess, along the corridor (which had gas lamps all the way along) and into the Billiard Room. He did it, and also took the animal back to the stables. Anyone who knows how stubborn these animals can be will appreciate the equestrian skill required.'

Rejoined 2nd RIR 10.6.1916. Joined 1st RIR, 18.12.1917, and was posted to C Coy. On sick leave with trench foot, 17.1.1918, and rejoined the battalion 6.7.1918. File ref: 9305, a destroyed file.

Chaworth-Musters Capt. Richard Hammond MC. Born at Annesley Park, Nottingham, 28.3.1895, and gazetted a 2/Lt. in 2nd Norfolk Regt, 16.12.1914, being later attached to 1st RIR.

He was transferred to the sick list, 2.3.1916, evacuated to England, 18.3.1916, and struck off the strength. Promoted to Lt., 30.7.1916, and was Adjutant of 1st Norfolk Regt, January 1918 to 8.1.1921. Wounded twice during the war, awarded the MC, and Mentioned in Despatches (*London Gazette* 30.5.1918). His entitlement to the 1914 Star with clasp indicates that he may have served in the ranks with the BEF. From 3.9.1921 until 19.5.1922 he was ADC Div. Command, Irish Command. He then acted as ADC to the Governor and Commander in Chief, Gibraltar, 1.11.1922 to 18.1.1924, being promoted to Capt. 1.1.1923. Resigned his commission in October 1925. Closed file, ref: (43956).

It appears that these men may have been his brothers: Lt. Patricius George Chaworth-Musters, 1st KRRC, died of wounds 11.1.1915, aged 26. He was the eldest son of the late Mr J.P. Chaworth-Musters DL, JP, of Annesley Park, Nottingham, and Mrs M.A. Chaworth-Musters, 13 Low Pavement, Nottingham. Capt. Philip Mundy Chaworth-Musters MC, 25th Division, RFA, died in Belgium, 18.7.1917, aged 22. Capt. Robert Chaworth-Musters MC, 12th KRRC, died at home while attached to 3rd Musketry Camp, 10.10.1918. Col. John Nevile Chaworth-Musters DSO, OBE, DL, JP (1890–1970), Royal Artillery.

Cinnamond Major Charles Henry Lalanne. Gazetted a 2/Lt., 15.11.1899, and served in the South African War 1900–02, taking part in operations in the Orange Free State, March–May 1900; Orange River Colony, May–November 1900 and November 1900 to 31.5.1902; Cape Colony 1900. Received the Queen's Medal with two clasps and the King's Medal with two clasps.

Promoted Lt. 10.3.1902, Capt. 28.6.1908, and served in India with 1st RIR. On 5.11.1914 he was suffering from lumbago and stayed behind when the battalion left for France. Joined 1st RIR 12.3.1915. Wounded at dawn, 6.4.1915, putting up barbed wire in front of his company and was taken to Princess Hospital, Boulogne. Promoted Major 1.9.1915. He later commanded 7th RWK, 24.6.1917 to 25.9.1917, and 6th RWK from 26.9.1917. Served on the Western Front, 20.2.1915 to 12.4.1915 and 28.10.1916 to 25.4.1918, being Mentioned in Despatches, *London Gazette* 28.12.1918. Served with 2nd RIR in Palestine. File missing.

Clendining Major Cecil Hamilton DSO. 'Joined 1st RIR from base on 2.4.1916 ... Admitted to hospital on 30.6.1916.' These are the only mentions of him in the War Diary and no first name or initial was given. This may be Hamilton Clendining who was gazetted a 2/Lt. in 17th RIR 23.8.1915. There was a C.H. Clendinning promoted to Lt. in 3rd RIR, 29.2.1916. Major H. Clendining assumed the duties of Second-in-Command of 2nd RIR, 11.6.1918. Took command of that battalion, 10.7.1918 to 25.8.1918. Left 2nd RIR, 27.9.1918, for England on leave prior to joining Senior Officers School at Aldershot. Awarded the DSO, *London Gazette* 1.1.1919. He attended the 36th (Ulster) Division Officers OCA annual dinner and signed the guest book as a past member of 10th RIR. Address in 1936 was Ulster Reform Club, Belfast. *Officers Serving 1920*: H. Clendining, Major RIR, MID 28.12.1918, and DSO. File missing.

Clery Capt. John Francis. Born 15.8.1897 at Middleton, Co. Cork, and educated at Clongowes Wood College, Co. Kildare (left 1913), and St Ignatius, Galway. Employed as a bank official with the National Bank, Galway. Attested Pte 26513, D Coy, 10th RDF, 19.3.1916, and joined at the Royal Barracks, Dublin, 26.3.1916. Applied for a commission in the infantry, 25.5.1916, expressing a preference for 8th RMF. Height 5 foot 10 inches, weight 144 pounds, chest 33½–35 inches. According to *Thom's Directory* for 1912, his father was manager of the National Bank at Middleton. Posted to No. 7 Officer Cadet Battalion, the Curragh, 24.6.1916, and discharged to a commission with 3rd RDF, 24.10.1916. Joined 1st RIR from 3rd RMF, 11.1.1917, and appointed acting Capt. 12.8.1917. Wounded and missing 16.8.1917.

Irish Times 4.9.1917: ' ... the eldest son of the late Mr W.J. Clery, manager of the National Bank, Galway. He received his commission from the Cadet Corps at Fermoy in October 1916, and went to France in January, 1917.'

Death accepted for official purposes 18.2.1918. Next of kin was his mother, Margaret Josephine Clery, 66 Hollybrook Road, Dublin. He had two younger sisters Margaret M. and Miriam C. Clery. There are contradictions in other paperwork in his file: the WO wrote to his mother, 3.3.1918, and broached the question of acceptance of his death; she replied 20 March and said that she had had reports from the CO and several men to the effect that Clery had been seen being stretchered off by the Germans and they therefore thought he was a POW in Germany. WO replied 24.3.1918 and said they wouldn't press the issue, but saw no evidence for POW being correct.

A WO letter, 29.12.1920, to his brother Gabriel M. Clery, stated that repeated letters to his mother regarding the disposal of effects had never been answered and the matter should now be cleared without delay. WO wrote to Cox's Shipping Agency, 26.5.1921, asking for an inventory of his effects held by them in storage. They replied 3 June. Gabriel Cleary wrote to the WO 27.9.1923 pointing out that his mother would never wind up John's affairs as she would not accept his death. He requested that this now be done as she was short of money and her mind was gone with regard to this issue. His letter is on headed paper from the National Bank Ltd., Secretary's Dept., 34 College Green, Dublin. WO replied, 20.11.1923, and acceded to Gabriel's request to by-pass his mother's approval. He wrote to the WO, 22.11.1923, asking for the effects and memorial to be issued to him as 'in her present state my mother would have nothing to do with them'. Gabriel wrote again, 5.2.1926, acknowledging that outstanding monies were paid to him near the end of 1923, as his mother had refused to wind up John's affairs 'her mind being deranged'. It had been discovered that a small sum was due on a life policy and a death certificate was requested. Tyne Cot Memorial. File ref: WO339/64692 139538.

Coey Lt. George Hamilton. Born 31.3.1895. Educated at Shrewsbury School where he was a Sgt in the OTC. Applied for a commission, 10.8.1914, expressing a preference for 3rd RIR. Gazetted a 2/Lt. in 3rd RIR, 15.8.1914. At that time he was single, employed in the linen trade and residing at Merville, Whitehouse, Belfast. This was the address of Edward Coey JP, who may have been his father. This would imply that he was the brother of Lt. James Arthur Coey.

Attached to 1st RIR and promoted to Lt., 8.5.1915. Wounded, 9.5.1915, embarked Boulogne–Southampton, 11 May, and admitted to No. 1 Western General Hospital, Fazakerly, Liverpool. On leave with medical certificate, 11.6.1915. There is a letter on his file dated 14.12.1915 which, though somewhat unclear, appears to be between private secretaries. It states that Sir Edward Carson would be obliged if Coey's discharge could be expedited so that he could take up a civil employment that had been held open for him.

The MB at Liverpool, 11.6.1915, noted he had a compound fracture of both bones, right forearm, extensive muscle damage and infection. Coey wrote to the WO from his home at Whitehouse, 31 October; the letter was written on black-edged mourning paper. Applied to resign his commission, 3.12.1915, as he was permanently unfit for service due to his severe wound. WO to Irish Command, 4.1.1916, advised that, as Coey was not classified as permanently unfit, he could not be granted retired pay if he resigned but he was eligible for a wound gratuity and possibly a wound pension. Under these circumstances did he still want his resignation application to stand? Applied for a wound gratuity, 8 January, and wrote a letter to the WO withdrawing his resignation saying 'but am now very glad that I can be made further use of in the army'. An RAMC Major at Fazakerly Hospital wrote to the WO, 6.3.1916, recommending that Coey be granted an extension of leave as he was to have further treatment in April. MB at Belfast, 20.6.1916, noted a considerable improvement but the radius bone had not fused and there was little finger movement – unfit for any service. MB at King George V Hospital, Dublin, 10.7.1917: wounds were healed but the radius had still not fused; had recently had another operation but the outcome was not yet clear – unfit for any service.

WO letter, 20.2.1918, stated that Coey was to be placed on the retired list as he was permanently unfit through wounds. Coey wrote to the WO, 12.3.1918, asking that he be 'supplied with a silver badge' (the Silver War Badge for those who had left the Army due to disability). WO to Irish Command, 16.5.1918, instructed that there should be another MB. Coey to WO, 18.5.1918, noted that he had a wound pension of £50 per anum until 8.5.1918 and asked if it would be renewed. Coey to WO, 15.7.1918, asked the outcome of the last MB and gave his address as Church Farm, Craigs, Co. Antrim. MB at Belfast, 26.5.1919, noted both bones of forearm were fused together, unable to extend or flex wrist, 'fair' use of fingers and thumb. MB at Belfast, 29.4.1920, condition unchanged. File ref: WO339/26048 3/83 (47219).

Coey Lt. James Arthur. Born 18.6.1893, the son of Edward Coey DL, JP, Merville, Whitehouse, Belfast. Educated at Campbell College (which he left in July 1906), and Shrewsbury School. Joined 1st RIR from 3rd RIR 1.4.1916. Struck off the strength of the battalion, 4.3.1919, having been demobilized while on leave. Ended the war as a Capt. in the North Irish Horse attached to 1st RIR. In 1938 his address was 15 Egerton Gardens, London SW3. Closed file, ref: 83 (102141). His brother, Capt. Edward Coey, 15th RIR, who was born 11.4.1892, also served in the war and died 29.4.1927.

Coffee 2/Lt. Francis Warren. Born 20.11.1888 in Whitechurch, Kilkenny, the son of Francis Richard and Evelyn Warren Coffee, *née* Warren. His father was a civil engineer. Entered Trinity College, Dublin, in April 1906. Applied for a commission in 5th RIR, 23.9.1915. At the time he was single and employed as a sub-manager for the Dunlop Rubber Company, Belfast. Granted a temporary commission in 3rd RIR, 22.10.1915, and sent for a course of instruction to Mersey Garrison, Liverpool, 2.11.1915. Joined 1st RIR in 1916. Struck off the strength 13.9.1916. Killed in action, 16.8.1917, 5th RIR attached to 14th RIR. Next of kin: father and sister Elizabeth Gladys Coffee.

Irish Life 5.10.1917: ' ... who was killed in an advanced position whilst gallantly leading his men forward during an attack on the enemy's lines on August 16th, 1917, was the eldest and only surviving son of Mr F.R. Coffee, Inspector, Board of Works, of 8 Fairfield Park, Rathgar. He was educated at Bishop Foy's School, Waterford; Fermoy College, and Trinity College. He was gazetted to the Royal Irish Rifles in October 1915, proceeded to France in June 1916 and went through the Somme campaign of that year. He again arrived in France in January last and was on active service there until his death.'

Tyne Cot Memorial. File ref: WO339/46037 115274.

Colles Capt. Arthur Grove. Born 12.2.1891 at 3 Elgin Road, Dublin, the only son of Alexander and Georgina Caroline Colles (daughter of Robert George Cullin). His father was Registrar of the Petty Sessions Office, Dublin Castle.

Educated at St Andrew's College, Dublin, and joined 4th RDF as a 2/Lt., 11.11.1910, being promoted to Lt., April 1912, and Capt., December 1914. He had been attached for a year to the Connaught Rangers at the Curragh. Went to the front with 1st RIR and was gazetted to that battalion, 2.3.1915. Killed by machine gun fire, 12.3.1915, while cutting barbed wire.

Bond of Sacrifice: 'In March 1915, he was gazetted to the 1st (Regular) Battalion of the Royal Irish Rifles as 2nd Lieutenant. 2nd Lieutenant Colles had been four months in the trenches.'

Irish Life 14.5.1915: 'In November last he was sent to the front with 1st Battalion, Royal Irish Rifles, to which regiment he was subsequently gazetted. Since he went out he had been continuously in the trenches until his last action.'

Irish Times 20.3.1915: 'No details are so far to hand but a fellow officer writes to say that the last he saw of him was "charging for all he was worth at the head of his men, taking Neuve Chapelle".'

Mother notified by telegram 17 March. The list of personal effects submitted by Capt. G.W. Edwards, 22 March, included a silver cigarette case and a leather purse containing a locket. Unmarried. A WO letter, 14.6.1915, stated his place of burial as Sheet 36 Belgium, Square M.35.D. – the orchard of the chateau at Neuve Chapelle. Le Touret Memorial, Pas de Calais. File ref: 44764.

Colles Lt. Edmond Brown Ramsay. Gazetted a 2/Lt. in 3rd RIR, 24.11.1915, and promoted Lt., 1.1.1917. Served on the Western Front 19.7.1916 to 3.9.1916 and 3.2.1918 to 8.5.1918. Army List for January 1917 shows him as serving with 1st or 2nd RIR. Joined 1st RIR, 16.2.1918, and was wounded 29.4.1918. Employed at the Depot according to the Army List of 1921. Medal Card shows RIR, RUR, attached Tank Corps. Closed file, ref: 83 (131096).

Cooke Lt. Ivan Chamrey. Born 24.10.1897, the son of Revd J.W. Cooke BD, Dromore Rectory, Co. Down. Attended Campbell College, Belfast, September 1910 to July 1915, when he enlisted into the RIR. Left the UK, 10.7.1916, and joined 1st RIR as a 2/Lt., 20.7.1916. Wounded, 25.9.1916, and took no further part in the war. Retired in 1922 with the rank of Lt. He then engaged in the commercial sector and in 1938 his address was 29 Lulworth Avenue, Osterley, Middlesex. Closed file, ref: 83 35/5 (132575)

Creighton 2/Lt. John Leslie. Gazetted a 2/Lt. in 5th RIF, 27.8.1915. Posted from 36th Divisional Reception Camp, 11.9.1918, he joined 1st RIR, 29.9.1918, and was appointed Battalion Burial Officer. Invalided to England, sick, 3.11.1918. Closed file, ref: (1097994).

Cullen Lt. Frank Neil. Born in India, 19.3.1896, the son of John Armstrong Cullen. Attested 24.5.1915 in 17th RIR at Annesley Barracks, Newcastle, Co. Down, and served as Rfn Cadet 17/787. His permanent address was 34 Kansas Avenue, Antrim Road, Belfast. Applied for a commission in 19th RIR 24.9.1915. Occupation student, 5 foot 2½ inches tall, weight 110 pounds, and chest 34–36 inches. Gazetted a 2/Lt. with 17th RIR 4.10.1915.

Posted to 10th RIR and wounded near Thiepval, 3.7.1916. Embarked Calais–Dover 7 July. His home address was then Rowerra (The Vicarage), Dundela Avenue, Strandtown, Belfast. The MB, Caxton Hall, London, 9 August, noted that he had been wounded by a high explosive shell suffering damage to his hip and a piece of shrapnel had damaged his right hand. It was recorded that he was improving but looked 'shaken and debilitated'. It was thought that he would be unfit for general service until early October 1916. Leave granted until 9.10.1916. The MB at Belfast, 16 October, stated that he had dislocated his right hip joint. Some improvement was recorded but he was certified unfit for another three months. A certificate by RAMC officer R.W. Harper, 20.11.1916, stated that he was wounded on 1 July. MB the next day noted a fair improvement but still unfit for general service for another two months. MB 10.2.1917: much improved but anaemic, unfit for general service for one month.

The MB at King George V Hospital, Dublin, 15.3.1917, stated that all wounds were healed but he was still anaemic and weighed only 109 pounds without clothes (he weighed 110 pounds at enlistment!) – unfit for general service for three months. The MB at Brocton Camp, Cannock Chase, Staffordshire, 4.5.1917, declared him fit for general service and ordered him to rejoin at Holywood Barracks. Promoted Lt. 1.7.1917.

He joined 1st RIR from 10th RIR, 2.4.1918, and transferred to 12th RIR 25.2.1919, serving in the Army of Occupation in Germany. Discharged 12.11.1919, medical A1, single, residing at The Vicarage, Holywood Road, Belfast. He appears to have applied for work with the Foreign Office. A letter to that office from the WO stated that a report, 6.1.1919, showed him to have 'good ability and professional knowledge, and to be a good disciplinarian with good powers of leadership'. File ref: 114771.

Cullen Capt. Patrick John MC. Born 1876, the son of Thomas Cullen, Carlow Town. Siblings were an elder brother Thomas and younger brothers and sisters – John, James, Michael, Robert, Mary, and Margaret. He had been a grocer's assistant.

Enlisted in the RDF, 7.9.1894, aged 18 years 6 months. Height 5 foot 7 inches, weight 122 pounds, and chest 33–34½ inches. Posted to 1st RDF, 24.11.1894, and 2nd RDF, 10.2.1896. L/Cpl 5.6.1897, Cpl 5.3.1898, Sgt 21.9.1899, Colour-Sgt 16.1.1901, Quartermaster Sgt 16.5.1903. Applied for an extension of his Army service to 21 years, 24.8.1905. Married Clara Helena Woods, 18.10.1905, at St John's, Kilkenny. Promoted Sgt Major 7.5.1910. Awarded Queen's South Africa Medal with six clasps and the King's South Africa Medal with two clasps, Long Service and Good Conduct Medals. Served Home 7.9.1894 to 9.2.1896, India 10.2.1896 to 17.5.1897, Africa 18.5.1897 to 11.2.1902, East Indies 12.2.1902 to 8.11.1903, Home 9.11.1903 to 7.4.1917. Joined the BEF 8.4.1917.

There is a note on his file from 2/Lt. H.M. Lee, acting Commandant of the Dollymount School of Musketry, to the Commandant of the Curragh School of Musketry. In it Cullen was commended for actions during the Easter Rising when he supplied good information regarding the movement of rebels by day and night.

Signed Army Form W.3125 at Keane Barracks, the Curragh, 7.9.1916, extending his service until the end of the war. 5th RDF.

5204 RSM Cullen was appointed a 2/Lt. in 8th RDF, 23.6.1917, and served with that unit and, later, 8/9th RDF. Admitted to No. 20 CCS, 2.11.1917, and to No. 2 Red Cross Hospital where he had a relapse, 4.11.1917. Embarked Rouen–Southampton aboard the *St George*, 6 November. He arrived at Manchester the following day, debilitated and anaemic. The MB at 2nd Western General Hospital, Manchester, 16 December, declared him fit for general service. He had been suffering from Trench Fever since 27.10.1917 at Bullencourt. Joined 1st RIR, 25.4.1918, and was made an a/Capt., 2.6.1918, while commanding A Coy and, later, D Coy. Awarded the MC for actions in September 1918 (*London Gazette* 1.2.1919, award noted 22.10.1918). See main text.

Granted leave to the UK, 22.10.1918, and this was extended to 24.11.1918. Attached Base HQ, Calais, 11.2.1919. He was struck off the strength of 1st RIR, 7.3.1919, having been appointed CO of No. 855 Area Employment Company (Labour Corps), Calais, 26.2.1919. Appointed Claims Officer, Calais Area, 30.4.1919. Admitted to No. 30 General Hospital, 22.7.1919, and discharged to duty 5.8.1919. Then ordered to proceed to England and to make a written application to the WO for retirement. This application was made 17.9.1919 and he requested that his gratuity of £1,000 should be issued as soon as possible as he envisaged that he would be taking up employment in South Africa at an early date. He was retired 4.10.1919 and placed in the Regular Army Reserve of Officers. Residing at Dagmar House, Vernon Avenue, Clontarf, Dublin. A change of address to 41 Wellington Road, Ballsbridge, Dublin, was notified to the WO, 10.3.1921.

On 7.11.1924 he was committed for trial at the next Kent Assizes on charges of embezzlement and falsification of accounts on his employer, Sydney Robson of the Associated Supply Company, St Peter's, Thanet. Two sums of £9 and £19.45 had been taken from his employer. Having pleaded guilty, he was convicted at Maidstone Assizes, 22.11.1924, and sentenced to twelve months imprisonment. No appeal was lodged. The Long Service, Good Service, and War Medals were forfeited and then restored by the WO (*London Gazette* 6.2.1925). The Prison Commission wrote and advised the WO, 14.2.1925, that Cullen had been notified that he had been deprived of his discharge rank. File ref: WO339/119052 223506.

Daniel Lt. Ernest. Born 19.9.1883 at Ashton, Cheshire. Educated at the Royal School, Dungannon, Co. Tyrone. Enlisted as Pte 6028 in 18th R. Fusiliers, 11.1.1915. Residing at Derryvale House, Coalisland, Dungannon – his father's address. Merchant by trade, unmarried, height 5 foot 8½ inches, chest 32–35 inches, weight 122 pounds. Applied for a commission 28.4.1915. Address at this time was 18th R. Fusiliers, Woodcote Park, Epsom, Surrey. Discharged to a commission, 17.5.1915, and ordered to report that day to 4th RIR at Holywood, Co. Down.

Served with 11th RIR until 1.7.1916. Embarked Boulogne–Dover, 7.7.1916, suffering from shell shock. Granted sick leave until 8.9.1916. The MB at Belfast, 4 September, declared him unfit for general service for two months and, on 9.10.1916, for a further two months. Rejoined 4th RIR for light duty 10.10.1916. MB at Belfast declared him fit for general service 20.1.1917.

He joined 1st RIR, 28.2.1917, and was wounded by gas poisoning, 31.7.1917. Embarked Le Havre–Southampton, 7 August, aboard the *Grantully Castle*. The MB at 3rd Southern General Hospital, Oxford, 23 August, declared him unfit for military duty for seven weeks from the date of wounding and was to remain in hospital because of heart symptoms. MB, 6 September, instructed him to rejoin 4th RIR at Carrickfergus in three weeks time. Later MBs: 29.10.1917 unfit for general service for four months; 28.12.1917 unfit for general service for one month; 30.1.1918 fit for general service. He rejoined 1st RIR, 7.8.1918, and was killed in action 21.10.1918.

Irish Times 29.10.1918: ' ... was a younger son of the late Mr Robert Daniel JP, Derryvale, Dungannon. Lieutenant Daniel, who had been associated with his father in the linen finishing business at Derryvale prior to the outbreak of war, was the Hon. Secretary of the Newmills Unionist Club, and the half-company commander of the Newmills Company, Dungannon Battalion, UVF, of which his late father was the company commander. He obtained a commission in 1915 in the Royal North Downs, and on going to the front was posted to the South Antrims, with whom he took part in the opening stages of the very memorable battle of the Somme, and sustained shell-shock opposite Thiepval. In the following year he was invalided home owing to gas poisoning. The late Mr Robert Daniel's five sons volunteered for service during the present war, and he was the recipient of a congratulatory letter from His Majesty on the subject.'

Harlebeke New British Cemetery, West-Vlaanderen, VI.B.5. File ref: 118167.

Darling Lt. William Oliver Fortesque. Eldest son of Revd Oliver Warner Darling (died 20.12.1914) and Edith Darling, *née* Dunn. (Revd Darling, Church of Ireland, was the third son of Richard Sisson Darling MIC, of Port of Spain, Lotherans, Trinidad. Having commenced his ministry in 1881 at Kinsale, he served in many parishes before he came to Duncannon in 1909.)

Applied for a commission, 18.10.1914, giving his permanent address as Killesk Rectory, Duncannon, Co. Wexford, and his correspondence address as c/o Miss Somerville, *Kilbarron*, Sandycove, Co. Dublin. He was single and had served 2½ years in the OTC, leaving 30.3.1910. From 1910 he served with the Mercantile Marine Service, and served under Messrs. Westcott and Laurence from November 1913. Gazetted to 14th RIR and transferred to 3rd RIR in April 1915.

Joined 1st RIR from 3rd RIR, 15.8.1915, and was promoted to Lt. during the same month. Killed, while on patrol, by rifle fire at 7 a.m., 16.10.1915. List of effects included a pair of dividers, a planimeter, a protractor, and a silk pocket containing hair.

Free Press, Wexford, 30.10.1915: 'Regret was felt by all classes in Duncannon and vicinity on receipt of the news of Lt. Darling's death at the front. The deceased was the eldest son of the late Revd Oliver Darling, rector of All Saints, Duncannon and obtained his commission last October in the 14th Rifles, Ulster Division. He was standing beside Capt. the Honourable A.S. Chichester when he observed a Corporal fall, wounded, and while endeavouring to effect his rescue, met his own death. His stepmother, Mrs Darling, Chelsea Lodge, Duncannon, is prostrate with grief at his untimely fate, and, following so soon after her husband's death, her grief is all the more poignant and has evoked the deepest sympathy.' Chichester appears to be Capt. the Hon. Arthur C.S. Chichester, Irish Guards, who was a Staff Officer and eldest son of Lord Templemore, Dunbrody Park, Co. Wexford.

Free Press 13.11.1915: 'Lt. W.O. Fortesque Darling: Mrs O.W. Darling has received a message of condolence from the King and Queen on the death of her stepson ... Lt. Darling was the grandson of Dr George Newman Dunn of Kinsale, Co. Cork. Born at Carham, Northumberland, on 11.9.1892, he was educated at Braidlea, Stoke Bishop, and at Haileybury College, Herts., where he became a member of the OTC. Subsequently he served as a cadet on the *Medway*, one of the Merchant Marine training vessels under Lord Brassey's scheme. He returned home to volunteer on the outbreak of the war and was gazetted to the 14th Bn Royal Irish Rifles in September 1914.'

Effects claim was signed by his stepmother 'with whom he made his home', 11.11.1915. A WO letter to her, 18.11.1915, stated that, as there was no will, effects would only be released to the nearest surviving blood-relative. She replied, 28 November, that the nearest blood relative was his brother, Lt. C.H.W. Darling, 3rd RIR attached 2nd RIR. The WO wrote to his brother asking whether the effects should be sent to his stepmother.

Irish Life 28.1.1916: '2/Lt. Claud Henry Whish Darling, 3rd Bn (attached 2nd) Royal Irish Rifles, who was killed in action in France on December 12th, 1915, was the second son of the late Revd Oliver W. Darling.'

The WO wrote to Mrs W. Stoyte, Greenhill, Kinsale, Co. Cork, 11.1.1916, saying they had been given her name as being the 'next surviving relative'. She submitted a next of kin form 14 January. A letter dated 13 January from the Revd William A. Darling, Lindley, Clevedon, Somerset, stated he was the eldest surviving brother of the late Revd Oliver Darling and, therefore, the nearest surviving male relative to W.O.F. Darling, who was his nephew. He then advised that he had an elder sister, Mrs H.B.O. Savile of 3 Rodney Place, Clifton, Bristol, and asked the WO to send the form for application for the effects to either him or his sister, whichever they consider to be the closest relative. He also informed the WO that it didn't really matter whether they gave the effects to him or his sister as they would, in any case, pass them straight to the stepmother, who had been a mother to the two boys since they were about six. The WO replied, 28.1.1916, mentioning the claim of Mrs Stoyte and asked for his comments.

Messrs. Ledbitter & Harvey, solicitors, wrote to the WO, 24.1.1916, saying that they were acting on behalf of the next of kin of the two officers and asked what the estate was due. At this stage they did not actually give the name of their client. Revd Darling replied to the WO, 31 January, advising that Mrs Stoyte was from the other side of the family but he didn't really mind where the effects went. The WO wrote to the solicitors, 16.2.1916, issuing another claim form. They replied, 18 February, stating that they would return the form in due course together with their views on Mrs Stoyte's request, but still did not say who their client was. They wrote again, 3 March, advising that their client was Mrs Violet Caroline Darling, the stepmother, and enclosed her signed application requesting that the WO now send her the effects. The WO wrote, 17.3.1916, confirming that they were going to get Cox & Co. to forward the effects to Violet Darling. On the same day they wrote to Mrs Stoyte advising her that her application had been cancelled.

A WO letter, 10.8.1916, told Mrs Darling that the grave was in Wye Farm Cemetery, Belgium, Map ref. H.35.b.7.2. Both brothers are remembered on a memorial plaque in St Multose Church of Ireland, Kinsale, Co. Cork. Y Farm Military Cemetery, Bois Grenier, Nord, K.30. File ref: WO339/22091 41889.

Daunt Lt.-Col. Richard Algernon Craigie DSO. Born 1.10.1872 at Dawlish, Devon, the son of Lt.-Col. Richard Daunt of Co. Cork, and Charlotte Isabella Craigie. Educated at Haileybury College. Gazetted to the RIR 7.3.1894, and served in Malta, India, Ireland, and South Africa. Served in the South African War, 1899–1902, and was on the Staff, as Divisional Signalling Officer, 3rd Division, South African Field Force, 1900. Operations in Orange Free State, February to May 1900, Orange River Colony, May to November 1900, Cape Colony, south of Orange River, 1899 to 1900, Transvaal, 30.11.1900 to 31.5.1902. Mentioned in Despatches (Lord Robert's Recommendation for Meritorious Service, 2.4.1901), *London Gazette* 16.4.1901; received the Queen's Medal with three clasps and the King's Medal with two clasps and was created a Companion of the Distinguished Service Order, *London Gazette* 19.4.1901, 'For services during operations in South Africa'. The insignia were presented there.

He was Adjutant of Militia and Special Reserve 2.1.1904 to 1.1.1909, being promoted Lt. 1.2.1897, Capt. 11.10.1902, Major 5.9.1912, and T/Lt.-Col. 19.10.1914. Joined the BEF, 14.8.1914, and commanded, as Major, 2nd RIR from 21.9.1914, being present at Mons, Le Cateau, the Marne, the Aisne, and the First Battle of Ypres. Suffered concussion as a result of shell fire, 24.10.1914, and invalided with shell shock to the UK. With 3rd RIR at Wellington Barracks, Dublin, 18.4.1915. Having been promoted Lt.-Col., 27.5.15, he returned to the front and took over command of 1st RIR, 13.6.1915, being placed on the sick list, 26.2.1916, suffering from shell shock. Mentioned in Despatches 15.6.1916 and assumed command of the battalion again 28.4.1917 to 27.6.1917. *Whitfeld*: 'E.C.L. has been replaced by Daunt. I am glad as I like Daunt very much ... 29 September 1917. Daunt has gone home. He didn't hit it off with Heneker [8th Division Commander].'

Returned to England on account of ill health, 30.8.1917, and was struck off the strength of the battalion on appointment to 4th Army HQ. At the end of 1918 he was commanding the Depot, RIR, Belfast. Retired August 1919. He married Ellen Georgina Ferozepore ('Feroze'), daughter of Capt. H.J. Cooper, Suffolk Regt, at Tarporley, Cheshire, 4.2.1903. They had two children: Richard Hubert, born 31.12.1903, and Moira Bridget. They lived at Lauston, Pentire, Newquay, Cornwall. Fellow of the Royal Astronomical Society. Died 4.7.1928.

Davies Lt. Percy John Llewellyn. 4th Royal Inniskilling Fusiliers attached to 1st RIR. He was transferred to 2nd RIR, 22.11.1914, and joined that unit three days later. To hospital, sick, 3.2.1915, and transferred to Berthen Convalescent Depot, 5.2.1915. Rejoined 16.2.1915. To hospital, sick, 2.4.1915. Later served with the Labour Corps. Closed file, ref: (45657).

Dawes Capt. Charles Reginald Bethel. Born 12.5.1888 at Osnaburg House, York Town, Frimley, Surrey, the son of Bethel Martin and Elizabeth Isabella Maud Dawes, *née* King. Later on his father was a Colonel on half pay at the RMC, Sandhurst. Joined 3rd RIR from the militia, being gazetted a 2/Lt., 11.12.1909, and promoted to Lt., 27.5.1914. At the outbreak of war he served with 2nd RIR and suffered bad gunshot wounds in the left arm and right thigh, 15.9.1914, at Veilly sur Aisne.

2nd RIR War Diary: 'Officers Patrol from D Coy under Lt. Dawes was ordered forward to ascertain whereabouts of enemy, came under heavy fire, Lt. Dawes and one man wounded.' Embarked at Rouen for the UK aboard the *St David*, 20 September. The MB declared, 9.12.1914, that the wounds were healed but that he was unfit for general service. Leave was granted 14.12.1914 to 3.3.1915. The MB again declared him unfit, 8.3.1915, as his elbow movement was still deficient. He wrote to the WO, 27 March, requesting a wound gratuity. The MB at Aldershot declared him fit for general service, 7.4.1915. At Wellington Barracks, Dublin, with 3rd RIR, 18 April. Returned to 2nd RIR and sent to hospital, sick, 29.6.1915, and rejoined 7.7.1915. On short leave 20–3.7.1915. To hospital, sick, 9.8.1915.

Contracted pneumonia in Paris, 25.8.1915, and returned to the UK on 9 September. The MB at Caxton Hall, London, 14.9.1915, declared him unfit for service. Arrested in Paris for being drunk, 2.11.1915. He was carrying papers which said that he had been granted one month's leave by a MB and had been ordered to wear plain clothes for this period. It is not actually stated on his file but it is inferred that he was in uniform when arrested. Court martialled at Rouen, 19 November, for drunkenness, pleaded guilty and received a severe reprimand. Ordered to return to the UK where he took up residence in the Jermyn Court Hotel, Piccadilly Circus, London.

The MB, 9.12.1915, declared him unfit for general service and, on 7.2.1916, that he was fit for light duties at home. Posted to 5th RIR in Belfast, 11.2.1916, and on 7 April was declared fit for general service. Joined 1st RIR, 20.7.1916, and was appointed Town Major of Fouqereuil, 4.8.1916. Struck off the strength of the battalion 13.1.1917. There is a very brief note on his file dated 2.12.1916 from Col. Lloyd, OC 1st RIR, which infers that there was an earlier confidential report from Lloyd to the GOC, France, reporting unsatisfactory performance by Dawes. Service at Border Redoubt is mentioned but not detailed. This probably refers to the German raid on the battalion's trench in August 1916.

A letter dated 22.12.1916 was sent from the Office of the C.-in-C., France, to the WO in London reporting Dawes as unfit (meaning unsatisfactory) for service with the Expeditionary Force: 'I request that he may not be sent to rejoin the forces under my command'. Another report, 25.1.1917, noted that his work as a Town Major had been unsatisfactory, and that 'he has previously received an adverse report when in the front line trenches'.

Went AWOL, 3.2.1917, and was arrested in uniform in London, 18.2.1917. Pleaded not guilty at a Court Martial held in Belfast, 27.3 to 4.4.1917. His plea was accepted but there is no explanation of the case on his file. He was severely reprimanded. He went AWOL 28.12.1917 to 6.1.1918 and again 23.1 to 10.2.1918. A note from the GOC Southern Command, 21.3.1918, stated that proceedings against Dawes had been delayed due to the need to investigate reports that cheques issued by Dawes were being returned unpaid. Court martialled at Perlam Down, 11.4.1918, found guilty and severely reprimanded.

Reported as owing a mess bill of £21, his CO gave him one day's leave to arrange finances. Instead he went AWOL on 16 August. Arrested at the Craven Hotel, London, 9 September. A note stated that he had said that 'his nerves were all wrong'. A further note said that his father, Col. Dawes, had called at the WO and said that his son's health had deteriorated and that he was not responsible for his actions. Court martialled at Durrington Camp, Salisbury Plain, 5.10.1918. Dawes claimed that he was shell-shocked but the MB examined him and declared him to be A1 physically, with no sign of any mental problems. Found guilty and dismissed from the Army.

Deane 2/Lt. Frederick William. Born in 1895, the son of Frederick Deane, *Sunnymead*, Knock, Co. Down. Attested at Perth, 11.9.1914, as Pte 2092 in 1/6th Black Watch (Royal Highlanders). Age 19 years and 4 months, 6 foot tall, chest 34–37 inches and good vision.

'Absent at Roll Call 20.1.1915, and confined to barracks for four days.' Embarked 2.5.1915 for the BEF in France. Appointed a substantive L/Cpl, 15.7.1915, and gazetted in the field as a 2/Lt., 7.11.1915. He went on leave 15.2.1916 and embarked Boulogne–Folkestone, 17.2.1916, aboard the SS *Onward*. A medical certificate extended this short leave by fourteen days to 8.3.1916. Wounded, 27.6.1916, while serving with 1st RIR and rejoined the battalion 16.7.1916. Having been attached to the RFC, he was struck off the strength of 1st RIR 14.9.1916. A report from the RAF School at Uxbridge, 2.4.1918, recorded the following: 'Gunnery – better than exams show due to nervousness; Bombing – fairly keen, but rather careless; Practice – good in theory but practice weak.'

Awarded the French Croix de Guerre. File ref: WO339/48492 118352.

Denson 2/Lt. Leonard Thomas. Born 28.11.1896 at Ealing, London, the son of Arthur Denson, *Hillside*, Maidenhead, Berkshire. Educated at the Modern School and County Boy's School, Maidenhead. Attested 16.9.1914 as Pte 1243, R. Fusiliers. Insurance clerk, single, height 5 foot 8 inches, weight 142 pounds, chest 30–34 inches. Posted to 18th R. Fusiliers 16.10.1914. Appointed L/Cpl, 24.2.1915, and transferred to the Depot 14.6.1915. Promoted to Cpl 14.7.1915. Transferred to 28th R. Fusiliers, 20.8.1915, with the rank of Sgt. Applied for a commission, 26.8.1915, expressing a preference for 3rd RMF. Transferred to MGC, 18.3.1916, as Sgt 29433 (machine gun school). Transferred to No. 7 Officer Cadet Battalion at the Curragh, 7.8.1916. Discharged to a commission in 3rd RMF, 18.12.1916. All service up to this date was at home.

Joined 1st RIR from 3rd RMF, 28.2.1917. Left 1st RIR 9.3.1917, and embarked Le Havre–Southampton aboard the Australian ship *Warilda*, 13 March. The MB at Caxton Hall, London, 26 March, recorded several shell splinter wounds, and there appeared to be nothing broken.

Currently in Mrs Mitchisons Hospital for Officers, Clock House, Chelsea. To be transferred to an auxiliary hospital in Cornwall. Unfit for general service for two months. The MB, 4.5.1917, noted that he had completely healed and his general health was good, fit for general service. Discharged 24.11.1919. Form shows as serving MGC, attached 3rd RMF, and last served with 10 Coy MT Army Service Corps. Single. Medical status A. Address 8 Beanford Mansions, Chelsea, London SW3. File ref: WO339/67923 143895.

Dent Lt. Edgar Dent. Born 26.7.1890 at Blackheath, London, the son of Alfred and Ada Margaret Schacht. His father was a stockbroker. His original name was Edgar Dent Schacht, which he changed by deed poll in August 1914. Served as a 2/Lt. in the 3rd Volunteer Bn, RWK, 16.12.1907 to 31.3.1908, continuing with 20th London Regt, following the Haldane Reforms, 1.4.1908 to 4.2.1914 when he resigned his commission. Promoted Lt. 4.5.1909.

Broke his nose, June 1911, after falling from a horse in British North Borneo. At that time he was acting ADC to the Governor. Transferred to England 1913 and joined 5th RDF. He went to France at the outbreak of the war having been gazetted to the RDF 12.8.1914. Applied for a transfer to the RFC, 2.1.1915, but this was not immediately granted. Height 6 foot 4 inches and weight 168 pounds. Joined 1st RIR, 26.3.1915, and was granted leave 22–8.6.1915. Wounded at Fleurbaix, 18.7.1915, by a gunshot wound to the neck. Embarked Le Havre–Southampton, 23 July, aboard the *Carisbrook Castle*. The MB at Caxton Hall, London, 31 July, declared him unfit for general service for two months. The MB at Woolwich, 27.10.1915, extended this for another two months. Joined the RFC at Montrose 19.11.1915. The MB declared him completely recovered, 15.12.1915. Reported to No. 6 Reserve Squadron, RFC, 6.1.1916. Promoted to Capt., 31.3.1916, and attached to 33 Squadron. He was in a flying accident, 7.5.1916, when he miscalculated the landing during a night flight. His nose was badly damaged, deflected nasal septum, which rendered him unfit for general service. On 13.7.1916 he was despatched to Africa in the hope that the better climate would assist his recovery. His nose, however, deteriorated on the voyage. Admitted to hospital in South Africa, 9.11.1916, but refused to allow them to operate on him there. Embarked aboard the *Durham Castle* for the UK on 21 November. When he reached Sierra Leone he made an unauthorised transfer to the SS *Saxon* and arrived at Devonport, 29.12.1916. This led to considerable confusion as he had no papers and, for a short time, was officially missing. He did write to the WO, 30.12.1916, notifying his arrival and contact details, but there appears to have been an internal breakdown in communication.

A MB at the Air Board, Strand, 21.2.1917, granted him leave until 14.3.1917. On 27.4.1917 he was declared fit for general service, being temporarily attached to 13th Reserve Squadron, RFC, at Dover. Ceased to belong to the RFC, 8.1.1918, and transferred to 2nd Irish Guards. Mentioned in a press communiqué 13.3.1918. Killed in action, 12.4.1918, and there is no record of his body having been recovered. He was part of No. 2 Coy's counterattack at Arrewage, Vieux-Berquin, and was hit by machine gun fire. The WO notified his wife, Mrs Isobel Dent, 85 Lansdowne Road, Old Charlton, Kent, 24 April. She later moved to 55 Lee Park, Blackheath, London SE. He died intestate and his estate was valued at £207.98. Merville Communal Cemetery Extension, Nord, III.F.40. File ref: 31576 339/15054 and AIR 76/301.

De Vine Lt. Harry. Born 19.4.1892 at Carrowfarnaham, Belturbet, Co. Cavan, and educated at Kildare Place College, Dublin. Enlisted as Pte 9280 in the Inns of Court OTC, 3.2.1916, giving his address as Wilson's Hospital, Multifarnham, Co. Westmeath, and signed Army Form E624 that day. Applied for a commission, 11.9.1916, and asked for 'Infantry, any Irish Regiment'. Unmarried at this time. Gave profession as Assistant Master. Height 5 foot 9 inches, weight 154 pounds, chest 37–39 inches. Father was a schoolmaster. To No. 7 Officer Cadet Battalion at Fermoy 3.11.1916. First posting was to 19th RIR, 28.2.1917. All service prior to this was at home. Joined 1st RIR on reposting, 6.4.1918, and was wounded 17.4.1918. Promoted Lt. 1.9.1918.

He was a patient in Dublin Castle Red Cross Hospital being treated for a GSW in the arm. His wife was staying in the Belvedere Hotel, North Great George's Street, Dublin, and had taken ill, so de Vine was granted 48 hours leave to visit her. While at the hotel he took ill with influenza and was too sick to be moved, so was treated there 10–17 February 1919, when he died. (The school roll of honour lists him as Henry deVere.) The WO had issued notice for the grant of a War Gratuity of £83.33, 14.2.1919. The Dublin Expeditionary Force Office notified the WO of his death on 1 March. The next of kin was his wife, Florence, 43 Dundonnald Road, Kilmarnock, Ayrshire.

The Belvedere Hotel submitted a bill, 10.3.1919, for bed linen and redecorating the hotel room, and loss of custom through there being illness in the hotel. The WO Committee of Adjustment rejected this claim, but approved a claim against the estate for the unpaid hotel bill. Belvedere Hotel to WO, 10 June: they had still not been paid and 'the limit of my patience is just now being reached'. Florence de Vine wrote to the WO, 17 June, requesting that her husband's affairs be settled as soon as possible as she was unable to meet her expenses. An undated internal WO note refers to 'threatening letters' from J.H.D. Molony, manager of the Belvedere Hotel. A further letter from Florence to the WO, 1.7.1919, asked for future correspondence to be sent to her at Dugort, Achill Island, Co. Mayo. The WO replied to the hotel, 14 July, saying nothing could be settled until the letters of administration were registered with them. Molony wrote to the WO, 16 July: 'I have not been treated fairly', and again asked for settlement of the account.

Florence to WO, 10.7.1919: 'I think it is shameful to be kept waiting so long for a settlement.' She again wrote, 27 July, advising that she paid the hotel bill and had a receipt. She strenuously disputed the hotel's other claims for decoration and loss of business, and believed them to be fraudulent. WO internal note 7.8.1919: 'FMR' asked 'Mr McNeill' what reply should be made to Florence's 'pathetic appeal'. Molony to WO, 14 August: he had written to Mrs De Vine but she 'declined' to tell him whether letters of administration had been issued. The WO replied to Molony, 12 September, telling him that it was none of their concern and he should settle the matter with 'the person who obtains a grant of probate or letters of administration'. Molony to WO, 22 September: he rejected their claim that they were not involved and said it was a military matter and therefore their responsibility. WO to Molony, 8.11.1919: de Vine was visiting the hotel for private reasons and it was therefore not a military matter. Messrs. O'Neill & Collins, solicitors, of 109 Great Brunswick Street, Dublin, to WO, 13 November, on behalf of Mr Molony, reiterated the military responsibility claim. WO replied, 12.1.1920, and again refuted the claim. Molony to WO, 16.6.1920, claimed that de Vine should have never been released from the military hospital and he considered it a military matter. He re-stated his claim. WO replied to Molony, 30 June, and repudiated his claim, adding that they thought he caught the flu in the hotel. A further WO letter to Molony, 9.12.1920, said the matter was closed and no further correspondence would be issued. Molony to WO, 19.10.1921, restated the whole claim. WO wrote to Molony, 1.2.1922, advising that they had nothing more to add. Molony, to WO 23.2.1922, wrote yet more variations on the 'military responsibility' claim. Molony to WO, 27.7.1922: still awaiting his money. Internal WO note stated that a reply was not necessary. Grangegorman Military Cemetery, Co. Dublin, CE Officers, 35. File ref: WO339/71861 83 149427.

Dickenson 2/Lt. Lawrence Aubrey Fiennes Wingfield. Born 1.2.1894 at Insworth Rectory, Kelvedon, Essex, the only son of the Revd Francis Wingfield and Florence A. Dickenson (daughter of the Revd Henry Battiscombe MA), and godson of Frederic Boughton Newton Dickenson JP, DL, of Siston Court, Gloucester. He was educated at Forest School, Walthamstow, and Selwyn College, Cambs., and was a Cambridge undergraduate where he served with the OTC. He had also served with the Junior OTC at Foust School. Gazetted into 4th Bedfordshire Regt, 1.9.1914. Height 5 foot 6¼ inches, chest 35–38¼ inches, and weight 142 pounds. This battalion was part of the Harwich Defence Force based at Dovercourt.

Left for the BEF, 19.3.1915, and was attached to 1st RIR which he joined 4.4.1915. Wounded 9.5.1915 and died the following day at No. 6 CCS, Merville. His personal effects included a horse-shoe. Unmarried. Merville Communal Cemetery, Nord, I.K.5. File ref: 33927.

Dixon 2/Lt. Charles George. Born 9.11.1896 at Bawnaglough, Clondulane, Fermoy, Co. Cork, the son of Major Charles Joseph and Mrs Sarah C. Dixon, *née* Jeffrey. His birth certificate noted that the family was English. Educated for three years at Cullens Collegiate School, Aldershot, and at King's School, Warwick, for four years. Applied for a commission, 19.8.1914, and was gazetted to 18th R. Irish. Height 5 foot 11¾ inches, chest 38½–42 inches, and weight 191 pounds.

Joined 1st RIR, 21.3.1915, and was appointed Machine Gun Officer. Killed in action 9.5.1915. A telegram was sent to his parents on 15 May. At that time his father was Camp Quartermaster, Stanhope Lines, Aldershot. Ploegsteert Memorial, Comines-Warneton, Hainault. File ref: 30217.

Doherty 2/Lt. Patrick. Born 9.1.1891 at Kilshanny, the son of John and Lizzie Doherty of Caherkalla, Kilshanny, Co. Clare. Educated at Kilshanny School, and Skerry's College, Dublin. His father was a farmer. Enlisted as Pte 7132 in 28th London Regt (Artists Rifles), 5.2.1916. Address given as 76 Calabria Road, Highbury, London. Civil Servant (Assistant Clerk, Seaman's Registry, Board of Trade), single, height 5 foot 5½ inches, chest 32½–35½ inches. No previous military experience yet he went to the BEF France 21.4.1916. Disembarked Rouen 22.4.1916. Joined his battalion in the field 25.5.1916. A later note on his file stated that he transferred from 2/28th to 1/28th Bn 'at own request' – it appears that he specifically asked for overseas service. Applied for a commission, 19.3.1917, asking for the infantry, 'any Irish unit preferably the Royal Munster Fusiliers'. Commissioned to 1st RIR, 3.4.1917, and joined the battalion that day. Wounded 31.7.1917. Died of wounds at No. 17 CCS the following day. Effects included a Rosary with crucifix (broken), religious tokens, and a watch that was also noted as broken. Next of kin list shows six brothers and four sisters. Lijssenthoek Military Cemetery, Poperinghe, XIV.A.18. File ref: WO339/101022 190852.

Dolan Lt. John Joseph MC. Gazetted a 2/Lt. in the RDF, 28.11.1917. He was reposted to 1st RIR 25.4.1918. The Army List for August 1919 shows him as a 2/Lt., RDF, attached Army Ordnance Corps, 9.7.1919. Closed file, ref: (230633).

Edwards Lt.-Col. George William. Served and wounded in the South African War as Colour Sergeant with 2nd RIR, 1899–1902. Employed with the mounted infantry operations in the Cape Colony, Orange River Colony, and the Transvaal, receiving the Queen's Medal with three clasps and the King's Medal with two clasps. Coronation Medal, 1911, having formed part of a representative detachment for the coronation of King George V. Joined 1st RIR 30.12.1914. Mentioned in Despatches, 22.6.1915, for the engagement at Neuve Chapelle. Also Mentioned in Despatches 1.1.1916, 25.5.1917, 24.5.1918, and 28.12.1918.

Quis Separabit, vol. 1, no. 3, 1929: 'G.W. Edwards enlisted in the Royal Irish Rifles in March, 1892, at the age of 18 and three months. After being stationed with the 1st Battalion at Fermoy, Newry, and Brighton, he joined the 2nd Battalion, with the rank of Corporal, at Malta in November, 1894, immediately proceeding with them to India, where he was promoted Sergeant. After various stations there, the battalion came home to Belfast in January, 1899, and in March, 1899, he was promoted Colour-Sergeant (which was the equivalent of the present rank of CSM and CQMS combined). Whilst undergoing a short course in mounted infantry duties at Canterbury in September, 1899, he was recalled as the battalion was mobilizing for the South African War – for which it embarked at Queenstown on October 25th, 1899 – landing at East London and shortly after taking part in the action of Stormberg (Dec. 10th), where Colour-Sergeant Edwards was wounded.

'On recovery he joined, with his company, the 9th Mounted Infantry, and served with it throughout the remainder of the war. The 2nd Royal Irish Rifles returned to Ireland, landing at

Dublin in February, 1903. During the period it was in Dublin Colour-Sergeant Edwards was in charge of the regimental football team which won the Irish Army Cup twice and the Dublin Garrison League three times, besides doing very well in civilian football. On the battalion going to Aldershot in October, 1906, where they won the Army Cup and were twice semi-finalists, he was posted to the permanent staff of the 6th Battalion, and served periods as RQMS with the Depot and the 5th Battalion (The South Down Militia, the Terrors of the Land), from which he was promoted to his old battalion, the 2nd, in Dover as Lieutenant and Quartermaster on March 30th, 1910, the 18th anniversary of his enlistment. On the battalion moving to Salisbury Plain in 1912 he again took over the Hon. Secretary of the regimental football team, which during its stay there won every cup available for competition in the Southern Command, and reached the fifth round of the Army Cup.

'On mobilization in August 1914, he, as QM of the Depot, mobilized the reservists of 1st and 2nd Battalions, and then the 3rd Battalion, proceeding to Dublin with headquarters of that unit. From there he went to the 1st Battalion ... He served with 1st Battalion on the Western Front throughout the war, being specially promoted to Captain and Major for distinguished service in the field, awarded the Belgian Croix de Guerre avec Brevete, and mentioned in despatches five times. On return from France he joined the Depot, serving with it at Belfast, Isle of Wight, and Armagh. During his stay in Armagh, while Hon. Secretary of the Depot football team, they won the Malocco Shield and reached the third round of the Army Cup. From there he joined the Boy's Technical School (Chepstow) in October, 1925, being promoted Lt.-Colonel last February, and now retires to take up recruiting duties at Nottingham ... We hope he may continue to be a contributor to *Quis Separabit* for many years to come.'

Quis Separabit, vol. 13, no. 1, May 1946: 'The announcement of the sudden death of Lt.-Col. G. Edwards will have come as a great shock to all those members of the Regt who served with him and loved his genial personality. I shall never forget my first encounter with George Edwards. Sent out to France in January 1915, to take over as Quarter-Master of the 1st Bn, he arrived at the transport lines near Estaires one evening on horseback. Riding bolt upright, with long stirrup leathers and with his fiercely waxed moustache, he looked the very picture of a cavalry man of the old school. His years in the M.I. in South Africa had left their mark. But his martial appearance was but a cloak to a kind and generous nature. Many a young officer avoided or escaped from the results of careless administration of his Coy when acting as Coy Commander pro tem, by profiting from the good advice and help often given to him by an understanding Quarter-Master. Similarly many a young Rifleman had to thank the same Quarter-Master for assistance given when kit inspection was looming near and deficiencies had to be made good ... and served in the South African War, where he was wounded and taken prisoner ... he became Chief Recruiting Officer at Nottingham, subsequently taking over the duties of secretary of the Regular Forces Employment Association, Nottingham, an appointment he only relinquished a few days before his death. The death of one of his sons as prisoner in Japanese hands was a terrible blow to him, and did much to hasten his end ... He is survived by his wife and son. — General Gartlan.' Closed file, ref: (15478).

Elliott Lt. Richard Joseph. Born Bessbrook, Co. Armagh, the son of Joseph and Sarah Elliott. Had an elder brother William. Enlisted as Rfn 5941 in RIR, 29.8.1899, aged 18 years. Height 5 foot 4½ inches, chest 34–36 inches, weight 115 pounds. Appointed L/Cpl, 27.3.1901, and based at the Depot. Promoted Cpl, 1.10.1902, and posted to 2nd RIR, 5.5.1904. All service to this point was at home. Married Kathleen Rogers at St Anne's, Belfast, 18.10.1904. Posted to 1st RIR in India, 13.1.1906, and appointed L/Sgt 29.4.1906. Promoted Sgt 24.1.1907. Posted to 2nd RIR, 1.4.1910, and to 5th RIR, 11.11.1911. Colour-Sgt 17.11.1914; acting CSM 6.11.1916. Posted to 1st RIR 29.1.1917. Reverted to Colour-Sgt, CQMS, 30.1.1917. Appointed to a commission as a

2/Lt. in 1st RIR, 18.8.1917. After the war he appears to have served with the RAF. Lt., Reserve of Officers, 1920. File ref: 1/83 RAF (236197) 126189.

Ennis 2/Lt. Reginald Joseph. Born 4.3.1896 at Sydenham, Kent, the son of Joseph and Eva Mimmie Ennis of 89 Merton Hall Road, Wimbledon, London SW. Educated at Wimbledon College. Attested as Pte 6796 (later 761483) in 1/28th London Regt (Artists Rifles), 9.12.1915. Single and residing with his parents at the above address. Height 5 foot 9½ inches, chest 32½–34½ inches. To Army Reserve 10.12.1915, mobilized for home service 24.1.1916 to 20.4.1916, then BEF 21.4.1916 to 2.4.1917. Disembarked Rouen 22.4.1916. Joined his battalion in the field 25 May.

Applied for a commission, 19.3.1917, specifying infantry, 'Any Irish Unit. Preferably Royal Munster Fusiliers.' Father was a civil servant. Gives own occupation as bank clerk. Joined 1st RIR from the Artists Rifles as a 2/Lt. 3.4.1917. Posted as wounded and missing 16.8.1917. WO telegram to father 26 August. Any further news would be transmitted.

Reports of death: 42405 D.H. Hayward, D Coy, Lewis Gun School, Etaples, 26.9.1917. Stated that Ennis was in charge of No. 13 and 14 platoons, D Coy, at Ypres. Shot through the body by a sniper and killed outright, at about 9 a.m. Body fell into a shell hole during a retreat, well over towards Zonnebeke Ridge. Hayward was about 20 yards away at the time. The casualty form contains a report, 30.10.1917, by the OC of the battalion stating he had interviewed Hayward and thought he had no grounds for assuming that Ennis was dead when he fell into the shell hole. A letter from 10868 James Fullerton, RIR, in Langensalza POW Camp, to his parents, 3.11.1917 – he asked that they write to the family of 'my Lieutenant' Ennis and tell them that he was shot through the heart and died instantly at Ypres. ' ... there was only three of us saw him killed. I do not know whether the other two got back or not.' (Another item gives Fullerton's number as 6407.)

The WO transmitted this statement to Ennis' father noting that they believed it to be accurate. The same day they also transmitted this news to Mrs James Ennis, 1a Auburn Terrace, Donaghadee, Co. Down, saying the original communication (from Fullerton) ' ... has been brought to the notice of the Secretary of the War Office by the Postal Censor'. No indication who this woman is. A further WO letter to the father, 18.12.1917, stated that further consideration had been given to Fullerton's letter and it was being accepted as factual. The father wrote to the WO, 21.12.1917, saying that Cox & Co. advised him that they had a package and that he should apply to the WO for authority for its release. The WO form shows Ennis died as a single man, no children, and the next of kin were his father and mother, brothers Wilfrid E. and Francis F., and sisters Gertrude M., Evelyn M., and Hilda. All were living at 89 Merton Hall Road. Will dated 14.8.1917 left all monies to his father and any other possessions to his mother. Tyne Cot Memorial. File ref: WO339/101023 190854.

Enright 2/Lt. Thomas. The son of Mary Enright of Ballineen, Co. Cork, and husband of Kathleen Enright of 4 Marwood Street, Cheetham, Manchester. Promoted from the ranks of 6th Connaught Rangers, after seven years service, to a commission in 1st RIR which he joined 3.10.1917. Wounded 27.3.1918 and died 20.4.1918, aged 27. Kensal Green (St Mary's) Roman Catholic Cemetery, London, C2424. Closed file, ref: (247181).

Farley 2/Lt. Thomas. Born 4.10.1894 in Navan, Co. Meath, the son of Thomas Farley, a forester of Kilmorony, Athy, Co. Kildare. He became a pupil at Wilson's Hospital School, Multyfarnham, Co. Westmeath, 12.10.1903. He went on to obtain an Assistant Scholarship from the Incorporated Society and completed his secondary education at Sligo Grammar School, and Mountjoy School, Dublin. Returned to Wilson's Hospital as an Assistant Master 29.9.1913.

Enlisted in 5th Leinster Regt (Candidate Company) 10.6.1916. Secondary School teacher, single, height 5 foot 5¾ inches, chest 33½–37½ inches, weight 133 pounds. Training was with B Coy, 5th Leinsters, at Gough Barracks, the Curragh. Applied for a commission, 20.9.1916, opting for the

RIR. This was overwritten in a different hand to the Connaught Rangers. Sent to No. 7 Officer Cadet Battalion at Fermoy, 4.11.1916. Appointed to a commission in 4th RIR 21.3.1917. Embarked Southampton, 11.5.1917, and joined the Base Depot at Le Havre the next day. Attached to 1st RIR 20.5.1917. Appointed Town Major of Red Lodge 15.10.1917. Granted leave to the UK 3–13.10.1917 and 17.2.1918 to 4.3.1918.

Took part in the defensive actions of March 1918. Wounded 17.4.1918. Admitted to No. 108 Field Ambulance that day with a GSW to his right leg. To No. 8 British Red Cross Hospital 18 April. Embarked Boulogne–Dover on HT *Brighton* 20 April. The MB, 4.6.1918, at Leith War Hospital, Seafield, Leith, noted that he had been wounded at St Julien. Granted three weeks leave and instructed to then report to 4th RIR at Larkhill. Embarked Southampton, 2.8.1918, arriving at 36th Divisional Reception Camp. Rejoined 1st RIR 9.8.1918. Admitted to No. 108 Field Ambulance, sick, 11.9.1918. To No. 11 CCS, 12 September, 'NYD'. Embarked Calais–Dover, 5 October, 'Sickness'. The file contains a report by Col. Hunt, OC 1st RIR, dated 11.10.1918, regarding 2/Lt. Farley: 'Inefficient ... He has no qualifications to render his service useful ... His employment as an officer would not be in the interests of the service.'

The Major-General commanding 36th Division recommended Farley's services as an officer be dispensed with, 25.10.1918. The Lt.-General commanding XI Corps recommended that Farley be deprived of his commission and be held to serve in the ranks, 27.10.1918. Field Marshal, C.-in-C., 6.11.1918, noted that Farley was evacuated to England and recommended a further trial at home. There is a note on the file to the effect that Farley had seen and signed the relevant correspondence. He was then attached to 3rd RIR and applied to resign his commission, 25.11.1918. On 13.12.1918 the GOC Southern Command was ordered to report on Farley in three months time. The OC of No. 1 Coy Repatriation Camp at Windsor reported, 13.3.1919: 'Works hard but is not up to standard required, was messing officer and did not carry out his duties satisfactorily.' Demobilized 2.4.1919 and resigned 24.5.1919.

Deeds not Words: 'He emigrated to India and began work on a tea estate in Assam. He did not forget his Alma Mater, making return visits to Multyfarnham in 1925 and 1929. The Warden reported that he was "doing very well".' File ref: WO339/76199 155081.

Fennell Lt. Percy Reginald Gilbert. Born 14.3.1898 at Templeogue, Co. Dublin, the son of Henry William Fennell, and was educated at the High School, Dublin. Served eight months in the school's Cadet Corps. His father was a senior clerk with the Engineering Dept., Dublin Port and Docks Board, and resided at 31 Grosvenor Place, Rathmines.

Enlisted from school, as Pte 1517, into the North Irish Horse, Antrim, 7.5.1915. He was sent before the CO, 21.8.1916, for 'making an improper reply to an NCO' and was admonished. Applied for a commission to 4th RIR, 18.10.1916. Height 5 foot 10½ inches, chest 34–37 inches, vision 6/6 in both eyes, and weight 156 pounds. Sent to No. 7 Officer Cadet Battalion, Fermoy, 31.1.1917, and had no overseas service up to that date. Appointed a 2/Lt. in the RIR, 10.5.1917.

Joined 1st RIR from 4th RIR, 30.6.1917, and was the Intelligence Officer during the German offensive on 27.3.1918. Admitted to hospital, sick, 3.7.1918; a MB report, made at No. 1 Base, Le Havre, 20.8.1918, noted that he was suffering from influenza and general debility and recommended three weeks leave in the UK. Acting Lt. 1.9.1918. Transferred to 12th RIR, 22.2.1919, and served in the Army of Occupation on the Rhine, being discharged 16.9.1919. Single and medical rating A1. Gazetted a Lt. in the Special Reserve 3.6.1920. File ref: 163629 339/82271.

Ferguson Major John Alex. Born 19.10.1872 in Belfast. Educated at the Royal Belfast Academical Institution and Queen's University, Belfast (Classics and Modern Languages), and the University of Louvain, Belgium. Served with 2nd South Staffordshire Regt from May 1900 to May 1902 when he resigned his commission. Joined 5th RIR, March 1907, and appointed an Honorary Capt. 17.3.1908. Married his wife Muriel 14.7.1915.

Arrived France, 22.5.1916, and joined 1st RIR three days later. Evacuated to the Base 8.6.1916. The arrival report, 27 June, gave his home address as 3 Kensington, Chichester Park, Belfast. Embarked Calais–Dover 17 June. Cause of return, varicose veins. Accompanying report from OC 25th Field Ambulance stated he was unfit for duty at the front and should be assigned to Base duty. The MB at Caxton Hall, 21 June, declared him permanently unfit for general service and unfit for home service for two months. His daughter Valerie was born 22.6.1916. The MB, 13 July, confirmed him unfit for general service but now fit for home service. Joined 5th RIR at Holywood 31.8.1916.

The MB at Belfast, 6.9.1916 and 16.10.1916, stated the varicose veins had been successfully operated on and he was now healed and fit for general service. Joined 2nd RIR, 19.11.1916, and left, 30.12.1916, 'over age for front line' to go to Rouen as a DCO (draft conducting officer). Embarked Le Havre–Southampton, 9.3.1917, on the *Gloucester Castle*. Cause, debility, having had influenza a short time previously. Home address, The Knoll, Craigavad, Co. Down. The MB at 5th Southern General Hospital, Portsmouth, 13 March, declared him fit for light duty. MBs at Belfast: 9 May, unfit for general service for one month, but fit for home service; 9 June, fit for general service and, 19.10.1917, in fair physical condition, but permanently unfit for general service due to age.

Certified fit for service with a Garrison or Labour unit abroad. The WO issued orders, 4.6.1919, that Ferguson (5th RIR attached 3rd RIR) was to report to the Embarkation Commandant at Folkestone, 9 June, for passage to France. He was to be an Officer Instructor, Army of the Rhine. Appointed 10th Royal Hussars Education Officer, 11 June, and Hussars Brigade Education Officer, 31.7.1919. Appointed Officer Instructor to 4th KRRC in India, 10.10.1919.

The MB at Belgaum (Poona Division), 30.8.1920, was ordered to examine Ferguson for fitness to serve in the Army Education Corps. Found fit, but WO letter, 6.12.1920, said his case had been carefully considered and it had been decided that he would not be appointed – 'educational qualifications good. No training as a teacher. Does not appreciate situation as regards Educational Training.' Permanent address at this time was 75 Eglantine Avenue, Malone Road, Belfast (father's address). MB, 12.2.1921, noted he was in good condition. Discharged 16.7.1921, 5th RUR attached 4th KRRC. Medical rating A. Honorary discharge rank of Major. Elected to demobilize in India. File ref: WO339/64227 138948.

Festing Major Arthur Hoskyns CMG, DSO, FRGS. Born 9.2.1870 at the residence of his grandfather, Richard James Todd, 4 Gloucester Road, Regent's Park, NW. He was the fourth son of Henry Blaythwayt Festing of Bois Hall, Addlestone, and Mary Eliza, eldest child of Richard James Todd of Great Eppleton Hall, Durham (Count of the Holy Roman Empire, created 1704; title not assumed in England). His other grandfather was Capt. Benjamin Norton Festing, RN, Knight of Hanover, who fought at Trafalgar. One of his uncles was Major-General Sir Francis Worgan Festing KCMG, GCB, ADC to Queen Victoria.

Educated privately on the continent and at Sandhurst. Gazetted to the RIR, 11.2.1888, and served with his regiment in the Nile Campaign of 1889. Seconded for service with the Royal Niger Company, 29.7.1895, and served as Adjutant to the Force in the Niger–Sudan Campaign of 1896–7, taking part in the expeditions to Egbon, Bida, and Ilorin. For his services, he was Mentioned in Despatches, *London Gazette* 11.6.1897, and received the West African Medal with clasp (Niger 1897). Promoted Lt. 3.7.1889, Capt. 15.1.1898, and Brevet Major 16.1.1898. Also received the Jubilee Medal. Served with the combined Imperial Troops (West African Frontier Force), and with the Royal Niger Company's troops in 1898 and 1899, being present at the operations on the Niger. Served in Borgu, and took part in the expeditions to Lapia, Argeyah, Ibouza, and Anam, being in command of the latter two. Again Mentioned in Despatches, *London Gazette* 7.3.1899; received a clasp to his medal, and was created a Companion of the Distinguished Service

Order, *London Gazette* 7.7.1899. 'In recognition of services whilst employed in the protected territories adjacent to the Gold Coast and Lagos and on the Niger.' The insignia were presented to him at Lokoja.

He was next on service in the South African War, 1899–1900. C Coy was converted to mounted infantry under his command, 4.2.1900. *Laurie*: 'This Company received horses and some bridles of sorts, and had to march 100 miles before they were issued with saddles.' Took part in the operations in the Orange Free State, February to May 1900; operations in the Cape Colony, south of the Orange River, 1900; in the operations in Rhodesia, May 1900; operations in the Transvaal, west of Pretoria, July to November 1900. For a time he was in command of the 11th Mounted Infantry Battalion, and on the Staff of the Rhodesian Field Force. Received the Queen's Medal with five clasps.

Served in West Africa (Southern Nigeria), 1901–2, and in the Aro Expedition, commanding various columns with the local rank of Lt.-Col. from January 1901. Mentioned in Despatches, *London Gazette* 12.9.1902; received the medal with clasp, and was created a CMG in 1902 for his services in the Aro Expedition. In 1903 he served as Base Commandant and Officer Commanding the Line of Communications in West Africa (Northern Nigeria), with the Kano–Sokoto Expeditionary Force. He was again Mentioned in Despatches, *London Gazette* 31.7.1903, and received a clasp. Retired to the Reserve, 6.9.1905, with the substantive rank of Capt., having received a civil appointment under the Colonial Office in appreciation of his service.

Retired from the Civil Service 1912, in which year he was awarded the Royal Humane Society's medal for saving two natives from drowning in a crocodile infested river, and was afterwards employed by the Royal Niger Company in the Cameroons. He married Victoria Eugénie Valentine, Comtesse de Valette, in 1912 but she died the following year.

At the beginning of the Great War he served with 3rd RIR in Dublin and went overseas in December 1914, joining 2nd RIR as Second-in-Command, 5 December. *Fr Gill*, December 1914: 'I made my first visit to the trenches under these conditions. As we made our way – I had a dear friend with me, Major Festing, afterwards killed – across open fields, bullets whistled past us. The consoling thing about bullets is that one does not hear the one which kills him! The major said with a chuckle – he was a little deaf – "You know, I can't hear 'em".'

The Burgoyne Diaries, 18.12.1914: 'He sent for two stretchers to come up to take the two wounded Gordons which were lying out in front of us. Festing and I went round to find the man who was to bring in these Gordons, but we discovered he could not induce his pals to volunteer to go out again. The dark frightened them, so Festing telling me to remain in the trench, off with his coat and crawled out. I at once followed and fell over him and nearly yelled with fright; thought I was on top of a huge corpse. After a hideous crawl on hands and knees through a turnip field we found the two men … Festing sat down with them and sent me for the stretchers. He remained an hour and then returned to me. No word of the stretchers. We dozed all through the night and at dawn I told him we must get them in in ground sheets. So out he and eight men went again, I staying inside to assist them over the parapet and after one hundred and fifteen hours lying wounded and starving out in the winter damp and cold, these poor fellows reached the dressing room station … Alston is a charming CO, and Festing all the men love; he's so cheery and hearty, but he can damn 'em too, as they know; but they all understand he'd never leave them in the lurch, and that's the sort of officer men like to follow, and will always follow … I am sending a post card to Aroon with some of Festing's nonsense rhymes on it. He is always making up rhymes on all and every kind of thing.

'*Nonsense Rhymes for Aroon.*
To me it is a dreadful wrench, / When I am told to leave my trench;
For up to date I've always found / It very pleasant underground.

Although I must admit as yet / I've found that same a trifle wet.
Still notwithstanding cold and stenches / I like my sojourn in the trenches.
A well directed German shell / May very likely give you Hell,
The only thing that we must say / You hear him coming all the way.
So if you're spry, with any luck, / You may avoid him if you duck.
Should you go out to shoot the Hun / You must not take your scatter gun,
And if you wish to down a partridge / You must not use an S.A. cartridge.
By Major Festing, RI Rifles.
(Re order: "Officers must not shoot game in front of the trenches!!!")'

John Lucy, 2nd RIR, wrote in *There's a Devil in the Drum*: 'The Second-in-Command – a big, fat, jolly major – came in from a trench inspection, and set them all laughing. He was wet to the waist, and told them his runner had let him down by guiding him into a shell hole full of water. He got his revenge crossing a water-logged old trench on the way back. Darkness had fallen and the major told the runner he would lead across the bridging duckboard, which he removed as he stepped to the other side. The runner, told to step lively, fell into the trench, and the officer cried "Quits". The major then fished his pet from the pocket of his British 'Warm' – a tiny, mewing kitten. This kitten accompanied him everywhere and was always in a blown up condition from drinking too much milk. The little animal was a minor nuisance to all except its master, who held up the war in his vicinity whenever the kitten wanted to feed or relieve itself.

'This major was a popular and gallant officer, and his many decorations included the Order of St Michael and St George. In the previous August he had made a spectacular escape from a German African possession, where he had been employed as British military attaché. He got the news of the outbreak of war by secret messenger while he was dining as a guest with the Germans, and was said to have taken to horse in Mess kit and to have reached the nearest British frontier ahead of his pursuing fellow diners. He was transferred from us to another battalion, and in a very short time he was shot dead leading an attack. His death was an occasion of outstanding sadness and loss to us all, and those of us who believed in a heavenly host hoped that he had joined the bright company of angels. We got no news about his little kitten.'

Commanded 2nd RIR, 10–17.1.1915, while the CO was on leave. Went on leave to the UK, 27.2.1915, and this was extended to 15.3.1915 due to illness. Joined 1st RIR, 21.3.1915, taking over the duties of Senior Major and Second-in-Command. He was killed in action, 9.5.1915.

Bond of Sacrifice: 'He was first wounded in the thigh, and was afterwards shot in the head and killed instantaneously while leading a charge ten yards from the German trenches.'

7875 Bugler Gough reported from the Maritime Hospital, Boulogne: 'He was the bravest officer I have ever seen. He went over the parapet with a revolver in one hand and a stick in the other, just as if nothing had happened, walking quite coolly. We took the trench, and that night we searched and searched for Major Festing's body and could not find it. I saw him fall, and he was shot dead instantly. The Germans bombarded the trench horribly, and that may account for his body not being found.'

The Burgoyne Diaries: 'He was lying wounded in a German trench and refusing to be taken prisoner he blew his brains out. A brave officer and a fine soldier.'

Lt. G.W. Edwards: 'The latter had had a very distinguished career, and throughout his service had been well known as a gallant and dashing Commander. He had held high posts in E and W Africa and could have had a staff job, but preferred fighting with his regiment.'

His favourite recreations were hunting, big game shooting, and polo. He was a brilliant linguist and a clever black and white artist. He was also a keen sportsman, and was a member of the Naval and Military, St James's, Bath, and Royal Societies' Clubs. Ploegsteert Memorial. He is named on a memorial tablet at Sandhurst. File missing.

ffrench-Mullen Capt. Ernest MC. Born in 1882, he lived at *Riversdale*, Templeogue, Co. Dublin, and was a rubber planter. Educated at Clongowes Wood College which he left in 1896. Gazetted a 2/Lt. in 4th RIR, 19.3.1905, and promoted Lt. 1.1.1908. School Certificate for Militia Subalterns. Served with 3rd RIR 28.6.1908 until 17.6.1913. Appointed to 1st RIR on promotion to Capt., 12.6.1915, and arrived in France 17.12.1915. He had taken no leave by the time his Coy, A, suffered heavy losses when the Germans raided their trenches 11.4.1916. See main text.

Transferred to the sick list 13 April and placed under arrest. A Court of Inquiry was assembled, 21 April, at Brigade HQ as a result of the raid. He was court-martialled at Henencourt 2–3 June. (A form from the Judge Advocate General's Office dated 8.7.1916 shows him as 3rd attached 1st Bn.) The charge was: 'Neglect to the prejudice of good order and Military Discipline'. Found not guilty and acquitted.

Capt. C.L.G. Powell, RAMC, the Medical Officer attached to 1st RIR, wrote a confidential note to the Adjutant, 4.6.1916: 'I beg to report that on several occasions lately I have visited Capt. ffrench-Mullen and that I have been much impressed by the change in his appearance during the last two months. I consider that the strain of awaiting a Court-Martial for so long has told most severely upon him and that he is now on the verge of a complete nervous collapse. On these grounds I strongly recommend that he be brought before a Medical Board as soon as possible with a view to granting him sick leave. I think that this should be done without delay.'

The following day Major Macnamara forwarded and recommended the request to Brigade. He went via No. 26 Field Ambulance to No. 5 CCS, Corbie, 8 June. The following note was also forwarded by ADMS, 8th Division: '7 June 1916. Capt. E. ffrench-Mullen, 1st RIR, has been sent to hospital by me today. This officer has been in France since 17th December 1915 and has had no leave. He has recently been through a GCM and, although honourably acquitted, the trial and the length of time he had to wait (7 weeks) has told on him. Previous to being put under arrest he had suffered on and off from malaria and although not on the sick list was not in a good state of health. Immediately after arrest he was in hospital for over a fortnight with symptoms of neurasthenia and insomnia. At present, although much better, he is in my opinion unfit for duties at the Front and I recommend his being sent to the Base with a view to appearing before a Medical Board. My remarks as being unfit for duty at present should be inserted on the H.F.A.36 accompanying him. Also please forward attached correspondence with him under confidential cover.'

He arrived back in the UK, 11 June, having sailed that day aboard HS *Panama*, and was admitted to No. 4 London Hospital with neurasthenia. A MB report 19.8.1916: 'Nervous debility ... he is now completely recovered'. Acting Major, 6th RIR, 24.12.1917. He was later attached to 1/10th London Regt, being wounded, and demobilized 19.6.1919. At that time he was single and medical category A, fit for active service. Awarded the MC, 12.12.1919, Mentioned in Despatches, 12.1.1920, and Egyptian Order of the Nile, 4th Class, 16.1.1920 (these medals were later stolen from his widow's home). Resigned his commission 5.3.1920. Worked on a rubber plantation, the Yam Seng Estate, in Kuala Lumpur, Malaya. He lived at Sydney House, Sandymount, Dublin, for two years during the 1920's. Died in 1929, the same year as his son, Jarlath, was born. File ref: WO339/9059. (*Riversdale* was owned by William Butler Yeats for the last six years of the poet's life, 1932–8.)

Field Capt. John William. Enlisted in 5th RIR as Rfn 3484 at Camp Drinagh, Wexford, 13.6.1892. At that time he was aged 17 years and 6 months, 5 foot 5 inches tall, chest 33–35 inches, and 114 pounds in weight. He had been a servant. Served in the South African War, 1901–2, receiving the King's Medal with clasps for Cape Colony and Orange Free State. He married his wife Elizabeth in Belfast, 10.12.1903, and they had five children. The family lived at Byron Villa, Holywood, Belfast.

Re-enlisted into 5th RIR 13.6.1904. His character statement at that time noted that he was 'exemplary' and 'greatly to the advantage of the battalion' if he was retained. Promoted from Sgt-

Major in 4th RIR to 2/Lt., 20.12.1914. Joined 1st RIR, 11.5.1915, and was promoted to Capt. 5.7.1915. Accidentally wounded and died, 20.9.1915, according to the War Diary. His file says wounded in action. A list of his effects included a watch, a gold ring, and a French phrase book. His wife was then living at 6 Marine Parade, Holywood. On 30.9.1915 the OC 5th RIR wrote to the Commander, Belfast Garrison, requesting urgent financial support for Field's wife and family. He, in turn, passed the request on to the WO with a strong recommendation. Mrs Field later remarried and the Ministry of Pensions gives her name as Mrs E. Fowles. Cabaret-Rouge British Cemetery, Souchez, Pas de Calais, XXI.C.6. File ref: 41803.

Finlay Lt. Robert Alexander. Born 2.2.1893, at Clondalkin, Co. Dublin, the son of Henry Thomas and Helen Lucy Finlay. Entered Trinity College, Dublin, 1910 and joined the OTC. Single. Promoted to Lt. in 5th RDF, August 1914. Joined 1st RIR, 26.3.1915, and was killed in action 9.5.1915. A WO telegram was sent to his father, 15 May, Lord Kitchener expressing his sympathy.

    Irish Life 30.7.1915: ' ... was the younger son of Colonel Henry T. Finlay DL, Corkagh, Clondalkin, High Sheriff of the Co. Dublin. Lieutenant Finlay was gazetted to the 3rd Royal Dublin Fusiliers in July 1913 and in March 1915 was attached to the 1st Royal Irish Rifles in Flanders where he was killed on May 9th, during an attack on the German trenches.' Ploegsteert Memorial, Comines-Warneton, Hainault. File ref: WO339/9100 19308.

Fitzmaurice Major Arthur Joseph William. Born 22.2.1885 at Laurel Lodge, Carlow, the son of William Fitzmaurice of Kelvin Grove, Athy Road, Carlow, and Mary Abigail, *née* Stopford, of Blackrock, Co. Cork. He spent his childhood at Kelvin Grove and attended Aravon School, Bray, Co. Wicklow, May 1897 to July 1903. Sporting past-times included rugby, soccer, tennis and rowing. His father was a magistrate and estate agent.

    Commissioned in 1905 in the Special Reserve and served with the 8th (Militia Bn) KRRC, known as the Carlow Rifles, stationed at Carlow Barracks. He had initially been attached to 6th RIR (Louth Militia) during his first year. Promoted Lt. 29.9.1906, and acted as Instructor of Musketry. The unit was disbanded under the Haldane Scheme, 28.1.1908, and he transferred to 5th RIR. Promoted to Capt. 18.5.1908, and Major 2.5.1914. Presented to HM King George V 10.7.1911. Specialised in Musketry and the Maxim Machine Gun and was a fully qualified instructor in these subjects. Mobilized in August 1914 and was later appointed Second-in-Command of 1st RIR, arriving in France from 5th RIR, 7.6.1916. Within hours of the start of the Battle of the Somme, 1.7.1916, he took over temporary command when the CO was fatally wounded. He was unfortunate to have Lt.-Col. Lloyd as his new CO. Lloyd proved to be a most unpopular and unsavoury character who was hated by most of his officers and men. *Whitfeld*: '17 November 1916. E.C. Lloyd and Fitzmaurice had a beastly row. Entirely E.C.L.'s fault, as usual ... 1 April 1917. I went to see Fitzmaurice and was sitting with him in a hut in a sunken road when the Hun let fly two whizz bangs and hit the corner of the hut. A very close shave for all of us ... E.C.L. very rude to Fitzmaurice.'

    Invalided home, 19.6.1917, due to an infection caused by trench conditions. Appointed Musketry Staff Officer. Second-in-Command of 5th RIR at Salisbury Plain 1918–19. Later served in France, 1919, as Second-in-Command of 7/8th Royal Inniskilling Fusiliers and, in July 1919, he was detailed to take part in the parade at the London and Paris Victory Marches. On 5.3.1918 he married Emilie Hilda Foot (1884–1977), living at *Everton*, Carlow, until they moved to Laurel Lodge in 1920 where they remained for the remainder of their lives. She was the second daughter of Albert Revell Foot, a barrister, 57 Northumberland Road, Dublin. They had one son A.W.R. (Brian) born 1923.

    Demobilized November 1919 and finally retired from the Army Reserve, 22.8.1935, on attaining the age limit, retaining the rank of Major. From 1919 he worked with his father, who at this time was High Sheriff for Carlow, in the family's insurance and estate agency at 1 Leinster Crescent, Carlow, and was later joined by his son. At one time he was the agent for the Carlow estate of George Bernard Shaw. His younger brother was Reginald Maurice Fitzmaurice who served with 4th Leinster Regt. He died in Carlow 14.7.1975, aged 90, the day before Major-General G.I. Gartlan who had been a Capt. under Fitzmaurice during the Somme attack. Closed file, ref: 5/83 (210502).

Fleming 2/Lt. Samuel Henry. Born at Letterkenny, Co. Donegal, 17.12.1888, the son of John R. Fleming, 33 Meadowbank Avenue, Londonderry. Educated at Hughes Academy, Londonderry; The Royal School, Raphoe, Co. Donegal, and Trinity College, Dublin, where he was in the OTC. Worked for five years at Scotts Shipbuilding & Engineering, Greenock; nine months at Dublin United Tramways; three years and nine months at the White Star and Red Star Lines, Liverpool, and seven months at Barclay Turbines, Glasgow. Applied for a commission, 24.4.1915, declaring no previous military experience; expressing a preference for motor transport, engineers, or any infantry regiment. Height 5 foot 8¾ inches, chest 33½–36 inches, weight 160 pounds, and 6/6 vision in both eyes.

Gazetted a 2/Lt. in 17th RIR, 10.7.1915, and left for overseas service with 1st RIR, 11.2.1916, reaching this unit 22.2.1916. Appointed T/Capt., 3.8.1916, and was gassed 4.3.1917. Transferred to the Royal Engineers, Inland Water Transport, 17.5.1917. Returned from overseas service and was discharged on arrival at Chatham 17.5.1919. During 1922 he was serving with the South Irish Coast Defences at Spike Island. Married 10.2.1923. An application for a regular commission, 21.11.1923, was rejected on the grounds of age.

Foley Capt. James Walter. Served in the ranks of the Tientsin Volunteer Corps, China 1900; relief of Pekin, medal with clasp. Gazetted a 2/Lt. 22.5.1909, and promoted Lt. 7.6.1910. Served in India and Aden with 1st RIR. At the start of the war he led a detachment, escorting German prize ships, from Aden to Bombay. Promoted Capt., 10.5.1915, and served with 7th RIR. Rejoined 1st RIR 9.1.1919. Closed file, ref: 83 (14701).

Forbes Major Murray. Born 1891, the eldest son of John and Annie Forbes, 72 Eglantine Avenue, Belfast, and brother of Robert Hogg Forbes. Known as Monk by his family. Entered Methodist College, Belfast, 1898. Won prizes in 1905 and 1908. Played rugby for the 1st XV, 1908, and left the college that year.

Served with 10th RIR. Promoted to Capt. 10.11.1915. He may have served with the R. Inniskilling Fusiliers. Joined 1st RIR 28.5.1918. Badly gassed during the war and suffered the effects for the rest of his life.

In 1927 and 1928 he attended the 36th (Ulster) Division Officers OCA annual dinner and signed himself as a past member of 10th RIR. Married Monica Hadon, daughter of Canon H.P. Hadon of Bristol 1929. Divorced 1941. Married Sybil Curran 1942. No children. Resided at Ava Cottage, Clandeboye, Co. Down, until 1965, and then at White Lodge, Cultra, Co. Down. Served during World War II in command of a searchlight battery in Northern Ireland. Died 21.11.1969.

News Letter, Belfast, Saturday 22.11.1969: 'At a nursing home, Murray, husband of Sybil, White Lodge, Cultra, Holywood, Co. Down. Service at Roselawn Crematorium on Monday at 2.30.'

News Letter, 25.11.1969: 'Major Murray Forbes, of Whitelodge, Cultra, who has died, was a well-known figure in the textile trade over a long number of years. Major Forbes, who was 78, was a director of the firm of Samuel Lamont & Sons Ltd., linen manufacturers, Strandmillis. He joined the company more than 40 years ago as a salesman. Throughout his years with the firm Major Forbes excelled in sales promotion and travelled to the United States where he sought orders for the company. Major Forbes fought in both World War I and II and was at the evacuation of Dunkirk. He was a former chairman of the Ulster club. He is survived by his wife.' File destroyed.

Forbes Lt.-Col. Robert Hogg OBE. Born 1894, the second son of John and Annie Forbes, 72 Eglantine Avenue, Belfast (later of *Sunbury*, Cadogan Park, Belfast) and brother of Murray Forbes. Entered Methodist College, Belfast, 1901, and won prizes in 1905, 1906, 1907, and 1909. Played cricket for the 1st XI, 1907–1910.

Gazetted a 2/Lt. in 5th RIR, being promoted Lt. 22.5.1915. He left for France, 26.5.1915, and joined 1st RIR 30 May. (His younger brother, 2/Lt. John Donald Forbes, born 1895, 10th Lancashire Fusiliers, died of wounds 29.9.1915.) Seconded for duty with 25th Brigade M.G. Coy, 19.1.1916, and later served with the MGC. Wounded 18.5.1916. Promoted to Capt. 27.8.1916. Remained on the Western Front until 17.6.1917, and was Mentioned in Despatches, *London Gazette* 25.5.1917. On 17.12.1917 he left the UK to join the Egyptian Expeditionary Force, where he remained until 31.10.1918. He was employed as Assistant Instructor at the Imperial School of Instruction from 20.2.1918. He had been gassed during the war and suffered the effects for the rest of his life. Married Gladys, youngest child of John and Margaret Pollock, Marino, Co. Down, in 1924. His son John was born 16.8.1925 and they also had a daughter Anne (who later married Kenneth Gumley of Edinburgh). During the inter-war years he owned a hem-stitching factory in Belfast.

During World War II he commanded an Ulster AA Battery which went to France. They were moved up to the Belgian border just before Dunkirk and were split in two. Robin, as he was popularly known, made it to Dunkirk and his half unit was evacuated in a destroyer. The other half, commanded by the Second-in-Command, Arthur Workman, was captured in the retreat. Then promoted to Lt.-Col. and given command of a mixed AA regiment, stationed in Kent, and was awarded the OBE. After the war he owned Sunray Ice Cream and then worked for the Electricity Board. Resided at Hillsea, Cultra, Co. Down, until 1938; Gortagreenan, Cultra, until 1953; Deramore, Craigavad, Co. Down, until 1970, when he moved to Edinburgh. Died 16.3.1977 at Barnton Court, Edinburgh.

News Letter, Belfast, 18.3.1977: 'March 16, 1977, in Edinburgh, Robert Hogg Forbes, OBE (late of Craigavad), beloved husband of the late Gladys M. Pollock and dear father of Vice-Admiral J.M. Forbes and Mrs Annie Gumley. Service in the Cloister Chapel, Warriston Crematorium, Edinburgh, on Monday, March 21, at 11.15 a.m.' His son, Vice-Admiral Sir John Morrison Forbes KCB, married Joyce Hadden of Wexford. Closed file, ref: (49103).

Furniss 2/Lt. James. Born 13.11.1888 in Cheshire, the son of John E. and Ellen Furniss of Straid, Ballynure, Co. Antrim. His father was a mine manager. Enlisted 9.1.1916 as Pte 9404 in the Inns of Court OTC. Bank clerk, height 5 foot 10 inches, weight 146 pounds, and chest 34–37 inches. Signed Army Form E624, 9.2.1916, and applied for the RIR. The OTC recommended him for a commission 19.9.1916.

Posted to No. 7 Officer Cadet Battalion, Fermoy, Co. Cork, 3.11.1916. Joined 1st RIR from 4th RIR, 23.5.1917. Killed in action 31.7.1917. A telegram was sent to his father, 5 August. The WO wrote to his brother, the Revd George Furniss, 16 August, in answer to his letter of 14 August, stating that no details of death were known to them and requested that he write to the battalion. A letter from John Furniss to the WO, 22.8.1917, asked for his son's effects to be sent on as soon as possible. He also requested details of death and burial: 'I understand his CO was killed at the same time, otherwise I would have written to him'. He then wrote to Sir Edward Carson saying that both he and his son had written to the WO but no information was forthcoming. This letter was passed on for comment. The WO replied, 9.10.1917, saying that the father had twice been advised to write to the battalion about this as they (WO) had no advice. Tyne Cot Memorial. File ref: 153050.

Galloway Lt. Robert Charles. Born 23.4.1886. Applied for a commission 5.5.1915. Permanent address on his file is unreadable, but ends Co. Donegal. Correspondence address 3 Rosemount Avenue, Londonderry. Single. Gazetted a 2/Lt. in 5th RIR 15.6.1915.

MB 28.3.1917, tonsillitis, now fit for general service. The MB at Belfast, 15.6.1917, German measles, now fit for general service. Joined 1st RIR, 10.11.1917, being struck off the strength of the battalion 18.2.1918, no reason given. To MGC Depot, Camiers, 28.5.1918. To 47th Bn MGC 6 June. Admitted to No. 4 London Field Ambulance, 16.8.1918, with scabies. To No. 25 Stationary Hospital 28 August. To No. 39 General Hospital 5 September. Returned to Base Depot, Camiers, 23.10.1918. To 56th Bn MGC three days later. Granted leave in the UK, 1–15.11.1918, leave in Paris 17–24.12.1918, and leave in the UK 31.1 to 14.2.1919, extended until 21.2.1919. Posted to duty in the UK 2.3.1919. On leave 9–22.3.1919. To 29th Bn MGC 27 March. To MG course 5 August. Returned 31.8.1919. Leave in UK 6–20.9.1919, extended until 23.10.1919. To dispersal camp prior to demobilization 16.2.1920. Discharged 5.3.1920. Address 19 Marlborough Terrace, Londonderry. 5th RIR, last served with 293rd MGC. Single. File ref: WO339/51793 5/83 & MGC 122525.

Galwey Capt. Arthur William. Born 6.5.1886 at Brompton Barracks, the son of Major (later Col.) W.J. Galwey, RE, and Ansonia Annie Galwey. His father received his first appointment 17.12.1862 and retired 27.3.1895. Col. Galwey applied for an Honorary King's Cadetship for his son 29.8.1905. This was granted and he was eventually gazetted 7.11.1906, being promoted Lt. 28.6.1908, and Capt. 13.3.1915. Height 6 foot 6½ inches, chest 33–36 inches, and weight 127 pounds. Having served in India with 1st RIR, he joined the BEF on the Western Front 7.11.1914. Wounded, 10.3.1915, by a GSW to the head and embarked from Le Havre to the UK 20 March. Granted leave, 17.4.1915 to 1.6.1915, and returned to France in November 1915, where he stayed until March 1916. Leave was granted 26.5.1916 to 25.6.1916. On 2.10.1916, while attached to 3rd RIR, he was declared fit for home service or Lines of Communication or the Base, but not fit for service with the BEF. In November 1916 he was stationed at Victoria Barracks, Belfast, and was offered an interview regarding the command of a company of Gentlemen Cadets at Sandhurst. In January 1917 he was serving as Commandant of the District School of Signalling, Newtownards. Injured during a hockey game at Larne, 29.12.1918, when his left patella was fractured. In July 1919 he was serving as District Musketry Officer in Cork. Went to Mesopotamia in January 1920 and moved to Egypt in May 1921, serving with 2nd RUR.

The MB declared him unfit for general service, 18.2.1922, due to wounds received during the war. That is the summary but the board papers actually give two reasons: the after effects of a gunshot wound to the head and 'acute peripheral neuritis (alcoholic)'. A WO minute attributes both problems to Great War service. Departed to the UK aboard the SS *Assaye* 17.4.1922. The GOC, Egypt, submitted his name for compulsory retirement, 16.6.1922, due to his being permanently unfit. When he arrived back in the UK, his address was Millbrook, Mallow, Co. Cork, and he was placed on the half pay list. A MB report made in Dublin, 28.12.1923, shows his home address as Summer Villa, Mallow. Both his wound and alcoholism are shown as disabilities. The scar on his head was one inch long and ¼ inch depressed. His physical condition was described as not particularly troublesome but his mental state displayed apparent loss of memory for recent events, excessive nervousness, and a lack of self-confidence. The Board stated that the alcoholism was attributable to service in the war and was not 'attributable to the officer's own negligence or misconduct'. Completed five years on the half pay list, 9.6.1927, and was retired to pension. Died 23.6.1956. File ref: WO339/6657 13070.

Gardiner 2/Lt. James Tatton. Born in 1899, the son of Thomas and Hannah Gardiner of Annagh House, Portadown, Co. Armagh. Wounded, 21.10.1918, while serving with 1st RIR and was taken prisoner. Died of wounds, 1.11.1918, aged 19. Schoonselhof Cemetery, Antwerpen, 54. File destroyed.

Gardiner Capt. William Craig. Born 21.10.1892 at Downpatrick, Co. Down, and educated at the Royal School, Dungannon, Co. Tyrone. In Canada from 1911, returning 11.10.1914. Married Dorothy Rachael Gardiner, 14.7.1915, and they had a son, Robert John, born 20.4.1916. Attested as Rfn 19/145 in 19th RIR at Belfast, 17.11.1915. Height 5 foot 7½ inches, weight 135 pounds, and chest 33–37 inches. Applied for a commission in 19th RIR, 21.3.1916, stating that he was an accountant and gave his father's occupation as being a Major in 16th RIR. Appointed a L/Cpl, 19th RIR, at Annesley Barracks, Newcastle, Co. Down, and was later promoted to Cpl. Moved to No. 7 Officer Cadet Battalion at the Curragh, 29.5.1916, and commissioned a 2/Lt. 4.8.1916. Joined 19th RIR, 21.8.1916, and left this unit, 29.12.1916, having being posted to 14th RIR, 109th Brigade, 36th Division. Then living at Irish Street, Downpatrick, Co. Down.

Embarked Le Havre–Portsmouth, 15.1.1917, suffering from 'nephritis'. A MB, 26 February, declared him unfit for general service for four months, and granted leave until 18 March. Rejoined 19th RIR at Co. Down, 30.3.1917, and was Musketry Officer. Declared fit for general service 26.5.1917. Promoted to Lt. 5.2.1918. Acting Adjutant until March 1918. Embarked Southampton –Le Havre, 29.5.1918, being posted to 1st RIR the following day and joined them 26.6.1918.

Wounded, 22.9.1918, by a gas shell and was admitted to No. 109 Field Ambulance and to No. 64 CCS the same day. Moved to No. 30 General Hospital 24 September. Wounded again, 2.10.1918, but rejoined the unit 9.10.1918. He took over the duties of Assistant Adjutant, 15–24.10.1918, and was appointed Demobilization Officer 10.12.1918. He went on leave to the UK 18.11.1918 to 9.12.1918. Appointed an Educational Officer of the battalion, 10.2.1919, he took over the duties of Acting Adjutant, 17.2.1919, and was appointed an acting Capt. On 22.2.1919 he was transferred to 12th RIR but remained attached to 1st RIR. 'To remain with 1st RIR on Cadre Establishment as a Special Case.' Transferred to 5th Army Area HQ, 19.5.1919, and appointed Staff Capt., HQ British Troops in France, 27.8.1919.

Relinquished his commission 11.12.1919, medical condition A1. Residing at Myholme, Downpatrick, Co. Down. He applied and was accepted into the Emergency Reserve of Officers, 21.11.1938. He regularly attended the 36th (Ulster) Division Officers OCA annual dinner up to 1947. Discharged from the Emergency Reserve due to age in October 1947. Address in 1950 was Coates Buildings, Castle Street, Belfast. File ref: WO339/61833 19/83 135733.

Gartlan Major-General Gerald Ion CBE, DSO, MC, JP, DL. Born 24.6.1889 at Newry, Co. Down, the son of Alexander Gartlan and Emily Hamill of Cabra House, Co. Down. Educated at Downside and at Sandhurst where he gained his blue for hockey and athletics, being a gentleman cadet, January 1908 to September 1909.

Commissioned into the RIR, 18.9.1909, and promoted Lt. 8.3.1910. *Laurie*, 24.1.1915: 'I was finishing my way round the trenches in the dark, when Mr Gartlan, RIR, a very nice boy, attached himself to me, and said he had orders to go to a certain place and did not know the road, and might he come with me. Of course I said "Yes", and we progressed till we came to a bridge, just a plank over a wide stream. I crossed it quietly after whispering to him to be careful. Next moment I heard a frantic struggle and fall, and discovered him clutching on for dear life to the plank, having slipped on it. We managed to rescue him from a watery grave. I must tell you that all of this was out in the open within 200 yards of the German trenches, as we were crossing from company to company.'

Twice wounded in the Great War (firstly 9.5.1915, returning to 1st RIR 17.8.1915.) and was awarded the DSO (*London Gazette* 1.1.1919). Gave up a staff appointment (4.2.1916 GSO 3, 8th Division), 22.5.1916, to return to 1st RIR for the Battle of the Somme. Commanded A Coy and was slightly wounded 1.7.1916.

Irish Times 5.7.1916: 'Mr Alex Gartlan, Newry, Sessional Crown Solicitor for the County Louth, has received a telegram from the War Office informing him that his son, Captain Gerald Gartlan, Staff Officer, Royal Irish Rifles, has been wounded.'

Left 1st RIR 5.9.1916, moving to 9th Brigade, 3rd Division, and served on the Staff as Brigade Major in France 1916–18; GSO 2 in France 1918–19; Brigade Major 1919–23 in the Rhine Army; Brigade Major 1926–8 in Egypt, and GSO 2 in the WO 1928–9. Appointed Brevet Major 1918 and Brevet Lt.-Col. 1932. He commanded the Regimental Depot at Armagh, 1929–33, and 2nd RUR in Gravesend, 1933–6. Lt.-Col. 1933, and Colonel 1937. Awarded the King's Silver Jubilee Medal, 1.5.1935. Married Dorothy Metcalfe 1933.

Quis Separabit, vol. VII, no. 2, November 1936: 'Colonel Gartlan was gazetted to the regiment 19 September 1909, and joined the 1st Battalion in India. Born with an eye for the ball, he has had a distinguished athletic career, being a high-class player at golf, hockey, tennis and polo, and representing the regiment in all of them. In his soldiering career he has been no less successful. Proceeding to France with the 1st Battalion, he took part in the Battles of Neuve Chapelle, Fromelles, and the Somme, being wounded in the first of these engagements. During the last two years of the war he held various Staff appointments, joining in 1918 the British Army on the Rhine as Brigade Major. After qualifying at the Staff College, he was appointed Brigade Major of the Canal Brigade, Egypt, and, after a tour of duty at the War Office, commanded the Regimental Depot before assuming command of the 2nd Batalion in March, 1933.'

Went to the Imperial Defence College 1937, and then commanded 5th Infantry Brigade 1937–40. Awarded the CBE and Mentioned in Despatches 1940. Commanded the Dorset Division 1941, and was GOC East Riding Area 1942. Retired from the Army in 1944.

His obituary appeared in the *Blackthorn*, vol. 2, no. 11, 1975: 'High Sheriff for Co. Down in 1954 and Honorary Colonel of 6th RUR (TA) 1950–6. JP 1955 Co. Down. Died in hospital 15.7.1975, aged 86, while residing at Castle Park, Ardglass, Co. Down. He was survived by his wife Dorothy and his two daughters, Jennifer Gartlan who was a Nursing Sister and Vanessa who was married to Michael Drake. His funeral and Requiem Mass was at St Mary's RC Church, Cabra. Pall bearers, bugler, and piper were from the Regimental Depot.

'Known universally as Jimmy he was a formidable figure to a newly joined second lieutenant and to many others for that matter. He was a highly competent soldier but he did not suffer fools gladly and many a tale can be told of his wrath descending on some luckless individual who had failed in some way. Nevertheless under a sometimes forbidding exterior he was a kindly man at heart who had the deepest affection for the regiment and its efficiency and well-being. — Major-General Norman Wheeler.'

Mentioned in Sir John French's despatch 4.4.1915 for the engagement at Neuve Chapelle; also three other mentions in despatches. Awarded the MC, *London Gazette* 23.6.1915 – it was one of the first quota of forty to be issued. Closed file, ref: (14939).

Gault 2/Lt. John Victor. Born 10.7.1887, the son of James and Maggie Gault, *née* Ferguson, Cogry, Co. Antrim. Attended Campbell College, Belfast, until July, 1903. Applied for a commission in the RIR, 8.10.1915, giving his permanent address as Strathavon, Cranmore Avenue, Belfast. The application form noted that he was formerly a rancher in Canada; height 6 foot 1 inch, chest 36–38 inches, and weight 156 pounds.

A WO telegram, sent to his parents 29.6.1916, advised that he had been admitted to No. 20 General Hospital, Etaples, 25 June, with a slight case of scabies. Joined 1st RIR from 5th RIR, 22.7.1916, and was killed in action 23.10.1916. His mother contacted the WO asking for details of his death and they told her that they had none, suggesting that she contact the Battalion Commander. The Death Plaque and scroll were sent to her in February 1919. His place of burial was noted as Map 57C SW, squares N.28.c and d. An inventory of his personal effects, returned via Cox & Co., included a wristwatch, an identity disc, two collar badges and two stars. Bancourt British Cemetery, Pas de Calais VI.B.3. File ref: WO339/44530 113280.

Gavin Lt. Robert Fitzaustin. Born 26.11.1889 at Fatehgarh, Bengal, India, the son of George Fitzaustin and Ann Bennett Gavin. The birth certificate noted that they were an Irish family. His father was a Capt. in the 6th Bombay Cavalry. Having been educated by private tutor and at Wellington College, Berks., 1902–7, he applied for admission to the Royal Military Academy, 6.5.1908. Gazetted a 2/Lt. 18.9.1909, and promoted to Lt. 15.4.1913. Served in India with 1st RIR and returned with them to join the BEF. After being wounded, 10.3.1915, he embarked Boulogne–Dover aboard the *St David*, 12 March. On 18 March, the MB reported that he had suffered gun shot wounds to his left foot and to his face – the bullet entered his left cheek, passed through his nose, behind the nostrils, and exited on the right side. There were no fractures in either case. On leave, 18.3.1915 to 28.4.1915, and joined 3rd RIR for light duty the following day. The leg wounds had healed but he still had some stiffness in his leg. The MB at King George V Hospital, Dublin, 27.5.1915 noted that he had completely recovered. Joined 2nd RIR 28.6.1915. Promoted to Capt., 28.7.1915, and went on short leave 8.8.1915. Killed in action, 25.9.1915, at Bellewarde while serving with 2nd RIR.

Witness reports: 7071 Cpl P. Murphy, 2nd RIR, was at Highfield Hall Red Cross Hospital, Southampton, 31.3.1916. He reported that Gavin went over the top for a second time and was hit by a shell in no-man's-land and that several men saw this. He did not know whether the body was recovered as the battalion never went back to the same trenches. CSM Field, while on leave at Boulogne, stated that he saw Gavin wounded before the attack but that he still led his men out. 20149 Rfn Darragh, while on leave at Boulogne, stated that he was told by Gavin's servant, Rfn Coleman, that he had been with Gavin when he was killed and took his watch so that he could give it to Gavin's mother the next time he went on leave.

Death was accepted for official purposes 19.8.1916. Ypres (Menin Gate) Memorial. He is named on a memorial tablet at Sandhurst. File ref: 14940.

Gibson Lt. Alfred James Edward MC. Born 12.9.1890, the son of the Revd Canon William Gibson LL D. His mother was Jane Ida, late Henderson, formerly Murray. Matriculated at Trinity College, Dublin, 1908 and served in the Dublin University OTC and the 35th Central Alberta Light Horse. Attested in the Canadian Overseas Expeditionary Force at Montreal 28.7.1915. No. 475859 in 3rd University Coy CEF. At that time he was a bank clerk, unmarried, 5 foot 8.7 inches tall, and chest 34–38 inches. Appointed L/Cpl 1915. Transferred from 11th Reserve Bn Princess Patricia's Canadian Light Infantry to No. 5 Officer Cadet Battalion, Trinity College, Cambridge, 14.4.1916, and nominated for a commission in 3rd RIR, 5.8.1916.

Joined 1st RIR 12.10.1916 and fell victim to shell shock during an attack 24.10.1916. Embarked Le Havre–Southampton, 1 November, aboard the *Gloucester Castle*. The MB at Osborne, Isle of Wight, 9 November, noted that he was practically recovered and granted him leave until 10.12.1916. The MB at the Military Hospital, Fermoy, declared him fit for general service 8.12.1916. Then served with 14th RIR and was awarded the MC. Promoted Lt. 5.2.1918. Applied for the transfer of his commission to the Army in India, 4.3.1918; this was forwarded to GHQ for consideration 17.3.1918.

Irish Times 11.4.1918: 'News has been received that Lieutenant A.J.E. Gibson MC, Royal Irish Rifles, has been wounded in France, and that when wounded was captured by the Germans. He is the second son of the Revd Canon Gibson LL D, The Rectory, New Ross. Early in the war he joined a Canadian regiment, and later was given a commission in the Rifles. He was in the engagements of the 7th June and 16th August, 1917, when the Ulster Division suffered heavily.'

Wounded at Ham, 24.3.1918. He suffered gunshot wounds to his left hip and abdomen and was taken prisoner the same day. POW in Germany from April to December 1918. There is a copy of the original German military registration form on his file. Embarked at Danzig, 9.12.1918, and arrived at Leith, Edinburgh, 13.12.1918. In his statement to the WO, he said that he was Second-in-Command of D Coy, supporting A and B. The Germans attacked at about 8 a.m. and D was ordered to cover the retreat of A and B. Bringing up the rear with his servant, he was hit by two machine gun bullets whilst crossing the Ham–Nesle Road, and was carried in by the German Red Cross at about 12.30 p.m.

He appeared before a MB at Dublin 23.6.1919. His address at that time was The Rectory, New Ross, Co. Wexford. A WO notification issued, 5.8.1919, exonerating him from responsibility for his capture. Discharged from 3rd RIR with the rank of Lt., 15.9.1919. He was single at this time. Resumed his career as a banker and gave his address as the Canadian Bank of Commerce, Alberta, Canada. Appeared before the MB at Calgary 27.10.1920. He was having problems walking and was suffering from discharges. He underwent a medical examination for an Imperial Pension at Calgary 20.9.1921. It appears that the continuation of his pension was agreed but the paperwork is not conclusive.

Applied for enrolment in the Army Officers Emergency Reserve, 12.1.1940, but did not return the application form sent to him 5.3.1940. At this time he was living at 3611, 1st Street SW, Calgary, Alberta., and was married with two sons aged 4 and 9. File ref: WO339/58109 3/83 & 83 130823.

Gillespie 2/Lt. He was struck off the strength of 1st RIR, 17.2.1918, no reason given. He is not mentioned anywhere else in the War Diary, nor is his regiment. Accordingly there is not enough information to make a positive identification.

Gilmore 2/Lt. Andrew. Born at Shankill, Belfast, 25.1.1877, the son of Richard and Catherine Gilmore. Attested as Pte 4674 in 1st RIR at Brighton, 25.11.1895. Height 5 foot 3¾ inches, weight 133 pounds, chest 35–37 inches, trade labourer. His parents, at this time, were living at 143 Nelson Street, Belfast. Appointed L/Cpl 29.9.1898.

Served in South Africa 25.4.1897 to 29.8.1899. With 1st RIR in India, 30.8.1899 to 4.10.1914. Severely reprimanded, 23.3.1900, in Calcutta, 'Insolence to Sgt Irvine'. Promoted to Cpl 5.3.1902, L/Sgt 11.7.1903, Sgt 6.4.1905, Colour-Sgt 10.1.1908, and CSM 1.5.1914. Employment Sheet dated 6.5.1914 states him to be 'Strictly honest and sober. An excellent accountant and capable clerk recommended for any position of trust.' He took a great interest in sports and temperance work in his battalion. Married Mary McLoughlin at the RC Church of St Peter, Belfast, 25.5.1904. Their son, Andrew, was born 30.4.1907 at Meerut, India. Awarded the Long Service and Good Conduct Medals (Army Order 99 of 1914). Home service 5.10.1914 to 4.11.1914, when he was gazetted a 2/Lt. and left for the BEF the next day. Will dated 1.11.1914 left his estate to his wife. Killed by GSW 11.3.1915.

Bond of Sacrifice: 'The CO wrote to his widow at *Kamptee*, 6 Rosapenna Drive, Belfast: "Your husband behaved with great gallantry on March the 10th, leading his men in the assault on the trenches in front of Neuve Chapelle and beyond the trenches through the town, which we captured. He was then in command of A Company, the other officers having fallen. His company then took up a position which we held till relieved next day. It was while leaving these trenches with his men that your husband was killed. He suffered no pain. I cannot tell you what a loss we have suffered. Your husband, for many years, had done his duty most nobly in the regiment, and had done everything possible for the good and credit of the Royal Irish Rifles. He was buried where he fell, about half a mile east of Neuve Chapelle."

'Another officer wrote: "I last saw him on the morning of the attack at about two o'clock. The attack took place at about 7.30 a.m. on the 10th instant, and he led his platoon in the charge which recaptured from the enemy the old trench which had been held by our 2nd Battalion last October, and where they suffered so heavily. His platoon had only very few casualties in this very gallant charge, and established themselves in the ground they had won and dug trenches to enable them to hold it. This they did, and kept the enemy at bay all night, repulsing two sharp counter-attacks with heavy loss to the Germans. On the morning of the second day of the operations (the 11th instant), our battalion was being withdrawn from the advanced trenches, being relieved by another corps, with a view to getting some short rest and food, and it was when superintending this operation by his platoon that Gilmore was shot. He was killed almost instantaneously." '

A letter from his mother to the WO, 20.3.1915, stated that his insurance company required proof of death and asked for a certificate. Address given was 16 Unity Street, Belfast. A letter from his wife to WO, 25.3.1915, asked what amount was due to the estate as she needed to make plans for the future. Address given was 3 Shandon Street, Belfast. His mother wrote to WO, 7.4.1915, asking for the death certificate without delay. The WO sent the certificate on 12 April. His wife wrote to WO, 14.6.1915, notifying her change of address to 34 Roe Street, Belfast. They wrote to her the same day, notifying the place of burial as Sheet 36 Belgium, Square M.35.D. The WO forwarded the will to Cox & Co., 29.7.1915. They, in turn, released £196.56 to his widow 23.7.1915. A widow's pension of £100 p.a. and child's 'compassionate allowance' of £24 p.a. was granted. Le Touret Memorial, Pas de Calais. File ref: WO339/18916 37111.

Glastonbury 2/Lt. Harold Mynett. Born in 1888. Married Irene Jennings at St Mary's, Taunton, 12.8.1913. They had no children. His address at the time of marriage and death was The School House, Thatcham, Berks. Attested 1.9.1914 as No. 2354 in 18th London Regt (London Irish Rifles). At enlistment he was aged 26 years 2 months. Height 5 foot 7 inches, chest 34½ inches expanded. Promoted to Cpl 18.9.1914, and to A/Sgt 4.11.1914. His service with the London Regt terminated 8.5.1915 when he was commissioned. No overseas service with that regiment.

Joined 1st RIR from 5th RIR, 27.6.1915, and was posted wounded and missing 1.7.1916. He had been C Coy Commander for the Somme attack and was recommended for gallantry by the CO. A telegram to his wife, 9 July, notified that he was wounded, details to follow. Another telegram, 12 July, advised that he was missing and further news would be sent upon receipt.

There are various reports on the file: 8187 Sgt Haycock, 1st RIR (writing from St Mark's Hospital, Chelsea), reported that Glastonbury was wounded in the leg and was bandaged up by a Gunner P. Dixon, but he couldn't be got back to the front line. 9978 L/Cpl W.J. Sharpe, No. 9 Platoon, saw him shot in the head at the parapet at about 7.40 a.m. and was later told by 9675 King of C Coy that he later saw him dead. 9138 Cpl W. Dawson, C Coy, said that he saw Glastonbury and other wounded in a shell hole between the British and German lines. Stated that a man of C Coy bandaged the wound, which he recalled as being to the leg. 8614 Rfn John Gorman said that Glastonbury was found in a trench with a piece of shell in his leg. The wound was not serious and he was apparently taken to a dressing station near Albert. 8193 Rfn J. Willott, No. 9 Platoon, stated that Glastonbury was wounded in the leg by a machine gun bullet in no-man's-land at about 9 a.m. and he last saw him crawling back towards the British front line.

He was presumed dead by the WO, 8.3.1917, but this was not consented to by his wife. On 5.7.1917 she requested that the WO take no further action as she hoped that there was a possibility that he was a POW. She requested an update from the WO, 24.10.1917, and, on 4.12.1917, asked that they wind up his affairs. 'Death accepted for official purposes' 20.12.1917. His will, dated 28.5.1916, left his estate to his wife (gross value at death was £174.36). Thiepval Memorial. File ref: 53594.

Graham Col. Fergus Reginald Winsford DSO, MC. Born 26.10.1884. Gazetted a 2/Lt. in the RIR 29.10.1905, and served in India, being promoted Lt. 5.12.1907, and Capt. 20.12.1914. He was one of four officers of 1st RIR who led the assault at Neuve Chapelle 10.3.1915, being wounded that day, and was awarded the MC. *Falls*: 'As they passed through the Lincolns, who cheered them, Captain Graham was blowing long blasts on a French postman's horn, and shouting hunting holloas.'

From 13.1.1916 to 14.9.1917 he served with 6th RIR as Second-in-Command in Greek Macedonia, Serbia, Bulgaria, European Turkey, and the islands of the Aegean Sea. Commanded 6th RIF, 4.8.1916 to 10.9.1916, and was appointed Brevet Major 4.6.1917. Served with the Egyptian Expeditionary Force, 18.9.1917 to 31.10.1918. A/Lt.-Col. commanding 6th RIR, 7.10.1917 to 11.10.1917; 6th Leinster Regt, 24.12.1917 to 22.1.1918, and T/Lt.-Col. commanding 10th London Regt, 9.7.1918 to 15.12.1919. During his war service he was wounded twice. Local Lt.-Col. 2.2.1922. Mentioned in Despatches 22.6.1915, 6.12.1916, 21.7.1917, 14.6.1918, and 11.6.1920, being awarded the DSO, 8.3.1919 (*London Gazette* 4.10.1919), and the French Croix de Guerre 17.8.1918. Promoted Major, 8.6.1923. Army List 1923 shows him serving as Commandant of the Malay States Volunteer Regt. Second-in-Command of 1st RUR at Aldershot in 1929. He was commanding the 1st Bn by 1931. In that year he was a guest of the 36th (Ulster) Division Officers OCA annual dinner. In 1932 he was appointed Commandant of the Shanghai Volunteer Corps and held this position until 1938.

Quis Separabit, vol. 32, no. 2, 1961: 'Fergus Graham died suddenly at his home near Carlisle on 3rd November, a few days after his seventy-seventh birthday. He had a common birthday with me though ten years my senior and he had already been that ten tears in the Regiment when I joined. I remember hearing stories of his "doings" both at home and abroad. Even in those early years the pattern of his character and his characteristics was emerging clear and strong. He became devoted to the regiment and to the Rifleman and he developed his sporting activities as a horseman and a fisherman outstandingly. Such a combination of qualities brought forth its inevitable reward – he won the confidence and love of the Rifleman to a remarkable degree and for what more can any of us ask?

'In the First World War he got the opportunity to display great powers of leadership and courage and the decorations which were bestowed on him were richly deserved. I think the younger generation will get a grand glimpse of him by re-reading the tribute which he paid to RSM Mulholland of the 6th Service Battalion in the last issue of *Quis Separabit*. I only served alongside Fergus Graham for a few months at Aldershot in 1929 but in that short time I could see with what pleasure he was looking forward to the crown of his service – command of the 1st Battalion. He took it to Palestine and there re-lived many experiences of his time with the 6th Battalion in the Palestine Campaign.

'We have all a heyday in our service – the command of the 1st Battalion was his – it was the culminating point of his hopes and aspirations; it was memorable in the life of the battalion. For a short time, in his subaltern days, he went "bush whacking" and here again he displayed the same qualities of leadership and flair for winning the confidence of his men. In the difficult appointment of Commandant of the Shanghai Volunteer Corps towards the end of his time in the Army he again showed his mettle and made his mark.

'He never gave up. I came across him in the Second World War when he was doing Yeoman service with the Royal Observer Corps in the Carlisle area. He left me in no doubt about what ought to be done. He never lost regimental interests. Each year on his fishing visits to Northern Ireland – which continued right up to the end – he was always keen to learn of friends and the activities of our units. His example should never be forgotten. We think particularly of his wife at this time and to her and the family the thoughts of many go out with special personal remembrance – the sympathy of all members of the Regiment is theirs.' Closed file.

Greene 2/Lt. Harry Caldwell. Born 27.4.1892, the son of Thomas G. and Mary Greene of Newtown House, Roscarberry, Co. Cork. Applied for a commission, 13.5.1915. Single. Address for correspondence: Kildare National School, Kildare. He was a teacher at this school. Requested infantry; a note in a different hand says RMF.

Joined 1st RIR from 5th RMF, 5.1.1917. The WO wrote to Thomas Greene, 3.2.1917, advising that his son has been admitted to 24th General Hospital, Etaples, 1 February, suffering from slight inflammation of the jaw. A further note informed that he had been discharged to the Base Depot, 20.2.1917. A letter was sent to the WO from the West End Clothiers Company Ltd., 28.6.1917, asking for the current whereabouts of Lt. H.C. Greene, RMF, no reason being given. Killed in action 29.4.1918. Very short list of effects included a wallet, correspondence, and a wristlet disc.

Irish Times 21.5.1918: 'The father of Lieutenant Harry Caldwell Greene, Royal Irish Rifles, has received a letter from Captain Tayler of the regiment in reference to the death in action of his son, in which he says: "Your son fell on 29th, when leading half a company to attack a hostile post. Being a young, gallant, and thorough officer, he was selected for this duty and it was performed, as the post was captured, and a German machine gun, too. Poor Greene – a friend of mine since January, 1917 – was sniped and instantly killed. His body was brought back and reverently buried on Hill Top Farm – our battalion headquarters – by the Revd W. Hutchinson, the regimental padre. Nothing I can say will lessen your loss, but it may, perhaps, be tinged with sad pride when I tell you that Greene was one of our brightest and best, well-beloved, cheerful, apt, and very capable. What he had not learned he got over with his own personality. Though he had moved away from the battalion as an Area Commandant for a long time, when he did return, his adaptability very soon led to his being temporarily in command of a company, and jolly well he did it too, as I personally know." '

A letter from his father to the WO, 18.7.1918, asked that all matters should be cleared 'so that I may be relieved once and for all of painful reminders about my dear son almost every day'. New Irish Farm Cemetery, Ieper, VI.F.4. File ref: WO339/33651 80823.

Gregg 2/Lt. William Henry. The son of John and Margaret Gregg, Deramore Park, Belfast. Gazetted a 2/Lt. 22.5.1915, and joined D Coy, 1st RIR, from 5th RIR, 6.6.1916. Killed in action 1.7.1916. A report dated 17.8.1916 by 8465 Cpl Beehan stated that Gregg (14 Platoon) fell shot between the first and second German lines. 8454 Rfn King (Gregg's servant) recorded that he was four to five yards away when Gregg was shot through the head. King was later wounded and was taken back by stretcher and stated that Gregg was still lying in the same place. The WO accepted his death for official purposes, 29.9.1916.

Irish Life 24.11.1916: 'He was a son of Mr John Gregg JP, of 3 Chichester Gardens, Belfast. He was educated at Rydal Mount, Colwyn Bay, and entered the business of the well-known firm of Gregg, Sons, and Phenix, Belfast, of which his father is a partner. He endeavoured to enter the army when the Ulster Division was formed, and was rejected no fewer than five times owing to eye weakness, but he was ultimately given his commission in May 1915.' Thiepval Memorial.

Griffith Lt. Henry Alfred Cullum. Gazetted a 2/Lt. in 3rd RIR 13.3.1918. First overseas date 29.5.1918 and joined 1st RIR, 13.6.1918. May also have served with the Royal Irish Regt. Closed file, ref: 18 83 (230196)

Gunnell 2/Lt. Frederick Charles MM. Previously served in the ranks. Joined 1st RIR and was posted to B Coy, 3.11.1917: the same day as his promotion. Struck off the strength of the battalion, 15.3.1918, on proceeding to England for six months. Rejoined the unit 17.11.1918. Returned to the UK, 10.2.1919, prior to going overseas with 2nd RIR. Closed file, ref: (251408).

Gwyn 2/Lt. Anthony Joseph Jermy. Born 8.9.1896. Educated at Clongowes Wood College, Co. Kildare. The college records include a note that three brothers were registered to come to the college but, in the event, only Anthony and his brother Reg arrived. They were the sons of Capt. R.P. Jermy Gwyn, 4th R. Fusiliers, Ballinderry, Mullingar, Co. Westmeath. Anthony attended the college from 14.1.1908 to December 1908. Reg, born 3.9.1897, attended from January to 30 June 1909. They were transferred to the Jesuit College at Stoneyhurst College, Lancashire, presumably when their father was promoted to Major, and moved to 185 Bidston Road, Oxton, Birkenhead.

3rd Norfolk Regt attached 1st RIR. He was shocked by shellfire 16.10.1915. Closed file, ref: (4925).

(CWGC records: 2/Lt. Reginald Augustine Jermy Gwyn, 2nd Lincolnshire Regt, was killed in action 3.3.1916, aged 18. Educated at Stoneyhurst and Sandhurst. A son of Major R.P. Jermy Gwyn, 7th R. Fusiliers, and Isabel Jermy Gwyn, 72 Lexham Gardens, Kensington, London. File ref: 10 3991.)

Haigh 2/Lt. John Caleb. Born 29.3.1890 at Kilmeaden, the son of Mr and Mrs J. Haigh of Kilmeaden, Waterford. Educated at Bishop Foy High School, Waterford. Enlisted as Pte 2859 in 24th R. Fusiliers at Waterford, 21.1.1915. Clerk, single, height 5 foot 9 inches, weight 123 pounds, chest 33–35 inches, vision 6/24 and 6/24, but a note stated that he had very good sight 'with glasses'. Next of kin mother, Mary Jane Haigh.

Admitted Gidea Park Camp, 4–8.5.1915, with measles. Transferred to 33rd Divisional Cyclist Corps 30.7.1915. Transferred back to 24th R. Fusiliers 14.9.1915. Home service 28.1.1915 to 14.11.1915. To BEF 15.11.1915. To hospital 'in the field' 4.3.1916, rejoining his unit 10.3.1916.

Admitted CCS 18.10.1916 with varicose ulcer right leg. Embarked Boulogne–England on the *St David*, 20 October. Admitted to the Italian Hospital, Queen Square, London, the next day and remained there until 21 November. Transferred to 4th London General Hospital until 25.1.1917. Posted 6th R. Fusiliers 30.4.1917.

Applied for a commission, 20.4.1917, requesting infantry, preferably 13th R. Fusiliers. Single. Father noted as deceased and had been manager of a Woolen Business. To No. 13 Officer Cadet Battalion at Newmarket, 8.9.1917. Discharged to a commission in 3rd RDF, 17.12.1917. Home service 21.10.1916 to 17.2.1917. Reposted to 1st RIR 25.4.1918. Wounded 11.9.1918. Killed in action 2.10.1918. A WO telegram was sent to 'Mrs Haigh', 6 October, at Kilmeaden. Another note says 'we have no record of this officer's body having been recovered.' Estate to wife Elsie, address then shown as 40 Ormiston Road, Greenwich, London SE10. There was some confusion here – the WO didn't seem to know whether they were dealing with the mother or the widow. A register form dated 8.10.1918 shows next of kin as 'Mrs Elsie Haigh (wife), Kilmeaden, Co. Waterford.' A WO letter to her, 12.2.1919, notified that Haigh was buried about 500 yards south-south-west of Panemolen, north of Gheluwe, east-south-east of Ypres. The grave was marked with an inscribed wooden cross. A further letter, 20.8.1920, informed her that the body had been exhumed and moved to Dadizeele New British Cemetery, Moorslede, West-Vlaanderen, V.B.1. File ref: WO339/106992 200239.

Hamilton 2/Lt. Douglas. Born in 1893 at Enniskerry, Co. Wicklow, and was a clerk. He later lived at Duncairn Terrace, Bray, Co. Wicklow, and moved to Vernon, British Columbia. Returned from Canada and enlisted at Westminster, London, as Guardsman 5084 in 1st Irish Guards 4.9.1914. Age 21 years 6 months, height 5 foot 11¾ inches, chest 33½–38½ inches, and weight 155 pounds. Appointed L/Cpl, 31.12.1914, and went overseas 3.1.1915. Gazetted to a commission in the RIR, 20.3.1915, and joined 1st RIR 26.3.1915. Killed in action 9.5.1915. He was unmarried and both of his parents were deceased. He left no will and the next of kin was his brother, Albert Hamilton, 20 Glebe Place, Chelsea, London. A WO telegram notifying death was sent 18 May.

There is also a WO minute on the file which refers to some forms having been returned by a L/Cpl C.R. Hamilton of 23 Carlyle Mansions, Cheyne Walk, Chelsea. This man appears on a later document as 2/Lt. Charles Robert Hamilton, Irish Guards. There is also reference to an aunt, Mrs Rooke of 2 Clarinda Park East, Kingstown, Co. Dublin. A further scribbled note says 'For A. Hamilton, who is on active service.' Ploegsteert Memorial. File ref: WO339/27850 1/83 49594.

Harper Lt. Louis. Born 21.1.1898 at Chichester House, Antrim Road, Belfast, the son of William and Jane Harper, *née* Moreland. His father was a solicitor. Louis worked in the linen industry and had been educated at the Ulster Provisional School, Lisburn; Portora Royal School, Enniskillen; Shaftsbury House Tutorial College, Belfast, and Queen's University, Belfast, where he was in the OTC. Applied for a commission in 5th RIR 22.11.1915. Height 5 foot 7 inches, chest 32–34 inches, and weight 128 pounds.

Joined 1st RIR from 5th RIR, 21.9.1916. Left the unit, 21.10.1916, and embarked for the UK, 29 October, appearing before the MB at Caxton Hall, London, 13 November. He was suffering from influenza, contracted during the Somme offensive 25.10.1916, when he was confined to bed for two weeks. The MB noted that he had recovered 12.2.1917. Promoted Lt. 1.7.1917. Demobilized from the RAF Pool of Officers 28.8.1919. File ref: WO339/50404 5/83 120771.

Hart Major John James MC. Born 1886. Served with 2nd RIR, 13.8.1914 to 13.1.1915, and with 1st RIR, 3.5.1915 to 16.1.1916. To hospital, sick, 11.12.1914. Promoted from Sgt to 2/Lt. in 2nd RIR 18.11.1914. Joined 1st RIR 18.5.1915. A/Adjutant of 1st RIR August 1915. Placed on the sick list 2.1.1916. Attached to the Nigeria Regt 19.12.1916. Served in British, German, and Portuguese East Africa, Nyasaland, and Northern Rhodesia. He was wounded and subsequently repatriated 14.2.1918, being awarded the MC, 4.3.1918. Promoted Capt. 24.4.1921. Left the Reserve of Officers 22.3.1936. In 1938 he was residing at Bramfield, Lower Green Road, Esher, Surrey.

Quis Separabit, vol. 37, no. 3, 1966: 'Major John James Hart MC (1886–1966) — A Tribute by General Steele … died in hospital near his home in Cobham, Surrey, on 22nd July 1966. He had been in failing health for some time and had just passed his eightieth birthday. He was one of a notable group who were commissioned in the regiment on the field of battle in France in November 1914, and I well remember the feeling of respect amounting almost to hero worship which I had when I met him early in 1915. Johnnie Hart was a Rifleman through and through and although he served in other regiments and corps there was never any doubt about where his true love lay. After a lengthy period of service in France and Belgium, he was transferred to German East Africa towards the end of 1916 and served with the Nigeria Regt WAFF and as Staff Captain of the West African Service Brigade. In these operations he was given the immediate award of the Military Cross.

'Not content with inaction after the Armistice, he managed to get to North Russia in 1919. On his return to England he was posted to the 1st Bn The Royal Ulster Rifles and in 1922 arrived in Cairo to serve with the 2nd Battalion. In 1927 he became adjutant of the Nilgiri Malabar Auxiliary Forces and on completion of that appointment he retired from the army in 1931. Johnnie Hart had always had a flair for administration and keeping accounts. Sure enough in 1936 he accepted an appointment in the Air Ministry as a Civilian Accountant officer. This led to his being commissioned in the RAFVR in September 1939 – he became a Squadron Leader and served until he was permitted to resign in May 1945. Thus he had a long and varied career in these two services: the Army and the Royal Air Force. You could not be very long in his presence without sensing his pride in such a record but, as I have mentioned, the regiment was what mattered most to him.

'Many of us older ones will remember him for the fun he diffused at regimental dinners, and I for one used to marvel at the knack he had of looking at a young officer and sizing him up pretty shrewdly. My wife and I recall the Hart's bungalow in the Nilgiri's S. India where hospitality was dispensed in true Irish style and naturally that also brings to mind the part which his wife, Corinne, played at that time in the happy regimental community at Wellington. Our deep sympathy goes out to her and to their daughter Joan at this sad time.'

His medals were donated to the RUR Museum by his widow. Also included were the medals of Supt. W. Hart: Egypt 1882 (Bars Tofrek and Suakin 1885) and the Khedive Star. Closed file, ref: 83 (41561).

Harte-Maxwell 2/Lt. Percival Maxwell. Born 20.12.1884 at Kingstown, Co. Dublin, the son of Samuel M. and Edith Maxwell Harte-Maxwell, *née* Carroll, Glen Albert, Roscrea, Co. Tipperary. Educated at Lismore College, Lismore, Co. Waterford, and the Civil Service College, Dublin. He was unmarried and had two brothers and a sister. Attested as Pte 3970, 5th Dragoon Guards, at Enniscorthy, 11.9.1914, giving his address as Bank of Ireland, Enniscorthy, Co. Wexford. Height 5 foot 7½ inches, chest 33–36 inches, and weight 127 pounds. Discharged to a commission 16.10.1914.

Free Press, Saturday 23.10.1915: 'Lt. P.M. Maxwell, formerly a member of the staff of the Bank of Ireland, Enniscorthy, was the guest of the Agent, Mr H.P. Evans, during the week. Early in the previous year Mr Maxwell joined the 6th Dragoon Guards as a private. After going through the usual course of training in England, he was offered and accepted a commission as a Second Lieutenant in the Connaught Rangers. Later he transferred to the Royal Irish Rifles in which he now holds the commission of Lieutenant. For the past five months Lt. Maxwell has been serving with his regiment in France. He went through several severe engagements and was fortunate to escape with a slight injury to his arm caused by a trench falling in. Lt. Maxwell, who is a member of the Protestant church speaks in terms of the warmest admiration of the devotion and heroism of the Irish priests. He said the conduct of the men of the battalion in responding to the appeals of the priests was exemplary. Lt. Maxwell left Enniscorthy on Thursday en route for the trenches in France.'

Irish Times 21.4.1916: 'The announcement in the casualty lists of the death of Lieutenant P. Maxwell Harte-Maxwell, a native of Glenalbert, Roscrea, Co. Tipperary, who had served four years as an official of the Bank of Ireland at Enniscorthy, when he volunteered for service in September, 1914, has evoked feelings of much regret in the latter town, where the deceased officer was very popular in commercial, sporting, and social circles. He joined the Connaught Rangers, but subsequently became attached to the Royal Irish Rifles.'

Joined 1st RIR from 4th Connaught Rangers, 25.5.1915, and was killed by shellfire, 11.4.1916, during a German raid on his trench. A WO letter to his father, 17 May, advised that he was buried at Becourt Wood, 2,500 yards east of Albert (Map 57D, Square X.25 central). A list of his effects dated 21 April included 'One German shell fuse'. The gross value of his estate was £724.65.

The Great War 1914–1918, Bank of Ireland Staff Service Record: 'He was educated at Fermoy Grammar School and entered the service of the Bank in June, 1905. He enlisted in the King's Own Dragoon Guards in September, 1914 and was subsequently commissioned in the Connaught Rangers.'

Bécourt Military Cemetery, Becordel-Bécourt, Somme. File ref: 339/30271 52820.

Haskett-Smith Lt.-Col. William Joseph Jerome Saccone. Gazetted into the RIR, 8.5.1901, and served in the South African War 1901–02, taking part in operations in Orange River Colony, August 1901 to 31.5.1902. Received the Queen's Medal with three clasps. Commanded G Coy. Promoted to Lt. 14.6.1905 (passing an exam in Tactics, Military Engineering, and Topography for Army Lieutenants), and Capt. 8.3.1910. Joined the BEF in France during October 1914, attached Leinster Regt, where he remained until February 1915. Returned to France, 5.7.1915, and joined 1st RIR 6.8.1915. Returned to the UK due to sickness, 19 October. Promoted Major 8.5.1916. Returned to the front, 5.9.1916, and joined 2nd RIR. Left to join 2nd South Lancashire Regt as acting Senior Major 5.10.1916. Served with 1st RIF, and was employed with the Tank Corps 1.1.1917 until August 1917. He resumed active service January 1918 until the end of the war, perhaps with 18th London Regt (London Irish).

Hon. Secretary of the RUR Regimental Association in the mid 1930's. In 1938 he was residing at Ellerton Lodge, Ellerton Road, Copse Hill, Wimbledon. Died at Jersey, Channel Islands, 1961. Closed file, ref: (98862).

Haslett 2/Lt. John MC. Born 22.2.1895. His father was a farmer. Educated at Belfast Mercantile College and Hughes Academy. Employed as a Customs and Excise Officer. Served with Army Cyclists Corps (25th Divisional Company) 9.12.1914. Appointed L/Cpl 27.11.1916. 'Permitted to enlist by Boards order of 16th February 1917' – as a Customs Officer his ability to enlist earlier had been restricted. Joined Belfast University OTC 14.3.1917. 'General efficiency very good. Will make a good leader.' Applied for a commission 12.6.1917 – 'Any unit in Ulster Division.' Height 5 foot 11¾ inches, weight 142 pounds, and chest 34–37 inches. To No. 7 Officer Cadet Battalion, Fermoy, 7.9.1917. Commissioned into 18th RIR 30.1.1918.

Joined 1st RIR, 7.8.1918, and was awarded the MC in September 1918 (*London Gazette* 11.1.1919). On 14.2.1919 he proceeded to the Concentration Camp prior to demobilization. Released from Military Duty 19.2.1919. Medical rating A1. His address at that time was Drumreagh, Ballygowan, Co. Down. File ref: WO339/114173.

Hatch Lt. Robert Pyne. Born 29.4.1888. Entered Trinity College, Dublin, 1913. Applied for a commission 15.6.1915. Single. Permanent address Hillsborough, Co. Down. Correspondence address, Wesley College, Dublin. Served with Dublin University OTC since November 1914. Applied for ASC Horse Transport. A second application for a commission was dated 2.9.1915; all details as above excepting that the branch applied for was changed to infantry. Gazetted a 2/Lt. in 15th R. Irish, October 1915. Joined 1st RIR 18.7.1916. Return report, 30.11.1916, shows 5th R. Irish attached 1st RIR. Left 1st RIR 5 November. Embarked Le Havre–Southampton, 12 November, aboard the *Panama* (P&O). 'Injury to left knee whilst in trenches.'

The MB at Oxford, 20.11.1916, noted that he had injured his knee while walking in a trench near Meaulte. The damage was severe but not permanent. Hatch wrote to the WO, 1.2.1917, requesting a MB. Stated he had applied to his CO for a transfer to a Garrison Battalion as he believed he was no longer fit for service in the field. Promoted Lt. 1917. A/Capt. at the Anti-Gas School 1918. He wrote to the WO, 27.4.1917, saying that he injured his knee while in the trenches and under fire near Le Transloy, and thought that he was due some compensation – would they let him know if this was correct and how much he was due. WO, 8.5.1917, ordered him to join the 3rd RIF. HQ Irish Command to WO, 23.5.1917, reported that Hatch was currently on a course of instruction and would join 3rd RIF on completion. This he did 25.6.1917. A WO letter, 12.3.1919, stated that, as Hatch had been declared permanently unfit for general service, his commission would be resigned on health grounds. To retain rank of Capt. A WO memo to Ministry of Pensions gave the disability as '1. Gonorrhoea 2. Cartilage knee'.

A WO letter, 17.5.1919, referred to a letter from Hatch concerning the issue of a Silver War Badge. They say that 'owing to the illness which led to the relinquishment of your commission, it is regretted that you are ineligible for the award of the badge and your claim therefore cannot be approved'. File ref: WO339/43891 112490.

Hellmers 2/Lt. Alfred. Born at Sydenham, Kent, in 1892, the son of Emile and Martha Hellmers, Ormeau House, Queen's Road, Forest Hill, London. His sister Tina was born in 1895. Attested as Pte 1182 in 28th London Regt (Artists Rifles), 1.4.1913, when he was aged 20 years and 7 months. At that time he was a clerk with Augustus Hellmers & Sons, Wine Merchants, 40 Great Tower Street, London EC. His papers noted that he was single, had served with Dulwich College OTC, height 5 foot 8 inches, chest 30–33 inches, and physical development moderate. He was embodied, 5.8.1914, and signed Army Form E624, 23.10.1914.

Embarked for France, 26.10.1914, and served until 2.3.1915. He was posted as a 2/Lt. to 1st RIR, 20.3.1915, and joined from the Cadet School, Bailleul, 26.3.1915. Wounded, 9.5.1915, and died of wounds at 10 p.m. (according to his father), 11 May, at No. 6 CCS, Merville. Intestate. His father wrote to the WO, 18 May, asking that they should convey his sincere thanks to Lord Kitchener for his expression of sympathy. Merville Communal Cemetery, Nord, I.LL.1. File ref: WO339/27921 49705.

Henderson Capt. Richard Lilburn. Born 1895, the youngest son of Sir James Henderson of Oakley House, Windsor Park, Belfast. He had three brothers and a sister. His father was proprietor of the *Belfast News-Letter*, JP and DL for Belfast and JP for Co. Antrim; called to the Bar, 1872, and was the first Lord Mayor of Greater Belfast, 1898; first High Sheriff of the county of the city of Belfast, 1900; eldest son of James Alexander Henderson, Norwood Tower, Co. Down. His mother, Martha, was a daughter of David Pollock, architect, of Newry.

Entered Methodist College, Belfast, 1904, and won prizes in 1907 and 1908. Gazetted to 4th RIR 12.2.1915. Joined 1st RIR as a 2/Lt. 18.5.1915. Struck off the strength of the battalion due to sickness, 18.7.1915. Promoted to Capt. 12.2.1916. Transferred to the sick list 11.5.1916. Struck off the strength of the battalion 3.6.1916. Later served with 7th RIR. He married Ruby Henderson and they had a daughter. Resided at 55 Gransha Road, Bangor, Co. Down. Died at Bangor Hospital 8.6.1960.

Belfast News-Letter 9.6.1960: 'We regret to announce the death of Captain Richard Lilburn Henderson, youngest son of the late Sir James Henderson and the late Lady Henderson, who were Lord Mayor and Lady Mayoress of Belfast in 1898. He was 65 years of age and had been seriously ill for nearly two years. A proprietor and joint managing director of the *Belfast News-Letter*, he earned the affection and respect of employees of the firm by his courtesy, kindliness, and interest in their welfare. He was responsible for a number of improvements in the production of the newspaper, which were greatly welcomed by its readers.

'His activities in the firm were mainly concerned with the commercial and mechanical departments, but he was also a frequent contributor to the paper and his weekly articles for 10 years under the pen name of *Kestrel* were enjoyed by a wide circle of readers. Outside his business career, Captain Henderson's interests were wide – the army, motor racing, flying, yachting, and the theatre were some of the fields in which he played an active part. Wherever he was engaged, he formed firm and lasting friendships and his passing will be mourned by all who knew him.

'Captain Henderson was educated at Methodist College, Belfast, and Bradfield College, Berkshire. On leaving school, he joined the *Belfast News-Letter* as an apprentice in the composing and printing department and also trained with the *Glasgow Herald* (Messrs. George Outram & Co.). Aged 19 at the outbreak of the 1914–18 war, he enlisted in the Army on August 4, 1914, being commissioned into the 4th Battalion the Royal Irish Rifles (Royal North Downs). He also served for two periods with the 1st Battalion the Royal Irish Rifles. During his service in France he was severely wounded.

'In 1926 Captain Henderson joined Queen's University Officer's Training Corps and commanded the infantry unit until 1933. He earned a reputation as an outstanding shot on the rifle range. After the war, he was engaged for some time in stockbroking and then returned to the *Belfast News-Letter* being appointed joint managing director in 1928. In association with Mr Harry Ferguson and the *News-Letter* motoring correspondent, the late Mr W.W. M'Leod, he was largely responsible for bringing the R.A.C. Tourist Trophy to Northern Ireland and continued to take an active interest in the race, both during its years on the Ards Circuit and later at Dundrod. He was president of the Ulster Automobile Club for several years, and resigned this position voluntarily in favour of Sir Milne Barbour. At the time of his death he held the office of vice-president.

'Captain Henderson was also a founder member of the provisional committee of the Flying Club of Ulster. In those days the *News-Letter* was a tireless advocate of the importance of aviation to Northern Ireland, and in 1934 co-operated with Sir Alan Cobham in arranging flying displays in various towns. In the early days of the Northern Ireland BBC station he was a frequent broadcaster on motoring, yachting, and naturalist topics, and for a time he gave a talk every month on current affairs in Northern Ireland.

'In Bangor, where he resided, Captain Henderson was known as a keen yachtsman, carrying on in this respect the traditions of the Henderson family. He was a member of the Royal Ulster

Yacht Club for many years, sailing several different classes of boats. He joined the club in 1912, was Rear-Commodore in 1928, and for many years was a member of committee. He was also a life member of the Royal Co. Down Golf Club. In March, 1931, he was elected a member of the Belfast Water Board, and was chairman of the Law Committee in 1940–1. He retired in March, 1947. He was also a member of the Belfast Chamber of Commerce and had been a member of the Council of the Chamber until 1953. For some years he was also a director of the Royal Hippodrome. Captain Henderson, who resided at Gransha Road, Bangor, is survived by his wife and daughter.'

Belfast News-Letter 10.6.1960: 'Funeral tomorrow (Saturday) at 11 a.m. from James Russell & Co.'s Funeral Parlour, Bingham Lane, Bangor, to Clandeboye Cemetery.' File destroyed.

Henke Lt. Frederick Ernest. Gazetted a 2/Lt. in 3rd RIR 27.6.1917. Joined 1st RIR, 12.9.1917, and proceeded to England on transfer to the Indian Army, 21.9.1917. Promoted Lt. 27.12.1918. Closed file, ref: 3/83 (181879).

Hill Lt. Douglas Bertram. Born 15.12.1895 and gazetted a 2/Lt. in 1st Norfolk Regt, 16.12.1914. Embarked for the BEF, 17.5.1915, and joined 1st RIR, 25.5.1915. Wounded 1.7.1916 and evacuated to the UK two days later. Promoted to Lt., 30.7.1916, with seniority to count from 30.7.1917. He also served with the BEF, Nov 1916 to Feb 1917, and March 1917 until the end of the war. Mentioned in Despatches 8.7.1919. Retired with a gratuity, 16.12.1924, and died 28.8.1972. Closed file.

Hodson Lt. Bertie John. Born 19.6.1882, married to Anna Hodson, and lived at 102 Broadhurst Gardens, London. They had two children, Carl and Rosemary. Served with the First Contingent Imperial Yeomanry during the South African War. He had enlisted January 1900 and was discharged August 1901 with the rank of L/Cpl. Awarded the Queen's South Africa Medal with three clasps. Worked as a war correspondent in Montenegro, Turkey, Belgium (siege of Antwerp), France, and the Dardanelles. Applied for a commission, 12.7.1915, answering the question 'Unit desirous of joining' with 'Preferably a corps fighting the Turks'. Gazetted a 2/Lt. in 5th R. Irish, 25.12.1915, and attached 1st RIR, 18.7.1916. A telegram was sent to his wife, 29.7.1916, stating that he had been wounded 27 July. Further details were sent, 30 July, advising that he had been admitted to No. 7 Stationary Hospital, Boulogne, with gun shot wounds to his head and shoulder, 'condition satisfactory'. Rejoined 1st RIR, 4.9.1916, and was promoted to Lt. 1.7.1917. Killed in action 21.3.1918. Telegram to wife 18 April. Personal effects sent to her included a leather wallet, correspondence, advance book, and sundry papers. Pozières Memorial.

Hogg Capt. William Frederick MC. Born 23.12.1896 at 189 Duncairn Gardens, Belfast, the son of William and Margaret Hogg, *née* Thompson. His father was an 'agent'. Applied for a commission, 14.3.1915, asking for 3rd RIR. Address *Sandon*, 63 Anglesea Road, Ballsbridge, Dublin. Student, height 6 foot 1 inch, weight 147 pounds, chest 32½–36 inches. Gazetted a 2/Lt. in 3rd RIR, 25.3.1915, posted to 14th RIR, and promoted to Lt. 29.2.1916. Wounded 1.7.1916. Awarded the MC, *London Gazette* 14.11.16. Left unit, 26.11.1916, having been wounded that day at Wulvenghem. Embarked Boulogne–Southampton, 2 December, on HMHS *St David*. GSW to the head.

Irish Life 24.11.1916: ' … is the eldest son of William Hogg, 63 Anglesea Road, Ballsbridge, and 23 Bachelor's Walk, Dublin. He was educated at the Endowed School, Bangor, and St Andrew's College, Dublin, from the latter entering Trinity, October, 1914 as a junior exhibitioner. After taking out his first year in Honours Mathematics in January, he was gazetted to the 3rd (Reserve) Royal Irish Rifles in March 1915 from Trinity Officer's Training Corps. He was promoted to his present rank in February 1916 and sent to France a month later, where he was attached to his present battalion with the 36th (Ulster) Division and was awarded the Military Cross for gallantry during the offensive on the Somme.'

The MB, 11 December, at 2nd Western General Hospital, Manchester, noted that he was looking through a trench periscope when it was hit and splintered – a fragment hit his head, flesh wound, no bone damage, now healed. Rejoined 3rd RIR, 3.1.1917. Rejoined the BEF. Wounded, 23.5.1917, and embarked Boulogne–Folkestone, 27 May, aboard the *St Patrick*. GSW – arms, hips, leg, and toe.

Irish Times 31.5.1917: ' … and served in Belfast before going to the front in the spring of 1916. He was wounded on the 1st July, 1916, when he won the Military Cross for gallantry in action. On that occasion he held a forward position in the enemy's trenches for eight hours under heavy enfilade and frontal fire. He had only about forty men, but repulsed several bombing attacks, only retiring when ordered to do so … It is a curious coincidence that Lieutenant W.G. Hogg, also of the Rifles, was killed on the day following the wounding of Lieutenant W.F. Hogg.'

The MB, 19.7.1917, at 2nd Southern General Hospital, Bristol, noted that he had been wounded at Wytschaete. The multiple wounds were caused by bomb fragments (grenade), some were healed, others not. Slight, not permanent. Discharged from hospital 11.8.1917. Applied to the WO, 8.10.1917, for a war wound gratuity. Joined 1st RIR 18.6.1918. Appointed a/Capt. 23.8.1918. Wounded, 15.10.1918, and embarked Calais–Dover, 18 October. GSW neck. Relinquished acting rank of Capt., 23.1.1919, and was disembodied the same day. Last served with 3rd RIR. Medical category C1. Single. Relinquished commission and retained the rank of Lt., 1.4.1920.

The WO received a letter from his wife Marion, 5.9.1927, asking for full details of her husband's service. They replied, 9 September, stating it was not normal to release such information, but if she would state the full reasons for the request then they would reconsider. His file contains a letter from S.W. Bell, Justice of the Peace, County of the City of Belfast, 14 September, to the WO (Headed paper, S.D. Bell & Co. Ltd., Tea and Coffee Merchants, 63 Ann Street, Belfast). He 'can vouch for the accuracy of Mrs Hogg's letter herewith'. Her second letter stated that her husband had suffered 'mental trouble which was brought on by his war service'. This had started with a breakdown four years ago. He was presently on his way home from Rhodesia where he had been sent in the hope that a change might effect a cure. His condition had not improved and she was now trying to have him admitted to the Sir Frederick Milner Home for Ex-Servicemen and she needed the service information in order to complete the application forms. The WO replied 'confidential', 5.10.1927, and gave an outline of his service. 'I am to state that his services were satisfactory and that nothing of an adverse nature is recorded against him.'

His brother, Charles E. Hogg, wrote to the WO, 24.6.1930, attaching what he believed to be William's record of service and asked if it was accurate. He gave no explanation of the purpose of the request. His statement said that the grenade wounding of May 1917 happened during 'a night investigation raid'. He also asked for a copy of the medical records. They replied, 3 July, giving a summary of service, 'confidential', but refused to give the medical records.

A Ministry of Defence letter, 31.8.1989, to a Mrs W.E. Hogg, 2 Castle Close, Sandycove, Co. Dublin, gave a standard reply to a next-of-kin enquiry of July 1989. It gave the absolute bare minimum and no detail at all about the medical matters mentioned, etc. File ref: WO339/45906 115089.

Holt 2/Lt. George Cyril. Born 21.2.1891 at Holywood, Co. Down. Enlisted 23.5.1912 at Belfast as Pte 1246 in 6th Black Watch. He had been a clerk with the Belfast Steam Company Ltd., and lived at 4 Woodland Avenue, Belfast. Height 5 foot 5½ inches, chest 30–32 inches. Signed Army Form E624 at North Queensferry, Edinburgh, 18.9.1914, while with 8th Black Watch. Embarked Folkestone 2.5.1915, writing out his will the next day and leaving everything to his father. Joined 6th Black Watch.

Admitted 1/2nd Highland Field Ambulance, Estaires, with scabies, 19.7.1915. Transferred to convalescence camp 25 July. Rejoined his unit 1 August. To 1/3rd Highland Field Ambulance with influenza, 23.9.1915, and moved to Etaples Base two days later. He transferred to England and was hospitalised at the Yacht Club, Gravesend, 26.9.1915 to 22.11.1915, due to bronchitis. Transferred to Orchard Convalescence Hospital, Dartford, until 11.2.1916. Applied for a commission 15.1.1916, at which time he was unmarried. He transferred from 3/6th Black Watch to No. 7 Officer Cadet Battalion, Curragh Camp, 6.4.1916 and was commissioned into 4th RIR, 6.6.1916. Home service 26.9.1915 to 7.7.1916.

Joined 1st RIR 30.9.1916. Wounded during an attack 25.10.1916. Embarked Calais–Dover aboard the *Dieppe*, 2 November. He was suffering from shell shock and scabies. His address was given as *Rosenberg*, Cliftonville Road, Belfast. Appeared before a MB at London, 3 November, and reported that he had been in the front line trench and was buried by an explosion. He did not lose consciousness. Symptoms were headaches, insomnia, bad nerves, and a slight tremor, but he was improving. Declared unfit for ten weeks. He wrote to the WO, 21.11.1916, apologising for the late return of a form – he had not been to his home in Belfast due to ill health. He gave his current address as 4th RIR, 177 Rathgar Road, Dublin. Appeared before the MB six times in 1917 and was always certified as unfit for general service. MB 11.2.1918: unfit for any category for nine months, in an officer's hospital. MB 13.5.1918 confirmed previous position.

He was married by the time of his discharge, 1.8.1919, medical classification C. Last served with 4th RIR in Ireland – OUTC Belfast. His civil occupation was stated to be that of an accountancy secretary. File ref: WO339/57671 130238.

Hoyle 2/Lt. Frederick William. He joined 1st RIR from 4th RIR 8.11.1917. Wounded 27.3.1918. Promoted to Lt. 19.6.1918. The Army List for December 1919 shows him as 4th RIR attached to 1st RIR. Closed file, ref: (143904).

Hubert 2/Lt. Donald F. He was on the Unattached List Indian Army and resided at 12 Victoria Crescent, St Helier, Jersey. Wounded, 10.3.1915, while attached to 1st RIR. GSW to his right foot but there were no fractures or bone damage. Embarked Boulogne–Dover aboard the *St David*, 12 March. Appeared before the MB at Caxton Hall, 18 March, and was granted leave until 28.4.1915. On that day he appeared before the MB at Jersey: his wound was healing but there was still some stiffness and was declared unfit for one month. Declared fit for light duties at home for one month, 27.5.1915, and was sent to 3rd RIR. The MB at King George V Hospital, Dublin, 27.8.1915, noted that he was recovered but that he had developed a large boil on the side of his left knee and was unfit for service at home for two weeks. Found to be fit for general service, 10.9.1915, and embarked for India, 12.10.1915. File ref: 47820.

Hudson Lt. Ewan Ronald Henry. Born 6.11.1897 at Bank House, Mozufferpore, Bengal, the son of Henry Ewan Hudson, an 'Independent Gentleman' who had been an Indigo Planter in India. Educated at the Private School, Hamilton House, Bath, and Marlborough College. Joined Marlborough OTC 20.1.1912. Applied for a cadetship at the RMC 18.8.1914. The application was counter-signed by his mother, Mary Katherine Moore Hudson. There is a note elsewhere on his file saying that the mother and father were separated. Height 5 foot 8½ inches, chest 36¼–38½ inches, weight 154 pounds. A confidential report from the headmaster included the comment 'He is rather immature at present'. Declared relatives with military connections as his grandfather, General Henry George Dela Fosse CB, and his cousin General Francis Boud, RE. Home address, The Dann, Seaford, Sussex. Admitted to Sandhurst 21.8.1914.

Commissioned a 2/Lt. in 3rd RMF, 16.12.1914. Served at Gallipoli with 1st RMF from 27.7.1915. Admitted to No. 15 Stationary Hospital, Murdos, 2.12.1915. Discharged to duty, 4.1.1916, 1st RMF in Egypt. To France with 1st RMF 23.3.1916. Left unit, 26.4.1916, and embarked Boulogne–Dover 1.5.1916. The MB at 1st London General Hospital, 8 May, recorded that he was suffering from neurasthenia: '14.4.16, during a bombardment, felt that he could not go up the line; became nervous and had severe headaches.' Unfit for general service for two months. Address at this time was 33 St Dunstan's Road, Barons Court, London W. MB, 7 July, 'he is now quite well'. Unfit for general service for one month but fit for service at home. Reported for duty with 3rd RMF, 8.7.1916. MB, 9.8.1916: 'He has now quite recovered' and fit for general service. Rejoined 1st RMF.

Left unit, 5.9.1916, and embarked Le Havre–Southampton, 10 September. Cause of return, shell-shock. The MB, 13 September, at 4th London General Hospital, recorded that he had been sent up the line at Guillemont, 5 September, and the next thing he remembered was being in a dressing station thirteen hours later. He had been back in France for one week. Unfit for general or home service for ten weeks. The MB, 13.11.1916, at Caxton Hall, noted that he had greatly improved and was fit for light duty at home. Reported for duty with 3rd RMF 15.11.1916. The MB at Queenstown, Co. Cork, 18 December: 'He is fit for general service'.

Left for France, 17.1.1917, and joined 1st RIR 20.1.1917. Left unit, 2.3.1917, and embarked Calais–Dover, 13 March. Cause of return, 'Poisoning. Gas shell.' The MB at Caxton Hall, 24 March, recorded that he was unconscious for several hours and sick continually for 24 hours. Unfit for general and home service for six weeks. The MB at the Princess of Wales Hospital for Convalescent Officers, 4.4.1917, declared him fit for light duty at home. MB at Queenstown, 11.6.1917, fit for general service. To Egyptian Expeditionary Force with 6th RMF, 2.9.1917.

At the beginning of 1918 there was correspondence from both his mother and father to the WO concerning where correspondence about their son should be sent. The father insisted that his address was the only valid one and the mother countered that she had divorced him and had legal custody of the children. The WO, 8.1.1918, stated that in this case they would send letters to both addresses. The MB at Abbassia Depot, Cairo, 26.2.1918, noted that he had been wounded, 30.12.1917, GSW to his lower leg. To BEF, France, May 1918 and joined 2nd RMF. Wounded 4.10.1918. The MB at 2nd General Hospital, Bristol, 21 October, recorded a shell splinter in the right heel. Likely to be incapacitated for two months from date of wounding. The MB report at the Military Hospital, Devonport, 10.5.1919, shows (1) GSW heel (2) gonorrhoea (3) scabies. Had been admitted to this hospital 19.2.1919. Healed and fit for general service. (2) was attributed to 'misconduct' and (3) to 'lack of personal hygiene'.

Resigned his commission 8.11.1919. The WO wrote to him, 8.11.1922, asking, as the RMF were to be disbanded, whether he wanted to be transferred to the General List Reserve of Officers or resign his commission. However, the Australian Embassy, London, wrote to the WO, 4.11.1922, saying that 'Stoker 2nd Class Hudson' of the Australian Navy wanted his time in the army counted towards his good conduct badges in the Australian Navy, and could the WO please confirm the service. WO reply, 25 November, giving an outline of Hudson's service. They also asked that the Australians should get Hudson to submit a formal resignation from the Reserve of Officers and enquired as to when he joined the Australian Navy. The Australian Embassy replied, 21.3.1923, that Hudson joined the Australian Navy, 15.8.1922, but had deserted 23.11.1922. Hudson was subsequently removed from the Reserve of Officers effective from 15.8.1922. File ref: WO339/3057 4271.

Hunt Lt.-Col. John Patrick CMG, DSO, DCM. Born in Dublin 8.3.1875, the son of Thomas and Sarah Hunt, and was educated at the Christian Brothers schools. He joined the RDF, 22.12.1891, achieving the rank of Colour-Sgt, and served in the ranks of the Imperial Yeomanry in the South African War 1899–1902. Received the Queen's Medal with six clasps (for Cape Colony, Talana, Tugela Heights, Orange Free State, Relief of Ladysmith, and Transvaal) and the King's Medal with two clasps, being Mentioned in Despatches, *London Gazette* 14.3.1900. He was wounded and subsequently awarded the DCM, 8.2.1901, as 4290 Sgt J. Hunt, 2nd RDF. Served in operations in the Aden Hinterland, 1902–3. In 1910 he was appointed instructor to the Dublin University

OTC, and later to St Columba's College OTC, claiming his discharge 31.3.1913. Re-enlisted in the RDF, 6.10.1914, and was given the number 8/15691. Stated he was then aged 41 and gave his trade as Drill Instructor. Height 5 foot 8½ inches and chest 34–36½ inches. Applied for a commission 15.9.1915. Promoted from Sgt-Major to 2/Lt. in 8th RDF 17.10.1915, to Lt. and Adjutant 1.11.1915, and to Capt. 16.4.1916. He was Adjutant of 8th RDF until 31.8.1916. Fought at Ginchy and got special praise for his formation of a defensive flank that he held for ten hours under heavy fire until relieved. Awarded the DSO, *London Gazette* 20.10.1916, and was appointed a/Major and Second-in-Command of 2nd RDF, 24.1.1917. Commanded 9th RDF, 4.6.1917 to 28.10.1917, and was employed as Commandant of VII Corps Reinforcement Camp 13.2.1918 until 19.4.1918. During the German offensive, 21.3.1918, he took command of 1st RDF and succeeded in holding the front centre of 48th Brigade throughout the early attacks.

Orange, Green and Khaki, 24.3.1918: 'In the absence of reinforcements, each corps trawled vigorously its own resources and mustered scratch units. In VII Corps this was known as "Hunt's Force", under newly promoted Lt.-Col. J.P. Hunt, 9th Dublins. Built around cadres from VII Corps Reinforcement Training Camp, it consisted of eight battalions, comprising 39th Division details; 24th Entrenching Battalion; two battalions of corps reinforcements; VII Corps school of instruction and a company of engineers; two battalions of men recalled from leave. Many, especially those from holding units, were mere recruits and the force had few automatic weapons except those salvaged from derelict tanks and manned by their crews. Despite these shortcomings, the force won a considerable fighting reputation.'

Served on the Western Front 19.12.1915 until the end of the war, being twice wounded. A/Lt.-Col. 20.4.1918 to 17.8.1918. Took over command of 1st RIR, 20.4.1918, and was awarded a Bar to his DSO, *London Gazette* 26.7.1918. Wounded at Punkah Farm 16.8.1918. Resumed command, 10.9.1918, and went to the UK on leave, 14.4.1919 to 9.5.1919. He transferred to the Labour Corps, 12.5.1919, with the rank of Lt.-Col., seniority to commence 25.10.1918. On 23.5.1919 he assumed command of No. 43 Labour Group HQ. Released, 29.10.1919, and relinquished his commission 1.9.1921. At that time he was living at 50 Rathdown Road, Dublin. Married to Bertha (Bridget) Moore, they had six sons and two daughters: Mary, Joseph, Leo, Thomas, Arthur, Bertha, John, and Denis. Mentioned in Despatches 20.10.1916, 4.1.1917, 21.12.1917, 28.12.1918, and 10.7.1919, and awarded the CMG 3.6.1919.

Commissioned into the Irish Free State Army, 24.4.1923, as a Colonel. As the Army reduced in size, following the end of the Civil War, he was made a Major, 29.2.1924, and appointed Chief Instructor A & I. On 24.4.1925 he was Officer in Charge of Training at the Curragh. Other duties during his career were: Adjutant 10th Reserve Bn 28.1.1931; OC 12th Reserve Bn 1933; Adjutant 10th Reserve Bn 1934, and Adjutant 1st Bn Regiment of Desmond 1935. He also passed the following courses: A.T. Curragh Field Officers 1930, Modified Infantry Course 1936, and Modified Infantry (C & S) Course 1937. *Quis Separabit* vol. VI, no. 2, noted that Col. Hunt attended the Dublin Branch annual reunion dinner of the RUR Association on 27.4.1935. 'Col. Hunt recalled the right hearty welcome he received when taking over command of the 1st Battalion, the Quartermaster at that time being his good old friend, George Edwards.' His civil employments included the Civil Service and accounts and book keeping at a Christian Brothers school in Dublin. He died at his residence, *Lynton*, Dundrum, Co. Dublin, 24.4.1938, 'occlusion of the coronary arteries', aged 63.

Quis Separabit, vol. IX, no, 1, May 1938: 'It is with regret we have to announce the death of Lt.-Colonel J.P. Hunt DSO. Colonel Hunt commanded the 1st Battalion during the concluding months of the war, and proved himself a very successful and popular commander. To his relatives we offer our sincere sympathy.'

His widow was turned down for a British Army pension, 19.7.1938, as he had not served five years as a substantive Warrant Officer and had not held a permanent Regular Army Commission.

A file note dated 23.9.1938 stated that his widow was receiving £2 a week from the Officer's Association. One of his sons, Henry, applied to be a Boy Soldier during 1938 but no further details are on the file. The Irish Army details were kindly provided by Comdt. V. Laing, OIC Military Archives. PRO file ref: WO339/43268.

Hutcheson Capt. Norman Heber. The son of Col. George Hutcheson, later the Inspector General of Civil Hospitals. Gazetted 23.5.1906, and promoted to Lt. 21.12.1907. He had been ADC to the Lt.-Governor of Burma and was unmarried. Joined 1st RIR 11.1.1915. Killed in action 12.3.1915. A telegram was sent to his sister at Charleton Villa, Newbridge, Co. Kildare, 18 March. The WO advised his father, 14.6.1915, that he was buried at Map 36 Belgium, Square M.35.b.6.o.

His file includes many reports of the circumstances of his death: 9777 Cpl Powell, 2 Chapel Street, Victoria Road, Bradford. While in Nell Lane Military Hospital, Manchester, 18.7.1915, he reported that he was in Capt. Hutcheson's Coy. During a bayonet charge he saw him shot and fall into a deep ditch between the second and third German trenches. Sgt C. Delury was at the Temporary Hospital, Warwick New Road, Leamington, 28.6.1915, and reported that at about noon, 12 March, he was ordered to take his platoon, No. 13, to reinforce the Notts and Derby Regt. 'A few of us succeeded in getting across.' Shortly afterwards Capt. Hutcheson and a few men of No. 15 platoon came across. A bullet passed through the parapet and went through Hutcheson's head, killing him. On the 14th he was in charge of a burial party of fifty men and he buried Hutcheson together with Lt. Laing, placing both names on one cross. He stated that Hutcheson had no equipment or private articles on him at this time. Rfn Vaughan reported from 4th Northern Hospital, Lincoln, 19.7.1915, that he saw Hutcheson shot through the head and afterwards buried him in a small churchyard at Neuve Chapelle. 7313 Rfn W.J. Myles, while at Parkgate Hospital, Neston, Cheshire, 3.7.1915, reported that during the attack he reached the German front line with Hutcheson who, while signalling for more men with his handkerchief, was shot through the head. Myles was one of the party who buried him that night and returned a few days later to erect a cross over his and other officers graves. L/Cpl Robinson, Magheralin, Lurgan, Co. Antrim, was at Raddon Court Hospital, Latchford, Warrington, 22.6.1915. He stated that Hutcheson was shot through the head by a sniper. He was also a member of the burial party. Cpl Kerr was at No. 3 General Hospital 18.6.1915. He said that he saw Hutcheson wounded in the eye before the charge on 12 March. He was not killed outright but was dazed and was led away to a dressing station. He did not know what happened to him after that. 7930 L/Cpl Duglas was at the VAD Hospital, Richmond Hill, Edgbaston, Birmingham, 18.6.1915, and reported that he buried Hutcheson in the Bois de Biez. He said that Sgt Whelan kept the burial records. 9302 L/Cpl Kennedy, 11 Lucknow Street, Kashmir Road, Belfast, while in the VAD Hospital, Barford Hill, Warwick, 21.5.1915, stated that he was with Hutcheson and Sgt Delury when they advanced into a trench. He saw Hutcheson shot through the head but did not witness the burial. 6728 Sgt Woolven, 312 Derby Road, Birdholme, Chesterfield, was in Hallegarth Hospital, Pickering, 22.5.1915. Between 16–20 March he was in the trenches immediately behind where Hutcheson had been killed. A party from 1st RIR and 2nd Lincolns buried him, 13.3.1915. 8307 Pte Luby of D Coy reported, while he was a patient in Colne House Red Cross Hospital, Cromer, that he was near Hutcheson when he was shot through the brain in a German trench. Sgt Gamble was at Casino Hospital, Boulogne, 10.5.1915. He said that Capt. Hutcheson went delirious on 8 March while under heavy shellfire. 'He is apt to go delirious at times like these, but recovers afterwards.' 9610 Pte Woodward, in Casino Hospital, 14.5.1915, said that Hutcheson and all the other officers of the regiment were buried just outside a wood at Neuve Chapelle, between the village and a wood. A large white cross was erected on the site. Capt. C.J. Newport was in the Canadian Hospital at Le Touquet and stated that the cross erected bore the inscription: 'Sacred to the memory of Capt. Norman Hutcheson, 1st Royal Irish Rifles, Killed in Action, March 12th'.

There is a letter to the WO on the file from Ranken & Co., of Calcutta pursuing a long standing debt for £6.94 and stating that attempts to contact his father had failed. Correspondence from Flights Ltd., Military Tailors, 90 High Street, Winchester, to the WO, made a claim against Hutcheson's estate due to an unpaid invoice for £89.86, part of which debt went back as far as 9.2.1907. The WO rejected this claim as the time elapsed was outside the time limits laid down in the Regimental Debts Act of 1893. In fact, Flights had first written to the WO about this 20.3.1916, stating that the father had refused to assist saying that there were no assets.

Cox's Shipping Agency wrote to the WO, 21.4.1922, asking for the address of the next of kin in order that they could forward his sword, which was left with them on 25.2.1915. The WO gave the father's address as c/o London County Westminster and Parr's Bank Ltd., Pavilion Buildings, Brighton. Le Touret Memorial, Pas de Calais. File ref: WO339/6501 12676.

Ingram Capt. Thomas Frederick. Born 1.3.1891 at Hillsboro, Lisburn, Co. Down, the son of Thomas and Agnes Ingram, *née* Crawford, of 46 Hardcastle Street, Belfast. His father was a post office sorter. Entered Methodist College, 1904, won a prize that year and left in January 1907. At that time his address was 24 Burmah Street, Belfast. Medical student at Queen's University having matriculated in 1911. Applied for a commission, 6.8.1914, stating that he had served as a Staff Sergeant in the OTC. He requested an appointment with 3rd The King's Royal Lancaster Regt. Height 5 foot 8 inches, chest 32½–35½ inches, weight 147 pounds. Still residing at Burmah Street.

Served at home from 8.8.1914 with 3rd RIR until he embarked for France, 4.1.1915. Wounded 12.3.1915 while attached to 1st RIR, taking no further part in the war. Embarked on the Hospital Ship *St Patrick*, 6 April, and was admitted to Guy's Hospital, London, being discharged and granted leave 3.7.1915 to 2.9.1915. He wrote to the WO, 19.11.1915, enquiring as to how much compensation he was entitled to, and how to claim it. At that time he was at the Hospital for Officers at 33 Upper Fitzwilliam Street, Dublin. Promoted to Lt., 27.11.1915, and attached to the Depot.

Awarded a £50 pension for one year from 7.4.1916, to be reassessed annually. He married, 27.6.1917, but his wife died 9.7.1918. Appeared before the MB at the Military Hospital, Stirling, 15.10.1918. His address was Forthside, Stirling, an Army Ordnance Base. Deemed permanently unfit for any form of overseas military service but fit for sedentary work and ordered to return to Forthside. The MB noted that his condition was unchanged, 15.1.1919, returning him to his unit at Durrington. Residing at 27 South Parade, Belfast, 26.2.1920, he appeared before a MB there. His disability was described as a gunshot wound to the arm. The right elbow joint had been excised making this arm three inches shorter than the other. 'The Board considers that this officer has been under-assessed at his previous Board.'

He wrote to the WO, 14.5.1921, saying that he was Clerk to the Petty Sessions 'to the important districts of Bangor' and asking for the honorary rank of Major. This request was rejected on the basis that he had insufficient commissioned service. He again wrote, 11.2.1924, saying he was clerk to the Justices of 'three very important districts' and requesting that he be given the honorary rank of Major as this would be more in keeping with his position. The address given was 76 Abbey Street, Bangor, Co. Down. He wrote again, 26.2.1924, asking for a reply stating that he was about to have stationery printed and was refused, 4.3.1924. Enrolled in the Officer's Emergency Reserve, 14.10.1938, with 3rd RUR and was discharged in March 1946. File ref: WO339/16107 33147.

Ivey Major Thomas Henry DSO. Born 20.9.1881. Served in the ranks of the Coldstream Guards on the Western Front, 12.8.1914 to 2.11.1914, and was Mentioned in Despatches 9.12.1914. Gazetted a 2/Lt. in the RIR, 1.10.1914, and promoted Lt. 15.3.1915. Returned to the front 29.6.1915 and was wounded at Bellewarde, 25.9.1915, while serving with 2nd RIR (being part of the machine gun section March 1915–March 1916). Promoted Capt. 1.1.1917, he returned to the front, 3.4.1917, and joined 1st RIR, 28.4.1917.

Took over the duties of Second-in-Command, 19.6.1917, and was appointed acting Major. He was in temporary command 1–9.8.1917, 9.10.1917 to 29.12.1917, and 4– 20.4.1918, being awarded the DSO and Mentioned in Despatches, 7.4.1918, *London Gazette* 3.6.1918. From 20.8.1918 he was employed as Commandant of 36th Divisional Reception Camp until the end of the war. Closed file, ref: (29458).

Jamison Lt. Samuel Miller. Born 10.10.1895 and educated at Belfast Technical and Carrickfergus Technical Schools. Enlisted 14.9.1914 as Pte 14982 in 14th RIR (YCV). Occupation wholesale draper, Presbyterian, height 5 foot 6 inches, weight 126 pounds, and chest 33–35 inches. Appointed an unpaid L/Cpl 24.6.1915. Admitted to the Surrey Home, Seaford, 1–6 September 1915, with scabies, and posted to the BEF France, 3.10.1915. Appointed a paid L/Cpl, 6.10.1915, he was granted leave 5–14 December 1916.

Applied for a commission in 4th RIR, 2.1.1917, and posted to the Depot, 16.2.1917. Transferred from 14th RIR to No. 10 Officer Cadet Battalion, 7.4.1917, and commissioned a 2/Lt., 31.7.1917. Joined 1st RIR from 3rd RIR, 28.9.1917, and was Signalling Officer, 27.3.1918, during the German offensive. He later commanded HQ Company. Promoted Lt. 1.2.1919. On leave to the UK 1.5.1919. Took over the duties of Acting Adjutant 19.5.1919. Discharged from 4th RIR, 20.6.1919, giving his home address as Burnside, Millisle, Co. Down. File ref: WO339/102275.

Jeffares Lt. Michael Henry. Born 29.4.1892 at Seskin House, Leighlinbridge, Co. Carlow, and educated at John Ivory College, New Ross. His father was a farmer. Enlisted at Carlow as Pte 11/27369 in 11th RDF, 25.7.1916. Height 6 foot 1 inch, chest 35–38 inches, and weight 152 pounds. His permanent address was Scarke House, New Ross, Co. Wexford. Occupation, chemist. Appointed an unpaid L/Cpl, 7.10.1916, and applied for a commission, 23.8.1916, specifying his choice as infantry, cavalry, artillery, ASC, and engineers with a preference for 4th RIR. Posted to 7th Officer Cadet Battalion, Fermoy, 4.11.1916, and appointed a 2/Lt. in 5th RIR, 28.2.1917.

Joined 1st RIR, 18.5.1917, and was wounded 31.7.1917 (GSW to the left thigh). The bullet passed through without damaging the bone and he embarked for the UK 3.8.1917.

Free Press, 11.8.1917: 'New Ross officer wounded. Lt. M. Jeffares, nephew of Mr J. Jeffares, Scarke House, New Ross, has been wounded.' Declared fit for home service at Belfast, 2.11.1917. His brother, Richard Thorpe Jeffares, was killed in action while serving with 2nd RIR.

Free Press, 3.11.1917: 'The death occurred in action on 6th October of Capt. R.T. Jeffares, nephew of John Jeffares of Scarke House, New Ross, and son of Mr M.H. Jeffares, Seskin, Leighlinbridge. He was wounded on the night of the 5th and died on the following day. Although only 27 years of age, he had a distinguished career. He received his early education in the John Ivory School, New Ross, after which he spent four years in the Kilkenny College, where he had a brilliant scholastic record. He received his commission in the Royal Irish Rifles in 1910 and, in 1912, was appointed to an important post in the Rhodesian Police. He was there until the outbreak of war in 1914 when he returned home to join his battalion and proceeded to Flanders shortly after his arrival. He went through several of the big engagements and was wounded in the early part of last August. He was on a visit home on a ten days leave in the latter part of September and shortly after returning to the firing line he received the fatal wound. For some time during 1916 he was Commandant of a bombing school in Ireland … Another brother, Lt. M.H. Jeffares, Scarke House, is at home at present having been wounded early last August. A second brother of the deceased is a paymaster in the Navy and a sister a VAD Nurse in England.'

Declared fit for general service 8.1.1918. By then he was at Palace Barracks, Holywood, Co. Down. Promoted Lt. 1.9.1918. Rejoined 1st RIR in September 1918 and was wounded again 14.10.1918. A bullet had fractured the upper third of his right thigh. Embarked for the UK 23 October. The MB at Caxton Hall, London, 1.7.1919, noted that he was walking with two sticks and sent him to the Officer's Military Convalescent Hospital, Mont Dore, Bournemouth. There being poor improvement to his right knee, he was sent for specialist treatment to Reading War Hospital, 30.7.1919, where he remained for many months. Placed on the retired list, due to his wounds, 23.7.1920. Died 22.5.1953.

Belfast News-Letter, 23.5.1953: ' ... at his residence, *Thornhill*, 28 Osborne Park, Bangor, Michael Henry, loved husband of Rebecca Jeffares. Deeply regretted by his sorrowing wife and family. House and funeral private.' File ref: WO339/76225 155117.

Jenings, Lt. Ulick C. Gazetted a 2/Lt. in the RDF 17.2.1902. Served with 4th RDF in South Africa 1902. Promoted Lt. 16.4.1904. He was attached to 1st RIR at the outbreak of war and went overseas November 1914. Joined 1st RIR 17.12.1914.

Confidential report from Lt.-Col. Laurie to HQ 25th Bde 25.12.1914: 'This officer only joined here about one week ago and I understand that he is quite useless ... I would request that this officer should be withdrawn from my Battalion as it is a danger to have incompetent officers on any duty in the field.' At the same time Laurie forwarded an application from Jenings for 'leave on private affairs'. A note on the file from Brigadier A. Lowry Cole, 28.12.1914, agreed that Jenings would be of no use in the field. Reports from Capt. A.J. Biscoe and Major H.C. Wright both refer to Jenings as 'ignorant' of military matters, etc., and were quite damning of him. They refer to the Sergeant under him as having to carry out the work and they want to be rid of him.

A letter from OC 4th RDF, 30.12.1914, stated that he had reported Jenings twice and that he lacked the mentality and initiative to have command. Another seven officers from the RDF were named as similarly incapable. He recommended that junior officers be promoted over the 'incapable' ones, but it appears that the WO blocked this in most instances. Another note included among these officers D.S. and E.F.T. Maunsell (see below).

Jenings left 1st RIR, 3.1.1915, and embarked Boulogne the following day. He stated that the cause of his return was 'leave' and gave his address as 13 Duke Street, St James's, Monkstown, Co. Dublin. A file note, 2.1.1915, stated that Jenings was ordered to England and to report to the WO on arrival. His father, Lt.-Col. Ulick A. Jenings, '(late) Army Medical Staff', wrote to the WO, 6.1.1915, stating that his son had protested about his supersession 'by no less than five officers' in his battalion. He referred to the death of his son, Lt. George Pierce Creagh Jenings, 1st Shropshire Light Infantry, on 6.11.1914 and that he had two other sons serving. His son Ulick thought that he was coming home on leave but had orders to rejoin 4th RDF at Sittingbourne, 19.1.1915. He sought redress but did not specify what was required. He gave his address as *Mervue*, 5 New Brighton, Monkstown, where his son also resided. *Thom's Directory* for 1912 gives an additional address as Ironpool, Co. Galway. Col. Jenings wrote again outlining the same points, 18.3.1915. The WO replied, 29.3.1915, referring to their letter of 18.12.1914 (not on file) to which they had nothing to add.

A confidential report from OC 4th RDF to HQ Thames and Medway Garrison, 16.3.1915, stated that Jenings was temperate and inoffensive in manner, but inefficient: 'His Company Commander reports he is unable to delegate the slightest duty to him'. Col. Jenings protested again on 30.3.1915. Lt. Jenings wrote to the Adjutant 4th RDF, 7.4.1915, applying to resign his commission as his position in the battalion was then 'most embarrassing'. OC 4th RDF certified, 21.4.1915, that he had no objection to the resignation being accepted. The WO confirmed the resignation acceptance, 8.5.1915, and this was gazetted 14.5.1915. There is no apparent evidence of further military service on his file.

Jenings wrote to the WO, 2.5.1921, acknowledging receipt of his war medals and asked what were the regulations for his wearing his uniform to events such as military balls, levees, and other functions. WO replied, 19.5.1921, stating that he did not hold military rank and had no right to wear a uniform as he didn't retain rank when his resignation was accepted. The situation had not changed since they had last written to him in this regard on 2.1.1919 (not on file). He then applied for a war gratuity but this was rejected due to his voluntary resignation. He wrote to the WO, 11.5.1922, requesting an interview with an MP on the issue of a gratuity. The WO replied, 30.5.1922, pointing out that they did not arrange such interviews. File ref: WO339/13810.

Jones Lt.-Col. Evan Bowen DL, JP. Born 13.2.1869, the eldest son of John and Lydia Ann Jones of Ynysfor, Penrhyndendreath, North Wales. Educated at Shrewsbury; Corpus Christi, Oxford, where he gained his BA.

Served in the South African War with the Imperial Yeomanry. Gazetted Hon. Capt. 18.10.1900. Serving with 3rd RWF at the outbreak of the Great War and temporarily attached to 1st RIR. He was transferred to 2nd RIR, 22.11.1914, but instead embarked Le Havre–Southampton, 13 December, suffering from frostbite. Leave was granted 14.12.14 to 31.1.1915. A MB, 1.2.1915, declared him unfit and extended his leave for two weeks and, 19.2.1915, being found fit for home service, ordered him to 3rd RWF at Wrexham which he rejoined 21 February. MB reports, 5.3.1915 and 5.4.1915, recorded that he was unfit for general service but fit for home service. Gazetted T/Capt. 29.4.1915. MB 7 May: unfit for general service and fit only for light duty at home for two months. MB at Colwyn Bay, 16.6.1915, noted he had completely recovered. Promoted T/Major (with effect from 26.4.1915), and was then gazetted, 31.12.1915, T/Major attached to a local Reserve Bn. MB 11.1.1916 granted leave for one month. At that time he was serving with 20th RWF.

A MB, 15.2.1916, noted that he 'flatly' refused to go to hospital and that disciplinary action was to be taken. His disability was shown as gonorrhoea. A letter from Jones, 26 February, to OC 20th RWF stated that he was being treated at home and was not fit to travel to hospital in Liverpool. He would obey, if ordered, but considered his treatment 'harsh and tyrannical'. Ordered to proceed to No. 1 Western General Hospital as soon as he was fit to travel. MB 6.5.1916 granted three weeks leave and advised him not to draw pay for that period. The WO advised Western Command, 16 May, that Jones would have to be told to resign on account of ill health and he relinquished his commission 3.11.1916.

A letter from Jones to the WO, 23.7.1917, stated that he had regained his health and applied to be re-employed, preferably with the Egyptian Expeditionary Force as his brother was there with 6th RWF. He noted that he had over 20 years service with the Militia and Special Reserve 'and served with the 8th Division in the 1st Bn Royal Irish Rifles at the commencement of the present war'. At that time he was the County Commandant of the Merionethshire Volunteer Regt with the rank of Lt.-Col. (gazetted 31.1.1917). This regiment was later designated 4th (Volunteer) Bn RWF.

MB at Bangor, 14.8.1917, noted that he had recovered but they did not consider him fit for general service. He would be suitable for a Garrison or Labour unit in service abroad. He was ordered to return to his home address at Ynysfor.

WO letters to Jones, 26.9.1917, said that there were openings for his reemployment. Relinquished his commission, 31.12.1917, and was granted the rank of Hon. Lt.-Col. He remained unmarried and died January 1940.

Who Was Who 1929–1940: 'Master of Ynysfor Hounds ... European War with 1st Bn R. Irish Rifles; in 8th Division and subsequently with 17th (S) Bn RWF; DL Merionethshire and Caernarvonshire. Recreations field sports generally.' File ref: WO339/23210.

Jones Capt. Oscar Wynne. Born 4.1.1889 at Portdinorwic, Carnarvonshire (now Y Felinhelli, Caernarfonshire), the son of William Edward Jones and Jane, *née* Jones. Father was a shipbuilder. Applied for a commission, 5.11.1915, expressing a preference for 2/7th RWF. Height 5 foot 10 inches, architect and surveyor, employed in Public Service, consent to enlist had been obtained. Signed Army Form E624. Commissioned a 2/Lt. in 7th RWF, 29.12.1915.

Joined 1st RIR from the RWF, 31.10.1916, and was struck off the strength of the battalion 1.4.1917. An undated medical case history sheet shows his unit as 1st RIR. It said that he had two attacks of bronchitis and was sent down the line in November 1916. Spent eight days in No. 1 New Zealand Hospital, then four days in No. 8 General Hospital at Rouen. Then sent to base, medical rating A, but, after two days there, he had another attack of bronchitis. Next had his tonsils removed. Spent two weeks in No. 2 General Hospital then returned to base for two weeks, again having an attack of bronchitis. MO suggested he should be sent to a warm climate.

Medical Boards at Le Havre: 23.3.1917, 7th RWF attached 1st RIR, chronic bronchitis, debilitated and anaemic, unfit for general service and to be retained at base for one month; 20 April, bronchial catarrh and laryngitis, unfit for general service and to be retained at base for one month; 17 May, debilitated and unfit for general service, to be retained at base for one month. MB, 14 June, at Lazarde Valley Camp, Le Havre (still noted as 7th RWF attached 1st RIR), debilitated and unfit for general service for one month, fit for Conducting duty.

Promoted to Lt. 1.7.1917. MB, 11 August, at Dieppe (now showing 7th RWF only), bronchitis, fit for general service. Seconded to the RE, 8.11.1917 to 23.12.1920. Appointed T/Capt. 15.10.1919 to 23.12.1920. Restored to the Territorial Force, 24.12.1920, and discharged the same day. T/Capt., Substantive Lt. Single. Last served with 7th RWF, attached Claims Commission, Whitchurch. Civil occupation, surveyor. Address, Wingdon, Pwllheli, North Wales. File ref: WO374/38401.

Jones 2/Lt. William Howard. Born 31.3.1894 at Beaumaris, Wales, the son of William Richard and Martha Emily Jones, *née* Williams. Having been educated at Beaumaris Grammar School, and Fryars School, Bangor, he was employed as an apprentice shipping clerk in Liverpool. Enlisted Pte 390, 2nd Welsh Horse Yeomanry, at Oswestry, 30.1.1915. Height 5 foot 7½ inches, chest 32–35 inches. Appointed L/Cpl 27.3.1915 and signed Army Form E624 31.3.1915. Commissioned a 2/Lt. in 3/6th RWF 21.12.1915. He served with this unit until he joined 6th RWF in Gallipoli where he was mentioned in the battalion war diary for helping the wounded during December 1915.

He was later attached to 1/24th London Regt, saw action in France and was wounded. Having spent time with 4th RWF, he was sent to 1st RIR, 31.10.1916, and attached to 25th TMB. Wrote to the WO, 25.5.1917, asking for an extension of his leave, giving his address as Buckley Hotel, Beaumaris, Anglesey. Wounded by shellfire, 16.8.1917, and embarked Le Havre–Southampton, 22 August, aboard the *Kalyan*. The MB at 1st Western General Hospital, Liverpool, 18 September, noted that his injuries – a shell wound to the left neck – were 'severe, not permanent', and that he was unfit for military duty for two months. (He asked the WO for a wound gratuity 5.10.1917, 13.11.1917, 21.10.1918, 4.12.1918, 11.1.1919, and 20.1.1919.) The MB at Liverpool, 19.10.1917, declared him unfit for general service for three months and home service for two months – now showing GSW left neck. MB 19.11.1917 at Prescott, Liverpool, noting GSW neck, declared him fit for home duty after three weeks leave. He was ordered to report to 4th RWF at Oswestry for duty when his leave was completed. His address at 20.2.1918 was the Military Convalescent Hospital, Ashton-in-Makerfield, Lancashire – headed paper showed 6th RWF. Headed paper, 4.12.1918, 3rd RWF, Redcar, Yorks.

The WO, 8.1.1919, advised that he was to be discharged as medically unfit and he relinquished his commission 21.1.1919. A WO letter, 23.4.1919, rejected his application for a wound gratuity and said that he has been told this on four separate occasions and must accept it as final. He replied 24.6.1919 and 11.8.1919 asking for reconsideration of granting a gratuity. His address at this time was *Tyddyn Fryan*, Llansadwon, Menai Bridge, Anglesey. He died 20.4.1984, leaving no widow, and was residing at *Rosemary*, Mayfield, Sussex. He had been in receipt of a pension of £599 p.a. and was suffering a 20 per cent disability. File ref: WO374/38553.

Keane 2/Lt. Edmond Patrick. Born 16.2.1893 at Charleville, Co. Cork, the son of Thomas Keane, National Bank, Ballygar, Co. Galway. Educated at St Munchin's College, Limerick, and Albert College, Dublin. Enlisted as Pte 9007 in Inns of Court OTC, 19.1.1916. Signed Army Form E624 that day. Height 5 foot 9¼ inches, weight 130 pounds, chest 32–36 inches, farmer, single. Father's occupation given as gentleman farmer. Applied for a commission, 31.5.1916, asking for infantry, 3rd RMF. To No. 5 Officer Cadet Battalion at Cambridge, 14.8.1916 to 21.11.1916. Discharged to a commission in 3rd RMF.

Joined 1st RIR, 20.1.1917, and left 16.2.1917. Embarked Calais–Dover, 6.4.1917, suffering from bronco pneumonia. At that time his address was Milltown Castle, Charleville, Co. Cork. The MB at Caxton Hall, 9 May, noted that he was improving but still weak – unfit for general service for three months and home service two months. MB at Caxton Hall, 20 June: unfit for general service for two months and home service six weeks. MB at King's Lancashire Military Convalescent Hospital, Blackpool, 19 July: unfit for general service, unspecified period, and unfit for home service for three months. MBs at Blackpool, 17 August and 17 September: unfit for general service, unspecified, unfit home service for three months. MB at Cork Military Hospital, 17 November: had also suffered from measles, from which he was recovered – unfit for general service for two months and home service for six weeks.

MB at Devonport Military Hospital: 15.1.1918 passed him fit for home service for two months; 18.3.1918 unfit for general service for three months; 22.11.1918 had made good progress, fit for general service. Attached No. 512 POW Coy, 89th Labour Group early 1919. To the UK on leave 19.6.1919. To No. 511 POW Coy, 89th Labour Group, Rivalla, Italy, 13.8.1919. Left for 14 days leave to the UK 13.9.1919. Demobilized 25.10.1919. Medical status A1. Single. File ref: WO339/62865 137151.

Kearns Capt. Michael Christopher. Served in the South African War 1899 during operations in Natal, receiving the Queen's Medal with clasps. He later served with 2nd RIR as CSM. Wounded in France and was promoted to 2/Lt. Rejoined from leave, 11.12.1914, and was attached to D Coy. Height 6 foot 4 inches.

The Burgoyne Diaries: '20.12.1914: Kearns is a very fine shot, and has done splendid work in the field. At Ypres, in November, during the attack by the Prussian Guards, he bowled over fourteen of them himself. A very cool man, a most trustworthy soldier and a fine officer … He was recommended for the DSO for taking up some men and holding a trench out of which the Gordons had bolted, but his name was not forwarded, to save the reputation of the "Jocks" … 7.1.1915: Damn! No officer at all now, to help me. Kearn's fool of a servant had made him tea from some foul water and given him bread on which some paraffin had soaked. Told him to go to Kemmel and report sick.'

Mentioned in Despatches 17.2.1915, and promoted to Lt., 15.3.1915, and Capt., 1.1.1917. Served with 7th RIR. Joined 1st RIR 16.2.1918 and was struck off the strength of the battalion 9.8.1918, no reason being stated. Died in hospital at Bath 21.12.1947. Closed file, ref: 2/83 (29457).

Keating Capt. Patrick William. Commissioned a 2/Lt. in 4th Connaught Rangers, 26.4.1913, and promoted to Lt., 1.5.1914. Attached to the RMF. Promoted to Capt. 10.7.1915. Appointed a Regular Capt. in the RIR 29.8.1916, and attached 7th RIR. Attached Tank Corps, 8.1.1917, as an Acting Major. Joined 2nd RIR 3.2.1918, and 1st RIR 21.10.1918. Went to the UK 14.2.1919 prior to going overseas with 2nd RIR. Mentioned in Despatches 3.2.1920. The regimental history of the Connaught Rangers incorrectly lists him as having 'Drowned in the wreck of the *Egypt*'. Employed at the Depot according to the Army List for 1923. Closed file, ref: (19537).

Kennedy 2/Lt. James. Born at Shankill, Belfast, 17.7.1896, the son of the Revd Professor Samuel Giuler Kennedy LL D, minister of Grosvenor Road Reformed Presbyterian Church, and Christine

Kennedy of Cromwell House, Cromwell Road, Belfast. Educated at the Royal Belfast Academical Institution, and apprenticed to a stationery business. Enlisted as Rfn 17/1793 in the Cadet Company of 17th RIR, 8.11.1915. His address at 31.7.1916, when he applied for a commission, was Ballykinlar, Co. Down. Height 5 foot 10 inches, weight 147 pounds, and 6/6 vision in both eyes. Moved to No. 7 Officer Cadet Battalion, 5.10.1916, and was discharged to a commission with 19th RIR, 28.2.1917. He may also have served with 8th RIR.

Killed in action while attached to 1st RIR 21.3.1918. The WO sent a telegram to his father, 18 April, advising of his son's death. A second telegram, 25 April, revised this to missing. The WO wrote to his mother, 20 June, advising that the second telegram should never have been sent as the information it contained 'does not refer to your son Second Lieutenant J. Kennedy, but to his brother Second Lieutenant J.A.C. Kennedy' who was serving with 12th RIR (J.A. Chancellor Kennedy was a past pupil of Methodist College, Belfast.) It seems that the other brother had firstly been reported a POW and that the revised status of missing had been for him, but the notification from France had only used the first initial and the WO clerk had assumed that (following so soon after the notification of James' death) that it was James who was being discussed. The matter was only clarified when notification was received that J.A.C. Kennedy was, in fact, a POW and the notification for him reverted to its original status. The WO letter expressed 'sincerest apologies' for the error. A WO letter to Revd Kennedy, 27.11.1918, said that a Red Cross list from the Germans showed Kennedy as 'Fallen and buried in the Castres Sector. Disc sent in 19.8.1918'. Grand-Séracourt British Cemetery, Aisne, II.F.13.

Kerr Lt. James. Born 2.7.1893. His father, Francis Kerr, was a solicitor with offices at Wellington Place, Belfast, and 13 Bachelor's Walk, Dublin. Attended Clongowes Wood College, Co. Kildare, 1908–10. Applied for a commission, 16.6.1915. Single. Permanent address *Altafort*, Myrtlefield Park, Malone Road, Belfast. Cadet at Queen's University OTC since January 1915. Applied for ASC but this was crossed out and infantry substituted in another hand. Posted to 7th RIR.

Irish Life 1.6.1917: ' ... has been awarded the parchment certificate of the Irish Division by Major-General W.B. Hickie CB, for gallant conduct and devotion to duty in the field. Lieutenant Kerr is the third son of Mr Frank Kerr ... He has been in France since the Irish Division went overseas and has seen a good deal of fighting.'

The Clongownian, 1917: 'He was at the taking of Guillemont and Ginchy in September last, and had previously been in several engagements north of the Somme.'

Left unit 20.7.1917. Embarked Boulogne–Dover, 24 July, on the *St Dennis*. Sprained right ankle. The MB at 2nd Western General Hospital, 15 August, noted that he sprained his ankle during an inter-regimental football match near St Omer, 19 July; now recovered, but marked unfit for general service and recommended three weeks leave. A statement from Major H.S. Allison, 7th RIR, noted that Kerr was knocked over and the other man fell on his ankle, 'I was present at the time'. There is an Army Form W.3428 on file, 'Report on accidental or self-inflicted injuries'. This showed Kerr was not to blame and the matter was accidental. MB at Belfast, 26.9.1917, declared him fit for general service and ordered him to return to Carrickfergus.

Joined 1st RIR from 5th RIR, 18.12.1917, and posted to C Coy. Played as a forward in the battalion soccer team, 17.3.1918, when they beat 2nd RIR by 2–1. He was in command of the Counter-Attack Trenches, C Coy, 21.3.1918, and was killed in action that day.

Irish Times 10.4.1918: 'He was in the service of Messrs. Thomas Somerset & Co. when he accepted a commission in the Rifles. He went overseas in 1916 and had service in the Irish Brigade. He was wounded, and was mentioned in despatches by Sir Douglas Haig in May, 1917.'

The Clongownian 1919: 'Jim Kerr ... was killed in action in France ... Only just a year ago his brother Jack was killed. Surely this cruel war has borne hard on this afflicted family.'

A letter from his father to the WO, 24 April, stated that he had received a telegram telling him that Pte J. Kerr, RIR, has been killed in action 21 March: 'I had a son J. Kerr in the Royal Irish

Rifles, but he was a Lieutenant, and I had not heard from him since the 21st, and would thank you to say if the telegram refers to him, and in that event I would like to get his personal belongings, and would like to know to whom I should apply.'

There are two WO telegrams on the file, both to his father. One refers to Pte J. Kerr and is date stamped 19.4.1918 and the second, dated 18.4.1918, refers to Lt. J. Kerr. The WO replied to father's letter, 30 April, stating the telegram referring to Pte J. Kerr was a telegraphic error and suggested that he write to OC 3rd RIR if he wanted details. Pozières Memorial. File ref: WO339/39903 6/83 107265.

Kingston 2/Lt. William MC. Joined 1st RIR from 3rd RMF, 28.2.1917. Wounded and missing 16.8.1917. Mentioned in Despatches. Age 25.

Irish Times 11.9.1917: 'Mr T.G. Kingston, Mount John, Greystones, has received intimation from the War Office that his brother, Second Lieutenant W. Kingston MC, Royal Munster Fusiliers, is wounded and missing since August 16th. Second Lieutenant Kingston joined the Inns of Court Officers Training Corps in November, 1915, and subsequently received his commission in the Royal Munster Fusiliers. On going to France last February he was attached to the Royal Irish Rifles.'

Irish Life 5.10.1917: 'He is the third son of the late Mr Richard Kingston and Mrs Kingston, Madame House, Clonakilty, Co. Cork, and was Mentioned in Despatches and awarded the Military Cross for gallantry in action at Ypres on July 31st.' Tyne Cot Memorial. File destroyed.

Kirkwood Lt.-Col. John Hendley Morrison DSO, JP. Born 11.5.1877, the only son of Major James Morrison Kirkwood, Yeo. Vale, Fairy Cross, North Devon, and Glencarha, Co. Mayo. Educated at Harrow and married to Gertrude, the daughter of Sir R. Lyle, Bt. They had two sons and one daughter. He had been a Lt. in 7th Dragoon Guards, Capt. in Royal North Devon Hussars, and T/Major in the Household Battalion. He served and was wounded in the South African War, 1899–1902, being Mentioned in Despatches (Lord Robert's Recommendation for Meritorious Service 2.4.1901). Received the Queen's Medal with three clasps and the King's Medal with two clasps. Conservative MP for SE Essex, 1910–12. Served with 4th Dragoon Guards, 1914–15, being wounded, and later with 1st Life Guards and Household Battalion. Awarded the DSO, *London Gazette*, 16.8.1917. He joined and assumed command of 1st RIR, 1.9.1917, but was placed on the sick list 9.10.1917. Transferred to England, 16.10.1917, and was struck off the strength of the battalion. He was also a JP in Devonshire. Resided at Yeo. Clubs: Turf and Carlton. Died 7.2.1924. File missing.

Knox Capt. Utred A. Frederick. Born 1.5.1885 and gazetted a 2/Lt. 20.11.1907; promoted Lt. 1.8.1909. Appointed Adjutant 4th RIR, 4.12.1914, and promoted Capt. 15.3.1915. Served at home until he joined 1st RIR, 25.12.1916. He transferred to hospital, sick, 23.1.1917, and rejoined two weeks later.

Whitfeld: '5.3.1917: We relieved 2nd Royal Berks at night. The CO and I went up "London Lane". We met Knox coming out with his company having gone up the wrong trench. He caught it properly from E.C.L. [Lloyd] who was in a furious temper.'

Rejoined the battalion from the sick list 19.4.1917. He returned home, 1.7.1917, and appeared before the MB, 30 July, suffering from pyorrhoea (teeth and gums) and was declared unfit for general service. Declared fit for home service 3.9.1917 and, 18.1.1918 at Belfast, fit for general service. Attached to 16th RIR. Returned to France, 6.4.1918, and remained there until 23.3.1919. Contracted influenza 21.2.1919. The MB at Cannock Chase Military Hospital, Staffordshire, noted that he had recovered 10 May. Resigned his commission, 21.11.1919, and went to the reserve list. His address was given as Carnathan Green Road, Knock, Co. Down. Removed from the Reserve of Officers, RUR, 1.5.1935, on account of his age. By then he was living at Hengas, St Tuay RSO, Cornwall.

Laing 2/Lt. Gilbert James. The son of George and Annie M. Laing of The Wilderness, Hadlow Down, Uckfield, Sussex. Unattached List Indian Army attached to 1st RIR. *Laurie*, 2.2.1915: 'Our General has had to go away this morning into hospital with fever. Mr Laing ... is now in bed with the same sort of complaint.'

Killed 12.3.1915 while serving with D Coy. At that time he was aged 19. A telegram was sent to his father, 18 March, notifying that that death had occurred on the 14th. This was corrected to 12 March on the 26th.

Witness statements: 7171 Rfn J. Scott, 1st RIR, at Cornelia Hospital, Poole, 21.5.1915, stated that he was with Laing when he was shot through the brain. Scott helped to stretcher the body to a grave where Laing was buried with Capt. Hutcheson.

Capt. C.H.L. Cinnamond at Princess Hospital, Boulogne, 9.5.1915, stated that, when he left the unit, news of Laing was not definite, but he believed that he was buried about 14 March. In an earlier statement, 21 April, he stated that Laing was killed about 2.45 p.m., 12 March, while leading his platoon. He had first been shot through the leg and was crawling towards the trench when he was shot through the eye and killed. He was buried beside Capt. Hutcheson about 100 yards left of Point 31 to the rear of the RIR trench. He also stated that he was in the trench in question when Laing was buried and that he thought that it was CQMS Walsh of D Coy who arranged the burial. 9165 Rfn Walsh, at Maritime Hospital, Boulogne, 13.4.1915, stated that Laing was shot while putting up wire entanglements in front of the trenches 'about three months ago'. 'We got his body and he was buried but I cannot say where.' The interviewer noted that 'This witness seemed afraid to tell me much, perhaps taking me for a spy'. Lt. Webb was at Westminster Hospital, Le Touquet, 10.5.1915: 'Lt. Laing was trying to cross the road with orders for men in another trench when he was riddled with machine gun fire. He was a very plucky officer.' An Irish Sergeant said to the informant that: 'Lt. Laing and Capt. Hutcheson were very brave and if it were not for them, and half a dozen like myself, Neuve Chapelle could never have been taken'.

A letter to his father from the WO, 14.6.1915, gave the burial place as Sheet 36 Belgium, Square M.35.B.6.0. A good proportion of his file is taken up with correspondence dealing with an overpayment of allowances to his estate, and subsequent dealings between various departments and the executor of the will to have money returned. The amount involved was 9s 6d (48p). His parents later lived at 28 The Avenue, Eastbourne, Sussex, and 80 Crescent Road, Reading, Berkshire. A WO letter was sent to the India Office, 8.10.1921, confirming Laing's eligibility for the Aug–Nov Bar to the 1914 Star. Neuve Chapelle Memorial, Pas de Calais. File ref: 47019.

Lake The Revd William Victor Cecil. Born 31.1.1892 at Preston Barracks, the son of Capt. Frederick Thomas Lake and Margaret Lake, *née* Maclennan. (His father ran away from home as a boy and joined the Cameron Highlanders at Fort George. Ended his career as a Capt. in the Army Pay Corps.) Spent most of his youth at the Rifle Depot in Winchester. Attended Coates Hall College, Edinburgh. Known as Cecil. He was planning on becoming an Anglican priest at the time war broke out. Enlisted August 1914 into the 1st (UPS) Bn Royal Fusiliers and rose to the rank of Platoon Sgt at Woodcote Park Camp. Requested a Special Reserve Commission in any regiment. At a medical inspection it was discovered that his heart was on the wrong side. Gazetted a 2/Lt. in 5th RIR, 14.5.1915, and trained at Holywood Barracks, Co. Down. While in Ireland he did a Musketry Instructors course at Dollymount, Co. Dublin, and a Mills Hand Grenade course. Sailed from Folkestone to Boulogne and on to Etaples, arriving in Flanders to join 1st RIR, B Coy billets, at Windy Farm Post. See main text.

During the Somme attack, 1.7.1916, he was the Bn Lewis Gun Officer and a member of B Coy. On the recommendation of the Adjutant, Lt. Whitfeld, he transferred to the Machine Gun Corps at Grantham, 22.8.1916.

'Before I had completed my course at Grantham on the Vickers machine gun, I had made the acquaintance of a Major Loftus of the Royal Irish Rifles, who was in command of the Receiving Depot at the Centre. He was keen to get me on to his staff and at the right moment secured me.'

Remained in England for the rest of the war. Promoted Lt. 1.7.1917. In August 1917 he married Emily Masters and they had three children, Cicele, Victor, and Dorothy. On demobilization he returned to college and trained for his ministry. Appointed to the Scottish Episcopal Church. Rector of St John's Episcopal Church, Selkirk. In 1924 he volunteered as a chaplain in the Territorial Army (CTA).

'By attaching me to a Medical unit that only took shape in the event of war, I was excused from attending the annual Territorial camps. But on being transferred to the Moray Diocese in 1929, I became attached to the 4th Battalion, the Seaforth Highlanders, whose Headquarters were in Dingwall.'

Ministered in charge at Dingwall and Strathpeffer. Reported for duty with the Highland Division in September 1939. Embarked January 1940 from Southampton to Le Havre and was captured at St Valery in May 1940. Made an early escape but was recaptured and interned in prison camps at Laufen, Schildburg, Rotenburg, and the majority of the time in Oflag IX A/H, Elbersdorf. Liberated by the Americans 4.4.1945.

He served a further period as padre at RAF Kinloss, 1952–3, and RAF South Cerney 1953–8. Died at Willersey 16.1.1978. His Great War memoirs are deposited with the Imperial War Museum. Closed file, ref: (118211). Sourced mainly from his unpublished autobiography with additional details being supplied by his son, Cdr. Victor M. Lake, RN (Rtd).

Lamont 2/Lt. Frank MC. Born 16.8.1892 at Ballymoney, Co. Antrim, the son of Thomas Lamont, a farmer and stock-keeper. Another form on his file shows his year of birth as 1891 – both entries are clear and signed by Lamont. Educated at Ballymoney Intermediate School and Queen's University, Belfast. Bank clerk.

Served as Pte 736305 in the Nova Scotia Regt, and was attested into the Canadian Overseas Expeditionary Force at Lethbridge, Alberta, 11.1.1916. He was single and had no previous military service. Height 5 foot 10 inches, chest 33–38 inches and weight 155 pounds. Applied for a commission in the RIR 28.5.1917. At this time he was serving with 17th Reserve Bn (Canadian) at Bramshott Camp, Hampshire. Sent to No. 7 Officer Cadet Battalion at Fermoy, 7.9.1917, and discharged on appointment to a commission in 18th RIR, 30.1.1918. His address was given as Cabra House, Ballymoney. Joined 1st RIR from 18th RIR, 12.7.1918.

War Diary, 4.10.1918: '6 a.m. One platoon of A Coy under 2/Lt. F. Lamont made an unsuccessful attack on two pill boxes … which was strongly held by the enemy with machine guns. The enemy counterattacked but was repulsed.'

He suffered a gunshot wound to his right leg, 23.10.1918, and embarked Boulogne–Dover, 30 October. Admitted to the Officer's War Hospital, Exeter, 31 October. The MB at Exeter, 18 November, recorded that he could walk with the aid of a stick and that he was improving, 18 December. Awarded the MC in November 1918. The MB at Belfast, 24.1.1919, noted that the wound was 'quite healed'. Ordered to rejoin the Reserve unit at Salisbury Plain. Having been discharged, 9.7.1919, he returned to Canada where he was employed by the Canadian Bank of Commerce, Lethbridge, Alberta. File ref: WO339/113156 213354.

La Nauze Lt. George Mansfield. Born 22.12.1891 at Manor, Highgate, Co. Fermanagh, the son of Thomas Story and Edith Emma, *née* Deering, La Nauze. Educated at Corrig School, Kingstown, Co. Dublin, and the Abbey Grammar School, Tipperary. Father's occupation 'Private Gentleman'.

Applied for a commission in 4th RIR 19.4.1911. Single, permanent address Island View, Clifden, Co. Galway, occupation 'none', height 5 foot 7½ inches, weight 132 pounds, and chest

33½–36 inches. He entered 4th RIR as a 2/Lt., 20.5.1911, being promoted to Lt., 13.2.1913. Letter from OC 4th RIR, Newtownards, 29.7.1913, to Staff Capt. No. 11 District, advised that La Nauze had secured a position in Malaya and wanted to try it before severing connections with the 4th Bn: may he have permission to miss training during 1914? The request was approved and permission granted to be abroad 10.8.1913 to 9.8.1914.

When war broke out he was employed in the Malay States but, returning as soon as possible, was sent to Holywood, near Belfast, to rejoin his battalion 31.10.1914, remaining there at duty until 16.3.1915. He then proceeded to France, joining 1st RIR 20.3.1915. Killed in action 9.5.1915. He was first wounded, and while waiting for a stretcher to be taken to a hospital, a shell burst, killing him instantly. He had taken command of his company a short time previously, Capt. O'Sullivan having been killed, and he was, at that time, the senior of his rank in the battalion. The WO telegram to his mother, 13 May, stated wounded, degree not known. Another telegram to her, 4 June, revised this to wounded and missing. There is a WO form on the file and seems to be a direct form of enquiry to the German Government, undated, asking if La Nauze was a POW. A German ink-stamp on the rear, and a stamped reply stated he was not on any POW list.

The WO wrote to his mother, Mrs G. Scott Mansfield, Hollywood House, Glenealy, Co. Wicklow, 6.5.1916, asking if she had any further news; if not then death on or since 9.5.1915 would have to be presumed for official purposes. She replied saying that she had news from a Major Kelets who had spoken to George on the battlefield after he had been wounded but had been unable to have him moved to safety. Shortly thereafter a shell burst nearby and the Major presumed him dead.

A statement by 6657 Cpl Carstairs, 14.10.1915, on leave at Boulogne, reported that La Nauze was wounded in the German front line trench and must have been taken prisoner or died after the battalion was driven back. Carstairs was in same platoon and was La Nauze's observer. Death accepted for official purposes 16.5.1916. A WO letter to C.-in-C., Forces in Ireland, 10.10.1916, noted that George joined for duty, 2.11.1914, from the Malay Federated States, and enquired if he had permission to reside abroad, and if so, under what authority. The Irish Command forwarded the original 1913 paperwork that approved the move abroad, 11.10.1916. Ploegsteert Memorial.

Irish Life 14.12.1917: 'Inspector C.D. La Nauze of the Royal North West Mounted Police, Canada, has just returned from a long patrol of two and a half years in the Arctic in search of the murderers of two French priests who were murdered in 1913 by the Eskimos. Inspector La Nauze and his men were successful ... He is the only surviving son of Mrs G. Scott Mansfield of Hollywood, Glenealy, Co. Wicklow. His two brothers were killed in action in France in May, 1915.'

Lt. William La Nauze, 4th RIR, was killed in action 16.5.1915 while attached to the RIF. Their sister, A. De La Nauze served with the VAD. The RUR Museum holds all three sets of medals. File ref: WO339/59630 132968.

Lanyon Capt. William Mortimer. Born 10.6.1880 at Lismara, Whiteabbey, Co. Antrim, the third son of Herbert Owen Lanyon, Northleigh, Fortwilliam Park, Belfast. His grandfather was Sir Charles Lanyon and his uncle Sir Owen Lanyon. Educated at Cheltenham, where he played in the Leconfield XV, afterward entering Sandhurst, from which he was gazetted to the RIR, 12.8.1899.

Promoted to Lt. 14.1.1901, and Capt. 7.2.1908. Served with 1st RIR in India and Burma until 1909, when he returned to the Depot at Belfast, and served there for three years. Appointed Adjutant of 5th RIR, 1.11.1913, with which he served after mobilization until he went to the front in March, 1915. Attached to 1st RIR. Shot in the head and killed instantly on the morning of 5.4.1915, sniped over the parapet. This was the day after he had entered the trenches for the first time. Major Baker wrote to Mrs Laurie 12.4.1915: 'We have now lost Capt. Lanyon, very sad, so soon after Capt. Biscoe being killed. They had been inseparable friends for years.'

He was married to Helen, youngest daughter of John McCance Blizard, of Donaghadee, Co. Down. They had two daughters: Joan Amy, born November 1913; and Elizabeth Helen, born December 1914. A member of the Junior Naval and Military Club, London, and of the Ulster Club, Belfast. He was a very good polo and hockey player, having played in the regimental teams during all the time he served with the battalion in India. He also hunted with the Co. Down Staghounds. Rue du Bacquerot (13th) London Graveyard, Laventie, Pas de Calais, G.1. File missing.

Laurie Lt.-Col. George Brenton. Born at Halifax, Nova Scotia, 13.10.1867. One of three sons of Lt.-General John Wimburn Laurie CB, MP, of 47 Porchester Terrace, London, and Mrs Laurie of Oakfield, Nova Scotia. Husband of Florence Clementina Vere-Laurie (Viscountess Masserene and Ferrard, eldest daughter of the Hon. Sydney William Skeffington) of Carlton Hall, Carlton-on-Trent, Newark, Notts. Married in September 1905, they had three children, George Haliburton 1906, Blanche 1907, and Sydney Vere 1910. Educated at Galt Collegiate Institute, Ontario, and the Picton Academy, from which he passed into the Royal Military College, Kingston, Canada in 1883. Commissioned into the RIR in 1885. He was the last officer to enter the British Army with the rank of full Lieutenant. Served in Gibraltar 1886, Egypt 1888, Nile Campaign 1889, Belfast, Malta, Sudan, and in the South African War. Promoted to Capt. 1893, and obtained an Adjutancy of Volunteers in Devonshire, October 1896. In March 1901 he was appointed a special service officer, including the command of a mounted infantry battalion for the South African War. He was present at operations in the Transvaal, Orange River Colony and Cape Colony, April 1901–May 1902, being Mentioned in Despatches 29.6.1902. Received the Queen's Medal with five clasps.

After the war he served in Ireland and, in 1903, was selected by HRH The Duke of Connaught to command a detachment of 50 men to represent the Army in Ireland at the funeral of HRH The Duke of Cambridge in London. Promoted Major in October 1904 and then served in England. In 1911 he commanded a representative detachment of the regiment at the coronation of King George V (Coronation Medal). Promoted Lt.-Col. in 1912 and went to India to take over command of 1st RIR. He was deeply engaged at this time in writing the Regimental History which was published in 1914. He had previously written a history of *The French in Morocco*.

Mentioned in Despatches 17.2.1915 and 4.4.1915. Killed in action 12.3.1915. See main text.

Irish Times 20.3.1915: 'The announcement of the death of Col. G.B. Laurie has occasioned much regret in Belfast where the deceased officer was well known as the head of the 1st Bn of the Royal Irish Rifles. He was closely connected by marriage with the north of Ireland having been married at Rostrevor in 1905 to Florence Clementina Vere, daughter of the Hon. Sydney Skeffington, third son of the 10th Viscount Massereene and Ferrard. Lady Ross of Bladensburg, Rostrevor, was a relative of the deceased officer who frequently visited Sir John and Lady Ross at their charming home at Carlingford Lough. Col. Laurie was the eldest son of the late Lt.-General Laurie CB.' Lt.-Col. Sir John Ross, Coldstream Guards, was Chief Commissioner to the Dublin Metropolitan Police 1901–14.

Irish Times 22.3.1915: 'His wife is a great granddaughter of Mr John Foster (Lord Oriel) the last speaker of the Irish House of Commons. He himself was the great grandson of an illustrious Irishman, Dr Inglis, the Bishop of Nova Scotia, who was the first Anglican Colonial Bishop ever consecrated – a Trinity College Dublin man and a rector of Ardara in Donegal … Col. Laurie's father, General J.W. Laurie CB, served with great distinction in the Crimea where he was twice wounded; in the Indian Mutiny and in the Transvaal. He was Hon. Colonel of the Royal Munster Fusiliers and, having sat for some years in the Canadian House of Commons, was from 1895 till 1906 Unionist member in the Imperial Parliament for the Pembroke Burghs, and a prime favourite with all sorts and conditions of men in the House of Commons.

'Col. Laurie's elder brother, Capt. Haliburton Laurie … fell in the Boer War in 1901. If he had not been a great soldier, Col. Laurie would have been a great historian. His knowledge of history was profound and his memory was singularly retentive. He had, moreover, a very sound judgement in the marshalling of facts. … Yours etc., J.G. Swift McNeill [MP for South Donegal], Dublin, March 20, 1915.'

Member of the Army and Navy and the United Services Clubs. Hunted with the Devon and Somerset hounds and played polo. His wife published his letters from the front in 1921. His son, Lt.-Col. George Haliburton Foster Peel Vere-Laurie DL, JP (1906–81), was Lord of the Manor at Carlton, and Willoughby in Norwell; Freeman of the City of London, and High Sheriff of Notts 1957–8. Pont-du-Hem Cemetery, La Gorgue, Nord, VI.L.15. File missing.

Law Capt. Reginald Owen H. MC. Gazetted a 2/Lt. in the Royal Warwickshire Regt. Appointed a 2/Lt. in 9th RIR, 6.10.1914, promoted Lt., 2.10.1915, and Capt., 14.10.1917. Served with 36th (Ulster) Division and was awarded the MC. He took part in the defence against the German offensive of March 1918, while serving with 1st RIR, and was awarded a Bar to his MC, 31.5.1918. Proceeded to England, 8.7.1918, for a six months tour of duty at home. Awarded a second Bar to his MC. In 1919 he was moved to the Reserve. Closed file, ref: (125336).

Lawler Capt. George. Born 26.1.1883 at 40 Lansdowne Road, Dublin, the son of William Vincent and Elizabeth Lawler, *née* Delahoyde. His father was a solicitor. Applied for a commission, 12.8.1914, and became a 2/Lt. in 4th RIR, 15.8.1914. At that time he was living at 5 Sorrento Terrace, Dalkey, Co. Dublin. He arrived at the front 4.7.1915, joining 1st RIR.

Wounded, 1.7.1916, and evacuated to the London Hospital (Officer's Section), Whitechapel, 7 July. Injuries were gunshot and shrapnel wounds. Certified fit to travel, 2 August, and proceeded to Dublin. The MB, 19 August, certified him as unfit for ten weeks. Being fit for home duties, he reported to 4th RIR at Carrickfergus, 27.10.1916. Promoted to Capt. 1.1.1917, he was retired as unfit 16.4.1919. Address, Officer's Mess, No. 11 Camp, Durrington Camp, Larkhill, Salisbury Plain. To Reserve of Officers 3.10.1919.

Leeper Capt. James Cyril. Born 5.2.1897, the son of William Leeper JP, Wellbrook, Cookstown, Co. Tyrone. Attended Campbell College, Belfast, being school prefect and on the 1st XV, 1915–16. P.S., OTC 1915. Attended the RMC and was gazetted a 2/Lt. in 1st RIR, going overseas 7.12.1916. Placed on the sick list, 14.4.1917, and rejoined 28.4.1917. Took over the duties of Assistant Adjutant until 12.7.1918 when he became Adjutant. Wounded 14.10.1918, he returned to the battalion, 24.10.1918, and was Mentioned in Despatches 28.12.1918. Awarded the Belgian Croix de Guerre in January 1919. On 10.2.1919 he went to the UK to attend an adjutants course at Cambridge. Later he was a Capt. in Queen's University OTC, Belfast. Director of John Gunning & Son, Cookstown, and resided at Forth Hill, Cookstown. He regularly attended the 36th (Ulster) Division Officers OCA annual dinner until 1938. Closed file, ref: (158008).

Lennard 2/Lt. Edward Wood. Born in Leicester 13.6.1891. His father, Edward Lennard, was a boot manufacturer. His mother Eliza lived at Shirley Lodge, Knighton, Leicester. Height 6 foot 2½ inches, 37 inches expanded chest measurement, and weighed 157 pounds. Enlisted as Pte PS/2950 in the 21st R. Fusiliers, 15.9.1914, and joined at Ashtead 25.9.1914, serving at home up to 12.11.1915. Served with the R. Fusiliers in France until 22.3.1916. Commissioned into 5th RIR, 4.7.1916, and joined 1st RIR, 17.9.1916.

Wounded, 24.10.1916, at Le Transloy, GSW right arm. Embarked for the UK 28 October. The MB declared him recovered, 1.2.1917. Rejoined 1st RIR 11.10.1917. On taking command of C Coy, he was mortally wounded, 30.11.1917, being first reported as wounded and missing. A WO letter, 8.2.1918, confirmed acceptance that he was killed in action. Tyne Cot Memorial.

Lewis 2/Lt. Frederick Homer. Born 22.5.1894 at Belfast, the son of Frederick William and Lizzie Blanche Lewis of 41 Shore Road, Belfast. His mother was sub-postmistress of Skegoniel and his father was an insurance agent. Educated at Belfast Royal Academy and later employed as an insurance inspector. Attested in Belfast, 24.10.1916, and posted to the Army Reserve. Joined Belfast University OTC 9.10.1916. The testimonial from his OC was very good. Applied for a commission, 12.12.1916, expressing a preference for Motor Machine Guns. Height 6 foot 2 inches, weight 162 pounds, chest 35½–38 inches. Mobilized, 27.2.1917, and posted to No. 2 MGC Cadet Bn at Pirbright, 1 March. 'Found to be unsuitable for appointment to Machine Gun Corps and therefore transferred to No. 9 Officer Cadet Bn, Gailes, on 7th June 1917.'

Re-attested at Ayr 10.8.1917, No. 19/1027, 'General Service' attached 9th Officer Cadet Bn. Commissioned to 19th RIR 28.8.1917. Joined 1st RIR from 10th RIR, 2.4.1918. Killed in action 29.4.1918. Effects to father at St Vincent Terrace, Shore Road, Belfast. Tyne Cot Memorial. File ref: WO339/ 83081 164825.

Linton Lt. William John MC. Born 21.9.1882 at Garvagh, Co. Derry, and educated at Coleraine Model School. His father was a farmer. Joined the Inns of Court OTC, 19.1.1916, as Pte 5/9009, and signed Army Form E624 (Imperial Service Obligation). Height 5 foot 8½ inches, weight 168 pounds, and chest 37½–40½ inches. Applied for a commission, 19.9.1916, stating that he was single and employed by the Ulster Bank Ltd., Belfast, as a bank official. Next of kin was his mother, Sarah Linton, Rockland Vale, Garvagh. Transferred from the Inns of Court OTC to No. 7 Officer Cadet Battalion, Fermoy, 3.11.1916. His record shows home service until 28.2.1917. Appointed a 2/Lt. in 19th RIR, *London Gazette* 5.4.1917.

Having been reposted to 1st RIR from 10th RIR, 28.4.1918, he was wounded at Courtrai 20.10.1918. Promoted Lt. 1.9.1918. He embarked Boulogne–Dover, 23 October, and was admitted to the 3rd London General Hospital the same day. Awarded the MC in November 1918. The MB at Military Hospital, Fargo, Salisbury Plain, 20.12.1918, noted that he had suffered two gunshot wounds but was recovered. He later served with 3rd RIR and was released from his commission 3.2.1919. Medical rating A1. File ref: WO339/71903 149494.

Liston Lt. William Gerard G. Joined 1st RIR from 4th RIR, 3.5.1917, and transferred to England, sick, during June 1917. Promoted Lt. 1.9.1918. File destroyed.

Lloyd Lt.-Col. Evan Colclough DSO. Born 4.1.1877, the son of J. Lloyd JP, DL, Gloster, Brosna, King's County (Offaly), and of Susan Lloyd, *née* Colclough, of Tintern Abbey, Co. Wexford. Educated at Wellington College, Berkshire. He married Mary, daughter of Sir Heffernan James Fitz Considine CB, MVO, DL, BA, Deputy Inspector-General, Royal Irish Constabulary (1900–11), Farm Hill, Dundrum, Co. Dublin, and Emily Mary Talbot, Ballytrent, Co. Wexford. They had one son. Gazetted a 2/Lt. in the R. Irish, 4.5.1898, and promoted Lt. 23.10.1899, Capt. 29.11.1904, and Major 25.8.1915. Served in the South African War, 1899–1902, and was Adjutant of the Mounted Infantry Bn, 12.6.1900 until 24.1.1901. He took part in the relief of Kimberley and operations in the Orange Free State, February–May 1900, including operations at Paardeberg (17–26 February), actions at Poplar Grove, Houtnek (Thoba Mountain), Vet River (5–6 May) and Zand River. Operations in the Transvaal in May–June 1900 including actions at Venterskroon. Operations in Orange River Colony including actions at Wittebergen (1–29 July), Ladybrand (2–5 September), Bothavill, and Caledon River (27–9 November). Operations in the Transvaal, January 1901–March 1902. Operations in Orange River Colony 30.11.1900 to January 1901 and March to 31.5.1902. Mentioned in Despatches 10.9.1901, he received the Queen's Medal with five clasps and the King's Medal with two clasps. At the Royal Irish Depot 1912.

Served with 1st R. Irish and later with 6th R. Irish where his CO was Lt.-Col. F.E.P. Curzon – an uncle of Lt. G.H.P. Whitfeld. Was Commander of D Coy, which was composed of members of the Guernsey Militia, March–October 1915, while they prepared to go overseas. Took over command of 1st RIR, 20.7.1916.

Whitfeld: 'September 1916. I am not impressed with him – he has a bad manner and a foul temper which he lost with Edwards the other day over billets, when it wasn't Edwards fault at all.

Jimmy [Gartlan] also hates him … 10 December 1916: E.C.L. and I have been to Paris, we had a top hole time and E.C.L. was very kind and not at all like he sometimes is.'

Major Fitzmaurice's son Brian told me: 'Many years ago he told me the story of the unpopular Lt.-Col. Lloyd, the way he was so intensely disliked by officers and men alike. On one occasion Lloyd was just off on leave, and my father was temporarily Officer in Charge and either the RSM or a CSM approached my father, asked a question, they did their business and my father said, in effect, "the Colonel has gone on a month's leave" and the instant reply was "Yes Sir, and I wish to God he had gone for six." I remember asking my father how he dealt with such a (truthful) reply from an NCO and my father intimated to me that the Sergeant Major "knew who he was talking to" and that the Colonel was universally disliked in the whole of his Command.'

2/Lt. Lake: 'For a little while we had an unsympathetic CO from the Berkshire Regiment who had no idea how to get the best out of war-weary, heart-broken troops. I nearly got court-martialled for resisting his impossible commands.' Lake, writing circa 1974, could have been referring to Major Sawyer of 2nd R. Berks who was in command for a short while after the April raid on La Boiselle. However, he was describing events after the Somme attack of 1 July. Lake himself left in August 1916 which may explain the short time reference.

Left 1st RIR, 28.4.1917, and took over command of a Territorial Battalion. *Whitfeld*: 'The RSM ventured to say goodbye to him and to say how sorry he was he was going. "I'll bet", said E.C.L. laughing.'. The Army List of March 1918 shows him as a Major with 6th RIR and acting Lt.-Col. 20.7.1916.

Wounded during the war and Mentioned in Despatches 1.1.1916, 18.12.1917, and 27.12.1918. Was CO of the R. Irish Depot at the end of the war and was present as the colours were handed over when the regiment was disbanded in 1922. 1914–15 Star. Awarded the DSO in the New Year's Honour List, 1.1.1918. Bar to DSO, *London Gazette* 26.7.1918: 'For conspicuous gallantry and devotion to duty in command of his battalion in action. In spite of very heavy enemy attacks, preceded by gas and accompanied by a dense bombardment, he succeeded in maintaining his position although nearly surrounded, a subsequent counter attack enabled him to withdraw the battalion, inflicting casualties on the enemy in doing so. His courage and tenacity gained valuable time to reorganise the defence in the rear of the battle zone. Later he was severely wounded.' File missing.

Longfield Major W.B.M. Born 26.11.1886. Gazetted a 2/Lt. in 5th RDF, 15.2.1907, mobilized 5.8.1914, and promoted to Capt. 4.3.1915. Joined 1st RIR 26.3.1915. On 29.11.1918 the MB granted him leave until 20.12.1918. Demobilized from 5th RDF 26.4.1919 with medical category A1. At that time he was noted as being domiciled in Australia. He relinquished his commission, 9.5.1922, with the honorary rank of Major. Died 23.7.1948. His widow, Mrs B. Longfield, *Oakley*, 11 Avebury Street, West End, Brisbane, Australia, wrote to the Ministry of Defence, 19.11.1965, advising that she thought that her husband had died from the effects of his war time service. Her request was sent to the Ministry of Pensions. No further details are on his file. File ref: 80716.

Love Capt. Castor Jennings. Born 8.12.1894 at Irish Street, Downpatrick, Co. Down, the son of George and Elizabeth Love, *née* Jennings. His father was a slater. Educated at Down Southwell National School, the Trade Preparatory School, and the Municipal Technical Institute, Belfast, serving two years with Belfast University OTC. Applied for a commission 7.8.1914, requesting 5th RIR. Architect's pupil, height 5 foot 10 inches, chest 30–33 inches, and weight 122 pounds.

Joined 1st RIR as a 2/Lt. from 3rd RIR, 30.5.1915, and developed varicose veins in October 1915. Promoted to Capt. 27.11.1915. Admitted to hospital, 27.6.1916, and returned to the UK aboard the *St Patrick*, via Rouen, 4 July. He went to Osborne, Isle of Wight, suffering from fever and gastritis and transferred to Queen Alexandra Hospital. Millbank, London SW, 17 July. He went on sick leave 11.9.1916, the MB detailing his illness as gonorrhoea, gastritis, and syphilis. His leave expired, 22.10.1916, and he appeared before the MB at Belfast, 1 November, when he was declared unfit for two months – gastritis and syphilis. On 13.12.1916 his disabilities were listed as varicose veins, gastritis, and syphilis. Rejoined 3rd RIR for home service, 13.12.1916. On 5.4.1917 and 29.5.1917 he appeared before the MB at Tipperary Military Hospital, still suffering from gastritis and syphilis, declared unfit for general service.

The WO wrote, 12.7.1917, to advise that he was not eligible for further sick leave. Love wrote to the WO, 28 August, complaining that he had been demobilized on 8.6.1917 due to his being in hospital in Dublin for an operation on his varicose veins. He had not been paid until 20.8.1917 and the WO did not reinstate him until 5.10.1917, when he rejoined 3rd RIR. Declared fit for home service 7.1.1918. The MB, 18.7.1918, noted that his condition pre-existed the war but had been aggravated by war service. He was ordered to return to 1st RIR immediately as he was now fit for general service.

Transferred to 12th RIR, 19.2.1919, and conducted a draft of men to the UK for demobilization. Requested an extension of his leave to 20.3.1919 so that he could receive dental treatment. He volunteered for service with the Army of Occupation in Germany with 12th RIR and was eventually demobilized from 3rd RIR, 13.11.1919. His address at that time was 30 Lothian Avenue, Antrim Road, Belfast. He regularly attended the 36th (Ulster) Division Officers OCA annual dinner until 1933. File ref: WO339/26053 47227.

Lucy Lt. Denis Joseph. Born 11.12.1893. Employed at the Woollen Mills, Blackpool, Cork, 1911–14. Address by 1917 was 77 Winchcombe Street, Cheltenham, where his wife Amy Fellon Lucy resided. 3rd RMF. Went to France in August 1915. Promoted to Lt., 28.2.1916. Joined 1st RIR 20.1.1917. To RFC as a Temporary Flight Officer, 16.12.1917. A note in Air 76, 16.7.1918, stated that he was fit for home service, ground duty only. Discharged at the Repatriation Camp, Shorncliffe, 11.1.1919. Service shown as RNAS, 3rd RMF, and RAF. File ref: 106445, a destroyed file, and Air 76.

Macaulay 2/Lt. Frank Robert Harms. Born 24.8.1898 at Kings Norton, near Birmingham, the son of Frederick William and Helena Macaulay, *née* Harms. His father was a civil engineer with Birmingham Water Dept. Applied for the RMC, 1.10.1916, stating that his family was Scots-Irish and that he had served with the Shrewsbury School Contingent OTC as a Sgt-Major.

Joined 1st RIR from 1st RDF, on reposting, 24.4.1918. Wounded while on patrol at Bailleul 14.8.1918. The MB at 2nd Western General Hospital, Manchester, 30.9.1918: the wounds to his left thigh were healed but that the limb was weak. MB at Grimsby, 18.12.1918, declared him healed. The MB at the Military Hospital, Safford, St Albans, 10.6.1919, noted that he had been admitted from Colchester Military Hospital the previous day. He was suffering from syphilis, attributable to his own neglect or misconduct, due to illicit sexual intercourse. Three months treatment was required. Overseas service noted as April–August 1918. Transferred to Hemel Hempstead Military Hospital, 2 August. Discharged, 18.8.1919, with instructions to report to 2nd RDF at Aldershot. Classed A fit.

He wrote to the Adjutant of 2nd RDF, 29.3.1920, applying to resign his commission as he could get a better job in civilian life and, seeing that he was so far down the Army List, he had no chance of promotion for years. He was willing to join the Reserve of Officers. His address on retirement would be Springfield House, Ludlow, Shropshire. At that time he was stationed in Turkey. The OC recommended acceptance of his request, 12.4.1920, and the WO was notified of his return to England, 23.5.1920. He served 'in the emergency' 9.4.1921 to 24.5.1921. File ref: WO339/89210 173809.

MacCarthy-O'Leary Brigadier Heffernan William Denis DSO, MC. Born 2.8.1885, the second son of Lt.-Col. William MacCarthy-O'Leary DL, Coomlagane, Millstreet, Co. Cork, an officer of

the South Lancashire Regt, who was killed in action while in command of the 1st Bn of his regiment at the assault on Pieter's Hill, Natal, during the South African War. His mother, Mary, was
the daughter of Heffernan Considine JP, DL, Derk, Co. Limerick. Educated at Stoneyhurst
College, Lancashire, and Sandhurst. Gazetted a 2/Lt. in 1st RIF, 16.8.1905, and joined this unit
in Dublin. Promoted to Lt. 24.2.1907, and Capt. 3.8.1912. Transferred to 2nd RIF and was
Adjutant at Quetta, India, 1913, and kept the position for three years. Served in France and
Belgium with 2nd RIF from December 1914 to November 1915 and in Salonika, December 1915
to October 1916, when he was wounded. On recovery from his wounds he proceeded to France in
June 1917, and joined 9th RIF. Joined 1st RIR, 9.8.1917, and took over command, having been
appointed a/Lt.-Col. He was wounded in the right shoulder 16.8.1917. Evacuated to England and
awarded the DSO (*London Gazette* 26.9.1917 with details 9.1.1918): 'Capt. (A/Lt.-Col.)
Heffernan William Denis McCarthy-O'Leary MC, R. Irish Fusiliers. For conspicuous gallantry
and devotion to duty. During a heavy hostile counter-attack, which had driven in his advance post
and recaptured part of the position, he went forward with one runner, rallied his men, and led
them forward again, driving the enemy back and restoring the situation. He remained encourag-
ing his men until he was himself severely wounded half an hour later, but he did not leave the field
until he had reported the situation to his brigadier.'

Rejoined 1st RIR and resumed command 29.12.1917. Appointed a/Lt.-Col. 12.1.1918, he was
wounded, 23.3.1918, but remained in command during the German offensive. Placed in charge of
all troops at Villerselve, 24.3.1918. Wounded again, 26.3.1918, and evacuated to England where
he remained until September 1918. Awarded a Bar to his DSO, *London Gazette* 16.9.1918.
Returned to France and was appointed a/Lt.-Col. of 1st RIF. He remained with that battalion
until he brought them home as a cadre in March 1919 and handed over command to Col. Greer.
Mentioned in Despatches 22.1.1915, 1.1.1916, 21.12.1917, 28.12.1918, and 17.7.1919, he was also
awarded the MC and the Ordre de la Couronne avec Croix de Guerre (Officier) Belge.

In August 1919 he joined 2nd RIF then reforming at Eastchurch. He served with 2nd RIF and
the amalgamated battalion at Dover and, later, at Ismailia. Promoted Major and Brevet Lt.-Col.
in 1925 and, shortly afterwards, assumed command of the Depot at Omagh, an appointment
which he held for a year. Rejoined the regiment at Cairo in 1926 and travelled with it to India, taking over command in March 1929.

Faugh-a-Ballagh, the regimental journal of the Royal Irish Fusiliers, April 1933: 'During the
period of his command the regiment has been unusually successful and happy. That this has been
so, despite the fact that Agra and Bombay leave much to be desired in most respects, has been due
largely to his power of leadership, devotion to duty, charming personality and efficiency. The welfare of the regiment has ever been foremost in his thoughts and he has worked unceasingly and
unsparingly, often under the most trying climatic conditions, in its interests.

'We congratulate him most heartily on his promotion to substantive Colonel and hope that we
may have the honour to serve under him again. Col. MacCarthy-O'Leary excelled in all branch-
es of sport, and represented the regiment at polo, cricket, football, hockey, and bayonet fighting.
He was, until he left, our best polo player and probably the soundest bat in the regiment. He was
also a keen rider to hounds and, in his younger days, a good boxer. Of him it may be asserted, with
truth, that nothing but good has ever been said about him. We miss him sadly, but his example
will remain as an inspiration to all of us while we live.'

CO 158th (Royal Welch) Infantry Brigade, TA, 1933–7. Retired pay 1937. Died at his home
in Co. Cork, where he lived with his sister, 23.2.1948, and was buried in Glasnevin Cemetery,
Dublin. Brig. Nelson Russell DSO, MC, attended the funeral representing the regiment and was
accompanied by Lt.-Col. E.K. Walkington. Members of the Dublin Branch of the OCA, of
which he was president, were present. His obituary appeared in the regimental journal in July
1948. Among the tributes were the following: 'As a young man, and throughout his life, he was

quiet and unassuming, but even then his was an outstanding personality. He excelled at games, particularly cricket and football, in both of which he played for the regiment. He was, moreover, a fearless horseman and a fine polo player ... He was wounded three times.

'It is also well known to many that, during the confusion of the Great Retreat of March, 1918, he was recommended for the VC by a senior officer, who could not find out his name ... and in 1933 he was promoted to a Territorial Brigade till 1937, when he retired. Called up again for service on the outbreak of the Hitler War in 1939, he was appointed to command the Blackdown Sub-area, and for the last two years of that war was employed with the Home Guard in Ulster, since he was considered too old for more active service ... In September, 1916, the Struma River (Greece) was crossed by our troops, in the face of heavy enemy resistance, the Irish Fusiliers being a unit of the attacking force. Donogh was left behind to act as Brigade-Major at Headquarters. Heavy enemy counter-attacks took place, day and night, for two or three days, and, just at dawn, on the last day, Donogh came forward from Brigade HQ, and rejoined the battalion. When asked why he had done so, he replied that he could not remain behind any longer, when his battalion was engaged in such heavy fighting, and asked how he could help. In carrying out an important duty, he was then severely wounded, and invalided home.' (W.T.G.).

'I had a tremendous admiration for him as one of the four or five outstanding regimental officers it has been my privilege to know. He had just that sense of personal leadership which Harold Alexander had and which I always think is required for Irish troops if you are to get the best out of them.' (Major-General Ian Grant).

'I say without hesitation or without fear of contradiction that no finer or braver officer or one more universally beloved, respected, and admired by all ranks has probably ever joined our regiment.' (Brig.-Gen. R.J. Kentish CMG, DSO).

Irish Winners of the Victoria Cross contains a section referring to some of those who should have been awarded the VC. In referring to his actions in March 1918, it concludes: 'Although he had done all that was required to earn a Victoria Cross, no award was ever made to him and there is no surviving evidence to suggest that a citation was ever written. A native of Glasnevin, Dublin, Donagh MacCarthy-O'Leary later commanded the Royal Irish Fusiliers in India where the father of one of the authors served under him.'

His medals are on display at the RIF Museum. He is commemorated in the RIF Chapel at Armagh Cathedral. Beneath four old regimental colours, the inscription reads: 'The Colours displayed above have been preserved by his family and friends as a memorial to a great Christian gentleman who served and loved his Regiment well.'

His younger brother, Lt. William Felix MacCarthy-O'Leary, 1st RMF, was killed in action at Ginchy, 7.9.1916. Closed file.

McClelland 2/Lt. Alfred. Born 23.10.1893 in the parish of St Ann's, Belfast, the son of James and Charlotte Marion McClelland of 105 Cavehill Road, Belfast. Formerly L/Cpl 1143 North Irish Horse. Enlisted 7.9.1914, at which time he had seven siblings ranging in age from thirty to eleven. Height 5 foot 9 inches, chest 33–36 inches, weight 126 pounds. Absent 10.10.1914 until 6 a.m., 12.10.1914. Deducted two days pay. 'Breaking out of camp and remaining absent till 10 p.m., 30.11.1914.' Deprived three days pay and awarded five days confined to barracks.

First overseas date 1.5.1915. Appointed L/Cpl 28.6.1915. Applied for a commission 17.5.1916. Single. Permanent address, Marsden Villa, Cavehill Road, Belfast. Correspondence address, D Squadron, North Irish Horse, BEF France. Pre-war employment, commercial traveller. Applied for Infantry, RIR; a further note in a different hand added Royal Inniskilling Fusiliers and Connaught Rangers. Admitted to hospital, 6.9.1916, and returned to duty 9.9.1916 – 'NYD'. Returned to the UK, 22.9.1916, and posted to No. 5 Officer Cadet Battalion at Cambridge, 4.11.1916. Gazetted to a commission in 5th RIR, 28.2.1917, and sent overseas the same day.

Joined 1st RIR from 5th RIR, 18.9.1917. Died of wounds, 13.10.1917, at No. 2 Australian CCS – shell wound left thigh, compound fracture. Short list of effects sent to his father included a wristwatch and strap, cigarette case, whistle and lanyard, and '90 centimes (souvenir)'. Trois Arbres Cemetery, Steenwerck, Nord, II.A.24. File ref: WO339/64891 139803.

McConnell Lt. Harold Jeffrey. Born 25.7.1893, the son of William and Mary McConnell of Spokane, Washington, USA, and Co. Down. Educated at Campbell College and Pyper's Academy, Belfast. He never married. Enlisted in the R. Fusiliers, 3.9.1914, and applied for a commission in the RIR, 28.4.1915, at which time he was Pte 1804 in C Coy, 18th R. Fusiliers (Public Schools Bn) stationed at Epsom, Surrey. His home address at this time was Kensington House, Knock, Co. Down, and he was employed by Messrs Cox & Co., Bankers, Charring Cross, London. Gazetted a 2/Lt. with 5th RIR, 15.6.1915, and arrived at the front, 6.6.1916, joining 1st RIR. Wounded 1.7.1916. The *Belfast Telegraph*, July 1916, stated that he was the son of the late William McConnell of Lisburn, and the nephew of Mrs Robson of The Mount, Hill Hall, Lisburn. (A telegram had previously been sent in error to John McConnell stating that his son Lt. J. Dunville McConnell had been wounded.)

Promoted Lt. 1.7.1917. Served with 7th RIR until it was absorbed by 2nd RIR, 14.11.1917. Joined the RFC at Reading 31.12.1917. After a one month course he went to the School of Navigation and Gunnery and commenced with No. 98 Squadron (D.H.9 day bombers), 6.4.1918, the same unit with which Lt. G.H.P. Whitfeld flew. Killed in action, 31.5.1918, and buried in Larch Wood (Railway Cutting) Cemetery, Ieper. Plot I.B.15. The next of kin was his sister, Miss J.S. McConnell, 12 Elmers Drive, Teddington, Middlesex.

McConnell Capt. John Dunville. Born 15.8.1885, the son of John McConnell, College Green House, Belfast. Applied for a commission, 17.8.1914, expressing a preference for the cavalry. Reapplied for a commission, 24.9.1914, no preference stated. Single. Home address College Green House. Correspondence address 9th RIR, Donard Lodge, Newcastle, Co. Down, but stated that he had no previous military training or experience. Height 5 foot 6 inches, chest 33½ –36½ inches, weight 126 pounds.

According to the War Diary of 1st RIR he proceeded to the MGC, Grantham, 18.6.1918. Discharged from No. 12 Reserve Bn MGC 15.11.1919. Medical category GS. Single. Occupation in civil life recorded as 'Independent'. Letter to WO, 12.7.1920, informed change of address to 1223 O'Farrell Street, San Francisco, California, USA. File ref: WO339/14402.

McCrum Lt. Robert Cowan. Born 31.5.1892, at Kilgreel, Templepatrick, Belfast. Enlisted as Rfn 19/307 in 19th RIR at Londonderry, 14.12.1915. Height 5 foot 7 inches, weight 139 pounds and chest 35–38 inches. His next of kin was his mother Elizabeth. His father had been a farmer and was deceased.

Applied for a commission in 19th RIR, 5.4.1916, and was posted to No. 7 Officer Cadet Battalion 29.5.1916. Commissioned into 19th RIR 4.9.1916. Appointed acting Lt. in 14th RIR according to the Army List of March 1917. Promoted Lt. 5.3.1918. Joined 1st RIR on reposting 9.4.1918. Sent to the Dispersal Camp for demobilization, 19.1.1919, and discharged 24.1.1919. He was single, medical A1, and still residing at Kilgreel. File ref: WO339/61847 135751.

McCullough Lt. David John MC. He was previously attached to 36th Division HQ and awarded the MC 1.1.1918. Joined 1st RIR, 28.5.1918, making an unsuccessful raid on the German trenches 19.7.1918. He went to the UK, 5.2.1919, prior to going overseas with 2nd RIR. Closed file, ref: (146195).

McDowell Lt. Albert C. Born 11.6.1893, his father, Mr M. McDowell, was manager of Messrs. William Ewart & Sons at Ballysillan. His address as of July 1916 was Glenbank, Ballysillan, Belfast.

Gazetted a 2/Lt., 22.5.1915, and wounded, 1.7.1916, while serving with 1st RIR. There are conflicting reports but it seems that a bullet grooved his throat and a shell fragment hit his helmet causing bruising to the left temple and internal bleeding about the eye. Evacuated to the UK, 4 July, aboard the *Lefranc* and was viewed by the MB, 9 July, at 2nd Southern General Hospital, Bristol. Leave was granted 10.7 to 10.8.1916. He reported to 5th RIR at Holywood Barracks, 10.8.1916, for light duty only. The MB at Belfast, 13.10.1916, declared him completely recovered. Later served with the King's African Rifles. Promoted Lt. 1.7.1917.

MacIlwaine Capt. Julian Mackay. Born 30.9.1888, the son of Edward Nangle MacIlwaine and Julia Alma Gaussen MacIlwaine of 69 Eglantine Avenue, Belfast. They later moved to 67 Eglantine Avenue. Educated at the Royal Belfast Academical Institution, he had been a Company Commander in the UVF and served with the Belfast University OTC for three years.

Applied for a commission 7.8.1914, expressing a preference for 5th RIR, 3rd RIR, 3rd RIF, or 'any Irish Regiment of Infantry'. Gazetted into 5th RIR. Promoted to Lt., 10.1.1915, and joined 1st RIR, 14.4.1915. Wounded, 27.4.1915, while putting up wire entanglements at night within 70 yards of the enemy. Embarked Le Havre–Southampton aboard SS *Asturious*, 6 May, and arrived the following day. The WO sent a telegram to his mother, 9 May, advising her that he had been admitted to 1st London General Hospital, 7 May, suffering from a GSW to the abdomen. Rejoined 5th RIR 5.7.1915. The MB at Belfast declared that he had recovered and was fit for general service 16.9.1915.

Transferred to the RFC at Oxford, 6.11.1916; No. 25 Reserve Squadron, Tretford, 24.1.1917, and to No. 18 Reserve Squadron for training 25.4.1917. The MB at the Air Ministry, 8.6.1917, noted that he had cardiac hypertrophy and 'a history of having been run over by a motor lorry' but declared him fit for flying training. To No. 60 T.S., 30.6.1917, on appointment as a Flying Officer. Joined the BEF at No. 12 Squadron, 28.7.1917, and was killed in action (missing), while serving as a pilot, 22.3.1918. His aircraft was an RE8, serial number B.4040, and his observer was 2/Lt. William M. Irvine. His mother was notified by telegram 25 March. Death was accepted for official purposes 24.9.1918. The executrix of his will was his sister, Miss Julia Thomasine Jane MacIlwaine. Arras Flying Services Memorial, Pas de Calais. File ref: 30384 and AIR 76.

McIntosh 2/Lt. Henry MC. Gazetted a 2/Lt. in 1st RIR, 3.9.1917. He was court-martialled in the field for drunkenness, 1.3.1918, and suffered forfeiture of seniority and a severe reprimand. Awarded the MC in November 1918. Army List for January 1919: 2/Lt. with seniority at 1.3.1918. He returned to the UK, 10.4.1919, prior to reporting for duty at the Depot. Closed file, ref: 1/83 (238629).

McKenna 2/Lt. John MC. Reposted from the RDF and joined 1st RIR 25.4.1918. He was attached to the L.M. Battery and awarded the MC in November 1918. Closed file, ref: (204420).

McLaughlin Lt. Arthur M. Born at Brookville, Belfast, 12.11.1894, the fourth son of William Henry McLaughlin DL, and Emily Sophia McLaughlin, *née* Dobbin, Macedon, Whitehouse, Co. Antrim. His father was a builder and contractor. Arthur was a brother of Major W. McLaughlin, 1st Garrison Battalion, RIR. Another brother, Trooper George McLaughlin, fell in action at Lindley, 30.7.1900, during the Boer War. His eldest brother, Henry McLaughlin, of Blackrock, acted on Lord Wimborne's Irish Recruiting Committee.

He was a member of the Public School's Alpine Club, and hunted with the East Antrim Hounds. After leaving Monkton Combe School, Bath, he entered Jesus College, Cambridge, and served in the OTC, October 1913 to May 1914. Reason for leaving, 'not enough spare time to attend parades'. Applied for a commission, 7.8.1914, requesting 3rd RIR. Occupation, university student, height 5 foot 7 inches, chest 34½–36 inches, and weight 139 pounds.

Left for the front and joined 1st RIR, 27.3.1915. Posted to B Coy and killed in action 9.5.1915. A telegram from his father to the WO, 15 May, asked if they had any news of Arthur, as he understood that many officers of the battalion had been killed or wounded during the past weeks fighting. He sent another telegram, 21 May, and said he had not received a reply from them, but had heard that Arthur had been killed – could they confirm? WO replied, 21 May, advising that Arthur was killed as per their telegram of 13.5.15, but the reference to May 13 was deleted – it appears that this telegram may never have been sent. Only three items appeared on the list of personal effects: a silver card case, a leather card case and a chequebook. These were sent to his father.

Witness statements: 13563 Rfn Percy Cox, in the Royal Sussex County Hospital, Brighton, 9.7.1915, had a letter from his friend 13562 Rfn Cherry, BEF France, saying that he saw Arthur killed. 9860 Rfn Brady of C Coy, Northumberland War Hospital, 16.7.1915, saw Arthur shot through the head and killed in the German trenches during an unsuccessful attack, before the regiment retreated. Brady's home address was given as 56 Mayfair Street, Old Park Road, Belfast. 9689 Pte Smith at No. 1 Canadian Hospital, Etaples, 7.7.1915, was Arthur's servant and had apparently sent an account of his death to a paper called *Ulster Saturday Night*. 4872 Cpl M. Lennon saw Arthur lying wounded during the advance. He saw him again the following morning lying in a trench and heard him giving his name to a Sgt who had asked for it. Lennon offered him some rum but he refused it, being a teetotaller, taking some tea instead. Lennon then spoke to an officer of the West Surrey Regt who came and spoke to Arthur and then sent for two stretcher-bearers who carried him off.

His father wrote to the WO, 8.6.1915, referring to Cpl Lennon having carried Arthur from the German trench and getting him to hospital. The WO replied, 8 July, stating that an inquiry had been held at Base and the following answer had been received: 'Corporal Lennon did not carry this officer to hospital. Lieutenant A. McLaughlin was killed in action 9th May. Confirmed.'

Irish Life 30.7.1915: ' …was a son of Mr W.H. McLaughlin … principal of the firm of McLaughlin and Harvey of Belfast and Dublin. He received his commission on 15th August and was posted to the 3rd Battalion of the Rifles at Dublin, in which regiment his brother, Captain McLaughlin, is also an officer.'

Irish Life 28.1.1916: 'He was educated at Monkton Combe School, Bath, and when he left school about a year before his death he was head prefect, captain of the football team and captain and "stoke" of the boat in the rowing team … His last words were "I'm all right; lead on, lead on". He died shortly afterwards.'

Bond of Sacrifice: 'He was in B Company, which was advancing to attack an enemy trench, and fell, with a bullet wound in the chest, into a trench partly filled with water. As his Sergeant passed him, he exclaimed, "I'm all right. Go on!" The Company went forward and occupied an enemy trench for a short time, but later were forced to retire. As they passed the disused trench, Lieutenant McLaughlin's body still lay there, and though his Sergeant and another tried twice to recover it, they were unable to do so. Lieutenant McLaughlin's promotion to that rank, to date from 8th May, was gazetted in June 1915, after his death.' Ploegsteert Memorial. File ref: 1/83 33148.

McManus Lt. Alexander Alfred Lambert. Gazetted a 2/Lt. 21.12.1917. He first went overseas and joined 1st RIR 13.6.1918. Reported missing 2.10.1918. He had been taken prisoner that day and was a POW until repatriated 13.12.1918. Promoted Lt. 21.6.1919. Closed file, ref: (173753).

MacMaster Lt. John Sinclair. Born 8.10.1896. Attested as a Cadet in 17th RIR at Belfast, 1.3.1915. Height 5 foot 7¼ inches, chest 30½–34 inches, weight 126 pounds, apprentice fitter, Presbyterian. Appointed a L/Cpl 22.7.1915. Applied for a commission, 27.7.1915, expressing a preference for 'Infantry 36th (Ulster) Division'. Permanent address 3 College Avenue, Londonderry, and correspondence address, Officer's School of Instruction, Queen's University, Belfast; presently serving with 17th RIR.

Gazetted a 2/Lt. in 17th RIR, 23.8.1915, and joined 1st RIR from the Base, 2.4.1916. Placed on the sick list, 19.5.1916, and embarked Dieppe–Dover, 24 May, aboard the SS *Dieppe*. Fractured humerus, above elbow joint. The MB at Caxton Hall, 26 June, gave the place of injury as Albert, 19 May, resulting from a fall while crossing a railway bridge on foot in the dark, 'on duty at the time'. 'Union taking place with the broken ends in a fair position.' Likely to be unfit for military duty for 3¼ months from date of injury. The MB at the Military Hospital, Londonderry, 29.8.1916, noted that the fracture was firmly united but declared him unfit for general service for another two months. Reported for duty to 17th RIR at Ballykinlar Camp, Co. Down, 30 August. MB at Belfast, 6.10.1916, noted some improvement but he still had restricted arm movement, unfit for general service for three months. MB at Reading War Hospital, 8.1.1917, unfit for general service for one month and, 8.2.1917, fit for general service. Promoted Lt. 1.7.1917.

Left 1st RIR, 27.1.1918, suffering from tonsillitis and embarked Rouen–Southampton. The MB at Caxton Hall, 19.3.1918, declared him unfit for general service for two months. MB at Fusehill War Hospital, Carlisle, 26.4.1918: unfit for general service for one month. MB at Fargo Military Hospital, Salisbury Plain, 17 June: fit for general service. Rejoined 1st RIR 28.8.1918. Discharged 19.11.1919, last serving with 12th RIR in Germany. Rated A1. Single. File ref: WO339/44458 17/83 113190.

McMillen Lt. John Nelson. Born 21.10.1897, educated at the Royal Belfast Academical Institution, and served in Belfast University OTC. Applied for a commission, 29.10.1915, stating that he had no previous military experience and that his civil occupation was that of a traveller. Expressed a preference for the infantry, 'Any unit. Irish preferred'. Unmarried and living at Knockfierna, Bloomfield, Belfast.

Joined 1st RIR from 18th RIR, 26.8.1916. Placed on the sick list, 13.9.1916, having been blown up and buried by a trench mortar at the Hohenzollern Redoubt. He lay buried for over an hour and lost the power of speech for nine days. Embarked Boulogne–Dover aboard the *St Patrick*, 21 September, and was admitted to the County of London War Hospital, Epsom, with 'shell shock, dilated heart, and ligaments of ankle stretched'. The MB at Hendon, London, noted that he was suffering from general pains and insomnia. The condition was severe, but not permanent, and was predicted to last three months.

Promoted Lt. 1.1.1917. Rejoined 3rd RIR at Belfast, 24.1.1917. The MB at Randalstown, 28.6.1918, reported: 'He states that he is slightly improved since last appearance. He is not fit for general service.' His address at that time was c/o Adjutant, Municipal Technical Institute, Belfast. Struck off the strength of Randalstown Depot, 2.7.1918, and attached to the Ministry of Labour, still noted as being 1st RIR. When he was released from the services, 1.8.1919, he was married and living at Hullock, Clonee Drive, Strandtown, Belfast. File ref: 116545.

McNeil Lt. William Niven. Born 4.5.1880 at Burnfoothill, Patna, Ayrshire, the son of a glass bottle manufacturer. Married his wife Daisy at Dumfries, Ayrshire, in 1900. A joiner by trade. Enlisted at Belfast, 8.2.1915, as Pte 64222 in the ranks of the RE. At that time his address was 27 Castlereagh Place, Belfast. Height 5 foot 8 inches, weight 182 pounds, and chest 37–41 inches. Appointed L/Cpl, 8.6.1915, and promoted to Cpl the next day. Went to France, 4.10.1915, and served with 121st Coy, RE. In August 1916 he applied for a commission in the RE. He made a second application for a commission, 28.12.1916, and expressed a preference for a pioneer or infantry battalion. Served as an acting Sgt from 30.1.1917 and returned to the UK 7.2.1917, reporting to No. 11 Officer Cadet Battalion at Pirbright, 9.3.1917. Gazetted a 2/Lt. in 19th RIR 17.6.1917. At this time his address was 29 Maidstone Avenue, Belfast. Returned to France, 27.6.1917, and presumably took up duty with 1st RIR. Wounded 23.3.1918 at St Simon with a slight GSW to his left leg. Evacuated to the UK, 27 March, and admitted to Leith War Hospital the following day. Later transferred to 16th RIR. Promoted Lt. 27.12.1918. Discharged, 1.2.1919, A1 medical condition. Belgian Ordre de la Couronne. File ref: 186347.

MacPherson 2/Lt. William Angus Smillie MC. Born 16.12.1894 at Bangor, Co. Down, and educated at Skegoniel and the Technical Institute. His father was a coal merchant. Joined Belfast University OTC, 13.11.1916, and was attested as 19/963 in 19th RIR, 27.11.1916. Address was *Edenview*, Earlswood Road, Knock, Belfast. Working in the linen business. Height 5 foot 6.6 inches and chest 33½ –36 inches. Transferred to the Army Reserve, 21.11.1916, and applied for a commission in 19th RIR, 20.2.1917. The Belfast University OTC report was: 'general efficiency very good; hardworking, keen and efficient cadet; will make a very good leader; thoroughly knows his work; 1st Class shot.'

Mobilized to 7th Officer Cadet Battalion, 5.5.1917, and commissioned in 19th RIR, 28.8.1917. Joined 1st RIR on reposting 6.4.1918. On 6.9.1918 he was appointed a/Capt. whilst commanding B Coy and was awarded the MC during September 1918. He relinquished the acting rank of Capt. (Additional) 9.12.1918. Released from service 5.2.1919, noted as single and medical rating A1. His address was 8 Cliftonville Avenue, Belfast. In 1933 he attended the 36th (Ulster) Division Officers OCA annual dinner. File ref: WO339/92542 178664.

Macausland 2/Lt. Oliver Babington. Born 28.11.1896 at Rawalpindi, Punjab, India, the younger son of Lt.-Col. Redmond Conyngham Samuel Macausland JP, late of the Indian Army, and Mrs Jane Isabella Macausland, daughter of the late Lt.-Col. R. Henry Keown, 15th King's Hussars and Royal North Down Militia. *Thom's Directory* for 1912 gave his father's address as Woodbrooke House, Garvagh, Co. Londonderry.

Passed out third in the order of merit at Sandhurst. Joined 1st RIR, 21.3.1915, and was appointed T/Lt. Killed in action, 9.5.1915, while leading his platoon.

de Ruvigny: 'His Commanding Officer wrote: "He was a young soldier with a soldierly faculty; gentle, just, and clear-sighted"; and the Adjutant wrote of him: "He was always more than ready to do any dangerous patrols that were to be done; and it was so nice to know that we could depend on him to do whatever was to be done without any further supervision. When he met his death, he was gallantly leading his platoon in the charge at Fromelles early on the 9th." '

Irish Life 30.7.1915: ' ... was the younger son of Lt.-Col. Macausland of Woodbank, Garvagh, Co. Derry. He was educated at Haileybury and the Royal Military College, Sandhurst (Prize Cadet), and was gazetted in August [8.11.1914] last as a Second Lieutenant on the unattached list for the Indian Army. He was, however, posted to the 4th Royal Irish Rifles and in March gazetted to the 1st Royal Irish Rifles in France.'

A marble tablet to his memory was placed in Errigal Church, Garvagh, Co. Derry. Neuve Chapelle Memorial, Pas de Calais. File missing.

Macky Lt. Whiteside. Born 14.4.1893. Served two years with Trinity College OTC, Dublin, and was gazetted a 2/Lt. in 17th RIR 28.1.1915. Joined 1st RIR, 16.2.1916, from 8th RIR. Wounded by a trench mortar in the right hand and knee, 13.4.1916. Evacuated to the UK aboard the *St Andrew* and remained home until December 1917. The middle finger of his right hand had been amputated the day after he was wounded. On 19.7.1916 he wrote from 17th RIR to the WO asking if he was entitled to compensation. His request was refused. Cleared by the MB, 9.3.1917, and promoted to Lt. 1.7.1917. Transferred to 3rd King's African Rifles, 29.12.1917, and relinquished his commission 26.5.1919. He was later an Assistant District Commissioner in Kenya but died from 'Kala-azar' 30.8.1921. File ref: 17/83 44090.

Macnamara Lt.-Col. Charles Carroll. Born 23.5.1875 at 13 Grosvenor Street, London, the elder son of Charles Nottidge Macnamara FRCS, Chorley Wood, Herts. On his father's side he was descended from members of the Macnamara clan of County Clare. His mother's great-grandfather was Chevalier De L'Etang, at one time page to Marie Antoinette, wife of Louis XVI of France. Height 6 foot 3 inches. Educated at Winchester, he left the Militia to receive a commission as a 2/Lt. in the RIR, 6.6.1896, being promoted to Lt. 23.1.1897. In April 1897 he arrived with his regiment at Ladysmith. While there he acted, for a time, as extra ADC to Lord Milner, who was then High Commissioner of South Africa.

Moved to India, 16.4.1899, and for the following four years was Adjutant (1.1.1900 to 31.12.1903) being promoted to Capt., 10.12.1902, and Major, 30.12.1902. From February 1904 to January 1905 he was employed as Staff Officer to the Colabra Depot, Bombay. Served as a Capt. in the Chinese Regiment, 2.2.1905 to 10.11.1906. While there he passed as an interpreter in Chinese. In November 1906 the Wei-hai-Wei Native Contingent was disbanded and he returned to his regiment at Meerut. He was admitted to hospital suffering from grave anaemia and was not certified fit again until 24.5.1907 and continued to serve in India. Seconded to the Egyptian Army, 20.6.1908, holding the rank of Kaimakan commanding the Equatorial Battalion, and remained in Sudan for seven years until 11.7.1915 when he got special leave to serve in the Dardanelles. Given temporary command of 1st Lancashire Fusiliers 27.8.1915. He was then appointed Brigade-Major of 126th Brigade, 42nd Division, being Staff Major to General Lord Hampden. Wounded in the leg by a rifle bullet 25.9.1915. Examined by the MB at 19th General Hospital, Alexandria, 24.10.1915, he was found to be suffering from dysentery and was certified unfit for two months. Returned to England 28.11.1915. While recovering he took over command of the Depot at Belfast and, in March 1916, was appointed BM of 203rd Brigade having its HQ at Bedford. After many requests he managed to get transferred to 1st RIR, arriving 25.5.1916, and in June 1916 took over command. He was severely wounded, 1.7.1916, and admitted to No. 24 General Hospital, Etaples, 3.7.1916. His file described him as being 'dangerously ill' with gunshot wounds to left eye, left arm, and ankle.

His father was, at this time, aged 83 and not able to travel. He applied for a visa for Carroll's sister to go to France to see him. She was Lady Bradford, wife of Admiral Sir Edward E. Bradford CVO. The visa was granted but not needed as Macnamara was transferred to Fishmonger's Hall Hospital, London, 6.7.1916, and died of his wounds 15 July at 10.45 p.m. Buried in Chorleywood (Christ Church) Churchyard, Hertfordshire.

A letter written by Capt. Gartlan told what happened: 'After that I lost sight of them as I had to bring my company along, and it was very slow work as the place was full of dead and wounded. But from what I can gather, the Colonel got to the head of the battalion and had just got clear of our wire, when he got hit. Nobody seems to know where he was hit at first, but he fell down and would not allow anyone to dress his wounds. His whole thought was to "go on, go on". He must have been hit once if not more, either lying on the ground or getting back to our trench, which he did shortly afterwards. Our Medical Officer, as soon as he heard that the CO was hit, came up and managed to get him down to the dressing station. The Colonel's whole anxiety, when he had sufficiently recovered to talk, was how the battalion had got on. Our doctor told me his courage was extraordinary. He never said a word about being in pain, but was full of enquiries for everyone else. Do you know if he received a letter from General Hudson before he died? The General told me he had written to him. I do so hope it arrived in time.'

The letter from General Hudson, 8th Division Commander, dated 5.7.1916, read: 'My Dear Macnamara, a few lines to say how sorry I am to hear that you are wounded and to express my admiration at the splendid conduct of your battalion so ably commanded and led by you. It was from all accounts magnificent – no hesitation, and every man doing his level best. It is a day of which the Royal Irish Rifles will rightly be proud. The men are full of heart and cheer, and will, I know, continue to do all that is asked of them. If you have any names you specially wish to bring forward, you may be sure that I will not forget them. A speedy recovery to you. Yours sincerely, H. Hudson.' The letter did not arrive until a few hours after Macnamara's death. The executor of his will was Lt.-Commander Patrick G. Macnamara, RN.

Macnamara Lt. Eric Thady. Born October 1884. Served two years with the Penang (Straights Settlements) Volunteers. Discharged at the beginning of the war to join the Honourable Artillery Company as Pte 1664 (attested 25.8.1914 and signed Army Form E624) and went to France with their 1st Bn (Machine Gun Section), 17.9.1914. Home address Beckford Road, Bath. Height 6 foot ¼ inch, chest 34½–37½ inches. A note in the attestation papers changed his next of kin from Dr. C.G. Macnamara, 95 St Stephen's Green, Dublin, to his mother, Mrs Isabel S. Macnamara, Beckford Road, Bath. (*Thom's Directory* for 1912 lists Dr Charles E. Macnamara LRCSI, Surgeon. Among others at the same address was Lt.-Col. Francis H. Macnamara, 5th RDF.)

His will dated 28.10.1914 left his entire estate to his mother. The WO received a letter from her, 20.11.1914, wanting to know exactly where he was and asked to be informed at once if he was taken ill or wounded so that she could go to him immediately.

Wounded at Locre, 14.12.1914, GSW right hand. Admitted No. 7 Field Ambulance the same day. To UK aboard the *St Patrick*, 16 December. Applied for a commission 23.2.1915. Single. Correspondence address 103 Hereford Road, Bayswater, London. Applied for 'Machine Guns Irish Rifles'. Commissioned to 4th RIR, 15.3.1915, and attached to 1st RIR. Casualty form for overseas service, post commission, shows 'Machine Gun Corps (1st RIR)'. Attached to 25th Brigade M.G. Coy, 28.2.1916, from 1st RIR and transferred 2.3.1916. Granted leave to UK 8–16.4.1916. Admitted to No. 26 Field Ambulance, 31.5.16, and later to Officer's Convalescence Home. Rejoined his company 9.6.1916. T/Lt. 1.11.1916. Sent for a machine gun course at Camiers 5.11.1916. Rejoined company 26.11.1916. To UK on leave 5–15.1.1917. Rejoined 21.1.17. To 5th Army rest camp, 22.6.1917, and rejoined 6.7.1917. Second-in-Command of No. 25 MG Coy, 11.7.1917. Leave to UK, 27.8.1917 to 6.9.1917, and extended until 24.9.1917. Rejoined company 27.9.1917. To artillery course 11.10.1917. Rejoined 16.10.1917. To machine gun training course at Grantham 18.10.1917.

A letter from the MO, Guy's Hospital, London SE1, 15.3.1918, stated that Macnamara had spent most of his life in tropical climes and that he had suffered chest problems ever since coming to northern Europe. Recommended a transfer to a more suitable climate. MB, 9 April, at Caxton Hall, noted that he was suffering from a corn, left foot, and bronchitis, recovering, but unfit for general or home service. MB at Colchester, 10 May: unfit general service for two months. MB at Grantham, 10 July: recovering but unfit general service for two months; to continue home duties with MGC. MB at Grantham, 26 July: declared fit for general service. Demobilized 8.4.1919. Single. Civil occupation, banker.

A letter to the WO, 4.4.1925, from Macnamara's wife, Cherrie, 5 Albert Terrace, Windsor, asked would it be possible for her husband to be called up under the new scheme for national defence. He was then in Morocco. WO replied, 22.4.1925, advising that he was not liable to recall. File ref: WO339/33460 80586.

Maddison Lt. Ralph. Joined 1st RIR, 6.4.1917, and was placed on the sick list ten days later. Transferred to England, 5.5.1917, and was struck off the strength of the battalion. Later served with the Tank Corps. Promoted Lt. 7.9.1918. Closed file, ref: (178684).

Mahoney 2/Lt. Edward Archibald. Born 15.4.1887 at 1 Portland Street, Dublin, the son of John Maunsell and Catherine Mahoney. His father was a medical student at the time of Edward's birth. He was sometimes referred to in his file as Ernest. *Irish Life* 26.10.17: ' ... the eldest son of the late Mr J. Maunsell Mahoney, Commissioner of Charitable Bequests, Dublin, and Castlegregory, Co. Kerry.'

Applied for a commission, 9.8.1915, at which time he was an assistant editor at the *Irish Times*. Attached to 3rd RIR. Wounded, 1.7.1916, while serving with 1st RIR.

Irish Times 10.7.1916: ' ... is in hospital in France suffering from a shrapnel wound to the shoulder ... His wound is not serious and he hopes to leave hospital shortly.' Returned to 1st RIR, 23.5.17, and was killed in action 16.8.1917.

Irish Times 22.8.1917: 'We regret to announce the death in action, on Thursday last, of Second Lieutenant Edward A. Mahony, Royal Irish Rifles. Mr Mahoney, who received his commission on 28th August 1915, had previously filled a responsible position on the editorial staff of the *Weekly Irish Times* for some years. He had seen a good deal of active service and was wounded on the 1st July 1916. When he recovered he returned to the front where he remained up to the time of his death.'

The executor of his will was his brother John Frederick Mahoney of 126 Cabra Park, Phibsborough, Dublin. Tyne Cot Memorial.

Maitland Capt. William Samuel MC. Born 12.10.1880, the son of George and Isabella Maitland of Murlough, Dundrum, Co. Down. He was a commercial traveller from Clough, Co. Down. Enlisted at Belfast 17.9.1914. Height 5 foot 6½ inches, chest 36 inches expanded, and weight 144 pounds. He had an anchor tattooed on his right wrist. Posted to 20th Public Schools Battalion, R. Fusiliers, at Epsom, Surrey, with Regimental Number 5286 and appointed L/Cpl, 6.2.1915. All his service with the R. Fusiliers was in the UK. Gazetted to 5th RIR 20.5.1915. By 1916 he also had a residence at Duncairn Gardens, Belfast, and was serving with 1st RIR.

Wounded, 1.7.1916, by a shell wound to the shoulder (first report) and was recommended for gallantry by the acting CO for his part in the attack. MC, 1.7.1916, Ovillers: 'For conspicuous gallantry. Although wounded he continued to lead his platoon in an attack in face of very heavy machine gun fire, until wounded a second time.'

Embarked Calais–Dover 7 July. Discharged from the Officers Hospital at Whitechapel, London, 15 July, with leave being granted 15.7.1916 to 31.8.1916; being certified fit to travel to Dundrum. The MB, 4 September, recorded a wound to his left leg. This was a bullet wound received 'later same day' – two pieces of a bullet were still embedded in his leg. Noted as fit for general service and posted back to 5th RIR at Holywood Barracks. At the Military Hospital, Belfast, 10.10.1916, the MB recorded that his shoulder had healed but the portions of bullet were still in his leg. 'Some stiffness.' Army List of March 1917 shows him serving with 7th RIR. Later attached 2nd RDF. Demobilized, 20.4.1919, and a pension was refused. Capt. Maitland attended the annual reunion dinner of the Dublin Branch of the RUR Association on 27.4.1935 and 30.4.1938. File ref: WO339/48381 5/83 118212.

Malcolmson, Lt. W.H.W.B. Gazetted a Lt. in 4th RDF, 20.4.1912. Left this battalion with three other officers (Colles, Jenings, and Maunsell), 19.10.1914, 'with orders to report himself' to 1st RIR, 'which he eventually did'. He advised the Adjutant, 'the late' A.O'H. Wright, 1st RIR, that he was going to hospital to report sick 'on or about the 3rd November 1914'. 'Disappeared' that day, going AWOL. He did not go overseas with the battalion. A railway warrant was exchanged at Winchester Station, journey 'value £2 11s 4d', 11.11.1914. The warrant was reported as mislaid by the railway company but it was thought to have been issued for a journey from Winchester to Dublin. Another note stated the journey was to Cork via Holyhead.

Lt.-Col. R.A.C. Daunt, OC 1st RIR, reported on 21.7.1915 that nothing further had been heard from Malcolmson. OC 4th RDF wrote to the WO, 30.7.1915, informing that Malcolmson's mother had written seeking his location. OC 4th RDF to WO, 30.7.1915, stated that Malcolmson had tendered his resignation immediately before mobilization but it was 'too late to be forwarded'.

WO recorded, 18.10.1915, that pay had been issued up to 30.9.1915. The RDF bankers stated that the last pay was drawn in February 1915 and that they had received no further communications. 'Ex-Lt. U.C. Jenings' (see above) complained, 10.8.1915, that although Malcolmson had disappeared from camp the previous November he still appeared on the Army Lists.

WO submission to King George V, 29.11.1915, recommended removal from the service. The King's initials are on the document 'Appd'. *London Gazette* 3.12.1915. File ref: WO339/33553.

Manico 2/Lt. Ernest Victor. Born 26.6.1892 at *Borcetti*, Bray, Co. Wicklow, the son of Ernest and Georgina Manico, *née* McClean. His father was a newspaper proprietor – Ernest Manico Ltd., Printers and Publishers, 2 D'Olier Street, Dublin, and Fleet Street, London. The publications included *Irish Society and Social Review* and *Irish Military Guide*. Educated at St Andrew's College, Dublin. Applied for a commission in 3rd RIR, 26.4.1915, giving his permanent address as *St Elmo*, Sutton, Co. Dublin, his parents' home, and his correspondence address as 7 Callow St, South Kensington, London SW. He was an insurance claims adjuster. Gazetted to 3rd RIR 15.6.1915.

He left 3rd RIR and was attached to 15th RIR, 36th (Ulster) Division. Wounded 1.7.1916 at Thiepval Wood. Embarked Boulogne–Southampton, 3 July, aboard the *St Andrew*, suffering from a GSW to his left thigh, and a shrapnel wound to his right thigh. The MB at Caxton Hall, London, 22 August, described the 4 by 3-inch wound to his right thigh as almost healed. The bullet had passed directly through his left thigh and caused no 'bone or nerve injury of importance'. The Board predicted that he would be unfit for 3¼ months from the date of his injury. The MB at King George V Hospital, Dublin, 4 October, noted that the left thigh had recovered but the right thigh 'is not yet strongly healed'. Rejoined 3rd RIR at Belfast 26 October. On 30.11.1916, 2.1.1917, and 6.3.1917, the MB at Dublin declared him fit for home service and unfit for general service for one month each time. Manico wrote to the WO, 12.2.1917, noting that he was still unfit for active service and repeated an earlier request for a wound gratuity. The MB at King George V Hospital, Dublin, declared him fit for general service 14.4.1917.

Joined 1st RIR 11.6.1917. Wounded at Guerbigny 27.3.1918. Embarked Le Havre–Southampton, 29 March, and was admitted to the Royal Victoria Hospital, Netley. The MB at Netley, 22 April, decreed the wound as 'slight' and predicted he would be unfit for service for three months. A report of an x-ray taken at Blackrock Orthopaedic Hospital, Co. Dublin, was made 17 May: 'fracture neck of scapula, slight displacement of fragments'. The MB at King George V Hospital, 28 June, stated that he was 'slowly improving'. It predicted that he would be unfit for another three months. Manico sent a letter to the WO, 29 July, noting that he had again been turned down for a wound gratuity and, seeing that he had a fractured neck, a bit of shrapnel in his head, and could only move one arm very slightly, he didn't quite understand why this was so. He asked for a review of his case. Mr James Ian MacPherson MP, wrote to the WO, 17 October, saying 'I cannot understand why his gratuity has been refused' and asked for the matter to be reviewed. The MB at Dublin, 16 November, declared that the wounds were 'severe and permanent'. The WO advised MacPherson, 12 December, that the classification 'severe' was not good enough, the classification had to be 'very severe' to qualify for a gratuity. The MB at Fargo, 14.2.1919, Salisbury Plain, declared 'he has practically recovered'.

Discharged from his commission 16.11.1919. At that time he was single and residing at *Plantation*, Monkstown, Co. Dublin. Applied for a permanent commission in 1st RIR, 30.12.1919, but was not selected. He sent a letter to the WO, 6.3.1920, advising that he intended to leave the UK during May; his new address would be 424 Ocean Park, near Los Angeles, California. File ref: WO339/55778 127651.

Marshall Lt. Joseph. *Irish Times* 21.7.1916: 'Second Lieutenant Joseph Marshall, wounded, joined the Royal Irish Rifles 15 years ago and served in South Africa and India. He came to England with the 1st Battalion from Aden in October 1914 and, after nine months in the field, was promoted to a commission from the rank of Company Sergeant-Major. He is a son of the late Mr W. Marshall, Fernamenagh, Co. Tyrone.'

Recommended for gallantry by the acting CO for his involvement in the attack of 1.7.1916.

There had been an earlier confusion with another 2/Lt. J. Marshall, 11th RIR, as can be seen from the following entry in the *Irish Times* 13.7.1916: 'Second Lieutenant James Marshall, Royal

Irish Rifles, son of Mr James Marshall, Ardenlea House, Ravenhill Road, Belfast, was reported as wounded in the press on Saturday, and his name appeared in the Official Casualty List. The WO had also wired that he was wounded. Yesterday, however, Mr Marshall was gratified to receive a letter from his son stating that he had come through the big advance without a scratch.'

Served as an officer with 1st RIR, 29.7.1915 to 1.7.1916, and 6.12.1916 to 17.1.1917. Later attached to the West African Frontier Force. Promoted Lt. 30.8.1916. Still serving in 1923. Closed file, ref: (105892).

Martin Lt. John Sinclair. Born 18.5.1896, the only son of Robert Thomas and Edith S. Martin, *née* Sinclair, of 14 College Gardens, Belfast, and grandson of Revd J.D. Martin, Co. Armagh, and John Sinclair, New York. Educated at Bilton Grange Preparatory School (near Rugby), 1906–10, where he gained a Foundation Scholarship in classics at Uppingham School, which he entered in 1910, and was captain of the school games, editor of the school magazine, and one of the first violins in the school orchestra. It was his intention, on leaving school in 1914, to enter University College, Oxford. He had been Senior NCO of the OTC at Uppingham.

Applied for a commission, 7.8.1914, expressing a preference for 5th RIR. Height 5 foot 11¼ inches, chest 34–37 inches, and weight 139 pounds. Gazetted a 2/Lt. in 5th RIR, 14.8.1914, being promoted to Lt., 10.1.1915, having completed a course of musketry in Dublin. Joined 1st RIR, 20.3.1915, and was killed in action 9.5.1915.

Bond of Sacrifice: 'His Commanding Officer at the front reported of him: "He was always ready to do more than his share of work in his company, and was most daring in any kind of patrol work that had to be done. I always admired the easy way and confidence he showed in commanding men, with whom he was very popular".'

A letter from his father, Robert T. Martin, solicitor, 7 Wellington Place, Belfast, to the WO, 2 June, referred to the WO advice of 13 May that John had been wounded on the 9th at Aubers Ridge. (The father also had an office at 41 Lower Sackville Street, Dublin.) Despite an earlier letter there had been no more official advice, but he had received letters from several officers saying that John was killed leading D Coy in the attack. Requested official confirmation of the true situation. The WO transmitted this request to DAG, 3rd Echelon, BEF, 4 June. DAG replied, 9 June, stating their report was that he was wounded – 'further enquiries being made'. WO transmitted this news to the father by letter dated 11 June.

Witness statements: 5369 Pte Hoey, No. 3 Stationary Hospital, Rouen, 9.6.1915, said that he was close to Lt. Martin when he was killed by a shell. He was buried in the graveyard which was set apart for officers. 4977 Rfn Patrick Thornberry, The Infirmary, Southport, 19.6.1915, said that Lt. Martin was wounded at Fromelles and his body was recovered and sent to hospital. 8505 L/Cpl Robinson, Raddon Court Hospital, Latchford, Warrington, 22.6.1915, said that he saw Lt. Martin, who was his company officer, shot through the body and fall, just after giving the order to charge at Fromelles and believed him to have been killed. 83181 Rfn W. McLaughlan, VAD Hospital, The Norlands, Erdington, Birmingham, 25.6.1915, said that he had a letter from Rfn Keogh, C Coy, saying that Lt. Martin was killed during the attack. 6963 Pte Burns, 1st Western General Hospital, Liverpool, 5.7.1915, said that he was beside Lt. Martin and saw him shot through the head and killed instantly. Lt. Martin fell within 15 yards of the German front line and a burial party couldn't reach him. 10994 A. Owens, B Coy, saw Martin shot through the forehead 'and appeared to lie as if dead'.

A WO letter to his father, 15.7.1915, stated that the OC, 1st RIR, reported that the death was not confirmed and 'evidence tends to show this officer was wounded and captured by Germans on 9th May, but no reliable information can be obtained.' A letter from OC, 5th RIR, at Holywood, 24.8.1915, advised that Lt. Martin was still appearing in the Army List but had been killed in action 9 May.

A letter from father to WO, 5.4.1916, asked if there was any further news. He himself had made enquiries with the American Embassy in New York and Paris, to no avail. He had also enquired of the Red Cross in Geneva, without result, and with the King of Spain who had established a bureau in his palace, but again without success. He then made enquiries through Professor Savory of Queen's University, Belfast. This led to contact with Dr Roediger, Director of the Royal University and Library at Marburg-on-the-Lahn, in Prussia. This apparently generated interest because Professor Savory had previously helped Dr Roediger by tracing his son, who was a German prisoner in Britain. A transcript of Dr Roediger's letter was attached. This was dated 14.12.1915 and addressed to Professor Savory, regretting that all his enquiries in Germany had failed and again thanked the Professor for his help in locating his son. Mr Martin asked the WO if a death certificate could then be issued. WO replied, 18.4.1916, and said enquiries were continuing. A WO letter, 9 May, asked Mr Martin if he had heard any further news – if not they will have to declare death accepted. Mr Martin had written that day asking the same question. He confirmed, 11 May, that no further news had been heard and that all enquiries had failed. He wrote again, 30 May, expressly stating that he wanted the death accepted. WO replied, 17 June, saying, that as all official reports stated that his son was wounded, they couldn't confirm death at that time as they didn't constitute proper evidence, but in view of the time lapsed since last news of him they were now constrained to accept death for official purposes. A notice issued 22.6.1916. Ploegsteert Memorial. File ref: WO339/14230 30382.

Maunsell, Lt. Douglas Slade. Born 22.4.1885 at Belfast, the son of Major Arthur Munro Maunsell, 2nd RMF, and May Isabel Maunsell (daughter of Charles Thomson) of 10 Galtrim Road, Bray, Co. Wicklow. Educated at the Royal School, Armagh.

Joined 4th RDF in 1911. Attached to 1st RIR and went overseas 5.11.1914. He is not mentioned in the War Diary but appeared on the Army List of February 1915 as RMF attached 1st RIR. See U.C. Jenings above. Apparently he was considered unsuitable by OC 1st RIR. Gazetted a 2/Lt. in 2nd RMF, 30.12.1914.

Promoted Lt. 28.8.1915. Invalided home in September 1915 and did light duty at Cork. He was serving in Dublin during the rebellion of April 1916. Returned to France 1.9.1916 and was attached to 1st RMF. Killed in action, 5.9.1916, between Guillemont and Ginchy, only five hours after joining the battalion. A note on his file gives the location about 500 yards east of Guillemont, north-west of Combles. His mother wrote to the WO, 20.12.1916, stating she had news that 2/Lt. F.M. Saunders, 1st RMF, had handed the effects in a rucksack to the Second in Command, Major Wilson, who himself had been killed two days later. There was then no trace of the effects. A memo from R.T. Baxter, QM 1st RMF, to WO, 17.1.1917, listed the effects (of which there was many) but advised that there was no trace of them. Medals were despatched to his brother Arthur Charles Stanley Maunsell.

de Ruvigny: 'Buried at Guillemont. Lt. Maunsell belonged to an old Limerick family, which had many distinguished soldiers from the eleventh century, when it came from France. Unmarried.'

Thiepval Memorial. File ref: WO339/9282.

Maxwell 2/Lt. John A. Joined 1st RIR 3.10.18. Wounded 15.10.1918. The only mentions in the War Diary are of a 2/Lt. J.A. Maxwell. The most likely appears to be John A. Maxwell, file ref: 2/83 (245700), a closed file. *London Gazette* 8.9.1935: '2/Lt. J. Maxwell having attained the age limit of liability to recall, ceases to belong to the Reserve of Officers.'

May Major Ernest Richard Hallam DSO. Born 16.10.1880. Applied for a regular commission, 11.9.1914, asking for infantry, 10th RIR. Married, permanent address, 16 Wellington Park Avenue, Belfast. Previously served with the 46th (Ulster) Imperial Yeomanry SAFF (South African Frontier Force).

Promoted Capt. 23.11.1914 and Major 7.1.1916. Left unit, 29.11.1917, to No. 24 General Hospital, Etaples. Embarked Calais–Dover, 28.12.1917, 'Sick'. The MB at Caxton Hall, 10.1.1918, noted his home address as Kilkeel, Co. Down. He had taken ill, 29.11.1917, with pyrexia; temperature now gone but he was 'shaky and run down' – unfit for general service for three months and home service for one month. The MB at Caxton Hall, 30.1.1918, unfit for general service for two months – recommended for three weeks leave, then fit for home service. MB at Belfast, 29 March, unfit for general service for one month but fit for home service; instructed to rejoin his unit. MB at Fargo Military Hospital, Salisbury Plain, 9 May, shows 5th RIR, fit for general service. Joined 1st RIR, 25.9.1918, from 15th RIR and took over the duties of Second-in-Command.

Awarded the DSO in November 1918, *London Gazette* 8.3.1919, details 4.10.1919. See main text. Went to 12th RIR, 19.2.1919, and took over as Second-in-Command. Discharged 25.4.1919. Last served with 12th RIR, rated A1, married, occupation shipping. Address, Kilkeel. Subscribed £1.05 towards the General Nugent Memorial Fund 1929. He regularly attended the 36th (Ulster) Division Officers OCA annual dinner until 1946 and signed himself as a past member of 10th RIR. File ref: WO339/45658 30435.

Mayne Major Edward Colburn. Commissioned as a Lt. into 3rd RIF, 24.2.1886, and promoted to Capt. 10.5.1893. Served in operations with the Sierra Leone Frontier Police, 1897–8, receiving a medal and clasp. Also served during the Boer War, 1899–1901, attached to 2nd RIF, and received the Queen's South Africa Medal, with clasps for Orange Free State, Transvaal, and Natal. Joined the Reserve of Officers 12.8.1903, Honorary Capt. in the Army (Honorary Major, ret. militia).

Joined 3rd RIF, 12.8.1914, and arrived with 2nd RIR 6.12.1914. On leave to UK 27.2.1915. Left 2nd RIR, 15.5.1915, and joined 1st RIR the next day. Mentioned in Despatches 22.6.1915. Temporary command of the battalion 20–4.10.1915. T/Major 3.2.1916. Took over command of the battalion, 26.2.1916 to 14.4.1916, just after the German raid at La Boiselle. Resumed command of his Coy and relinquished temporary rank of Major, 19.5.1916. Took over the duties of Town Major at Millencourt and Vermelles, 23 June. To 25th Field Ambulance, 13 August, and discharged to duty, 4 September.

Whitfeld, at Dernancourt, 25.10.1916: 'The RTO [Railway Transport Officer] was old Mayne who had once been with us and incidentally as CO used to award NCO's C.B. much to Browne's astonishment and annoyance.'

To Etaples, 19.11.1916, as Instructor at No. 2 Training School. Arrived VIII Corps reinforcement camp from Etaples, 5.1.1918. Area Commandant Hipshoek and St Jan-Ter-Biezen, 21.10.1918. Granted leave to the UK, 7–21.12.1918. Ordered to proceed to England and report to WO in writing upon arrival, 16.3.1919. Demobilized with the honorary rank of Major, 22.9.1919. Occupation in civil life, 'Nil'. Served during 'The Emergency' 9.4.1921 to 26.4.1921, 'Unposted'. Home address 11 Holland Road, London W14. 'Station', Horse Guards, London. Unit, RIF. Presently employed with the Ministry of Labour. During his service he passed the School of Instruction and qualified as Instructor of Musketry. File ref: WO339/25047.

Mercer 2/Lt. Samuel. Born 16.2.1895. Enlisted at Belfast, 1.6.1915, as Pte 17/1066 in 17th RIR. Draper, height 6 foot ½ inch, weight 140 pounds, chest 33–35 inches, single. Applied for a commission, 27.9.1915, asking for infantry, 19th RIR, address 276 Shankhill Road, Belfast, single, presently serving with 17th RIR at Newcastle as a L/Cpl (Cadet). Gazetted a Temp. 2/Lt. in 17th RIR, 4.10.1915.

Joined 1st RIR from 17th RIR, 16.8.1916. Left unit, 11.11.1916, and embarked Le Havre–Southampton, 18 November, aboard SS *Dunluce Castle*. 'Trench Fever and General Debility.' The MB at 2nd Western General Hospital, Manchester, 18.12.1916, noted that he was on the Somme sector: pains began 2.11.1916, head and abdomen. 'He is now better. Has occasional pains in legs. But is still weak.' Unfit for general or home service for one month. T/Lt. 1.1.1917. MB at Belfast, 18.1.1917, improving, unfit for general service for one month, fit for home service, and, 19.2.1917, fit for general service.

Joined 2nd RIR, 7.5.1917, and was wounded 18.6.1917. Embarked Boulogne–Dover, 22 June, GSW both legs. Seemed to have been one bullet passing from side to side, no bone damage. Wrote to the WO, 21.9.1917, stating that he was shot through both thighs at Warniton. The wounds were healed but his left leg was useless and he had to use crutches. Applied for wound gratuity. At this time he was in the Ulster Volunteer Force Officers Hospital, 60 Botanic Avenue, Belfast. He wrote again, 15.10.1917, advising that he was then in the West Down Branch of the Ulster Volunteer Force Hospital, Dunbarton House, Gilford, Co. Down, and again asked for a wound gratuity. Another application, 1.1.1918, advised that he was now walking with the aid of a 'stout stick'.

A note dated 6 June states that Mercer was serving with an Armoured Car Section in Belfast. He was living at Claremorris, Co. Mayo, 28.6.1918, when he again asked for a wound gratuity. His address was the Free Library, Edward Street, Portadown, 12.8.1919, when he complained about the lack of action to his requests for the gratuity. Discharged 11.7.1919. Last served attached Ministry of Labour. Civil occupation, civil servant. Address was given as 7 Albert Street, Bangor, Co. Down. Medical rating C1. Single. The MB at Belfast, 25.2.1920, rated his disability at less than 20 per cent. A note gave overseas service period as August–November 1916 and May–October 1917 – this is obviously incorrect as he returned to the UK in June 1917. File ref: WO339/45658 114770.

Meredith-Jones Capt. H.D. Served in the South African War, 1901–02, Commandant Britstown. Operations in Cape Colony, Orange River Colony, and the Transvaal. Received the Queen's Medal with five clasps. Joined 1st RIR as a 2/Lt. from the RWF, 31.10.1916, and was struck off the strength of the battalion, 10.11.1916. File missing. Capt., Reserve of Officers, 1920.

Merriman Lt.-Col. Arthur Drummond Nairn DSO. Born 1876. Took part in operations in Sierra Leone, 1898–9, receiving a medal with clasp. Commissioned in August 1899. Transferred to the RIR from the Manchester Regt, 1908. He served in the South African War 1899–1902, being wounded twice (slightly and severely). Took part in operations in Natal, 1899, including action at Lombard's Kop; Defence of Ladysmith, including the action on 6.1.1900; operations in Natal, March–June 1900, including action at Laings Nek (6–9 June), operations in the Transvaal, East of Pretoria, July to 29.11.1900, including actions at Belfast (26–7 August) and Lydenberg (5–8 September) and operations in the Transvaal (1900–02) employed with mounted infantry. Mentioned in Despatches 10.9.1901 and 17.1.1902. Received the Queen's Medal with three clasps and the King's Medal with two clasps. Promoted to Capt. 20.5.1908, and Major 17.4.1915. Joined and took over command of 1st RIR, 17.5.1915 to 13.6.1915.

War Diary, 25.9.1915: '10 a.m. Major Merriman led 2 platoons of A Coy across to the German trenches just east of Bridoux Fort ... Eventually under an avalanche of bombs the Lincolns retired and our men with them. In the retirement Major Merriman was wounded.'

He lost an arm in this action. Awarded the DSO, *London Gazette* 3.6.1916, and Mentioned in Despatches, 1.1.1916, 15.6.1916, and 9.9.1921. On 8.6.1919 he succeeded to the command of 2nd RIR and, not long afterwards, was leading it on active service in the Arab Rebellion of 1920 in Mesopotamia. He completed his period of command at the Citadel in Cairo, 7.6.1923, and retired the same year. In 1939 he was commanding and teaching rifle drill to the local Home Guard. He died 14.4.1966 in a nursing home in Taunton, three miles north of his residence at Corfe in Somerset. He had two daughters, Sheila and Penelope. His obituary appeared in *Quis Separabit*, vol. 37, 1966.

Mew 2/Lt. Gordon Morrison. Born 1895 at Reigate, Surrey, and resided at Dudley House, Redhill, Surrey. A dental student at Guy's Hospital, London, and had served in Eastbourne College OTC. Attested and embodied Pte 1585 in 28th London Regt (Artists Rifles), 6.8.1914. Age 19 years 5 months; height 5 foot 11 inches, and chest 30½–36 inches. Signed Army Form E624, 23.10.1914, at Abbotts Langley. Served overseas with the London Regt, 26.10.1914, until he was gazetted a 2/Lt. in the RIR, 3.3.1915. Joined 1st RIR, 18.3.15, from the Cadet School, Bailleul.

Injured 9.5.1915, GSW to the leg, and embarked for the UK aboard the *St Patrick*, 11 May. Promoted to Lt., 13.11.1915, and three days later appeared before the MB at Croydon. It reported that he could then walk short distances without the aid of a stick and recommended a further two months leave. A letter sent to the WO, 8.1.1916, reported that he was at King Edward VII Hospital, 5 Grosvenor Gardens, Victoria, London, and had had an operation to his thigh. Mew wrote to the WO, 9 February, asking for a wound gratuity, giving his address as Lady Carnarvon's Hospital for Officers, 48 Bryanston Square, Paddington, London. He notified the WO of the expiry of his leave, 8.5.1916, while staying at the Red Cross Convalescent Home, 11 Chichester Terrace, Brighton. Awarded a wound pension of £50 for the year to 8.5.1917. The MB noted, 18.5.1916, that he could then get about on crutches and, 20.7.1916, that he had made excellent progress and a full recovery was expected. He could walk up to half a mile at a time with the aid of a stick. On 11 August he was staying at the Regent's Hotel, Brighton. The MB reported, 25 August, that there had been no further progress and his condition was considered stationary. Rejoined 3rd RIR at Victoria Barracks, Belfast, 28.8.1916. The MB, 31.5.1917, reported that there had been an improvement and that he could then walk without difficulty but 'tires easily and can't take active service'. Transferred to the Labour Corps, 21.6.1917, and relinquished his commission due to ill health, 19.1.1919. By 3.12.1923 he was practising as a dentist at Morley House, Bruce Road, Bow, London E3. File ref: WO339/27948 49737.

Miles Capt. Robert Patrick. Born 11.12.1879 at The Lawn, Shirehampton, Gloucestershire, the son of Robert Fenton Miles, The Old Bank (Union of London and Smith's), Bristol. He was related to Sir Henry Robert Miles, Bt., of Leigh Court, and was a godson of General Sir Patrick Macdougall, at one time C.-in-C. in Canada. Educated at Marlborough, where he gained some athletic distinction, and joined the Yorkshire Light Infantry in August 1899, becoming a Lt. in January 1901. Served in the South African War, being present at operations in the Orange Free State and at Paardeberg; actions at Poplar Grove, Driefontein, Houtnek (Thoba Mountain), Vet and Zand Rivers; in the Orange River Colony, Cape Colony, and the Transvaal. Received the Queen's medal with four clasps and the King's Medal with two clasps. He also had the medal for King George V's Durbar in India. In October, 1907, he was appointed Superintendent of Gymnasia for the Southern Army, India, where he served for ten years. Belonged to 2nd The King's (Shropshire Light Infantry). Promoted Capt. 6.3.1909. Appeared on the WO list of officers who were qualified as French speakers. *Thom's Directory* for 1912 shows him with 9th (Secunderabad) Division, Ootacamund, Southern Army, India.

He was a good all-round athlete and very interested in Army boxing, he was also fond of big-game shooting, in which he was indulging while on leave in British East Africa when the war broke out. On his return he was attached to 1st RIR, as 1st SLI, to which he had been transferred, had already gone to the front.

Laurie, 30.12.1914: ' ... poor Capt. Miles, attached to me, was shot in the head. Being close by, I waded to him, but it was hopeless from the first. Such a place to die in! – but Heaven will be Heaven after that. His poor wife, too. I must write to her. He was a very nice man. I had plenty of morphia given to him, and he is now dying without any pain quite peacefully. PS ... I have just been to see poor Capt. Miles carried out on a stretcher dead ... He was a talented man, and used to write for papers. When the war broke out he was running a cinematograph film-collecting expedition in German East Africa, and just managed to get away. Poor fellow!'

Strangely enough, he was not mentioned in the War Diary. Married to Nora Passy, formerly Miles, 69, Philbeach Gardens, Earls Court, London. Estaires Communal Cemetery, Nord, I.D.3. File missing.

Millar 2/Lt. James Lytton. Born 7.11.1897, the only son of the Revd Ross Millar and Mrs Ida Frances Millar of Hillmount, Letterkenny, Co. Donegal. Served in Campbell College OTC for one year and two terms. Matriculated at Queen's University, Belfast, June 1915, Faculty of Medicine. Applied for a commission, 21.6.1915, expressing a preference for the Royal Garrison Artillery. A second application, 8.10.1915, changed his preference to 5th RIR. Single, Presbyterian, height 5 foot 9½ inches, chest 35–37 inches, and weight 144 pounds. Commissioned to 5th RIR and attached to 1st RIR. Killed in action 29.7.1916. His effects were sent to his father.

Irish Life 24.11.1916: 'He received his commission in November 1915 and had only been six weeks at the front when he was killed.'

Vermelles British Cemetery, Pas de Calais, IV.H.1. File ref: WO339/47770 117434.

Miller Lt. Joseph Ewing Bruce. The only son of Dr Joseph Ewing Miller MB, B.Ch, JP, and Helen Stewart Miller, *née* Bruce, of 18 Pump Street, Londonderry. His father was Hon. Surgeon for the County and County Borough Infirmary of Londonderry, in addition to being the Medical Officer on the Visiting Committee of HM Prison, Londonderry.

Applied for a commission, 12.8.1914, expressing a preference for 5th RIR. Single, medical student at Edinburgh University (enrolled 15.4.1913), height 6 foot, weight 158 pounds, and chest 35–37½ inches. Joined 1st RIR from 5th RIR, 28.3.1915. Wounded 9.5.1915. A WO telegram was sent to his father, 13 May. Father sent a telegram to the WO, 14 May, asking that they please wire his son's condition and whereabouts as soon as possible.

Irish Times 15.5.1915: 'Soon after the war started Lt. Miller got a commission in the 5th Battalion of the Royal Irish Rifles; and was stationed in Belfast. He left for the front some time ago, being attached to the 1st Battalion of the Rifles. His brother-in-law, Capt. Charles Norman DL, has been at the front since the commencement of the war, and his uncle, Capt. J.T. Miller, is with the 10th (Service) Battalion, Royal Inniskilling Fusiliers (Ulster Division).'

WO reply, 18.5.1915: 'Lt. J.E.B. Miller Royal Irish Rifles admitted to Stationary Hospital St Omer suffering from gunshot wound thorax and shoulder. Seriously ill.' WO telegram to father, 21 May: 'Lt. J.E.B. Miller Royal Irish Fusiliers. Condition reported dangerously ill 21st May.' OC, No. 10 Stationary Hospital, sent a telegram to the WO, 23 May, advising that Miller was critical and 'may be visited'. WO telegram to father, 24 May: 'Lt. J.E.B. Miller Royal Irish Rifles No. 10 Stationary Hospital St Omer reported yesterday. Condition critical. May be visited.' Father sent a telegram to the WO: 'Please wire immediately locality of No. 10 Stationary Hospital ... and if I could get there.' Died of wounds, 24.5.1915, at No. 10 Stationary Hospital. WO telegram to father, 26 May, reported the death, Lord Kitchener expressing his sympathy.

Irish Life 30.7.1915: 'Lieutenant J.E. Bruce Miller ... grandson of the late Major Stewart Hervey Bruce, Argyll and Sutherland Highlanders. He was 20 years of age and was gazetted to a Lieutenancy in the 5th Royal Irish Rifles in January last, and shortly afterwards proceeded with his regiment to France.'

Longuesnes (St Omer) Souvenir Cemetery, Pas de Calais, I.A.133. File ref: WO339/14233 30385.

Miller Lt. William (John Paterson). A certified extract from birth records, produced in May 1927, shows John Paterson born 28.5.1885 in Govan, Glasgow. His file contains letters from various members of his family using the spelling Paterson or Patterson. First attested as John

Patterson, Pte 8233 in the RIF, Belfast, 19.12.1903. Age 18 years 7 months, labourer, Presbyterian, height 5 foot 4¼ inches, weight 123 pounds, chest 33–35½ inches, anchor tattoo left forearm, shamrock left hand and harp right hand, serving with 4th RIR Militia. Next of kin parents John and Sarah Patterson, 116 Dee Street, Belfast.

Seven days confined to barracks, 26.4.1904, for being absent from roll call and deficient of regimental necessities (Holywood). Three days confined to barracks for being absent from tattoo, 28.12.1904 (Holywood). Appointed L/Cpl 16.3.1905. Reverted to Pte, 19.7.1905, having been deprived of rank due to being improperly dressed in town, not complying with an order from Military Police, and giving false name to Military Police (Fermoy). Seven days confined to barracks, 22.11.1906, for improper conduct in town (Dublin). To Army Reserve 18.12.1906.

Enlisted as Pte 3458 in 8th Hussars at Belfast, 16.11.1908, as William Miller. Gave age as 20 years 5 months, trade labourer. Held awaiting trial by court martial (DCM) at Colchester 8.2.1909. Sentenced to 14 days detention for 'making a wilfully false answer etc.' Ten days confined to barracks, 8.2.1909, for 'absent from gymnasium' (Colchester). Convicted and 'Held to serve on last attestation', 2.3.1909. Awarded 14 days detention (Belfast). Letter from OC 8th Hussars to Cavalry Records, 11.3.1909, notified conviction. Returned to duty, 16.3.1909, and posted to India, 29.9.1909. Admitted to hospital at Lucknow, 4.2.1910, slight wound to leg. Admitted to hospital at Lucknow, 17.10.1910, sprained ankle, 'trivial'. Appointed L/Cpl 25.11.1911. Admitted to hospital at Lucknow, 17.3.1913, broken arm, accidental. Promoted Cpl 18.3.1913.

To France 15.10.1914. Severely reprimanded for being absent from parade 19.11.1914 (Marseilles). Promoted Sgt 1.11.1915. Severely reprimanded, 8.9.1916, for being absent from line of march ('field'). To 4th Army Gas School 25.10.1916. Rejoined 31.10.1916. To duty at 5th Cavalry School 9.11.1916. Recommendations for a commission are very good – 'thoroughly reliable, intelligent', etc. Preference was for a commission in the RE Gas Services Branch, later amended to Infantry, preferably RIR. Promoted from Sgt H/3458, 8th Hussars. Took up duties as a 2/Lt. in 1st RIR, 15.10.1917. Went to the UK 16.2.1918. Posted to 52nd R. Sussex Regt at Thetford 16.3.1918. Returned to France, 8.11.1918, and rejoined 1st RIR, 12 November. Left the battalion, 11.2.1919, and granted leave to the UK. Promoted Lt. 15.4.1919. Joined 3rd RIR at Rugeley, 22 April. Posted to 2nd RIR at Thetford, 2 May. Embarked for Mesopotamia 18 September. Admitted to hospital February 1920. The MB, Egypt, 19.7.1920, declared him unfit A1 for twelve months and unfit C1 for six months. Miller applied for return to the UK, 12.3.1922, for retirement with a gratuity. Willing to serve on Army Reserve. This was forwarded by OC 2nd RUR, 31.3.1922.

WO telegram, 15.5.1922, to Mrs Paterson, 8 Ravenhill Road, Belfast, warned that they had a report dated 9 May that Miller was admitted to Abbassia Officer's Hospital and was dangerously ill. WO memo, 23 May, stated that technically the RIF service was never struck out and would therefore qualify towards service for a gratuity, but as Paterson/Miller denied it when he joined the Hussars it could also be disregarded. Telegram from Egypt Force to WO, 20.5.1922, 'Regret to report death of Lieutenant W. Miller, 2nd Ulster Rifles, 18th May, cause Alcoholism'. WO reported his death to Mrs Paterson, 22 May, but said nothing about the cause. A note at this time showed Miller as Battalion Transport Officer. Many of the papers on the file relate to bills and receipts re Millers' debts (many of them in Arabic or French). Buried in the British Protestant Cemetery, Cairo.

Letter from David Paterson, 8 Ravenhill Road, 27 July, to the Adjustment Committee 2nd RUR in Cairo: Regretted that 'my mother' could do nothing to contribute to the debts of 'her son'. His father died 21.7.1922. David stated that the father never had a nights sleep since hearing of the death and 'the cause of death broke his heart' (the death certificate stated alcoholism). David went on to say that he may be able to pay off some of the debts 'when my wounds are better'. (Death certificate for father, John Patterson, showed that he was aged 63, a fitter by trade, and died of heart failure at the Royal Victoria Hospital.) The unbalanced debts amounted to £101.91. The file contains a very long list of personal effects – four foolscap pages – including two RIR collar badges, his WW1 trio of medals, 8th Hussars badges, and a RIF sports medal – all that kind of thing going to the next of kin. Other items such as furniture, revolver and holster, suits, linen, books, etc., are marked sold, with amounts noted against every item. These funds were offset against outstanding debts. A small addendum list shows items as 'unserviceable' which were destroyed – odd socks and the like.

A very long letter from his mother to the Ministry of Pensions, 21.3.1927, asked for a pension. She said Millar died due to malaria, 18.5.1922. She confirmed his false name enlistment stating he enlisted with the 8th Hussars as William John Millar but his correct name was John Paterson. It may be that she never actually saw the WO notification of cause of death, and that the malaria story is what her husband and other son had told her. M.o.P. passed this letter to the WO who replied, 6.4.1927, saying there was no entitlement to a dependant's pension as the death was not service attributable – they didn't actually state the cause of death. They did say, however, that there was a small relief fund and she may be eligible to a grant from that – an application form was provided. Relief fund application form completed and countersigned by a Belfast magistrate, 19.4.1927. This showed an annual income of £13 from a lodger and £26 from the family. Mother was then aged 63 years. There were three married sons aged 39, 34, and 26 years. Five married daughters were aged 43, 36, 32, 30, and 28. WO relief fund granted £20, 17.5.1927, and advised that grants could not be issued more frequently than once every three years. A supplementary grant of £10 was issued 24.3.1928. Daughter-in-law, Mrs S. Paterson, applied for a grant on her behalf, 27.5.1930, and a grant of £20 was made 23.6.1930. Daughter Mrs Sarah Coard applied for a grant on behalf of her mother, 21.6.1933, and a grant of £20 was made 1.7.1933. Sarah again applied 24.5.1936 – award £20 issued 4.7.1936; 4.6.1939 – award £10, 13.7.1939. File ref: WO339/129592 1/83 (248762).

Minchin 2/Lt. Reginald Humphry Loder. Born 1896, the son of Lt.-Col. Hugh Dillon Massey Minchin, Indian Army. Unattached List Indian Army. Joined 1st RIR, 26.3.1915, but there are no further references to him in the War Diary. Married Miss Annie McFerran Ferris, 7.7.1915. May have later served with the Australian Imperial Forces.

' Glenahilty and Dublin line of the family. His brother, Lt. Hubert Charles Minchin, was killed in France 1916. Another brother, Brigadier Hugh Charles Stephens Minchin, born 1893, was Assistant QMG at Western District Headquarters, UK, during World War II. This information comes from *Saga of the Minchins* compiled by Wendy Sawyer and kindly provided by Paul Minchin McKay of Bangor. I could only locate a Lt. H. Minchin on the CWGC database – killed at Neuve Chapelle, 20.12.1914, while serving with 125th Napier's Rifles, Indian Army. File missing.

Mitchell 2/Lt. A. Joined 1st RIR from 6th RIR, 18.6.1917. Transferred to England and struck off the strength of the battalion, 27.8.1917. The War Diary entry for this man could read as A. or R. Mitchell. He could not be traced from the available information.

Mockett Capt. Gordon. He had originally been commissioned as a 2/Lt. in the Special Reserve and served with the 8th (Militia Battalion) KRRC, known as the Carlow Rifles, stationed at Carlow Barracks. Qualified for appointment as Instructor of Musketry. School Certificate for Militia Subalterns. The unit was disbanded under the Haldane Scheme, 28.1.1908, and he transferred to 5th RIR. Made an Honorary Capt., 2.5.1914, and had been Adjutant of 5th RIR. Joined 1st RIR at La Plateau, Camp 107, 29.12.1916. Transferred to the sick list 14.4.1917. Wounded 31.7.1917. During this day he had command of the battalion for a while. Officer Cadet Bn, 1918. Closed file, ref: 5/83 (42162).

Mole Brigadier Gerard Herbert Leo DSO, MC. Born 24.10.1897, the son of Philip Charles Mole and Nina O'Dea. Educated St Xavier's College, Calcutta, and Mount St Mary's College, Sprinkhill, Derbyshire. Married Claire Marie Kassapian and they had three sons and two daughters.

Joined RIR 1916. Went overseas, 1.7.1916, and joined 1st RIR as a 2/Lt., 20.7.1916. Struck off the strength, 13.9.1916, no reason given, and returned to the UK, 26.9.1916. Resumed active service on the Western Front from 1.12.1916 until 6.9.1918, with the MGC. Promoted Lt. 7.10.1917. Awarded the MC. Took part in the Archangel Relief Force in 1919 and described his experiences in *Quis Separabit* issues for May and November 1935.

Served until 1923 with the West African Frontier Force; in Cologne and India with 2nd RUR to 1933. Promoted Capt., 17.9.1925, and was Garrison Adjutant, Bordon, in 1936. Promoted to Major 22.3.1937. Served at home until the Second World War, and went to France with the BEF and also served in North-West Europe. 129th Infantry Brigade, Home Forces. Awarded the DSO and Bar, Mentioned in Despatches. Recreations golf, shooting, and travel. Address c/o Lloyds Bank Ltd., 6 Pall Mall, London SW1. Died November 1944. Closed file, ref: 83 & MGC (132677).

Moore 2/Lt. Robert McConnell MM. Born 23.3.1895 at Shankill, Belfast, the son of Thomas and Sarah Moore of 227 Springfield Road, Belfast. Enlisted as Pte 9/15621 in the RIR, 9.9.1914. Presbyterian, a fitter by trade, height 5 foot 7 inches, weight 135 pounds, and chest 33–36 inches. Appointed a L/Cpl 11.9.1914, promoted Cpl 1.7.1915, and Sgt 21.9.1915. Served at home to 1.10.1915 and with 9th RIR in the BEF France until 23.12.1916. He received a severe reprimand, 14.3.1916: 'when on active service, neglect of duty when in charge of a billet' – 'not paying compliments to a sentry' – 'insolent conduct'. Severely reprimanded again, 26.4.1916: 'when on active service neglect of duty'. Awarded the MM 21.12.1916.

Applied for a commission in the RIR, 11.12.1916, and joined No. 5 Officer Cadet Battalion at Trinity College, Cambridge, 6.2.1917. Commissioned into 17th RIR, 29.5.1917, and returned to the front. Killed in action, 27.3.1918, while serving with 1st RIR. His father wrote to the WO, 17 November: 'Last April I received a wire from the War Office saying my son, 2/Lt. Robert McConnell Moore, R. I. Rifles, was wounded and missing on 27th March. Since then I have heard nothing of him, then on 11th November received the enclosed postcard. On the 13th November I got a letter from a lady in Switzerland which she wrote at the request of a German officer, to say he buried R.M. Moore, he photographed his grave and sent us a copy. Could you make any enquiry as to which communication is correct.'

There is a WO enclosure envelope attached to this but it is torn open and empty – no photo and no postcard. The WO replied, 20.11.1918, stating that nothing was known. There is a sketch in the file that is said to be a copy of the photo of Moore's grave. It shows a wooden cross, Brodie Helmet, and crossed rifles, but there is no text on the cross. A facsimile of a letter from Liny Toedtli, the Swiss lady, states that the German officer got the family address from papers on Moore's body. There is a sketch map showing the supposed location of the grave, apparently made by the German officer. The WO wrote to his father, 29.5.1919, stating that they currently had no record of a grave and, 29.6.1919, issued a notice of acceptance of death for official purposes. They wrote again to his father, 11.12.1919, advising that the grave had been discovered 500 yards west of Erches, and that the remains had been re-interred in Mezieres Communal Cemetery Extension, north-west of La Quesnel, Somme, Plot B.22. File ref: WO339/91112 176561.

Morrow Capt. Hugh Gelston MC. Born 16.4.1894, the son of Andrew John Morrow of 2 Avonmore Terrace, Balmoral, Belfast. Enlisted, 5.6.1915, as Cadet 17/1060 in 17th RIR. Linen warehouseman, height 5 foot 9 inches, weight 119 pounds, and chest 31–33 inches. Next of kin, father. Unpaid L/Cpl, 7.12.1915. Applied for a commission 27.1.1916. Single, Presbyterian, permanent address Avonmore Terrace, correspondence address 17th RIR, Ballykinlar Camp, Co. Down. Preference was 19th RIR. Posted to No. 7 Officer Cadet Battalion, 5.4.1916, and commissioned a 2/Lt., 6.7.1916. Struck off the strength of 1st RIR, 1.11.1916, no reason given. A WO telegram to his father, 26.10.1918, informed that Hugh was wounded 20 October. Killed in action, 22.10.1918, while serving with 15th RIR as an A/Capt. Single and died intestate.

A scribbled note on the file noted that he was first reported wounded and missing 20.10.1918. Another field service report gives killed in action 20.10.1918. A WO letter to his mother, 29 October, advised that nothing more was known since the telegram notifying Hugh as wounded on the 20th. They shall investigate and advise. WO telegram to the home address, 6 November, regretted to advise that the reply to their investigations was that Morrow was in fact killed in action 22.10.1918. A Graves Registration Department form, 12.2.1919, stated that he was buried about one mile north-west of Deerlyck, north-east of Courtrai. A WO letter to the father, 14.10.1920, states that Hugh was exhumed and re-buried in Harlebeke New British Cemetery, Harlebeke, West-Vlaanderen, VII.B.18. File ref: WO339/57731 19/83 130318.

Morrow 2/Lt. James. Born 22.2.1891. Applied for a commission 8.9.1915; single and residing at 19 Ashley Avenue, Belfast. Being unable to ride, he applied for any infantry unit. Had been a member of Queen's University OTC and classed good in all report sections. Gazetted to 5th R. Irish and attached to 1st RIR, 18.7.1916. Left this unit, 17.10.1916, suffering from trench fever, embarking Calais–Dover, 1 November, aboard *City of Antwerp*. Address was given as Rehola Terrace, Ashley Avenue, Belfast. Appeared before the MB at the Research Hospital, Cambridge, 4.11.1916.

There is no record on his file but it appears that he was badly wounded while serving with the MGC. Reported to 4th R. Irish at Queenstown, Co. Cork, 6.3.1917. He wrote to the WO from the Ulster Volunteer Force Hospital, Dunbarton House, Gilford, Co. Down, 22.9.1917, saying that he was still hospitalised and applied for a war gratuity. The hospital wrote to the WO, 5.1.1918, stating that Morrow was permanently unfit for service. File ref: 6-5/18 MGC-113741 44896.

Muir Capt. James Lennox MC. Gazetted to 4th RIR, 10.10.1914. Joined 1st RIR as a 2/Lt., 30.6.1915. Posted to the sick list, 27.12.1915, and rejoined 25.3.1916. On 22.4.1916 he took out a party of twenty men to raid the German trenches opposite Bécourt Wood. His objective was a machine gun post in the enemy's line, 120 yards from the British wire. He was the only one to enter their trench and he shot two Germans. He was not supported by his men as they were held up by machine gun fire. The raid failed and one man was killed and several wounded. Promoted Lt., 30.5.1916, and awarded the MC 24.6.1916. Struck off the strength of the battalion, 19.2.1917, no reason given. Served with 2nd RUR in Palestine and awarded a Bar to his MC, 10.8.1921. Employed at the Depot 1923. Attended the Regimental Reunion Tea with his wife, 21.6.1935.

Quis Separabit vol. 16, no. 1, 1949: 'Captain James Lennox Muir, whose death at Rotura, New Zealand, was announced recently … He was awarded the MC for conspicuous gallantry in leading an attack against the German trenches in 1916 prior to the Somme offensive.' Closed file, ref: (44873).

Mulholland Colonel James Alan MBE, MC. Born 11.10.1885, the son of James H. Mulholland, Strathclyde, Donaghadee. He was a pupil at Campbell College, Belfast, until December, 1901. For the next ten years he was employed with Henry Matier & Co., Belfast.

Promoted to Capt. in 14th R.I.R., 9.4.1915, and appointed Adjutant 22.8.1915.

Irish Times 20.10.1916: 'Capt. J.A. Mulholland, Royal Irish Rifles (slightly wounded), is … one of three brothers holding commissions in the Army. He was formerly associated with the Young Citizen Volunteer Movement and had been Adjutant of his battalion since 22.8.1915.'

His brothers were Capt. Henry Holmes Mulholland, RAMC, Sqn/Ldr Denis Osmond Mulholland, AFC, and Flying Officer George Philip Mulholland. Commanded 14th RIR in 1917. In that same year he was awarded the MC. Joined 1st RIR and took over the duties of Second-in-Command, 29.4.1918. Rejoined from hospital 30 May. Proceeded to Bonninques to take over command of the Battalion School, 31.7.1918. Assumed command of 1st RIR 16.8.1918. Proceeded to the UK for a six months tour of duty, 18.9.1918. Promoted to Lt.-Col. in 1918. Served on the WO Staff 1918–21. Awarded the Legion of Honour, French Croix de Guerre and Palm. In 1929 he subscribed £1.05 towards the General Nugent Memorial Fund. During 1927–34 he commanded 18th London Regt. Promoted to Colonel 1934. Resigned his commission 8.5.1935. In 1938 he was residing at 4 Kensington Park Gardens, London W11, and was a councillor on Westminster City Council.

Quis Separabit vol. 37, no. 2, 1966: 'Colonel Mulholland, who died at his London home, was an outstanding member of the Ulster community in London and a former Mayor of Westminster. He was aged 80. After his term of office as Mayor in 1949–50, he became an Alderman. His 31 years of service with the Council ended in 1964 when the Westminster City Council was absorbed into the Greater London Council.

'Born in Donaghadee, he was educated at Stockport Grammar School, and Campbell College, Belfast. After extended service with the Army during the First World War he began a successful advertising business career in London. After service with the 6th Black Watch he transferred to the 14th Royal Irish Rifles and fought with the Ulster Division. He was promoted to the command of this battalion before taking over as Commanding Officer of the 1st Battalion The Royal Irish Rifles in 1917. He was awarded the MC and the French Croix de Guerre. He later spent three years at the War Office.

'Between the wars he was Commanding Officer of the London Irish Rifles and in 1939 was again in uniform. For his further services he was awarded an MBE. Colonel Mulholland was a leading member of the London Ulster Association and a City Liveryman. He acted as a Conservative Chief Whip on Westminster City Council, and during his Mayoralty was appointed to the Legion of Honour upon receiving the French President in London. We extend our deepest sympathy to Mrs Mulholland.' File destroyed.

Mulock-Bentley Capt. Michael Aubrey. Born 18.11.1896, the son of Thomas Mulock-Bentley, a doctor. Matriculated at Cape of Good Hope University in 1914. From 1908 he had been in the South African Cadet Corps and was discharged with the rank of Sgt, 30.6.1914, being overage. Attended Trinity College, Dublin, 1914. Gazetted a 2/Lt. in 3rd RIR, 20.7.1915. Certified fit for appointment to the Regular Army in 1916 and served in Dublin with 3rd RIR from April to May 1916 at Portobello Barracks – the time of the Easter Rising.

Joined 1st RIR, 30.5.1916, and served with B Coy. Appointed T/Capt. 4.9.1916. Arrived back in the UK, 22.2.1917, having been suffering from a cold and cough since January 1917. Attended the MB, 11 April, and was granted three weeks leave (unfit) and declared fit for home service only. Declared fit for general service with the Expeditionary Force 5.6.1917. Later attached to the 1st King's African Rifles and served in Nyasaland and Portuguese East Africa, December 1917 to September 1920, and was demobilized with the rank of Capt., 29.6.1923.

Murphy 2/Lt. Robert. Born 31.10.1896, the fourth son of Clarke and Martha Murphy of Main Street, Ballymoney, Co. Antrim. Educated at the Academical Institution, Coleraine. Enlisted as Rfn 19/678 in 19th RIR at Belfast, 1.9.1916. Bank clerk, Protestant, height 5 foot 5¼ inches, chest 32–35 inches. Appointed a L/Cpl, 30.4.1917, and posted to No. 7 Officer Cadet Battalion at Fermoy, 5.5.1917.

Ballymoney Heroes 1914–1918: 'The family lived about half-way down Main Street on the town clock side. Clarke had a coopering business at his house in Main Street and was one of the practical jokers of the town. His sense of humour was well known and woe betide anyone who tried to pull a fast one on him. This sense of humour was to stand him in good stead over the years because, as can be seen in the following few sentences, life was not easy.

'The family at home had had more than their fair share of grief. On 31st December 1876, their daughter, Martha, died aged sixteen months. Fourteen years later, another daughter, Mary, died. This was on 6th September 1890, at the age of thirteen. On 12th October 1891 Clarke's wife, Lizzie, died, and then on 3rd April 1897, their son Clarke died aged 10. On the 12th January 1915 Clarke married Matilda McMichael in St James's Presbyterian Church, Ballymoney. He was very interested in the well-being of the town and was a member of the Urban District Council.

'On 1st July 1916, another son, Johnston, was killed in action at Thiepval. The following year, in September 1917, Clarke became a JP and he adjudicated at the local Petty Sessions. Soon after this, on 3rd July 1918, he died at the age of 65. Their son Robert was home on leave for the funeral, and a short time after he went back, on 2nd October 1918, he was killed in action.'

After Lizzie died, Clarke married Robert's mother, Martha, who died 11.11.1913. Appointed to a commission in 19th RIR, 28.8.1917, being sent to 8th RIR. Joined 1st RIR from 14th RIR, 25.4.1918, and died of wounds sustained during an attack on 2.10.1918. Not knowing that his father had died, the WO sent a telegram, 6 October, advising that his son had been killed. They also wrote to him, 22.1.1919, notifying that Robert had been buried at Terhand Military Cemetery and that the grave had been marked with a durable wooden cross. A further letter in October 1920 advised his body had been exhumed and reburied at Dadizeele New British Cemetery, Plot I.E.4. File ref: 19/83 188167. (His brother, Lt. Johnston Murphy, 6th RIR attached 8th RIR, died 2.7.1916, aged 24.)

Neill Lt. Robert Larmour. Born 16.7.1893 at 62 Wellington Park, Belfast, the younger son of Sharman Dermot and Annie Symonds Neill, *née* Tomlin, of Ardmoyle, Holywood, Co. Down. Served in the OTC of Campbell College, Belfast, leaving in 1911, and had been a Company Commander in the UVF. Applied for a commission, 7.8.1914, expressing a preference for 5th RIR. Single, permanent address Ardmoyle, Cultra, Co. Down, profession – auditing and accounting, height 5 foot 7 inches, chest 33½–36½ inches, and weight 145 pounds.

Gazetted a 2/Lt. in 3rd RIR, August, 1914, and transferred to 5th RIR. Promoted to Lt., January 1915, and posted to France, 22.3.1915, joining 1st RIR, 1.4.1915. Killed in action, 9.5.1915, at the head of his platoon, after reaching the first German trench. A WO telegram was sent to his father, 15 May.

Irish Times 18.5.1915: 'He was the younger son of Mr Sharman D. Neill, the well-known jeweller and silversmith, of 22 Donegall Place, Belfast.'

Effects were sent to his father (aged 57 at the time) whose company letterhead was Sharman D. Neill Ltd., and incorporated a Royal Warrant 'By Appointment to His Majesty The King'.

Irish Life 30.7.1915: 'He was educated at Campbell College, where he joined the Officer's Training Corps and completed his studies at Neuchâtel, Switzerland. On his return home he joined the Holywood contingent of the 1st Battalion North Down Regiment, Ulster Volunteer Force. He obtained a commission in the Royal South Downs early in August and left for the front on March 22nd to join 1st Battalion, taking out a draft of Princess Charlotte of Wales's Royal Berkshire Regiment.'

He was a promising golfer and cricketer, an enthusiastic yachtsman, and a popular member of the Royal North of Ireland Yacht Club. At the time of his death he had a brother and three sisters. His brother was James Dermot Neill, age 27, on 'active service BEF, France'. Ploegsteert Memorial. File ref: WO339/14231 30383.

Newport Lt.-Col. Charles Johnstone OBE. Born 11.6.1888 at Inistioge, Co. Kilkenny. Went to Harrow School 1901. Gazetted a 2/Lt., 2.2.1905, in 3rd R. Irish. Granted a regular commission in the RIR 27.5.1908, promoted to Lt. 5.1.1910, and Capt. 10.4.1915. Served in India with 1st RIR. Wounded, 10.5.1915, and arrived back in the UK, 12 May. See main text.

Irish Life 16.7.1915: ' ... who has been undergoing treatment for some weeks in Mrs Falkner's Hospital, 6 Montpelier Square, London, having sustained wounds in action on May 10th, when he lay for fifteen hours before he was rescued. Though dangerously ill for some time, he is improving under skilled care.'

Irish Life 31.3.1916: ' ... has been Mentioned in Despatches [1.1.1916] for conspicuous gallantry in the battle of May 9th last in the advance trenches when, being the senior surviving officer of his regiment, he resisted all efforts of the enemy to dislodge him, though heavily pressed and attacked on both flanks, until his command was reduced to 20 or 30 men, whom he managed to withdraw safely, being himself dangerously wounded. Captain Newport is the eldest son of Mrs Edith Newport, Ballygallon, Inistioge, Co. Kilkenny.'

Irish Times 22.9.1916: 'Capt. H.G. Newport, 2nd Leinster Regiment, son of Mr G.B. Newport of Ballygallon, Inistioge, was dangerously wounded in action in France on August 31st. His brother, Capt. C.J. Newport, who was severely wounded last year, has now sufficiently recovered to be able to undertake the duties of Staff Captain in an important military district. These officers are the nephews of Col. Edgeworth-Johnstone, Chief Commissioner of the DMP, and of Major Robert Johnstone VC, Commandant of the Prisoners Camp, Oldcastle, who gained his enviable distinction for his heroism in the South African War.'

His address in 1938 was Matthouse, Ropley, Hants.

Blackthorn, vol. 2, no. 11, 1975: 'After leaving school he joined the Wexford Militia (3rd Bn The Royal Irish Regiment) and was commissioned 2/Lt. on 23rd January 1905 ... and served throughout World War I, being mentioned twice in despatches. At the end of the Great War he held an appointment as an Assistant Commandant in the Prison Service, retiring as a Major (RUR) in 1923.

'He was recalled from the Reserve in 1939 and served throughout the Second World War as a Commandant of various Military Corrective Establishments, being awarded the OBE in 1947, finally retiring as Lt.-Col. on 12th February 1948.

'In 1946 his son, Patrick, was commissioned into the Royal Ulster Rifles, later transferring to the RASC.'

Col. Newport died at his home, 11.5.1975, aged 86. His address at this time was Flat D, 203 Sandgate Road, Folkestone, Kent. Closed file, ref: (14106).

Nicholson Lt. Alexander Howard. Born 8.7.1890 at 52 Brookhill Avenue, Belfast, the son of Samuel and Margaret Nicholson, *née* Lyons. Father was a warehouseman. Educated at Royal Academical Institution, Belfast.

Home address at enlistment Frankfort, Deramore Park, Belfast. Applied for a commission, 3.6.1915, expressing a preference for 5th RIR. Single, wholesale warehouseman. 2/Lt. 3.7.1915. To School of Instruction, Cork, 7.7.1915. Joined 1st RIR from 5th RIR, 25.8.1916, and was wounded during an attack, 23.10.1916. Embarked Calais–Dover, 30 October, aboard *Stad Antwerpen*. Wounded through both buttocks, machine gun fire at Lesbeufs. MB at Caxton Hall, London, 6 December: wounds now healed but still considerable tenderness, unfit for general service for three months. Granted leave 6.12.1916 to 17.1.1917. MB at Belfast, 17 January, fit for general service. Rejoined 5th RIR at Holywood the next day. Promoted Lt. 1.7.1917.

Rejoined 1st RIR, 13.9.1917, and was wounded, 27.10.1917 (his file states that he was wounded at Messines Ridge, 28.10.1917). Left unit 28 October. Embarked Rouen–Southampton, 5 November. Rifle grenade grazing wound leading to an infection of the right knee; another note has this as a GSW. MB, 19 November, at 3rd Southern General Hospital, Oxford: unfit for general service for two months and to remain in hospital. MB at the same hospital, 11.12.1917: fit for home service, to report to 5th RIR, 3.1.1918. MB at Belfast, 30.1.1918: knee still causing problems with walking distances, unfit for general service for one month. MB at Belfast, 19 March: 'Has become quite well'. Ordered to rejoin his unit.

Rejoined 1st RIR, 3.10.1918, and was wounded again, 14.10.1918, leaving the unit that day. Embarked Calais–Dover, 22 October, gunshot wounds left thigh. MB at Red Cross Hospital, Dublin Castle, 9.1.1919, still had difficulty taking exercise. Demobilized 12.2.1919, medical category C1. Single. Application to resign commission was approved, 16.2.1920. In the War Diary he is named as A. Howard-Nicholson. File ref: WO339/52942.

Nolan 2/Lt. William Anthony Gerard. Born 13.7.1897 at Limerick, the son of William Michael Nolan JP, and Ellen Mary Nolan, *née* Murphy. Father was Limerick Town Clerk and Secretary of Committees who, according to *Thom's Directory* for 1912, was residing at 4 Melrose Villas, O'Connell Avenue, Limerick.

Left Clongowes Wood College in 1914. Applied for a commission, 3.9.1915, expressing a preference for 3rd RMF. Single. Home address 7 Newenham Street, Limerick. Served with 1st RMF. Wounded at Ginchy, 9.9.1916, and embarked Calais–Dover 13 September. GSW left shoulder. Address, Mentana, Laurel Hill Avenue, Limerick. Arrival report 21.9.1916. Admitted Queen Alexandra's Hospital for Officers, Millfield Lane, Highgate, London N. The MB, 21.9.1916, noted that the bullet had passed straight through without damaging bones or nerves. Discharged from hospital 30 September and granted two months leave. Letter from Nolan's father to the WO, 9 November (headed paper, Wm. M. Nolan, Town Clerk's Office, Town Hall, Limerick), advised that a notification had been received telling his son to report to the WO, but he hadn't been feeling too well and had gone away with his mother for a change of air, but would be back the following week. Nolan wrote to the WO, 17 November, complaining that he had been instructed to report to 4th RMF once his sick leave had ended, but he was 3rd RMF. He also noted that he had recently appeared in a gazette as 4th Bn, 'I presume there must be some mistake'. MB at Limerick, 21.11.1916: the wound had greatly improved but he was suffering from bronchitis, unfit for general service for two months. Nolan applied to the WO for a wound gratuity, 28 November. MB at Limerick, 20 December: he was recovering but unfit for general service for 'probably' two months. Rejoined 3rd RMF 21 December. MB at Queenstown, 20.1.1917: fit for general service. Joined 1st RIR 28.2.1917. Letter from father to WO, 28.2.1917, said that Nolan was now attached to 1st RIR and was at Etaples and queried why no wound gratuity had yet been issued. Struck off the strength of 1st RIR, 21.2.1918. Through Dispersal Depot at Alexandria, 29.6.1921. Papers show 3rd RMF, Egyptian Expeditionary Force. Medical status A1. Single. Demobilized 9.8.1921. Partial correspondence on file, April 1922, which indicates that Nolan had been turned down for a wound gratuity. His father and Lord Carson both wrote to the WO asking for a special grant so that Nolan could resume his medical studies. WO passed this on to the Ministry of Labour. No other details on that matter. Employed on home service with the RUR during WW2. File ref: WO339/42331 (110494).

Noonan 2/Lt. Vincent Patrick. Joined 1st RIR from the Leinster Regt, 25.7.1916, and was wounded during an attack 23–6 October 1916. Closed file, ref: (123829).

Northfield 2/Lt. Wilfrid Benjamin. Born 16.8.1898 at Beville House, High Street, March, Cambs. (the family home), the son of Benjamin John and Adelaide Northfield, *née* Allen. His father was a Baptist Minister. Educated at the Grammar School, Newport, Isle of Wight, April 1907–July 1915. Applied for admission to Sandhurst, 21.12.1915, and had no OTC service. Passed entrance examination, February 1916, and awarded a Prize Cadetship. Height 5 foot 5 inches, chest 31–34 inches, weight 114 pounds; '½ inch under chest. Likely to develop'. Commissioned a 2/Lt. from Sandhurst to the ASC, 27.10.1916. To France with the ASC, January

1917, and returned to the UK the following month as under-age. Course of Infantry instruction at Bedford, June 1917. Attached to 1st RIR from the ASC, 6.10.1917. Admitted to hospital with a fungal heart problem, 22.11.1917. Embarked Boulogne–Dover 'approximately' 28 November, 'Sick'.

The MB at 4th London General Hospital, 14.2.1918, declared him permanently unfit for service and placed him on the half-pay list for twelve months. A letter from Northfield to the WO, 14 September, asked if he was eligible for any gratuity. Address 9 Burrowmoor Road, March, Cambs. WO refused as he held a permanent commission. Northfield to WO, 25 October, quoted pay regulations to them and said he was entitled to full pay for twelve months, not half pay. WO replied, 2 December, stating, because he was declared permanently unfit, that circumnavigated the regulations he had quoted. Northfield to WO, 10 December, claimed that he was due out-standing money from his prize Cadetship to Sandhurst and requested payment. WO replied, 28.12.1918, informing that this money could not be paid until the end of the war, and at the moment it had merely been 'suspended'. Formally discharged 23.6.1919. Last attachment listed as RASC attached 1st RIR. Address at discharge given as Burrowmoor Road. File ref: WO339/77453 156913.

O'Connor 2/Lt. Gerald. Joined 1st RIR from 6th RIR, 28.2.1917. Had also served with the Royal Irish Regt. Closed file, ref: 6/83 & 18 (115773).

O'Kane Lt. Paul. The third son of Joseph Patrick O'Kane JP, and Kate O'Kane of Ballycastle, Co. Antrim. His father was a journalist. Gazetted a 2/Lt. in 4th RIR, 8.10.1915, and joined 1st RIR, 5.1.1917. Transferred to England, sick, June 1917. Rejoined 11.10.1917. Rejoined from 25th TMB, 29.1.1918. Died of wounds at No. 109 Field Ambulance, 21.3.1918. Age 23. 1st RIR attached No. 107th TMB.

Irish Life 26.4.1918: ' ... went to the front in December 1916. He took part in many engage-ments including the Cambrai offensive and the battle of the Somme and was promoted to Lieutenant in December last.'

The WO telegram, 23 March, notifying death was addressed 'O'Kane, 2 Granville Villas, Sandhurst Road, Belfast'. Unmarried and died intestate. A short list of effects included a silver identity disc, a religious emblem, and a 'worsted' trench mortar badge. His mother applied for a pension, undated, giving her address as 5 The Glen, Limestone Road, Belfast. His father wrote to the WO, 25.5.1918, stating that he had received a letter from Paul's Colonel advising that he had been promoted a full Lt., 1.7.1917, and presumed that back pay was therefore now due. Letter to WO from the father, 8.7.1918, stated that he had wound up Paul's affairs. His address was given as 35 Cliftonville Road, Belfast. This is also the address that appeared on the letters of adminis-tration as being Paul's home address. Pozières Memorial. Also named on the Ballycastle War Memorial. File ref: WO339/43513 112025.

Oliver Lt. Harold. The Medal Card shows first service as CQMS 2/7351. First overseas date is May 1917. Promoted from the ranks of 7th RIR, 7.10.1917, and joined 1st RIR, 8.10.1917. Wounded, 21.3.1918. Promoted Lt. 7.4.1919. File missing.

O'Neill 2/Lt. Herbert John. Born 12.9.1894, the son of John O'Neill. Educated at Belvedere College, Dublin. His father was clerk of the North Dublin Union and Rural District Council of Dublin, address *Derrylavin*, 60 North Circular Road, Dublin. Applied for a commission, 14.10.1915, giving preferences for the Army Pay Department or ASC. A different hand had added Royal Field Artillery. Single, address *Derrylavin*, no previous military service. It is not clear from his file what happened to this application. Another application for a commission, 17.2.1917: against a question as to whether any application for a commission had previously been made, he answered 'No'. Preference, 'Infantry, an Irish Regiment only', single, bank official, height 5 foot

6½ inches, chest 33–35 inches, weight 119 pounds. Had served three months as a Cadet in Belfast University Contingent OTC (joined 13.11.1916). A report dated 20.2.1917 noted that he was still serving. Attested, 2.3.1917, at Belfast as Rfn 20/297 in 20th RIR and placed on the Army Reserve the same day.

To No. 7 Officer Cadet Battalion at Fermoy, 5.5.1917. Commissioned to 5th RIR, 28.8.1917. OC 5th RIR to WO, 1.10.1917, reported O'Neill's arrival at the battalion that day, 'on first appointment'. Joined 1st RIR from 5th RIR, 10.11.1917. Left the unit 22.11.1917. The MB at Boulogne Base, 7 December, noted 'He is suffering from debility following a severe and prolonged attack of diarrhoea. The board recommended three weeks sick leave to England'. Embarked Boulogne–Folkestone, 8 December, due to 'sickness'. The MB at King George V Hospital, Dublin, 5.1.1918, declared him fit for general service and ordered him to rejoin 5th RIR at Holywood. He submitted an application to his CO, 5th RIR, 13 February, to be allowed to transfer to the RFC. This was forwarded to Irish Command with a recommendation on 21 February. The application was turned down by the RAF standing medical board, 23.3.18, no explanation was given in the letter. The MB at Fargo Military Hospital, Salisbury Plain, 20 June, noted that he fell from a bicycle, April 1918, and hurt his neck. Admitted to King George V Hospital, Dublin, for three weeks. MB stated he was category A but had reported to his unit medical officer that he still had a stiff neck. An x-ray showed no abnormality. Disability rated at zero per cent. Ordered to rejoin unit for duty.

Joined 16th RIR. Left unit suffering from bronchitis, 19.9.1918. Embarked Calais–Dover, 24 September. The MB at 1st Western General Hospital, Liverpool, 10 October, noted that the physical symptoms had all cleared. Granted three weeks sick leave and ordered to report to 5th RIR at Larkhill. Discharged 25.8.1919, last served with 1st RIR, fit for general service, single. Relinquished commission in Special Reserve, 5th RIR, 1.4.1920. Address at this time was *Derrylavin*. File ref: WO339/92544   178667.

O'Riordan Capt. Henry Michael OBE. Born 29.9.1883. Educated at Christian College, Cork. Attested as Pte 8186 in the Inns of Court OTC, 6.12.1915. Address 6 Morrison's Island, Cork; next of kin mother, M. O'Riordan, same address; height 5 foot 8½ inches, weight 131 pounds, chest 36–38 inches, manager. Signed Army Form E624, 19.2.1916. Applied for a commission, 3.7.1916, stating a preference for the infantry, 3rd RMF. To No. 7 Officer Cadet Battalion at Fermoy, 11.8.1916 to 18.12.1916. 3rd RMF attached 1st RIR, 19.2.1917. Joined Base Depot, Le Havre, 24 February.

Joined 1st RIR 3 March. To No. 26 Field Ambulance, sick, 23.3.1917. To No. 25 Field Ambulance, 4 April, with trench fever. Rejoined 1st RIR, 13 May. Struck off the strength, 25.8.1917. Classified medically unfit and proceeded to Base, 26 August. The MB at Etaples, 17 October, declared him unfit for general service for six months. No explanation is on his file. Rejoined No. 16 Infantry Brigade Depot from UK leave, 31 October. To St Omer on POW Duty, 4.11.1917. Discharged with the honorary rank of Capt., 16.10.1919, address still Morrison's Island. The sheet shows H.M. O'Riordan OBE. Last served with RMF attached to No. 270 POW Coy. Married, medical status B2. File ref: 3/101 LC 142800.

O'Sullivan Capt. Arthur Moore. Born at Ootacamund, India, 19.8.1878, the only son of Patrick and Sydney Jane O'Sullivan (daughter of William Daniel Moore MD). Unmarried.

Quis Separabit, vol. 3, no. 1, described the preparations for leaving Aden: 'I can still see "Amos" (Captain A.M. O'Sullivan), our PMC, singing "We're going to war, we're going to b—y war" whilst he and the Mess Staff lightly tossed mess property and mess plate into the boxes. This "lightly tossing" cost us in 1919 £300 for repair of silver.'

Irish Life 30.7.1915: ' … son of the late Mr Patrick O'Sullivan, Advocate General, Madras Presidency … and was educated at Bedford Grammar School and Hertford College, Oxford. He enlisted in 1900 in the Oxfordshire Light Infantry and served in the South African War, receiving the Queen's Medal with four clasps. He obtained a commission in the Royal Irish Rifles in 1902 … and was Adjutant of his regiment in 1910–12. In 1905–7 he was seconded for service with the Northern Nigeria Regiment of the West African Frontier Force [1.10.1905 to 22.11.1907]. Captain O'Sullivan went to the front with his regiment in November 1914 and was wounded at Neuve Chapelle and Mentioned in Despatches [31.5.1915 for gallant and distinguished conduct in the field.]'

During the South African War he was present at operations in the Cape and Orange River Colonies and the Transvaal, April 1900–April 1901. Received a commission in 1st RIR, 23.7.1902, being promoted to Lt. 9.7.1906, and Capt. 11.3.1910. It was he who fired his revolver at midnight, 25/26 December 1914, to signal the end of the Christmas truce in his part of the line. Wounded by machine gun fire while cutting barbed wire, 11.3.1915. Killed in action 9.5.1915. Royal Irish Rifles Graveyard, Laventie, Pas de Calais I.C.1. The CWGC note that he was the son of Mrs E.J. O'Sullivan of Auburn, Greystones, Co. Wicklow. File destroyed.

O'Sullivan, Lt. John Joseph. Born 12.6.1891, the son of Michael J. O'Sullivan. Educated at the National School, Macroom, Co. Cork. Enlisted in the ASC at Clarecastle, 19.2.1916, and appointed Staff Sgt the same day. Father's occupation given as 'rate collector, farmer, etc.'. Appointed Staff Sgt-Major, 8.5.1916. Applied for a commission, 30.9.1916, stating a preference for the ASC, Forage Department. Permanent address Main Street, Macroom, and correspondence address 13 Church Street, Ennis, Co. Clare. Occupation farmer. Presently serving in the ASC Forage Dept. Discharged from the ranks of the ASC, 9 October. Home service only up to this time. Height 5 foot 10½ inches, chest 33½–37½ inches. Commissioned a 2/Lt. in the ASC Forage Dept., 10.10.1916. To No. 2 School of Instruction for Infantry, Elstowe, Bedfordshire, 16.6.1917. Joined 1st RIR, 6.10.1917. Acting rank of Capt., 16.10.1918, relinquished 16.11.1918.

Took over the duties of Transport Officer 8.2.1919. Left unit, 24.3.1919, and embarked Calais–Dover, 26 March, on leave. Wrote a letter to the WO, 5 April, stating that he was presently on UK leave from the Army of Occupation in Germany. His leave would expire 9 April but he was unwell and asked for his leave to be extended. A doctor's certificate was attached certifying bronchitis. The WO extended his leave until 19 April. He applied again for another extension due to an attack of dyspepsia. WO extended his leave until 24 April. Temporarily took command of HQ Coy, 1st RIR, 1.5.1919. Transferred to 15th RIR 22.5.1919. Discharged from RASC Supply Depot, Cologne, 6.5.1920. Lt., acting Capt. Married. File ref: WO339/74294 152618.

Palethorpe 2/Lt. Mervin A. According to the Army List for 1915 he was with 17th RIR having been commissioned 28.1.15. With 8th RIR at Bramshott, 1915. The War Diary noted that he arrived and joined 1st RIR at the front from 13th RIR, 16.2.1916. Wounded 1 July.

Irish Times 10.7.1916: '2/Lt. M.A. Palethorpe, wounded, was sent to a regular battalion at the front from the reserve of the Ulster Division at Ballykinlar. He is a son of Captain A.H. Palethorpe, ASC.'

Promoted to Lt., 1.7.1917, and became Transport Officer, 3.11.17. Closed file, ref: 17/83 (44097).

Palmer Lt. Geoffrey James Head. Born 15.10.1896 at Glenlo Abbey, Bushypark, Galway, the son of James Elliott and Maude Palmer, *née* Head. His father was a merchant and magistrate. Spent four years at Baymount Preparatory School and four at Shrewsbury School. At a medical inspection in London, 25.11.1914, he was noted as being 5 foot 8½ inches tall, chest 33–36 inches, weight 133 pounds, teeth good, and vision 6/6. Nominated for a commission by the headmaster at Shrewsbury, 11.12.1914. This was approved and he was granted a Cadetship at the Royal Military Academy. Gazetted to 3rd R. Irish and attached to 1st RIR, which he joined 18.7.1916.

War Diary, Hohenzollern Redoubt: '9 October 1916. 3 a.m. 2/Lt. Palmer with 12 ORs carried out a most successful enterprise against the hostile trenches. He and 5 men got to within 5 yards of the German parapet but were unfortunately seen, never the less he shot two Germans and several bombs were thrown.'

Whitfeld: 'Palmer did a good "show" last night. He attempted to raid the Hun who, as bad luck would have it, was on the look out and opened fire. Palmer, however, slew two Huns.'

He was wounded in this action and embarked Boulogne–Southampton, 15 October, aboard the *Panama*. A MB at No. 2 Western General Hospital, Manchester, 5 November, recorded that he had suffered multiple grenade wounds to the right loin and left knee. The injuries were described as slight and not permanent, a full recovery was expected in two months. Appeared before a MB at Galway, 28 December, where it was recorded that his knee was still stiff and that he was unfit for general service for three months. There are no further notes on his file until he arrived at Southampton from Rouen, 26.3.1918, having been wounded, 21.3.1918, while attached to 2nd R. Irish, 49th Brigade. The MB, 24 April, noted that he had a bullet wound to the left ankle, there being a clean entry and exit, which was then quite well healed. 'He is able to walk well.' Declared fit for home service. Appeared before a General Court Martial at Durrington Camp, 22.7.1918, charged with absenting himself, 18 June, when he failed to report to 3rd R. Irish at Durrington until 23 June. Pleaded guilty and was sentenced to be reprimanded. Posted to the Labour Corps Base Depot at Boulogne, 19 September, and to No. 239 POW Coy, 27 September. Admitted to No. 51 General Hospital, 17 October, '(VDG)M' and discharged to '3EBN', 19.11.1918.

Applied to resign his commission, 26.7.1919, explaining that he was an only son and that, as his father was dead, he was required to run the family estate. He was, at that time, serving with 3rd R. Irish at Rugeley Camp. The CO backed his application and the WO approved, 12.9.1919, transferring him to the Reserve of Officers. His address at discharge was Glenlo Abbey. File ref: 128656 56443.

Panter Lt.-Col. George William MBE, MP. Educated at Sedburgh School, Yorkshire; Trinity College, Dublin (entered 1912 and served with the OTC), and Sandhurst. Gazetted, 16.12.1914, and joined 1st RIR, 20.3.1915. Joined 2nd RIR, 8.12.1915, at Le Bizet. Promoted Lt. in 1915. 2nd RIR War Diary, 8.3.1916: '2/Lt. G.W. Panter transferred as observer (temporary) to R. Flying Corps.' Wounded and lost his left arm. Mentioned in Despatches, 1.6.1916.

Irish Life 9.6.1916: ' ... is the second son of George William Panter MA, of The Bawn, Foxrock, Co. Dublin.' Later served with the RFC/RAF 1916–18. Appointed T/Capt. and Adjutant 1917. Employed Air Ministry 1918. Awarded the MBE 3.6.1919. Adjutant 3rd RUR 1.9.1921. Capt. in the Regular Army 1.1.1923. Served 1919–35 with the RUR in Italy and the Sudan, reaching the rank of Lt.-Col. He had been appointed Adjutant of 3rd RIR, 1.1.1921, and promoted Capt. 1.1.1923. In 1936 he was residing at Clooneavin, Warrenpoint, Co. Down.

Quis Separabit vol. IX, no. 1, May 1938: 'We were delighted to see Major G.W. Panter MBE, MP, successfully contested the Mourne Division for the Northern Ireland Parliament. It will be interesting to know if Major Panter is the first retired regular officer who has achieved this distinction.'

He had, in fact, been elected unopposed. Attended the Annual Dinner, Dublin Branch, of the Regimental Association 30.4.1938. A daughter was born 15.9.1938. Later resided at Enniskeen, Newcastle, Co. Down. Retired as MP 1945 and died the same year. Closed file, ref: 83rd RFC (44011).

Parke 2/Lt. William Edward. Born 30.12.1894, the son of Kate Parke of 70 Millbrae Road, Langside, Glasgow. Educated at Queen's Park High School, and Kerry's College, Glasgow. Attested, 28.6.1915, in the Queen's Own Royal Glasgow Yeomanry as Pte 2984, later 95689, and signed Army Form E624. Student teacher, height 5 foot 3 inches, weight 119 pounds, chest 32–35 inches, single, next of kin mother, and residing with her. Embarked Southampton–Rouen, 1.2.1916, and joined A Squadron, 14 February. Admitted to No. 73 Field Ambulance, 28 February, and discharged back to his unit, 4 March, no reason stated. Applied for a commission, 5.2.1917, preference infantry. Struck off the strength, 21 April, and posted to the UK for an Infantry Cadet Unit. To No. 8 Officer Cadet Battalion at Lichfield, 5 July. Commissioned a 2/Lt. in 17th RIR, 31 October. On reposting to 1st RIR from 10th RIR, he reported at Detail Camp, 8.4.1918. Wounded, 20 July, and embarked Calais–Dover, 6 August. GSW right elbow. The MB at 2nd London General Hospital, 10 September: the wound was caused by a small piece of shrapnel that had been removed. The wounds were healed and his general condition was good. Recommended one month at a convalescent hospital. The MB at Falmouth Military Hospital, 14 October (admitted 21.9.1918), noted that he 'has made no progress' and was unfit for general or home service for one month. The same MB, 28 October, noted he 'has made a good recovery', fit for general service. Discharged 28.3.1919. Last served with 3rd RIR. Single. Rated A1. Address still at Millbrae Road. File ref: WO339/110996 11/83 209076.

Parkes Lt. Herbert Percy. Born 1893, the son of Mr H.C. Parkes, Carleton, Sherwood Park Road, Sutton, Surrey. Served with Dulwich College OTC. Enlisted as Pte 1006 in 28th London Regt (Artists Rifles), 7.11.1911. Dental medical student at Guy's Hospital, age 18 years 7 months, height 5 foot 8 inches, and chest 30–33½ inches. Embodied, 5.8.1914, and signed Army Form E624 at Abbott's Langley, 23.10.1914. Embarked from Southampton for France, 26.10.1914. Gazetted a 2/Lt., 3.3.1915, and joined 1st RIR from the Cadet School, Bailleul, 18.3.1915.

Wounded, 9.5.1915, and embarked Boulogne–Dover aboard the *St Andrew*, 11 May. He was on leave, 16.5.1915 to 26.6.1915, mainly at O Ward, No. 3 General Hospital, Wandsworth, London SW. The MB report refers to a gun shot wound to his right leg: 'wound gaping and very dirty'. Still attending hospital, 16.1.1916, but was discharged at the end of February from the same hospital. There is a reference at this stage of his file that he was 1st RIR attached to 9th DCLI and residing at Bournemouth.

Arrested at 9.30 p.m., 17.3.1916, for being drunk in the Hippodrome Theatre, Boscombe, and twice gave the wrong name to APM. A WO letter, 10 April, to GOCIC Southern Command, Salisbury, stated that Parkes was to be court-martialled. Parkes wrote to the WO, 17 April, and noted that he had been placed under arrest, 15 March, and was released the following day. He also reported that he was then being paid daily in arrears. Tried at Wareham, 16 June, and found guilty, receiving a severe reprimand.

The MB at Wandsworth, 25 July, reported that his wound was very nearly healed and that he could walk 100 yards. Joined 3rd RIR at Belfast, 30.9.1916, and applied for a wound pension, 20.10.1916. Promoted Lt. 17.8.1917. A note dated 27.5.1918 stated that he was still doing duty at Alexandra Dock, Belfast, and did not go to England with 3rd RIR. The MB at Belfast, 30.5.1918, found that his condition remained stationary and returned him to Alexandra Dock. He was then deemed permanently unfit and marked to relinquish his commission due to ill health. The release date is unclear but he had left the Army by December 1918. File ref: 49743.

Patterson Capt. William Reginald Lambert. Born 4.3.1893, the son of George B. and Mary E. Patterson, *née* Meek. His father was a bank cashier. Entered Trinity College, Dublin, 1911. Applied for a commission, 29.3.1912. Gazetted a 2/Lt., Supplementary Reserve, 2nd R. Scots Fusiliers, April 1912. Permanent address Bank of Ireland, Londonderry. Had served with the Junior OTC at St Bees School, Camberley. Height 5 foot 10 inches and chest 32½–35½ inches. Accepted for training on condition that his chest measurement increased within six months to meet the minimum height/chest ratio. His chest was half an inch below requirement.

Joined the BEF with 1st R. Scots Fusiliers, 13.8.1914. Left the unit, 6.9.1914, and disembarked Southampton, 16 September. Had suffered a 'nervous breakdown with complications'. He wrote to the WO, 19.9.1914, giving his new address as Cloonaslea, Portrush, Co. Antrim. Held the rank of Capt. by 10.10.1914. His file contains a series of references to medical boards, but there is no paperwork giving details. The OC, 8th RIR, Ballykinlar Camp, wrote a memo, 27.4.1915, to HQ Scottish Command requesting the transfer of Patterson to the Special Reserve, RIR. No. 2 District, Scottish Command, Hamilton, replied granting the request, 9 May. They said that the transfer did not reflect any cause for concern with Patterson's honour, character, or professional efficiency. Patterson wrote to the WO confirming that he wanted the transfer to be near his home, financial reasons, and he knew several officers in the RIR. The MB, 6 June, certified him fit for home duties, and on 17 June, fit for general service. The OC, Ulster Division, 25.6.1915, passed a recommendation to the WO for Patterson to be promoted to Lt. and appointed Adjutant of 8th RIR. ADMS Ulster Division, 10 July, notified the WO that Patterson, 8th RIR, was unfit for active service due to neuritis in his left arm and leg. A request was made for an urgent medical board. Patterson reported for duty with 3rd RIR in Dublin, 19 July. The MB at King George V Hospital, Dublin, 31 August, did not think that he would ever again be fit for general service.

In October 1915 he was a speaker, organiser, and recruiting officer in Ireland and was appointed Adjutant of Command Depot, 12.10.1915. Patterson wrote to the WO, 13 November, requesting a war gratuity. The MB at Cork, 27 November: he had lost his sight in his left eye, but was fit for home duty. He wrote to the WO in July 1916 asking if he had to apply to renew his pension after 11.8.1916. The MB at Belfast, 11.4.1917: he had much improved but was still unfit for general service. Appointed OC Brigade Bombing and Lewis Gun School in France, 31.8.1917, and later posted to 1st RIR. Wounded (GSW) at Passchendaele, 30.11.1917, while in command of A Coy. Embarked Boulogne–Dover, 5 December. Admitted to hospital in Dublin, 22.2.1918, reason unclear. Placed on the retired list due to ill health, 10.6.1918. His address was given as Craiglockhart War Hospital, Edinburgh.

Called to the Irish Bar, 1921, and became a solicitor in 1930. Applied for a job in the Colonial Office during 1932. The WO gave a satisfactory reference. Patterson wrote to the WO in 1936 and offered his services to the Army or Air Force in a legal capacity. The WO replied that there was a very long waiting list. Applied for the Emergency Reserve of Officers, 8.3.1940, but was not accepted. File ref: WO339/8718 18310.

Patton Capt. Edward MC. Gazetted a 2/Lt., 21.10.1917, and joined 1st RIR the same day. Appointed Adjutant and a/Capt. 9.11.1917. Awarded a Bar to his MC in May 1918. Relinquished the position of Adjutant, 12.7.1918. Promoted Lt. 21.4.1919. Closed file, ref: (249383).

Phillips 2/Lt. Joined 1st RIR from the RWF, 31.10.1916, and was struck off the strength of the battalion, 14.11.1916, no reason being given. There is not enough information in the War Diary to make a positive identification.

Pollin 2/Lt. Robert Kelly. Born Shankill, Antrim, 16.6.1897, the eldest son of James Moore Pollin (a member of the firm of Robert Kelly & Son, solicitors, 43 Lr Sackville Street, Dublin, and Belfast), and Martha Pollin, *née* Corbitt, of *Westhoek*, Taunton Avenue, Belfast. Articled as a solicitor. Enlisted at Belfast, 8.1.1916, as Rfn 19/346 in 19th RIR. Height 5 foot 8 inches, weight 125 pounds, chest 32½–34½ inches. Applied for a commission, 21.3.1916, giving his first preference for the ASC, and his second for 19th RIR. With 19th RIR Cadet Corps, November 1915–May 1916. To No. 7 Officer Cadet Battalion at the Curragh, 29.5.1916. Commissioned a 2/Lt. in 4th RIR, 4.9.1916. Joined 1st RIR from 4th RIR, 12.3.1917. Admitted to No. 39 General Hospital at Le Havre, 18.3.1917, 'sick, a slight case'. No explanation given but discharged to 'Reinforcements Havre', 27.5.1917.

A will dated 27.7.1917 left his estate to his father, James Moore Pollin, *Albertville*, Taunton Avenue, Lansdowne Road, Belfast. Killed in action 31.7.1917. A letter from his father to the WO, 29 August, complained that all of Robert's effects (including his revolver and wristlet watch) had not been returned to him by Messrs Cox & Co. 'May you be good enough to tell me why? Surely all my poor lad's effects ought to be returned?' WO replied, 5 September, stating that, as far as they were aware, everything that was sent to Cox & Co. had been forwarded to him. If anything else is sent in then it will also be returned to him.

Irish Life 31.8.1917: ' … was educated at the Belfast Royal Academy and was a law apprentice with his father when he volunteered for service, obtaining his commission in the Royal Irish Rifles in September 1916. He was a very capable officer and was killed whilst bravely leading his platoon in an attack.' Tyne Cot Memorial. File ref: WO339/110996 135780.

Pollock Lt. Norman Varien. Born 27.4.1894, the son of Hugh McDowell Pollock JP, and Annie M. Pollock, *née* Marshall, 11 College Gardens, Belfast. Educated at Felsted School; Campbell College, Belfast (until July 1911), and in Switzerland. His father was a member of the Belfast Board of Trade, Marine Dept. (one of the members elected by ship owners), Belfast Chamber of Commerce, a city magistrate, and later became MP for South Belfast and the first Minister of Finance in the Government of Northern Ireland. Applied for a commission, 9.9.1914, requesting 'a Reserve unit of infantry'. Single, no previous military experience, address 11 College Gardens, profession 'Gentleman'. Height 5 foot 10¾ inches, chest 33½–36½ inches, weight 149 pounds. Left unit, 3rd RIR, 30.7.1915, and embarked Dublin–Southampton the next day. Promoted to Lt. 31.7.1915. Joined 1st RIR 7.8.1915. Struck off the strength of the battalion, 23 October, suffering from Catarrh and Jaundice. Wrote to the WO, 8 November, advising that his leave would expire on 19 November and asked for a further MB. The OC 3rd RIR wrote to the WO, 2.12.1915, advising that Pollock reported for duty, 29 November, and was found fit for general service. Posted to 2nd RIR which he joined 13.8.1916. Left unit, 27.1.1917, on leave to the UK. A letter to WO, 5.2.1917, from James Graham MD, headed paper from the City of Belfast Coroners Office, advised that he had examined Pollock at home and found him to be suffering from acute bronchial catarrh, Pollock being currently on leave from 2nd RIR. Leave was extended to 14 February. ADMS, Belfast District, to Military Hospital, Belfast, 16 February: a medical officer was to be sent to visit Pollock at home and report. The report on the same day stated that his cardiac action was very poor and that he was unfit to travel. The MB at Coomassie, 14.1.1918: Pollock now shown as Lt., Gold Coast Regt, West African Frontier Force. Very thin and anaemic. Poor physique. Numerous attacks of fever had left him lacking both physical and mental energy. Unsuitable for service in Africa and unlikely to recover there; recommend evacuation to the UK.

A letter from the Governor, Accra, to WO, 8.2.1918: Pollock had been granted leave of absence to the UK on medical grounds. A letter from the Colonial Office to WO, 16 March: Pollock's appointment to the Gold Coast Regt was terminated and they asked for details of his re-absorption into the Home Army. A reply from WO, 30 April, stated that there was a MB, 4 April, and he was declared unfit for duty. The point they were making was that, as Pollock had been with the Gold Coast Regt, they presumed that it would be the Colonial Office who would sanction his sick leave, and therefore be responsible for his pay of 57p per day. MB, 30.10.1918: fit for general service. From this date he came under Army funds for pay. WO instructions to Pollock ordered him to report to 3rd RIR at Larkhill, Salisbury Plain, 'forthwith'. A telegram from Pollock to WO, 11.12.1918, stated he was 'Unfit to travel for period 12 days. Please grant extension. Medical certificate follows'. This was forwarded to OC 3rd RIR. WO to Director of Operations, Salisbury, 1.1.1919, asked whether Pollock had yet rejoined. This was repeated, 17 January. WO to Salisbury, 4 February: orders for Pollock to rejoin 3rd RIR were cancelled. WO to Pollock, same date, orders to rejoin cancelled, 'Please return railway warrant sent you'. WO to Pollock, 22.2.1919, referred to a MB on 9.1.1919 and stated that he was to be retired on account of ill health.

A letter from Jacqueline Sefton, his daughter, 22 Stormont Park, Belfast, to M.o.D., 4.9.1984, asked for details of his service as they were needed for her admission to the UVF Hospital,

Circular Road, Belfast. M.o.D. replied, 20.9.1984, advising that he served with the RIR, 15.8.1914 to 3.3.1919, and retired due to ill health, 4.3.1919. File ref: WO339/61870 5701.

Quilliam Brigadier Cyril David OBE. Born 11.6.1898 in Dublin. To RMC, August 1916. Gazetted a 2/Lt. in the RIR, 1.5.1917. Joined 1st RIR from Base, 24.6.1917, and was wounded, 16.8.1917.

Falls: 'The important "pill box", known as Anzac Farm gave some trouble, but was finally surrounded and captured with a number of prisoners, by Lt. C.D. Quilliam and his platoon, and held until the counter-attack.' Promoted Lt. 1.11.1918.

Employed Ministry of Pensions. British Military Mission to the Interallied Armies, Occupation Forces, Constantinople, Turkey, February 1919 to October 1921. Promoted Capt., 19.5.1927. D Coy Commander in 2nd RUR until 1936 when he left for an appointment with the forces in Palestine. Promoted to Major in 1938.

Blackthorn, vol. 2, no. 7, 1972: 'Cyril Quilliam died at his home in Ontario, Canada, on March 28, 1972. He was 73. His service to his country was both unusual and distinguished. It developed in three spheres; the military phase; the politico–military years and finally the period he spent on the Editorial Staff of *The Times* as its Middle East correspondent. The second and third spheres seemed to emerge naturally as his special talents unfolded.

'The purely military record shows that he was commissioned in the Royal Irish Rifles in 1917; was wounded in France in the same year and then had periods of regimental service in 2nd Battalion, The Royal Ulster Rifles, in South India and in Poona, Madras, and Khartoum from 1929–33. He attended the Staff College at Camberley in 1934–5. His politico–military years were (i) from 1919 to 1923 when he was engaged on Intelligence work in Constantinople with the Inter-Allied Armies and, as well, did some service with the Turkish Gendarmerie; (ii) from 1924–9 when he served with the Royal Corps of Signals on intelligence and cypher duties in Baghdad, Teheran, and Palestine and (iii) from 1936–45 mostly spent in Palestine or Egypt on intelligence work.

'In the war years (1939–45) he held successively appointments as GSO (1) Greece, DDMI GHQ Cairo, DDMI Baghdad and finally (1943–5) the very important post of Head of Military Intelligence (PICME). By any standards, this is a most impressive record. His outstanding gift for languages, an obsession, almost, to get to the bottom of things and his interest in people led inevitably to the specialisation in Intelligence in which, I make out he spent 18 of his 28 years of Army Service. Without doubt he made a considerable contribution to the successful military operations in the Middle East. Having worked closely with him in 1942–3 and having had a hand in his selection as head of PICME I was not surprised when *The Times* tempted him with the offer of a post on their Editorial Staff as Middle East correspondent. His acceptance of this plum job in 1945 necessitated his retirement from the Army. For seven strenuous years he served in this appointment and certainly made his mark. In its obituary notice *The Times* noted his "abiding loyalty to those he served combined with a willingness to rebel against authority in private when he believed it necessary", "the unpopularity of his opinions never caused him to alter them" and "the depth of the knowledge of the area which produced many despatches more profound than those his competitors could offer".

'He never lost interest in the regiment. It is the picture of him as a regimental soldier that I think most as I write. We admired his intellectual equipment, his skill as a musician and the zest with which he took part in regimental life. It was a joy to me and others to see him last year at the Royal Irish Rangers' dinner in London. My wife and I were looking forward to seeing him and his wife at our home this summer. He married Helen when he was doing duty in Teheran. When news came through there was the usual speculation. When we saw her we all fell in love with her. I wager that the sentiment still stands today amongst those who came under her spell in regimental life. In reference to this marriage *The Times* mentioned that "thereafter their home became a salon of military, social, and political discussion". We mourn with Helen the loss of Cyril – we extend our deepest sympathy. — General J.S. Steele.' Closed file, ref: 83 MGC (147644).

Quinn Lt. John Peter. Born 2.8.1887. Applied for a commission, 31.7.1915, requesting infantry. Single, present address for correspondence, 29142, No. 2 Coy, 30th Reserve Bn, Napier Barracks, Shorncliffe, Kent. Previously served 6.2.1907 to 24.2.1907 'approximately' in the RDF – purchased discharge. Currently serving with 30th Reserve Bn, Canadian Expeditionary Force, having transferred with a draft from the Machine Gun Section, 47th Bn, CEF. Gazetted a 2/Lt. in 6th RMF, October 1915.

Left 2nd RMF, 26.8.1916, and embarked Le Havre–Southampton, 2 September. Wounded right arm. Address: The Donahies, Raheny, Co. Dublin. Medical Boards: 8 September, unfit for general or home service one month; 11 October, unfit for one month; 14 November, unfit for another month. Joined 1st RIR from 6th RMF, 20.1.1917. Left unit, 5.3.1917, embarked Boulogne –Dover, 9 March, aboard the *St Denis*. Sprained ankle. Later joined 5th RMF. Promoted Lt., 1917, and returned to 2nd RMF. Left unit, 15.3.1918, and embarked Le Havre–Southampton, 24 March. 'Wounded'. MB, 30 April, unfit for general or home service for six weeks. MB, 31 May, declared A1 fit and granted three weeks leave and then to report to 5th RMF at Fort George.

Court-martialled at Harfleur, 25.1.1919, for impeding an officer legally exercising his authority. Sentence: dismissal commuted to a severe reprimand. Discharged 31.3.1919. Last served with 7/8th Royal Inniskilling Fusiliers. Occupation in civil life, sugar planter. Medical category A1. Married. Entered Trinity College, Dublin, 1919. Commission in Special Reserve relinquished 1.4.1920. About 1930 he was still residing at The Donahies. File ref: WO339/43830 112418.

Reed Capt. Charles Henry Rowe MC. Born 17.10.1896, the son of Arthur Fasnell Graham Reed, a stockbroker, and Alice Clay Reed. Educated at Sidcup Hall College, and Cranbourne School of Mines, serving with the Sidcup OTC, which he left in 1912. Enlisted as Pte 3628 in 5th RWK, 6.8.1914. Mining student, height 5 foot 8½ inches, chest 31–33 inches. Transferred to 4th RWK, 24.10.1914, and had no overseas service with this regiment. Applied for a commission at Tilbury Fort, 23.6.1915. His first appointment was 25.9.1915. Joined 1st RIR as a 2/Lt. from 3rd Leinster Regt, 25.7.1916, and took part in the attack of 23.10.16.

Whitfeld: 'E.C. Lloyd in one of his nasty moods. He lived up to his reputation in this attack, so I am told, by saying to young Reed, who was an exceedingly brave fellow and who merely asked E.C.L. if he should wait awhile till the shelling died down before advancing. This brought from E.C.L. the remark, "Are you afraid to die?" while he, so saying, dived into a dugout.'

Wounded, 31.7.1917, rejoined, 13.8.1917, and appointed acting Capt. Proceeded to England, 8.7.1918, for a six months tour of duty at home and was demobilized, 14.3.1919, medical class A1. At that time his address was given as *Barcaldene*, Granville Road, Sidcup, Kent. File ref: 3/100 83 110498.

Reid Lt.-Col. Alexander Daniel DSO. Born in Edinburgh 2.2.1882, the son of Capt. William Thomas Reid JP, of Ardmeallie and Hazelwood, Banffshire, and Mrs Margaret Grieg Reid (daughter of James Grey) of Cowickan Station, Vancouver, BC, Canada. Educated at Westminster and Sandhurst. He was a Lt. in the Indian Army from 28.10.1902, serving on the Staff Corps and retired 26.4.1909.

Residing in Canada at the outbreak of war, he rejoined and was appointed to 7th Royal Inniskilling Fusiliers as a Major. In February 1915 he went to France with this unit. When they were at Leuze Wood, he had been left out of the battle but came forward on a visit during the night of 5.9.1916. The next day his CO, Lt.-Col. H.N. Young DSO, was seriously wounded and Reid assumed command. He himself was wounded soon afterwards. A WO telegram was sent to his mother, 11 September, advising that her son had been admitted to hospital in Rouen, 8 September, 'with slight gunshot wound right eye'. Admitted to hospital in London, 12 September, with his name appearing on the wounded list in the *Morning Post*, 18 September. Rejoined his unit, 31.12.1916, and acted as CO until the return of Col. Young. Then served continuously as Second-in-Command with this battalion until 7.7.1917, and was awarded the DSO, 4.6.1917. 'Not invested. Warrant not sent.' Took over command of 1st RIR, 8.7.1917.

Whitfeld: 'He arrived with the BM and got to work at once. Rather frightened us all and sacked some of the HQ Staff right away. I liked him very much. He was very thorough indeed.'

Killed in action, 31.7.1917. See main text. A telegram was sent to his mother, 3 August. She administered his will and requested that his DSO should be given to her other son, Lt. Henry Francis Reid 'now serving in France' with 7th Inniskillings. He had a sister Rachel Duff Reid also residing at the Vancouver address. Mentioned in Despatches, 22.5.1917, and awarded the Silver Medal for Military Valour (Italy), *London Gazette* 26.5.1917. Ypres (Menin Gate) Memorial.

Riddell Capt. Roderick Cranstoun. Commissioned a 2/Lt. in 7th RWF, 9.10.1915, and served with 3/7th RWF. Later attached to 1/24th (County of London) London Regt, joining the battalion in France where he saw action. Joined 1st RIR from 4th RWF, 31.10.1916. Struck off the strength, 25.7.1917, when he rejoined 4th RWF. Promoted to Lt., 1.7.1917, and remained in France until the end of the war. He commanded a company from 21.4.1918 to 14.6.1918 with the rank of a/Capt. File missing.

Robb Capt. George Cyril. Born 9.12.1894, the son of John Robb, *Tivoli*, Castle Avenue, Clontarf, Dublin. Attended Campbell College, Belfast, until July 1912, when he went to Trinity College, Dublin. He was a medical student at the time of his enlistment and a cadet in the OTC. Applied for a commission, 5.8.1914, and was gazetted a 2/Lt. in 3rd RIR, 15.8.1914. Promoted to Lt., 8.5.1915, and joined 1st RIR, 18.5.1915. Returned to the UK suffering with pleurisy, 5.11.1915. The MB declared him fit, 6.6.1916. Joined 2nd RIR, 13.8.1916. Developed acute rheumatism at Thiepval, 27.9.1916, and left the unit, 30 September. Returned to the UK, 3.10.1916, and was not declared fit again until 20.4.1917. Promoted Capt. 16.3.1917. Rejoined 1st RIR and took over command of C Coy, 20.8.1917.

Wounded, 19.9.1917, GSW right forearm, and rejoined from hospital, 5.10.1917, as an a/Capt., resuming command of C Coy. Wounded again, 30.11.1917, by shell fire and transferred to England, 14 December. Demobilized, 25.2.1918, and remobilized, 27.8.1918. Rejoined 1st RIR, 7.12.1918, transferring to 12th RIR, 22.2.1919, and served in Germany. Discharged, 19.11.1919, and returned to Trinity College 1920, receiving his BA and BDS 1922. Enrolled in the Officers Emergency Reserve, 27.10.1938, but there is no indication on his file that he was ever called up. At that time he was practising as a dental surgeon and residing at 22 Hoghton Street, Southport, Lancs. File ref: 47225.

Rodney Major Lennox George Brydges. Gazetted a 2/Lt., 4.5.1898, and served in the South African War, 1899–1901, with operations in the Transvaal (May and June 1900); Orange River Colony (June to 29.11.1900); Cape Colony, South of the Orange River (1899–1900). Taken prisoner by the Boers at Stormberg. Received the Queen's Medal with three clasps. Promoted Lt. 24.2.1900, and Capt. 16.6.1906. Wounded during the battle of Neuve Chapelle, 10–13 March 1915, while serving with 1st RIR.

The Burgoyne Diaries: 'Rodney got a very bad wound shattering his wrist. He held it up to his men, "Look what the … have done, boys – have at 'em".'

Promoted to Major, 27.5.1915. Attached to 3rd RIR in 1917 on recruiting duties. He was on retired pay 1919. In 1938 his address was Royal Portsmouth Corinthian Y.C., 62 Clarence Parade, Southsea, Hants. File missing.

Roe 2/Lt. Patrick Joseph. Born 11.4.1893. Matriculated at the Royal University of Ireland, June 1909. Had applied for a commission in the ASC, 17.8.1915. Applied again, 8.9.1915, expressing a preference for 'Infantry, any unit in Irish Brigade'. Single, home address, Seatown Place, Dundalk, Co. Louth. Practised as a solicitor in Francis Street, Dundalk.

Dundalk Democrat, 25.9.1915: 'Mr Patrick J. Roe BA, solicitor, son of the late Mr Thomas Roe, proprietor and editor of the *Democrat*, has received a commission as 2nd Lieutenant in the 6th Leinsters and leaves for Cork next week to commence his training. Mr Roe surrenders for the time being a fine and promising practice at the local Bar, built up by ability, character, and that close attention to detail which is the chief element in the making of a successful career. It is no small sacrifice that he makes in relinquishing, even for a time, so fine a prospect. It is, however, a sacrifice that has been made by many high spirited and patriotic young Irishmen of his profession, who have followed the insistent call of conscience from a life of ease and comfort to one of unaccustomed hardship and danger. We know that whatever lies before him Mr Roe will acquit himself well; and that when he returns to civil life at the end of this war he will have done credit to his name and to his native town.

'We think that the example given by Lt. Roe will not be lost upon other young men of his class who are free to join the army, but who show no sign of being alive to their responsibility in this crisis. Every man, of course, is free to serve or refuse service; and many who would gladly lend a hand are deterred by duties that cannot be evaded. But there are others who prefer ease and personal safety to a higher call of service and sacrifice. They do not lack good example. Mr John Redmond's only son is with the Irish Brigade. Mr John Fitzgibbon's son, a class-fellow of Lt. Roe, has given his life gloriously in the cause of liberty at the Dardanelles.'

Joined 1st RIR from the Leinster Regt, 25.7.1916. (6th Leinsters transferred to General List, attached No. 25 TMB.) *Dundalk Democrat* 23.12.1916: ' ... was in Dundalk during the week on a few days leave from the front. Lt. Roe has been in the trenches for several months, with a trench mortar battery, in the region of the famous Hohenzollern redoubt and on the Somme. His many friends were delighted to see him in the pink of condition and in excellent spirits.'

Left unit 4.3.1917. 'Wounded 4th March.' Home address Hampton Terrace, Dublin. Embarked Boulogne–Dover, 8 March, aboard the *St Denis. Dundalk Democrat*, 10.3.1917: 'Intimation was received during this week that Lt. P.J. Roe, solicitor (son of the late Mr Thomas Roe, editor and proprietor of this paper), has been wounded. A subsequent cheery letter from Lt. Roe himself relieved his family and friends of apprehension. He "stopped a piece of shrapnel" is his own cheerful way of putting the matter; and he wrote on his way to a home hospital. Lt. Roe has been nearly a year in France with a trench mortar battery.'

The MB at King George V Hospital, Dublin, 23 April, recorded two superficial bullet wounds, left loin, almost healed. Unfit for military duty for ten weeks from date of wounding. Letter to WO, 7 May, applied for a wound gratuity. MB at the Tipperary Military Hospital, 29 June: wounds now recovered but had been suffering attacks of bronchitis; fit for light duty, unfit for general service for two months. Granted three weeks leave and told to report to Irish Command, Dublin. Leave address, Seatown Place. Joined 3rd Leinsters at Cork, 23 July. MB, 31.8.1917, at Limerick, 'he has now quite recovered'. Ordered to stay with 3rd Leinsters and await further orders. *Dundalk Democrat*, 7.9.1918: ' ... who is home on leave ... served in Egypt and Palestine after his recovery and was subsequently sent back to the Western Front, where he has been for some months.' Slightly wounded, 9.10.1918, while attached to a TMB. Discharged 15.1.1919. Single. Rated A1. File ref: WO339/43624.

Ross Sqd./Ldr Alexander Jacob Myer MBE. Born 28.2.1885 at 224 Upper Parliament Street, Liverpool. There is a copy of his birth certificate on file that shows his parents as David Rosenbaum and Leah Ann Rosenbaum (formerly Schonstadt). His father was as a cabinetmaker.

Educated at Liverpool Institute, and Merchant Taylors. He was a Trooper with the Liverpool Troop, King's Colonials (Imperial Yeomanry), about 1907. Using the name A. Murray Ross, he wrote to the WO, 22.11.1915, on headed paper, 'The London Aerodrome, Hendon NW'. He had called to see Major Warner on the 12th regarding a commission as Assistant Equipment Officer in the RFC. Unfortunately the Grahame White Aviation Company would not release him from his position as manager of the flying school, for the time being. Major Warner replied, 25.11.1915, and told him to get in touch when the company was prepared to let him go. A letter to Major Warner, 14.3.1916, asked if he could spare a few minutes to see him.

Applied for a commission, 27.3.1916, stating a preference for the RFC. He was then called Alexander Jacob Myer Ross, but was still the manager of the Grahame White Flying School. Permanent address Grove Road, Wallasey, Cheshire. Address for correspondence, Colin Park, The Hyde, London NW. A WO letter, 28.3.1916, noted that Ross apparently had multiple personalities, and requested that he please explain what was going on. Ross replied, 29.3.1916: Rosenbaum was changed to Ross by deed poll. He had never used the first names Jacob Myer but forgot, when he filled in the application for a commission, and included them. Murray was a family name of his mother and he used it at her request. His correct name was Alexander Jacob Myer Ross.

Appointed a 2/Lt. in the RFC Special Reserve, 17.5.1916, joining at South Farnborough the same day. Left the Southern Aircraft Depot, Farnborough, and embarked for France, 15.6.1916. Promoted to Lt., RFC, 1.7.1917. Sent on three months attachment to 1st RIR, 22.8.1917, and was recalled to the RFC, 10.11.1917. T/Capt. RAF, 1.4.1918. For the remainder of the war he served with R.F. Salvage Section. Mentioned in Despatches, 31.12.1918 and 11.7.1919, and made a Member of the Order of the British Empire, 3.6.1919. After the war he served mostly with Stores Depots in India, Egypt, and the Mediterranean. Subsequent promotions were Flying Officer (Stores) 17.6.1920, Flight Lt. (Stores) 1.1.1921, and Sqn./Ldr (Stores) 1.7.1926. From 1928 to 1932 he worked on stores staff duties with 10 Group HQ, Lee-on-Solent. Placed on the Retired List, 28.2.1935. File ref: 136745.

Ross Capt. Arthur John. Born 22.5.1876 at Busby House, Renfrewshire, the eldest son of Charles John and Clarissa Findlay Ross (daughter of I. Wyllie Guild, Park Terrace, Glasgow), Oaken Holt, Oxfordshire, and Grosvenor Street, London SW. Educated at Britannia and had been a Mercantile Marine Officer, 1892–9, joining Paget's House 1899.

Fought in the South African War (3.2.1900 to 24.6.1901) with the Imperial Yeomanry and later served as a Lt. with the 18th London Regt TF (London Irish Rifles). Married the Hon. Una Mary Dawson (later Lady Una Ross), 30.7.1904, at St Stephen's Church, Kensington, daughter of the Hon. Anthony Lucius Dawson (son of the 1st Earl of Dartrey) and Mary Frances, Baroness de Ros (Premier Baroness of England), Old Court, Strangford, Co. Down, and 22 Wellington Court, Knightsbridge, SW. His address was Busby House, Renfrew. They had two sons: Peter, 8.8.1906, and Charles Dudley Anthony, 5.10.1907. Gazetted to 5th RIR in August 1904 and promoted to Capt., 7.6.1914. According to *Thom's Directory*, 1912, he was a magistrate for Co. Down residing at Old Court.

Joined 1st RIR, 8.5.1915, the day before the unit suffered severe casualties at Rouges Bancs, but did not take part in the attack. He was Battalion Commander at Bac St Maur in the Divisional Reserve billets, 11–17 May 1915. One of the officers presiding at the FGCM of L/Cpl P. Sands, 30.8.1915 (later executed).

B Coy Commander. Wounded, 1.7.1916. 'Fragments of metal above and below left elbow, no bone damage, damage to left hand', and 'He is also suffering from shock'. See main text. Evacuated to the UK, 6 July.

The MB declared him unfit for two months, 12 July. This was extended for a further two months, 12 September. A report, 1 November, said that he had been in a nursing home for six weeks and was still exhibiting shock symptoms. The MB at Kensington General Hospital, London, 2 November: unfit for another three months. The MB, 31.1.1917: unfit for general service for a further two months. It added another two months, 3 March, but, on examination 10 April, declared him fit. Rejoined the battalion, 4 May. During the attack of 31.7.1917 he was the acting liaison officer to 2nd Lincs.

Killed in action, 16.8.1917, and there are conflicting reports as to what happened. 25711 Cpl P.I. O'Connor, at No. 1 War Hospital, Reading, 18.9.1917: ' ... killed by a shell crossing parapet in charge at Armentiers. His leg was blown off and he could not possibly have lived.' 7184 Cpl Toner, Etaples, 10.9.1917: 'He had his head blown off in the affair at Ypres on 16th August. I saw his headless body lying in a shell hole about 400 yards out from our front line, as I went past in the action.' 43893 J. Jeffcott referred to Capt. Ross' tattooed arm being found whilst going over the lines at 7 a.m. on the 16th. 7870 Rfn A. Madaine had him killed by a shell at 4 a.m., 'head was cut clean off'. Against Madaine's report had been typed 'a very clear and intelligent informant'. 8978 Rfn W. Reilly, 1st RIR Bn Transport: 'I took his body down to be buried to a spot about ¾ of a mile to the right of Ypres. It is about 100 yards off the main rood on the left going into Ypres from Menin. When I left there was no name put on that grave.'

A telegram was sent to his wife, 20 August, reporting Ross as missing on the 16th. His death was accepted for official purposes, 18.4.1918. An estate of £3,697.90 was left to his widow. Tyne Cot Memorial.

Samman Major James Galloway Stanley Wood. Born 30.9.1884. Gazetted a 2/Lt. in 5th Rifle Bde, 18.12.1901. Served in the South African War: operations in Cape Colony and Orange River Colony (14.1.1902 to 31.5.1902). Received the Queen's Medal with three clasps, and was made an honorary 2/Lt. in 3rd RIR, 4.10.1902, being promoted to Lt., 29.6.1903, and Capt., 15.12.1907. Transferred to 3rd RIR, 8.4.1905. Mobilized, 5.8.1914, and promoted to Major, 18.9.1915. Joined 1st RIR, 19.5.1916, and went sick, 29.6.1916, being admitted to hospital the following day. Embarked for the UK, 2 July, aboard the *Panama*. Suffering from trench foot and general debility, being granted leave 6.7.1916 to 6.8.1916.

The MB at Belfast, 17.2.1917, noted that he had recovered. However, he appeared again before the Board, 17 March, as he was then recovering from an attack of hepatitis and was in a very weak and debilitated state. MB, 21 April: unfit for two months. The hepatitis was caused by 'chill and exposure'. MB, 15.6.1917: 'he is now fit for general service', and ordered him to rejoin at Belfast.

Demobilized from command of 2/4th The Queen's, 8.11.1919. Had last served with the Army of Occupation in Germany. Medical category A, married, home address *Cliffholme*, Tynemouth, Northumberland. Mobilized 9–26.4.1921. At that time his home address was 62 Church Road, Richmond, Surrey. Applied to resign his commission, 24.10.1921. File ref: WO339/65355 140408.

Sargent 2/Lt. Reginald William Fitzgerald. Born 20.6.1882 at Exeter, son of the Revd John FitzGerald Sargent, Clerk in Holy Orders, and Clara Catherine Sargent. Enlisted at Brighton, 25.8.1914, as Pte 235 in 8th R. Sussex Regt. This set of attachment papers shows his name as Reginald Fizgerald Sargent, and declared age as 29 years 66 days. Single, height 5 foot 9½ inches, chest 35–37 inches, tattooed on both arms.

His will dated 26.5.1915 left his estate to his father, mother, brothers, and sisters to divide as they saw fit. First overseas date 31.5.1915 to 7th R. Sussex Regt. To No. 36 Field Ambulance, 17.10.1915, 'NYD'. To No. 33 CCS, 21 October, with influenza. Admitted to No. 9 General Hospital, Rouen, 29 October. To Hospital Ship *St Patrick* for passage to the UK, 16 November. To Military Hospital at Brockhurst. Discharged 8.1.1916. Applied for a commission, 26.12.1915. The papers show his name as Reginald William Fitzgerald Sargent. Preference infantry, 18th R. Irish or The Buffs. Single. Occupation, solicitor and notary public in the Province of British Columbia.

Presently serving as a L/Cpl in 7th R. Sussex Regt. A note said that he previously applied for an infantry commission in September 1915. Another note recorded that he was admitted to hospital that month, but no details were given. Family address, Raglan, Dane Road, Seaford, Sussex. Returned to the UK, 20 January. Ordered to join Oxford University OTC, 26 January. On probationary attachment, 5th R. Irish attached 3rd Bn. Joined 1st RIR from the R. Irish, 18.7.1916. Struck off the strength of the battalion, 22.8.1916, no reason given – presumably to attend a MGC training course at Grantham. Embarked Southampton–Le Havre, 17.3.1917, and posted to 220th Coy, MGC. On leave to the UK, 28.9.1917, and rejoined his unit 30.9.1917. Killed in action, 5.10.1917. Buttes New British Cemetery, Polygon Wood, Zonnebeke, West-Vlaanderen, Special Memorial, A.12. File ref: WO339/53383 5/18 MGC 124477.

Sawyer Lt.-Col. Guy Henry DSO. Born 18.5.1882. Gazetted a 2/Lt. in the R. Berkshire Regt 8.5.1901. Served in the South African War, 1901–2, during operations in Cape Colony (October 1901 to 31.5.1902), receiving the Queen's Medal with three clasps. Promoted to Capt. 1.8.1910, and Major 8.5.1916. Served on the Western Front 4.11.1914 to 30.1.1915; May to 25 September 1915 (being wounded in the attack at Bois Grenier while serving with 2nd R. Berks); February to 1 July 1916 (wounded while Second-in-Command of 2nd R. Berks), and November 1917 to the end of the war.

Commanded 1st RIR, 8.5.1916 to 17.6.1916; 3/4th R. West Surrey Regt (TF), 6.12.1917 to 26.1.1918, and 7th Leicester Regt from 27.1.1918. Awarded the DSO (3.6.1916) and Bar (24.9.1918). Mentioned in Despatches, 1.1.1916, 4.1.1917, and 28.12.1918. French Croix de Guerre. Closed file, ref: (98918).

Schroeder Capt. Eric Douglas. Born 17.2.1894 at 32 Chippenham Road, Paddington, London, the son of Philip Eyre and Anice Eyre, *née* Summers. His father was a journalist. Educated at Pelinborough School, Hampstead; Sunbury House School, Wilsden Green, and University College School, Hampstead, Sept 1909 to July 1911. Applied for a commission, 24.9.1914, requesting 6th Middlesex Regt. The application was named Eric Douglas Schroeder. Single. Currently serving as a Pte in the London Scottish (14th London Regt). WO to OC 6th Middlesex Regt, 31.10.1914: acknowledged Schroeder's application, but the birth certificate was for a man called E.D. Eyre. It seems that, on 23.2.1895, a Mr W.F. Schroeder married Anice Eyre. Since that time the boy was known as Eric Douglas Schroeder, at school and in private and public life. The fact of his real name was not known to Eric or to his half sisters until very recently (1914 was implied). It is unclear from his file what happened next, but the WO accepted Schroeder to be the correct name. However, at some stage he must have reverted to Eric Douglas Eyre, as some of the subsequent papers refer to E.D. Eyre. The application for a commission doesn't seem to have gone anywhere, and there is no paperwork on file for the London Regt enlistment and service. A second application for a commission was made, 3.10.1915, expressing preferences for the R. West Surrey, RIR, or the Border Regt; Machine Gun Section in any case. This was still as Eric Douglas Schroeder. Promoted Lt. 28.12.1915.

Embarked Southampton–Le Havre, 11.8.1916. To Base Depot, MGC, Etaples, 15 August. Admitted to No. 20 General Hospital, with intestinal colic, 30 August, and discharged to duty, 7 September. To No. 20 General Hospital, 12 September, with scabies, being discharged to duty, 15 September. Readmitted to No. 20 General Hospital, 19 September, scabies, and discharged to duty, 28 September. Rejoined Base Depot, 29 September. Posted to No. 18 Battery, 4 October, and to Base Depot, MGC, at Camiers, 9 November. Posted to A Battalion, Heavy Branch (Tanks), 16 November. To No. 12 Stationary Hospital, 26 December, with a compound fracture and dislocated right elbow, caused by his horse rolling onto him. To the UK aboard HS *Dunluce Castle*, 7.1.1917. Applied for a wound gratuity, 30.4.1917 and 11.8.1917. His letters stated RIR attached MGC. MB at Bodmin Military Hospital, 6 June: unfit for general service for four months.

A memo from Officer Superintending Instruction Hospitals to the Tank Corps, Woolwich, 8.10.1917, noted Schroeder as RIR attached Tank Corps: the MB, 18.9.1917, had passed him fit for light duty. Asked to keep him as an Assistant Instructor. A memo to Schroeder, 9 October, told him to report to the Officers Convalescent Hospital at Osborne, Isle of Wight, where he would be attached to the Instructional Staff. Position as Instructor ceased, 21.4.1918, and he was ordered to rejoin 'his reserve unit' the next day.

Taken on the strength of 1st RIR, 18.6.1918. Rejoined from II Corps Temporary Works Bn, 22 July. Left 1st RIR, 15 September, due to sickness and embarked Calais–Dover, 20 September. '1st R. I. Rifles 36th Div & Tank Corps'. A letter dated 15 September from Schroeder to the Adjutant of 1st RIR requested that he should be assigned back to the Tank Corps. This request was passed from OC, 36th Division, to II Corps, 21 September, and from II Corps to 2nd Army the next day. They passed on the request to the WO, 2 October. WO to C.-in-C., BEF, France, 8 November, advised that it was a mistake that Schroeder was sent to the RIR and should have returned to the Tank Corps. Admitted to Queen Alexandra Military Hospital, Millbank, London, 27 December, 'NYD'. On leave from Salisbury. Discharged to duty without being boarded, 3.1.1919. WO to Southern Command, 20.12.1918, asked for a MB on 2/Lt. E.D. Eyre of 1st RIR. Southern Command replied, 23.12.1918, agreeing but the papers that had been received were for Capt. E.D. Schroeder. MB, 11.12.1920, at Hillah, Mesopotamia, while serving with 2nd RIR: named as Eyre but the injury referred to is the 26.12.1916 horse incident. The Board noted that the injury was severe and permanent, but he was fit for duty as an officer. The MB at the Citadel Military Hospital, Cairo, 29.11.1921, granted sick leave to Capt. Eyre for an unspecified reason. Left 2nd RUR, 9.1.1922, and embarked Port Said–Southampton aboard HMT *Huntsgreen* on sick leave for six months. Disembarked 21 January. Nothing on file about discharge. File ref: WO339/57571 83 Att 1/87 130116.

Shaw 2/Lt. William. Born 23.10.1893 at Belfast, the son of George and Elizabeth Shaw, 80 Cromwell Road, Belfast. 'Privately educated.' Applied for a commission, 9.2.1916, stating a preference for 3rd RIR. Currently serving with Queen's University OTC, Belfast. Enlisted as Pte 5910 in the 5th Cadet Battalion, Pembroke College, Cambridge (18th City of London Regt), 31.3.1916. Chartered accountant, single, height 5 foot 9.88 inches, chest 33½–36 inches, weight 122 pounds. Next of kin, parents. Discharged to a commission in 3rd RIR, 4.8.1916. All service to this time was at home.

Joined 1st RIR., 11.10.1916. Left unit, 4.12.1916, and embarked Le Havre–Southampton, 30 December, aboard the *Glenart Castle*. 'Sickness (trench fever).' Home address 30 Cromwell Road, Belfast. MB at 2nd Western General Hospital, Manchester, 22.1.1917, granted one months leave. MBs at Belfast: 17 February, unfit general service for two months and home service for one month; 17 March, unfit for general and home service for two months; 17 April, unfit general service one month but fit for home service. A letter from HQ Irish Command to the WO, 6.3.1918, advised that Shaw had been transferred to Command Depot, Tipperary. A letter from Southern Command to WO, 10 May, stated that Shaw was serving at the Curragh as OC, Messing, Cheshire Yeomanry. A note, 17 July, from the Adjutant, 2/1st Cheshire Yeomanry, to the Adjutant, 3rd RIR, Belfast, stated that Shaw was no longer with the Yeomanry. OC 3rd RIR to OC 2/1st Cheshire Yeomanry, 22 July, asked if he actually knew where Shaw was. MB, 5 October: unfit for categories A and B for three months, but fit for category C and ordered to report to the Ministry of Labour, Gresham House, London EC. Discharged, 30.5.1919, medical status C1, single. Last served with the RIR attached to the Ministry of Munitions. File ref: WO339/56008 3/83 127993.

Sinclair 2/Lt. George Stanley. Born 24.4.1897, the son of Samuel and Edith Mary Sinclair, *née* Darbishire, of *Inglewood*, Adelaide Park, Belfast. A brother of Lt. H.D. Sinclair. Father was a merchant. Educated at Castle Park, Dublin; Royal Belfast Academical Institution, and Queen's University, Belfast. Served with Belfast University OTC. Applied for a commission, 20.4.1915, expressing a preference for 5th RIR. Single, medical student, height 5 foot 8½ inches, chest 35–37½ inches, weight 154 pounds. Gazetted a 2/Lt. in 5th RIR, 30.4.1915. Joined 1st RIR, 5.7.1916. Wounded during an attack, 23.10.1916. A WO telegram to his mother, 27 October, notified that her son had been slightly wounded, but remained at duty.

Died of wounds received accidentally while instructing the battalion bombers, 28.5.1917. *Whitfeld*: 'Poor young Sinclair had been killed at bomb practice, saving another man's life really – he was a charming fellow and never cared a damn. I was awfully sorry to have lost him.' Death reported by OC 24th Field Ambulance. Cause, 'accidental bomb wounds'. Intestate, single, had one sister and five brothers. Next of kin was his mother.

Statements of witnesses to accident: 9790 Sgt Hyland. Attended a bombing practice commanded by Sinclair. At about 3.40 p.m. he was near the trench where the bombs were being thrown and saw Rfn Abraham draw back his arm to throw a bomb. The lever flew off but Abraham still had the bomb in his hand and it exploded. A few seconds later another bomb exploded but he didn't see where it was. Abraham and another man were throwing at the time and Sinclair was standing on their right and Sgt Irvine was standing behind them. Hyland ran to the spot and found all four wounded. 8719 Sgt J. Greene. Gave the time as 3.45 p.m. He was two traverses away when he heard the first explosion. Looked over the top and saw a man with his arm back in the act of throwing, then there was a second explosion. He ran to the trench and found the man he had just seen, with his right arm blown off. Another man and Sinclair were also lying wounded. There were two holes less than a yard apart in the bottom of the trench 'and from the position in which Lt. Sinclair was lying it seemed as if he had made an attempt to pick up something'. 14901 Sgt A.H. Richards. Gave the time as 3.30 p.m. He was one traverse away from the throwing position. Named the other man throwing as Rfn Neill. Said that, when Abraham drew back his arm to throw, it hit Neill. Richards dropped down below the traverse and heard an explosion. He then stood up and saw Sgt Irvine climb out the trench; 'He came to me shouting for bandages. He was wounded in the face.' Richards started towards the trench and saw Rfn Neill jump up to the parapet and almost immediately another bomb went off and Neill fell back in, wounded in the leg. Richards looked into the trench and saw Sinclair and Abraham; 'Both were badly wounded'. 9946 Cpl A. Murray. Gave the time as 3.40 p.m. He was standing with Sgt Richards. Said Abraham's hand caught on Neill's sleeve and he saw the bomb go off in his hand. There was a second explosion a few seconds later. Murray used his field dressing on Sgt Irvine, who was wounded near the eye. Then he ran to the trench and saw Neill wounded in the trunk and both legs. Abraham was lying on his back and Sinclair was stooped against the traverse, badly wounded in the face and chest.

Capt. H.H. Elliot, RAMC, medical officer to 1st RIR: he was near the trench when the accident happened and, when he saw stretcher-bearers running to the spot, he followed. When he got there the stretcher-bearers were attending to Abraham, Neill, and Sinclair. Sinclair was severely wounded in the head and chest. Abraham was severely wounded in the face and right leg, and had lost his right hand. Neill had numerous small wounds in the body and left leg, and a wound to the abdomen which 'might prove severe'. Irvine was wounded in the face and arm, but these appeared to be slight. All four were sent to No. 24 Field Ambulance. All the witness statements were counter-signed by Capt. G. Mockett, 1st RIR.

A WO telegram to his mother, 29 May, advised of death due to accidental bomb wounds. Effects, which were sent to his mother, included a whistle and lanyard, a wristwatch (broken), cigarette case and holder.

A Court of Enquiry, 10 June, decided that Sinclair not to blame for the accident. Query: was anyone else to blame? – 'impossible on the evidence to say'. That was the opinion of OC 1st RIR when he signed his report, 29 May, but OC 25th Brigade (the following day) wrote: 'In my opinion the accident was due to the disregard of the instructions contained in Sec II, Para 12 of the Training and Employment of Bombers, Sept 16'. OC 8th Division added his comments, 8 June, saying that 'Although instructions were disregarded, no action proposed'.

Sinclair was originally buried in Nurlu British Cemetery, north-east of Peronne. Later re-interred at Peronne Communal Cemetery Extension, Ste Radegonde, V.M. File ref: WO339/48385 118216.

Sinclair Lt. Herbert Darbishire. Born 30.5.1894, a brother of 2/Lt. G.S. Sinclair. Applied for a commission, 21.11.1914. His application noted that he was fluent in French and German; occupation clerk. Educated at the Royal Belfast Academical Institution, and the Ecole de Commerce, Neuchâtel. No previous military experience but had served 18 months in the UVF. Height 5 foot 9 inches, weight 144 pounds, eyesight 6/9 right and 6/6 left. Gazetted a 2/Lt. in 5th RIR, 2.12.1914.

Joined 2nd RIR, 10.6.1916, at Bailleul aux Cornailles. Left that unit, 'sick', 24.7.1916. Returned to the UK, 15 August, suffering from bronchitis. The MBs at Belfast declared him as unfit for any service until he was declared fit for light duties, 9.1.1917. Declared fit for general service, 19 January. Promoted Lt. 1.7.1917.

Joined 1st RIR and was posted to C Coy, 18.12.1917. Severely wounded in the head and right forearm by a grenade when the Germans raided his trench, 1.3.1918. Admitted to No. 2 Red Cross Hospital at Rouen and transferred to No. 3 Southern General Hospital, Oxford, 26 March. Moved to the Cottage Hospital, Southport, 2 May. Transferred to the Irish Command Depot at Tipperary, 2 August. Underwent a further operation at the Central Military Hospital, Belfast, 4 September. Presented to the MB, 21.1.1919, for a war wound assessment and was demobilized, 28.1.1919, medical status C1. Later lived at 100 Broomielaw, Glasgow.

Smith Lt. Samuel Donard Irvine. Born 14.2.1891 at Arkeen, Newcastle, the son of Irvine and Margaret J. Smith, Annesley Mansions, Newcastle, Co. Down. He resided at Arkeen and was single. Enlisted with 5th RIR at Belfast, 26.8.1914, and was a member of the battalion rugby team. At that time his mother was widowed and living at 53 Leinster Square, Bayswater, London. Had previously served one year with the North Vancouver Engineers and returned from Canada in July 1914. He was a member of the UVF and applied to the RIR for a commission, 12.10.1914. No vacancies were available and he was put on the waiting list. On the application he answered the query regarding profession or occupation with 'private income'.

Joined 1st RIR, 25.5.1915, and was D Coy Commander for the Somme attack, being killed in action, 1.7.1916. A report by 6700 Rfn T. Carey, 1st RIR, stated that Smith was hit by machine gun fire near the third German line. 2282 L/Cpl C. Burns said that Smith was seen by him near the second German line with a bayonet wound to the chest, but was still throwing grenades. Recommended for gallantry by the acting CO for his part in the attack. Originally buried at 'Map ref. 57.d.X.b.0.8. Reported by OC 6th R. W. Kents'. This is just a few yards west of the British trench Longridge Street so it is probable that the body was brought in by that unit. His ID discs were returned to base, 16.7.1917, with a note stating that no other effects were recovered.

Irish Life 29.9.16: 'S. Donard Irvine-Smith ... was the only son of the late Mr J. Irvine-Smith BL and Mrs Irvine-Smith, Glenmore, Newcastle, Co. Down, and 53 Leinster Square, London, and grandson of the late Revd J.A. McMordie, of Seaforde, Co. Down.'

On 10.12.1919 the Graves Registration advised that the body had been exhumed and had been reverently treated and re-buried in Blighty Valley Military Cemetery, B.L.111.J.8.

Smyth Lt. Albert John. Joined 1st RIR, 22.7.1916. On 19.9.1916 he proceeded to Grantham (MGC) and was struck off the strength of the battalion. Promoted to Lt. 8.1.1917. The Army List for November 1918 shows him as still serving with the MGC. Closed file, ref: (131246).

Soulby Capt. Alfred Christopher. Born 8.11.1892 in London, and was an architect and surveyor. Height 5 foot 7 inches. The son of Mrs J.W. Soulby, 20 Sheen Park, Richmond, Surrey, he had a sister, V.R. Soulby. Enlisted, 6.8.1914, in the 25th London Regt as Pte 1519 and served in the ranks with the BEF, 26.10.1914 to 2.3.1915. Gazetted a 2/Lt. in the RIR, 3.3.1915, and joined 1st RIR, 18.3.1915, from the Cadet School, Bailleul. Wounded, 27.4.1915, while putting up wire entanglements at night within 70 yards of the enemy and was severely wounded again (GSW) 9.5.1915. Transferred to hospital in the UK, 12 May, being discharged 3 June. On leave until he was sent for light duties to 7th RIR. The MB declared him still unfit, 11.12.1915. Later he transferred to the Heavy Branch MGC and embarked at Devonport, 9.12.1916, disembarking at Alexandria, 9.1.1917. Transferred to the Tank Corps, 28 July, and was gazetted an a/Capt. the same day. Sent to No. 66 CCS, 27 August, with an undiagnosed fever. From there he went to No. 4 Stationary Hospital the following day. Discharged from hospital, 25 September, and rejoined the Tank Corps two days later. Embarked from Alexandria for the UK, 4.7.1918. This appears to be the end of his overseas service and he last served as a Capt. in the Tank Corps. Discharged 24.2.1920. He described his post-war occupation as 'Illustrator and periodical artist (student)'. File ref: 49755.

Stapleton Lt. Albin John Patrick. Gazetted a 2/Lt. in 3rd RIR, 26.9.1917. Joined 1st RIR from 3rd RIR, 20.12.1917, and was struck off the strength of the battalion, sick, 18.3.1918. Promoted Lt. 26.3.1919. Closed file, ref: 3/83 (209982).

Steavenson Capt. Alexander Arthur Frederick T. Joined 6th RIR (Louth Militia) as a 2/Lt., 1903. Promoted Lt., 1905. When the old 6th RIR was disbanded under the Haldane Scheme in 1908, he transferred to 3rd RIR. Moved to 4th RIR. Completed a course of musketry in Dublin, January 1915. Promoted to Capt., 13.10.1915, and attached to 1st RIR. Placed on the sick list, 12.4.1916, and struck off the strength of the battalion, 23.4.1916. Closed file, ref: (18565).

Steele-Nicholson Capt. Alfred Francis James. Born 5.11.1885, the son of James Steele-Nicholson, Ballow House, Bangor, Co. Down, and Falmore House, Co. Donegal. His mother was Maria J., daughter of George Augustus Chichester Macartney, Holywood House, Co. Down, and great-granddaughter of Sir John Macartney, Bt., Lish, Co. Armagh.

His baptism certificate, 11.4.1886, shows his surname as Nicholson only. Attended Bangor Grammar School. His father's trade or profession was shown as 'Gentleman'. He was single and running a timber and creosoting business at the time of enlistment. By then his father was deceased and his brother, William Herbert Hamilton Steele-Nicholson, born 27.11.1875, was a consulting engineer who lived at 35 Botanic Avenue, Belfast. Gazetted a 2/Lt. with 5th RIR, 15.6.1915, and joined 1st RIR, 6.6.1916. Appointed an a/Capt., 12.8.1917, and reported as wounded and missing, 16.8.1917. The WO wrote to his mother at Ballow House, 3.3.1918, advising that the process for death being accepted for official purposes was being put in hand.

Irish Times, 16.4.1918, reported on the death of his brother: 'Lieutenant W.H.H. Steele-Nicholson, Royal Engineers, who died in Endsleigh Palace Hospital, London, on 13th inst., was the second son of the late Mr James Steele-Nicholson ... The deceased officer, who came over with the Canadian Expeditionary Force, was severely wounded on 8th August, 1916, during the battle of the Somme, and had since been in hospital.' Tyne Cot Memorial.

Tate Capt. Thomas Marshall. Gazetted a 2/Lt. in 5th RIR, 15.8.1914, and joined 1st RIR, 25.5.1915. He was the Battalion Transport Officer. Promoted Lt., 4.11.1917. Awarded the French Croix de Guerre a l'Ordre Regiment (Bronze Star), December 1918. Went to the UK, 8.2.1919, and employed as Musketry Officer with 4th RIR. Later went overseas with 2nd RIR. Promoted Capt. 23.6.1923. Closed file, ref: 1/83 (50809).

Tayler Major Harry Francis MC. Joined 1st RIR from 4th RIR as a 2/Lt., 18.5.1915. Promoted to Capt., 18.12.1915, and Mentioned in Despatches, 15.6.1916. D Coy Commander. Placed on the sick list, 4.3.1916, rejoining 9.1.1917. Sent to hospital, sick, 23.1.1917, and struck off the strength of the battalion, 1 April. Rejoined, 1 October, and commanded C Coy but took over command of B Coy, 5 October. Assumed the duties of Second-in-Command, 31.10.1917. Wounded, 2.10.1918, transferred to England two days later. Awarded the MC in November 1918. Musketry Officer, 4th RIR, in 1919. Closed file, ref: (37266).

Taylor Capt. Archibald Cotton. Born Wimbledon, London SW, 23.4.1883. The ward of E.J. Cotton, Elsinore, Whiteabbey. Attended Campbell College, Belfast (until April 1895), and Thanet College, Cliftonville, Kent. From 1900 he was working as a clerk in the London Stock Exchange. Married Della Jessie Rose Allen, spinster, 28.11.1913, at Holy Trinity Church, Selhurst, Surrey. Enlisted as Pte 22598 in the 5th Rifle Bde, 9.9.1914, at Winchester. Height 6 foot, weight 136 pounds, chest 35–39 inches. Medical examination noted that the first toe of his right foot had been amputated but this was not detrimental to military service. Next of kin wife, Della Cotton Taylor, 2 Hurst Road, Bexley, Kent. Posted to 5th Rifle Bde 17.9.1914. All Rifle Bde service was at home. Applied for a commission, 10.2.1915, expressing a preference for 4th RIR. Address, Helston House, Margate, Kent. Discharged to a commission in 4th RIR, 18.3.1915.

Posted to 1st RIR, 2.12.1915, arrived France, 4 December, and 'To Front', 8 December. Attached to 25th TMB as a T/Lt., 7.2.1916. 'Posted' to 25th TMB 18 April. Appointed OC 25th TMB, 17 June, with the temporary rank of Capt. Mentioned in Despatches, 13.11.1916 and 21.12.1917. Leave to UK, 3–13.10.1917. To England on a six-month tour of duty, 1.11.1917, and struck off strength of battalion the same day. Ordered to rejoin BEF, 4.1.1918, and posted to 25th TMB. Posted to 1st RIR, 28 January. Rejoined TMB, 6 February, and returned to 1st RIR five days later.

To Liverpool Merchants Mobile Hospital at Etaples, 13 February, with myalgia. Discharged to Base, 26 February. The MB at Etaples, 27 February, noted debility and recommended three weeks leave to the UK. He wrote from 10 Dalby Square, Margate, Kent, to the WO, 20 March: 'I am returning to France on the 23rd inst.' His wife was at Strathearn, Strandtown, Co. Down. The MB in France, 1 April, graded him B2 and instructed that he was to be retained at a base or in lines of communication for three months. Granted leave 13–27.8.1918. Posted to No. 231 POW Coy (Labour Corps), 14.9.1918, and struck off the strength of 1st RIR the same day. MB, 30.1.1919, declared him unfit for twelve months and granted UK leave, 22 February to 8 March 1919. Rejoined his Coy, 8.3.1919. Granted leave 20 June to 4 July 1919. Returned to the UK for demobilization, 1 November. Discharged 2.11.1919, rated B2. In 1933 he attended the 36th (Ulster) Division Officers OCA annual dinner. By 1938 his address was Essex House, Barnes, London SW13. File ref: WO339/43330 111778.

Tee Major Charles Clifford OBE, MC. Transferred to 1st RIR from the R. Warwick Regt and was promoted to Lt., 27.4.1907, and Capt., 1.10.1914. Served in India and was a member of the Rifles team that won the Burma Rugby Cup in 1911.

Quis Separabit, vol. 3, no. 1, May 1932, contained an article describing the voyage home from Aden: 'By 11 p.m. we had the whole lot on board, and went ashore for a last farewell at the Club. An amusing story is told about Charles Tee that night. Charles, coming off to the ship about 3 a.m., very tired and sleepy, found his cabin unbearably hot, so carted his bed up on deck. Somehow in the dark he got to the ladies' side of the deck by mistake, and finding a vacant place dumped down his mattress, only noticing that there was a sleeping form on each side of him and quite oblivious to the fact that they weren't of the same sex as himself. The ship put to sea about 4 a.m., and the wind blew the lady's plait of hair right across his face. The Officer of the Watch – I believe Fitz Gavin – going his rounds, in the early morning, was horrified on passing to see

Charles fast asleep, lying on his back with his mouth open, snoring loudly and coughing and choking every time the hair blew into his mouth. Fitz thought he had better do something about it, so tried to waken him. At any time it was difficult to waken Charles Tee, and after hitting and kicking him (which had not the slightest effect) he only succeeded in waking the two damsels. This adventure had repercussions throughout the ship, and for several days relations between ourselves and the Indian Army (the women being the wives of Indian Army officers) were somewhat strained. They were convinced that Charles had done it on purpose.'

In December 1914 he was the battalion machine gun officer. *Laurie*: 'January 18, 1915: Capt. Tee had a couple of narrow escapes while he was out with us.' Wounded 9.5.1915. Later served with the MGC and was awarded the MC, 3.6.1918. Mentioned in Despatches, 28.11.1917 and 3.2.1920; awarded the OBE, Class IV, 3.2.1920. Also awarded the Russian Order of St Stanislaus, 2nd Class. Appears to have died in the 1920s. Closed file, ref: 83 MGC (11106).

Thompson 2/Lt. Henry. Born 10.4.1881 at Portrush, Co. Antrim, the son of Mona Thompson, Muckamore Abbey, Co. Antrim. (There is a Robert Thompson JP, Muckamore Abbey, listed in *Thom's Directory* for 1912, who may have been his father). Attested in Bury St Edmunds as Rifleman Cadet 17/1975 in 17th RIR, 30.3.1916. Address at that time, Estate Office, Elveden, Thetford, Suffolk. Single, estate agent, height 5 foot 8½ inches, chest 36½–39 inches, weight 145 pounds. Next of kin, mother. Applied for a commission, 2.8.1916, stating a preference for 4th RIR. Address, Ballykinlar Camp, Co. Down. Attached No. 7 Officer Cadet Battalion at Fermoy, 5.10.1916.

Transferred to No. 2 MGC Officer Cadet Battalion at Pirbright, 3 December. 'Not suitable for MGC returned to former Cadet Bn.' No date on that note. Appointed to a commission in 4th RIR, 27.4.1917. Joined 1st RIR from 4th RIR, 30.6.1917. Left unit, 8.8.1917, and embarked for the UK, 16 August, with trench fever. Examined by the MB at Caxton Hall, 26 October. Address as of 7 November was Endsleigh Palace Hospital, Euston Square, London NW1. MB, 8.4.1918: permanently unfit for any form of service and to be placed on the retired list. Address, The Grange, Muckamore, Co. Antrim. File ref: WO339/73136 151110.

Thompson 2/Lt. John Crawford. Born 26.4.1898 at Shankill, Co. Antrim, the only son of John Butler Thompson and Mrs O.G. Thompson of *Gayerville*, 7 Chlorine Gardens, Belfast. Attended Wesley College, Dublin, and Methodist College, Belfast (1909–June 1912), during which time his address was 98 Malone Avenue; played rugby for the Med. XV 1912. Unmarried. Joined Queen's University OTC, 9.9.1914, and applied for a commission in March 1916 but was refused on the grounds of age. At that time he was a student and woollen manufacturer's agent in the service of Messrs. James Ireland & Co., May Street, Belfast. Attested and marked as a reserve, 25.8.1916. Mobilized, 19.12.1916, and posted to No. 7 Officer Cadet Battalion. He was also required to make a general enlistment at the same time, choosing 5th RIR with the allocated number D/10402. His standard at OTC, Queen's University, Belfast, was recorded as 'General efficiency B. Musketry, failed in Table A. Signalling nil'. Under general remarks is recorded 'Efficiency, very fair. Leadership, good'. Height 5 foot 10.6 inches and 37 inches expanded chest measurement. After a period of training there and at Fermoy he was gazetted into the Royal South Downs, 26.4.1917. Proceeded overseas and joined 1st RIR, 11 September.

War Diary: '16.1.1918. A party from D Coy under 2/Lt. J.C. Thompson ... doing much good work in digging buried men out.' Killed in action, 21.3.1918.

M.C.B., June 1920: 'It is with pride and sorrow that the college accepts for the Assembly Room the portraits of two O.M.C.'s who fell in the Great War. Crawford Thompson came to M.C.B. when quite young and was a most enthusiastic supporter of all the college activities. After some years spent in Dublin he renewed his old friendships and was often up with us in the college. He enlisted quite early and in former numbers we have spoken of his work in the Army.' Pozières Memorial.

Turkington 2/Lt. Isaac Henry. Gazetted a 2/Lt., 3.5.1917. Joined 1st RIR from 19th RIR, 11.10.1917. Not on the Army List of January 1919. File destroyed.

Tutty 2/Lt. Arthur Samuel Buchanan. Born 2.6.1895, the son of Edward and Annie M. Tutty, 2 Whitehall Terrace, Clontarf, Dublin. Educated at Howth Road School, Clontarf. Enlisted as Trooper 1699 in South Irish Horse, 12.11.1915. Occupation, clerk and motor driver, Wesleyan, height 5 foot 6 inches, weight 112 pounds, chest 32½–34½ inches. Next of kin, mother. Appointed Trumpeter, 11.3.1916. Absent from barracks, 6.10.1916, and fined two days pay. First overseas date 20.11.1916. To Base Depot, Rouen. Overstayed his pass by half an hour, 10.12.1916, and fined three days loss of pay. Applied for a commission the next day, expressing a preference for the RIR. Permanent address 2 Whitehall Terrace, Clontarf. Correspondence address, Trooper 1699, South Irish Horse, 5th General Cavalry Base, BEF (Rouen). Returned to the UK, 26.1.1917. To No. 21 Officer Cadet Battalion, Crookham, 9 March. Discharged to a commission in 19th RIR, 26.6.1917. Posted to 8th RIR. Left unit 14 September. Embarked Le Havre–Southampton, 20 September. 'Sickness, vomiting, abdominal pain and diarrhoea.' See later report by Major Mulholland. MB, 23 October: fit for general service after three weeks leave. A doctor's note, 11.2.1918, implied that Tutty was at Newtownards Camp. A memo, 5 July, from OC 3rd RIR, Durrington Camp, to the WO, reported that Tutty was AWOL.

Letter from Tutty to WO, 6 July; address is partly obliterated: John Mc ?, Chemists and Druggist, High Street, Newtownards. He was 'greatly perturbed' to have received their letter of 4 July and saw that 'it is impossible to accept my resignation'. He wanted to be demobilized for a time as his wife 'is laid up and I am busy in the shop, there being nobody here to keep the shop going. I simply throw myself on the mercy of the WO in granting this. It means everything to me. Thanking you for past kindness. I have the honour to be, Sir, your obedient servant.'

WO telegram to Embarkation Officer, Folkestone, 19 July: 'wire any trace Second Lieutenant A.S.B. Tutty Irish Rifles embarking for France since 29 May'. WO telegram, same date, to DAG Base, France: 'wire any trace Second Lieutenant A.S.B. Tutty Irish Rifles'. Folkestone reply, 20 July, no trace. Rouen Base reply, 22 July, no trace.

A WO internal note, 24 July: 'this officer … appears to be a slippery customer … We have wired APM Ireland to arrest him and return him to his unit at Durrington.' Provost Marshal memo to WO, 27 July, reported that Tutty was in possession of a WO telegram extending his leave to 31 July. In fact various notes on the file indicate that this extension, though technically valid, was a mistake as Tutty never had leave in the first place. He told the WO that he was on leave and asked for a short extension, and they took this at face value and extended that which did not exist in the first place. Note from OC Irish Reserve Brigade, Durrington, to Southern Command, 2 August: Tutty was to be regarded as AWOL from 31 July. Letter from Tutty to WO, 17 August: he had orders to go to France that day but had come to London to see the WO instead. Said it was a matter of life or death. His wife was ill, 'threatened miscarriage', and while he was in England she had to 'stand on her feet from 8 o'clock in the morning till 7 o'clock at night'. Letter goes on at length; rambling, sentimental and irrational. Asked to resign or have six months unpaid leave. Another letter from Tutty to the WO, but undated, virtually repeats the above. At one point he asked if they could spare him seeing 'we're now doing so well' at the front. An undated letter, from Tutty to the WO, refers to a meeting with General Davis at the WO on the previous Tuesday. Again asked for his resignation to be accepted. He went on and on about how worried he was, very repetitive. Another letter seems to be a continuation. Said he had been ordered to France. Then said that if an officer did something wrong he was invariably dismissed from the service, he had done nothing wrong, but surely they could spare him as well. His life could be in danger. The letter ran to four pages of this, repeating the same plea over and over. A WO note, undated, 'Probably of little value as an officer but even if allowed to resign would be caught up again as he is fit and of age'.

Telegram from Dublin Command to WO, 17 September, said Tutty was admitted to Holywood Hospital, 31 July, 'from leave' and was discharged to duty at Salisbury Plain, 12 August. Embarked Southampton–Le Havre, 24 August, and joined Base Depot the following day. Joined 1st RIR in the field, 30 August. Admitted to No. 109 Field Ambulance, sick, 6 September, to No. 11 CCS the same day, and sent to England, 21 September. Cause given as shell shock and neurasthenia.

Letter from Lt.-Col. Hunt, OC 1st RIR, to OC 19th RIR, 16 September: '2nd Lieut A.S.B. Tutty, who recently joined the battalion under my command, has proved himself to be absolutely inefficient and incapable of commanding men. Would you please forward a report on this officer and, if possible, state the Cadet Battalion at which he was granted a Commission in the Army.'

Staff Capt., 107th Brigade, to OC 1st RIR, 17 September, advised that 19th RIR no longer existed, and to send the reports to him. There is an inference here that Col. Hunt had in fact reported on 'Officers', not just Tutty: the plural was used three times, the singular was not used at all. By a process of deduction, the likely officers would appear to be Lt. Chandler and 2/Lts Branford and Farley. A report, 17 September, signed by Capt. W.A.S. Macpherson, OC B Coy, and Capt. and Adjutant J.C. Leeper: Macpherson says of Tutty: 'I consider him as altogether inefficient as an officer' and recounted how he encountered Tutty when he joined the battalion near St Marie Cappelle. Then, east of Neuve Eglise, he sent Tutty to post his platoon in various posts. When he went to check he found Tutty and the whole platoon in one post. Asking Tutty why he hadn't carried out the order Tutty said he felt very nervous and would like to see the doctor. Macpherson sent Tutty to an aid post and put the platoon under the command of a Corporal. 'During the time he [Tutty] was with the Coy he lacked initiative and had absolutely no control of men.' A copy of this, and all other confidential reports were sent to Tutty.

Confidential report by Major J.A. Mulholland, 13.11.1918: Tutty was incapable of commanding men. His services 'could not possibly be of any value to the Army. I strongly recommend his removal from the Service with Ignominy'. An attached report by Mulholland referred to the Messines incident: Said it was about 7 September. About 6 p.m. he saw a figure being led down the road by a soldier. When they reached him the soldier said he had been ordered by Capt. Macpherson to bring down Mr Tutty. Mulholland questioned Tutty 'about the disgraceful state he was in'. Tutty said that a shell had burst and hit a Sergeant beside him 'and he could not stand any more'. Mulholland threatened to send Tutty back to the line but Tutty 'beseeched me not to send him back. I later on received a report from Captain McPherson that he had found Mr Tutty grovelling in the trench calling on his men to save him as he was an only child and had a wife.'

Mulholland said that if he had had Macpherson's report earlier then Tutty would have been sent down 'under arrest on a charge of cowardice'. Said Tutty had only served a few weeks abroad and had never 'been under undue strain or hardship'. Tutty wrote to the Ministry of Pensions, 14 November, from Bretwood, Shore Road, Newtownards, Co. Down. Applied for a wound pension due to shell shock. Said he was partly buried by a shell at Messines, 4.9.1918. Then spent fourteen days in No. 14 CCS, and No. 35 General Hospital at Calais. Then to the UK, and on to the UVF Hospital, 14.10.1918.

Confidential report by Capt. Maxwell, late Adjutant 19th RIR, to 1st RIR, 16.11.1918: said that Tutty was taken ill during the train journey to the front, winter 1917. Was 19th RIR gas officer until ordered to proceed to Egypt, but a medical examination said he was unfit and the orders were cancelled. The battalion moved from Newtownards to Clandeboye, March 1918. Tutty had recently married and was allowed to live out of camp. Fourth week in April, the battalion moved to Salisbury Plain, but Tutty 'lay in bed saying unfit to travel'. Examined by two medical officers who found nothing wrong with him. 'An officer was ordered to bring him to the station of entrainment, which was carried out.' Shortly after arriving at Salisbury he absented himself and attempted to reach Ireland. Surrendered to arrest and brought back to Salisbury Plain where he was remanded for trial by General Court Martial. Then posted to 4th RIR at Salisbury as 19th RIR was being disbanded. Trial by GCM did not take place 'and I learned later that he had been severely censured by the Brigadier General Commanding Irish Reserve Brigade at Larkhill'.

Since severing his connection with 19th RIR 'I have heard various rumours reflecting to his discredit as an officer'. In Maxwell's opinion Tutty was unfit to be an officer and was a malingerer. 'I have reason to believe that 2/Lt. Tutty's record is known to almost the whole of the civilian element in this locality [Newtownards].' Memo from Col. Hunt to HQ 107th Brigade, 26 November, strongly recommended that Tutty be dismissed from the service. A scribble on a WO sheet, 28.11.1918: 'The sooner he is out of the Army the better.' Report by OC 36th Division (Major General C. Coffin), 14 December, stated that in his opinion Tutty should be tried by FGCM for cowardice on 6 September but may get away with it because he was admitted to a Field Ambulance and sent home. If he was tried then Mulholland and Macpherson would be required as witnesses, and also Rfn 20323 Bell, 1st RIR (presumably the soldier on the road). In any case Tutty was not fit to be an officer. Memo by OC XV Corps, 18 December, stated: 'I think it would meet the case if this officer were deprived of his commission.'

MB at Belfast, 31.12.1918: neurasthenia, was improving. One months leave. Letter from Office of C.-in-C., GHQ, France, to WO, 4.1.1919, said that due to the lapse of time, and proper procedures not being followed, the best thing to do would be to just dispense with Tutty's services. Tutty had in fact already been allowed to resign his commission. A scribbled internal WO file note, 10.1.1919, said of Tutty: 'He was a miserable creature, we saw him frequently in this passage trying to get extensions of leave and we had a shrewd suspicion that he was endeavouring to evade service ... It is unfortunate that he has got away with the retention of rank but of course that could not be helped and is due to delay in France.'

On the same sheet, but in a different hand and dated 13.1.1919, a note instructed that the papers were to be kept on file in case the question of a pension ever cropped up. A letter dated 27.5.1919, with no connecting correspondence, from the WO to Tutty: regarding his letter, 15 May, there was no opportunity of utilising his services. There is no clue as to what they were referring. File ref: WO339/96985 10/83 185198.

Tyrrell Lt. William Upton. Entered Trinity College, Dublin, 1913, and joined the OTC. Gazetted a 2/Lt. in 3rd RIR, August 1915. May have been involved in the Easter Rebellion in Dublin as he was with 3rd RIR and did not arrive at the front until 19.5.1916. Wounded, 1.7.16, while serving with 1st RIR.

Irish Times 15.7.1916: ' ... received his commission in the Royal Irish Rifles from the Royal Military College, Sandhurst, on 11th August [1915] and served with the Special Reserve in Dublin before going to the front. He comes from Ballindoolin, Edenderry, Kings County.'

Promoted Lt. 24.11.1916. At Victoria Barracks, 13.11.1916. Later served with the Royal Corps of Signals, and then with 22 Squadron (Bristol Fighters), RAF, 1918. RAF Communiqué No. 26, 26.9.1918: 'Weather: fine – 25½ tons of bombs dropped by night and 21 tons by day – Considerable enemy aircraft activity ... Lts C.W.M. Thompson and W.U. Tyrrell, 22 Sqn, when returning from escort duty to the above raid became engaged with a number of Fokker biplanes, two of which they shot down out of control and were observed to crash by other pilots.' His pilot in this action was Lt. L.C. Rowney. Returned to the RIR, June 1919. Closed file, ref: (129511).

Valentine Lt. Thomas Arthur. Born January 1898, the son of Thomas Arthur Valentine, 23 South Anne Street, Dublin. Enlisted, 10.3.1915, at the Old Town Hall, Belfast, as Rfn 17/10 in 17th RIR. Residing at 96 Langside Avenue, Langside, Glasgow, and employed as a clerk. Age 17 years 2 months, height 5 foot 6½ inches, weight 134 pounds, and chest 31–34½ inches. Appointed L/Cpl, 20.8.1915. Applied for a commission in 19th RIR, 27.9.1915, giving his address as Donard Camp, Newcastle, Co. Down. Transferred to No. 7 Officer Cadet Battalion at the Curragh, 7.8.1916. Commissioned a 2/Lt. in 17th RIR, 18.12.1916.

Wounded, 21.3.1918, while serving with 1st RIR. Embarked Rouen–Southampton, 29 March. The MB at No. 3 London General Hospital, 8 April, recorded that he had a fractured skull that was healed and a gunshot wound to his thigh which was gaping and in need of stitches. Certified unfit for general service for four months. Valentine wrote to the WO, 7 May, applying for a war gratuity. The MB, 6 June, noted all wounds were healed but that he was suffering from giddiness, headaches and loss of memory: unfit for general service for four months. Promoted Lt. 19.6.1918. Wrote to the WO, 10 August, from Cawdor Auxiliary Hospital, Bishopbriggs, Glasgow, applying for a further gratuity.

The MB at Yorkhill War Hospital, Glasgow, 13 August, noted that he had greatly improved but complained of occasional headaches: unfit for general service for three months. His address was still at Langside and he was ordered to report to Larkhill, 4 September. MB at the Military Hospital, Fargo, Salisbury Plain, 26 October: condition unchanged, fit for home duty with 5th RIR at No. 13 Camp, Durrington. MB Fargo, 7.1.1919: GSW head and left thigh. Condition unchanged, could march ten miles. Ordered to return to duty at Durrington, but unfit for general service. MB, 10.3.1920, classes the head wound as severe and permanent. Discharged, 27.3.1919. Last served with 3rd RIR. Occupation welder, single, and medical category C1. File ref: WO339/67962 14/83 143952.

Veitch Lt. Robert Alexander. Born at Belfast, 31.10.1895, and educated at Belfast Mercantile College. His father, Robert, was Scottish. Enlisted in the TF, 6th Home Service Bn, Black Watch, 24.11.1914. Pte 2611, later 265787. Address 26 Madison Avenue, Belfast. Height 5 foot 6½ inches, weight 143 pounds and chest 32–35 inches. Insurance clerk. Transferred to 4th Black Watch, 20.5.1916. Signed Army Form E624, 25.8.1916 (overseas service obligation, a very late signing). Applied for a commission in the Special Reserve (infantry), 12.10.1916. Transferred to No. 4 Officer Cadet Battalion, 9 Alfred Street, Oxford, 4.11.1916. Discharged to a commission in 3rd RIR, 28.2.1917. Joined 1st RIR, 24.4.1917. Wounded, 31.7.1917, left the unit, 2 August, and embarked Calais–Dover, 20 August, being admitted to 3rd London General Hospital, Wandsworth. The MB at the hospital, 15 October, noted a GSW to the right foot, two toes had been amputated. Unfit for service for three months. The MB at Reading War Hospital, 28.5.1918: he could walk a mile with the aid of a stick, disability at the time 40 per cent, unfit for a further three months. MB at the Officer's Command Depot, Ripon, 1 August: no improvement, unfit for general service for six months and to be admitted to the Command Depot. Promoted Lt. 1.9.1918. MB at Ripon, 3 October, noted an improvement, unfit for general service for one month. MB, 12 November, as before. Discharged, 17.4.1919. Last service was with 3rd RIR. Unmarried at the time. MB at Belfast, 17.6.1919: unfit for general service (already demobilized). File ref: WO339/76684 83 155729.

Wainwright 2/Lt. Christopher. Gazetted a Regular 2/Lt. in the RIR, 21.4.1917. Joined 1st RIR, 24.4.1917. Transferred to England and struck off the strength of the battalion, 27.8.1917. The Army List for February 1918 stated that he was Assistant Adjutant and Orderly Room Officer Convalescent Camp. Acting Capt. 12.9.1918. To Reserve of Officers 26.8.1919. Closed file, ref: 2/102, 2/83 (271279), which indicates service with 2nd RDF and 2nd RIR.

Walker 2/Lt. Arthur Walton. Born 5.9.1891. His father was Lawrence Walker, a lecturer in music at Belfast University. Attended the Royal Academy, and Queen's University, Belfast, where he obtained a first class BA in French and German. Employed as senior French and German master at Colston's School, Bristol. L/Sgt in No. 16 Training Reserve Bn. Attested for the Gloucester Regt at Bristol, 18.11.1915, and applied for a commission in the Intelligence Dept., 1.12.1916. On 10.8.1917 he was accepted into the Officer Cadet Bn at Newmarket being commissioned and posted to 17th RIR, 11.12.1917. At that time his home address was 75 Cliftonville Road, Belfast. Went to France in February 1918 and was wounded at Roye, 27.3.1918, receiving a flesh GSW to his right back and was sent to the Prince of Wales Hospital, Marylebone, London NW1, 2 April. A medical report, 8 May, stated that he was unfit for another six weeks. Returned to France in July and joined 1st RIR, 30 August. Received a GSW and was captured, 2 October, near Dadizeele. He was a POW in Germany, being repatriated, 3.12.1918, and arrived back in the UK, 9.12.1918. In a statement to the WO, 14.4.1919, he said that he was shot while advancing during an attack which was to fail. 'The enemy then came out from the farm house and carried me off on a stretcher.' He appears to have been attached to No. 21 Entrenching Battalion at the time. He suffered a 30 per cent disability and relinquished his commission, 7.5.1919. Exonerated by the WO of responsibility for his capture, 2.9.1919. File ref: WO339/102623 193438.

Wallace Lt.-Col. Frederic Campbell DSO, MC. Gazetted a 2/Lt. in 5th RIR, 15.8.1914, and joined 1st RIR, 25.5.1915. *War Diary*, 25.9.1915: '6.30 a.m. 2/Lt. Wallace and 24 Brigade bombers were sent to assist the Lincolns. Finding that the Germans could out throw us, 2/Lt. Wallace returned to the breastwork for his 8 catapults and with them did excellent work clearing the German trenches.'

Mentioned in Despatches, 15.6.1916, 4.1.1917, 20.5.1918, and 20.12.1918. Lt. Wallace was appointed Staff Capt., 24th Infantry Brigade, 16 January–30 July 1917; being struck off the strength of 1st RIR, 22.2.1917. Promoted Capt. 16.3.1917. From 31 July 1917 to 18 October 1918 he was Brigade-Major and was awarded the MC, 1.1.1918. He then returned to the UK and received a Bar to MC, 24.9.1918, and was awarded the DSO, 1.1.1919. In 1924 he attended the 36th (Ulster) Division Officers OCA annual dinner. Closed file, ref: (49123).

Whelan 2/Lt. William Clement. Joined 1st RIR, 13.6.1918. Appointed Assistant Adjutant, 12.7.1918. Took over duties of Acting Adjutant, 15–24 October 1918, and again on 10.2.1919. Went to the UK, 17.2.1919, prior to going overseas with 2nd RIR. File destroyed.

White Lt. Randal Merrick. Born 15.9.1896, educated at Wesley College, and entered Trinity College, Dublin, 1912. Living at 48 Leeson Park, Dublin, as a student when he applied for a commission, 19.8.1915. Gazetted a 2/Lt. in 3rd Leinster Regt, September 1915. Joined 1st RIR from 3rd Leinster Regt, 24.7.1916. Gassed 11.2.1917. Left 1st RIR, 21 February. Embarked Calais–Dover, 10 March, aboard SS *Brighton*. His address was stated as Carnashee, Bailey, Co. Dublin (Carnashee, Carrickbrack Road, Sutton, according to *Thom's Directory* for 1912, was owned by R.H. White). Admitted to the Military Hospital, York, 12 March, suffering from bronchial pneumonia. Promoted Lt., 1917. Arrived at the Base Depot, France, 14.4.1918. Joined 2nd Leinster Regt, 14 June. Transferred to 2nd Army School, 30 August. Granted leave to the UK, 11–31.10.1918. Discharged, 20.1.1919, last serving with 2nd Leinster Regt. Medical category A1. Obtained his MA from Trinity College 1919. Married Kathleen Emily, 1.9.1920, and predeceased her 4.1.1978. File ref: 3/100 110505.

Whitfeld Brigadier Gerald Herbert Penn OBE, MC, DL. Born 5.3.1896 at Little Easton (near Dunmow), Essex. His parents were the Revd Arthur Lewis Whitfeld of Hamsey House, Lewes, and Mary Ellen, who was the daughter of Col. the Hon. Ernest George Curzon, 52nd Foot, sixth son of the Earl of Howe. Educated at Malvern College (1910–13) and Sandhurst where he was a Gentleman Cadet (November 1914 to April 1915). His brother, Lt. Arthur Noel Whitfeld, 2/RIR, was killed in action, 14.10.1914. Another brother was Lt.-Col. Ernest Hamilton Whitfeld MC of the Oxfordshire and Buckinghamshire Light Infantry. His uncle, Col. Fitzroy Edmund Penn Curzon, RIR, was killed in action while commanding 6th R. Irish at Ginchy, 9.9.1916.

Appointed a 2/Lt., 17.4.1915, spending some time with 3rd RIR in Dublin. Promoted Lt. 28.12.1915. Joined 1st RIR in France, 10.3.1916. Appointed Assistant Adjutant, 3.4.1916, and took over as Adjutant, 2.7.1916. Transferred to hospital, 23.1.1917, and rejoined the battalion two weeks later. Sole surviving officer of the attack, 31.7.1917, he was temporary CO on that day and after the attack of 16.8.1917. Mentioned in Despatches 25.5.1917. After being on leave for a month he relinquished his position as Adjutant, 9.11.1917, being sent to take over a company in the 8th Division Training Wing. Awarded the MC 1.1.1918. By this time he had been appointed a/Capt. Rejoined 1st RIR as Second-in-Command, 3.2.1918, and left the battalion to join the RAF, 6.4.1918. Trained as a pilot in England and was commissioned into the RAF, 6.7.1918.

Flew in a DH 9, as an observer, with 98 Squadron in France, his pilot being Capt. O.W.C. Johnsen. RAF Communiqué No. 16, 15–21 July 1918, credited them with bringing down two enemy aircraft. During a bombing raid on the rail yards at Valenciennes, 8.8.1918, he was shot down and wounded by a Fokker D VII from Jagdgeschwader 1 (JG 1 whose commander was Herman Goering) based at St Christ. Spent the remainder of the war as a POW in Germany.

Completed a full tour as Adjutant of 1st RIR in the Isle of Wight (1919–22). In 1922 he married Joan Marguerite Hughes D'Aeth, daughter of Capt. and Lady Nina Hughes D'Aethe of Beaulieu. He was on the staff at Sandhurst, 1922–8. Promoted Capt. 1.1.1923. During this time he assisted Cyril Falls, who was writing *The History of the First Seven Battalions*. His war memoirs are held by the Imperial War Museum. In 1929 he was with 2nd RUR at Poona and then went as Assistant Military Secretary to the Commander in Chief, Southern Command, India. Left 1st RIR, 1934, and had been a member of their polo team.

He was the OC Regimental Depot, Armagh, and editor of *Quis Separabit* 1936–8. Gold Staff Officer, HM Coronation, 1937. Spent three months at the Senior Officer's School at Sheerness in the spring of 1938 and was then promoted Lt.-Col. Took command of 2nd RUR in Palestine. He returned home in 1939 in time to lead the battalion to France soon after the outbreak of war. Visitors to the battalion at this time included Major-Gen. B.L. Montgomery, the Duke of Windsor, the Duke of Gloucester, General Georges, General Sir Edmund Ironside, and HM King George VI. The history of the RUR contains the following entry: 'On April 14th the plot thickened. The battalion was put on short notice to move east. But any question of flurry among the young officers was immediately eliminated by Lt.-Col. Whitfeld. Clad most incorrectly in his black Rifles' greatcoat, he said: "It would be just typical of Hitler to attack on a Sunday." Then, turning to the PMC, he continued, "I hope there is going to be no stupidity about luncheon".'

He just missed commanding 2nd RUR in the advance into and the withdrawal from Belgium in May 1940 for, a week before the flag fell, 2 May, he was appointed AAG, GHQ, BEF. Served on the staff of the French Admiral during the evacuation of Dunkirk. For this work he was awarded the OBE. In the rebuilding of the Army in the summer of 1940 he became a Brigadier and an Infantry Brigade Commander in the 43rd Wessex Division. Became Commander of the 'Phantom' Division whose role was to carry out deception schemes in the Central Mediterranean Theatre in 1944. He wrote a report for the WO Historical Branch about the activities of this Division. During 1945–6 he had a Staff appointment in East Africa. Deputy Commander Mid-West District in Shrewsbury, 1947–9. At this time he assisted Charles Graves in writing the history of the RUR. Retired from the Army in May 1950.

His daughter Angela was born in 1927 and his son Anthony in 1940. They lived at The Red House, Hartsbourne Ave., Bushey Heath, Herts. Deputy Lieutenant for Hertfordshire and a county councillor there, 1956–69. He died in hospital, 18.2.1975, after a lingering illness. Closed file.

Whitla Major George Townshend. 3rd RIR attached to 1st RIR. Promoted to Capt. 8.5.1915. Transferred to the sick list, 6 January to 5 February 1916. Evacuated to England and struck off the strength of the battalion, 6.4.1916. There is an RAF index card that shows his address as Crinken Cottage, Shankill, Co. Dublin. Major. Born 7.6.1882. Came from Halifax, Canada, 17.1.1915, 'passage paid by Canadian Government for service with the RI Rifles'. To No. 193

Training Squadron, 1.4.1918. No. 69 Training Wing, 21.4.1919. The Army List for April 1919 shows him attached to 1st Garrison Battalion. To Unemployed List 22.1.1920. Closed file, ref: RGR 83 RAF (9736).

Wilkie 2/Lt. Alexander Buchan. Promoted from the ranks of 7th RIR. Joined 1st RIR 8.10.1917. Died of wounds received from shell fire at 8.30 p.m., 30.11.1917, Somme Point, Passchendaele. Ypres Reservoir Cemetery, III.B.21. Closed file, ref: (247183).

Williams Lt. Ernest Joseph. Born 11.10.1892 in Londonderry, the son of James A. and Emily K. Williams of The Willows, Northland Road, Londonderry. Father was a bank manager. Educated at Hoyle College, Londonderry, and Strand School, London. Matriculated at the University of London. Had a medical examination at Regina, Canada, 25.1.1915. Height 5 foot 11 inches, weight 154 pounds, chest 38½–41½ inches. At enlistment, joined 46th Bn Canadian Infantry as Pte 26440. Transferred to 10th Bn Canadian Infantry, 28.8.1915, apparently on arrival in France. Applied for a commission, 23.12.1915, expressing a preference for 3rd RIR. Single, bank clerk, address in Londonderry as above. Correspondence address: L/Cpl 26440, 10th Bn, Canadian Expeditionary Force, France. To No. 2 Officer Cadet Bn at Pembroke College, Cambridge, 25.2.1916. Commissioned a 2/Lt. in 3rd RIR. Joined 2nd RIR, 13.9.1916. *War Diary 2nd RIR*, 15.2.1917: '2/Lt. E.J. Williams slightly injured, remained at duty. Cause of accident: premature explosion of No. 5 Mills Bomb.'

Irish Times 23.2.1917: 'Mr J.A. Williams, actuary, Londonderry Savings Bank, has been notified that his second son, Lieutenant Ernest J. Williams, Royal Irish Rifles, has been accidentally wounded in France. Second Lieutenant Williams was in the service of the Bank of Montreal when the war broke out. He joined the Canadian Expeditionary Force, and after a winter's active service in France received his commission in the Royal Irish Rifles, going to the front again last August. His only surviving brother, Temporary Captain H.B. Williams, Royal Inniskilling Fusiliers, is at present on active service. His two other brothers, Captain C.E. Williams and Second Lieutenant Alfie Williams, both of the Royal Irish Rifles, were killed in action last year.'

Rejoined 2nd RIR from leave, 3.6.1917, and posted to C Coy. Wounded again 7.6.1917. Embarked Boulogne–Dover, 15 June, aboard *St David*. Cause, GSW right elbow. The MB at 1st Western General Hospital, Fazakerly, Liverpool, 3 July, stated Messines as the place of wounding. There was no damage to bones or nerves. Unfit for general service for two months from date of wounding. MBs at Belfast: 25 July, still considerable stiffness of right arm, unfit for general service for three months; 25 August, three weeks leave and then to rejoin unit at Holywood for home service, unfit for general service for one month; 24 October, now fit for general service and ordered to rejoin unit.

Killed in action at Gulleghem, 15.10.1918, while serving with 1st RIR. Died a bachelor, intestate. WO telegram to father, 20 October. Effects in total consisted of an advance book, a cheque book, and a 'disc', sent to father. Various papers for his death show him as 5th RIR attached 2nd RIR. The actual death report is from OC 1st RIR. Burial report to father, 10.2.1919, stated Military Cemetery, near Ledeghem, west-north-west of Courtrai. This report also incorrectly shows 5th RIR attached 2nd RIR. Dadizeele New British Cemetery, Moorslede, II.B.1. File ref: WO339/77314 156719.

A Ministry of Defence letter to Major M.D.C. Devlin, 8.6.1995, in reply to his letter of 4.1.1995, gave the service record as: Appointed to commission as 2/Lt. in 3rd RIR, 25.2.1916. Posted 5th Bn and attached 2nd Bn 'unknown date'.

Wilson 2/Lt. John Edward Goodwin. Born at Derby, 23.8.1885, the son of Edward Wilson. Married to Alice Maude Sarah Spencer Wilson and they lived at 5 Haughton Villas, Welshwall, Oswestry, Shropshire. A medical examination, 25.11.1915, noted that he had a breakdown twelve months previously: 'Is a bank cashier. Was greatly overworked. Open air life should be beneficial'. Height 5 foot 3 inches. Signed up for overseas service, 27.11.1915. Commissioned a 2/Lt. in the 7th RWF, 2.1.1916, and served for a time with 3/7th RWF. Later attached to 24th London Regt. Joined 1st RIR from 4th RWF, 31.10.1916, and was killed in action 16.8.1917. Tyne Cot Memorial.

Windle 2/Lt. Philip. Born Chesterfield, 25.2.1893, the son of Henry Job and Annie Windle, *née* Billinge. Father was a banker's clerk. Educated at Gresham's School, Holt, Norfolk (September 1907 to December 1909). Applied for a commission, 17.6.1915, expressing a preference for 4th RIR. Address, Bank House, Heanor, RSO, Derbyshire. Single, clerk in Parrs Bank Ltd. Gazetted a 2/Lt. in 4th RIR, 26.7.1915.

Joined 2nd RIR at Averdoingt, 23.5.1916. Wounded, 9.7.1916, at La Boiselle. Left unit, 9 August, and embarked Calais–Dover, 13 August, aboard the *Dieppe*. The MB at Caxton Hall, 21 August, noted that he was wounded at La Boiselle, 8.8.1916. Superficial shrapnel fragment wound to right chest, six inches long by one inch wide, 'Now healed'. Unfit for general service for two months. Sick leave expired on 20 October. There is some confusion above. He is listed as being wounded at La Boiselle, 9.7.1916, in Fall's history and not 8.8.1916 when the battalion was at Auchonvillers. Joined 4th RIR for duty at Carrickfergus, 14 November. Still at Carrickfergus, 10.1.1917 (dental treatment). MB same date shows fit for home service but unfit for general service for two months. MB, 19 February: fit for general service. Joined 1st RIR from 4th RIR, 8 November. Wounded again, left hand, 27.11.1917, and left unit two days later. Embarked Calais–Dover, 4 December. MB at 4th London General Hospital, 25.1.1918, noted a shrapnel wound left hand, and declared him unfit for general service for three months from that date. Wrote to the WO asking for a wound gratuity, 29 January, 19 June, and 27 September. Address, Atlantic Hydro, Blackpool. Still hospitalised. Had lost ring finger left hand and the second finger was 'useless'.

MB at Blackpool, 9 October, graded him as medical rating F and sent him home. Classed medically unfit for further service and put forward to go on the retired list. MB, 24.1.1919, at the WO: the disability was severe and permanent; no longer serving. He wrote to WO, 12 February, thanking them for granting a £250 wound gratuity. Strong letter from John Andrews JP, Heanor, Derbyshire, to WO, 2 June: he was involved in local pensions administration and complained that Windle still hadn't received any money. He had 'never known a case where a man has been so badly used by the authorities as Lt. Windle has been by your office'. Requested immediate action. WO replied, 20 June, and referred to the £250 award in February. 'The information on which your letter was written is therefore incorrect.' MB at Leeds, 16 October: there had been no improvement since the last board. File ref: WO339/34543 100238.

Windus 2/Lt. Charles Eric. Born 1893, the son of Thomas Charles Windus of 52 Thorsold Road, Bowes Park, London N. Had served with Bedford OTC until he left school in June 1912. On 7.8.1914 he joined 28th County of London (Artists Rifles) as Pte 1663, aged 20 years 11 months. Height 5 foot 11 inches and expanded chest measurement 37½ inches. Served overseas with the Artists Rifles, 26.10.1914 to 2.3.1915, when he was appointed to a commission in 1st RIR. His address was 24 Queensdale Road, Holland Park, West London.

Joined 1st RIR, 18.3.1915, from the Cadet School, Bailleul, and was killed in action, 9.5.1915. A telegram was sent to his father, 13 May, reporting that he was missing. A subsequent telegram, 24 July, advised that he had been killed. Miss B. Davies, 28 Elms Road, Clapham Common, London SW, wrote to the WO, 18 May, stating that she had seen Windus' name in the missing lists and enquired for more news. The WO replied, 22 May, that no other information was known. In his will he left his wrist watch and silver cigarette case to Miss E.M. Rhodes, 33 Westminster Palace, London SW. Ploegsteert Memorial. File ref: 49764.

Wolfe Lt. George Frederick. Born 1882. Joined 1st RIR from 6th RDF, 11.9.1916. Wounded during an attack, 23.10.1916. Left unit the same day and embarked Le Havre–Southampton on HS *Cornwallis Castle*, 2 November. GSW right leg. MB at 3rd Southern General Hospital, Oxford, 4 December: unfit for any service for eight weeks. MB at King George V Hospital, Dublin, 1.2.1917: unfit for general service for three months and home service for two months. Admitted to King George V Hospital, 21 February. He wrote a letter to the WO, 25 February, enquiring about a wound gratuity. MB at King George V Hospital, 1 March: unfit for home or general service two months. Letter to WO, 18 March, asking when his next medical board would be. Address, 14 Park View Avenue, Harolds Cross, Dublin. MB at King George V Hospital, 25 April: unfit for general service for three months and home service two months. Letter to WO, 21 May, advised that he was sent to King George V Hospital, 25 April, and then sent on to Dublin Castle Red Cross Hospital where he had been ever since. Again enquired about a wound gratuity.

Letter to WO, 10 July, from the barracks, Tipperary: said that he was there, marked as unfit for duty, and only had limited movement on crutches. Asked for a further wound gratuity. Gave his unit as 6th RDF and MGC. Another letter, 27 August, basically had the same content as the previous letter. MB, 24 September, at the Military Hospital, Tipperary: wound broken down slightly so he could not have a massage; walking with crutches, unfit for any duty for three months.

Another letter to WO, 1 October, still at Tipperary, titled himself 'Lieutenant MGC'. Struck off the strength of Tipperary Base upon admission to hospital, 6 November. MB that date declared him unfit for any service for four months. Letter to WO, 21 December, advised that he had a MB at Dublin Castle, 6 November, and was ordered to Dublin Castle Red Cross Hospital where he had been bed-bound to date. Again asked for a wound gratuity. MB, 31.1.1918: unfit for home service for three months and general service for six months. Letter to WO, 18 April, still at Dublin Castle. Said his health was excellent except that he could not route-march. Advised that, pre-war, he worked on the railways and would be suitable for that kind of employment in the Army. Would prefer to resume duty without convalescence. Said that he had three operations. Again signed himself as Lt. MGC. Letter from Irish Command to WO, 25 April, asked to be allowed to have Wolfe classified C2, as the opinion was that he would never be fit for a higher category. He could then be employed as an Assistant Railway Transport Officer. Discharged from hospital 2 May. MB that date noted he was steadily improving. Three weeks leave then instructed to join MGC Training Centre at Grantham. Letter to WO, 12 May, asked for another wound gratuity. WO replied, 25 May, and told him that the £250 he had received was the maximum for his rank. MB at Grantham, 7 August: he was walking fairly well with a stick. Doing mainly sedentary work. 'Quite unfit for active duty with troops.' Letter to Ministry of Pensions, 29 November, writing from E 53 Mess, MGTC, Grantham, asked for a disability pension. They referred him back to the WO. Wrote to WO, from Grantham, 3 December. Demobilized, 20.1.1919, medical class C2, married. Occupation in civil life, railway clerk. Letter to WO, 3.3.1919, from 1 Le Bass Terrace, Leinster Road, Rathmines, Dublin. His demobilization gratuity had not been credited to his account; his wife was ill and he was having to 're-start' his house, which was broken up when he entered the Army. Would they please expedite the payment. File ref: WO339/43831 112419.

Workman Capt. Arthur Coates. The son of Robert E. Workman of Cultra, Co. Down. Gazetted a 2/Lt. in 5th RIR, 17.10.1914, and promoted Lt., 22.5.1915. Joined 1st RIR, 4.7.1915, and was wounded, 13.10.1915, while attached to 2nd Home Counties RE. Joined 10th RIR, 1916, and transferred to the RFC later the same year. Adjutant to 84 Squadron RFC. Adjutant at Stockbridge, 1917. Adjutant of the Sea Plane Station at Plymouth, 1918, and demobilized there.

During World War II he served as Second-in-Command of an Ulster AA battery which went to France. His CO was Robert Hogg Forbes. They were moved up to the Belgian Border just before Dunkirk and split in two, Arthur commanding one half. He was captured during the retreat.

Died, 19.10.1979, aged 84. *Blackthorn*, vol. 3, no. 16, 1980: 'During World War 2 he was with the Royal Artillery (Supplementary Reserve) and was a POW for several years. He was a widower living in Newcastle, Co. Down, and is survived by his son Mr Ian W. Workman and daughter Mrs Sonia Cotton.' Ian Workman died in Vancouver, Canada, 1999. Closed file, ref: (50815).

Workman Lt. Edward MC. Born 4.12.1886 at Belfast, the only son of Frank and Sarah (daughter of John M'Causland) Workman of The Moat, Strandtown, Co. Down. Educated at Charterhouse and Trinity College, Cambridge, where he graduated BA in Engineering with Honours, 1908.

de Ruvigny: ' ... was a member of the Ulster Club and of the Royal Ulster and the Royal North of Ireland Yacht Clubs, and steered his owns yacht successfully on many occasions. He was also a member of the County Down Staghounds and a keen motorist. Before the war he had been an enthusiastic member of the Ulster Volunteer Force, and during the grave political crisis of Easter, 1914, he rendered most practical valuable service to the Unionist cause.'

He had been an officer in 6th Bn, East Belfast Regiment, UVF. Applied for a commission, 19.8.1914, expressing a preference for 5th RIR. Single, 'Shipbuilder', height 5 foot 7¾ inches, weight 139 pounds, chest 34–36½ inches. Gazetted a 2/Lt. in 5th RIR. Promoted to Lt. 22.5.1915. The War Diary noted that he joined 1st RIR on 5.6.1915, but his file states that he joined in the field, 9.5.1915. Attached to A Coy, 2nd RIR, 24 August, and was involved in their attack at Hooge, 25 September, and was one of only three officers of the battalion who came out uninjured. Mentioned in Despatches (*London Gazette* 1.1.1916) for his gallantry on this occasion.

On 19.1.1916 he was in a raid at Le Touquet, River Lys, to gain information on the German trenches and was wounded by a blow to the head from a rifle butt. Admitted to No. 1 Red Cross Hospital, Le Touquet, 21 January. Telegram from the hospital to WO, 22 January, warned that he was 'now dangerous' and 'may be visited'. WO telegram, 22 January, to Embarkation Officer, Folkestone, granted permission for his father to visit. Telegram to father same date confirmed this. Telegram from WO, 23 January, granted the same permission for his mother.

Telegram from No. 1 Red Cross Hospital to WO, 24 January, advised that the parents of Lt. Workman had arrived, and advised WO would also allow their daughter and husband, Capt. Lindsay, to travel to France. 'Recommend permission be granted, parents aged, please wire Lindsay, Pavilion Hotel, Folkestone.' WO telegram, the same day, to Embarkation Officer, Folkestone, advised that permission was granted to Capt. D.C. Lindsay, RIR, and his wife to visit Workman at No. 1 Red Cross Hospital. Explained that they were his brother-in-law and sister respectively. Telegram to Lindsay confirmed this had been done. Told him to take the telegram with him and be able to prove his identity to the embarkation officers.

Irish Times 25.1.1916: 'He was reported to be dangerously wounded, but a letter received from him yesterday, written since he was wounded, does not put so serious a complexion on his condition.'

Died of wounds at No. 1 British Red Cross Hospital (Duchess of Westminster's), Le Touquet, 26.1.1916. Cause of death, 'Meningitis following wound on head by rifle butt'. (Compound fracture of skull). Bachelor, died intestate.

Irish Times 28.1.1916: ' ... his condition from the first was critical, and septic poisoning intervened. His father and mother, who left Belfast on Saturday night, reached the hospital on Monday, and were in constant attendance on him until the end ... was a director of the well-known shipbuilding firm of Workman, Clark and Co. Ltd., of which his father, Councillor Frank Workman, an ex-High Sheriff of Belfast, was one of the founders, and he resided with his parents at The Moat, Strandtown. Prior to the outbreak of war he took an active part in the affairs of the firm with which he was associated, and was held in the highest esteem by all the employees with whom he came in contact. He obtained his commission in the Royal South Downs on 15th

August 1914 ... He had been serving at the front for a considerable period, and in the last despatch received from Field-Marshal French he was recommended for gallant and distinguished service in the field.'

Effects 'handed to relatives of deceased by OC No. 1 British Red Cross Hospital'. Awarded the MC, 15.3.1916.

Irish Life 31.3.1916: ' ... of wounds received in action on the 19th, for his valuable services in which he was awarded the Military Cross, having been Mentioned in Despatches for gallantry at Hooge ... He went to the front on May 1st, 1915.'

WO letter to father, 10.4.1916, advised of the burial in Camiers Road Cemetery, Etaples, grave A. 41.

de Ruvigny: 'His CO, Lt.-Col. Sprague, wrote to his parents: "The enterprise was considered very successful, and the success was, to my mind, mainly due to the exceptional coolness, good leading, and pluck of your poor son. I knew him well, and I looked on him as one of my best officers, who served me in a most heroic and loyal manner." The Adjutant, Capt. Norman: "He did magnificently, and, as everyone says, the success of his party was due entirely to him." Sgt Field: "I have lost the finest company officer in the Army, the best soldier I ever met." ' Etaples Military Cemetery, I.B.21. File ref: 49124.

Wright Capt. Allan O'Halloran. Born at Mill Terrace, Rose Ward, Adelaide, 27.4.1886, the youngest son of Frederick Wright JP, Consul at Adelaide, Australia, and of Frances Jane Wright (daughter of Major, the Hon., Thomas Shuldham O'Halloran, 97th Regt) of Clanferzeal, Woodlands Road, Red Hill, Surrey. His father was a financial agent. Educated at St Peter's College, Adelaide, and at Bedford Grammar School. Although only fourteen years of age at the time, he served in the South African War with the South Australian Mounted Rifles, and received the Queen's Medal with three clasps. In 1902 he joined the Bedford Royal Engineers (Volunteers), and was appointed to the Sussex Royal Garrison Artillery (Militia), 1903, and promoted Lt., 1905. From the Militia he was gazetted a 2/Lt. in 1st RIR, 29.5.1907, and promoted Lt., 22.1.1909. Served in India with 1st RIR and was Adjutant from 1.1.1913, being promoted T/Capt., 15.11.1914.

Shot at 5.30 a.m., 13.3.1915. Mentioned in Despatches, 31.5.1915, for gallant and distinguished service in the field.

He was extremely musical, composing military marches and other compositions, and went in extensively for polo and all sports. He was a qualified instructor of gunnery, musketry, signalling and scouts, being for several years Scout Officer of the battalion. Unmarried and died intestate. A WO telegram was sent to his sister, Helen, 16 March. Personal items to be returned included two pipes, one whistle, and two shrapnel pellets. A WO letter to the family, 14.6.1915, stated that he was buried at map reference Sheet 36 M.35.b3.0., which is just south of Lafone Redoubt, about 200 yards from the British front line. Peculiarly enough, the letter goes on to say that 'this map can be obtained from any map shop'. Le Touret Memorial. File ref: WO339/6822 13486.

Wright Major Henry Coram. Gazetted to the RIR 12.3.1892. Promoted to Lt. 17.3.1896, Capt. 30.11.1901, and Major 2.11.1911. Served in the South African War 1899–1900. Operations in Orange Free State (March–May 1900); Orange River Colony (May–November 1900); Cape Colony, South of Orange River (1899–1900). Received the Queen's Medal with two clasps. Served in India with 1st RIR.

Laurie, 7.2.1915: 'Only Major Wright was hit on the head by a splinter, which did not hurt him, as his skull is fairly resisting!' Wounded, 12.3.1915, and took no further part in the war. The Army List for March 1917 shows him employed with 1st (Garrison) Bn Worcester Regt. Later at the Records Office, Dublin. By 1919 he was on retired pay. File missing.

MEDICAL OFFICERS

These are the only men that I have been able to establish as being Medical Officers to the battalion. Files for Royal Army Medical Corps officers who did not get a permanent commission are not very common at the Public Records Office. Capt. Powell was the sole regular officer, the others having only war time commissions.

Cameron Capt. J.R. Joined 1st RIR 14.9.1917. Wounded 22.10.1918. File missing.

Elliot Capt. H.H. MC, MB. Serving with 1st RIR, 28.5.1917. Mentioned in Despatches and awarded the MC while serving with 8th Division. File missing.

Hawes Capt. A.J. MC, MB. Mentioned in Despatches and awarded the MC while serving with 8th Division.
   Whitfeld: '5.7.1917: We got in safe but a company of the Worcestershires got caught and had casualties, and many of them brought into our mess room and laid on the mess table while Hawes helped the MO to dress them … 14.9.1917: Hawes, the MO, goes to England. He was a splendid little fellow.' File missing.

Maclean Capt. Ivan Clarkson DSO, MC, MD. Son of Major-General H.I. Maclean and Frances Maclean, *née* Clarkson. Only identified by a mention in Whitfeld's personal diary entry for 31.10.1916: 'A man said to have died of exposure in the night. McClean, however, has examined him and it transpires he has drunk half a jar of rum and has really nearly killed himself.'
   Mentioned in Despatches and awarded the DSO, MC, and Bar while serving with 8th Division. DSO awarded for his activities near Westhoek Ridge, 31 July and 1 August 1917 (*London Gazette* 9.1.1918): 'For conspicuous gallantry and devotion to duty in clearing the wounded. He took his stretcher bearers well in advance of our forward positions and behaved with the most exemplary courage and devotion throughout, sparing no efforts to collect the wounded men. After his battalion was relieved he continued to work under the heaviest fire for another twenty-four hours, and was severely wounded on his way back after all the cases had been cleared. He set a splendid example of energy and contempt of danger.'
   Died of wounds as a POW, 4.4.1918, aged 36 At that time he was attached to 2nd Rifle Bde. Premont British Cemetery, Aisne, IV.B.33. File missing.

Powell Capt. Charles Leslie Grove MC. Born 17.2.1892. Served three years each with Westminster School OTC and London University OTC. Applied for RAMC appointment, 20.4.1915. Declared no previous or present employment but had served four months on an Indian Hospital Ship and was just completing his training at St Thomas' Hospital, London. The letter of recommendation to the WO was from his uncle, J.L.G. Powell, OC 6th East Surrey Regt (Territorials based at Kingston, Surrey. His uncle, however, was actually on the retired list and the battalion had long since gone to India.)
   At the time of his commission, his address was 2 Old Palace Lane, Richmond, Surrey. Went to France, 17.5.1915, and was attached to 1st RIR as MO. Witnessed and certified the death by firing squad of L/Cpl P. Sands, 15.9.1915. Mentioned in Despatches, *London Gazette* 15.6.1916. His name was forwarded to Brigade by the acting CO for his bravery on 1.7.1916. He appears to have left 1st RIR in the autumn of 1916 and served with No. 6 CCS. Later moved to 1st DCLI until the end of his tour in France, 15.12.1917, when he went to Italy as MO for 1st East Surrey Regt. His service there ended, 16.2.1918, when he fell down stone steps at his billet and fractured his right tibia. The bone had to be joined with a metal plate. The incident was accepted as accidental, one note stated that part of the stairs had been 'shot away' by artillery and that his lamp had gone out. In hospital, 26.3.1918 to 30.10.1918. The MB at Chatham, 16.12.1918, noted that he had recovered and ordered him to rejoin his unit.

Applied for a wound gratuity, 28.3.1919. Married Ethel Stockley (born 11.10.1889) at Hampstead, London, 27.10.1920. Transferred to India, 25.1.1921, and died from heat-stroke at 9 a.m., 18.7.1922, at the British Station Hospital, Multan, India. His death was directly attributable to service. Wife's address at the time was Kasula, India. WO letter to widow at 46 King Henry's Road, Hampstead, London NW3, 21.12.1922, notified that she would receive a double pension of £100 per anum. She married Major James Russell Yousell, 23.6.1938. At this time she was receiving £100 p.a. widow's pension.

RAMC Medical Journal, 1922: 'On July 18, at Multan, Capt. C.L.G. Powell MC, aged 30. He entered the Army as a temporary Lieutenant on May 7, 1915, becoming Captain after a year's service, and received a permanent commission, ranking as Captain from November 7, 1918. He served in the recent war, was mentioned in dispatches in the *London Gazette* on June 15, 1916, and received the Military Cross on November 17, 1917.'

His RAMC papers state that he was Mentioned in Despatches, 17.12.1917. They also state Lt., T/Capt., 7.5.1915; Capt. (T.C.), 7.5.1916; Capt., 7.11.1918, but not to reckon for pay or allowances prior to 1.7.1919. Served Home, 7.5.1915 to 23.5.1915; France, 24.5.1915 to 16.12.1917; Italy, 17.12.1917 to 26.3.1918; Home, 27.3.1918 to 25.1.1921; India from 26.1.1921. File ref: 183694.

Stallard Lt. J.P. Present at the C.-in-C. inspection at Bac St Maur, 17.4.1915. Took part in the attack of 9.5.1915. File destroyed.

CHAPLAINS

The full list of chaplains that served with the battalion is not available. I have set out below the details for those that I know were attached to 1st RIR. The Royal Army Chaplain Corps had two departments. In general terms, one of these selected four Church of England chaplains to a brigade. Another four chaplains came from the second department which was composed of members of the Roman Catholic, Presbyterian, Wesleyan, and 'United Board' denominations. Although some chaplains, but not all, were attached to particular battalions, they were flexible and would often minister throughout their brigade or division.

Hutchison Capt. Revd William Holmes MC, BA. Born in Dublin, 21.1.1882. Studied at Queen's College, Belfast, and graduated in Arts at the Royal University of Ireland, 1904. Took his theological course at the Presbyterian College, Belfast, and was licensed by the Belfast Presbytery, 26.5.1908. After a period as Assistant to Dr Charles Davey in Fisherwick, he received a call to the Cuningham Memorial Church, Cullybackey, Co. Antrim, where he was ordained by the Ballymena Presbytery, 5.5.1910.

He was Moderator of the Synod of Ballymena and Coleraine in 1914. Enlisted as Pte M2/222351 in the ASC (despatch rider), Motor Transport, 15.9.1916. Address, Cullybacky. 'Clergyman', also noted that he was a motorcyclist. Height 5 foot 8¾ inches, chest 36½–39 inches, distinctive marks shown as 'a crown, an anchor, and 1887 tattoo on back of left forearm'. Next of kin was his sister, Miss May Elizabeth Hutchison. All ASC service was at home. Applied for a commission as an Army Chaplain, 30.11.1916.

Discharged to a commission as Army Chaplain, 1.2.1917, while serving at Larkhill Camp, Salisbury Plain. Served with 1st RIR. Army contract renewed, 15.1.1918. Gassed, 14 April, and returned to duty, 23 August. Awarded the MC for bravery in the field, 1.9.1918. GSW right arm, 20 October, and returned to duty, 26 October. Appointed Educational Officer to the battalion, 10.2.1919. Left 1st RIR, 28 March, and was posted to Calais for duty. Ordered home for demobilization, 30.6.1919. Last served with 5/6th Scottish Rifles. Single. Medical rating A. Home address given as Cullybacky. Asked for an appointment in the east, 14.12.1920. WO acknowledged, 18 December, and said that they would advise if anything came up. Letter to Army Chaplain's Dept., 3.3.1921, enquired whether there might be an appointment for him 'in the East' within the next six months. Appointed Honorary Chaplain, 4th Class, 4.10.1921.

In 1932 he was called to Ballywillan, and was there installed by the Presbytery of Coleraine on 26.5.1932. In 1932 and 1933 he attended the 36th (Ulster) Division OCA annual dinner. Died 24.8.1953. His widow was Dr Isobel Alexander of Portrush. His obituary appeared in the Annual Reports for 1954: 'He was deeply absorbed in his work as a minister of the Gospel. To his calling he brought not only a sense of commitment, but also ability and discrimination in the use of the written and spoken word. His warm-hearted disposition and ready spirits made him welcome wherever he went, both in times of prosperity and of stress. In his ministries he made and retained many warm friendships, and these were more lasting because their background was that of a living faith.' File ref: WO339/89915.

Knapp, Capt. Revd Fr Simon Stock OCD, DSO, MC. Born 1858. Posted to 6th Inniskilling Dragoons and served in the South African War. *The Cross on the Sword* tells us that his CO, later Field-Marshal Lord Allenby, wrote that he was not only 'quite the best specimen of Army Chaplain I've ever met but a charming companion'.

Signed army service contract 10.10.1914. Address given as Carmelite Priory, Church Street, Kensington. Ordered to report to Revd R.H. Nash, senior Roman Catholic Chaplain, Salisbury Plain District, Tidworth. Appointed to 25th Bde, serving with 1st RIR.

Returned to the UK, 11.1.1915, and appeared before a MB at Queen Alexandra Military Hospital, London, six days later. It was noted that he was aged 56 and suffering from debility and influenza that began at Estaires 28.12.1914. Cause recorded as exposure on military service: unfit for general service for one month. A WO letter, 11.2.1915, instructed Fr Knapp to regard himself as being on leave until instructions are issued regarding the results of his medical examination. His address at that time was 61 Warwick Street, London SW. MB 18.2.1915: presently unfit for any kind of service. WO letter, 23.2.1915, extended his leave for another three weeks. MB at Caxton Hall, 12.3.1915: fit for general service. The next day the WO requested him to report to France as soon as possible and issued a railway warrant.

Rfn S. O'Neill (probably No. 6867) had a letter published in the *Cork Examiner* early 1915: 'Our chaplain is not an Army chaplain, but a Volunteer who came from Winchester with us, and a regular saint. He is the Revd S.S. Knapp, and he is always in the trenches with the regiment. He has faced death at least forty times since we came out. No other clergyman have I seen in the front trenches but him – hearing confessions, with bullets, in showers like hailstones, passing over the heads of the penitents and confessor. This is what makes soldiers fight well and die calm.'

Temporarily attached to 1st Irish Guards, 24.5.1915. Rejoined 1st RIR, 16.7.1915, until he was attached to 2nd Irish Guards 30.8.1915. Renewed army service contract 13.7.1915 and 5.11.1916. Awarded the DSO, MC, and two Mentions in Despatches. Died of wounds received while attending to the wounded at an ADS at Boesinghe, 1.8.1917. A Field Service Report dated 6.8.1917 stated that he died at No. 47 CCS.

A WO telegram was sent to Mrs O'Brien, 10 South Parade, Bath, 2.8.1917, notifying the death and asked for relationship of the next of kin. Effects request form was signed by his sister-in-law, Jeannette O'Brien. Another note stated she was the next of kin and that the effects should be sent to the Prior at Kensington. The WO asked for details of a blood relative. Mrs O'Brien replied that she was the only kin. Fr Knapp's parents both died when he was a child. She had married his elder brother who died in 1882. He was noted as having taken the name O'Brien (no explanation given) and had been a Captain in the 3rd Middlesex Regt. Another brother had been killed in the South African War, no name supplied. The WO told Mrs O'Brien that, as there was no will in her favour, she had no claim to the effects. Outstanding debts were 'servant's wages 7s/4d and groom's wages 8s/9d'.

A note, 3.8.1917, referred to the Irish Guards sending men to a Requiem. There are two undated and unattributed newspaper articles on the file. The first refers to Viscount French unveiling a stained glass window at the Carmelite Priory. This memorial was subscribed by the officers, NCO's, and men of the 2nd Irish Guards. The second article refers to Fr Knapp being known to the 2nd Irish Guards as 'The Saint of Kensington'.

The Cross on the Sword: 'He had been in a front-line battalion constantly since 1914. The denial of the Victoria Cross to another Catholic chaplain has been adversely commented upon by Professor O'Rahilly. But if ever a British soldier deserved the highest award for gallantry, it was Fr Simon Knapp ... But how a gentle Carmelite monk, such as Fr Knapp, could adapt himself in two wars to both cavalry and infantry units in the field, and distinguish himself in each, is incredible. After the war the Irish Guards commissioned a memorial window to Fr Knapp, and it was erected in the Carmelite church, Kensington. Sadly this stained glass window was destroyed in 1944 during the German flying-bomb bombardment.

'Fr Rawlinson, in a letter to the Father Prior, Carmelite church, Kensington, said: "No words can express what a loss he is to the Chaplain's Dept., or how highly he was thought of by the whole of the Guards Division ... He is the greatest loss we could have sustained." There is no doubt that had he lived, the Victoria Cross could not have been denied Fr Knapp; the Guards Division would have seen to that.'

Dozinghem Military Cemetery, Poperinghe, II.C.1. File ref: WO339/23030.

Matthews Revd Fr. Attached temporarily while Fr Murphy was sick, 18.6.1916 to 13.10.1916. There is not enough information to make a positive identification.

Murphy Capt. Revd Fr Bruno. Born 1862. He had previously been a soldier in the R. Irish and served in Egypt and the Sudan. *The Cross on the Sword*: 'Possibly he was on the Nile Expedition to relieve General Gordon and was inspired by Fr Brindle, his regimental chaplain. After army service he became a Trappist monk and was ordained at Roscrea in 1907.'

A WO letter, 7.8.1915, notified Murphy of his selection to serve with the BEF. Address was Mount St Joseph's Abbey, Roscrea, Co. Tipperary: a Cistercian Abbey. He was probably the only Trappist monk on the Western Front. His acceptance form is dated 10 August. Confirmed ordained priest in the Roman Catholic Church. Form witnessed by Fr Boniface Ryan, same address.

WO letter, 14.8.1915, advised him to proceed to Folkestone and report to the Embarkation Officer as soon as possible. As this was his first appointment, travelling expenses to Folkestone could not be claimed against public funds. Next of kin shown as Michael Murphy, Ballyhindon, Fermoy, Co. Cork. Embarked 5 September and joined 1st RIR three days later. Form to renew army contract, 3.6.1916, was witnessed by Capt. G.I. Gartlan, 1st RIR. To Sick List 3 June. Officer's sailing list for HS *Panama*, 11 June, from Le Havre, included Fr Murphy and Capt. E. ffrench-Mullen, 1st RIR. Admitted Mrs Mitchison's Hospital, The Clock House, Chelsea, SW, 11 June, with iritis. Medical note to WO, 19 June, stated that he had severe conjunctivitis and it was impossible to predict when he would again be fit for service. The MB at Caxton Hall, 21 July: conjunctivitis (left eye) and cystitis; unfit for general or home service for six weeks.

MB at Fermoy Military Hospital, 4 September: fit for general service. Age given as 53 years 11 months. WO telegram, 6 September, ordered him to report to the Chaplains Department at the WO, Friday 8th, with a view to departing for France 'early Saturday'. Caught 7.50 a.m. train from Charring Cross, 9 September. Rejoined 1st RIR, 13 October. Moved to Base on Staff Billet, 2 December. On list for No. 7 Ambulance Train to England, 28.3.1917, with iritis. Sailed for the UK aboard HS *Warilda*, 29 March. MB at No. 2 London General Hospital, 27 April: left eye again, problem developed at Rouen, unfit for general service for three weeks. MB at No. 2 Red Cross Hospital, Rouen, 2.7.1918: he had an operation to remove a dermoid cyst from left side of his chest; three weeks UK leave recommended. Demobilized, 2.2.1920, medically classified A. Appointed Chaplain to the Forces, 4th Class, 13.10.1921. *The Cross on the Sword*: 'He did not return to his monastery. Instead, he was accepted by the Aberdeen diocese in 1927.' File ref: WO339/64129.

Nolan Capt. Revd Fr James. Born 1887, the son of John Nolan, Newbliss, Co. Monaghan. Notified of acceptance as Acting Chaplain, 18.7.1916, and ordered to report to GOC 58th London Division at Sutton Veny as soon as possible. Reported for duty, 9.8.1916. Ordered to embark for France on 26 September. On arrival was posted to 15th Brigade, 5th Division. Joined 1st RIR, 9.12.1916. He appears to have remained with 25th Brigade when 1st RIR transferred to 107th Brigade.

Captured 'unwounded', 27.5.1918, while attached to No. 25 Field Ambulance at Bouvancourt. His report, on repatriation, explained what happened: he was having a meal in the officer's mess about 10 p.m. (a house in the village) when someone reported that the Germans had surrounded the village. The CO went out, came back shortly and said everyone must make their way out as best they could. He didn't see the CO again. Decided that some attempt would probably be made to evacuate the unit and wounded and that if he left before then it would be injurious to his standing as a chaplain. Went to dugout where wounded and RAMC men were. Heard sound of a large party of Germans about 250 yards away. Officers in dugout were consulting what to do. Went out with Capt. Hughes of 25th Field Ambulance to see if the way out of the village was clear for escape. A party of Germans shouted at them and they were taken prisoner.

A memo from the WO to the Chaplains Department, BEF, 19.9.1918, stated that an application to renew his appointment had been received from Fr Nolan and asked if they recommended this renewal. Reply dated 23 September from Revd B.S. Rawlinson CMG, stated 'I should be sorry after all he has been through not to recommend him for such a renewal. At the same time, he was not looked upon as a very suitable man, and I am not anxious to have him back in France when he is released. He would probably be more fitted elsewhere than in France.'

WO to Revd Rawlinson, 7 October, asked if the unsuitability 'is a matter of health or of some other nature½' Rawlinson to WO, 10 October: 'His unsuitability was not a matter of health, but rather of temperament. There was nothing absolutely against him, except that he was not wanted at the units he went to, and was not regarded as a suitable Chaplain.'

WO to Fr Nolan, October 1918, advised that his temporary position was retained and the question of permanence would be addressed when he was returned to the UK. Fr Nolan was at Nr.12394 Stube 4, Bar.B, Offiziere-gefangenenlager, Stralsund, Danholm, Germany. There is a note on his file about recent representations objecting to the Germans holding British clergy as POWs. Repatriated, 1.11.1918. MB, 2 November, at the Prince of Wales Hospital for Officers, Marelybone, London NW1. Address, Ballyshannon, Co. Donegal. Disability: 'Debility. Exchanged prisoner of war.' General health good. Recommended two months leave.

Fr Nolan wrote to the WO, 21.11.1918, stating that he was applying for a discharge and asked for an extension of his leave. Gave the Newbliss address. WO replied, 2 December, saying that they would not object if he pressed for a discharge, but there was a shortage of RC Chaplains and, if he wanted to extend his service for a while, they would be pleased. Fr Nolan to WO, 6 December: due to his Bishop's orders he wanted the resignation to go through. WO, 6 January, confirmed that his discharge would be effective from 7.1.1919. Appointed Honorary Chaplain to the Forces, 4th Class. No blame for his capture and placed on Exonerated Officers List. File ref: WO374/50787.

SOME OTHER RANKS

Most files for other ranks were destroyed by a fire during the Blitz in World War II. Below are some soldiers whose details came to light during the course of my research.

Carroll Capt. William MC. Born 1879, the son of Thomas Carroll, 21 Byron Street, Knowsley Road, Bootle, Liverpool. While working as a painter he was a member of the 5th Volunteer Battalion, Liverpool Regt. Height 5 foot 6½ inches. Enlisted as No. 5710 in the RIR, 17.11.1898, and served in South Africa with 2nd RIR, 16.12.1899 until 11.11.1902. Medals: Queen's South Africa Medal, clasps Cape Colony, Orange Free State, and Transvaal. King's South Africa Medal, clasps 1901 and 1902. He then served in India with 1st RIR. Promotions: Cpl 1.8.1902, L/Sgt 2.2.1904, Sgt 13.1.1906, C/Sgt 29.12.1911, CSM 1.5.1914, RSM 4.11.1914 – the day he joined the BEF.

Laurie: 'January 18th, 1915 ... my Sergeant-Major, Master Cook, and Sergeant-Bugler, all trembling with cold ... shut themselves up last night with a charcoal fire, and we found them about four o'clock insensible from the fumes, and had a certain amount of difficulty in bringing them round. Here in the war these people do different things ... The Sergeant-Major, instead of drilling the battalion, arrives up with 8 mules and three ammunition carts.'

Mentioned in the Despatches of Field Marshal Sir John French, 4.4.1915, for the engagement at Neuve Chapelle.

Dundalk Democrat, 25.12.1915: 'Another Irish VC ... We are able to state that Regimental Sergeant Major W. Carroll, 1st Battalion Royal Irish Rifles, has been recommended for the Victoria Cross for conspicuous bravery.

'On the 9th of May, just two months after Neuve Chapelle, the Royal Irish Rifles marched out to take up a position in the assembly trenches. On this occasion the 1st Battalion was allotted the leading position, with the Rifle Brigade on the right. It was here that Regimental Sergeant Major Carroll, who had previously distinguished himself at Neuve Chapelle, won further fame. Brigadier-General Lowry-Cole was killed on this day, and Major Clinton Baker (since killed) the commander, was wounded. He had taken a party of 20 men to the right flank to try and stop the enfilading from that flank, and had sent Sergeant Major Carroll with a party of 20 men to do the same on the left flank. Both these parties were wiped out to a man, except Sergeant Major Carroll, who had several bullet holes in his clothing and equipment, but was only slightly wounded in the hand.

'The Sergeant Major's party included two men who had got the DCM for cutting the wire entanglements at Neuve Chapelle. For this gallant deed, in which he faced death all the way across to the enfilading forces, Sergeant Major Carroll has been awarded the Military Cross – the medal of St George, 2nd Class. He has since been recommended for the Victoria Cross.'

Awarded the MC, 23.6.1915, with a gratuity of £20. Wounded, 25.9.1915, and returned to the UK. He was at the Depot, 1 October, and awarded the Russian Medal of St George, 1st Class, the following day. RSM of 3rd RIR, 16 December. The War Diary, 9.1.1916, stated that he rejoined the battalion near Estaires having recovered from wounds received at Bois Grenier (shrapnel wound to right thigh).

Whitfeld: 'June 1916. RSM Carroll is a wonderful man and a splendid RSM, one could not wish for a better one anywhere ... November 1916. Carroll has decided to go and to take a commission. He does not move with the times I am afraid and I don't doubt that my policy displeases him.'

Left the battalion, 21.11.1916, having been promoted a 2/Lt. in the East Yorkshire Regt. While serving as an a/Capt. with the 12th Bn, he was killed in action, 3.5.1917, aged 38. He never married and his eldest brother, 31572 Pte Thomas Boyd Carroll, C Coy, 2nd Garrison Bn,

Cheshire Regt, Egyptian Expeditionary Force, and 6 Halford Street, Liverpool, administered the estate of £152.10. Albuera Cemetery, Bailleul-Sire-Berthoult (N), C.15, Pas de Calais.

Clarke RSM W. DCM. 8519 See main text. CSM Clarke was awarded the DCM, 3.6.1918, and the Croix de Guerre, 12.7.1918. By May 1934 he was RSM of 1st RUR.

Driscoll Lt. James MC, DCM. Born St Patrick's, Cork, 3.7.1879, the son of Eugene and Mary Driscoll. Enlisted as Rfn 5420 in the RIR, 3.1.1898. Labourer, height 5 foot 4¾ inches, weight 117 pounds, chest 32–34 inches. At the Depot, 3.1.1898 to 24.10.1889. Served in the South African War, 25.10.1889 to 4.2.1903. Married Mary Hogarty at St James', Dublin, 1.11.1903. Their children were Mary Josie (3.2.1905 Dublin); Gregory Michael (23.8.1906 Dublin); Margaret Mary (28.10.1908); James Patrick (23.11.1910 Dover) and Rosina Elizabeth (2.12.1902 Tidworth). Served at home, 5.2.1903 to 10.12.1913. Posted to 2nd RIR, 1.5.1904.

Appointed L/Cpl, 23.7.1907, and sent to 3rd RIR, 28.8.1908. Promoted Cpl, 17.11.1909, and returned to 2nd RIR, 27.1.1910. Appointed L/Sgt, 19.6.1911, and promoted Sgt, 1.9.1913. Served in India with 1st RIR, 11.12.1913 to 4.10.1914. Served at home, 5.10.1914 to 5.11.1914. To France with 1st RIR, 6.11.1914. Acting CSM, 10.3.1915, and CSM, 29.3.1915.

DCM, 14.1.1916: 'For conspicuous gallantry. When all his officers had been killed or wounded, he exhibited conspicuous courage and ability in leading his company out of action, and throughout the operations invariably showed the greatest devotion to duty.' (*London Gazette* 11.3.1916). CSM C Coy in the attack of 1.7.1916 and his name was forwarded for gallantry by the acting CO. Acting RSM, 21.11.1916 to 5.1.1917.

Granted a commission and posted to 23rd R. Fusiliers, 6.3.1917, where he was awarded the MC. Left unit, 'wounded (gas shell)', 15.3.1918, and embarked Rouen–Southampton, 19 March. MB, 27 March, noted that he had a cough and congestion, unfit for general service for two months from date of wounding. MB at Dover, 31 May, shows 23rd R. Fusiliers attached 5th Bn, 'He has recovered', instructed to report for duty.

Letter from WO, 29.5.1922, advised Lt. Driscoll MC, DCM, R. Fusiliers, that his retirement would be enforced in ten days time. He could opt for retired pay of £200 p.a. or a gratuity of £2,300. Removed from the Reserve of Officers due to age, 3.7.1929. File ref: WO339/98342.

Graham 8796 Cpl James MM. Born Saintfield, Co. Down. Enlisted and resided Belfast. As a L/Cpl he was awarded the MM for 'Gallantry in action on July 1st 1916'. Transferred to 2nd RIR and promoted Cpl. Killed in action, 22.10.1918. Tyne Cot Memorial.

Henniker Major Charles H.D. MBE. 9562 Sgt Henniker was awarded the French Medal Militaire, 15.12.1919. By May 1934 he was RQMS of 1st RUR.

Quis Separabit, vol. 37, Spring 1966: 'It was with deep regret we learned that Charles Henniker had died at his home in London on 6th December 1965. Charles joined the regiment as a band boy from the Duke of York's School in 1910. He served with the regiment as a Sergeant during the 1914–18 War in France and was awarded the French Medaille Militaire for gallantry at Passchendaele in 1917. Between the two Great Wars Charles was with either the 1st or 2nd Bns. in Parkhurst, Isle of Wight, with the 1st Bn in the Army of Occupation on the Rhine, in Victoria Barracks, Belfast, in Palestine, in Alexandria, in the Far East in Hong Kong and Shanghai and on the NW frontier in India. During this period he was awarded the Long Service and Good Conduct Medal in 1931 and became RSM in 1937.

'Charles Henniker was commissioned as a Lt. QM in 1939 just about the time I joined the 2nd Bn stationed in Parkhurst Barracks on the Isle of Wight. Charles had the difficult task of mobilizing the Bn and then all the problems connected with the move to France in 1939. He remained our QM throughout the war, in France with the BEF and evacuation at Dunkirk, during the long months of training in England, the landings in Normandy and through to VE Day in Bremen. For his services during the war he was awarded the MBE in 1946.

'It was during this wartime period that I got to know him well and as a company commander I found that I got the utmost co-operation from him even in the most difficult and exposed positions. As a brother officer I valued his advice and friendship as I am sure we all did; even his smoking a pipe at 5.30 a.m. in the morning immediately after he awoke could not annoy his friends. Charles left the 2nd Bn in 1946 to look after a prisoner of war camp at Abergavenny from 1947 to 1951. His last year of service was with the London Irish Rifles, thus finishing his career as a Major at the Duke of York's where he started it some 41 years before as a boy. He retired in 1951 and lived quietly in South London "counting the milestones of his career". Many of us were delighted to see him on the perhaps too rare occasions of regimental functions in London.

'The funeral took place at Raynes Park with full regimental honours on the 10th December 1965 ... I am sure that all members of the regiment who served with him would like to join with me in saying how much we mourn him and extend to his wife and family our most heartfelt sympathies. — D.E.L.'

McCourt RSM D. MM. Went overseas with 1st RIR to join the BEF. While serving as a L/Sgt he was recommended for gallantry for his part in the attack of 1.7.1916. Military Medal, *London Gazette* 9.11.1916. *War Diary*, 11.1.1917, noted MM to 9405 Sgt McCourt of B Coy. French Croix de Guerre. Later RSM 7006428.

McFaull, Major W.R. MBE. Regimental number 9280. *Quis Separabit*, vol. 38, 1967: 'It is with deep regret that we heard of the death of Major McFaull at his home in Larne on 14 May, 1967. He left his home in Glynn and joined the Regiment in March, 1909, with the 2nd Battalion in Aldershot, and subsequently served with the 3rd (Res) Battalion, and afterwards in France and Belgium with the 1st and 2nd Battalions respectively, being awarded the French Croix de Guerre (Silver Star) in 1918.

'On the cessation of hostilities he again served for a short period with the 3rd (Res) Battalion, later being posted to the 1st Battalion, where he was promoted WOII and appointed Regimental Quartermaster Sergeant in 1921. In the same year he was posted to the Regimental Depot in Armagh. He served for over 14 years at the Depot, being promoted WO Class I (RSM) in 1928. During his tour of duty at the Depot he was active in his interest in the welfare of the recruits and Depot staff. He made a large circle of friends amongst the civilian population, and being a keen angler, he was for a time President of the Armagh Angling Club.

'In June 1935 he was commissioned Lieutenant (Quartermaster) and posted to the 2nd Battalion Gravesend and the following period of three years proved to be a very busy period with frequent camps, including the Aldershot Tattoo and Bisley Ranges. It was at the latter place he was called upon to represent Ireland in the Small Bore Competition when they won the competition.

'He left the 2nd Battalion in Palestine prior to joining the 1st Battalion in India where he served on the N.W. Frontier, returning home in 1940. Leaving the 1st Battalion, he was employed on the Staff of Combined operations, until demobilization. He retired in 1948. For his services he was awarded the MBE in July 1941.

'Residing in Larne, he was unable to take an active part in the affairs of the Regimental Association, but was always actively identified with the organisation of the Annual Appeal in aid of the Benevolent Fund and for SSAFA. With Captain R. Lyttle, the Town Clerk, he played a large part in the organisation of the fund for the victims of the Princess Victoria which sank in 1953. Shortly after, he joined the Larne Borough Council as Secretary of the Entertainments Committee. He resigned in 1965 and as a tribute for his services he was appointed the first official Mace Bearer to the Mayor, Aldermen and Councillors of the Larne Borough Council.

'To his wife Florence, and his son and daughter, he offer our sincere sympathy.'

Simner 7095 CSM William H. DCM, MM. DCM, *London Gazette* 5.8.1915: 'For conspicuous gallantry on 9th May 1915 near Rouges Bancs, when he, with great courage and determination, captured a German machine gun, thereby materially assisting to repel several counter attacks.'

Tried by FGCM at Lercus, 7.12.1915, on a charge of drunkenness. Found guilty and reduced from CSM to Sgt. Recommended for gallantry for his part in the attack of 1.7.1916. Restored to CSM July 1916. Awarded the MM for 'Gallantry in action on July 1st 1916'. Rejoined 1st RIR from 1st RIF, 8.11.1918.

Stovin 2/Lt. Charles Ernest DCM. Mentioned in Despatches of Field Marshal Sir John French dated 4.4.1915 for the engagement at Neuve Chapelle. 7323 CSM Stovin, B Coy, had his name forwarded for gallantry by the acting CO for his part in the attack of 1.7.1916. DCM, *London Gazette*, 13.2.1917: 'For conspicuous gallantry and devotion to duty. He has performed consistent good work throughout, and has at all times set a splendid example.' Left 1st RIR, 5.3.1917, having been gazetted a 2/Lt. in the East Yorkshire Regt. Closed file ref: (164062).

Tonge 7270 CSM John. D Coy. Born St Pancras, Middlesex, the son of Fred and Alice Tonge. Husband of Lily Tonge, 7 Hales Buildings, St George's Road, Southwark, London. Enlisted London. Tried by FGCM at Lercus, 7.12.1915, on a charge of drunkenness. Found guilty and reduced to Sgt. Later restored to CSM. Recommended for gallantry for his part in the attack of 1.7.1916, being killed in action that day. Age 29. Thiepval Memorial. File destroyed.

THE FIRST CASUALTIES

Orr 6795 Rfn Hamilton. Born Newtownards, Co. Down, the son of James and Lizzie Orr, 50 James Street, Newtownards. Had served twelve years, ten of these in India. Returned with 1st RIR to join the BEF and was killed in action, 15.11.1914, while occupying the trenches for the first time at Rue Tilleloy. B Coy. Aged 30. Rue du Bacquerot (13th) London Graveyard, Laventie, plot G2. File destroyed.

Sparrow 9838 Rfn Robert Charles. His is one of the 'burned series' of files and is incomplete. Born St Ann's, Dublin, 1893, the son of Robert and Mary Sparrow, 33 Kildare Street, Dublin. Enlisted in 2nd RIR, 17.11.1911, aged 18 years 1 month, Church of Ireland (Anglican), gardener, height 5 foot 7½ inches, weight 125 pounds, chest 32–34½ inches.

To hospital, 10.3.1912, and discharged, 13.3.1912, 'Wound scalp'. Three days confined to barracks for 'rusty rifle on parade', Tidworth, 31.10.1912. Three days confined to barracks for 'absent from parade', Tidworth, 30.4.1913. Posted to 1st RIR in India, 11.12.1913.

In hospital, 18.4.1914 to 6.5.1914, and 21.7.1914 for 26 days. Note of Court of Enquiry, 20.5.1914, at Kirkee: 'In no way to blame' This is a very damaged document but it appears that he was on company training, 16.4.1914, ran around a tree and into a branch, hurting his wrist and thigh.

Returned with 1st RIR to join the BEF and was killed in action, 15.11.1914, while occupying the trenches for the first time at Rue Tilleloy. Identity disc dispatched to Mrs M. Sparrow, 33 Kildare Street, Dublin. Receipt for war medals signed by Mary E. Sparrow, 9 Pembroke Gardens, Ballsbridge, Dublin. Le Touret Memorial. File ref: WO364/S2294.

THE COMMANDING OFFICERS

Whitfeld: 'As far as Commanding Officers were concerned, I have always imagined that there was no battalion in France so unlucky. I may be wrong. We never seemed to be able to keep one and it made Adjutant a very difficult and responsible position. To most people not acquainted with military life, it would not appear to be of much importance whether Commanding Officers changed frequently or not; provided they were competent. That is not so. There is nothing worse for a battalion than frequent changes of Commanding Officers. Efficiency, discipline, esprit de corps all suffer. Efficiency, because there is no continuity of orders or command generally. Discipline, because there is no continuity of system. Esprit de corps, because as so often happened, the new CO did not belong to the Regiment and the men took little interest in the CO and the CO took less interest in the men. This was more than true in the battalion and unfortunately the person concerned stayed with us for a long time and I always thought, did untold damage.' These bitter comments, written in December 1918, are directed against Lt.-Col. E.C. Lloyd, for whom I could hardly find a complimentary word in any of my research.

Lt.-Col. George Brenton Laurie	6.8.1914 to 12.3.1915.
Lt.-Col. Osbert Clinton Baker	12.3.1915 to 9.5.1915.
Lt.-Col. Arthur Drummond Nairn Merriman	17.5.1915 to 13.6.1915.
Lt.-Col. Richard Algernon Craigie Daunt	13.6.1915 to 26.2.1916.
Major Edward Colburn Mayne	26.2.1916 to 14.4.1916. Royal Irish Fusiliers.
Lt.-Col. Guy Henry Sawyer	14.4.1916 to 17.6.1916. Royal Berkshire Regiment.
Lt.-Col. Charles Carroll Macnamara	18.6.1916 to 1.7.1916.
Major Arthur Joseph William Fitzmaurice	1.7.1916 to 20.7.1916.
Lt.-Col. Evan Colclough Lloyd	20.7.1916 to 28.4.1917. Royal Irish Regiment.
Lt.-Col. Richard Algernon Craigie Daunt	28.4.1917 to 27.6.1917.
Major Thomas Henry Ivey	27.6.1917 to 8.7.1917.
Lt.-Col. Alexander Daniel Reid	8.7.1917 to 31.7.1917. Royal Inniskilling Fusiliers.
Major Thomas Henry Ivey	1.8.1917 to 9.8.1917.
Lt.-Col. Heffernan William Denis MacCarthy-O'Leary	9.8.1917 to 16.8.1917. Royal Irish Fusiliers.
Major Thomas Henry Ivey	16.8.1917 to 1.9.1917.
Lt.-Col. John Hendley Morrison Kirkwood	1.9.1917 to 9.10.1917. Household Battalion.
Major Thomas Henry Ivey	9.10.1917 to 29.12.1917.
Lt.-Col. Heffernan William Denis MacCarthy-O'Leary	29.12.1917 to 3.4.1918. Royal Irish Fusiliers.
Major Thomas Henry Ivey	4.4.1918 to 20.4.1918.
Lt.-Col. John Patrick Hunt	20.4.1918 to 16.8.1918. Royal Dublin Fusiliers.
Major James Alan Mulholland	16.8.1918 to 10.9.1918.
Lt.-Col. John Patrick Hunt	10.9.1918 to 12.5.1919. Royal Dublin Fusiliers.

Bibliography

Blackthorn (1969 —) Regimental Journal of the Royal Irish Rangers and the Royal Irish Regiment.

Boraston, Lieutenant Colonel J.H. CB, OBE and Captain Cyril E.O. Bax (1926), *The Eight Division in War, 1914–1918*, London.

Bowman, Timothy (1999), '*The Administration of British Military Justice, 1914–18*', Limerick: Royal Munster Fusiliers Association Magazine, Issue No. 15.

Brown, Malcolm, and Shirley Seaton (Revised 1994), *Christmas Truce*, London.

Burgoyne, Gerald Achilles (1985), *The Burgoyne Diaries*, London.

The Campbell College Register, 1894 to 1938 (1938), Belfast.

'*Clongowes Wood College, War List, Revised to January 1918*' (1918), Kildare: The Clongownian.

The Clongownian (1917, 1918, and 1919).

Corbally, Lt.-Col. M.J.P.M. (1961), *The Royal Ulster Rifles 1793–1960*, Glasgow.

Clutterbuck, Colonel L.A., editor, in association with Colonel W.T. Dooner and Commander the Hon. C.A. Denison (1916), *The Bond of Sacrifice*, 2 vols, London.

Creagh, General Sir O'Moore VC, GCB, GCSI and E.M. Humphris (1924), *The Distinguished Service Order 1886–1923*, London.

Donnelly, Edward (1916), letters in the author's collection.

Falls, Cyril (1925), *The History of the First Seven Battalions: The Royal Irish Rifles in the Great War*, Aldershot.

— (1922), *The History of the 36th (Ulster) Division*, Belfast and London.

Gill, Fr H.V. SJ, DSO, MC, *War Reminiscences of, 1914–1918*, held by Irish Jesuit Archives, Dublin, unpublished.

Graves, Charles (1950), *The Royal Ulster Rifles*, Belfast.

The Great War 1914–1918, Bank of Ireland Staff Service Record (1920), compiled by Thomas F. Hennessy, Dublin.

Hall, Brendan & Donal Hall (2000), *The Louth Rifles, 1877–1908*, Genealogical Society of Ireland, Dún Laoghaire, Co. Dublin.

Harbison, John F. (1973), *The Ulster Unionist Party 1882–1973*, Belfast.

Irish Life (1914–19), weekly magazine published in Dublin.

Irish Times (1914–19), daily newspaper published in Dublin.

Johnstone, Tom (1992), *Orange, Green and Khaki*, Dublin.

Johnstone, Tom & James Hagerty (1996), *The Cross on the Sword: Catholic Chaplains in the Forces*, London.

The King's Royal Rifle Corps Chronicle 1915 (1916), Lt.-Col. R. Byron DSO, editor, Winchester.

Kipling, Rudyard (1923), *The Irish Guards in the Great War*, London.

Lake, Revd W.V.C. (c.1974), unpublished autobiography.

Laurie, The Letters of Lt.-Col. G.B., edited by Florence Vere Laurie (1921), Aldershot.

Laurie, Lt.-Col. George Brenton (1914), *History of the Royal Irish Rifles*, Aldershot.

Lucy, John F., *There's a Devil in the Drum*, reprinted London (1992).

In Memory of Lt.-Colonel C.C. Macnamara, Royal Irish Rifles (1916), published for private circulation.

Methodist College, Belfast, '*M. C. B.*' (1915–23).

Middlebrook, Martin (1971), *The First Day on the Somme*, London.

——(1978), *The Kaiser's Battle*, London.

Quis Separabit (1928–68), Regimental Journal of the Royal Ulster Rifles, Belfast.

Register of the Alumni of Trinity College (Second Edition) (1930), Dublin.

Robertson, David (1998), *Deeds Not Words*, Westmeath.

Royal Air Force Communiqués 1918 (1990), edited by Christopher Cole, London.

Royal Irish Academy (1999), *The Royal Irish Academy's Dictionary of Irish Biography*, Dublin.

Ruvigny, Marquis de, *The Roll of Honour: A Biographical Record of Members of His Majesty's Naval & Military Forces who Fell in the Great War*, reprinted London (2000).

Services of Military Officers 1920 (1920), Suffolk.

Soldiers Died in the Great War 1914–19, Part 67: The Royal Irish Rifles, H.M. Stationery Office (1921).

South African War Honours & Awards, 1899–1902, reprinted London (1971).

Tallow (1918), *Hints for Adjutants in the Field*, Aldershot.

Thompson, Robert (1999), *Ballymoney Heroes, 1914–1918*, Bushmills.

——(1998), *Bushmills Heroes, 1914–1918*.

——(2001), *Portrush Heroes, 1914–1918*.

Thom's Official Directory, 1912 (1912), Dublin.

36th (Ulster) Division Officers' (Old Comrades') Association (1924–48), a scrapbook of the annual dinner; in private hands.

University of Dublin, Trinity College, War List, February 1922 (1922), Dublin.

War Diary of the 1st Battalion The Royal Irish Rifles, Public Record Office WO95/1730 and WO95/2502.

War Diary of the 2nd Battalion The Royal Irish Rifles, Public Record Office WO95/1415, WO95/2247 and WO95/2502.

War Diary of the 25th Infantry Brigade, Public Record Office WO95/1726.

War Diary of the 107th Infantry Brigade, Public Record Office WO95/2502.

War Diary of the 8th Division's General Staff, Public Record Office WO95/1675.

Weekly Irish Times (1998), *1916 Rebellion Handbook*, Dublin.

Whitfeld, Diary of Brigadier G.H.P., held by the Imperial War Museum, unpublished.

Who Was Who 1897–1990 (1991), London.

Note: Every effort has been made to obtain permission from the relevant copyright holders.

Index